AF658505

ADVANCED MACROECONOMICS

ADVANCED MACROECONOMICS

Volume I

K.R. Gupta

Published by

ATLANTIC

PUBLISHERS & DISTRIBUTORS (P) LTD

7/22, Ansari Road, Darya Ganj,
New Delhi-110002
Phones : +91-11-40775252, 23273880, 23275880, 23280451
Fax : +91-11-23285873
Web : www.atlanticbooks.com
E-mail : orders@atlanticbooks.com

Branch Office
5, Nallathambi Street, Wallajah Road,
Chennai-600002
Phones : +91-44-64611085, 32413319
E-mail : chennai@atlanticbooks.com

Printed in India at Glorious Printers, A-13, D.S.I.D.C.,
Jhilmil Industrial Area, Delhi-110095

Preface

Macroeconomics is very essential for understanding the functioning of an economy and for proper formulation of economic policies. It gains additional importance as economic issues and events impact the everyday life of common people. The intermediate target variables, crucial for macroeconomic policies and outcomes are fiscal balance, savings and investment, while the ultimate targets are growth, inflation and external balance.

Advanced Macroeconomics has a wide coverage and comprehensively studies all the topics normally included in the subject, viz. Concept and Calculation of National Income, Classical Theory of Employment, Determination of Income, Output and Employment, Savings, Investment and Multiplier, Consumption Function, Marginal Efficiency of Capital, Rate of Interest, IS-LM Analysis of Demand, Saving-Investment Equality, Principle of Acceleration, Unemployment in an Undeveloped Economy, Secular Stagnation, Money and Prices, Inflation and Deflation, Inflation and Unemployment: Trade-off, Credit Creation and Credit Control, Business Cycles, Economic Stabilization, Monetary Policy, Fiscal Policy, Deficit Financing, Public Debt, Open Economy Macroeconomics, etc. It does not include Growth Models because I have published a separate book on this subject. The students should refer to that book for Growth Models. The book incorporates the latest developments in the subject and the chapters are organised in topics that are more or less self-contained.

The focus of this book is on developing simple theoretical models that provide insight into the reasons for fluctuations in aggregate variables such as an economy's total production of various goods and services, the aggregate level of unemployment, the general level of interest rates, and the overall level of prices. These models explore how shocks or impulses to the economy influence individuals' behavior in specific markets and analyze the resulting implications in terms of changes in aggregate variables.

Throughout the book, the aim is to present a clear and rigorous, primarily graphical and mathematical, analysis. It is an exhaustive and elaborate presentation of all the concepts along with various theories and laws, written in a lucid, accessible style and will be an indispensable tool for all students who wish to gain a firm grounding in the complexities of macroeconomic theories.

A major objective of this book is to encourage students to think of policy issues in terms of macroeconomic models. It includes detailed discussion of the unemployment problem in terms of models involving perfect and imperfect competition and endogenous rigidities, with an emphasis on open-economy issues of relevance to small economies.

The book will meet the requirements of B.A. (Hons.) and M.A. Economics students of all the Indian universities. It will also be useful for the students of MBA, CA, ICWA, CS as well as those preparing for competitive examinations such as Indian Administrative Services, Indian Economic Services, etc.

K.R. Gupta

Contents

Micro and Macroeconomics

WHY STUDY MACROECONOMICS

As we have entered the new millennium, it has turned out that economic issues are gaining more and more importance everyday. The economic events have started affecting the everyday life of a common man. An office goer earns Rs. 12,000 per month and after a month's hard work he finds out that his meagre income cannot satisfy even his basic needs as the prices of different goods and services are continuously rising. He wonders why the prices keep rising all the time while his own income does not rise at the same rate. An engineering student comes out of college, and hopes to get a handsome job with a fat paycheck. His efforts to find a job get frustrated because there is general unemployment in the country. He wonders why he cannot succeed in getting a job with his first class degree and good performances at the interviews?

Sometimes you experience that certain goods have disappeared from the market while certain other goods are available in large quantities. Have you not wondered why this is so? Have you noticed that different type of goods have shown more or less a permanent tendency to disappear from the market just few weeks before the Central Government presents its budget every year and have you not wondered why the Central Government has to keep on increasing the doses of taxation in every budget?

All these issues concern the basic functioning of the economy. By the word 'economy' we mean an organized system through which a society performs different types of economic activities, i.e. produces different types of goods and services which it requires and distributes them among its members for consumption. In a way, economics is the study of how the economy works.

The economy is composed of individuals, households, and business firms. An individual is the smallest unit of economy. Many decisions that he takes in his life, e.g. what profession to enter?

Where to work and where to live? etc. are largely governed by economic considerations. The next larger unit of economy is the household which is a group of individuals who fulfil their needs in unison. A common definition household accepted in our country is that household basically constitutes all those persons who are either related by blood or by bonds of marriage and share a common kitchen establishment. A household is basically a consumption unit. A firm, on the other hand, is also a household but it is basically a production unit. A firm is a collection of individuals, or of a group of individuals who produce some goods or services required by individuals or households for consumption. In other words, the firm is a productive household. The firm performs its economic functions, not as a social service but as a business proposition. It organizes production, hires workers, purchases raw materials and machinery, and thus produces goods. The cost it has incurred on producing goods, is known as cost of production. The firm sells its product at a price which is most often substantially, and sometimes marginally higher than the cost of production. This surplus or difference between the selling price of a unit of product and its per unit cost of production is called profit, which is firm's earning. In other words, this is the reward a firm gets of performing the socially useful function of organization of productive forces.

The next larger unit of the economy is the industry. An industry is a collection of several firms turning out identical or closely identical products. Thus, cotton textile industry refers to a number of firms, all of whom produce cotton textiles, and cosmetics industry refers to a number of firms, all of whom produce different varieties of cosmetic products.

Closely linked to the concept of industry, is the concept of market. A market, in economics, does not mean a marketplace such as Connaught Place, or Sabzi Mandi, as is the usual connotation in everyday language. In economics, the term 'market', refers to an area over which the buyers and sellers of a particular commodity are spread and they determine the price of that commodity through mutual competition and bargain. The market for any good may be local, regional, national or international. Different types of fruits, vegetables, milk, curds etc. have only local markets in our country as these goods are perishable. But the same goods have a national market in the United States because they could be frozen, transported quickly and are sold in the completely airconditioned shops which are scattered throughout the continent. This reveals an interesting fact that extent of market could be changed by technological advance. Some goods which may be sold in one region but could not be sold in other regions have regional markets. The goods which are bought and sold within the national frontiers of a country have a national market. A good example of this would be the government securities issued by the Government of India which hold good only in India and in no other country. Then, there are goods like wheat, rice, gold, drugs, steel, aircraft, guns, tanks, tractors, etc. which have international markets, because they can be bought and sold across the national frontiers.

A collection of several industries turning out products which may have some common characteristics is called a sector. The nomenclature of sector depends upon what purpose one has in mind. For example, all industries producing consumer goods may be called consumer goods sector. All industries producing for export may be called export sector. All firms engaged in export import business may be classified as foreign trade sector. There may be a number of sectors in an economy.

What we have been describing in preceding paragraphs, is known in technical language as aggregation procedure. Industry is an aggregation of firms. Sector is an aggregation of industries and economy is an aggregation of sectors. The relationship between different levels of aggregation of economic unit is shown in Fig. 1.1. Panel (a) depicts the production side of economy and Panel (b) shows consumption side. The production side constitutes firms,

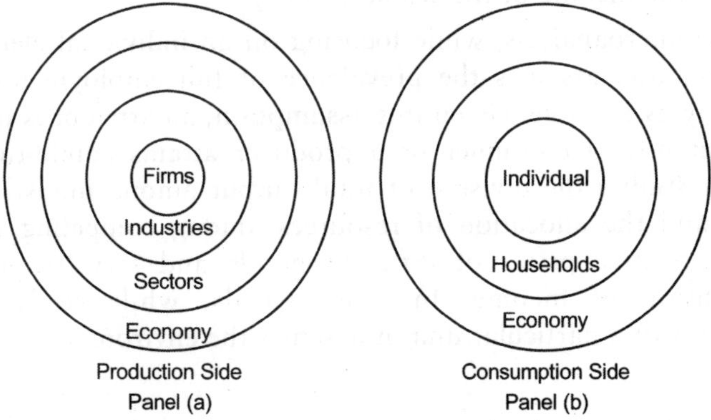

Fig. 1.1: Relationship Between Different Levels of Aggregation

industries and sectors. A sector is a subset of economy. An industry is a subset of sectors and so on. Similarly, on the consumption side, household is a subset of economy and individual is a subset of household.

MACROECONOMICS AND MICROECONOMICS DISTINGUISHED

The terms microeconomics and macroeconomics were coined by Prof. Ragnar Frisch of Oslo University in 1933 and since then these terms have gained popularity. Now they are being widely used by the economists and have become an integral part of economic terminology.

The word 'micro' means a millionth part. Microeconomics means study of a small part or component of the whole economy. Microeconomics is the opposite of macroeconomics. It deals with the analysis of the constituent elements of an economy. It studies economic motives and behaviour of individual consumers and producers and the principles involved in organising and operating the individual firms and industries. It studies how an individual person, firm, or industry attains the equilibrium position. It may be the study of an individual consumer's behaviour or that of an individual firm or of a particular industry. In price analysis, for instance, under microeconomics, we study the price of a product or a factor of production and not the general price level. Similarly, in a demand analysis, we study demand of an individual person or that of an individual household, or that of a firm or industry and not the aggregate demand of the entire community. In income analysis, we study the income of an individual or household, or firm or industry and not the income of the whole country.

The microanalysis, while focusing on an individual element of the economy, assumes the prevalence of full employment in the economy as a whole. Given this assumption, an attempt is made to find out how a consumer or a producer attains equilibrium. As such, it studies the division of total output among industries and firms, and the allocation of resources among competing uses. It studies relative prices of different goods and services, and the distribution of income. In other words, while studying the behaviour of a particular unit, it assumes the environmental data as given.

Macro and microeconomics are two different branches of the same tree. Though there is a great deal of interdependence between them, they have many distinctions in their respective approaches.

The term microeconomics is derived from the Greek word, 'Mikros' meaning small and the term macroeconomics from the Greek word, 'Makros' meaning large. K.E. Boulding makes the distinction between them more clear and more specific when he says, "Microeconomics is the study of particular firms, particular households, individual prices, wages, incomes, individual industries, particular commodities" (K.E. Boulding, *A Reconstruction of Economics*, 1950, p. 3). "Macroeconomics deals not with individual quantities as such, but with aggregates of these quantities; not with individual incomes, but with the national income; not with individual prices, but with the price level; not with the individual outputs, but with the national output" (K.E. Boulding, *Economic Analysis*, p. 25).

Microeconomics should be carefully distinguished from macroeconomics. Microeconomics also does deal with some 'aggregates', but not of the type with which macroeconomics is concerned. Microeconomics determines the product price, output and employment of an industry. Industry is also an aggregate of the various firms producing the same product. It also explains the determination of price of a product through the interaction of demand and supply of the market for that product. Market demand is the aggregate of individual demands of all consumers while the market supply is the aggregate of individual productions of all the firms producing the same product.

But the aggregates with which macroeconomics concerns are somewhat different from the aggregates with which microeconomics deals with. Macroeconomics deals with those aggregates, which relate to the whole economy. It also discusses the sub-aggregates. But these sub-aggregates are not like the sub-aggregates with which microeconomics deals with. Examples of sub-aggregates with which macroeconomics concerns, are the total production of consumer goods, total production of capital goods, etc.

Therefore, the subject matter of macroeconomics is to study aggregates or averages of the entire economy such as national income, output and employment, total consumption, total savings and investment, aggregate demand and aggregate supply, etc. The macro-approach is essential, for what it is true of the parts may not be true of the whole. Prof. Ackley says, "Macroeconomics also uses aggregates smaller than for the whole economy, but only in a context which makes them sub-divisions of an economy-wide total. Microeconomics also uses aggregates, but not in a context which relates them to an economy-wide total."

A separate and distinct microeconomic and macroeconomic analysis are essential to understand the true and actual function of the economic system of a country as a whole. None of these two approaches, viz. micro and macroeconomics, alone is adequate for the analysis of a economy. Thus, it is very much essential to integrate the two approaches to arrive at a correct solution for better understanding of the economic problems.

IMPORTANCE AND USES OF MACROECONOMICS

There are several reasons for which we have to study macroeconomics separately. What are the main justifications in having it as a separate branch of modern economic theory? Is microeconomics not adequate in itself? To give answer to these questions we have to take into account the following:

(a) We cannot obtain the laws governing the macroeconomic variables such as total national product, total employment and total income, general price level, etc. by simply adding up, multiplying or averaging the results obtained from microeconomic variables. The macroeconomic aggregate is not merely a matter of addition or multiplication or averaging of microeconomic variables. Therefore, a separate macroanalysis is needed to study the behaviour of the economic system as a whole in respect of variables of macroeconomic aggregates.

(b) Macroeconomic analysis takes into account many relationships which are not applicable to individual parts at all. For instance, an individual may save more than what he invests or he may invest more than he saves, but for the economy as a whole it is one of the important principles of Keynesian Macroeconomics that actual savings are always equal to actual investment. Likewise, for an individual or a group of individuals, expenditure may be more or less than his income, but the national expenditure of the economy must be equal to the national income. In fact, the national expenditure and national income are two identical things.

(c) The study of macroeconomics becomes indispensable for the formulation and successful execution of government's economic policies. Governments are concerned with the regulation of aggregates of the economic system such as the general price-level, the general level of production, the general volume of trade and so on. Macroeconomics studies these statistics of the aggregative variables accurately and reliably to formulate the sound governmental policies.

(d) The study of macroeconomics is indispensable even for the purpose of building and developing microeconomics. No microeconomic law can be formulated without a pre-study of aggregates.

(e) The popularity of macroeconomics has greatly increased in recent years on account of the fact that it deals with most of the controversial and challenging issues of the day such as unemployment, deficit financing, inflation, taxation, planning and economic development. It is helpful in understanding the functioning of complicated economic system. It seeks to explain fluctuation in the level of national income, output, employment, etc.

Although macroeconomics has got lot of popularity, yet it has some drawbacks which may not be avoidable. It may be discussed in several ways.

(a) The aggregation may not influence all the sectors at a time in same direction. Some sections will be benefited and some sections affected adversely, for example, a general rise in prices for which some industries may be benefited more than other industries.

(b) Sometimes the aggregative study gives us misleading conceptions. Suppose, thc price of agricultural products falls by 50 percent while that of industrial products rises by 50 percent. These two types of price changes neutralize each other showing that the general price level remains the same. One guided by macro analysis alone needs no new policy to help the agriculturist.

(c) It takes into account an excessive generalization from individual experiences to the system as a whole. What is true of an individual component may not necessarily be true of the aggregate.

(d) The attempt of aggregation of variables which are considered homogeneous in nature may not be true in many cases. Sometimes, we may have to take into account aggregates which are rather heterogeneous in character.

(e) The techniques of measurement of aggregates are very complicated. Many times they create problems.

INTERDEPENDENCE BETWEEN MICRO AND MACROECONOMICS

Microeconomics and macroeconomics are complementary to each other rather than being competitive. Actually micro and macroeconomics are so interdependent that one cannot be approached studied without the other. Again we cannot attain a complete understanding of the functioning of the economic system unless we integrate the two approaches in a judicious manner. Let us now examine this.

Macroeconomics Depends on Microeconomics

The theories regarding the behaviour of some macroeconomic aggregates are derived from the theories of individual behaviour, i.e. theories of microeconomics. The theory of relative prices of products and factors is essential for the explanation of the determination of general price level. Even Keynes used microeconomic theory to explain the rise in price as a result of the increase in the money supply of the country. According to Keynes, as a result of the increase in money supply and consequently the aggregate demand, more goods are produced and, the cost of production rises. With the rise in the cost of production, the price rises. According to him, cost of production rises because of (a) the law of diminishing returns operates, and (b) wages and prices of raw materials may rise as the economy approaches full employment. Now, the influence of cost of production, diminishing returns, etc. to determine the general price level are the parts of microeconomics. So, microeconomic theory contributes to macroeconomic theory in many ways.

Microeconomics Depends on Macroeconomics

The microeconomic topics, the determination of the rate of profit and the rate of interest depend greatly upon the macroeconomic aggregates.

The magnitude of profits depends upon the level of aggregate demand, national income and the general price level, which are the macroeconomic topics.

In the determination of rate of interest Keynes showed that the rate of interest is determined by the liquidity preference function and the stock (or supply) of money, both are macroeconomic topics. Again in the modern interest theory (i.e. intersection of IS-LM curves) along with liquidity preference and supply of money, the other two forces, saving and investment functions, which are macro terms, are used to explain the determination of interest. Thus, microeconomics depends to some extent upon macroeconomics.

Therefore, there is a good deal of interdependence between micro and macroeconomics. Microeconomics contributes to macroeconomics and macroeconomics, in turn, contributes to microeconomics. It is very essential to integrate the two approaches to get correct solution of our main economic problems.

THE NATURE OF MACROECONOMICS

The study of economy can be made at different levels of aggregation. For the sake of convenience, economic theory is classified into two separate branches—microeconomics and macro-economics. Microeconomics is that branch of economic theory which analyses the economic phenomenon at small units of aggregation. It studies such issues as: How an individual spends his income? How should he allocate his scarce resources to satisfy his competing wants? How can individual demand of a commodity be converted into market demand? How the price of a commodity is determined? Under what circumstance this price is stable? How firm decides what to produce, how much to produce and what technique of production to adopt? Is it better to have competition in one industry or monopoly or vice versa. All these questions have one common attribute—they are either concerned with the economic decisions of one single individual, or one single firm or one single market. Thus, microeconomics is the study of either a single individual (such as theory of firm) or of a single market (such as perfect competition).

Macroeconomics, in contrast, is a study of aggregates of the entire economy, e.g. national income, output, employment, total consumption, savings, investment, aggregate demand, supply, general price level, etc.

Macro means big or large. Hence, in macroeconomics we study the economy as a whole. In this branch of economic enquiry, we deal with aggregate economic variables such as national income, price level and employment level. It deals with questions such as: How is the level of income determined in an economy? Why does it fluctuate? Why the prices of all commodities rise at some time and fall at some other time? How the excess capacity develops? How the employment is determined and how can unemployment be reduced? In the analysis of all these issues, the basic unit of study is the economy itself. Hence, all this comes under the scope of macroeconomics.

Microeconomics is not necessarily restricted to individual units, say, a household or a firm. It also covers aggregates, e.g. study of an industry which consists of several firms. For example, consumer demand for cotton is an aggregate of the demands of several households. But the difference is that aggregates in microeconomics relate to only a part of the economy while the aggregates in macroeconomics cover the entire economy.

SOME MISCONCEPTIONS ABOUT MACROECONOMICS

The classification of economic theory into microeconomics and macroeconomics should not be taken as water-tight compartments. In many ways, they overlap each other. In fact, there cannot be any meaningful macroeconomics without microeconomics. It is just like group behaviour is not always the same as individual behaviour. Hence, with good reason, they should be kept separate for analytical purposes. It does not mean that group behaviour shall always be different from individual behaviour. In fact, many things which are said to be true about the individual behaviour may also hold good for the group behaviour. However, some economists like Gary Becker do think that this classification is unnecessary and there is no need for separate theories in order to deal with macro and microeconomic issues. Instead, both types of issues could very well be handled with what they call 'economic theory' encompassing both micro and macro theories. However, in this book we shall adhere to the distinction between micro and macroeconomic issues for several reasons: firstly, this is a book specifically dealing with macroeconomic issues and we shall not have to say much about the microeconomic issues as such, except occasionally. Secondly, this is in line not only with age-old tradition in economic analysis but also in conformity with the standard practice at the university departments where courses in micro and macroeconomics are offered separately.

It shall not be out of place to clear some of the misconceptions which people hold about the relative significance of micro and macroeconomics. It is not correct to say that macroeconomics is more useful, more relevant, and more realistic than microeconomics. Both of them are useful. Both are relevant and both may be equally realistic or unrealistic.

The truth of the matter is that micro and macroeconomics are two different approaches to study the economic phenomenon. Sometimes, it is useful to adopt a micro approach to reach any meaningful conclusion. In treatment of some other problems the micro approach may not prove so useful and so productive. Consequently, a macro approach is required. It does not mean that one has become unimportant, irrelevant, or useless in comparison to the other; both types of approaches are useful for the analysis of different type of issues.

METHODS OF MACROECONOMICS

The methods of analysis commonly used in economic analysis may be classified into three categories: (i) static method, (ii) comparative static method, and (iii) dynamic method.

The equilibrium in a model is defined as the balancing of some opposite forces involving some selected variables of the model in such a manner that there is no inherent tendency in the system to change. The analysis of equilibrium in this sense is referred to as statics. Thus static analysis is characterized with the lack of change, i.e. once the variables in the model assume a certain value, these values are adhered to until the position of equilibrium is reached. That is why static analysis is dubbed as analysis of how equilibrium is obtained. It does not concern itself with the questions such as: Whether the equilibrium will be stable or unstable? What if there are changes in the parameters? Whether a new equilibrium will be established or not? How shall it compare with the original level of equilibrium, etc. The static analysis is centered on a point of time. The moment the equilibrium is achieved, its job is done. Probably, this was the consideration which led professor Hicks to remark: "...we call economic statics those parts of economic theory where we do not trouble about dating"[1] meaning thereby that time is not taken into account in static analysis.

Comparative statics is concerned with the comparison of two equilibrium positions. It addresses itself to the questions which have been raised above in pointing out the limitations of static analysis. In static method, certain initial values to parameters are assumed to be given, then the attainment of equilibrium is investigated. In comparative static analysis, it is assumed that initial equilibrium exists and there is a given change in the original parameters. Suppose we can obtain a new equilibrium position with some values of parameters, then it is the function of comparative statics to compare the new equilibrium position with the original equilibrium.

A dynamic analysis is one in which all variables of an economic model change with time in such a manner that their rate of change also becomes variable. The dynamic techniques of analysis are used in growth models. However, we shall remain concerned only with statics and comparative statics in the whole of this book.

Partial and General Equilibrium

Most of the economic activities do not depend only upon a single factor. They depend upon a number of factors. So in analysing a particular economic phenomenon, we may adopt any of the two different approaches available to us. One way is to consider all the possible relevant factors affecting the phenomenon. This is general equilibrium approach. The other way, sometimes more simple and straightforward, is to consider a few selected factors which are considered to be crucial for the study of the problem. This is called partial equilibrium approach. Let us take the familiar example of a demand function for a commodity, X. Let

Q_x = Quantity demanded for X,

P_x = Price of the commodity X,

P_y = Price of the commodity Y,

$P_z ,\ldots P_n$ = Price of the commodity Z and prices of all other commodities in the economy,

Y = Income, and

T = Tastes, fashion etc.

Now the demand function of the commodity X can be written as:

$$Q_x = f(P_x, P_y, P_z, \ldots\ldots\ P_n, Y, T) \qquad \ldots(1.1)$$

Equation (1.1) describes a demand function with a general equilibrium approach. It states that quantity demanded of goods X depends not only upon price of goods but also upon the prices of all other goods as well as upon income and tastes. The basic assumption in general equilibrium approach is that everything depends upon every thing. However, price of several goods may not affect the quantity demanded of goods X at all and it may be better to drop them from the model. Similarly, income, tastes, and other price may not change in course of time when we are studying the effect of a change in P_x upon Q_x. Therefore, equation (1.1) can be rewritten as:

$$Q_x = f(P_x, \overline{P}_y, \overline{P}_z, \ldots\ldots \overline{P}_n, \overline{Y}, \overline{T}) \qquad \ldots(1.2)$$

where, the bar on the variables indicates that these variables remain constant. Therefore, equation (1.2) can be further rewritten as follows:

$$Q_x = f(P_x) \qquad \ldots(1.3)$$

Equation (1.3) states that quantity demanded of goods X depends upon its price. Thus, statement is valid only if we add another phrase 'other things remaining the same' implying that all other factors which may possibly influence the quantity demanded of goods X do not change in course of analysis. This is partial equilibrium approach which invokes assumption *ceteris paribus* which means nothing, but 'other things remaining the same'.

In course of study of macroeconomics we shall adopt a general equilibrium approach and employ the methods of static and comparative static analysis.

Aggregate Economic Variables

We have learnt above that macroeconomics is the study of aggregate economic activity. It studies the complete economy in its operation. How income is created? What governs investment and so on. Studying aggregate economic activity, macroeconomics deals with economic variables in their aggregate form. So let us explain what do we mean by aggregate economic variables. Here we are concerned with the variables such as income, consumption, investment, saving, employment, interest rate, etc.

In aggregate form these variables are related to the economy as a whole. By consumption expenditure we do not mean consumption expenditure of a single individual, or of a single family or household. It means the expenditure which the whole society incurs upon its consumption needs. Similarly, saving refers to total savings by the economy and investment is not amount invested by any single firm but is the total amount invested by all the firms. Price level refers to price of all goods and services. Of course, the economy is still divided into segments and sectors and some variables relate to the specific sectors. The basic function of macroeconomics is to study the interrelationships between different sectors and shed light on the working of the whole economy.

Macro-Dynamics and Macro-Statics

The traditional theory, when dealing with the economy as a whole, is concerned with certain aggregative relations which obtain in the stationary position without attempting to show how the economy reached there, temporally or spatially. This type of study is called 'macro-statics'. In contrast to this traditional theory of static equilibrium, Keynes considered his analysis 'dynamic', calling it "the theory of shifting equilibrium."[2] Keynes' theory is considered dynamic in the sense that it explains "a system in which changing views about the future are capable of influencing the present situation."[3] His emphasis on the role of 'expectations' lends some plausibility to his claim. Probably a more cogent interpretation of the 'dynamic' nature of Keynes' theory of shifting equilibrium is that he is thinking dynamically, because there can be no shift from one position of equilibrium to another without prior movement of variables through time. Keynes, however, made no formal attempt to trace the process of transition from one position of equilibrium to another. His method of comparing different equilibrium levels of income corresponding to changes in the consumption and investment variables, that is, changes in the values of macro-variables, has been termed "comparative statics".

Macro-dynamics, in contrast, is concerned with discrete movements or rates of change of macro-variables. This method analyses the discrete or continuous changes in aggregates, the sequence of cause-and-effect events arising from some initial disturbance, and the time paths of macro-variables and aggregative relationships. Thus, the macro-dynamic method enables one to see a 'progressive whole'. This technique has been developed by economists like D.H. Robertson, R. Frisch, M. Kalecki, J. Tinbergen, P.A. Samuelson, R.F. Harrod, J.R. Hicks etc. If Keynes "comparative statistics" is concerned with the level of employment 'at any time' the macro-dynamics of those other economists is concerned with the fluctuations of employment "at instants of time". If the former is interested in the precise effects of change in some aggregate upon the stationary or equilibrium position of the economy as a whole, the latter may be said to describe the temporal process of deviations or disequilibria.

HISTORICAL DEVELOPMENT

Pre-classical Contribution: Even before Adam Smith, a group of economic thinkers known as 'Mercantilists' had been by and large concerned with the functioning of the whole economic system. They studied the cause and relation between a favourable balance of trade and national prosperity, between inflow of gold and the domestic rate of interest, between the rate of interest and the volume of investment and the level of employment. They were interested in practical policies aimed at promoting domestic prosperity and progress.

Classical Contribution: T.R. Malthus, better known for his *Essays on Population* (1798) than for his *Principles of Political Economy* (1820), was an important forerunner of macroeconomics. He ventured to put forward the view that aggregate demand could be inadequate in contrast to the then prevailing view of an automatic self-adjusting economy. He challenged Say's law on the reasoning that the parsimony which Adam Smith and others had sanctioned would, if pushed to excess, "destroy the motive to production" and lead to the 'stagnation of capital, and subsequent stagnation in the demand for labour'.

Karl Marx is probably the most important exception to the classical tradition roughly from Adam Smith to John Stuart Mill in more than one ways. He made the first attempt to deal with the problems of the whole economic system and to build a picture of economic life and relationships as a whole. Marx's aggregative analysis is considered predominantly 'organistic' in the sense that it is concerned with the organism of capitalism as a developing whole.

In contrast, Keynes' analysis runs mainly in terms of 'mechanistic' equilibrium analysis since his method consists it investigating the equilibrium mechanism of capitalism in a historically given situation.

Neo-classicals: The neo-classical economists were concerned by and large with micro-analysis which culminated with Marshall. They took the economy as whole for granted and thus studied the determination of individual prices, outputs and employments, ignoring the general level of prices, output and employment.

Modern Contribution: Though modern macroeconomic theory is associated with the name of Keynes, there are other writers also who before or along with Keynes contributed to macroeconomics, e.g. L. Walras, K. Wicksell, I. Fisher, etc.

EQUILIBRIUM IN MACRO-ANALYSIS AND MICRO-ANALYSIS

Though the objectives are different, both the macroeconomics and microeconomics make use of the concepts of supply and demand and the equilibrium that may be established between the two. In micro-analysis, we study the market for a particular commodity. The buyers demand different quantities at different prices. Similarly, the sellers offer different quantities at different prices. The equilibrium is reached at the point where the demand and supply are equal and no one has the incentive to upset the position. If the price thus reached is so high that even the producers with the highest cost of production can earn abnormal profits, new firms will be attracted in the market which would result in an increase in supply. To induce the buyers to purchase the additional supplies, the price would have to be reduced. In this way the equilibrium would be attained by changes in price and in the quantities demanded and supplied.

In macro-analysis we study equilibrium between demand and supply for the economy as a whole. Supply consists of all types of goods and services available in the country while the demand is the aggregate of demands for all commodities. Since different commodities (e.g. cloth, shoes, wheat, cars) cannot be measured in terms of a single unit, in macroeconomics, the demand and supply are expressed in terms of money. The equilibrium will be reached where the aggregate demand is equal to aggregate supply. Inequality between aggregate demand and aggregate supply will cause changes in production and prices, and perhaps also in the volume of employment because less labour will be required if the level of production declines. It cannot be said with certainty, however, whether or not these changes will lead the economy towards an equilibrium position. Herein lies the difference between the single-commodity market and the economy as a whole.

This is because there are underlying relationships between demand and supply which can be ignored in micro-analysis but which are of vital importance when the economy as a whole is under study. In a single-commodity market, it is not unreasonable to assume that the buyers and sellers act independent of each other and the two sets of people influence each other's decisions only through the market itself. If the number of workers employed in a particular industry increases, it would be paying more wages and hence the recipients of wages would be in a position to spend more; but the effect of this on the product of the industry concerned may not be appreciable barring the exceptional cases when the industry employs an important portion of the community's workers or when the product of the industry is so important that the workers spend a considerable portion of their income on it. We can, therefore, safely ignore such behind-the-scenes 'feedback' of purchasing power from the supply side to the demand side. When, however, the supply of and demand for all the products are aggregated, the 'feedback' cannot be ignored; the buyers and sellers are more or less the same persons. The money obtained in exchange for goods and services on the supply side of the economy passes into the hands of spenders who appear on the demand side.

The aggregate demand and supply are thus linked through the intermediary of income. If the buyers, for instance, decide to spend less, the value of the commodities and hence the incomes of the suppliers of those commodities would decline which would cause a further decline in expenditure. Similarly, if the buyers decide to spend more, the value of the commodities and hence the incomes of the suppliers would rise which would lead to a further rise in expenditure. Thus while the market for a single commodity can be viewed to work in terms of the confrontation of the two forces of demand and supply, the functioning of the entire economy is to be conceived in terms of a triangular relationship—the three corners of the triangle being respectively aggregate supply, aggregate income and aggregate demand.

NEED FOR MACRO APPROACH

The need for a separate macro approach to the study of several economic problems arises from the fact that micro approach is not only inadequate but may lead to entirely misleading conclusions. In economics what is true of parts may not necessarily be true of the whole. The problem of aggregate is not simply a matter of adding or multiplying what happens in respect of the various individual parts of the whole. For example, in a period of recession, savings by an individual may increase his prosperity but savings by all the people would accentuate depression and bring misery for the country as a whole.

Wage cutting in a particular firm would increase employment in that firm but general wage cutting may fail to expand employment in the economy as a whole. An individual would become richer if he finds a few currency notes but the country as a whole cannot become richer by printing more notes. An individual depositor may withdraw his funds from the bank without doing any harm to it but if all the depositors act in the same manner simultaneously, the entire banking system would collapse.

Neither of the two approaches alone are adequate to analyse the multifarious problems facing an economy. To arrive at correct solutions, it is very necessary to integrate the two approaches. Even during the boom period, for instance, some industries may be dying because of a lack of effective demand for the products owing to number of reasons. Similarly, during a recession period, some industries may prosper fast. To apply solutions suggested by the micro-analysis to such industries would obviously be wrong. It would be equally wrong to apply solutions suggested by the micro-analysis of such industries to the economy as a whole. There are few macro problems which have no micro elements involved and there are hardly any micro problems without macro aspects. What is, therefore, required is a proper integration of the two approaches both in analysing economic problems and in prescribing policy measures for tackling them.

MEANINGFUL MACROECONOMICS

There arises the question whether a meaningful macroeconomics is possible.[4] It would be futile if confined solely to definitional relationships among macroeconomic variables. It must also study relationships among economic variables which express motivation and behaviour. Theories involving such relationships would obviously depend upon hypotheses concerning the behaviour of the individuals, families and firms which comprise the economy. The usefulness of macroeconomics would, therefore, depend on whether or not aggregative theories of behaviour are possible.

Experience tells us that individuals do react in certain generally common ways to changes in circumstances that confront them. With the increase in their incomes, other things remaining the same, for instance, most of the individuals will increase their expenditure. But the ratio of increase in expenditure to a certain increase in income would differ from person to person depending on a number of factors like total income, size of family, likely future needs for money, expected future income, thriftiness etc. It is not possible to have a theory which would accurately predict the behaviour of individuals to increase in their incomes. But while dealing with aggregates, the law of large numbers comes to our help. The law tells us that the vagaries of individual behaviour have a tendency to appear in a regular mass behaviour. While dealing with aggregates for the whole economy, we take advantage of greater regularity of mass than of individual behaviour.

The differences in individual behaviour may not, however, be of a random nature. There may be systematic and measureable differences of consumption behaviour as income changes between high and low income families, between rural and urban families, between wage-earning families and families living on profits etc. Even if each group of families reacted to changes in income in a regular and predictable manner, there may be no systematic and predictable response of aggregate consumer expenditure to a change in aggregate consumer income. If a given increase in aggregate income was received at one time primarily by one group and at another time mainly by another group, no reliable generalization would be possible in regard to the effect of a certain aggregate increase in income on aggregate increase in expenditure.

A regular aggregative relationship would exist only if the income distribution among groups with different responses remains unchanged or change in some systematic and regular way as the aggregate consumption-income relationship would be compound or product of two kinds of laws viz. (i) laws relating to consumer behaviour or several groups and (ii) the laws relating to distribution of income. Fortunately, experience tells us that composition of several of our most important aggregates is fairly stable or systematic to allow meaningful aggregate theories and measurements.

Meaning is added to macroeconomics by another law, that is many variables that are important for explaining individual behaviour have a tendency to cancel out when we deal with aggregates. This is more true in the short run. Consumption behaviour of the individual family, for instance, depends, in addition to income, on many other things, *e.g.*, size of the family, age of the family head, age of its automobile and other durable goods, births, deaths, weddings, age-groups of children. While considering behaviour of aggregate families, many of these variables cancel out particularly in the short run. Birth and death rates of individual families, for instance, vary substantially but are fairly stable and predictable for the whole population. Similarly, the age structure of the total population changes very slowly.

The above discussion shows that macroeconomics is not meaningless. It can exist at least as a first approximation of reality because (a) it can depend upon certain macroeconomic truisms; (b) the composition of many aggregates is relatively stable, or varies systematically and regularly with changes in the magnitudes of the aggregates; and (c) many of the variables most significant in explaining individual economic behaviour cancel out, at least roughly when dealing with the entire economy.

IMPORTANCE

Macroeconomics is very essential for understanding the functioning of an economy and for proper formulation of economic policies. The causes of inflation, deflation, business fluctuations and underdevelopment, for instance, can be properly discovered only by techniques of macro-analysis and not by studying individual units. Similarly, the steps for remedying these maladies are based on macroanalysis.

LIMITATIONS

Macroanalysis cannot be very precise because of heterogeneous nature of different elements constituting an aggregate. For instance, 2 mangoes + 4 mangoes = 6 mangoes is a meaningful aggregate; but 2 mangoes + 4 books is a meaningless aggregate. The introduction of money as a common measuring rod has, however, added meaning to macroanalysis. The aggregate income, consumption, saving and investment are measured in terms of money and not in terms of heterogeneous goods and services. But the value of money itself continues changing which renders difficult comparisons of economic aggregates over time. But such limitations are more in the nature of practical difficulties in formulating meaningful aggregates rather than factors invalidating macroeconomic analysis.

STOCK AND FLOW VARIABLES

All the aggregate economic variables with whom we shall be dealing in this book may be classified into two kinds of variables: (i) stock variables; and (ii) flow variables. The distinction between these variables shall be basic to our understanding of functioning of aggregate economy.

Stock variables are those which are measured at a point of time. Flow variables are those which are measured in a period of time. A period is nothing but the difference between two points of time. Some examples may be helpful in making the distinction between these two concepts. The weight of a car is a stock as it is measured at a point of time but its speed (e.g. 80 km. per hour) is measured in a period of time. A student's weight on 1st January, 1983 was 65 kg. So the weight is a stock variable. Suppose that in preceding year he registered an increase of two kg. in his weight. This is a flow. Therefore, all changes in stock are flow as they have a time dimension.

Suppose that you keep Rs. 10,000 in a fixed deposit account in a bank. This is stock as its amounts shall be measured on a specific point of time. If you keep on receiving an annual interest payment the stock would remain the same even after several years. However, if you have instructed your bank to credit the interest payment in the same account, your stock of deposit will grow and change in deposit will be regarded as flow. Now, suppose that bank pays interest at the rate of 5 percent per year on its deposit, after one year you will earn Rs. 500 as interest payment. This is a flow as it is measured in a period of time, i.e., one year. Since interest is a type of income, you can generalize that all types of incomes are flow variables. But the amount of capital for an economy has, at any given moment of time, is a stock.

CIRCULAR FLOW OF INCOME

We have seen above that income is flow variable. Now, let us see how flow of income is generated in an economy. Let us assume that there is a simple economy composed of households and business firms. This is a two sector model of economy. It is assumed that there is no government which may impose taxes and incur expenditure. It is also assumed that there is no foreign trade sector, i.e. nothing is imported from abroad and nothing is exported to foreign countries. A model of economy in which foreign trade sector is not taken into account is known as a model of closed economy.

There will be two markets in our simple economy—factor market and product market. Factor market is one in which the productive services of factors of production are bought and sold. Households are also the owners of factors of production. They own labour power, capital stocks, buildings and lands and shares in the companies. They sell these services to firms who appear as buyers in the factor market. Thus, money is transferred from firms to households. The firms get productive services of factors of production in return of their money. The money paid by firms to the households, for exchange of factor services becomes income for households. This income is in the form of wages, interest, rent and profits.

The firms carry on the productive process with the help of factor services which they buy in the factor market. They produce various types of goods and services and sell in the product market. The households are the buyers of these products and they spend their income which they earned in the factors market to buy these goods and services in the product market. Thus, money is transferred from households to the firms in the product market. The firms get their income in the product market from the households which obtain goods and services in exchange for their money. These flows have been depicted in Fig. 1.2 and direction of arrows show from whom to whom goods and income are flowing. Also notice that there is not one flow but there are two flows—one is the flow of goods and services, and factor services. And the other is the corresponding flow of income. The flow of goods and factor services is sometimes called the real flow and flow of income is called the money flow. The money flow is always in the opposite direction of real flow.

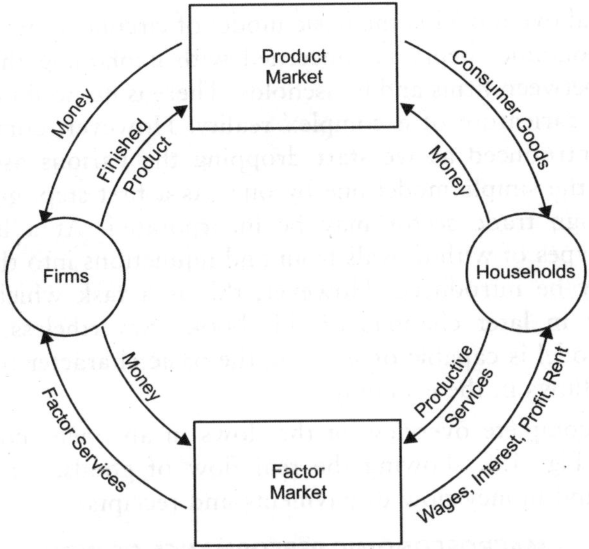

Fig. 1.2: Circular Flow of Income.

It is also necessary to recognize the dual role of households and firms in order to understand the circular flow of income. These dual roles are explicitly shown in Fig. 1.3. The households are sellers of factors services and at the same time they are buyers of products. Similarly, firms are buyers of factor services and sellers of products. They switch over their respective roles in the factor market and product market. Thus, sellers in the product market become buyers in the factor market and vice versa.

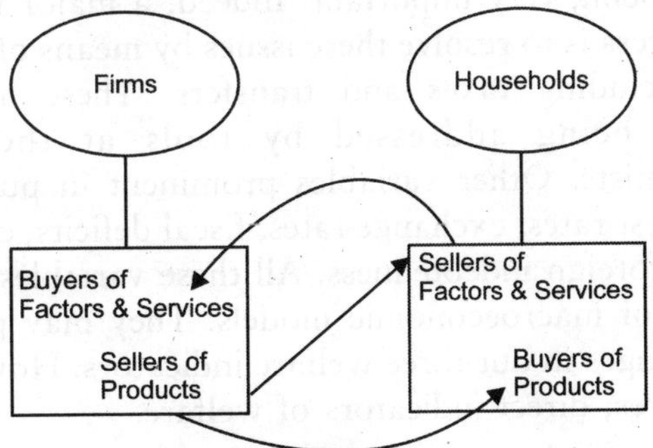

Fig. 1.3: Dual Role of Firms and Households.

The above model is the basic model of circular flow of income. Macroeconomic theory is concerned with explaining this flow of income between firms and households. There is no doubt that this is a simple caricature of a complex reality. However, complications can be introduced as we start dropping the various assumptions made in the simple model one by one. As a first step, government and foreign trade sector may be incorporated. At a later stage various types of withdrawals from and injunctions into the circular flow may be introduced. However, this is a task which shall be taken up in later chapters of this book. Nevertheless, even the simple model is capable of showing the basic character of different types of flows in the economy.

The complete overview of the flows in an open economy are given in Fig. 1.4, showing the real flow of goods, services, and factors, and money flow of payments and receipts.

MACROECONOMIC PERFORMANCE OF INDIA

In general, the performance of a national economy can be judged by the well-being of the country's citizens. From the perspective of model building in macroeconomics, we must be much more precise, and choose specific variables as indicators of welfare. In this book, our focus is on three familiar variables—the level of real gross domestic product (GDP), the rate of unemployment and the rate of inflation.

It is important to note that a number of off-cited variables did not make it onto our list. One is the distribution of income. Economists recognise that society regards income-distribution question as being very important. Indeed, a major function of the political process is to resolve these issues by means of various policy measures including taxes and transfers. These are not issues, capable of being addressed by tools at the disposal of macroeconomists. Other variables prominent in public discussion include interest rates, exchange rates, fiscal deficits, current account deficits and foreign indebtedness. All these variables are important components of macroeconomic models. They may provide signals of future changes in our three welfare indicators. However, they are not, themselves, direct indicators of welfare.

Now turn to the recent performance of India in terms of the three welfare indicators. Since the beginning of the last decade of

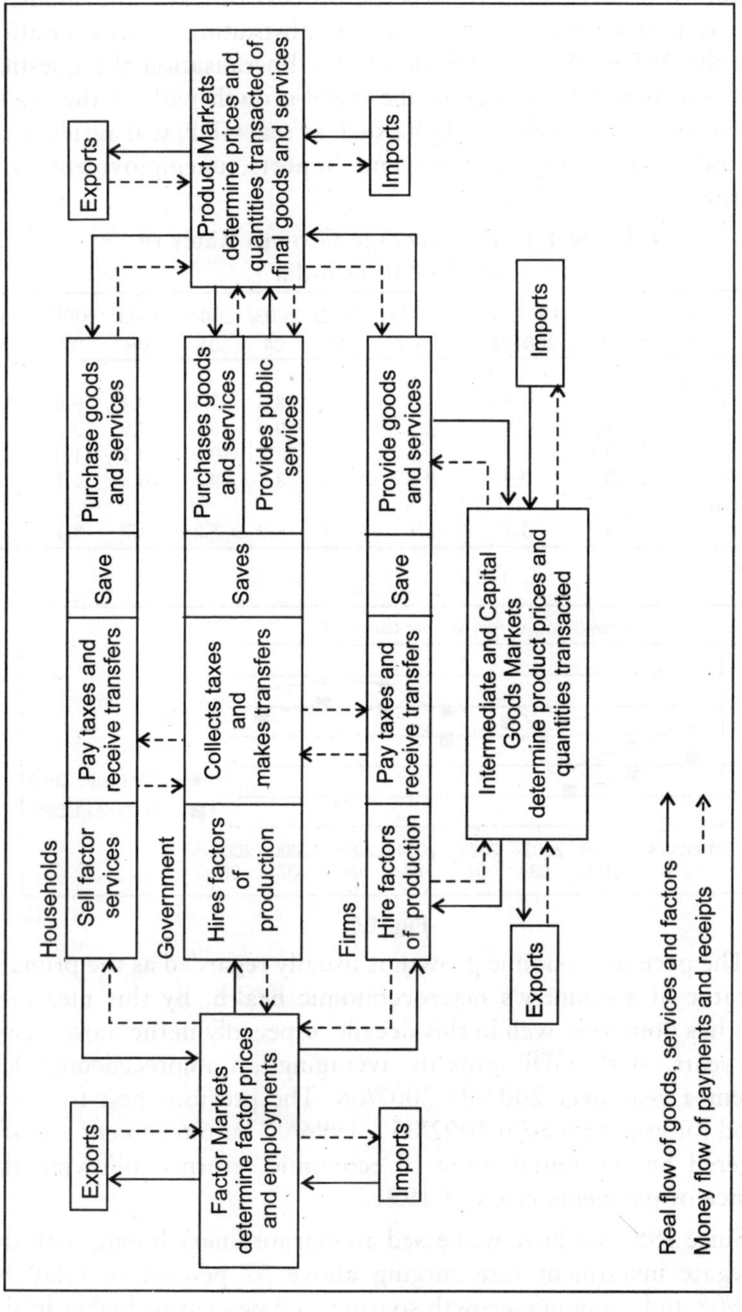

Fig. 1.4: Overview of the Economy.

the 20th centaury, India started the process of trade and financial liberalisation after decades of import-substituting industrialisation since the 1950s. After a decade of this liberalisation the question arises—is there any change in the trend-growth path of the major macroeconomic variables of India such as real GDP, real agricultural and industrial output, exports and imports, unemployment rate, inflation etc.?

Table 1.1: The Average Growth Rates of Real GDP in India

	1992/93-1996/97	1997/98-2001/02	2002/03-2006/07	2002/03	2003/04	2004/05	2005/06	2006/07	2007/08
GDP (factor cost)	6.6	5.5	7.8	3.8	8.5	7.5	9.4	9.6	9.0
Agriculture	4.8	2.5	2.5	– 7.2	10.0	0.0	5.9	3.8	4.5
Industry	7.3	4.3	9.2	7.1	7.4	10.3	10.1	11.0	8.5
Services	7.3	7.9	9.3	7.5	8.5	9.1	10.3	11.1	10.8
Per Capita GDP	4.4	3.5	6.1	2.3	6.9	5.8	7.7	8.1	7.5

Source: CSO

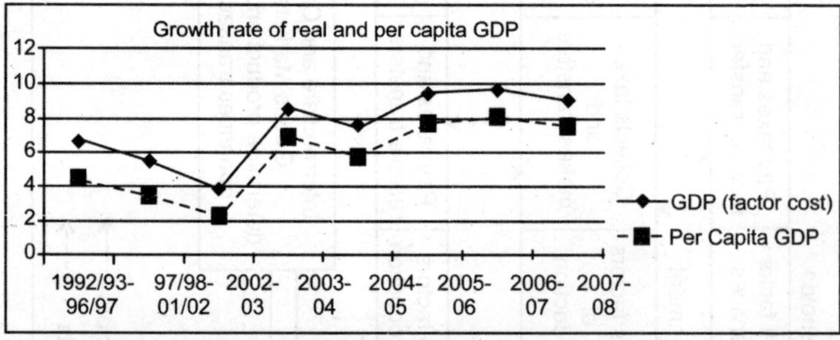

Fig. 1.5

The pace of economic growth is usually regarded as the primary indicator of a country's macroeconomic health. By this measures India has done very well in this decade, especially in the most recent five years, with GDP growth averaging an unprecedented 8.8 percent a year over 2003/04-2007/08. The previous best five-year period for growth was in 1992/03 – 1996/07 (at 6.6 percent a year), triggered by the initial burst of economic reforms following the balance of payments crisis of 1991.

Since 1991 we have witnessed an extraordinary boom, with the aggregate investment rate surging above 37 percent of GDP by 2007/08 and economic growth soaring to 9 percent or higher in the last three years, 2005/06 – 2007/08. The proximate drivers of this growth spurt included the sustained investment boom, cumulative productivity enhancing effects of reforms, an unusually buoyant international economic environment and a demand-and-technology driven acceleration of modern services output.

Now we shall consider the composition of GDP growth from the expenditure side. The following table gives the expenditure composition of growth.

Table 1.2

	Shares in real GDP (%)		Contribution to GDP growth (%)		
	Average of 1994-97	Average of 2004-07	1991/92 to 1996/97	1996/97 to 2001/02	2001/02 to 2007/08
Investment	23.9	32.6	29.2	20.4	57.3
Government Final Consumption	11.1	10.2	8.2	16.7	5.3
Private Final Consumption	65.7	59.6	54.3	60.2	47.9
Net Exports of Goods and Services (including Discrepancies)	–0.7	–2.4	8.4	2.7	–10.5
GDP (Factor Cost)	100.0	100.0	100.0	100.0	100.0

Source: CSO

The increase in aggregate investment expenditure between 1991/92 and 1996/97 accounted for nearly 30 percent of GDP growth achieved during these years and reflected a significant rise in the share of investment in GDP. With the investment ratio declining in the next five years the contribution to growth from investment demand dropped to just 20 percent. However, what is truly remarkable is the surge in investment between 2001/02 and 2007/08, which raised the investment rate above 37 percent of GDP by 2007/08 and contributed an extraordinary 57 percent of total GDP growth over this period. Conversely, the contributions of government and private final consumption expenditure to growth show an opposite pattern, rising in the period between 1996/97 and 2001/02 and falling markedly thereafter.

If GDP is the primary indicator of a country's macroeconomic performance, inflation must surely be a close second. India has three separate consumer price indices (CPI) for different categories of workers, of which, the one for industrial workers is the most commonly cited. The wholesale price index (WPI), published every week, is the most widely monitored indicator of headline inflation. It suffers from the obvious limitation of being confined to commodities in an increasingly service-driven economy. A subindex of manufactured products, WPI (MP), is sometimes monitored as a proxy for 'core' inflation. Against this background the best indicator of inflation over the years may be the implicit GDP deflator. However, it is only available for annual and quarterly data and that too with considerable lags. The following table shows the inflation trends of India since 1992.

Table 1.3

	WPI (AC)	CPI (IW)	WPI (MP)	GDP (deflator)
1992/93-1996/97 (average)	8.7	9.3	8.3	9.1
1997/98-2001/02 (average)	4.9	6.3	3.0	5.0
2002/03-2007/08 (average)	5.0	4.9	4.5	4.4
2002-03	3.4	4.1	2.6	3.8
2003-04	5.5	3.7	5.7	3.4
2004-05	6.5	4.0	6.3	5.5
2005-06	4.4	4.2	3.1	4.1
2006-07	5.7	6.8	4.6	5.5
2007-08	4.6	6.4	4.9	4.1

WPI (AC) = Wholesale Price Index (All Commodities) 1993/94 = 100

CPI (IW) = Consumer Price Index (Industrial Workers) For 1992/93 – 2006/07, 1993/94 = 100. For 2007/08, 2001 = 100.

WPI (MP) = Wholesale Price Index (Manufactured Products) 1993/94 = 100.

Table 1.3 and Fig. 1.6 present the basic information on annual inflation trends since 2001/02. The data support the following broad generalizations. First and most importantly, inflation has been in the 'comfort zone' of around 5 percent or less in nearly every year since 1989/99. Second, if one focuses on the WPI or five-year averages of any index, inflation has been subdued since 1996/97. Third, in the current decade, the GDP deflator has averaged just over 4 percent, with only two years in which the rate has crept above 5 percent. Even in 2007/08 and despite the global commodity price shock, which hit India by the first quarter of 2008, the annual rate on inflation reflected in the GDP deflator was only 4.1 percent.

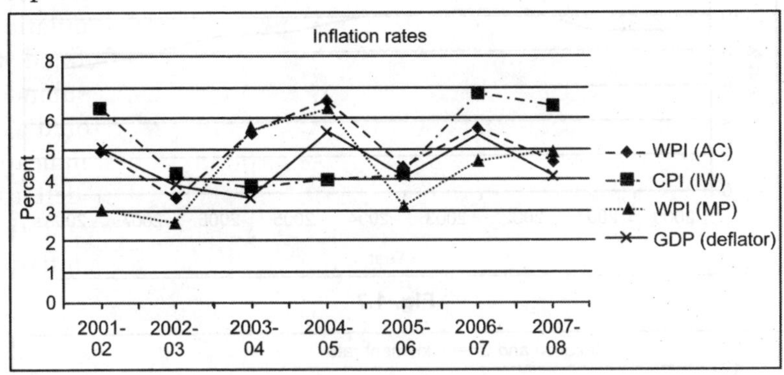

Fig. 1.6

The following table shows the annual rates of unemployment in India.

Table 1.4

Year	2000	2001	2002	2003	2004	2005	2006	2007	2008
%	9.2	9.2	10.5	10.4	10.1	9.20	8.90	7.80	7.20

Table 1.4 shows the unemployment rate for each year since 2000. The unemployment rate is the percent of the labour force that is not employed. In between 2000 and 2008 we see that unemployment rate was highest in 2002 and it decreases to 7.20 in 2008.

From the data of Table 1.4 we can draw the Fig. 1.7 showing the trend of unemloyment in India. The figure shows that unemployment rate is decreasing over the time.

Now let us consider the inflation and unemployment rate in a single diagram. In this diagram we will consider the Wholesale Price Index for all commodities.

Fig. 1.8 shows a negative relationship between inflation rate and unemployment rate. Years of relatively high rates of inflation are years of relatively low unemployment. Here we see that after 2002 unemployment rate is continously decreasing while there is much fluctuation in the inflation rate.

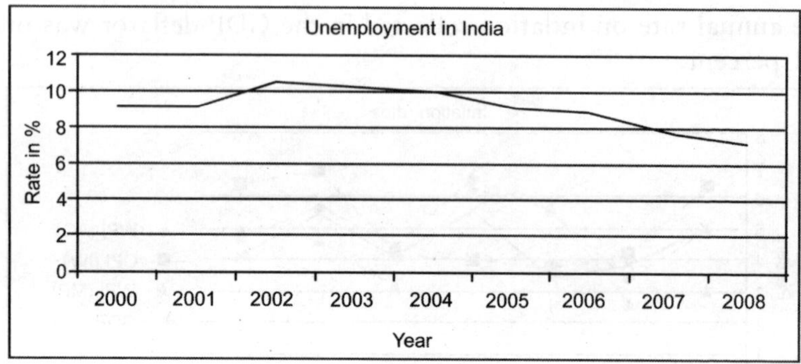

Fig. 1.7

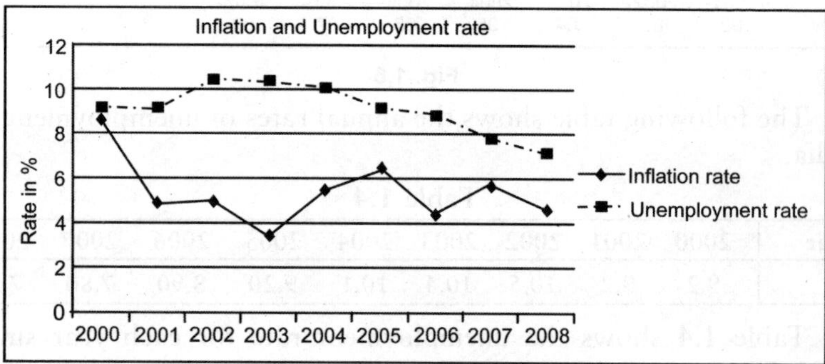

Fig. 1.8

Usually, the current account balance is the single most widely monitored indicator of a nation's external balance position. In India too, the rise of the current deficit to a record 3 percent of GDP in 1990/91 preceded the balance of payments crisis of 1991. By this measure, India's external balance position has been comfortable throughout the period 2000/01 – 2007/08, ranging between a high of 2.3 percent of GDP in 2003/04 and low of minus 1.5 percent in 2007/08. Moreover, the relative health of current account balance has been concurrent with a marked rise of India's merchandise trade to GDP ratio from 23 percent in 2000/01 to 35 percent in 2007/08, as the country continued to deepen its integration with world economy and, more recently, rising oil prices bloated the import bill.

Growth, inflation, and external balance are the main ultimate targets of macroeconomic policy. They are the outcome variables by which an economy's macroeconomic performance is generally evaluated. There is also much interest in a set of intermediate target variables, which are crucial for macroeconomic policies and outcomes. These are the fiscal balance, savings, and investment.

By 2007/08, sixteen years had passed since the external payments crisis of 1991/92 and the initial burst of economic reforms it triggered. It is instructive to look at how major macroeconomic indicators have evolved over this period. Table 1.5 presents the data for three successive sub-periods, with the first two corresponding to the eighth and ninth Five Year Plans and the third period spanning the Tenth Plan plus the year 2007/08.

Table 1.5: Comparative Overview of Macro Indicators

	1992/93-1996/97	1997/98-2001/02	2002/03-2007/08	2003/04-2007/08
Economic Growth (% per year)	6.6	5.5	7.9	8.8
Inflation (GDP deflator, % per year)	9.1	5.0	4.4	4.5
Current Account Deficit (% of GDP)	1.1	0.6	0.1	0.4
Combined Fiscal Deficit (% of GDP)	7.1	9.0	7.2	6.7
Gross Domestic Investment (% of GDP)	24.2	24.3	32.2	33.6

In the above table we see that the last five-year period, 2003/04-2007/08 boasts the best average outcomes with regard to all the major macro indicators of economic growth, inflation, external balance, fiscal imbalance and aggregate investment, when compared to any other five-year period since 1991. Furthermore, this superiority in macroeconomic performance would hold up on all counts, even if we took such comparison back to 1980.

It is important to note that the combination of a global slowdown, a world-wide commodity price shock (especially energy and food), stalled domestic economic reforms and fiscal laxity seems to have marked 2008 as the end of this "golden era", with economic growth slowing, inflation soaring the current account and fiscal deficits widening sharply and gross investment faltering.

Judging by the outcomes in terms of the exchange rate, strong trade expansion, low inflation, investment buoyancy, and record economic growth, strategy of the RBI & government for managing the unprecedented capital surge appeared to have been remarkably successful. However, one significant weakness might have been the rapid increase in domestic liquidity over this period, since sterilization of capital inflows was only partial. This may have exacerbated the impact of the global commodity price shock that hit India in early

2008, resulting in a sharp acceleration in inflation from March onwards.

CONCLUDING NOTE

The major part of the chapter has given an overview of the development of macroeconomics. Economics, like other disciplines, is sometimes prone to a 'herd mentality' in its approach to research. In these situations, it is useful to have a longer-term view of the important issues. There is an enormous literature on the history of economic thought, but it is often a rewarding experience, if time permits, to read the original material. An alternative approach to this literature can be made using *The New Palgrave Dictionary of Economics* and *The New Palgrave Dictionary of Money and Finance*. These volumes can be consulted on a huge variety of current and historical topics, and each of the articles provides a bibliography for those who want to pursue their quarry more closely.

To solve the economic problems we construct models, which are more complicated, using numerous equations and variables. The models illustrates the point—economists, like other scientists, attempt to develop theories, or coherent explanations of reality, that, when confirmed by the evidence, can provide insight into the complexities of the human behaviors observed. In this book we will construct another kind of economic model to illustrate a dilemma facing every nation—the tradeoff between the standard of living and national defence.

Keynes remarked that, in referring to such disparate economists as Ricardo, Mill and Marshall by the single term '*classical*', he was perhaps perpetrating a solecism. To apply the term 'new classical' to the advocates of market-clearing macroeconomics may simply be to compound the error a stage further. In this book we will investigate the relationship between the new classical school and some other schools, a full inquiry along those lines would take us too deeply into the history of economic thought and well beyond the purposes of this book. It is nevertheless appropriate to ask exactly what is *new* and what is *classical* about the new classical economics. To answer this question it is useful to survey the competing schools of macroeconomic thought in order to discern better how the new classical macroeconomics is distinguished from them. Any attempt to assign economists to particular well-defined schools is bound to be a procrustean enterprise. Any economist is described most fully by a vector of characteristics. A definition emphasizes some elements of this vector, while playing down related ones. Another definition might take the related elements to be more important. The borders of such categories are bound to be poorly defined. Definitions may necessarily by arbitrary to some degree. Still, the attempts to formulate them need not be sterile. The members of a school may bear only a family resemblance to each other; nevertheless, the attempt to classify them yields clarification of the nature of alternative views of the economic process as a by-product.

NOTES

1. J.R. Hicks, *Value and Capital* (1939), Oxford University Press, New York, p. 115.
2. J.M. Keynes, *The General Theory of Employment, Interest and Money* (London, 1936), p. 293.
3. *Ibid.*
4. Gardner Ackley, *Macroeconomic Theory* (Tokyo, 1971), pp. 19-23.

National Income

2

The macroeconomics theory deals with broad national aggregates like national income, consumption, saving and investment. For a proper understanding of this theory, it is very necessary to be clear about the meaning of such terms. This is what we propose to do in this chapter.

During the World War II Keynes published a pamphlet *How to Pay for the War,* in 1940. In that small tract, he identified the inflation gap created by resource constraints during the war effort, and promoted the device of compulsory saving and rationing to prevent price inflation, proposals that were adopted in 1941. *How to Pay for the War* is notable for it provided the seeds of a theory of inflation to complement the depression economics of the *General Theory*. One of the advantages of Keynes's *General Theory* was the provision of a closed, interdependent general equilibrium theory based on a few simple, essential relationships such as those between consumption and income, investment and interest rates, etc. It was fortuitous that national income accounts, which began to be collected in the 1920s by institutions and economists such as Simon Kuznets in the US and Colin Clark, Richard Stone and James Meade in the UK, contained within them these very categories. John Maynard Keynes joined the British Treasury in 1915 and was involved in the design and implementation of the policies used to finance World War I. In Keynes's view, an important goal of war finance was to avoid the high inflation that had occurred during World War I. He predicted that inflation would increase as wartime output and incomes rose, while resources were diverted away from the production of consumer goods and services. To prevent inflation, he argued that the only viable options were to institute price controls, to borrow or to tax away consumer's spending power. Keynes recommended raising taxes to finance the war and that these taxes should be borne by the wealthy. Since, this would not be sufficient to raise revenue for the war, Keynes proposed a "system of sharply rising levies on all incomes in excess of a small minimum, with the highest incomes paying 85 percent marginal rates" and compulsory savings for the working classes. This is deferred pay, which would be rebated with interest after the war beginning in the first post-war recession. Keynes's approach to wartime finance was first based on constructing a consistent set of national income accounts capable of providing the structure needed to understand the public finance problem presented by the war. James Meade and Richard Stone further developed this theory.

Simon Kuznets was the founder of national income measurement. He was invited to join National Bureau of Economics Research (NBER) where he did research on national income and product accounts. He was responsible for the publication of the nation's first national income estimates for 1929-1932. In his book *National Income and its Composition, 1919 to 1938* published in 1941, he explains the concept of national income which is now the basis for the modern national income accounting. The term "Gross Domestic Product" was created by Simon Kuznets during World War II to quantify final aggregate demand according to the new economics of Keynes. As such, GDP ignores all intermediate spending in the economy, based on the tenuous argument that earlier stages of production constitute double counting. Kuznets's life work was the collection and organization of the national income accounts of the United States, an accomplishment paralleling that of Richard Stone and James Meade in Great Britain. Kuznets's work was similar to the two other developments at the time: the emergence of econometrics and the Keynesian Revolution, both of which found in Kuznets's data an important resource for their advancement. The system of national accounts built by Kuznets was the empirical scaffolding for Keynes's theory of national income determination.

A major contributor to the development of national income accounting was Sir John Richard Nicholas Stone. He also won the Nobel Prize for economics for developing an accounting model that could be used to track economic activities on national and international levels. The first official estimates of British National Income and expenditures were made according to Stone's method in 1941. Stone had also published a complete set of accounts for the United States in 1942, and together with Meade, had produced textbook, *National Income and Expenditure*, which was illustrated with estimates from Britain and America. He offered the first statistical model to calculate investment, government spending and consumption. Stone organised national accounting on the basis of an extensive transaction matrix which was then used to construct different types of models by imposing various kinds of restrictions on it and combining it with a response matrix. In other words, national accounts structures were used for the model construction such as Keynesian macro models, which emphasise factor markets, international trade models and input-output models, special cases of transaction models. World War I and World War II brought about the statistical revolution, which introduced national income estimates both in United States and in Britain as an example of a technological improvement stimulated by war.

MEASUREMENT OF AGGREGATE ECONOMIC ACTIVITY

It is by now clear that macroeconomics is the study of aggregate economic activity. Therefore, we need a measure by which we could determine the performance of aggregate economy. The total production of economy would be one such measure. But the problems of measurement and of aggregation are involved here.

An economy is an organization of the process of production and distribution where, in co-operation with others, people produce and acquire goods and services for the satisfaction of their wants. An economy is a collection of all the farms, factories, workshops, mines, roads, railways, banks, schools, cinema, houses and hospitals, etc. which provide the people with the goods which either they consume or use for further production or export to the foreign countries. Not only goods are produced, but services are also rendered by professional people, like doctors, teachers, lawyers, musicians, etc. These services are directly consumed by the members of the society. Each one of these individuals, who renders services, is an important production unit. Thus, the economy produces hundreds of thousands types of goods and services. These goods and services are measured in different types of units. Some goods like television sets, radios, fans etc. are measured in number. Foodgrains, rice, wheat, etc. are measured in quintals. Cement and steel are measured in metric tons. Then economy produces different types of machinery which manufacture cloth, television sets, radio, steel, and tractors. How all these could be aggregated to arrive at a single measure of aggregate economic activity? An easy way out of this problem is to calculate the value of all goods and services (Value = price × quantity) and sum them over all goods and services produced in economy in a given period of time. The figure, thus arrived at, is a measure of aggregate economic activity and is known as gross national product or GNP, of which a more formal definition is given below:

GNP or gross national product is the value of all final goods and services produced by any economy during a given period of time, usually a year, and valued at current market prices.

We must keep the following facts in mind about GNP:

(a) GNP is the value of all final goods and services. A good or service is considered final when it reaches the consumer who finally consumes it. For example, bread is a final good. The value of all bread shall be included in GNP. The baker uses flour, sugar, egg, and coal to make bread, but the values of these things are not included in the calculation of GNP. The reason is that the value of all these inputs is included in the price of bread. There are some goods which are final products of one industry but are used in production in some other industry as inputs. These goods are called intermediate goods. All intermediate goods are excluded from the accounting system of gross national product. It is necessary to do so to avoid double counting which shall greatly inflate our measure of aggregate economic activity and misrepresent the productive capacity of the economy. Consequently, to avoid double counting, intermediate products are neglected and only final products are counted. In the above example, flour, sugar, eggs and coal shall be included in GNP accounting only if they are bought by households for final consumption.

(b) We should note that GNP includes only such economic activities which are produced for market. In other words, only those goods and services which have a price tag on them are included in the calculation of GNP. Some economic activities may be performed outside the scope of market system, e.g. a housewife prepares meals in her kitchen, an amateur gardener grows vegetables in his backyard, a test star cricketer participates in a friendly match in his home town, a film actor appears at a charity show in aid of a hospital, etc. All these activities shall not be included in GNP. However, if the same activities were performed on a commercial basis, they would have been included in GNP. Now, we can state as a rule that activities performed due to love, charity, entertainment and pleasure, patriotism, etc. are not included in GNP, but if the same activities were performed for a price, they would be included in GNP.

(c) It should also be clear that only legal economic activities are included in GNP. The illegal economic activities such as smuggled goods and services, the amount of goods stolen, the income obtained by theft, dacoity, cheating, etc. are not included in GNP.

We can establish an identity between gross national product (GNP) and gross national income (GNI) of an economy. GNP is the money measure of all the final goods and services produced during the year. Thus, if q_1, q_2, q_3;..., q_n are the qualities of all the final goods and services produced during the year and p_1, p_2, p_3..., p_n are their per unit prices, then

$$GNP = q_1 p_1 + q_2 p_2 + q_3 p_3 + \ldots + q_n p_n$$

Corresponding to every flow of goods, there is a flow of factor incomes. Production is a joint effort of factors like labour, land, capital and organisation which, in turn, for their contribution to production receive wages (W), rent (R), interest (I) and profits (P). The national income being a sum total of factor incomes can be expressed as,

$$GNI = W + R + I + P$$

Since both the production of final goods and the income of the factors arise out of the same production process, they are identically equal to each other. This can be proved by the following set of equations:

$$GNP = p_1 q_1 + p_2 q_2 + p_3 q_3 + \ldots + p_n q_n \quad \ldots(2.1)$$

$$GNI = W + R + I + P \quad \ldots(2.2)$$

In the equation (2.2) P represents the profits of the entrepreneurs. The profits are a residue left over with the entrepreneurs after making payment to all the other factors viz. land, labour and capital from his total sale proceeds. Thus,

$$P = p_1 q_1 + p_2 q_2 + p_3 q_3 + \ldots + p_n q_n - (W + R + I) \quad \ldots(2.3)$$

By transposing the last point of the equation (2.3) to the left hand side we get,

$$W + R + I + P = p_1 q_1 + p_2 q_2 + p_3 q_3 + \ldots + p_n q_n \quad \ldots(2.4)$$

Now the left hand side of the equation (2.4) denotes national income while the right hand side is the gross national product. Thus,

GNI = GNP

In other words, on the basis of the simplifying assumptions that we have made, the aggregate value of all the final goods and services produced in an economy during a given year is always equal to the aggregate of factor incomes generated during the year.

NNP AND NATIONAL INCOME

GNP can be produced by a combination of three factors of production—land, labour, and capital. Land is assumed to be fixed. Let us also assume that withdrawal from labour force (persons who retire every year) is exactly matched by new arrivals (persons who attain the working age and thus enter the job market). Thus, we are assuming that labour force is also constant. Thus GNP would depend mainly upon the capital stock. If the economy started with a given amount of capital stock in one year, in the next year GNP would decline. This will happen because capital stock will decline. There will be wear and tear of machinery in course of production. So the capital stock cannot remain constant. This is also called capital consumption meaning thereby that some amount of capital shall be consumed (lost) in the productive process. Unless some provision is made to replace this lost capital, the capital stock cannot remain intact at the initial level. Therefore, a special allowance is made to replace the capital and make up for the wear and tear of machinery. This is known as depreciation allowance or capital consumption allowance.

The Net National Product (NNP) is obtained from GNP after deducting the depreciation allowance:

NNP + D = GNP

or, GNP – D = NNP ...(2.5)

where,

NNP = Net National Product,

GNP = Gross National Product,

D = Depreciation or capital consumption allowance.

Closely related to the concept of NNP is the more popular concept of National Income which is the sum total of income of all individuals of the society. In fact, conceptually NNP and national income are the same thing.

DEFINITION OF NATIONAL INCOME

The national income has been defined by different persons in different ways. There is nothing absolutely right or wrong about any of these definitions. The most suitable definition of income would depend mainly on the purpose for which income estimate is required. Marshall defines national income as below:

> The labour and capital of a country, acting on its natural resources, produce annually a certain net aggregate of commodities, material and immaterial, including services of all kinds...and net income due on account of foreign investments must be added in. This is true net annual income or revenue of the country, or the national dividend.

Though, this definition is theoretically sound, simple and comprehensive, it has serious practical limitations. It is not easy to make statistically correct estimates of the total production of goods and services particularly because of the difficulties of double counting and portion of the produce which is retained for personal consumption.

In the words of Prof. Pigou, "...the national dividend is that part of the objective income of the community including, of course, income derived from abroad, which can be measured in money...". According to Prof. Pigou, only those goods and services are to be counted, avoiding double counting, of course, which are actually exchanged for money. Pigou's definition is practicable and convenient and avoids the difficulties of measuring national dividend inherent in Marshall's definition. But it has its own shortcomings.

National Income at Factor Cost

The sum total of goods and services are produced by the cooperation of the factors of production and as such their money value is distributed among those factors of production. The national income can, therefore, also be conceived as the total incomes received by the factors of production for their contribution of land, labour, capital and entrepreneurship. Such receipts take the form of wages, rent, interest and profits.

The income of an individual may be defined as the amount of his earnings from the productive services currently rendered by him or by his property. National income is simply the sum of incomes of all individuals. It is a flow concept and relates to a definite period, normally a year.

Income defined as earnings should be distinguished from income receipts. The income earned during a certain period may not be received during the same period either because it is taxed away before receipts or is retained to be paid at a later date. Income received during a certain period may also exceed the income earned during that period either because delayed payment of past earnings exceeds current retentions or because of receipt of "transfer payment" which does not represent payment for productive services rendered in the present or past period, e.g. relief payments which represent "government transfer payments", bad debts of consumers to business are a form of "business transfer payments", gifts in kind or money exchanged among individuals are a type of "interpersonal transfer payments".

Income should also be distinguished from simple asset transformation. The sale proceeds of a house, bonds, patent rights, for instance, are not income. Similarly, the amount received as a result of repayment of a debt is not income. All that has happened in such cases is the transformation of wealth from one form to another, that is, cash. In contrast, the current flow of services from the house, interest from the bond and royalties from the payment are income.

A special problem arises in case of capital gains resulting from sale of assets at prices higher than their purchase prices. This difference represents neither an asset transformation nor true income except in case of a person whose profession is buying and selling assets and who earns his livelihood by his ability to buy at prices lower than the sale prices. Normally capital gains, which are of the nature of a windfall and not earnings from current productive services, are not considered a part of income.

Theoretically, any costs which the individual incurs in earning his income should be deducted from his gross earnings. Examples of such costs are provided by the cost of tools which he must himself supply, union dues, travel to and back from the place of work, etc. In practice, however, most of these costs are not deducted because of the practical difficulties involved in clearly separating between expenses incurred in earning income and those for using or enjoying income. Part of the travel expenses, for instance, may be because the worker prefers to live at a distance from his place of work. In order to be able to work, a worker must have some clothing to wear, food to eat and shelter to live. To be efficient, he must have some entertainment and relaxation. If this argument is stretched further, we will reach the conclusion that a considerable portion of consumer expenditure is cost of earning income and should be deducted from the gross income. But the widely adopted convention is not to deduct such expenditure on the plea that the workers earn in order to consume and not consume in order to live. It would, however, be fair to deduct from gross income, at least, that expenditure which is obviously incurred for earning income, e.g. cost of workers' tools.

In case of business enterprises, the expenses incurred in earning income are easily defined and are quite important and must be deducted from the gross income. Unlike most of consumer expenditures, most of business expenses are incurred for earning income. The usual practice, therefore, is to deduct business expenses in order to arrive at earnings of the business enterprise.

In short, national income is the sum of (i) wages, salaries, commissions, bonuses and other forms of employee earnings before deduction of taxes or social security contributions; (ii) net income from rentals and royalties; (iii) interest income; and (iv) profits before deduction of taxes based on income.

The major significance of the concept of national income lies in revealing the distribution side of national economic activity or the manner in which the total product is allocated to the factors of production relatively to the productive services rendered. National income proper is considered to be the most satisfactory single measure of overall economic activity, not only because it has all the merits of net national product mentioned in the following pages but also because it shows how much total expenditure on consumer goods and capital goods (the latter being in excess of replacements) there must be in order to offset the total income of productive factors (total cost of production from the point of view of the producers).

PERSONAL INCOME

It is the total of incomes received by individuals from all sources. It consists of wages and salaries, interest, rent, dividends, incomes of self-employed people like farmers, doctors and shopkeepers, and receipts which are not payments for current productive services (i.e. government and business transfers). National income that is, total income earned and personal income, that is, total income received must be different because some income which is earned is not actually received (e.g. undistributed corporate profits, corporate income taxes, social security contributions) and conversely some income which is received is not currently earned (e.g. transfer payments). Thus,

Personal Income = National Income – Social Security Contributions – Corporate Income Taxes – Undistributed Corporate Profits + Transfer Payments.

The concept of personal income is helpful for the specific purpose of knowing the potential purchasing power of the household sector of the economy in a given period. Those inclined to regard consumer welfare both as a paramount economic end and as an essential means to national prosperity usually attach great importance to personal income data. But the concept of personal income fails to indicate what is actually available to the household sector for spending and saving purposes. This lacuna of the concept has necessitated another concept viz., Disposable Income.

DISPOSABLE INCOME

A person does not have complete command over the personal income, as defined above, to spend, to save, to give away in any manner he chooses. He must pay taxes like income-tax, property tax etc. and other obligatory payments like national insurance contributions. The income which a person is free to dispose of in any manner he likes, therefore, is personal income minus taxes and other obligatory payments. This income is called disposable income. A person's freedom to dispose of even this income is limited by his contractual obligations, e.g. life insurance policies, mortgages, instalment contracts.

The total of disposable income of all sectors must add up to the same total as the national income itselt because the effect of the various taxes and transfer is merely one of redistribution. This process does not generate any new income. The only income available is that originally accruing to the owners of the factors of production.

The major usefulness of the concept of disposable income lies in the light it throws on the government's fiscal policy as an important factor affecting individual decisions to spend and to save.

REAL INCOME

The national income is expressed in terms of money but the purchasing power of money changes over time as a consequence of changes in the general level of prices. If the intention is to find out what the national income of any period is worth in terms of goods and services, then its 'normal' or 'money' value will have to be converted into its 'real' value by an adjustment or correction process known as 'deflating'. The money income can be deflated so as to obtain real income by the formula given below:

$$\text{Real income in terms of constant money} = \frac{\text{Nominal income in current money}}{\text{Price index for current period}}$$

ECONOMIC VERSUS ACCOUNTING INCOME

To understand the concepts of economic income and accounting income, let us consider the following figure.

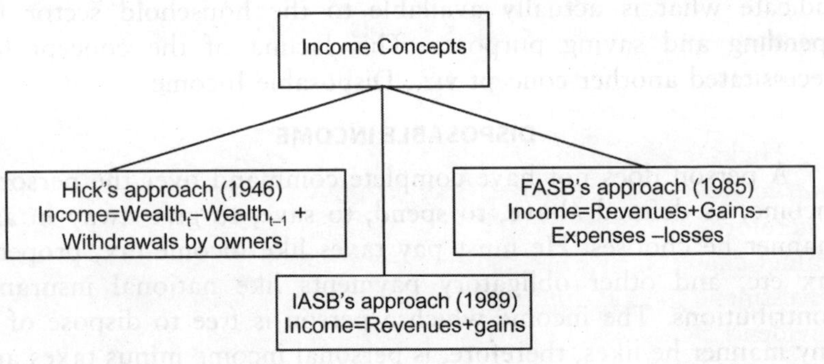

Hicks' Approach

According to Hicks, income is the change in wealth adjusted for withdrawals by owners. Change in wealth depends on measuring income and withdrawals by owners during the period, i.e.,

Change in wealth = income – withdrawals by owners. ...(2.6)

And change in wealth depends on measuring wealth at the beginning and end of the period, i.e.,

Change in wealth = wealth $_t$ – wealth $_{t-1}$. ...(2.7)

Both mathematical sentences have something in common on the left side. Simplifying equation (2.6) and equation (2.7) we have

$$\text{Income} = \text{wealth}_t - \text{wealth}_{t-1} + \text{withdrawals by owners} \quad ...(2.8)$$

Economists have adopted a wealth maintenance concept. They measure income by the difference between wealth at two points in time. They subtract beginning wealth from ending wealth and adjust for any withdrawals by owners during the period. Economic income consists of withdrawals by owners, which is consumption, and change in owners' wealth, which is saving. Under the wealth maintenance concept, income is the maximum amount that can be consumed during a period and still leave the owners with the same amount of wealth at the end of the period as at the beginning. Hicks' classical definition states that enterprise can measure economic income, which is based on some valuation (e.g. historical cost, fair market value, or discounted future cash flows) as a measure of increase or decrease in net wealth. The accounting of the *Off-balance-sheet assets* is vital to the information-era enterprise. Human resources, information systems, R&D play key roles in the net wealth of owners. For example, if the manager leaves the enterprise, the difficulty lies in the recognition and measurement of the gain or loss. The investor's ability to evaluate the qualitative factors (e.g. decision-making ability of managers) is as important as the investment decision itself.

Hicks' wealth is determined with reference to the *current market values of equity* at the beginning and end of the period. Therefore, the economic income would fully incorporate market value changes in the determination of periodic return on an investment. Thus, financial return on an investment consists of dividend and change in market value, i.e.,

$$\text{Periodic return} = \text{dividend} + [(\text{market value})_t - (\text{market value})_{t-1}] \quad ...(2.9)$$

The periodic return shareholders get on an investment comes in two forms. First, shareholders may receive some cash from the enterprise during the year, called a dividend, which is a realised component of periodic return. In addition, a market value change of equity represents an unrealised component of periodic return. If shareholders sold the investment at the end of the period, both dividend and market value changes of equity are realised components of periodic return.

Financial Accounting Standards Board's (FASB's) Approach

The continuous process of earnings is conceptually straightforward, but application of *wealth maintenance concept* to short periods is difficult. The opposite of the continuous process approach is the complete process approach, which is the accountants' approach for income measurement. The key reason for the disparity between the economic and accounting measures of income relates to the need for periodic reporting. Investors believe that information can be useful in investment decision-making only if it is relevant and reliable. Since fluctuations in market values are often a matter of conjecture, accountants preclude the recognitions of market value changes until these are realised by a transaction. Accountants have concluded that there must be guidelines for revenue and expense recognition.

Accountants have defined income by reference to specific events that give rise to recognisable elements of revenue and expense during a reporting period. The events that produce reportable items of revenue and expense comprise a subset of economic events that determine *economic income*. Changes in the market value of wealth components are often deliberately excluded from the measurement of accounting income but are included in the measurement of economic income.

Both accountants and economists understand that the earnings process occurs throughout the various stages of production, sales, and final delivery of the product. However, the difficulty in measuring the precise rate at which this earnings process is taking place has led accountants to conclude that income should normally be recognised only when it is fully realised. Realisation generally implies that the enterprise producing the item has completed all of its obligations relating to the product and that collection of the resulting receivable is assured beyond reasonable doubt. For very sound reasons, accountants have developed a reliable system of income recognition that is based on generally accepted accounting principles applied consistently from period to period. The interplay between recognition and realization generally means that values on the balance sheet are recognised only when realised through an income statement transaction. The FASB's definition of comprehensive income of business enterprises is discussed in Statement of Financial Accounting Concept No. 6, *Elements of*

Financial Statements—Comprehensive income is the change in equity of a business enterprise during a period from transactions and other events and circumstances from non-owner sources. It includes all changes in equity during a period except those resulting from investments by owners and distributions to owners (SFAC 6 paragraph 70). Comprehensive income results from (a) exchange transaction and other transfers between the enterprise and other entities that are not its owners, (b) the enterprise's productive efforts, and (c) price changes, casualties, and other effects of interactions between the enterprise and the economic, legal, social, political, and physical environment of which it is a part (SFAC 6 paragraph 74).

Comprehensive income result from revenues and gains, expenses and losses, which are classified according to business activities—operating income, non-operating income, and price level changes. Revenues and expenses are gross concepts, whereas gains and losses are net concepts. The income statement reports gains and losses at net instead of gross amounts because owners do not need information on the components of either peripheral or gross amounts because owners do not need information on the components of either peripheral or non-recurring income items. Currently, Hicksian income is probably the understanding of the FASB's comprehensive income from the viewpoint of the preferred and common shareholders. The appropriate measurement of income is partially dependent on the vantage point of the party doing the measuring. From the perspective of outside investors taken as a whole, income might be defined as earnings before any payments to those investors, including bondholders and preferred shareholders, as well as common shareholders. On the other hand, from the viewpoint of the common shareholders, income might better be defined as earning after payments to other investors, including creditors and preferred shareholders. Companies have issued various capital share classes that differ in their priority ranking in bankruptcy proceedings. Also, accounting standard-setting bodies have issued pronouncements that create new shareholders' equity accounts. An effective analysis of the profitability and risk of an enterprise requires an understanding of the accounting for shareholders' equity.

International Accounting Standards Board's (IASB's) Approach

According to the IASB's framework income of business enterprises is defined as "Income is increases in economic benefits, during the accounting period in the form of inflows or enhancements of assets or decreases of liabilities that result in increases in equity, other than those relating to contributions from equity participants (IASB's Framework paragraph 70 (a)).

The IASB's Framework owes much of its development and direction to the prior work of the Financial Accounting Standards Board. The IASB emphasises this definition of income encompasses both revenue and gains. The IASB's Framework states that profit is used as a measure of business enterprise's economic performance. The basic elements directly related to the measurement of profit are income and expenses. The IASB's Framework has an Anglo-Saxon influence. In the U.S., it is usual to use the term income for a net amount after the deduction of expenses. In Britain, this restriction is not so observed. In this sense, the term income is more general and can be applied to a person or to an enterprise.

According to economic substance over form, income reporting should be the same regardless of legal form. Revenues-gains and expenses-losses of a corporation are separated from the revenues-gains and expenses-losses of the shareholders. In both the sole proprietors and partnership form of business enterprise, the revenues-gains and expenses-losses identification process is more difficult. Items such as salaries paid to owners or partners may by thought of as distributions of profit rather than expenses. So, the income of owners depends on legal form of entity. The IASB approach does not focus only on the income of owners but also focuses on the income of the business enterprise.

Hicks and the Concept of 'Income' in the Conceptual Framework

Starting with the overriding objective of usefulness in making economic decisions, and thereby of usefulness in assessing cash flow prospects, the Boards' frameworks focus on 'enterprise resources, claims to those resources, and changes in them'. This leads to definitions of the elements of financial statements, beginning with assets, which are (in FASB's current version) characterised as 'probable future economic benefits obtained or controlled by a particular entity as the result of past transactions or other events'. It is argued that all other elements can be derived from the definitions of assets, which gives assets 'conceptual primacy' and leads to the 'asset/liability' view of income measurement, in which income is a measure of the increase in the net resources of the enterprise during a period, defined primarily in terms of increases in assets and decreases in liabilities.

At a joint FASB and IASB meeting it was tentatively decided for the new joint framework that, as a working definition, 'an asset of an entity is a present economic resource to which, through an enforceable right or other means, the entity has access or can limit the access of others'. This definition, which is in substance like the definitions in the existing individual FASB and IASB frameworks, stands in contrast with 'earlier efforts that included deferred debits among assets'.

Deferred debits are allegedly indefinable independently and are simply the result of the 'revenue and expense', or 'matching', approach to measuring income. But, at least in principle, the accusation that traditional accounting conventions allow into the balance sheet items that would not meet the FASB/IASB asset definition appears to be false. Deferred debits as traditionally understood, must also represent probable future economic benefits.

It is at this point that the framework purports to be grounded in a theory prevalent in economics—that an entity's income can be objectively determined from the change in its wealth plus what it consumed during a period. It is on this foundation that the 'conceptual primacy' of assets, and the superiority of the 'asset or liability' view over the 'revenue and expense view' in measuring a business's income, are purportedly based. The Boards' attempt to ground their converged framework of accounting theory and principles on a sound economics foundation is to be welcomed. Unfortunately, their foundation will not support the particular structure that the Boards wish to erect. Although Hicks was concerned here only with individuals' income, his definition of 'Income No. 1' can be translated for a company as equal to 'the maximum amount that could be distributed to the equity shareholders in a period and leave intact the capital value of the company's prospective receipts as at the beginning of the period'. *Ex ante* this will be based on what was expected about cash flows and interest rates at the beginning of the period, and *ex post* on what actually occurs during the period and on revised expectations about the future at the end of the period.

According to Hicks, so long as we confine our attention to income from property, and leave out of account any increment or decrement in the value of prospects due to changes in people's own earning power (accumulation or decumulation of "Human Capital"), Income no. 1 *ex post* is not a subjective affair, like other kinds of income; it is almost completely objective.

The concept of income as 'current cash flow plus increase in the net present value of the entity's expected future cash flows' (excluding transaction with owners), or 'cash flow plus actual capital accumulation', has long been advanced in writing for practitioners by many leading academic accounting authors. However this concept of income is only fully determinable and objective where there are 'complete and perfect markets'—i.e. where every resource and claim on future cash flows has been 'commoditised' into fully exchangeable assets and where everyone faces the same prices (including interest—the 'price' of future versus current commodities). In this situation there is no doubt about the magnitude of wealth and therefore about the magnitude of changes in it (income no. 1) both *ex ante* and *ex post*. So the reporting of income is redundant.

In the real world, markets are neither complete nor perfect, so there will in the case of business enterprises, be a large element of the value of their future cash flow prospects that is not captured in the value of their net assets, however good the markets in which the value of those assets and liabilities ay be measured. This element of value depends *inter alia* on the skill with which management and the workforce can exploit an enterprise's resources and its markets, and its business, social and political opportunities—what Hicks labels 'Human Capital'.

In general, therefore, an 'objective' version of Hicks's No. 1 *ex post* concept of the business income of a listed enterprise is more likely to be found in the measure of its 'shareholder return' (dividend plus/minus change in share price), i.e. the change in its 'capital value' at the stock market level, than in the change in the enterprise's net assets. But if firms are merely to report their stock price return (plus dividends) at their income, their accounts are again redundant, at least for valuation or investment decision purposes.

In the real world of incomplete and imperfect markets, there is no justification for the FASB/IASB (2005) paper's rendering of Hicks's 'capital value' as 'in accounting terms, its assets and liabilities'. There is of course an extensive academic literature exploring how far concepts and measures of asset and liability value that are consistent with (while not generally capturing all of) Hicks's underlying model of 'capital value' may be developed; and how changes in such net asset values may be related to Hicks's notion of 'Income No.1'. Any such links require considerable further restrictive assumptions to handle *inter alia* what are identified in the FASB/IASB 2005 paper as the 'cross-cutting issues' of 'uncertainty', 'unit of account' and 'management intentions'.

In the work cited in FASB/IASB 2005, Hicks confines himself to the individual person who wishes to measure his or her income and he does not actually discuss firms there at all. However, he does in Hicks (1979). Here he revisits his earlier analysis and begins by commenting that an early nineteenth-century millowner, in trying to estimate the profitability of his business, would be seeking to ascertain 'the *maximum* that could be *safely* taken out of the business...without damaging the prospects of the business. But that, it is clear, would be a matter of judgement'. He argues that, with the advent of the income tax, and of the joint-stock corporation, there are other parties now interested in knowing the business's profitability and 'at this point the accountant enters'.

Hicks observes that the accountant's approach needs to be as objective as possible to minimise disagreements; so it cannot measure profit in the way the mill-owner himself would think of it. According to Hicks, the accountant's approach naturally draws on the 'mercantile' tradition with which accountancy is already familiar, whereby the problem of sales and costs and inventory for each item of trade overlapping accounting period-ends can be relatively simply solved by carrying forward the inventory at cost. This, however, requires adaptation for industrialisation, as one has also to deal with plant and machinery and measure periodic cost of use. To Hicks: "It is just the same problem as the allocation of overheads, and to that, as is well known, there is no firm economic solution. Neither has the accountant found a solution—only a name and a set of, essentially arbitrary, rules. There is thus no reason why there should be any simple rule, which would cause the profits that are calculated by its use to have any correspondence with the income that would be assessed by the criterion with which we began—the maximum that can be safely taken out of the business".

Hicks then turns to exploring what the depreciation for a period (e.g. period 1) would be following this criterion. He is only able to do so by postulating a purchase of the whole business at time 0 and a sale of the whole business at time 1, to obtain an objective measure. However Hicks does not find a satisfactory, practical way of defining a business firm's income, whether *ex ante* or *ex post.*

Whatever the relation between asset/liability measures in accounting statements and Hicks's 'capital value', and whether or not 'Income No. 1 *ex post*' can be 'objective', there is however an even greater problem with the FASB/IASB (2005) paper's reliance on Hicks's concept as the bedrock of its approach to the conceptual framework. Hicks does concede some role for his 'Income No. 1 *ex post*': such calculations 'have their place in economic and statistical history; they are a useful measuring rod for economic progress; but they have no significance for conduct'.

However, it may be argued that one cannot expect to be able to predict the future and income *ex ante* without some knowledge based in past experience (e.g. as hypothesised in Friedman, 1957). Hicks discussed further the role of accounting here in a book review for the *Economic Journal* (Hicks, 1948). As explained by Brief (1982), with extensive quotations, Hicks here endorsed what he thought to be an important argument (buried in the compilation of miscellaneous articles, etc. constituting the book being reviewed), namely the importance of the underlying objectivity of the 'statistics' that the accounts record: hence the justification for historical cost and the dubious value of introducing subjective adjustments (e.g. to lower market value). So, for example, the bias introduced by historical cost in inflationary times is a matter for correction by users in their interpretation of the accounting numbers.

However, Hicks added his own observation that 'bare' statistics are never sufficient: so what is to be done for external shareholders? The accountant 'has thus some public obligation to pack into his figures the maximum of information even if he can only do this, within the limits prescribed, by some sacrifice of objectivity. How ought this difficulty to be got over? Should it be laid down that companies must publish an audited report as well as audited accounts? Or would this make the accountant, more than ever, master of the destinies of us all?' So the main issue with Income *ex post* is 'how much of the future is it useful to bring into accounts of the past if they are to be helpful in forming expectations about future Income *ex ante*? This must be primarily an empirical question, to which the answer may vary according to how far 'permanent' and 'transitory' elements can be distinguished, and according to different types of business activity; while also being subject to different users' needs and trade-offs of 'relevance' and reliability'. There is no necessary merit in simply tracking Hicks's 'Income No. 1 *ex post*'.

The FASB/IASB 2005 paper says that a concept of income founded ultimately on the definition of 'assets' is necessary because, among the proponents of the alternative (the 'revenue and expense') view, "none could meet the challenge' of defining 'income directly, without reference to assets or liabilities or recourse to highly subjective terminology like *proper matching*'. Hicks himself could 'meet the challenge'. Dissatisfied with his 'No. 1' version he had already offered 'Income No.2', defined as the amount that an entity can consume in a period and still expect to be able to consume the same amount in each ensuing period. In the case of a joint stock company this translates as 'the maximum dividend the company could pay this period to its current equity shareholders and expect to be able to be able to pay them the same dividend in all future periods', which is equivalent to what financial analysts call its 'maintainable (or 'permanent') income'.

It was this 'No.2' concept of income that underlay the proposals in the UK's Sandilands Report (1975) for 'current cost accounting'. Sandilands said: "no accounting system can predict a company's future prospects. However, an accounting system can at least ensure that the profit figure reported is such that, if the profit for the year were fully distributed, it would not prejudice the ability of the company to continue to generate the same profit in future years". Scott argues for the importance of assisting users to estimate '(real) standard stream income' (alongside 'gain') and, while critical of much of the methodology proposed by Sandilands, suggests ways in which accounts can be best adapted under changing prices to achieve this, many of which must inevitably be subjective. Scott concludes (drawing on his own experience as an investment Trustee for a charity): 'First, there is a strong practical need for estimates of standard stream income and, second, useful estimates can be provided—but not, so far, or perhaps ever, by accountants *qua* accountants'. This conclusion appears close to Hicks's (1948) view that adjustment to the basic historical cost accounting records should be made, as far as possible, by those using and interpreting the accounts, rather than within the accounts themselves.

Given the 'maintainable income' one can, under further restrictive assumptions, also derive definitions and measures of 'assets' and 'liabilities' that would be consistent with this concept, but they are to be derived from it, not it from them. Thus, more recently, Ohlson (2006) argues that investors like to have a natural starting point in the income statement as they try to forecast subsequent periods' sustainable earnings. This concept of sustainable earnings is again consistent with Hicks's (1946) 'No. 2 Income'. Ohlson argues that reporting such maintainable earnings would require that assets and liabilities be derived from income and not *vice versa* (as in his formulation of an 'accounting rule' for deriving a period's closing net operating assets and its periodic operating expense). However, it remains unclear how far Ohlson's resulting balance sheet figures would be subject to any 'reality check' (as his proposed system would prohibit immediate write-downs: they would be accounted for 'prospectively').

Ohlson's approach also takes as non-problematic 'fair value' accounting for financial assets and liabilities, but in fact the problem of changing interest rates (and risk) causes equal difficulty here, at least in a 'second best' world where not all values and changes in them can be captured in the accounts. So here too a 'Hicks No. 2' rather than a 'Hicks No. 1' approach may often be needed. Finally we may note that, given the conceptual tension between 'Income No. 1' (expressed in terms of capital value) and 'Income No. 2' (expressed in terms of maintainable income), there are also conceptual grounds for believing that the most relevant income concept for users and their economic decisions will often vary with their individual circumstances and conditions. Thus, someone facing a major expenditure (e.g. a family wedding or an unexpected, uninsured medical operation and hospitalization) would be concerned more about the effect of changes in the value of their wealth (No. 1); while someone facing retirement might be more concerned with how much maintainable pension they are entitled to or can obtain from their investments (No. 2). This insight can go a long way towards explaining why the underlying motivations of those who identify with the 'asset/liability' view and those who identify with the 'revenue/expense' (or 'matching') view are sometimes complementary, but are often seen as in opposition with regard to what is the most useful approach to measuring enterprise income in the context of individual accounting standards. Neither approach should therefore necessarily be preferred in principle over the other as the basis for accounting standard setting: in each case the relevant approach should be chosen on its merits in that context.

FASB/IASB (2005) sees the conceptual framework project as a crusade against conventions. 'To be principles-based, standards cannot be a collection of conventions but rather must be rooted in fundamental concepts.' Economists writing about accounting have generally been very respectful of accounting conventions. As noted above, Hicks argued that the accountant's solution to 'depreciation' was a natural development from merchandise accounting. He also credited the accountant's view of capital as a 'fund' with a profound influence on English Classical economists; and noted that Marshall seemed content with the accountants' approach to depreciation (Hicks, 1974). While more recent inflationary pressures and tax policy changes have put the conventions under great strain, as noted above Hicks appeared to believe that the necessary adjustments could best be made by those using and interpreting the accounts rather than by expecting reform of the accounts themselves. Indeed this could interfere with the underlying, objective statistical record (Hicks, 1948; Brief, 1982).

Kaldor too (1955) noted that 'the accountant is rightly in search therefore of a concept of income *ex post* which is as near a counterpart as can be found to the investor's income *ex ante*. In the light of the foregoing analysis, it is not surprising that the accountant's definition of income *ex post* is based, as it can only be based, on a series of admittedly arbitrary conventions whose value depends, to a large extent, on their status as time-honoured conventions—i.e. on their steady and consistent application.' There may of course also be value in 'sticking to agreed rules' for purposes of contractual and other 'settling up' such as taxation, bonuses, partners' profit shares, loan covenants, etc., where Lindahl's 'restatement with hindsight' would never allow closure. Similarly Solomons' (1989) *Guidelines* do not deal with this difficulty. That is not to say accounting conventions cannot be improved: the economists had perhaps an overindulgent view of accounting's achievements which may not be surprising given that they were generally writing before the advent of UK standards and the wider understanding of just how inconsistent many accounting practices are. But it is naïve of FASB/IASB to overlook the power of conventions, and their surrounding myths, in maintaining the ordinary fabric of social structure and interaction.

It is well known that in 1961 Solomons predicted the 'twilight' of income measurement within 25 years, but in 1989 was writing his *Guidelines* for the UK's Accounting Standards Board ('ASB') on how best to report it. Similarly Ohlson (1987), in his commentary on Beaver &Demski (1979), argued that the reporting of income is too embedded in accounting tradition to be abandoned, despite the inescapable conceptual limitations. So rather than pursue the FASB/IASB (2005) direction of seeking to replace 'conventions' with 'concepts' the focus should rather be on deepening understanding of how and why those conventions have emerged and thereby of how best to adapt them, where necessary, to new situations and purposes in the light of relevant conceptual considerations. While much of the academic discussion reviewed here, as well as the FASB/IASB (2005) paper itself, appears to recycle arguments from more than 50 years ago, there have been interesting recent practical developments in alternative ways of setting out 'income' and 'value' in accounting reports, given dissatisfaction with existing conventions. The most conspicuous of these at the present time is the developments in supplementary reporting of life insurance profitability according to a '(Market Consistent) Embedded Value' model which bears structural similarity to a 'Hicks No.1 *ex ante-ex post*' cycle. This emerging practice has been developed to overcome the severe limitations of the traditional approach in a new world, where there is extensive restructuring of financial institutions together with changes in both their market opportunities and in their regulation. But, as ASB has recognised, the new approach has potentially major implications for the conception of performance measurement and reporting in other industries. It is to such experiments and their consequences that standard setters should be looking to find a basis for improvement in their conceptual framework, rather than to further attempted refinement of concepts such as 'income' or 'assets'.

GROSS NATIONAL PRODUCT (GNP)

The gross national product is a basic social accounting measure of the total output or aggregate supply of goods and services. It is the total value of goods and services produced during a period, say, a year, at the market prices. Two things should be carefully noted in regard to GNP. In the first place, it is a monetary measure of the total goods and services produced during the period. There is no other way of adding up the heterogeneous types of goods and services. With a view to accurately measure the changes in physical output during different periods, the figures of gross national product are adjusted for price changes.

Secondly, in calculating gross national product, all goods and services produced during the period should be counted only once. Most of the goods pass through several processes of production before reaching the final market. Cotton, for instance, is spun into yarn which in turn is woven into cloth. Now while counting cloth in the GNP, we should be careful to avoid counting value of cotton which has gone into yarn and that of yarn which has gone into cloth. Similarly, if cloth is converted into ready-made garments and they are included in the GNP, we should avoid counting the value of cloth which has gone into the ready-made garments. Thus the GNP includes the market value of only final goods and ignores transactions involving intermediate goods, because the value of final goods includes the value of intermediate goods which have gone into their production.

The gross national product at market prices may be obtained by adding up the following:

(a) Expenditure of private persons on consumption or what is called personal consumption expenditure;

(b) Expenditure of business enterprises on replacement, renewal and new investment or what is called gross domestic private investment;

(c) Expenditure of the government on the purchase of goods and services, i.e., government purchase; and

(d) Expenditure of the rest of the world on the output of the national economy over and above what this economy spends on the output of the rest of the world, i.e. export surplus or net foreign investment.

The definition of GNP mentioned above assumes the existence of markets in which buyers are free to buy as much or as little as they desire, and in which the price is both a condition of supply and a reflection of the intensity of the buyer's desire for the commodity. But this is not true in case of some services, an important case being that of public services like education, external defence and the maintenance of internal law and order etc. Such services are normally provided without collecting a direct charge from the beneficiaries and cost of such services is met from the revenue of taxes, payment of which is compulsory, and whose amount in case of each citizen is not necessarily related to the value of the services rendered to him. It is not, therefore, possible to find out the market price of such services. As such their value can be measured only in terms of their cost. In the absence of evidence to the contrary, there is no alternative but to assume that the cost of provision of such services represents the value which the community attaches to these services.

A second case is that of owner-occupied houses, which obviously provide a service to the owner. Had the owners not owned those houses, they would have had to pay rent to others. Although no rent is paid in actual practice, the value of service can be assessed in money terms by assuming it to be equal to the rent paid by non-owning tenants who occupy houses of similar size and amenities. Logically, a similar procedure should be followed for all durable goods which are used by their owners, e.g., motor-cars, radios, television sets, etc. If a person hires a car on 'self-drive' terms, or rents a radio or a television set, the payment can be regarded as representing the value of the services rendered and counted as a part of the economy's production. The question arises why not count on a similar basis the imputed value of services yielded by cars and television sets used by their owners. This is, however, not done because of the obvious difficulties involved in calculating the imputed values.

A third case relates to the services rendered by housewives to their families. The housewives render valuable services by cooking, washing clothes, cleaning house, etc. Logically, these should be included in the aggregate output. Since the services of housewives are not sold in the free market for a wage, it is very difficult to impute proper money value to them. As such, the official statisticians normally do not take them into account.

There is further the difficulty of separating current from capital expenditure. The Department of Commerce of the United States arbitrarily defines as capital all expenditure on items that have a useful life of greater than one year. Before we can classify an expenditure as current or capital, we must know the life of the item for which the expenditure is being incurred. In case of many items, it is not possible to say with certainty as to whether or not their life will exceed one year till they are completely worn out. The Department of Commerce, for instance, excludes expenditure on repairs and maintenance from the definition of capital expenditure but some repairs may last for more than one year. In fact some of the Scandinavian countries use the concept of capital in a much broader sense than the United States. Maintenance of plant and machinery may considerably vary from period to period. There is a tendency to postpone repairs during periods of low profits and to catch up during periods of high profits when the firm can easily afford to spend on repairs and maintenance. The exclusion of maintenance and repairs from gross national product would underestimate true fluctuations in economic activity from prosperity to depression.

There also arises the problem of distinguishing between intermediate and final goods and services in regard to the services provided by the government. They may be considered as final products given to the economy or may partly represent intermediate products given to business firms. In both cases, since normally they are provided free of any charge, it is debatable as to whether or not they should be included at cost in the gross national product. Things like roads, conservation and information services provided by the government can be considered primarily as services consumed by producers in the process of their production. It could be argued that if business firms were required to directly pay for these services the market prices of the goods requiring such services would rise and as such these items should be included in gross national product at their cost. On the other hand, it could also be argued that business firms to pay for these services in the form of several taxes, or that the consumers would shift their choices to low-priced goods, if the cost of government services were included in the price of the goods and, therefore, the cost of government services should not be included. The normal practice, however, is to include in gross national product all government services valued at cost.

The GNP concept has the merit that it reflects more accurately than any derived statistical concept, the actual conditions of production and employment during the period in question. In this concept the total production in the current period is not underestimated as would be in a derived figure excluding replacement investment nor is the total employment, considered as function of total production, understated, as it would be if the number of those employed in producing the new capital goods destined to replace the old depreciated one were to be excluded from the calculation. Another advantage of the GNP concept is that it avoids many conceptual and statistical difficulties involved in estimating the value of capital consumed or depreciated as well as many arbitrary assumptions involved in reducing a product figure to an income figure. But the concept of GNP has also its weaknesses. The most important weakness is that it obscures the current net gain in production over and above the capital consumed and replaced. To conclude, the concept of GNP is particularly useful for the purpose of analysing national economic activity during a relatively short period, that is, for the type of analysis which proceeds by taking the physical stock of capital, technology and other fundamental conditions of supply as given.

VALUE ADDED

The Gross National Product can also be defined as the sum of 'values added' over a given period by the various branches of economic activity. This definition eliminates the problem of multiple counting. The increase in value which each sector imparts in the course of production to the materials which it uses as inputs is estimated. The sum of such increases in value for all sectors gives the value of Gross National Product. The economy is considered to be like a huge assembly line. At its starting point, agriculture and mining at home, and imports from abroad, provide primary materials. The primary products pass from one process to another until they emerge at the end in the final form of clothing, furniture, radios, machine tools and other durable instruments of production. Each process through which the materials pass adds to their value. The process need not necessarily be such as to change the form of the commodities. Transportation services, for instance, increase value of the commodities by carrying them from less to more convenient places without changing their form. Banks and other financial institutions, though not handling physical commodities, provide useful services which ease the process of production. Similar is the nature of services provided by the government and other public authorities. At each stage along the line, imports will be joining the stream of commodities emerging from anterior stages, and exports will be leaving the line instead of going on the next process.

The value added by a process to the commodities passing through it during a given period can be found by deducting the value of the inputs from the value of the products leaving the process. The sum of the values added by all the processes would give us the value of the gross national product.

The gross national product calculated by this method does not include the value of imports because the cost of imported materials is automatically deducted from the value of output of the industries using them. In computing value added, the value of stocks used in production is deducted from the value of products made from them; but the stocks accumulated during the period constitute a part of the current output which has not been sold by the end of the period.

To arrive at net national product, depreciation would have to be deducted from the sum of values added. In computing the value added, the value of the inputs of materials is deducted from the value of commodities at each stage of production. It is assumed that the materials are completely absorbed into the process to which they are submitted. But plant and machinery, which wears out partially and is not completely absorbed into the product, should also be treated as an input similar to the input of materials and accordingly deducted from the value of output.

The 'value added' method and the 'final products' method give the same results. While the former counts the flow of output past each process along the assembly line, the 'final products' method counts the quantity of commodities which are delivered at the end of the line during the given period, with appropriate adjustments for the goods still in transit at the beginning and the end of the period, and with a deduction to eliminate inputs of imported goods and services.

The 'value added' method is in accordance with the normal business accounting procedures because every firm must for its own purpose record the value of its output and value of materials used. The 'final products' method involves serious difficulties in that it requires a division of actual output into consumers' and producers' goods. Certain grades of coal, for instance, may be used by domestic consumers as well as the industry. It is difficult to say what part of coal output is to be classified as consumers' goods until it is actually in the possession of consumers. Motor-cars are mostly used by private consumers but a good number is also used for commercial purposes which would constitute producers' goods. Such examples can be easily multiplied. In fact, there are not many products whose entire output can confidently be put into one or the other of the two categories of goods. The only way to be sure whether or not a particular product is consumers' goods is to find out as to whether or not it is in fact bought by consumers. But this is a classification of expenditures rather than of products and since expenditures belong to a different side of the economy, they should not be included in an account which aims at estimating output.

In actual practice, however, it is very difficult to precisely estimate the depreciation during a particular period, say, a year. The depreciation during a year, for instance, can be calculated by dividing the value of equipment by the number of years of its life. But it is difficult to ascertain the life of equipment till it is finished. Further, if the price of the equipment rises over the year, there arises the problem as to whether it is the old or book value of the equipment or the current market price of that which is to be taken into account. Similarly, there arises a problem if the equipment becomes technically obsolete and has to be scrapped halfway through its previously expected life.

The major merit of the concept of Net National Product is that it clarifies the net increase in total production over and above current consumption and current replacement investment. Another merit lies in stressing the long-run significance of maintaining and improving the physical productivity of capital for economic growth.

It is these merits which make the NNP concept highly useful for the purposes of 'growth economics'.

RELATION BETWEEN NNP AT MARKET PRICES AND NATIONAL INCOME AT FACTOR COST

The difference between national income at factor cost and net national product arises because indirect taxes and subsidies cause market prices of output to be different from the factor incomes resulting therefrom. For illustration, suppose that the actual cost of production of a table is Rs. 40 which is the payment made to different factors of production as wages, rents interests and profits. The government imposes a tax of Rs. 10 on the production of a table. The table would obviously be sold in the market for Rs. 50. Thus the market value of this output is Rs. 50 while the income payments received by the different factors of production amount to Rs. 40 only. Similarly, if the government gives a subsidy of Rs. 10 on the production of a table, the market value of the table would be Rs. 30 while the income receipt of different factors of production would be Rs. 40. It follows, therefore, that the national income at factor cost is equal to net national product minus indirect taxes plus subsidies.

Sometimes the government also renders productive services and earns profits. Since these profits do not go to the factors of production as incomes and are appropriated by the government treasury, they must also be deducted from the net national product in order to obtain national income at factor cost. Thus,

National Income at Factor Cost = { Net National Product at Market Prices – Indirect Taxes + Subsidies – Profit earned by Government.

NATIONAL EXPENDITURE

Gross National Expenditure is the sum of all 'final' expenditures during a certain period by the residents of the country. It consists of consumers' expenditure (C), public authorities' current expenditure on goods and services (G), gross capital formation at home (I) and the difference between exports (E) and imports (M). When these expenditures are shown at market prices, it is necessary to deduct indirect taxes minus subsidies.

National expenditure is not the sum of all expenditures made in the country during a given period. To count not only consumers' expenditure on bread but also manufacturers' expenditure on wheat, wheat flour, fuel etc. would involve the problem of multiple counting similar to that we eliminated in the calculation of Gross National Product. It is, therefore, necessary to exclude all purchases which are 'intermediate' in the sense that they are offset, within the same period, by the release of commodities bought, either in their original or after processing and absorption into other commodities. Thus only those transactions would be counted which relate to purchases of final goods and services which do not change hands again during the same period. Some final commodities will be completely used up in consumption or in public authorities' activities. Others may take the form of stocks of semi-finished goods or of durable plant and machinery which has been bought during the period but has not yet been absorbed into the commodities produced with its aid. Expenditure on new equipment and on increasing stocks is known as capital formation.

There arises a question as to whether 'stocks of materials' consist of goods held at the input end of each process, such as raw jute in case of jute mills, or also of stocks of finished products which the mills have not yet sold. Obviously, the purchases of 'input' materials must be counted but it is difficult to understand how the 'output' stocks can be counted since they have not been purchased by anybody and, therefore, no expenditure has been incurred. Nevertheless, the normal practice is to count them by assuming that the firms themselves have bought their stocks of finished commodities.

The second question relates to depreciation of old machinery and plant bought in the past years. To the extent the value of old equipment, is being embodied in current output, it would require to be replaced, and the amount spent on replacement can be thought of as 'intermediate' expenditure. But because of the usual difficulties involved in distinguishing the part of capital expenditure devoted to replacement and that devoted to expansion of productive capacity, business expenditure on new equipment is generally given "gross of depreciation" and the National Expenditure estimated on this basis is called Gross National Expenditure.

All expenditure on goods and services and capital formation by consumers as well as by public authorities does not constitute National Expenditure because it also includes payments for imported commodities. The National Expenditure generally includes only that part of expenditure which is spent on national products. At the same time, the National Expenditure includes expenditure by foreigners on the goods and services produced by the country concerned.

RELATIONSHIP BETWEEN INCOME AND EXPENDITURE

There exists a close relationship between income (Y) and expenditure (E). Income is the major source for incurring expenditure and expenditure necessarily generates income. But while expenditure necessarily generates income, all income need not necessarily be spent. The total money expenditure is not necessarily restricted to the income received in the preceding period. The aggregate expenditure may exceed aggregate income in the preceding period as a result of activisation of past hoardings or as a result of borrowing from the banks. Similarly, aggregate expenditure may be less than the aggregate income in the preceding period because a part of the income is hoarded of being spent. Thus the expenditure can be more or less than the income of the previous period.

RELATIONSHIP BETWEEN OUTPUT AND EMPLOYMENT

The flow of goods and services which constitute the national product can be increased either by employing larger quantities of labour and capital or using the existing resources in a more efficient way through improvements in the methods of production. Improved methods of production are partly the result of chance discoveries and partly of sustained operational research which is a very slow process and whose outcome cannot be guaranteed in advance. Even when improved methods have been devised, it takes time to implement these at the factory level. The changes in methods of production, therefore, cannot be much depended upon for increasing production in the short period. Over a short period, the techniques of production must be taken as more or less fixed and an increase in production can be obtained by increasing input of labour or capital equipment or both.

Though an individual firm can increase its capital equipment quickly, this is not possible for the economy as a whole. Before the economy as a whole can expand its capital equipment, the machines must be produced, buildings must be constructed to house them, sources of power must be installed, and provision for various ancillary services must be made, which requires time. Thus when a substantial increase (say 12 percent) in production over a short period (say months) is under consideration, the total stock of capital equipment, like the techniques of production, must be taken more or less fixed.

Labour remains the only factor whose input can be increased rapidly. To attain a fast increase in production, more workers can be employed, or those already in employment can be asked to work longer hours or the two can be combined. Similarly, if output is to be decreased, some of the workers can be removed, or their hours of work can be reduced or both. Thus in the short period, during which techniques of production and the total stock of capital equipment are more or less fixed, changes in output are primarily attributed to the changes in the volume of labour employed.

An objection may, however, be raised that labour and capital are not being treated in the same manner. If the input of labour can be varied by the working of more or less man-hours, why can't the input of services of capital equipment be varied by use of more or less machine-hours? Fixed capital has been regarded as a stock of productive capacity. If labour is dealt with in the same manner, it would appear as a stock of 'labour power' rather than flow of services. Just as the country's total labour-power employed is measured by the number of man-hours worked, the stock of capital could be regarded as being used more or less intensively according to the number of machine-hours involved. Closing down the factory would be similar to the firing of a worker. According to this view, production will vary not only with the input of labour but with man-hours and machine hours taken together.

The above view is not entirely wrong but it does not invalidate our previous conclusion that, in the short period, the volume of output primarily depends on the input of labour. The capital equipment is owned by the enterprises and they have to bear its cost of maintenance whether or not it is put to use. In contrast, the labourers are not owned by them and they can hire as much labour as they desire within the limits of what is available. Neither the owners of capital equipment nor the owners of labour-power would like to allow their resources to remain unutilised. But since the control of production is in the hands of the owners of capital equipment they would make every effort to make utmost use of their equipment as possible, even when they have decided to decrease production, by employing less labour and spreading it thinly over all the available equipment. In such a situation, output per worker may be fairly low because the volume of labour is too small to take the best advantage of the available equipment. If more man-hours are worked, output will increase in greater proportion because it will lead to a better utilisation of the equipment. If the input of labour is further increased so that the plant has to work above its capacity, the output would still increase but the increase will not be in proportion to the increase in man-hours. Finally, a stage would be reached at which further additions of labour would not lead to any increase in output at all. This sequence exemplifies the 'law of variable proportions', according to which successive additions of one factor of production to fixed quantities of other factors will lead to first increasing, then constant, then diminishing and finally zero marginal returns.

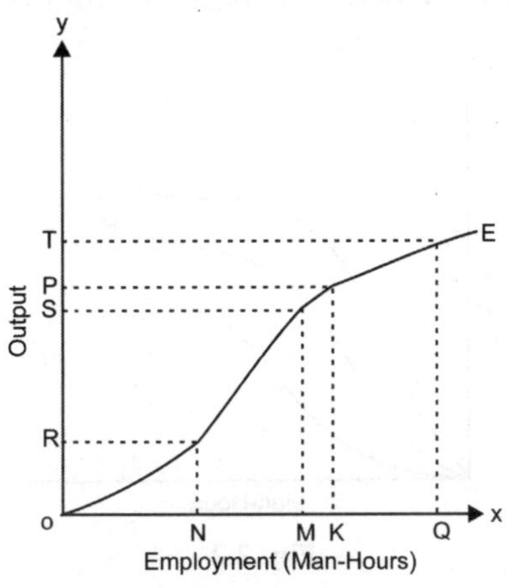

Fig. 2.1

In Fig. 2.1 the curve OE represents the relation between employment and output. At a low level of employment, say at ON, the output is small, that is, OR; at this level of employment, output per man-hour is OR/ON. As the volume of employment increases to OM, output rises to OS, and the proportionate increase in output is obviously greater than the proportionate increase in employment i.e. $\frac{RS}{OR} > \frac{NM}{ON}$. At this level of employment, output per man-hour is OS/OM and obviously exceeds OR/ON. If the employment further increases to OQ, the output rises to OT, and the proportionate increase in output is smaller than the proportionate increase in employment i.e. $\frac{ST}{OR} < \frac{MO}{OM}$. At this level of employment, output per man-hour has declined to $\frac{OT}{OQ}$ which is smaller than $\frac{OS}{OM}$. The flattening of the OE curve as it moves towards right indicates that input of additional man-hours will increase output by smaller and smaller amounts. Since the amount of capital equipment is fixed, only at one point the labour and capital will be in their most productive relationship, or in other words, only at one point the output per man-hour would be maximum; this point is represented at K. Where the volume of employment is less than OK, the number of man-hours is too small to make the best use of the available equipment; where more than OK man-hours are worked, the plant becomes inadequate to take the best advantage of the employed man-power.

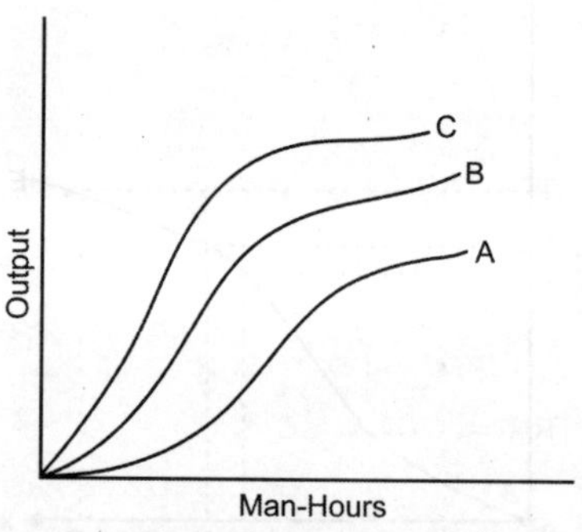

Fig. 2.2

If the time perspective were lengthened beyond the short period, it would be necessary to take into account the possible changes in the economy's stock of capital equipment and its techniques of production. This would give rise to a whole family of curves as shown in Fig. 2.2. Each curve shows the employment-output relationship for a given stock of capital equipment and given techniques of production. The larger the amount of capital equipment and the better the techniques of production, the higher would be the curve.

MEASUREMENT OF NATIONAL INCOME

The concept of national income, as seen above, has three interpretations. It represents a receipts total, it represents an expenditure total and it represents a total value of production. Thus three-fold interpretation arises; and if the goods and services bought are valued received equals the value paid, both of which equal the value of goods and services exchanged. Corresponding to this three-fold interpretation of income, there are three methods of measuring national income viz. (i) Product method, (ii) Income method, and (iii) Expenditure method.

Product Method

This method is also known as 'Inventory Method' or 'Commodity Service Method'. Under this method, the value of the gross product (sales + self-consumption + increase in stocks) of all the producers in an industry is summed up and from this total are deducted the purchases of these producers from other producers (i.e. value of intermediate products), and the depreciation of equipment involved in the process of production. This gives the net value contributed by these producers to the net value of aggregate national output. Such an estimate is made for each industry. The sum of all these estimates gives the net domestic product at factor cost classified by industrial origin. The addition of net income from abroad to this total gives net national product or national income at factor cost.

To measure national income by this method, we should consider the following points:

(a) We include only final products in the estimation of national income. We exclude intermediate products. Otherwise, there will be double counting. On way to avoid this problem of double counting is the value added method. In the value added method, we consider the value at each stage of production and add them up. This method will give us the value of the final products.

(b) Inventories i.e., unsold stocks of goods are to be valued at the existing market price and included in the national income.

(c) Services of owner-occupied houses are to be evaluated on the basis of imputed rents and these rents should be included in GNP.

(d) The values of household services rendered by the members of the family is not included in the GNP. But the value of services rendered by paid workers in the household sector is to be included. Wages paid to such workers are taken as the value of such services.

(e) Goods consumed by the producers themselves should be included in national income.

(f) The values of the services of self-employed persons are to be included in GNP.

(g) The cost of provision of public services, such as, defence, police, medical, education, etc. should be included in GNP.

In this way, in the product method, the problems of valuation of non-marketed goods are overcome. The money value of all final goods and services produced during the year are taken. By adding them, GNP of the country is obtained. We get NNP or national income by substracting depreciation of capital from GNP.

Income Method

Under this method, all incomes accruing to the various factors of production are added. This gives the national income classified by distributive shares as specified by the following equation:

$$Y = W + R + I + P \quad \text{...(2.10)}$$

where,

Y = National income,

W = Total wages before tax,

R = Total Rents,

I = Total Interest, and

P = Total Profits.

Thus, national income is the sum total of all wages, all rental payments, all interest payments and all profits in the economy during a year. The idea behind income received approach is that every earner in the society is the owner of at least one factor of production for which he receives payment—Wage is the reward for labour. Rent is the payment for the use of land. Interest is the payment for capital. Profits are the residual income for entrepreneurs. Thus, if we add the income payments of all the four kinds, we will arrive at an estimate of national income.

In modern times, profit accrues to business firms and companies. These firms retain a part of total profits which they may use for further investment in the next period. The other part of the profit is distributed among the shareholders and is known as distributed profits or dividends.

This is shown in the following equation

$$P = P_r + P_d \quad ...(2.11)$$

where,

P = Total Profits,

P_r = Retained Profits,

P_d = Distributed Profits or Dividends.

Substituting equation (2.11) into equation (2.10), we get

$$Y = W + R + I + P_r + P_d \quad ...(2.12)$$

which shows that both retained profits and distributed profits are included in national income. However, we must note carefully, that national income is not the amount of income which is available to the individuals of a country for spending. The income which is available for spending is called disposable income and is defined below.

$$Y_d = Y - P_r - T_x + T_r \quad ...(2.13)$$

where,

Y_d = Disposable Income,

Y = National Income,

P_r = Retained Profits,

T_x = Taxes,

T_r = Transfer Payments.

Disposable income as explained above is a measure of maximum purchasing power of household. This is the income which is available for spending. Since retained profits lie with the firms and are not distributed they are subtracted from national income. Next thing to be deducted is the tax paid to the government. Taxes which are paid to the government by the individuals and business firms constitute government income. They are included in national income as will be shown below but are excluded from disposable income. However, government pays some amount to individuals as old age pensions, scholarships, help to poors and unemployment compensations, etc. These types of payments are called transfer payments because they transfer income from government to the individuals. Since individuals are at liberty to spend this income also, transfer payments are also included in disposable income.

The composition of disposable income shall become clear if we substitute equation (2.12) into equation (2.13)

$$Y_d = W + R + I + P_d - T_x + T_r \qquad ...(2.14)$$

Equation (2.14) states that disposable income is the total of wages, rents, interest, dividends, and transfer payments minus total taxes.

There is another way to look at it. We can define net taxes imposed by the government as a difference between total tax revenue and transfer payment.

$$T = T_x + T_r \qquad ...(2.15)$$

where,

T = Net Taxes,

T_x = Total Tax Revenue, and

T_r = Total Transfer Payment.

New disposable income can be viewed as

$$Y_d = Y - P_r - T \qquad ...(2.16)$$

Equation (2.16) states that disposable income is obtained after deducting retained profits and net taxes from the GNP.

Alternatively, the GNP can be viewed as

$$Y = Y_d + P_r + T \qquad ...(2.17)$$

which tells that GNP is the sum total of disposable income, retained profits and net taxes. From the point of view of use, the disposable income has only two possible uses. Either it may be spent on consumption or it may be saved. From a macro point of view, it is more likely that a part of disposable income will be spent upon consumption and other part of it will be saved. This can be shown as follows:

$$Y_d = C + S \qquad ...(2.18)$$

where,

Y_d = Disposable Income,

C = Consumption Expenditure, and

S = Saving.

Substituting equation (2.18) into equation (2.17), the GNP can be seen as

$$Y = C + S + P_r + T \qquad ...(2.19)$$

where a part of GNP is shown as expenditure on the right hand side which takes us to expenditure approach for the estimation of national income.

Expenditure Method

Under this method, we obtain 'gross national product at market prices' by adding up personal consumption expenditures, gross private domestic investment, net foreign investment and government purchases of goods and services.

The basic idea behind expenditure approach towards the estimation of national income is that total expenditure and total income would be the same for economy as a whole. Thus, an estimate of national expenditure would also be an estimate of national income. It may be possible for individuals to spend more than what they earn but it is not possible for the whole economy to do so. Imagine a simple economy with only two members—A and B. Suppose A and B earn one thousand rupees each and spend the whole of it without saving anything. Thus, national income as well as national expenditure of this simple economy would be the same Rs. 2000. However, if B spends Rs. 1500 and he borrows Rs. 500 from A then A's spending will be reduced by Rs. 500. Thus, A in the new situations, will spend Rs. 500 and B will spend Rs. 1500. Their total expenditure is still Rs. 2000 which is equal to their total income. Thus, the national expenditure of any economy is by definition equal to its national income.

The society spends a major part of its income upon satisfying consumption needs such as food, clothing, shelters, entertainment etc. The expenditure on such items is called consumption expenditure and is a major component of national expenditure. The other most important component of national expenditure is investment expenditure. This is that part of expenditure which is incurred upon production, upon buying land, machinery, and raw materials, etc. So that production of goods and services as well as the production of more machinery etc. may be carried out. Here only net investment is counted because gross investment is component of GNP. Therefore, depreciation is not included in national income.

The total of consumption and investment expenditure by private individuals may be called private expenditure. But government also incurs some expenditure. First of all, this government has to buy different types of goods for its own consumption from the private economy, e.g., government buys paper for use in its offices, cloth to provide uniform to its soldiers and police, etc. It also buys services of individuals who could run the administration, etc. Sometime, the government undertakes production also and makes investment expenditure. Thus, total government expenditure can be looked as:

$$G = G_c + G_i \qquad ...(2.20)$$

where,

G = Total Government Expenditure,

G_c = Government's Consumption, and

G_i = Government's Investment.

Thus, it is conceptually possible to distinguish between government's consumption and government's investment. However, to keep the analysis simple, we shall not make this distinction in this book and treat all government expenditure together.

A society not only produces goods and machines for its own use but also for sale to other countries. The amount of goods, services, and machines, which are sold to other countries by one country is called export. All exports transfer goods and services from producing country to the buying country and money income from buying country to producing country. Thus, exports raises a country's national income. However, the country may also have to buy goods, services, and machines etc. from other countries. Such purchases are called imports. Imports bring in goods and services in the buying country and transfer money income from buying country to the selling country. Thus, net increase in income by exports can be known only if we subtract import from it. Suppose that we denote exports by the symbol X, and imports by the symbol M, then (X – M) would represent net exports. If exports are greater than imports, then net exports would be positive and it would raise income. However, if exports are greater than exports then net exports (X – M) would be negative and it would cause income to decline. Thus, expenditure approach can be summarized in the following equation:

$$Y = C + I + G + X - M \qquad ...(2.21)$$

where,

Y = National Income = National Expenditure,
C = Consumption Expenditure,
I = Investment Expenditure,
G = Government Expenditure,
X = Earning from Exports,
M = Expenditure on Imports, and
X – M = Net Exports.

In the theoretical model of macro-economic activities we shall make the following assumptions:

(a) Retained profits are zero. In other words, it shall be assumed that all profits are distributed in the form of dividend. This assumption is necessary to investigate the investment behaviour of the private firms.

(b) We also assume closed economy. This assumption does not mean that there is no foreign trade. There is foreign trade but we only assume that net exports (X – M) are zero, which means exports and imports all just equal to each other.

$$X = M \qquad ...(2.22)$$

Thus, in effect, we are assuming that foreign trade sector have no influence upon our economy. Thus, we abstract from the problems of balance of payment, exchange rate and money and other problems which are studied in international economics.

SOCIAL ACCOUNTING

Accounts maintained by private individuals are called "Private Accounting." Similarly, the accounts for the entire economy are known as "Social Accounting." Thus social accounting refers to that part of the descriptive economics which relates the production and distribution of national income. It is concerned with the statistical classification of the activities of human beings and human institutions in ways which help us to understand the operation of the economy as a whole. It helps us to understand how the entire economic system works and what are the relationships among the various sectors of the economy. Social accounts reflect changes in the health of the economy. They indicate fluctuations in economic activity and the performance of the economy. They help us in assessing the impact of government policy on various sectors. They also help us in knowing about the distribution of income among the various classes. Proper maintenance of detailed social or national accounts is very essential for having an idea of economic progress in different sectors and sub-sectors of an economy. Social accounts are helpful in comparing the prosperity, past and present, of nations, and of the various groups of persons and institutions comprising nations. In recent years they have been used for forecasting changes in the economic state of nations and in assessing the more probable economic consequences of government action.

Social or national accounts refer to a number of bodies of systematically arranged data, which have as their focus the economic activities taking place within a nation. The major five such bodies of data, treating different aspects of the nation's economic activity, are:

(i) *National Income and Product Accounts.* In their simplest forms, national income accounts are no more than measurements of production, consumption and investment arranged in such a way as to emphasize the distinction between the decisions of people concerned with, the consumption of what has been produced. They are a statistical statement of national output or receipts, e.g. gross national product, net national product, personal income and disposable income. These accounts include consolidated business income and product account, personal income and expenditure account, rest of the world account, and gross savings and investment account.

(ii) *Input-Output Tables.* They are concerned with the current productive activity of the economy and focus attention on inter-industry relationships. They are also known as inter-industry analysis. It is a detailed and systematic analysis of the inter-relationship between an industry's or an economy's output of goods and services and the volume of goods and services required to attain a given volume of production. It shows the flow of goods and services represented by their money value during a given period (say a year) between different sectors (generally known as industry).

(iii) *Flow of Funds Statements.* They cover all money and credit transactions in the economy. They contain information on the creation of bank credit, the purchase of securities and other changes in the assets and liabilities of the different sectors of the economy, as well as on payments and receipts of income.

(iv) *Balance of Payments Tables.* They show foreign trade statistics by country of origin and destination of the commodity, as well as foreign financial transactions.

(v) *National Balance Sheet.* It shows the assets and liabilities of the different sectors of the economy. The assets included are both tangible and intangible. While the flow of funds statements deal with flows, the national balance sheet deals with stocks.

Sectoral Breakdown in Social Accounting

National income estimates for social accounting can be presented in several ways. One of such ways is to divide the economy in four sectors, namely: (i) personal (household and institution) sector, (ii) business sector, (iii) government sector, and (iv) foreign (rest-of-the-world) sector. We have already seen that gross national product at market prices can be obtained by adding up the following: (i) expenditure of private persons on consumption or what is called personal consumption expenditure, (ii) expenditure of business enterprises on replacement, renewal and new investment or what is called gross domestic private investment, (iii) expenditure of government on purchase of goods and services, i.e., government purchase, and (iv) expenditure of the rest of the world on the output of the national economy over and above what this economy spends on the output of the rest of the world, i.e., export surplus or net foreign investment.

Personal Sector. This sector considers income and product originating not only in the households in the usual sense of the terms but also the income and product originating in non-profit institutions such as schools, colleges and hospitals, voluntary associations like temples, clubs and 'funds' like the Red Cross; trust funds benefiting consumers and private pension and welfare funds. When an institution—say a hospital—pays wages and buys supplies, these are considered as personal expenditure. The charges made by a private non-profit hospital and the donations received by it from private households to meet its deficits are considered as interpersonal transfers and, therefore, are not incorporated in the account. Gifts from business concerns will, however, be shown as business transfer payments. Similarly, the payments made by a private pension or welfare funds to its beneficiaries are treated as interpersonal transfers and not shown in the account. The payment made by an employer into the funds, however, is treated as personal income (supplements to wages and salaries). Similarly, the interest earned by the funds on its investments is treated as personal income. Table 2.1 shows the form of personal income and outlay account.

Table 2.1: Personal Income and Outlay Account

Personal consumption expenditures:	Wages, salaries, and Supplements from:
Purchases from business	business
Wages, salaries, and supplements	government
Purchases abroad	households
Interest paid	abroad
Personal taxes	less: employee and employer social insurance contributions.
Personal saving	Rental income of persons
	Proprietor's income:
	business and professional farm
	Dividends
	Personal interest income
	Government transfer payments
	Business transfer payments
Personal Outlay and Saving (total)	Personal Income (total)

In personal sector, there is no two-fold measurement in terms of both product and cost, as in case of business sector account shown below. This is because there is no transaction representing the sale of a product of a teacher employed by a private non-profit school or of a doctor employed by a charitable hospital and their product is measured by the wages received by them.

Business Sector. The business sector is defined to include in addition to corporate enterprise, all organisations producing goods and services sold at a price intended to cover at least the cost of production. The definition is broad enough to include government enterprises. It also includes unincorporated business enterprises like family businesses farm operators, independent professional practitioners, lessors of real property etc. Table 2.2 shows the income and product account for the business sector.

It is clear from Table 2.2 that for business sector gross national product equals national income plus certain 'adjustment' and plus depreciation. Or net national product equals national income plus the adjustments.

Table 2.2: Business Income and Product Account

National income originating in business:	Consolidated net sales:
Compensation of employee	to persons
Wages and salaries	to government
Supplements*	to abroad
Net interest	to business on capital account
Net dividends	Increase in inventories
Corporate profits tax liability	
Proprietors' income	
Rental income of persons	
Adjustments to market price	
Indirect business tax liability**	
Business transfer payment***	
Current surplus of government enterprises	
Less: subsidies	
Net national product originating in business (sub-total)	
Depreciation	
Charges against business gross (Total)	Business gross product (Total)

* Supplements include employer's contribution to social insurance, employer's contributions to private pension and welfare funds, and miscellaneous kinds of 'other labour income'.

** All business taxes not based upon business profits. This includes, of course, all real estate taxes, even those paid by owner-occupants. All included are minor non-tax liabilities.

*** Includes bad debts inter-business bad debts out; this leaves net bad debts by persons to business, charitable contributions by business prizes, etc.

Government Sector. The national product and income originating in government sector can be presented by a simple statement of government receipts and expenditures which is shown in Table 2.3.

Table 2.3: Government Receipt and Expenditure Accounts

Purchases of goods and services:	Taxes:
from business	personal tax receipts
from abroad	corporate profits tax accruals
Transfer payments:	Contributions for social insurance:
to persons	
foreign	employer
Net interest paid	personal
Subsidies	
Less: current surplus of government enterprises	
Surplus or deficit (–) on income and product account	
Government outlays and surplus (total)	Government receipts (total)

The above is a consolidated statement, netting out all transactions among various levels of the government. Similarly, the social insurance funds are consolidated with other government accounts. The statement excludes all transactions in existing assets like government purchase or sale of land or buildings. The account also excludes government lending transactions as well as the current accounts of government enterprises. The purchases of capital goods by the government enterprises and the interest payments on any obligations of these enterprises are, however, included in the general government budget on the expenditure side. The current surplus of these enterprises forms a source of government revenues. It is, however, shown as a negative item on the expenditure side, instead.

Foreign Sector. Some of the income and product originating in a country say India accrues to foreigners who own the factors of production located in India. Similarly, some of the income originating abroad accrues to Indian residents who own the factors or production located in foreign countries. Income and product originating in the rest of the world sector is defined as the net foreign investment from the India side. Table 2.4 shows the foreign sector accounts.

Table 2.4: Rest-of-World Account

Net purchase of factor services (by rest-of world from India)	Net disinvestment (by rest of-world) in India
Wages and salaries	Transfer payments from Indian government
Interest	
Dividends	
Branch profits	
Net purchases from (Indian) business	
Net purchases from (Indian) government	
Net purchases from (Indian) households	
Net current payments to India (Total)	Sources of net current (Total)

Combining Four Sector Accounts. By combining the accounts in the four sectors, we can obtain the total national income. From business sector we have wages, salaries, and supplements; net interest; corporate profits, income of unincorporated enterprises, and rental income of persons. To this we add the wages, salaries, and supplements earned in government, and the same items earned in households, plus household interest payments. We further add net factor earnings from the rest-of-world sector.

Similarly, we can obtain the total national product by combining the sector national products. The gross national product tabulated by sector of origin is shown below:

(i) Household output:
- (a) wages, salaries, and supplements
- (b) interest paid

(ii) Business output:
- (a) sales to consumers
- (b) sales to government
- (c) net sales abroad
- (d) sales to business on capital account
- (e) change in inventories

(iii) Government output:
- (a) wages, salaries and supplements

(iv) Rest-of-world output:
- (a) wages and salaries
- (b) interest
- (c) dividends
- (d) branch profits.

The above breakdown of national product is not, however, the more useful for analytical purposes. We, therefore, generally rearrange these items into a tabulation of gross national product by type of expenditure, as is shown below:

(i) Consumer expenditures
- (a) on business products
- (b) on household services
- (c) on imports

(ii) Government expenditures
- (a) purchases from business
- (b) purchases from abroad
- (c) wages, salaries and supplements

(iii) Gross private domestic investment
- (i) sales to business on capital account
- (ii) change in inventories

(iv) Net exports of goods and services.

DIFFICULTIES IN THE MEASUREMENT OF NATIONAL INCOME

Measurement of national income involves certain conceptual and statistical difficulties. A few years ago, when the national income studies were not extensive, the difficulties were numerous. But in recent years some of the conceptual problems have been successfully solved. Simon Kuznets mentions the following theoretical or conceptual difficulties in the estimation of national income:

(a) The definition of the term 'nation' as such in national income.

(b) The method to be used in the measurement of national income.

(c) The stage of economic activity at which national income should be measured.

(d) The type of goods and services which the national income should include.

The first three of these difficulties have been resolved to a large extent. It is now generally agreed among economists that the concept 'nation' in national income measurement does not mean country as such and the national income is not restricted to income produced within the territorial boundaries of a country. The concept of national income cuts across political boundaries and includes, in addition to income produced within territorial boundaries of the country concerned, income earned by its nationals abroad by way of interest, banking, insurance, shipping charges, etc. minus any such payments made to foreigners. This broad definition of the concept of 'nation' is now accepted by all economists.

The second problem relating to the choice between methods to be adopted for measuring national income has also been resolved. It is now generally believed that anyone or all of them should be used simultaneously depending upon the availability of relevant data.

In regard to the third problem, there exists common consensus that any stage of economic activity—production, consumption, or distribution—may be adopted depending upon the purpose of measurement of national income. If the purpose of measuring the national income is to assess the economic strength and potentiality of an economy, the production stage would be more suitable. If the objective is to assess the economic welfare of individuals as reflected by their incomes consumed, it would be better to adopt the consumption stage.

The problem which has not been successfully resolved is the fourth one which relates to the type of goods and services to be included in the national income. The problem particularly relates to the goods and services which are not exchanged against money, e.g. services rendered by housewives, owner-occupied houses. Since we have already discussed this problem in detail earlier, we will not dwell on it here any further.

The fifth difficulty relates to the problem of avoiding double or multiple counting in the calculation of national income. This problem has also been discussed above.

The sixth problem to the transfer payments, which is connected with the measurement of national income by income method. All transfer payments must be excluded from national income because they simply represent redistribution of income and not accrual of income as such. For instance, a person may earn an income of Rs. 50,000 and out of it pay Rs. 10,000 as income-tax to the government. It would be double counting if we include in national income the individual's income of Rs. 50,000 and also government's income of Rs. 10,000. Thus all transfers of money between different persons, or groups of persons should be excluded from national income. This can best be done by taking into account only disposable incomes.

The seventh problem relates to the income generated by forcing firms. Is this income to be included in the national income of the country in which they are located or in that of the country which owns them? In this connection, the I.M.F.'s suggestion is that the income flowing from foreign firms should be ascribed to the country in which the production takes place but the profits earned by the foreign firms should be credited to their parent concerns.

The eighth problem relates to the value of services rendered by the government. This problem has also been discussed above.

DIFFICULTIES IN MEASUREMENT OF NATIONAL INCOME IN UNDERDEVELOPED COUNTRIES

The underdeveloped countries are characterised a marked degree of self-sufficiency in households. As such a considerable portion of their produce is consumed within the family and does not come to the market. This is particularly true of the small farmers who grow just enough for their family. A further portion of the produce is exchanged on barter basis without the introduction of money. It is very difficult to make a fairly reliable estimate of the value of the produce that is consumed within the family or exchanged on barter basis. This difficulty is particularly marked in the agricultural sector.

A large number of producers are illiterate and do not follow the practice of keeping regular accounts. The national income statistician, therefore, finds it difficult to get reliable information from them.

It is difficult to estimate national income by industrial origin because people lack specialisation of functions and occupational classification is not scientific. Many persons simultaneously engage in several economic activities. A farmer, for instance, may engage himself in some manufacturing business at home or take employment in a factory during the slack season in agriculture.

There is a general lack of statistical data which adds to the difficulties involved in estimating national income.

IMPORTANCE OF NATIONAL INCOME STATISTICS

National income statistics are a valuable instrument of economic analysis and a guide to economic policy. The emergence of planning and state intervention have further added to their value. A knowledge of national income trends is very essential for forming a realistic plan. National income statistics give us an idea about the structure of the economy. They throw light on the relative importance of various sectors in the economy. They help us in knowing about the distribution of incomes among the various classes. They indicate the manner in which national expenditure is divided between consumption expenditure and investment expenditure. This enables us to know whether or not reasonable provision is being made for depreciation to maintain the capital stock of a community. This also indicates the rate at which the economy would grow. The national income statistics help the government in knowing whether the economy or any of its sectors need any stimulus or regulation or control. They help in assessing the impact of government policy on various sectors. They help us in comparing the standard of living of people in different countries and at different times in the same country. They help in determining equitable contributions of different member countries towards the expenditure of international organisations like the United Nations International Monetary Fund and International Bank for Reconstruction and Development.

NATIONAL INCOME AS AN INDEX OF WELFARE: CONTROVERSIAL ISSUES

Generally, national income of a country is regarded as an index of welfare. According to Haberler, other things being equal, higher the level of national income, higher will be the level of welfare. But this idea has been now changed and put into question. That is why, national income is not a good measure of welfare for the following reasons:

(a) GNP includes final output valued at market prices. But the services which are not valued at market prices, such as, service of a housewife, mother, sister, leisure, etc. are not considered as part of national income. But these affect welfare.

(b) Distribution of wealth and income, stabilization of government, etc. are the factors which contribute to economic welfare. But these factors are not considered in national income. That is why, national income of a country is high, but her total welfare may less.

(c) There are some social costs of industrialization, such as, air pollution, industrial disease, etc. These social costs reduce social welfare. Higher industrial output implies higher national income and higher welfare. At the same time, it implies more social cost and hence less welfare. Thus, more output does not necessarily imply more welfare.

(d) If people have been forced to work against their will to increase national output, we cannot say that the welfare of the economy has increased with the increase in output.

For all these above reasons, GNP of an economy does not give a true welfare index. To make GNP a good welfare index Samuelson has suggested some modifications' in GNP measure. He has given a new concept called Net Economic Welfare (NEW) which takes into account all the major factors affecting welfare. For example, leisure should be counted as one which contributes to welfare and air-pollution as one which should be subtracted from GNP to get the value of NEW.

In the measure of economic welfare, William Nordhaus and James Tobin have also evolved a new concept called Measure of Economic Welfare (MEW). It is similar to Semuelson's NEW. They have classified some items as regrettables and some items as intermediaries. Regrettables items are those items which have no direct utility but may be regrettably necessary and are counted as final products and included in GNP. These items should be excluded from the Measure of Economic Welfare (MEW). Intermediaries items are those items such as, defence, diplomacy, etc. which do not directly contribute to welfare.

If these modifications are made, national income may serve as an index of welfare.

CONTROVERSIES AMONG MODERN MONETARY THEORIES AND NATIONAL ACCOUNTING

Recent developments in monetary theory offer great challenges to national accounting. Some monetary theories, those based fundamentally on the quantity theory of money, assert that changes in 'costless' fiat money cannot have effects on such real phenomenon as the distribution of national income. Yet, as national balance sheets and wealth accounts show, outside fiat monies is becoming increasingly marginal.

National income reflects differences in the underlying classical, neoclassical and Keynesian theories. Keynesian models of unemployment rest upon the empirical and theoretical unimportance of outside or fiat money. Friedman argues, against the Keynesian position, that with real capital gains (losses) accruing to holders of money because of Keynesian disequilibria, real national income will tend to equilibrate at classical economic levels. Thus, if prices are falling because of unemployment, then according to Friedman the real income of people, holding given nominal amounts of outside fiat money, will be positive, and will rise faster and faster and become bigger and bigger the more quickly prices fall, thus causing the unemployment to vanish. As monetary economies are characterized with less and less outside or fiat money, the less and less important is the Friedman counter to Keynes. The question which must be asked is: Is it meaningful to introduce capital gains and losses associated with deflations and inflations and the holding of fiat money into national income revaluation accounts when under modern monetary and central banking theory, such holdings, at least in the form of reserves with central banks, are vanishing?

The basic problem is that current national accounts is that we do not have meaningful measures of the output of private banks nor, even more importantly, of the output of central banks. Since the banks are the principal purveyors of transactions services, and therefore affect monetary production technologies, it follows that the inability of the national accounts to arrive at satisfactory measures of the output of banks means that they cannot measure satisfactorily production in monetary economies. Thus, though one of the central questions dividing Keynesian and neoclassical analyses and the effects of monetary developments on the concepts and measures of national income cannot be currently understood using the current national income accounts, even deeper questions emerge.

Disregarding how macroeconomic aggregates are constructed and their structural definitional problems, what we know about the behaviour of macroeconomic variables is just our understanding from empiricism and we have rarely found the laws of the interrelationship among macroeconomic variables. Perhaps it can be said that Fisher's original quantity theory of money is just our main progress at macroeconomics. He tries to express equilibrium rather than going through supply and demand. Disregarding the definition of aggregate and sub-aggregate variables, national income accounting and identities among total income and total expenditures and total production is an elegant theoretical base for macroeconomic analysis. It seems that to improve macroeconomic theories and policies we need redirect researches to basic philosophical thinking about macroeconomic theoretical foundation and try to rebuild a new concrete base for macroeconomics.

Classical Theory of Employment

3

The role of theory in economics can be summarised in the following three statements:

(a) The purpose of a theory is to understand the world better. It is built on the critical variables that explain and predict the phenomenon under consideration.

(b) The process of focusing on a limited number of variables to explain or predict an event is called abstraction.

(c) A theory is better judged by its prediction than by its assumptions.

All theories are abstract and all theories make assumptions, and it is better to judge a theory by how well it predicts than by its assumptions, level of abstraction, or anything else. Theories have names, or labels. Four macroeconomic theories or schools of thought are called classical, Keynesian, monetarist, and new classical.

In this chapter, we present the classical theory as it relates to unemployment and production. The classical economics view of how our economy behaves is this: If the economy were left on its own—without the interference of government—it would move toward an equilibrium rate of growth that would produce, with only minor interruptions, full employment without inflation. This discussion is important for three reasons:

(a) First, it gives us knowledge of an important school of economics, the classical school. The term classical economics was applied to a school of economic thought that began with Adam Smith's writing of the Wealth of Nations in 1776. Interestingly enough, the creator of the term was Marx, and it was further perpetuated by John Maynard Keynes in his General Theory. The classical school of economic thought was the dominant school of thought until the time of the great depression. Some of the most famous economists of the classical school include Adam Smith, Jean Baptiste Say, David Ricardo, W. Jevons, John Stuart Mill, Professor Pigou, and Alfred Marshall.

(b) Second, classical theory provides the backdrop for the development of Keynesian theory.

(c) Third, classical theory makes up a large part of the intellectual heritage of monetarism and the new classical school of economics. Neither development can be fully understood without knowing something about the classical theory on which they are based.

The classical theory assumes that the economy is always close to or on its production possibilities frontier. This means that the economy is always close to or at the point of producing natural real GNP or the full-employment real GNP. Another way to say this is that the economy is always on or near its long run average supply curve.

The economy is always close to or at full employment, or the natural unemployment rate. This follows from the above statement, since if the economy is producing natural real GNP, it does so at the natural unemployment rate. And whatever real GNP is produced and supplied will be demanded.

Overall, the classical economists believed that the economy is a self-adjusting mechanism that stabilizes itself at full-employment output, or natural real GNP. This position is based on (a) Say's law, (b) interest rate flexibility, and (c) wage-price flexibility.

The Classical argued that the aggregate labour market determines total employment, and can be summarised by two postulates:

(a) Wage = MPL (marginal product of labour).

This equality holds under the assumptions—(i) the wage is real, (ii) everyone receives the MPL as their wage, and (iii) diminishing returns to a fixed factor exists, in this case, capital is fixed in the long run. Consider the following figure for the employment (L) and output (Y).

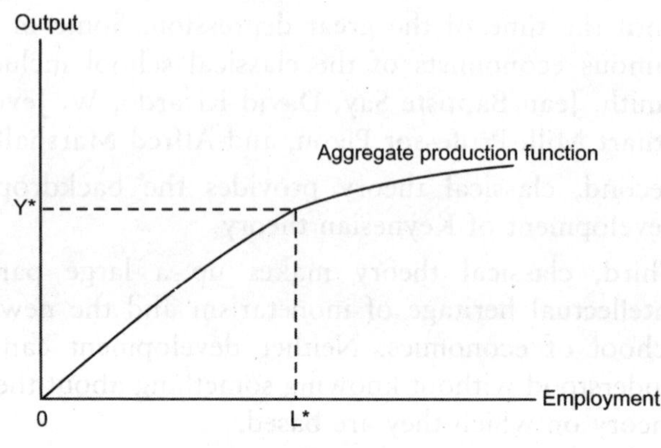

Fig. 3.1

In the above figure, we see that the curve is downward sloping, which implies that the second derivative is negative. There are several possible causes of this—(i) the first and most prominent reason is that diseconomies of scale set in, (ii) the second could be a skill argument (e.g. firms are forced to hire less and less productive workers, as the pool of available workers shrinks.), and (iii) long run fixed capital argument—represents fixed plant equipment.

We assume one productive sector making both an output and a consumption good. This means that the real wage is same for both producers and consumers. Consider the following figure.

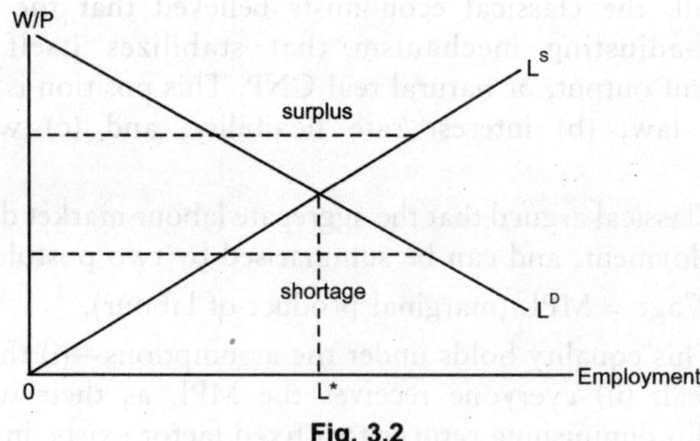

Fig. 3.2

Here we can see that demand is downward sloping—this is a consequence of profit maximisation. This leads us to our second postulate.

(b) Utility of wage = Surrendered leisure time or marginal disutility of work.

If we have voluntary contracting in the economy (no forced labour), maximum employment is the intersection, L*. Maximum employment therefore yields maximum output. At wages below L*, we have a shortage and the level of labour and output is less, as determined by the supply curve. At wages above L*, we have a surplus and labour/output are determined by the demand curve.

According to Classical there are two types of unemployment—frictional (time lag between jobs) and voluntary (people not actively seeking jobs). During the great depression, Pigou and Marshall claimed that the real wage was too high. Workers needed to accept a lower wage—they are in effect claiming some sort of sticky wage. This however requires workers to be acting irrationally.

In classical economics, the economic system is self-adjusting to full employment. Classical view that forces or mechanisms exist to restore a position of full employment. If we did not have any interference or government intervention, we would have a tendency to move to full employment. They would still admit there could be lags or leaks in the system.

Money is neutral in the classical economy. If we increase the quantity of money, it only influences the general level of prices. It will have no effect on relative prices. It will have no effect on the real output and employment of the economy. The interest rate functions to clear the loanable funds market. Interest rates should bring savings and investment in conjunction with one another, but it does not affect the real output of the economy.

Savings drive economic growth. Income that is not spent for consumption purposes is savings (That which is left over from the expenditure screen of consumers). Saving would then go to capital accumulation.

Saving → Capital Accumulation → Growth

Therefore, the higher the rate of saving, the higher the rate of growth.

Classical theories revolved mainly around the role of markets in the economy. If markets worked freely and nothing prevented their rapid clearing then the economy would prosper. Any imperfections in the market that prevented this process should be dealt with by government. The main roles of government are therefore to ensure the free workings of markets using 'supply side policies' and to ensure a balanced budget. The main theories used to justify this view are:

(a) Free market theory
(b) Say's law
(c) Quantity theory of money

FREE MARKET THEORY

In a free market—one in which the forces of demand and supply have the opportunity to alter the price—a market equilibrium tends to appear, although shifts in demand and/or supply cause the equilibrium state to be a moving targets.

The freedom to pursue one's economic self-interest is an intrinsic part of the capitalist system. Men and women are free to choose their line of work with few or no governmental restraints or subsidies, and businesspeople are free to combine any resources at their command to produce products and services for profit. Labour and consumers are free to produce, purchase, and exchange any good or service so long as their activity does not infringe on other's rights. However, it should be noted that participants are also not free of the constraints of limited resources and unlimited wants. Free market, in sum, means that

(a) Labour are free to work at any job for which they are qualified;
(b) Business firms and entrepreneurs can freely combine resources, at competitive market prices, to take advantage of profit opportunities;
(c) Consumers can decide what products and services will be produced; and
(d) There is freedom within constraints (for example, within a rule of law).

Classical economists assumed that if the economy was left to itself, then it would tend to full employment equilibrium. This would happen if the labour market worked properly. If there was any unemployment, then the following would happen:

Unemployment → Fall in wages → Increased demand for labour → Equilibrium restored at full employment.

As the demand curve illustrates, it is argued that there is an inverse relationship between the wage rate (or price of labour), depicted on the vertical (price) axis P, and the quantity of labour demanded, which is depicted (as quantity of any other goods) on the horizontal (quantity) axis Q. There is also a supply of labour curve S in this diagram.

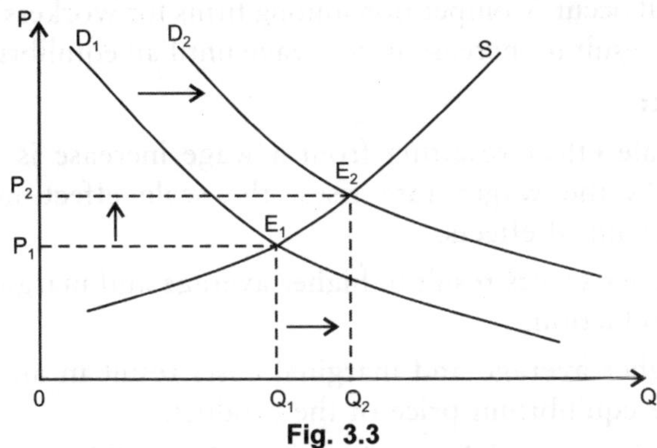

Fig. 3.3

This negative relationship between the wage and the quantity of labour demanded is the result of two effects.

Substitution Effect

Let the wage (P) mean price per combination of products 1 and 2, while quantity of labour (Q) is the total output of product 1 and product 2. Let us now assume that the price of product 2 that uses the same technology, ingredients, know-how, buildings and so forth decreases, which reduces the opportunity cost of making product 1.

Hence, some product 2 makers move into the product 1 business to substitute for the lag in the overall demand for product 1. At this point, the original equilibrium point E_1 = intersection of P_1 and Q_1, with constant wages on the line (P_1, E_1) moves to the right to intersect with D_2, which is the expected optimum output of product 1. Hence, for some time, before the equilibrium is restored at (P_2, D_2), the quantity of labour demand is reduced, or is, at the best, constant (apparently content with the lower wages on the line (P_1, E_1) while, at all times, the labour supply is constant as seen in equilibria (P_1, D_1) and (P_2, D_2).

Eventually, an equilibrium occurs in a labour market at the combination of wages and employment at which market demand and supply intersect.

(a) If the wage rate is above the equilibrium, the quantity of labour supplied exceeds the quantity demanded and a surplus occurs. In this case, the existence of unemployed workers will be expected to result in downward pressure on the wage rate until an equilibrium is restored.

(b) If the wage rate is below the equilibrium, a labour shortage will occur. Competition among firms for workers is expected to result in increase in the wage until an equilibrium occurs.

Scale Effect

The scale effect resulting from a wage increase is a bit more complex. As the wager rate rises, the scale effect involves the following chain of effects:

(a) higher wages result in higher average and marginal costs of production,

(b) higher average and marginal costs result in an increase in the equilibrium price of the product,

(c) as the price of the product rises, the equilibrium quantity of the product demanded declines (a reduction in the 'scale' of production), and

(d) the reduction in output results in a reduction in the quantity of all inputs used to produce this product (including this category of labour).

Hence, classical economists were of the view that the economy is self-adjusting. In fact, in their view, because the economy tends to full-employment, there is no need for government to actively intervene. In fact, intervention may simply be destabilising and inflationary. The key to long-term stable economic growth is therefore to ensure free markets with no imperfections (through supply side policies) and control the growth of the money supply to ensure low inflation.

The effect of supply side policies can be seen in the Figure 3.3 where we assume only one price level, say P_1, and we increase the level of output from Q_1 to Q_2, while the price level P_1 remains stable. Supply side policies as we have said are ones that reduce market imperfections. They may include:

(a) improving education and training to make the work-force more occupationally mobile,

(b) reducing the level of benefits to increase the incentive for people to work,

(c) reducing taxation to encourage enterprise and encourage hard work,
(d) policies to make people more geographically mobile (ending rent controls, simplifying house buying, and so forth),
(e) reducing the power of trade unions to allow wages to be more flexible,
(f) removing any capital controls, and
(g) removing unnecessary regulations.

The hands-off view rests upon two simple propositions about markets—(a) all markets are basically competitive, and (b) as a result, all prices are flexible upward and downward, approaching equilibrium, if they are not already there.

In classical view, unemployment is only a temporary condition, caused by wage rates climbing above the equilibrium rate. In the long run, however, these above-equilibrium wage rates cannot last. The excess labour supply, the unemployed, competes with those who have jobs, driving the wage rates down to equilibrium and employment levels to full employment.

If classical economists insist that unemployment is only temporary, why do we find unemployment stubbornly persisting in the real world? Because, they argue, people interfere with the competitive process, preventing wage rates from reaching equilibrium. The interference creates the unemployment. Labour unions, for example, might use their market power to push wage rates above equilibrium levels, but they can only do so at the expense of employment.

Government, too, gets into the act. They create unemployment by imposing minimum wage laws that necessarily cut people out of jobs they otherwise would have taken at less than the minimum wage. The unintended result is painfully clear. The unskilled labour force is the big loser. Therefore, the most appropriate countercyclical policy, or stabilization policy, in terms of unemployment, according to classical economists, is for the government to do nothing. The competitive market should be allowed to work its way to equilibrium.

Free market economics is closely associated with laissez-faire economic philosophy, which advocates approximating this condition in the real world by mostly confining government intervention in economic matters to regulating against force and fraud among market participants. Some free market advocates oppose taxation as well, claiming that the market is more efficient at providing all valuable services of which defence and law are no exception, that such services can be provided without direct taxation and that consent would be the basis of legitimacy making it a morally consistent system.

While some economists regard the free market as a useful if simplistic model in developing economic policies to attain social goals, others regard the free market as a normative rather than descriptive concept, and claim that policies which deviate from the ideal free market solution are 'wrong' even if they are believed to have some immediate social benefit.

In political economics, one opposite extreme to the free market economy is the command economy, where decisions regarding production, distribution, and pricing are a matter of the state. Other opposite are the gift economy and the subsistence economy. The mixed economy is intermediate between the position of a planned economy and market economy. And in social philosophy, a free market economy is a system for allocating goods within a society—purchasing power mediated by supply and demand within the market determines who gets what and what is produced, rather than the state. Early proponents of a free-market economy in 18th century Europe contrasted it with the medieval, early modern, and mercantilist economies which preceded it.

SAY'S LAW

The classical economists' belief in full employment as a normal condition of a free market economy is based on Say's Law of Markets. It was on the basis of this law that the classical economists thought that general over-production and hence general unemployment were impossible. The law (named after the French) economist, J.B. Say, (1767-1832) is very simple. It states "supply creates its own demand." In other words, every supply of output creates an equivalent demand for output so that there can never be a problem of general over-production. Thus the law denies the possibility of a deficiency of aggregate effective demand. It describes an important fact about the working of the free exchange economy that the main source of demand is the sum of incomes earned by various productive factors in the process of production itself. The employment of hitherto unutilised productive resources makes its own way because it simultaneously enlarges the market demand for goods by an amount equivalent to the income created and the value of output produced. Ricardo expressed Say's Law of Market as below:

> No man produces but with a view to consume or sell, and he never sells but with an intention to purchase some other commodity which may be useful to him, or which may contribute to future production. By producing them, he necessarily becomes either the consumer of his own goods, or the purchaser and consumer of the goods of some other person. . . . Productions are always bought by productions, or by services; money is only the medium by which the exchange is effected.[1]

Say stated the law as below:

> . . . . a product is no sooner created than it, from that instant, affords a market for other products to the full extent of its own value. When the producer has put the finishing hand to his product, he is most anxious to sell it immediately lest its value should vanish in his hands. Nor is he less anxious to dispose of the money he may get for it; for the value of money is also perishable. But the only way of getting rid of money is in the purchase of some product or other. Thus the more circumstance of the creation of one product immediately opens a vent for other products.[2]

J.S. Mill states the law as below:

> What constitutes the means of payment for commodities is simply commodities. Each person's means of paying for the production of other people consist of those which he himself possesses. All sellers are inevitably and by the meaning of the word, buyers. Could we suddenly double the productive powers of the country, we should double the supply of commodities in every market; but we should, by the same stroke, double the purchasing power. Everybody would bring a double demand as well as supply; everybody would be able to buy twice as much, because every one would have twice as much to offer in exchange.[3]

As a corollary of the Say's law, it has been supposed that any individual act of abstaining from consumption necessarily leads to, and amounts to the same thing as, causing the labour and commodities thus released from supplying consumption to be invested in the production of capital wealth. In the words of Marshall:

> The whole of a man's income is expended in the purchase of services and of commodities. It is indeed commonly said that a man spends some portion of his income and saves another. But it is a familiar economic axiom that a man purchases labour and commodities with that portion of his income which he saves just as much as he does with that he is said to spend. He is said to spend when he seeks to obtain present enjoyment from the services and commodities which he purchases. He is said to save when he causes the labour and the commodities which he purchases to be devoted to the production of wealth from which he expects to derive the means of enjoyment in the future.[4]

According to the writings of Henry Hazlitt (1959), "whenever business was bad, the average merchant had two explanations at hand—the evil was caused by a scarcity of money and by general overproduction. Adam Smith, in a famous passage in *The Wealth of Nations*, exploded the first of these myths. Say devoted himself to a refutation of the second".

In other words, Say was not attempting to create a doctrine, which said that business downturns or recessions were impossible, but rather tried to explain why he believed that recessions were not caused by a general overproduction of goods. In fact, any unbiased reader can see that Say was actually describing what one might call recession conditions.

Say's Law involves six major proportions:

(a) The total factor payments received for producing a given volume (or value) of output are necessarily sufficient to purchase that volume (or value) of output.

(b) There is no loss of purchasing power anywhere in the economy. In other words, there are no Keynesian leakages in the economy. People save only to the extent of their desire to invest and do not hold money beyond their transactions need during the current period.

(c) Investment is only an internal transfer, not a net reduction, of aggregate demand.

(d) In real terms, supply equals demand *ex ante*, since each individual produces only because of, and to the extent of, his demand for other goods.

(e) A higher rate of savings will cause a higher rate of subsequent growth in aggregate output.

(f) Disequilibrium in the economy can exist only because the internal proportions of output differ from consumer's preferred mix--not because output is excessive in the aggregate.

Even the critics held to the first three propositions. It was the last three that created the controversy. It should also be noted that the last proposition helps from the basis for the Austrian Business Cycle Theory as outlined by Ludwing von Mises, F.A. Hayek, and Murray N. Rothbard. As might be expected the real source of the conflict between supporters of Say's Law and its opponents came with the controversy over whether or not gluts—unsold inventories—were proportional or general. Proponents of Say's Law believed the former, while Malthus and others held to the latter, which falls the aegis of theories of underconsumption.

The doctrine is easily seen to be true in a barter economy, although its application was not supposed to be restricted to such an economy. What Say had in mind was that people work not for its own sake but only to obtain goods and services which yield satisfaction. The total production was limited by the fact that, at some point, or each individual, the satisfaction obtainable from a little leisure would outweigh the satisfaction obtainable from the consumption of goods and services which can be produced by foregoing that leisure, but such unemployment will be voluntary and not involuntary. If some productive resources are involuntarily unemployed, additional production will be undertaken which would yield an equivalent amount of income; whole of this additional income will be spent in the purchase of additional production. Say assumed that money is simply a medium of exchange and is never hoarded. As such the law framed in terms of barter economy would hold true in an economy using money. Money economy would behave in the same way as barter economy because rational individuals will not hold idle money. But in actual practice money is more than simply a medium of exchange. It is also a medium of store. Individuals as well as business firms have a tendency to hold cash for a number of purposes. If a part of the total supply of money is held as cash and not spent, the identity between buying and selling presumed in a barter economy will not hold true.

, Say's Law can be illustrated with a three person, three commodity, barter economy. Let our three persons be Mahesh, who produces books, Verinder, who produces cloths, and Jayaprakash, who produces foods. Mahesh will produce books for two reasons, either because he wants to use them himself, or because he wants to trade them for cloths and food. Verinder and Jayaparkash also work either to consume their own output or to trade it. If initially each unit of food and cloths is worth one book, Mahesh may plan to trade five books for two units of cloths and three units of food. In the table below these plans are shown with a positive number indicating that a person plans to supply a commodity to the marketplace and a negative number indicating that a person plans to demand a commodity from the marketplace. The numbers show what each wants to do at the existing set of prices, not necessarily what each actually does.

Planned Sales and Purchases

	Mahesh	Verinder	Jayaprakash	Summation
Books	+5	–1	–2	+2
Cloths	–2	+5	–3	0
Food	–3	–4	+5	–2
Summation	0	0	0	0

In a barter world, buying cannot be done unless one sells at the same time, and selling cannot be done unless one buys at the same time. In this system, the only way one can finance purchases is by selling, and there is no reason to sell except to finance purchases. It is for this reason that Say's Law implies that a column should sum to zero. The act of supplying is also an act of demanding; supply creates its own demand.

The table contains the plans of Verinder and Jayaprakash in addition to Mahesh. Notice that adding each of their columns results in a total of zero. If, however, rows are added, there is no need to sum to zero, and the rows for books and food do not sum to zero. A non-zero total here means that plans will not be realised. The +2 in the books row indicates that at the original prices there will be an oversupply or surplus of books. The –2 in the food row means that at the original prices there will be an overdemand or a shortage of food. To make the markets clear, the price of books should fall and the price of food should rise. In turn, the new prices will affect future plans. Most economists have believed that, with repeated changes in prices and plans, eventually an equilibrium situation will be reached so that all rows will sum to zero—that quantity supplied will equal quantity demanded in each market.

The logic of the table implies that there can be no general glut or oversupply of goods, which was the point Say and others were arguing. It is possible for 'gluts' of particular goods, but counterbalancing this is a shortage or undersupply of other goods. It is not possible, given the assumption that columns must sum to zero, for an oversupply (or underdemand) of all goods to exist. This conclusion won the debate in the early 19th century and remained unchallenged until the 20th century.

The logic of the table also implies that if all markets except one are balanced, then the last one also must balance. This conclusion was named after Leon Walras and has become known as Walras' Law which says that if a system has n markets, and n—1 of them are in equilibrium, then the final n^{th} market must also be in equilibrium.

If we want to get a more accurate understanding of Say's Law, perhaps we should consult what Say himself had to say about his supposed law. In the passage where he gets at the insight behind the notion that supply creates its own demand, Say writes—it is production, which opens a demand for products. Thus, the mere circumstance of the creation of one product immediately opens a vent for other products. Put another way, Say was making the claim that production is the source of demand. One's ability to demand goods and services from others derives from the income produced by one's own acts of production. Wealth is created by production not by consumption. My ability to demand food, clothing, and shelter derives from the productivity of my labour or my non-labour assets. The higher the productivity, the higher is my power to demand.

In his book on Say's Law, Hutt states this as: All power to demand is derived from production and supply. The process of supplying, i.e., the production and appropriate pricing of service or assets for replacement or growth—keeps the flow of demands flowing steadily or expanding. Later, Hutt was to be somewhat more precise with his definition—the demand for any commodity is a function of the supply of noncompeting commodities. The addition of the modifier noncompeting is important. If I sell my services as a content developer, it is presumed that my resulting demands will be for goods and for services other than those of a content developer (or something similar). The goods or services competing with those that I sell can always be obtained by applying my labour directly, so I am unlikely to demand them. The demand for my services as a content developer is a result of the supplying activities of everyone but content developers.

This way of viewing Say's Law gets at the interconnections between the various sectors of a market economy. In particular, it makes sense of the claim that the employment of all is the employment of each. As each worker finds employment, he or she is able to turn around and demand goods and services from all other noncompeting suppliers, creating the opportunity for their employment. From this perspective, Say's Law has nothing to do with an equilibrium between aggregate supply and aggregate demand, but rather it describes the process by which supplies in general are turned into demands in general. It is always the level of production which determines the ability to demand.

Say's law, of course, recognises the possibility that the individuals may not correctly direct their production in accordance with one another's wants. The person producing toys may produce more than people want to buy at the price which he assumed while deciding the number of toys to be produced. As a consequence, the toys would fetch in return quantities of other goods smaller than those he anticipated. This would lead him to produce some other goods which are in more demand or to have more leisure. But such maladjustments of relative outputs would be temporary and would be corrected soon by the operation of market forces.

This process can be seen in the difference between small, poor, rural towns and wealthier suburbans areas. In the small town, the fact that less value is being produced by residents means that their ability to demand goods and services is correspondingly limited. As a result, the selection of products, the number and diversity of sellers, and the degree of specialization among producers is quite limited. By contrast, in the wealthier suburb, there is an amazing array of products, with a large number of diverse sellers all offering very specialised goods. Perhaps most important is that in the wealthier area, there is a greater degree of competition, as the market can support multiple sellers of particular goods given the level of wealth being generated by producers. Say points out that this explains why a seller will likely get more business as one among a large number of competitors in a big city than the sole seller of an item in the more sparsely populated countryside. The key to understanding Say's Law of Markets is that it is production that must come first. Demand, or consumption, follows from the production of wealth.

To a degree, Say's Law is just an extension of Adam Smith's insight that the division of labour is limited by the extent of the market. Smith's point was that the degree of specialisation that one would see in a given market depends upon how much demand there was for the specialised product. Thus, small towns rarely have five star restaurants beyond the very popular small *dhabas*, nor do they have radio stations that specialise in very narrow musical formats (classical from the 1950s only, for example). Larger, wealthier communities can support this degree of specialisation because there is sufficient demand, deriving from a larger population and a larger degree of wealth being produced. It is in this sense that production is the source of demand.

Because all movements between supplying and demanding have to take place through the medium of money, it is somewhat oversimplified to say that production is the source of demand. Actually demanding products requires the possession of money, which in turn requires a previous act of supply. We sell assets or labour services for money, which we then use to demand. Money is an intermediate good that enables us to buy the things we ultimately desire. However, we have to be careful to remember that what enables us to purchase is not the possession of money, per se, but the possession of productive assets that can fetch money's worth on the market. When we sell that asset (or our labour services) we receive wealth in the form of money. As we spend that money, we demand from the wealth our production created. However, because we do not spend all of our wealth that we temporarily store as money, but choose to continue to hold some of it in the monetary form, the demand for current goods and services will not precisely match the value of what has been produced, as some money remains in the producers' possession. Thus it looks as though, given the existence and use of money, Say's Law, even rightly understood, leaves open the possibility that aggregate demand is insufficient to purchase what has been supplied.

However, if the monetary wealth is stored in the form of bank-created money, such as a checking account (but not Reserve Bank of India Notes), then that withheld consumption power will be transferred to those who borrow money from the bank that created it. The money I leave sitting in my checking account is the basis for my bank's ability to lend to others. The power to consume that I choose not to utilise by leaving my production-generated wealth as money is transferred to the borrower. When he spends his loan, his addition to aggregate demand fills in for the missing consumption demand resulting from my decision to hold money. There is, therefore, no excess or deficiency in aggregate demand, as long as the banking system is free to perform this process of turning the saving of depositors into the spending of borrowers. Say's Law of markets cannot be fully appreciated unless one understands the working of the banking system and its role in intertemporal coordination.

Because all market exchanges are of goods or services for money, all markets are money markets, and the only way there can be an excess supply or demand for goods is if there is an opposite excess supply or demand for money. Take the more obvious case of a glut of goods, such as one might find in a recession. Say's Law, properly understood, suggests that the explanation for an excess supply of goods is an excess demand for money. Goods are going unsold because buyers cannot get their hands on the money they need to buy them despite being potentially productive suppliers of labour. Conversely, a general shortage, or excess demand for goods, can only arise if there is an excess supply of the goods trade against, which can only be money. Recessions and inflations are, therefore, fundamentally monetary phenomena, as Say's Law points us in the direction of looking at what is going on in the production of money to explain the breakdown of the translation process of production into demand.

Assumptions of Say's Law

Say's law as described above is based on the following assumptions:

(a) There is no state intervention in economic activities because this obstructs the automatic and self-adjusting mechanism of the economy.

(b) The size of the market is capable of expansion. It expands with the increase in the volume of products offered in exchange.

(c) In an expanding economy new firms and workers make their way into the productive process not by supplanting others but by offering their products in exchange.

(d) The free enterprise system based on price mechanism provides opportunities for the growing population and increase in capital.

(e) All savings are automatically invested and this equality between savings and investment is brought about by interest flexibility.

Implications of Say's Law

(a) Since there is automatic adjustment of every element with the working of the economy, there is no need for government intervention in the functioning of the economic system.

(b) General over-production and general unemployment are not possible.

(c) So long as there exist unemployed resources in the economy, it is profitable to employ them because they can pay their own way. In other words, when the unemployed resources are employed, they lead to more production which covers their own costs.

(d) The mechanism of interest flexibility brings about an equality between savings and investment.

(e) The mechanism of wage-flexibility brings about full employment. Any unemployment would disappear if the workers are ready to accept a wage rate equal to their marginal productivity.

(f) Money is no more than an instrument of overcoming the inconveniences of barter. It is simply a veil which conceals the fact what constitutes the means of payment for commodities is simply commodities.

Say's Law and Mercantilism

The period of growing commercial activity, falling roughly between the Thirteenth and Sixteenth Centuries, was more a period of economic action than of economic thought. At least, it is difficult to find a figure whose ideas seem at all representative of the economic developments of that time. However, the influx of gold from America and the problems associated with it seemed to foster extensive efforts to understand and appraise the rapidly changing economic scene. The literature of the Fifteenth Century is filled with observations on the necessity of increasing exports in order to increase the stock of money within a nation. For those nations which lacked mines, a favourable balance of trade was thought to be the only means whereby coin might be secured. Those who accepted the fact of an important interrelation between wealth, an abundance of money, and foreign trade were the mercantilists.

A few of the Mercantilists such as Mun, Davenant, Petty, and Steuart clearly distinguished between wealth and money, but by and large the mercantilist writers either considered the two identical or avoided a clear statement of their relationship. It seems fair to say, however, that the complete identification of money with wealth was an extreme position of mercantilist thought, exaggerated by critics of Mercantilism.

Although the assumption that wealth consisted in an abundance of money may now appear unreasonable, strong arguments were offered to support it. The financial stability of the state in those days depended largely upon a ready supply of precious metals. Since public borrowing was still undeveloped, and taxation was not as flexible as it is today, the security of a government was naturally assumed to lie in an accumulated reserve of coin and bullion.

The issues aroused by the Mercantilists were numerous. Not a few of them continued in one form or another to engage the attention of eminent economists of later years even down to the present day. Such questions as a nation's supply of gold, the use of paper money, the relation of money to prices, and the extension and control of credit have not been solved to the satisfaction of all; and not a little of present day public policy emanates from the careless interpretation of these key points in economic thought.

In attempting to reach such a judgment, an obvious starting point is the proposition (that is, Say's Law of markets) that supply creates its own demand. This has come to epitomize classical economics, for the simple reason that it was selected by Keynes for sacrifice to his new principle of effective demand. Jean Baptiste Say had expounded and elaborated upon Adam Smith's great work (The Wealth of Nations, 1776); and the significance of Say's Law of markets rests with its contradiction of the mercantilist case against free trade.

Mercantilism originated during the transition from the feudal economy to merchant capitalism and international commerce, in the sixteenth and seventeenth centuries. A strong central authority was considered essential to the expansion of markets and it was a mercantilist imperative that the power of the state should be enhanced by an accumulation of national wealth. Here, a general concern with business recession had become focused in a particular fear that productivity might outstrip consumers' purchasing power. Mercantilists argued that nations compete for business opportunities; they asserted that a nation prospers only at the expense of other nations and they concluded that a trade surplus provides the wealth necessary to support the international prestige and power of the state.

According to Say's Law, the mercantilist fear of a general glut is unfounded, for the reason that individuals produce goods either for personal consumption or to buy other goods. Supply and demand concepts that relate to a nexus of diverse commodities, so the idea of general overproduction is rendered meaningless. Recessions resulted, not from any general overproduction, but from the overproduction of a particular items beyond their levels of demand. In a market system, this implied a deficiency in the production of some other items, so that business recessions were symptomatic of a necessity to redeploy (or to reprice) productive factors.

The argument against mercantilism and in favour of free trade applied to domestic and international market alike. The efficiency gains from specialisation and the division of labour implied that variety in the composition of consumption was almost entirely dependent on trade. Consumption and investment goods were acquired generally through the production of other items with the implication that production created not only a supply of goods but also a demand for goods. Free trade allowed the creation and distribution of a greater diversity of goods, and export sales were retarded only by a refusal to allow foreign goods access to home markets. As a corollary, the mercantilist assertion, that prosperity requires preferential access to foreign markets and the protection of domestic markets, was also phony.

Criticism of Say's Law

As the depression of 1929 deepened and years passed without signs of recovery, the validity of Say's law was called into question. The producers found it difficult to sell their entire output and there was a general glut in the economy. In 1936, Lord J.M. Keynes came forward with his *General Theory of Employment, Interest and Money* which rejected Say's Law on the ground that aggregate demand need not necessarily be equal to aggregate supply at full employment.

The incomes of the factors of production are necessarily equal to the value added in the productive process but this does not mean that the entire income will be automatically spent in goods and services created in a given time period. The recipients of the income spend a part of their incomes on consumer goods and save the other part. Unless the investors are willing to invest an amount equivalent to the amount of savings, the total effective demand which consists of demand for consumers' goods and producers' goods will not be sufficient to absorb the entire available supply of output. In such a situation, the producers will not be able to sell their entire output, their profits will fall and they will be compelled to reduce their production which will create unemployment. The savings and investment being done by different persons and for different motives, in the absence of any agency to ensure equality between intended savings and intended investment, a discrepancy between the two will not be an uncommon phenomenon. In contrast to the classical view that full employment equilibrium is the normal situation, Keynes, therefore, believed that in a free enterprise economy, there are more chances for the equilibrium to be established at less than full employment level. It may, however, be pointed out that rejection of Say's law by Keynes was not a new thing. It was rejected by Karl Marx much before Keynes.

Say's Law and Classical Theory

The classical economists like David Recardo and Adam Smith believe that in a competitive capitalist economy there exists an automatic mechanism which brings about full employment of labour. This automatic mechanism is known as the 'invisible hand.' According to the classical theory, levels of income and employment are governed by fixed capital stock on the one hand and wage-goods fund on the other. The belief of classical theory regarding the existence of full employment in the economy is based on Say's Law propound by a French economist J.B. Say. According to Say's law, "Supply creates its own demand." This shows that every increase in production, will be sold in the market and hence there will be no problem of lack of demand.

In this way, classical economists rule out the possibility of overproduction. Say's Law states that over production automatically leads to a greater money income which creates the market for the greater flow of goods produced. In this way, deficiency in demand being no problem, the process of capital accumulation and expansion of productive capacity will continue till all people are employed. Thus, the income, which is not spent on consumer goods, is saved and will be invested in the production process. Therefore, investment equals savings. Thus, a given productive capacity continues to be fully utilized and no problem of deficiency of demand arises.

As per opinion of classical economists, there is always a tendency towards full-employment in a capitalist economy, if price mechanism is allowed to work freely without any interference by the government. Thus, the classical theory of employment is based upon two basic assumptions: (i) There is always enough expenditure or aggregate demand to purchase the total production at full-employment level of resources. (ii) Even when deficiency of aggregate expenditure or demand arises, the prices and wages would change in such a way that real production, employment and income will not decline. The classical economist thinks that there is no problem of deficiency of expenditure. Demand for goods was based upon Say's law.

Say's law says that every production of goods creates income equal to the value of goods produced and this income is spent on purchasing these goods. It can be said in other way that every production creates its own purchasing power, i.e., 'Supply creates its own demand.' Thus, the problem of over production does not arise. J.B. Say's argument is that when a new entrepreneur employs some factors of production and pay them their monetary rewards. The unemployed labourers when employed create their own demand. Thus, the new entrepreneur increases not only the supply of goods but also at the same time creates the demand for them. Production is the only source of demand. Dillard rightly writes that "'Say's Law of Markets' is the denial of the possibility of deficiency of aggregate demand. Therefore, employment of more resources will always be profitable and will take place to the point of full-employment, subject to the limitation that the contributors of the resources are willing to accept rewards not greater than their physical productivity justifies. There could be no general unemployment, according to this view, if workers will account what they are worth."*

Wages and Employment

The classical economists believed that there could be no involuntary unemployment in a labour market characterised by free and unhindered competition. In such a market, wage-rates would have a tendency to fall under the pressure of unemployment until all those who are willing to work can find employment. This follows from the definition of unemployment, for any man who is not in employment and who does not try to get work at a lower rate is no more considered to be unemployed than the man who refuses to work overtime or on Sundays. At the ruling wage, he prefers leisure to employment. He is idle but not involuntarily unemployed. If he really wanted employment, he would have offered himself at a lower wage which would have reduced the level of wages. Unemployment thus is incompatible with equilibrium. It can persist only if the State, or the trade unions, or some other institution prevents the unemployed from seeking employment at lower wages and thereby setting in motion the automatic mechanism which leads to equilibrium and full employment.

Prof. Pigou diagnosed the ills of depression mainly due to two causes viz., (i) an improper allocation of people among jobs and (ii) the prevalence of wage-rates above the level warranted by the general demand conditions. He, therefore, advocated a policy of wage cuts to cure unemployment. He held that given flexible wage-rates, the economic system has an automatic tendency towards full employment and the more rigid wages are, the larger would be the fluctuations in employment. He stated:

* D. Dillard, "Economics of J.M. Keynes."

> With perfectly free competition among work people and labour perfectly mobile, the nature of the relation (i.e., between the real wage-rates for which people stipulate and the demand function for labour) will be very simple. There will always be at work a strong tendency for wage-rates to be so related to demand that everybody is employed. Hence in stable conditions everyone will actually be employed. The implication is that such unemployment as exists at any time is due wholly to the fact that changes in demand conditions are continually taking place and that frictional resistances prevent the appropriate wage adjustments from being made instantaneously.[5]

The process by which the reduction in wage-rates cures unemployment is described by the classical economists as below. In a free market economy, a reduction in wage-rates lowers the cost of production and hence prices which lead to an increase in sales. Increase in sales leads to increase in production which leads to an expansion of employment of the workers. Reduction in costs as a result of lower wages also increases profits of businessmen. Profits increase because it is assumed that the decline in wage-rates is larger than that in prices. The process of declining wages accompanied by rising profits and employment continues till equilibrium is reached at full employment. Thus the classical equilibrium is always at full employment equilibrium.

The main fallacy in the classical argument arises from the fact that the classical economists ignored the effect of a reduction in wages on the aggregate effective demand. They wrongly presumed that wage cuts leave the aggregate demand unaffected. They tried to extend to the whole economy the logic that was actually applicable to a single firm or industry. The classical theory is certainly true when applied to a single firm or industry. Take, for illustration, the case of a reduction in wage-rates in the watch industry alone. The reduction in wages will lower cost of production and hence prices in the watch industry. Decline in the prices of watches will lead to an increase in demand for them which will necessitate larger employment in the watch industry. No doubt, the reduction in the incomes of workers employed in the watch industry will decrease their demand for all goods including watches, but the effect of this will be insignificant because they constitute a very small portion of the total buyers of watches.

In contrast, if the wage rates are reduced uniformly in all industries, the incomes of the buyers of watches as well as other goods will decline which would lead to a decline in the demand for all goods including watches. Thus the logic which is true in case of a single industry will not hold for the economy as a whole. While the reduction in wages in a single industry will not significantly reduce the demand for the product of that industry, the increased employment in that industry will also not significantly increase the aggregate employment in the economy as a whole. In fact, the increased employment in watch industry will be offset by small decreases in employment in all the industries whose products are bought by the workers employed in watch industry because reduction in their incomes as a result of wage cuts leads to a reduction in their demand for most of the goods they normally buy. Since one person's expenditure constitutes another person's income, the money incomes fall to the extent the general cut in wages reduces expenditure.

Decline in money wages may not necessarily result into a decline in real wages because the general fall in price resulting from a general reduction in wages may offset the decline in money wages and thus leave real wages unchanged. Keynes does assume that prices fall in proportion to the fall in wages. On this assumption, real wages will not decline and if real wages do not decline, profits cannot rise. If profits do not increase, there is no incentive for entrepreneurs to increase production. We again come to the same conclusion that the classical logic suffers from the drawback that it tries to extend to the whole economy what is true in case of only a single firm or industry.

Another version of the classical theory rests on the belief that the demand for labour is elastic. It is argued that a reduction in wage-rate per hour will increase the total earnings of workers because this will be more than offset by the increased volume of employment that results from it. The increased earnings would mean larger effective demand and hence greater volume of employment. Even if the profit per unit of output does not increase, total profits would increase as a result of greater output. This version of the classical theory also suffers from the same basic drawback as other versions. It assumes that supply creates its own demand for both consumption and investment output. We have already seen that Say's law is not valid and if that is so, wage-cut theory will not hold. No doubt, additional workers and others who share the newly created income will bring additional buying power in the market for consumption goods, it will not be adequate to absorb the entire output. A part of the additional income will naturally be saved and if this is not matched by additional investment, employment will not increase. But there is nothing automatic about increases in investment. This is the simple and basic point of Keynes' reaction to the classical theory of employment.

Keynes rejected the classical theory of employment more strongly on practical grounds. It is very difficult to implement a general cut in wage-rates because collective bargaining by labour unions, unemployment insurance minimum wage laws, etc., have come to stay. Keynes considered such a step immoral and anti-social.

According to Keynes, the volume of employment depends upon the volume of effective demand which in turn depends upon the propensity to consume and the relation between the marginal efficiency of capital and the rate of interest. A reduction in wage rates would, therefore, lead to an increase in employment only if it leads to an increase in the propensity to consume, or an increase in the marginal efficiency of capital, or a decline in the rate of interest. Let us briefly examine below the effect of a general reduction in wage-rates on these three independent variables.

Propensity to Consume: Consumption is the most important constituent of effective demand. Wage cuts lead to a transfer of income from wage-earners to rentiers, interest-recipients and enterpreneurs or, in other words, from the poorer classes towards the richer classes. Since the propensity to consume of the poorer classes is higher than that of the richer classes, the effect of wage cuts on consumption would be unfavourable. The decline in prices following wage cuts would, however, increase the purchasing power of people's fixed money wealth and thereby tend to increase their consumption.

Marginal Efficiency of Capital: The effect of wage cuts on the marginal efficiency of capital depends on what the entrepreneurs expect in regard to future wage-rates. If the reduction in wage-rates is once-for-all and is not expected to be followed by further wage cuts, the effect on the marginal efficiency of capital would be favourable. The entrepreneurs will be encouraged to make alterations and additions to plant and equipment and to build new plant when the wages are at the minimum. In case the entrepreneurs expect the reduction in wages to be followed by further wage cuts at a later date, the marginal efficiency of capital will be lowered because the entrepreneurs will have a tendency to postpone investment till the wages have fallen to still lower levels.

Once-for-all wage cuts are possible only in an authoritarian economy. Under a system of free labour and management, there is no way to ensure that a reduction in wages is not followed by further reductions in wages. Normally in such matters labour and management do not act as a whole and if labour is strongly organised, it would be almost impossible to effect reduction in wages. Generally, the weaker unions will be cut first and others will follow gradually. A gradually declining wage level will have adverse effects on the marginal efficiency of capital. A rigid wage policy will perhaps have more favourable effects on the marginal efficiency of capital than a policy of gradually declining wages.

Rate of Interest: A general reduction in wage-rates lowers the price level and thereby reduces the demand for money for transactions purpose. The total supply of money remaining unchanged, a decline in the demand for money for transactions purpose would release more money for inactive balances which would lead to decline in the rate of interest. Given the marginal efficiency of capital, a decline in the rate of interest will stimulate investment.

If money-wage reductions are expected to continue, people's liquidity-preference will probably increase, particularly to satisfy the speculative motive, that is, to hold money as a 'store of wealth' against the increasing uncertainty that deflation of wages generates. This may lead to two things. Firstly, the demand for consumer goods may be cut down in favour of the demand for money as a 'store of wealth', i.e., to save and hold a larger portion of consumer income in the form of liquid assets. Secondly, the liquidity function may become so elastic with respect to interest that the monetary authority may not succeed in lowering the interest rate by varying the quantity of money. The first of these possible results obviously affects the consumption function whereas the second affects the investment function to the extent that investment decisions require a favourable 'monetary atmosphere'.

Open Economy: In an open economy, a change in the general wage rate and price level will affect the balance of trade. A cut in wage rates would lower the cost of production and hence prices. A decline in the price level would stimulate exports and discourage imports. A surplus in the balance of trade would be equivalent to an increase in real investment which would have multiplier effect on domestic real income and employment. This effect may be strengthened by a worsening of the terms of trade, which increases the employment necessary to obtain the equilibrium level of real income and real saving. These favourable effects may, however, be counteracted by similar wage adjustments or changes in exchange rates in other countries.

Public and Private Debt: Reduction in wage rates is also objectionable on the ground that the decline in the price level that follows it increases the real burden of private as well as public debt. Entrepreneurs find it difficult to meet their obligations and to pay the stipulated sums to the debenture holders. The real burden of the public debt is also increased which necessitates increased taxation.

Pigou Effect: Prof. Pigou contended that a decline in the price level raises the real value of the stock of liquid assets held by the people. As a result, the people would have a tendency to increase their consumption and to reduce savings because after the prices fall, a smaller amount of savings would be required to make purchases planned for the future. This means that so long as the market remains uncleared, wages and prices will fall, so that consumption will continue to increase until full employment is restored. This process has come to be known as 'Pigou effect'. But the modern economists have questioned the validity of the 'Pigou effect' on a number of grounds. In the first place, a large number of persons do not possess money assets. Secondly, those who possess money assets want to possess still more. Thirdly, since the 'Pigou effect' has only modest influence, considerable wage cuts would be required to affect employment appreciably, which would not be acceptable to trade unions. Fourthly, if the wages and prices are expected to decline further, expenditure may be postponed leading to an increase in unemployment. Fifthly, if the consumption changes only in response to changes in 'permanent' wealth and if the price level is expected to return to its previous level, the increase in wealth would be considered transitory and, therefore, the consumption may not increase. Sixthly, if there is a money illusion and people feel that a 'Rupee is a Rupee', consumption will not increase. Seventhly, with the decline in wages and prices, consumers' over-all asset position may be so impaired as to strengthen their desire to add more to their assets and less to their consumption, particularly if the real value of consumer durables and non-monetary assets is reduced much more than that of liquid assets is increased. Eighthly, although the value of liquid assets held by creditors increases with the decline in prices, there are also corresponding debtors, the real value of whose obligations increases. As such, the Pigou effect would fail to materialise at all if the "wealth effects" of price changes affect debtors and creditors symmetrically. It is, however, argued that the effects are not symmetrical because a large portion of the liquid assets held by the public is in the form of government obligations—the currency and governmental debt. Since government consumption is not supposed to be affected by a change in the real value of government obligations, there will be a net change in consumption resulting from a decline in the price level.

QUANTITY THEORY OF MONEY

Crucial to the understanding of classical economics is an understanding of how money works. Money is just something that can value goods, used to exchange those goods among individuals in an economy. The quantity theory of money is the theory dealing with money and prices. It states that the price level in an economy depends on how much money is in the economy. In classical economics, the quantity theory of money centers around the equation "(Quantity of money) × (velocity of money) = (price level) × (quantity of goods sold)." Thus, in simplest form the equation is $MV = PQ$, where M stands for the quantity of money in the economy, V stands for its velocity of circulation, P stands for the price level, and Q stands for the quantity of real output for the year.

According to the quantity theory of money there is a direct relationship between prices, income, and the amount of money circulating in the economy. The quantity theory was first propounded in its most basic form by French philosopher Jean Bodin (1530—1596), who observed that the large amounts of gold and silver being brought back from the other parts of the world were driving up prices across Europe. Later two British philosophers, John Locke

(1632-1704) and David Hume (1711-1776), noted that when the quantity of money grew, so did purchasing power and economic activity. Thus, if a government wanted to lower prices to combat inflation, according to the quantity theory, all it had to do was decrease the amount of money in circulation. Consumers would have less money to spend, demand would fall, and prices would drop. Over the next two centuries other economists elaborated on this basic interconnection between the quantity of money, income, and prices, and until the 1930s it remained the dominant theory for explaining inflation, deflation, and the nature of business cycles. Henry Thornton in 1802 assumed that more money equals more inflation and that an increase in money supply does not necessarily mean an increase in economic output.

During the 1930s the quantity theory came under attack because its opponents argued that government attempts to increase the amount of money in circulation during the early years of the Great Depression (1929-1939) had almost no affect on consumer demand. The primary opponent of the quantity theory was British economist John Maynard Keynes (1883-1946). He claimed that increasing the money supply alone would never be enough to stimulate a contracting economy. Only high levels of employment could resuscitate demand and that meant the government had to create jobs for unemployed workers if the private economy could not.

Keynes's 'fiscal policy' approach to economic growth ruled the world of economics until the 1960s when a new quantity theory of money arose to take its place. Let by U.S. economists Milton Friedman, the new quantity-of-money theorists agreed with Keynes that government fiscal policy had an important role to play in stimulating the economy. However, they showed that during the Great Depression government officials had not really expanded the money supply fast enough or in large enough quantities to get the economy growing, so the Depression did not really disprove the quantity theory of money after all. Moreover, using new tools of economic research, the Friedman school of economists showed that increasing and decreasing the money supply did in fact have a direct effect on inflation and deflation.

An Aggregate-Demand and Aggregate-Supply View of the Quantity Theory

The equation of exchange can be rearranged to become a statement about the aggregate quantity of goods and services demanded in an economy. If we let Q in the equation represent the aggregate quantity of goods and services demanded, the equation of exchange says that Q = MV/P. In this arrangement, q and P are inversely related, that is, a decrease in P (the price level) is associated with an increase in Q (real national income and product demanded) provided that there is no change in either M (the money supply) or V (the velocity of circulation of money). This inverse relationship is illustrated in Figure 3.4.

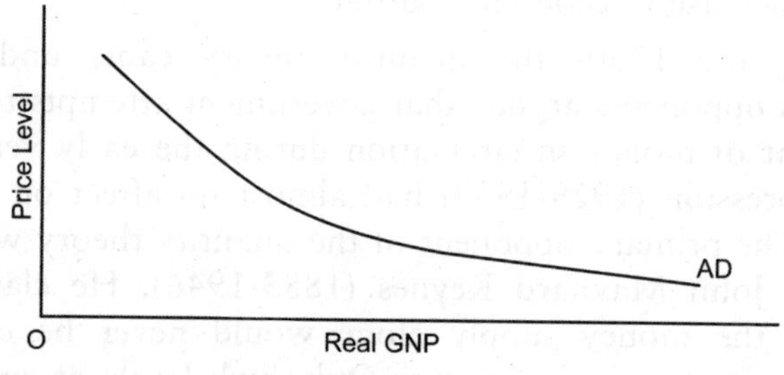

Fig. 3.4

Although the 'AD' curve in Figure 3.4 is not a true aggregate-demand curve, it is helpful in understanding the economics of the quantity theory of money. In drawing the curve, the money supply (M) and the velocity of money (V) are held constant. Changes in either of these variables, therefore, will shift the curve. Increasing the value of these variables shifts the curve to the right and decreasing their values shifts it to the left.

According to the quantity theory of money, the velocity of money circulation is constant and there is a one-to-one relationship between percentage changes in the money supply and percentage changes in the price level—a 10 percent increase in M causes a 10 percent increase in the price level, and so on. What does this say about the aggregate quantity supplied? It says that the aggregate quantity supplied does not change when the price level changes. This is illustrated in Figure 3.5.

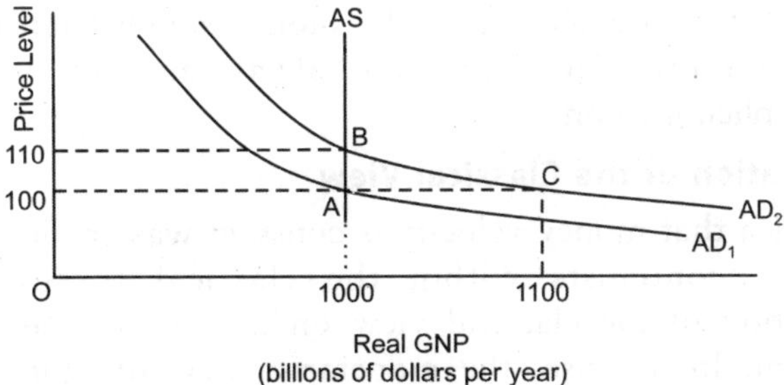

Fig. 3.5

The AD_1 curve shows the relationship between aggregate quantity or real GNP demanded and the price level according to the equation of exchange, assuming the money supply and the velocity of its circulation are constant. The AD_2 curve illustrates a 10 percent increase in the money supply, with velocity remaining constant. Since the quantity theory of money states that a 10 percent increase in the money supply is associated with a 10 percent increase in the price level, the implicit aggregate supply curve is a vertical line, labeled AS.

According to the quantity theory of money, the velocity of the money circulation is constant, and there is a one-to-one relationship between percentage changes in the money supply and percentage changes in the price level.

According to the quantity theory of money, the vertical aggregate supply curve represents the full employment level of output for the economy and incorporates the view that this level of output is the same regardless of the price level. In other words, change in the money supply affect only the price level and do not affect real output.

Is there any truth in the classical view that changes in the money supply affect only the price level? Time and again throughout history, when governments have printed large amounts of money or when large quantities of gold or silver have been discovered, the resulting increase in the money supply have been followed by increase in prices. As a result, it is widely accepted that there is some truth in the quantity theory, although many believe that money-supply increases affect more than just the price level. Milton Friedman states that although there are significant and variable time lags between a change in the money supply and a resulting change in the price level, inflation "always and everywhere" is a monetary phenomenon.

A Modification of the Classical View

The idea that money velocity is constant was challenged in the 1970s by economists within the classical tradition. Their reformulation of the classical view on money became known as monetarism. In a sense, the monetarist view of money was an attempt to rescue the classical view from the onslaught of empirical evidence that showed that M1 money velocity was anything but constant.

Monetarists accept the idea that velocity is not constant, nonetheless they believe that it is still highly predictable, well-behaved, and independent of money supply.

They explain the steady increase in money velocity since the 1950s by pointing to the technological changes associated with the transactions demand for money. For example, the use of computers speeds up the banking process. Also, the widespread use of credit cards allows people to buy and sell goods and services with less cash and lower bank balances relative to nominal GDP. The result is higher money velocity. Since technologies in money and banking are still developing and pay periods are becoming more frequent, monetarists believe it is reasonable to predict increases in velocity over time, and for the short run at least, they believe the increases will be well-behaved.

If money velocity is known—that is, relatively stable and highly predictable—and if Q is at full-employment real GDP, then the quantity theory of money—expressing the relationship between money and prices remains intact. In the end the monetarist version of the quantity theory of money still leads to the same classical conditions—although money cannot influence how much we produce, it does influence the prices of the goods and services we produce.

We stop our discussion on quantity theory of money here and will again come back on this topic with more details in latter chapters.

ASSUMPTIONS OF KEYNES

Keynes' money-wage theory is based on a number of assumptions, the important of which are[6]: (a) that labour is the only variable factor of production, (b) that pure competition exists throughout the economy or that the degree of monopoly is constant, (c) that "money illusion" affects the supply function for labour and (d) that "money illusion" does not occur in other supply and demand functions. It is necessary to remove these assumptions because they clash with other basic assumptions.

No Variable Factors Other than Labour: By assuming that labour is the only variable factor, Keynes rules out the possibility of substitution as a result of changes in money-wage rates. A reduction in wages, the prices of other variable factors remaining unchanged, would stimulate substitution of labour for other factors of production. Such a substitution would not only directly expand employment of labour but would also check or even reverse the transfer of income from labour to non-wage-earners and thereby raise the propensity to consume which would indirectly expand employment. In case the owners of other variable factors tried to avoid such substitution, they would reduce their prices in the same proportion as wage-rate and as a result their income would not increase at the cost of labour.

Pure Competition or Constant Degree of Monopoly: Keynes assumes that prices rise or fall in the same ratio as the changes in money-wage rates. This would be true only if there prevails pure competition or, under monopolistic conditions, if the degree of monopoly—the ratio of the difference between price and marginal cost to price—remains unchanged. Monopolistic conditions lead to price rigidity and stickiness. As such, a cut in money-wage rates will increase the degree of monopoly which would, other things remaining same, increase the relative share of national income going to non-wage-earners. Since the marginal propensity to consume of the wage-earners is usually higher than that of the non-wage-earners, such a redistribution of income reduces the real demand for goods and services, and thereby adversely affects the volume of output and employment.

Money Illusion in the Supply of Labour: Economic theory is usually based on the assumption that the people behave in a rational and consistent manner. A consumer, for instance, is not expected to change his pattern of expenditure if his income doubles and simultaneously the prices of all the goods he buys also double. Similarly, a business firm is not expected to change its output when the price of its product and the prices of all the factors which it employs change in the same ratio. The real wage being a ratio between the money-wage rate and the current price level of goods consumed by wage-earners, it would be expected that at a particular real wage the same amount of labour would be forthcoming irrespective of the level of money-wage-rate.

But, because of a number of reasons, the "money illusion" does influence the labour supply function. In other words, the labour does attach importance to the money-wages rate, and more labour would be forthcoming at the same real wage, the higher is the money wage. Let us briefly state such reasons. In the first place, high money-wages-rates are a concrete and immediate accomplishment of the leadership of individual unions. The object of each individual union is to protect, and if possible to advance, their wages relative to other unions. The cost of living is a remote phenomenon over which a single bargaining unit has hardly any control. The unions have to bargain money wages for periods during which the cost of living may frequently change. Secondly, the wage-earners have obligations fixed in terms of money, *e.g.*, debts, taxes, contractual payments like insurance payments. A reduction in wages, even if accompanied by a proportionate decline in current prices, would increase the burden of such obligations. Thirdly, the labour may have inelastic price expectations. They may expect a certain 'normal' price level, or range of price levels, to prevail in the future irrespective of the current level of prices. With such price expectations, it is obviously in the interest of wage-earners to have, with the same current real income, the highest possible current money income. The higher are their money incomes, the larger would be their money saving and, therefore, their expected command over future goods. They will resist reductions in money wages even when prices are falling, not only because of their fear that wages will not rise again when prices rise but also because the expected price rise would reduce the real value of their current savings. Fourthly, the labour may be actually ignorant of the course of prices or naively deceived by the "money illusion." This argument might have some force in the past but in recent years the workers have become very much conscious of the cost of living and as such this argument does not carry much weight.

The "money illusion" may frequently affect not only labourers but also the suppliers of other factors of production. As such there can be price rigidities in all markets and consequently fluctuations in the use of all factors of production. In such an economy, the money-wage-rate is an independent determinant of the volume of employment.

The wage-earners may be affected by the 'money illusion' not only when they are selling their labour but also when they are acting as consumers. Not only wage-earners but all consumers may be influenced by the 'money illusion'. The Keynesian consumption function, which is crucial to the Keynesian solution to the money wage problem, however, is formulated in real terms. The real consumption expenditure is considered to be determined by real income. This is the significance of Keynes' use of wage-units. If 'money illusion' influences consumption and saving decisions, real consumption expenditure would depend on the level of money income as well as that of real income.

KEYNESIAN EMPLOYMENT FUNCTION

Suppose our aggregate supply function is $Y = f(N)$, which relates the employment N with the aggregate supply price of the corresponding output. The employment function only differs from the aggregate supply function in that it is, in effect, its inverse function and is defined in terms of the wage-unit; the object of the employment function being to relate the amount of the effective demand, measured in terms of the wage-unit, directed to a given firm or industry or to industry as a whole with the amount of employment, the supply price of the output of which will compare to that amount of effective demand. Thus, if an amount of effective demand D_{wr}, measured in wage-units, directed to a firm or industry calls forth an amount of employment N_r in that firm or industry, the employment function is given by $N_r = f_r(D_{wr})$. Or, more generally, if we are entitled to assume that D_{wr} is a unique function of the total effective demand D_w, the employment function is given by $N_r = f_r(D_{wr})$. That is to say, N_r men will be employed in industry r when effective demand is D_w.

There are two reasons why the substitution of the employment function for the ordinary supply curve has been considered. In the first place, it expresses the relevant facts in terms of the units to which we have restricted ourselves, without introducing any of the units which have a dubious quantitive character. And secondly, it lends itself to the problems of industry and output as a whole, as distinct from the problems of a single industry or firm in a given environment, more easily than does the ordinary supply curve.

The ordinary demand curve for a particular commodity is drawn on some assumption as to the incomes of members of the public, and has to be re-drawn if the incomes change. In the same way the ordinary supply curve for a particular commodity is drawn on some assumption as to the output of industry as a whole and is liable to change if the aggregate output of industry is changed. When, therefore, we are examining the response of individual industries to changes in aggregate employment, we are necessarily concerned, not with a single demand curve for each industry, in conjunction with a single supply curve, but with two families of such curves corresponding to different assumptions as to the aggregate employment. In the case of the employment function, however, the task of arriving at a function for industry as a whole which will reflect changes in employment as a whole is more practicable.

Now assume that propensity to consume is given as well as the other factors which we have taken as given in above, and that we are considering changes in employment in response to changes in the rate of investment. Subject to this assumption, for every level of effective demand in terms of wage-units there will be a corresponding aggregate employment and this effective demand will be divided in determinate proportions between consumption and investment. Moreover, each level of effective demand will correspond to a given distribution of income. It is reasonable, therefore, further to assume that corresponding to a given level of aggregate effective demand there is a unique distribution of it between different industries. This enables us to determine what amount of employment in each industry will correspond to a given level of aggregate employment. This is to say, it gives us the amount of employment in each particular industry corresponding to each level of aggregate effective demand measured in terms of wage-units, so that the conditions are satisfied for the second form of the employment function for the industry, namely $N_r = f_r(D_w)$. Thus we have the advantage that, in these conditions, the individual employment functions are additive in the sense that the employment function for industry as a whole, corresponding to a given level of effective demand, is equal to the sum of the employment functions for each separate industry. Thus, we have

$$f_r(D_w) = N = \sum N_r = \sum f_r(D_w)$$

Next, let us define the elasticity of employment. The elasticity of employment for a given industry is

$$e_{er} = \frac{dN_r}{dD_{wr}} \cdot \frac{D_{wr}}{N_r}$$

Since, it measures the response of the number of labour-units employed in the industry to changes in the number of wages-units which are expected to be spent on purchasing its output. The elasticity of employment for industry as a whole we shall write

$$e_e = \frac{dN}{dD_w} \cdot \frac{D_w}{N_r}$$

Provided that we can find some sufficiently satisfactory method of measuring output, it is also useful to define what may be called the elasticity of output or production, which measures the rate at which output in any industry increases when more effective demand in terms of wage-units is directed towards it, namely

$$e_{or} = \frac{dO_r}{dD_{wr}} \cdot \frac{D_{wr}}{O_r}$$

Provided we can assume that the price is equal to the marginal prime cost, we then have

$$\Delta D_{wr} = \frac{1}{1 - e_{or}} \cdot DP_r$$

where P_r is the expected profit. It follows from this that if $e_{or} = 0$, i.e. if the output of the industry is perfectly inelastic, the whole of the increased effective demand (in terms of wage-units) is expected to accrue to the entrepreneur as profit, i.e. $\Delta D_{wr} = \Delta P_r$; whilst if $e_{pr} = 1$, i.e. if the elasticity of output is unity, no part of the increased effective demand is expected to accrue as profit, the whole of it being absorbed by the elements entering into marginal prime cost.

Moreover, if the output of an industry is a function $f(N_r)$ of the labour employed in it, we have

$$\frac{1-e_{or}}{e_{er}} = -\frac{N_r f''(N_r)}{p_{wr}\{f'(N_r)\}^2}$$

where p_{wr} is the expected price of a unit of output in terms of the wage-unit. Thus, the condition $e_{or} = 1$ means that $f''(N_r) = 0$, i.e. that there are constant returns in response to increased employment.

Now, insofar as the classical theory assumes that real wages are always equal to the marginal disutility of labour and that the latter increases when employment increases, so that the labour supply will fall off; if real wages are reduced, it is assuming that in practice it is impossible to increase expenditure in terms of wage-units. If this were true, the concept of elasticity of employment would have no field of application.

Moreover, it would, in this event, be impossible to increase employment by increasing expenditure in terms of money; for money-wages would rise proportionately to the increased money expenditure so that there would be no increase of expenditure in terms of wage-units and consequently no increase in employment. But if the classical assumption does not hold good, it will be possible to increase employment by increasing expenditure in terms of money until real wages have fallen to equality with the marginal disutility of labour, at which point there will, by definition, be full employment.

Generally, e_{or} will have a value intermediate between zero and unity. The extent to which prices (in terms of wage-units) will rise, i.e. the extent to which real wages will fall, when money expenditure is increased, depends, therefore, on the elasticity of output in response to expenditure in terms of wage-units.

Let the elasticity of the expected price p_{wr} in response to changes in effective demand D_{wr}, namely $(dp_{wr}/dD_{wr}) \times (D_{wr}/p_{wr})$, be written as e'_{pr}.

Since, $O_r \times p_{wr} = D_{wr}$, we have

$$\frac{dO_r}{dD_{wr}} \times \frac{D_{wr}}{O_r} + \frac{dp_{wr}}{dD_{wr}} \times \frac{D_{wr}}{p_{wr}} = 1$$

or, $e'_{pr} + e_{or} = 1$

This implies that the sum of the elasticities of price and of output in response to changes in effective demand (measured in terms of wage-units) is equal to unity. Effective demand spends itself, partly in affecting output and partly in affecting price, according to this law.

In case of an industry if we assume that we have a unit in which output as a whole can be measured, the same line of argument applies, so that $e'_p + e_o = 1$, where the elasticities without a suffix r apply to industry as a whole.

Let us now measure values in money instead of wage-units and extend to this case our conclusions in respect of industry as a whole.

If W stands for the money-wages of a unit of labour and p for the expected price of a unit of output as a whole in terms of money, we can write e_p (= (Ddp)/pdD)) for the elasticity of money-prices in response to changes in effective demand measured in terms of money, and e_w (= (DdW)/WdD)) for the elasticity of money-wages in response to changes in effective demand in terms of money. Thus, we can show that $e_p = 1 = e_o(1 - e_w)$.

If $e_o = 0$ or if $e_w = 1$, output will be unaltered and prices will rise in the same proportion as effective demand in terms of money. Otherwise, they will rise in a smaller proportion.

So far we have seen that to every level or aggregate effective demand there corresponds a unique distribution of effective demand between the products of each individual industry. Now, as aggregate expenditure changes, the corresponding expenditure on the products of an individual industry will not, in general, change in the same proportion—partly because individuals will not, as their incomes rise, increase the amount of the products of each separate industry, which they purchase, in the same proportion, and partly because the prices of different commodities will respond in different degrees to increases in expenditure upon them.

The assumption that changes in employment depend solely on changes in aggregate effective demand (in terms of wage-units), is no better than a first approximation, if we admit that there is more than one way in which an increase of income can be spent. For the way in which we suppose the increase in aggregate demand to be distributed between different commodities may considerably influence the volume of employment. If, for example, the increased demand is largely directed towards products which have a high elasticity of employment, the aggregate increase in employment will be greater than if it is largely directed towards products which have a low elasticity of employment. In the same way employment may fall off without there having been any change in aggregate demand, if the direction of demand is changed in favour of products having a relatively low elasticity of employment.

These considerations are particularly important if we are concerned with short-period phenomena in the sense of changes in the amount or direction of demand which are not foreseen some time ahead. Some products take time to produce, so that it is practically impossible to increase the supply of them quickly. Thus, if additional demand is directed to them without notice, they will show a low elasticity of employment; although it may be that, given sufficient notice, their elasticity of employment approaches unity.

Suppose a product has a period of production n if n time-units of notice of changes in the demand for it have to be given if it is to offer its maximum elasticity of employment. Obviously consumption-goods, taken as a whole, have in this sense the longest period of production, since of every productive process they constitute the last stage. Thus if the first impulse towards the increase in effective demand comes from an increase in consumption, the initial elasticity of employment will be further below its eventual equilibrium-level than if the impulse comes from an increase in investment. Moreover, if the increased demand is directed to products with a relatively low elasticity of employment, a larger proportion of it will go to swell the incomes of entrepreneurs and a smaller proportion to swell the incomes of wage-earners and other prime-cost factors; with the possible result that the repercussions may be somewhat less favourable to expenditure, owing to the likelihood of entrepreneurs saving more of their increment of income than wage-earners would. Nevertheless the distinction between the two cases must not be over-stated, since a large part of the reactions will be much the same in both.

However, long the notice given to entrepreneurs of a prospective change in demand, it is not possible for the initial elasticity of employment, in response to a given increase of investment, to be as great as its eventual equilibrium value, unless there are surplus stocks and surplus capacity at every stage of production. On the other hand, the depletion of the surplus stocks will have an offsetting effect on the amount by which investment increases. If we suppose that there are initially some surpluses at every point, the initial elasticity of employment may approximate to unity; then after the stocks have been absorbed, but before an increased supply is coming forward at an adequate rate from the earlier stages of production, the elasticity will fall away; rising again towards unity as the new position of equilibrium is approached. This is subject, however, to some qualification insofar as there are rent factors which absorb more expenditure as employment increases, or if the rate of interest increases. For these reasons perfect stability of prices is impossible in an economy subject to change—unless, indeed, there is some peculiar mechanism which ensures temporary fluctuations of just the right degree in the propensity to consume. But price-instability arising in this way does not lead to the kind of profit stimulus which is liable to bring into existence excess capacity. For the windfall gain will wholly accrue to those entrepreneurs who happen to possess products at a relatively advanced stage of production, and there is nothing which the entrepreneur, who does not possess specialised resources of the right kind, can do to attract this gain to himself. Thus the inevitable price-instability due to change cannot affect the actions of entrepreneurs, but merely directs a *de facto* windfall of wealth into the laps of the lucky ones.

When effective demand is deficient, there is under-employment of labour in the sense that there are men unemployed who would be willing to work at less than the existing real wage. Consequently, as effective demand increases, employment increases, though at a real wage equal to or less than the existing one, until a point comes at which there is no surplus of labour available at the then existing real wage; i.e. no more men (or hours of labour) available unless money-wages rise (from this point onwards) faster than prices. The next problem is to consider what will happen if, when this point has been reached, expenditure still continues to increase. Up to this point the decreasing return from applying more labour to a given capital equipment has been offset by the acquiescence of labour in a diminishing real wage. But after this point a unit of labour would require the inducement of the equivalent of an increased quantity of product, whereas the yield from applying a further unit would be a diminished quantity of product. The conditions of strict equilibrium require, therefore, that wages and prices, and consequently profits also, should all rise in the same proportion as expenditure, the 'real' position, including the volume of output and employment, being left unchanged in all respects.

Nevertheless there are certain practical qualifications to this conclusion which must be borne in mind in applying it to an actual case:

(a) For a time at least, rising prices may delude entrepreneurs into increasing employment beyond the level which maximises their individual profits measured in terms of the product. For they are so accustomed to regard rising sale-proceeds in terms of money as a signal for expanding production, that they may continue to do so when this policy has in fact ceased to be to their best advantage; i.e. they may underestimate their marginal user cost in the new price environment.

(b) Since, that part of his profit which the entrepreneur has to hand on to the rentier is fixed in terms of money, rising prices, even though unaccompained by any change in output, will redistribute incomes to the advantage of the entrepreneur and to the disadvantage of the rentier, which may have a reaction on the propensity to consume. This, however, is not a process which will have only begun when full employment has been attained; it will have been making steady progress all the time that the expenditure was increasing. If the rentier is less prone to spend than the entrepreneur, the gradual withdrawal of real income from the resources will mean that full employment will be reached with a smaller increase in the quantity of money and a smaller reduction in the rate of interest than will be the case if the opposite hypothesis holds. After full employment has been reached, a further rise of prices will, if the first hypothesis continues to hold, mean that the rate of interest will have to rise somewhat to prevent prices from rising indefinitely, and that the increase in the quantity of money will be less than in proportion to the increase in expenditure; whilst if the second hypothesis holds, the opposite will be the case. It may be that, as the

> real income of the rentier is diminished, a point will come when, as a result of his growing relative impoverishment, there will be a change-over from the first hypothesis to the second, which point may be reached either before or after full employment has been attained.

There is, perhaps, something a little perplexing in the apparent asymmetry between inflation and deflation. For whilst a deflation of effective demand below the level required for full employment will diminish employment as well as prices, an inflation of it above this level will merely affect prices. This asymmetry is, however, merely a reflection of the fact that, whilst labour is always in a position to refuse to work on a scale involving a real wage which is less than the marginal disutility of that amount of employment, it is not in a position to insist on being offered work on a scale involving a real wage which is not greater than the marginal disutility of that amount of employment.

Conclusion

It is not easy to work out a clear-cut relationship between wage-cuts and employment. "Even Keynes found no simple answer. His analysis is pragmatic and leads to an agnostic position. In some circumstances, the effect will be favourable; in others not. All we can do is to apply our analysis to a variety of assumed conditions."[7] To cite from another book of Hansen, "there are few, if indeed any, economists now who will dogmatically assert either that wage cuts will surely increase employment or that such cuts cannot possibly have any favourable effect. There are too many unknowns that vary with special conditions and circumstances."[8] But there is certainly no simple rule as the classical economists envisage relating the level of employment to the money wage rates.

WAGE-BOOSTS

We have seen that a reduction in wages cannot cure unemployment. At the other extreme is what may be called the "trade unionist argument" that the way out of depression is to raise money wages. It is held that an increase in wages will increase total effective demand and hence employment. This argument, however, has the same flaw as the one for reduction of wages. The rise in costs and prices that follows the rise in wages will offset the nominal increase in purchasing power. The increase will thus be only in nominal effective demand and not in real effective demand or, in other words, in employment.

As regards the indirect effects, rise in wages would redistribute income in favour of the wages-earners which would raise the propensity to consume. But it would have adverse effects on the marginal efficiency of capital and the rate of interest. An increase in wages at a time when the business is suffering losses from costs in excess of revenues would further impair the confidence of the business community in the prospects for profitable operations. Higher prices resulting from higher wages would increase the demand for money for transaction purpose. Unless there is an expansion in the total quantity of money, it will decrease the quantity available as a store of value which will lead to a rise in the rate of interest. A rise in the rate of interest will discourage investment and thus adversely affect the total volume of employment.

FLEXIBLE WAGE POLICY VERSUS FLEXIBLE MONETARY POLICY

The process whereby wage cuts lead to a decline in interest rates is not different from that whereby the total quantity of money is increased in order to increase the amount of money available for inactive balances. Both do the same thing. In the words of Keynes himself, "We can......theoretically......produce precisely the same effects on the rate of interest by reducing wages, whilst leaving the quantity of money unchanged, that we can produce by increasing the quantity of money whilst leaving the level of wages unchanged."[9]

Though, theoretically wage policy and monetary policy are very much the same, there is a world of difference between the two in actual practice. According to Keynes only "a foolish person........ would prefer a flexible wage policy to a flexible money policy; unless he can point to advantages from the former which are not obtainable from the latter."[10] There are important practical difficulties with the flexible wage policy which do not apply to flexible monetary policy. Important of such difficulties are mentioned below.

It is almost impossible to affect a general wage cut. This is possible only in a dictatorial society. In democratic countries, the wages are determined by the system of collective bargaining between individual labour unions and employers' unions which means that the wage reductions, if any, would be only piecemeal, that is, the workers with weak trade unions would be the first and the largest victims of cut in wages. In contrast, it is very easy for the government to increase the quantity of money to lower the rate of interest.

Even if labourers can be compelled to accept a general cut in wages, such a step would go against the democratic ideal of social justice. The non-wage-earners, particularly the rentiers receiving incomes from land rents, bonds and other forms of contractual securities would benefit at the cost of wage-earners. In contrast, an increase in the supply of money would cause a reduction in the real income of all sections by raising the prices of almost all goods.

Lower prices brought about by a general cut in wage-rate increases the burden of private as well as public debt. As against this, an increase in the supply of money reduces such burden. The existence of a large public or private debt is often an important objection to a policy of general reduction in wages and prices.

In an open economy, a general wage cut, though strengthens the balance of payments position, would deteriorate the terms of trade and thus lead to a reduction in the real income of the country.

A flexible wage policy would cause great instability of prices which would make business calculations difficult and thus be injurious to the smooth functioning of the economy. In contrast, the use of monetary policy for attaining the same purpose would create less instability and thereby promote proper functioning of the economy.

Keynes was of the opinion that a flexible monetary policy is an alternative to and on both economic and political grounds preferable to a flexible wage policy. According to him, under certain conditions money wage cuts might lead to a small increase in employment but anything that can be attained by reducing wages, as a matter of practical policy, can be attained better by monetary policy. In the words of Prof. Lerner, "To seek alleviation of depression by reducing money wages, rather than directly reducing the rate of interest or otherwise encouraging investment or consumption, is to abandon the high road for a devious, dark, difficult and unreliable path, for no better reason than that the dangers that await one at the common destination are more clearly seen when it is approached by the broad way."[11]

KEYNES' WAGE POLICY

Keynes was of the opinion that for a closed economy the best short run policy was to keep money wages as stable as possible. As seen above, besides the serious practical difficulties, steadily declining wages adversely affect the marginal efficiency of capital and thereby the volume of employment. Stable wages would remove this type of adverse effect on the volume of investment. In the long run, when productivity is likely to increase steadily, a choice can be made between stable wage-rates and gradually declining prices or stable prices and gradually rising money wages. Keynes preferred the latter alternative because it will (i) have favourable effects upon the expectations of the entrepreneurs and hence upon the inducement to invest, (ii) lighten the real burden of debt, (iii) provide greater psychological encouragement to the active working class than will the real wages in the form of stable money wages and falling prices, and (iv) facilitate the transfer of resources out of declining industries into growing industries by raising money wages in the latter without having to lower them in the former.

WAGE-PRICE POLICY DURING DEPRESSION

During the depression period, the decline in aggregate demand exhibits itself immediately in a decline in output and prices. The decline in prices is greater in highly competitive industries where commodities are bought and sold in organized markets. In contrast, in oligopolistic industries, where firms have some control over the prices they charge, prices, at first, decline slowly or not at all. The result is that the decline in economic activity normally leads to distortions in the price structure. The past depressions show that farm prices have declined more than industrial prices and the costs and prices in construction industry (and also in other capital-goods industries) have tended to be sticky and to remain high when the demand for building falls off. A more balanced fall in prices, and particularly lower prices for investment goods, would tend to moderate the severity of a depression. This indicates the scope for government intervention in the field of prices. The government should take steps to prevent a demoralising decline in prices in competitive industries (particularly agriculture) and force down costs and prices in monopolistic industries (particularly in construction and other investment goods industries).

FULL EMPLOYMENT AND INFLATION

The inflationary aspect of the wage-price problem raises two critical and related questions. Firstly, when aggregate demand rises, whether during the natural course of a business upswing or as a consequence of government measures, is the increase in spending likely to push up wages and prices? Secondly, is there danger, if full employment is continuously maintained, that the demand of strong labour unions and other organised groups will cause wages and prices to rise steadily, so that the objective of price stability becomes unattainable? Or to put in a more simple way, may not full employment and price stability be incompatible as objectives of policy?

A continuously maintained full employment is likely to lead to a steady rise in wages and prices. If the fear of unemployment disappears and the government undertakes to take measures to stimulate aggregate demand in case there appears any unemployment, the trade unions are likely to press steadily for higher wages. In case, as is very likely, the resulting wage increases are in excess of the normal improvements in productivity, labour costs will rise and businessmen will raise their prices. With the rise in the prices of industrial products the farm groups will demand government help in raising agricultural prices. And the general rise in prices will lead to a fresh round of rise in wage rates.

It is widely accepted that a continuously maintained full employment policy invariably leads to one of the two results. Either the goal of price stability must be abandoned or else full employment can be maintained without involving open inflation only if the government interferes with the traditional economic liberties by depriving labour of its right to bargain freely with employers, by imposing wage and price controls, and by direct control of consumer and business spending through rationing, allocations, and similar devices. On the other hand, some economists are more hopeful and believe that organized labour and other groups can be educated to keep their demands within limits so that full employment can be maintained without a steady rise in the price level. Some people, while accepting that a full employment policy leads to inflation in the absence of controls, prefer to restrict the power of labour and other groups if necessary to attain both price stability and full employment.

MOVEMENT OF REAL AND MONEY WAGES

The theory of the firm teaches us that a firm in a competitive industry will hire workers up to the point where the value of the marginal product (marginal product multiplied by the price of output) just equals the cost of the factor. Assuming that pure competition prevails, this profit maximization condition may be written as:

$$w = px_n$$

or,

$$w/p = x_n$$

where w stands for the money wage, p for the price level, w/p for the real wage, and X_n for the marginal product of labour. The demand for labour may therefore be written as:

$$N_d = D\left[\frac{w}{p}\right]$$

which states that demand for labour is a function of the real wage. Since the law of diminishing returns suggests that the marginal product of labour declines as more workers are hired, increase in employment cannot be brought about without a decline in the real wage. Most of the economists, accepting the labour demand function as written above, assume that a decline in real wages is a natural consequence of emergence from depression. Noting that money wages rise with an increase in output, Keynes expressed the opinion that "the change in real wages associated with a change in money wages, so far from being usually in the same direction, is almost always in the opposite direction."[12] In other words, Keynes and most economists believed that, even though money wages rise during recovery, prices rise even faster so that real wages fall. The empirical, analysis, however, showed that the real wages actually rise with the increase in output and employment.[13] Apparently there is something wrong with the idea that the demand for labour is a decreasing function of the real wage.

In a later article[14] Keynes conceded that real wages seem to increase, though he refused to abandon the assumption of diminishing returns in the short run. He suggested instead that real wage increases would be consistent with employment increases if the assumptions of pure competition were abandoned. While under pure competition a producer would hire workers up to the point at which the wage rate is equal to the value of the marginal product (marginal product multiplied by price), under monopoly he would hire workers up to the point at which the wage rate equals the marginal revenue product (marginal product multiplied by marginal revenue). Since marginal revenue (mr) can be written as

$$mr = p\left[1 - \frac{1}{e}\right]$$

where p is the price of output and *e* is the price elasticity of demand, we may write

$$w = p\left[1 - \frac{1}{e}\right]X_n$$

or,

$$\frac{w}{p} = \left[1 - \frac{1}{e}\right]X_n$$

as the condition for maximum profit. This means that we can write the demand for labour as

$$N_d = D\left[\frac{w}{p}, e\right]$$

Under these conditions output increases are compatible with real wage increases so long as demand elasticities increase with increases in aggregate demand. In fact, under imperfect competition, even if demand elasticities remain unchanged, increases in employment are not inconsistent with the increases in real wage rates.

It should be recognised that though a certain stock of capital goods exists, this does not, unless the stock of capital goods is indivisible, mean that whole of it will necessarily be employed in the sense that it is utilised in the production process. A factory having 40 machines may, for instance, in times of slack demand use only 30 machines because substitution between labour and machines is not perfect. 'The firm may, therefore, use only 30 machines together with some labour even though labour costs are variable while the machine costs are fixed in the short run'.

If the period of slack demand persists, the idle equipment may gradually be reduced. But since this can normally take place only by a slow process of depreciation and obsolescence, the typical depression can be expected to be characterised by widespread excess capacity, which, if equipment is divisible and production function is characterised by ranges of zero returns, may for purposes of analysis be considered unemployed. From this it follows that output can be expanded by hiring more labour, by bringing additional existing machines into use or by both. This means that there is more than one attainable marginal productivity of labour schedule and that enployment can be increased both by a shift in the schedule and by a movement along it. From this it follows that there may be many possible real wage rates that are compatible with labour market equilibrium.

Keynes ruled out, in the short run, the possibility of changes in organisation, equipment and techniques. In fact, changes in techniques go on year after year with sufficient speed and as such an expansion in output may be accompanied by constant real wages even if we assume rising cost curves. This is so because improvements in technology may counteract the increase in marginal cost arising from the shape of the cost functions.

Contrary to Keynes' view, it is now widely believed that the variable and marginal cost curves are substantially flat over wide ranges of output. If this is accepted, the process of increase in output and employment may not lead to a decline in real wage rates even if improvements in technology are ruled out in the short period. In case the possibilities of improvements in techniques are taken into consideration, there may even be an increase in real wages.

The classical theory supposes that a reduction in money-wages is quite capable in certain circumstances of affording a stimulus to output. Keynesian difference from this theory is primarily a difference of analysis. The generally accepted explanation is quite a simple one. It does not depend on roundabout repercussions, such as we shall discuss below. The argument simply is that a reduction in money-wages will stimulate demand by diminishing the price of the finished product, and will therefore increase output and employment up to the point where the reduction which labour has agreed to accept in its money-wages is just offset by the diminishing marginal efficiency of labour as output is increased.

The reduction in money-wages may have some effect on aggregate demand through its reducing the purchasing power of some of the workers, but that the real demand of other factors, whose money incomes have not been reduced, will be stimulated by the fall in prices, and that the aggregate demand of the workers themselves will be very likely increased as a result of the increased volume of employment, unless the elasticity of demand for labour in response to changes in money-wages is less than unity. Thus in the new equilibrium there will be more employment than there would have been otherwise except, perhaps, in some unusual limiting case which has no reality in practice.

In any given industry we have a demand schedule for the product relating the quantities which can be sold to the prices asked; we have a series of supply schedules relating the prices which will be asked for the sale of different quantities on various bases of cost; and these schedules between them lead up to a further schedule which, on the assumption that other costs are unchanged (except as a result of the change in output), gives us the demand schedule for labour in the industry relating the quantity of employment to different levels of wages, the shape of the curve at any point furnishing the elasticity of demand for labour. This conception is then transferred without substantial modification to industry as a whole; and it is supposed, by a parity of reasoning, that we have a demand schedule for labour in industry as a whole relating the quantity of employment to different levels of wages. It is held that it makes no material difference to this argument whether it is in terms of money-wages or of real wages. If we are thinking in terms of money-wages, we must, of course, correct for changes in the value of money; but this leaves the general tendency of the argument unchanged, since prices certainly do not change in exact proportion to changes in money-wages.

If this is the groundwork of the argument surely it is fallacious. For the demand schedules for particular industries can only be constructed on some fixed assumption as to the nature of the demand and supply schedules of other industries and as to the amount of the aggregate effective demand. It is invalid, therefore, to transfer the argument to industry as a whole unless we also transfer our assumption that the aggregate effective demand is fixed. Yet this assumption reduces the argument to an *ignoratio elenchi*. For, whilst no one would wish to deny the proposition that a reduction in money-wages accompanied by the same aggregate effective demand as before will be associated with an increase in employment, the precise question at issue is whether the reduction in money-wages will or will not be accompanied by the same aggregate effective demand as before measured in money, or, at any rate, by an aggregate effective demand which is not reduced in full proportion to the reduction in money-wages. But if the classical theory is not allowed to extend by analogy its conclusions in respect of a particular industry to industry as a whole, it is wholly unable to answer the question what effect on employment a reduction in money-wages will have. For it has no method of analysis wherewith to tackle the problem. Professor Pigou's *Theory of Unemployment* seems to be get out of the classical theory all that can be got out of it; with the result that the book becomes a striking demonstration that this theory has nothing to offer, when it is applied to the problem of what determines the volume of actual employment as a whole.

Let us apply the Keynesian method of analysis to answering the problem. It falls into two parts:

(a) Does a reduction in money-wages have a direct tendency, to increase employment, being taken to mean that the propensity to consume, the schedule of the marginal efficiency of capital and the rate of interest are the same as before for the community as a whole?

(b) Does a reduction in money-wages have a certain or probable tendency to affect employment in a particular direction through its certain or probable repercussion on these three factors?

The volume of employment is uniquely correlated with the volume of effective demand measured in wage-units, and that the effective demand, being the sum of the expected consumption and the expected investment, cannot change, if the propensity to consume, the schedule of marginal efficiency of capital and the rate of interest are all unchanged. If, without any change in these factors, the entrepreneurs were to increase employment as a whole, their proceeds will necessarily fall short of their supply-price.

Perhaps it will help to rebut the crude conclusion that a reduction in money-wages will increase employment 'because it reduces the cost of production', if we follow up the course of events on the hypothesis most favourable to this view, namely that at the outset entrepreneurs *expect* the reduction in money-wages to have this effect. It is indeed not unlikely that the individual entrepreneur, seeing his own costs reduced, will overlook at the outset the repercussions on the demand for his product and will act on the assumption that he will be able to sell at a profit a larger output than before. If, then, entrepreneurs generally act on this expectation, will they in fact succeed in increasing their profits? Only if the community's marginal propensity to consume is equal to unity, so that there is no gap between the increment of income and the increment of consumption; or if there is an increase in investment, corresponding to the gap between the increment of income and the increment of consumption, which will only occur if the schedule of marginal efficiencies of capital has increased relatively to the rate of interest. Thus the proceeds realised from the increased output will disappoint the entrepreneurs and employment will fall back again to its previous figure, unless the marginal propensity to consume is equal to unity or the reduction in money-wages has had the effect of increasing the schedule of marginal efficiencies of capital relatively to the rate of interest and hence the amount of investment. For if entrepreneurs offer employment on a scale which, if they could sell their output at the expected price, would provide the public with incomes out of which they would save more than the amount of current investment, entrepreneurs are bound to make a loss equal to the difference; and this will be the case absolutely irrespective of the level of money-wages. At the best, the date of their disappointment can only be delayed for the interval during which their own investment in increased working capital is filling the gap.

Thus, the reduction in money-wages will have no lasting tendency to increase employment except by virtue of its repercussion either on the propensity to consume for the community as a whole, or on the schedule of marginal efficiencies of capital, or on the rate of interest. There is no method of analysing the effect of a reduction in money-wages, except by following up its possible effects on these three factors.

The most important repercussions on these factors are likely, in practice, to be the following:

(a) A reduction of money-wages will somewhat reduce prices. It will, therefore, involve some redistribution of real income—(i) from wage-earners to other factors entering into marginal prime cost whose remuneration has not been reduced and (ii) from entrepreneurs to rentiers to whom a certain income fixed in terms of money has been guranteed.

What will be the effect of this redistribution on the propensity to consume for the community as a whole? The transfer from wage-earners to other factors is likely to diminish the propensity to consume. But if rentiers represent on the whole the richer section of the community and those whose standard of life is least flexible, then the effect of this also will be unfavourable. What the net result will be on a balance of considerations, we can only guess. Probably it is more likely to be adverse than favourable.

(b) If we are dealing with an open system, and the reduction of money-wages is a reduction relatively to money-wages abroad when both are reduced to a common unit, it is evident that the changes will be favourable to investment, since it will tend to increase the balance of trade. This assumes that the advantage is not offset by a change in tariffs, quotas, etc.

(c) In the case of an open system, a reduction of money-wages, though it increases the favourable balance of trade, is likely to worsen the terms of trade. Thus there will be a reduction in real incomes, except in the case of the newly employed, which may tend to increase the propensity to consume.

(d) If the reduction of money-wages is expected to be a reduction relatively to money-wages in the future, the change will be favourable to investment, because as we have seen above, it will increase the marginal efficiency of capital; whilst for the same reason it may be favourable to consumption. If, on the other hand, the reduction leads to the expectation, or even to the serious possibility, of a further wage-reduction in prospect, it will have precisely the opposite effect. For it will diminish the marginal efficiency of capital and will lead to the postponement both of investment and of consumption.

(e) The reduction in the wages-bill, accompanied by some reduction in prices and in money-incomes generally, will diminish the need for cash for income and business purposes; and it will therefore reduce *pro tanto* the schedule of liquidity-preference for the community as a whole, *cetri paribus*, this will reduce the rate of interest and thus prove favourable to investment. In this case, however, the effect of expectation concerning the future will be of an opposite tendency to those just considered under (d). For, if wages and prices are expected to rise again later on, the favourable reaction will be much less pronounced in the case of long-term loans than in that of short-term loans. If, moreover, the reduction in wages disturb political confidence by causing popular discontent, the increase in liquidity-preference due to this cause may more than offset the relase of cash from the active circulation.

(f) Since a special reduction of money-wages is always advantageous to an individual entrepreneur or industry, a general reduction may also produce an optimistic tone in the minds of entrepreneurs, which may break through a vicious circle of unduly pessimistic estimates of the marginal efficiency of capital and set things moving again on a more normal basis of expectation. On the other hand, if the workers makes the same mistake as their employers about the effects of a general reduction, labour troubles may offset this favourable factor; apart from which, since there is, as a rule, no means of securing a simultaneous and equal reduction of money-wages in all industries, it is in the interest of all workers to resist a reduction in their own particular case. In fact, a movement by employers to revise money-wage bargains downward will be much more strongly resisted than a gradual and automatic lowering of real wages as a result of rising prices.

(g) On the other hand, the depressing influence on entrepreneurs of their greater burden of debt may partly offset any cheerful reactions from the reduction of wages. Indeed if the fall of wages and prices goes far, the embarrassment of those entrepreneurs who are heavily indebted may soon reach the point of insolvency, with severely adverse effects on investment. Moreover the effect of the lower price-level on the real burden of the national debt and hence on taxation is likely to prove very adverse to business confidence.

If, therefore, we restrict our argument to the case of a closed system, and assume that there is nothing to be hoped, but if anything the contrary, from the repercussions of the new distribution of real incomes on the community's propensity to spend, it follows that we must base any hopes of favourable results to employment from a reduction in money-wages mainly on an improvement in investment due either to an increased marginal efficiency of capital under (d) or a decreased rate of interest under (f). Let us consider these two possibilities in further detail.

The contingency, which is favourable to an increase in the marginal efficiency of capital, is that in which money-wages are believed to have touched bottom, so that further changes are expected to be in the upward direction. The most unfavourable contingency is that in which money-wages are slowly sagging downwards and each reduction in wages serves to diminish confidence in the prospective maintenance of wages. When we enter on a period of weakening effective demand, a sudden large reduction of money-wages to a level so low that no one believes in its indefinite continuance would be the event most favourable to a strengthening of effective demand. But this could only be accomplished by administrative decree and is scarcely practical politics under a system of free wage-bargaining. On the other hand, it would be much better that wages should be rigidly fixed and deemed incapable of material changes, than that depressions should be accompanied by a gradual downward tendency of money-wages, a further moderate wage reduction being expected to signalise each increase of; say, 1 percent in the amount of unemployment. For example, the effect of an expectation that wages are going to sag by, say, 2 percent in the coming year will be roughly equivalent to the effect of a rise of 2 percent in the amount of interest payable for the same period. The same observations apply *mutatis mutandis* to the case of a boom.

It follows that with the actual practices and institutions of the contemporary world it is more expedient to aim at a rigid money-wage policy than at a flexible policy responding by easy stages to changes in the amount of unemployment; so far, that is to say, as the marginal efficiency of capital is concerned. But is this conclusion upset when we turn to the rate of interest follows?

If the quantity of money is itself a function of the wage- and price-level, there is indeed, nothing to hope in this direction. But if the quantity of money is virtually fixed, it is evident that its quantity in terms of wage-units can be indefinitely increased by a sufficient reduction in money-wages; and that its quantity in proportion to incomes generally can be largely increased, the limit to this increase depending on the proportion of wage-cost to marginal prime cost and on the response of other elements of marginal prime cost to the falling wage-unit.

We can, therefore, theoretically at least, produce precisely the same effects on the rate of interest by reducing wages, whilst leaving the quantity of money unchanged, that we can produce by increasing the quantity of money whilst leaving the level of wages unchanged. It follows that wage reductions, as a method of securing full employment, are also subject to the same limitations as the method of increasing the quantity of money. The same reasons as those mentioned above, which limit the efficacy of increases in the quantity of money as a means of increasing investment to the optimum figure, apply *mutatis mutandis* to wage reductions. Just as a moderate increase in the quantity of money may exert an inadequate influence over the long-term rate of interest, whilst an immoderate increase may offset its other advantages by its disturbing effect on confidence; so a moderate reduction in money-wages may prove inadequate, whilst an immoderate reduction might shatter confidence even if it were practicable.

There is, therefore, no ground for the belief that a flexible wage policy is capable of maintaining a state of continuous full employment—any more than for the belief that an open-market monetary policy is capable, unaided, of achieving this result. The economic system cannot be made self-adjusting along these lines.

If, indeed, labour were always in a position to take action (and were to do so), whenever there was less than full employment, to reduce its money demands by concerted action to whatever point was required to make money so abundant relatively to the wage-unit that the rate of interest would fall to a level compatible with full employment, we should, in effect, have monetary management by the trade unions, aimed at full employment, instead of by the banking system.

Nevertheless while a flexible wage policy and a flexible money policy come to the same thing, in as much as they are alternative means of changing the quantity of money in terms of wage-units, in other respects there is, of course, a world of difference between them. Let us consider the four outstanding considerations:

(a) Except in a socialised community where wage-policy is settled by decree, there is no means of securing uniform wage reductions for every class of labour. The result can only be brought about by a series of gradual, irregular changes, justifiable on no criterion of social justice or economic expedience, and probably completed only after wasteful and disastrous struggles, where those in the weakest bargaining position will suffer relatively to the rest. A change in the quantity of money, on the other hand, is already within the power of most governments by open-market policy or analogous measures. Having regard to human nature and our institutions, it can only be a foolish person who would prefer a flexible wage policy to a flexible money policy, unless he can point to advantages from the former which are not obtainable from the latter. Moreover, other things being equal, a method which it is comparatively easy to apply should be deemed preferable to a method which is probably so difficult as to be impracticable.

(b) If money-wages are inflexible, such changes in prices as occur will mainly correspond to the diminishing marginal productivity of the existing equipment as the output from it is increased. Thus the greatest practicable fairness will be maintained between labour and the factors whose remuneration is contractually fixed in terms of money, in particular the rentier class and persons with fixed salaries on the permanent establishment of a firm, an institution or the State. If important classes are to have their remuneration fixed in terms of money in any case, social justice and social expediency are best served if the remunerations of all factors are somewhat inflexible in terms of money. Having regard to the large groups of incomes which are comparatively inflexible in terms of money, it can only be an unjust person who would prefer a flexible wage policy to a flexible money policy, unless he can point to advantages from the former which are not obtainable from the latter.

(c) The method of increasing the quantity of money in terms of wage-units by decreasing the wage-unit increases proportionately the burden of debt; whereas the method of producing the same result by increasing the quantity of money of producing the same result by increasing the quantity of money whilst leaving the wage-unit unchanged has the opposite effect. Having regard to the excessive burden of many types of debt, it can only be an inexperienced person who would prefer the former.

(d) If a sagging rate of interest has to be brought about by a sagging wage-level, there is, for the reasons given above, a double drag on the marginal efficiency of capital and a double reason for putting off investment and thus postponing recovery.

It follows, therefore, that if labour were to respond to conditions of gradually diminishing employment by offering its services at a gradually diminishing money-wage, this would not, as a rule, have the effect of reducing real wages and might even have the effect of increasing them, through its adverse influence on the volume of output. The chief result of this policy would be to cause a great instability of prices, so violent perhaps as to make business calculations futile in an economic society functioning after the manner of that in which we live. To suppose that a flexible wage policy is a right and proper adjunct of a system which on the whole is one of *laissez-faire*, is the opposite of the truth. It is only in a highly authoritarian society, where sudden, substantial, all-round changes could be decreed that a flexible wage policy could function with success.

This policy will result in a fair degree of stability in the price-level—greater stability, at least, than with a flexible wage policy. Apart from 'administered' or monopoly prices, the price-level will only change in the short period in response to the extent that changes in the volume of employment affect marginal prime costs; whilst in the long period they will only change in response to changes in the cost of production due to new techniques and new or increased equipment.

It is true that, if there are, nevertheless, large fluctuations in employment, substantial fluctuations in the price-level will accompany them. But the fluctuations will be less, as I have said above, than with a flexible wage policy.

Thus, with a rigid wage policy the stability of prices will be bound up in the short period with the avoidance of fluctuations in employment. In the long period, on the other hand, we are still left with the choice between a policy of allowing prices to fall slowly with the progress of technique and equipment whilst keeping wages stable, or of allowing wages to rise slowly whilst keeping prices stable. On the whole my preference is for the latter alternative, on account of the fact that it is easier with an expectation of higher wages in future to keep the actual level of employment within a given range of full employment than with an expectation of lower wages in future, and on account also of the social advantages of gradually diminishing the burden of debt, the greater ease of adjustment from decaying to growing industries, and the psychological encouragement likely to be felt from a moderate tendency for money-wages to increase.

WAGE POLICY FOR FULL EMPLOYMENT

The full employment situation that would be reached through a simple application of functional finance would be one of low full employment. Whenever the number of unemployed falls below a fairly high figure, as already seen, the bargaining power of labour becomes strong which leads to a rise in wage rates and consequently to inflationary pressures even though there is no technical reason, in terms of real limitations on the mobility of labour, why unemployment should not be reduced to a much lower figure. Attainment of high full employment requires a wage policy which prevents inflationary wage increases.

Such a wage policy should be directed not at real wages but at money wages. Basically real wages are much more important than money wage rates but it is only the money wage rates that policy can directly affect. It is possible to raise (or to lower) a money wage rate and to know that it is in fact raised (or lowered). The same is not true of real wage. An attempt to change the real wage by changing the money wage may be defeated. If an increase in money wage rate leads to an equal increase in the prices of goods, and services bought by the workers, the real wage will not in fact have been raised at all. And this type of phenomena is not unlikely in actual practice. Raising money wage rates always increases costs which naturally leads to a rise in prices.

Secondly, the wage policy should be directed not at the general level of money wage rates but at specific wage rates in particular industries, trades and regions. This is because an over-all change in wages in general without any change in the relation of particular money wage rates to each other brings about a proportional change in prices, leaves the real wage rates unchanged, and has no effect on the volume of employment.

Though the wage policy should be directed at particular wage rates in particular labour markets, it must be such as results in desirable general effects on the general level of wages and on the general level of prices and incomes.

An important effect of a rise in the general level of money wages and the resultant rise in prices is the effect on the relationship between debtors and creditors because of the reduction in the real value of the debts. There is also a monetary effect. At a higher level of money wages, prices, and incomes, a larger volume of money is required to carry on with the same convenience as before, the same level of real economic activity, that is, in employing the same number of men and producing the same quantity of goods and services.

If the monetary authorities do not increase the stock of money, money will become tight. The tightness of money can lead to curtailment of investment and other economic activity which would result in unemployment and a reduction in real output and income. Many people would hold increase in money wage rate responsible for such unemployment. But other would put the blame for unemployment on the monetary authorities for their failure to increase the stock of money. It would, of course, be easier and more practicable to increase the supply of money than to lower all wages and prices. Increase in the supply of money would keep the wages and prices at a higher level without any real change in the production and consumption of goods and services or in the volume of employment in comparison with the situation before the money wages were raised.

The raising or lowering the general level of wages and prices can be very disturbing not only to the debtors and creditors but to those in charge of monetary policy and to investors and all who are concerned about what wages and prices are going to be in future. The wage policy, therefore, should be such as keeps the prices and the value of money stable.

It is not possible to have a wage policy which would stabilise both the general level of wages and the general level of prices. This is because productivity is continually increasing. Improvements in techniques of production resulting from a continuous process of inventions and scientific discoveries reduce the costs and prices of products in relation to the wage rate. If with the improvements in productivity, a choice is to be made between stable wages with declining prices and stable prices with rising wages, the latter course would be preferable. The latter course makes the financial management of the economy much easier and most probably the workers would like to see their increased real income over time taking the form of more money in their pay envelopes rather than the less tangible form of being able to buy more goods with the same amount of money.

The function of wages is to induce workers to work and to make them do the kind of work that is most effective in satisfying the needs of consumers—to make them produce the goods and services which the consumers prefer. Higher wages are the means of attracting workers where they are needed more. Similarly, lower wages are the means of persuading workers to leave places where they are needed less.

Higher wages have to be offered to induce workers to go where there is an increase in demand for their product or to go where they would otherwise not like to go because the conditions of work are not very congenial or the nature of work is not to their taste.

According to Lerner, wage policy can be based on indices of relative attractiveness.[15] An index of relative attractiveness of any occupation is provided by the ratio between the number of people who are qualified and ready to work in the occupation but have not been able to get a job there and the number of people actually employed in the occupation. For the economy as a whole the corresponding figure is an average that may be called the "national average index" of attractiveness of all occupations. The wage policy consists of rules indicating that wages should in general rise at a rate equal to the rate of increase in productivity, that wages should rise faster where the index of relative attractiveness is sufficiently less than the national average, and that wages should be frozen where the index of relative attractiveness is sufficiently greater than the national average.

The increases in wages suggested above can be effected either frequently (say quarterly, half-yearly or yearly) or infrequently (say after every three years). The increases in wages would be small in the former case and large in the latter one. The method of adjustment to be followed would depend on what is more satisfactory to the workers and to the employers and could very well be one of the matters for collective bargaining. The more continuous adjustment would involve least dislocation and would mean more complete adjustment to the current conditions. It is also felt that the workers would prefer less frequent but more exciting increases in wages. There might be some advantage in annual adjustments which could be considered together with other issues in the course of the collective bargaining agreements.

Some people may consider wage policy to be unfair to labour in that it seeks to check the inflationary spiral of wages and prices by checking the increases in wages. They may raise the question as to why not to check inflation by checking price increases instead of checking increase in wages. It is better to stabilise wages than to stabilise prices for two reasons. In the first place, a policy of stabilising wages does not impair the effectiveness of price mechanism. The price level can also be stabilised without fixing individual prices if it is done by rationing spending in general or by limiting total spending in some other manner. But this brings us to the second reason for preferring stabilisation of wages. If we stabilise prices by limiting spending, we are in fact keeping prices from rising by keeping demand down to the level where the bargaining power of the workers is no longer excessive. We are then back at the low level of full employment with the reserve army of unemployed that we want to avoid. We can attain high full employment only by checking inflation through wages instead of through prices.

PRICE FLEXIBILITY AND FULL EMPLOYMENT

The phrase "price flexibility" can be interpreted in two different ways, viz. (i) structural price flexibility, and (ii) cyclical price flexibility. Structural price flexibility means the long-term secular adjustment in the price structure. It is concerned not with the level of prices but with the interrelation of individual prices. Changes in technology and the methods of production, for instance, continually alter the relative unit costs of production of different commodities. Structural price flexibility means an adjustment of prices to change in relative unit costs resulting from unequal rates of technological progress in different industries or from shifts in the pattern of wants. A structurally flexible price system operates to direct the productive resources into channels which will yield the largest social product. In the absence of structural price flexibility, there would prevail an uneconomic allocation of resources and as a result it would not be possible to realise the full gains of economic progress.

Cyclical price flexibility refers to the sensitivity of prices to fluctuations of the business cycle. Commodities whose prices move swiftly in response to changes in the national income and whose amplitude of fluctuations is relatively large are said to be cycle-sensitive commodities in regard to price. Experience shows that raw materials, agricultural as well as industrial, are to a large extent cyclically price sensitive while finished manufactured products are, by and large, insensitive to cyclical changes in employment, output and income. In the case of farm products the sensitivity is limited to price responses, while in the case of certain industrial raw materials the sensitivity relates both to price and to fluctuations in output.

There exists more or less consensus of opinion in regard to the desirability of structural price flexibility. Absence of structural price flexibility would lead to an uneconomic utilization of resources. Further, any marked dearrangement in the structural adjustment of the prices of important commodities in relation to unit costs may have a disrupting effect upon consumption and investment expenditures, contributing to the initiation of a decline in industrial activity. Thus, at times, structural price adjustments may contribute to cyclical movements.

Price Flexibility and the Cycle: There, however, exists a sharp controversy in regard to cyclical price flexibility. It is held that unemployment is caused, or at least intensified, by the depression insensitivity of a large and important group of commodities. It is suggested that depression might, to a large extent, be prevented or mitigated by making all commodities as price sensitive as per most raw materials. The deflationary movements cannot be remedied by chasing administered prices and wage rates down the level of agricultural and other flexible prices. If in the industry as a whole, and particularly in the capital goods and durable consumers' goods industries, prices and wages were reduced drastically to an extent commensurate with decline in the prices of cyclically flexible commodities—agricultural and other raw materials—it is to be expected that, by and large, such price and wage declines would merely reduce the gross volume of monetary expenditures made in capital goods industries and durable consumers' goods area, without appreciably affecting the physical volume of output. Since these cost payments are also income receipts of individuals, incomes fall along with a decline in costs. Further, cyclical price flexibility all round under conditions prevailing at the end of a boom might accentuate the downswing. The expectation by business and consumers that prices will fall tends to generate a cumulative decline in expenditures and to intensify the downswing. There results not only inventory disinvestment, but also the curtailment of investment and durable consumers' expenditures in the expectation of further fall in the national income and in costs and prices. It was not altogether an accident that the most violent deflationary movement in the Great Depression came in 1931 in the midst of wholesale wage cuts. A high degree of wage stability during the business cycle, therefore, is considered to be preferable to a policy of wage adjustments.

The effect would, of course, be different if the income and effective demand could be maintained or expanded at the moment the costs are reduced. Combined with monetary and fiscal policies designed to maintain the total volume of consumption and investment opportunities, an orderly programme of cost-price readjustment does facilitate recovery.

Just as forced cyclical downward adjustments of administrative prices are to be avoided, so also an increase in administrative prices in the upswing is to be avoided. Such an increase similarly creates business expectations which tend to cause the accumulation of excessive inventories, leading to subsequent relapses.

It is sometimes asserted that chronic unemployment of resources must indicate that prices are too high in relation to the level of purchasing power and the situation can be rectified by progressive reduction of prices. This type of reasoning is meaningful only in case of monopoly prices and technological innovations reducing the unit cost of production. High monopoly prices have a tendency to reduce the volume of employment. They tend to reduce the real purchasing power of wage earners and to enhance profits. The increase in inequalities in the distribution of income tends to reduce consumption expenditure and to increase savings. As such, a reduction in monopoly prices will stimulate consumption and raise the level of employment.

Level of employment would also rise when consumer goods prices fall as a result of technological innovation which reduces the unit cost of production. The cost-reducing innovation induces new investment, and this results in an increase in employment while the new investment is made, and, subsequently, in a reduction in consumer goods prices after the new investment yields increased supply of goods.

In the absence of monopoly prices or of technological change, price reductions can be used as a means of increasing employment. If competitive prices are arbitrarily reduced, wage rates remaining unchanged, marginal firms will be driven out of business, and disinvestment will occur, causing a reduction in employment. It is not possible to solve this problem of unemployment by relying upon the potentially larger purchasing power which, it is assumed, will appear if prices are arbitrarily reduced below the point determined by competition.

Conclusion. While the price policy does play an important role, it does not constitute an adequate remedy for the business cycle and for chronic underutilisation of resources. Price policy must be integrated with monetary and fiscal policies. It is by and large upon these latter that reliance must be placed to prevent any large decline in business activity and in the national income. If this is done, cyclical price dispersion between cycle-sensitive commodities and cycle-insensitive commodities will be minimised to a large extent. From the long-run point of view, a reasonably full utilization of resources will facilitate the adaptation of individual prices to structural changes incident to the differential rates of technical progress in different industries.

NOTES

1. *Principles of Political Economy* (Gonner ed.), pp. 273-75.
2. Jean, B. Say, *Treatise on Political Economy* (Princep edition), (Boston 1921).
3. J.S. Mill, *Principles of Political Economy*, Book III, Chap. XIV, p. 2.
4. Alfred Marshall, *Pure Theory of Domestic Values*, p. 34.
5. A.C. Pigou, *The Theory of Unemployment*, p. 252.
6. James Tobin, "Money-Wage Rates and Employment" in S.E. Harris (ed.) *The New Economics* (London, 1947), pp. 577-82.
7. Alvin H. Hansen, *A Guide of Kenyes* (New York, 1953), p. 175.
8. ——, *Monetary Theory and Fiscal Policy* (New York, 1949), p. 128.
9. J.M. Keynes, *The General Theory of Employment, Interest and Money* (London, 1936), p. 266.
10. *Ibid.*, p. 268.
11. A.P. Lerner, "The General Theory (1)" in Seymour E. Harris (ed.), *The New Economics* (London, 1960), p. 132.
12. J.M. Keynes, *The General Theory of Employment, Interest and Money* (London, 1936), p. 10.
13. L. Tarshis, "Changes in Real and Money Wages", *Economic Journal*, 1939, pp. 150-54.
14. J.M. Keynes, "Relative Movement of Real Wages and Output", *Economic Journal*, 1939, pp. 34-51.
15. Abba P. Lerner, *Economics of Employment* (New York, 1951).

A Pure Exchange Walrasian Economy

4

The idea that prices adjust to clear markets is common to much of a new classical macroeconomics. Therefore we consider an economy consisting of perfectly competitive markets in which individuals take prices at which exchange can be made as parametric, and prices adjust to eliminate excess demands so that individuals' plans at given prices are feasible. This characterises the 'Walrasian' economy, which is described by the process by which prices adjust to excess demand or supply as a groping process.

In our analysis we consider three characteristics of the economy:

(a) Our economy is a pure barter economy.

(b) It is an exchange economy.

(c) It is a timeless economy.

The economy is defined by m consumers characterised by their consumption sets and their preferences, n producers characterised by their production sets, and the total resources, the available quantities of the various commodities which are *a priori* given. In our given economy the production is absent, instead, individuals have initial fixed endowments of various commodities. The following assumptions are made for the simple Walrasian economy:

(a) There are m individuals, (a = 1, 2, ..., m), and T commodities, (i = 1, 2, ..., T), in the economy. Agent a's initial endowment of commodity i is given by $\overline{c}_{ai}$, $\overline{c}_{ai} \geq 0, i = 1, \ldots\ldots, T$. Therefore, we have

$$\sum_{a=1}^{m} \overline{c}_{ai} = \overline{c}_i > 0$$

(b) All exchanges occur at a single point in time.

(c) Each individual faces the same known set of prices at which exchange can occur. A relative (purchase) price of commodity i indicates the units of commodity j required to purchase one unit of commodity i. A relative (sale) price of commodity i indicates units of commodity j received when one unit of commodity i is sold.

(d) Purchase and sale prices are identical for each commodity. It implies that there are no 'price spreads' which would suggest either a gain to an individual buying and selling the same commodity or the presence of costs to making an exchange. Thus, for the T commodities there are T^2 exchange rates, or relative prices, taking two commodities at a time.

(e) Individual a's preferences are described by his utility function $u^a(c_{a1},...,c_{aT})$ where $c_{a1},......,c_{aT}$ denote agent a's consumption bundle, $c_{ai} \geq 0, i = 1,......., T$.

(f) Individual a will choose the most preferred consumption bundle from the set of feasible alternatives. Given the possibility of costless exchange at the set of relative prices represented by $(\pi_1,.....,\pi_{T-1})$, feasible consumption bundles or sets $(c_{a1},......,c_{aT})$ are defined by

$$\sum_{i=1}^{T} \pi_i \overline{c}_{ai} - \sum_{i=1}^{T} \pi_i c_{ai} \geq 0,$$

where $\sum_{i=1}^{T} \pi_i \overline{c}_{ai}$ denotes the initial endowment of individual a in terms of commodity T. This expression defines the budget set.

Now we will consider the problem of the consumer. From assumption (e) and (f), individual a's optimum bundle is the solution to the problem

$$\max_{c_{a1},....,c_{aT}} u^a(c_{a1},....,c_{aT})$$

subject to

$$\sum_{i=1}^{T} \pi_i \overline{c}_{ai} - \sum_{i=1}^{T} \pi_i c_{ai} \geq 0, \quad c_{ai} \geq 0, \quad i=1,.......,T$$

The Lagrangian form of the above maximisation problem can be written as:

$$\max_{c_{a1},\ldots,c_{aT},\lambda} L(c_{a1},\ldots\ldots,c_{aT},\lambda) = u^{a}(c_{a1},\ldots\ldots,c_{aT}) + \lambda\left(\sum_{i=1}^{T}\pi_i\,\bar{c}_{ai} - \sum_{i=1}^{T}\pi_i\,c_{ai}\right)$$

First order necessary conditions are

$$\frac{\partial L}{\partial c_{ai}} \le 0,\ i = 1,\ldots\ldots,T$$

$$\frac{\partial L}{\partial c_{ai}}\,c_{ai} = 0,\ i = 1,\ldots\ldots,T$$

$$c_{ai} \ge 0,\ i = 1,\ldots\ldots,T$$

$$\frac{\partial L}{\partial \lambda} \ge 0$$

$$\lambda\,\frac{\partial L}{\partial \lambda} = 0 \text{ and } \lambda \ge 0$$

The constrained maximisation problem can be written into the unconstrained Lagrangian form as

$$\max_{c_{a1},\ldots,c_{aT},\lambda,\mu_1,\ldots\ldots,\mu_T} \bar{L}(c_{a1},\ldots\ldots,c_{aT},\lambda,\mu_1,\ldots\ldots,\mu_T) = u^{a}(c_{a1},\ldots\ldots,c_{aT}) + \lambda\left(\sum_{i=1}^{T}\pi_i\,\bar{c}_{ai} - \sum_{i=1}^{T}\pi_i\,c_{ai}\right)$$

The necessary conditions for maximisation are

$$\frac{\partial \bar{L}}{\partial c_{ai}} = 0,\ i = 1,\ldots\ldots,T$$

$$\frac{\partial \bar{L}}{\partial \lambda} \ge 0$$

$$\lambda\,\frac{\partial \bar{L}}{\partial \lambda} = 0$$

$$\frac{\partial \bar{L}}{\partial \mu_i} \geq 0, i = 1, \ldots\ldots, T$$

$$\mu_i \frac{\partial \bar{L}}{\partial \mu_i} = 0, i = 1, \ldots\ldots, T$$

$$\lambda \geq 0$$

$$\mu_i \geq 0, i = 1, \ldots\ldots, T$$

Now we can define the optimal consumption bundle for agent a by the above first-order conditions and will be denoted by the expression:

$(c_{a1}, \ldots\ldots, c_{aT})$, where $c_{ai} \geq 0$, i = 1,......,T.

Individual a's demand functions will be of the form:

$$c^d_{ai}\left(\pi_1, \ldots\ldots, \pi_{T-1}, \sum_{i=1}^{T} \pi_i \, \bar{c}_{ai}\right), i = 1, \ldots\ldots, T$$

That is, individual a's demand of commodity i depends on the T -1 relative prices of commodities and the initial endowment. Note that the form of the utility function implies the utility maximizing consumption bundle meets the budget constraint with equality. At the optimal bundle we have

$$\frac{\partial L}{\partial \lambda} = \sum_{i=1}^{T} \pi_i \, \bar{c}_{ai} - \sum_{i=1}^{T} \pi_i \, c^d_{ai} = 0$$

The demand functions are homogenous of degree zero in what might be called accounting prices. Accounting prices are defined such that $p_i = \pi_i \cdot p_T, i = 1, \ldots\ldots, T$, so it is clear that if all prices increase by the multiple θ, relative prices and the initial endowment are unchanged.

Then individual a's excess demand function for commodity i is defined by $z_{ai} = c^d_{ai} - \bar{c}_{ai}$. If z_{ai} is positive, agent a is a net buyer of commodity i, while if z_{ai} is negative, the agent is a net seller of commodity i. The market value (in terms of the numeraire) of the quantity of the ith commodity that individuals a seeks to exchange is then given by $\pi_i z_{ai}$. From the budget constraint, we know that

$$\sum_{i=1}^{T} \pi_i \left(c_{ai}^d - \bar{c}_{ai}\right) = 0$$

or
$$\sum_{i=1}^{T} \pi_i z_{ai} = 0$$

In other words, for each individual the market value, in terms of commodity T, of individual excess demands must sum to zero.

Now suppose that there are m individuals in the market. Aggregating or summing individual demand functions, we obtain an aggregate or market demand function for commodity i of the form

$$c_i^d \left(\pi_1, \ldots\ldots, \pi_{T-1}, \sum_{i=1}^{T} \pi_i \bar{c}_{i1}, \ldots, \sum_{i=1}^{T} \pi_i \right) = \sum_{a=1}^{m} c_{ai}^d(\cdot)$$

Similarly, we can get the aggregate or market excess demand function for the commodity i by summing the agents' excess demand functions for the commodity i as

$$z_i = \sum_{a=1}^{m} (z_{ai}) = \sum_{a=1}^{m} \left(c_{ai}^d - \bar{c}_{ai}\right)$$

Here one point should be noted that a zero aggregate excess demand for commodity i does not imply that no exchange of commodity i occurs among the m agents. However, a zero individual excess demand for commodity i does imply no exchange of commodity i by that particular individual.

In the case of macroeconomic analysis, the effects of the distribution of initial endowments across individuals on market demands is ignored such that the market demand function for commodity i is assumed to be of the form

$$c_i^d \left(\pi_1, \ldots\ldots, \pi_{T-1}, \sum_{i=1}^{T} \pi_i \bar{c}_i \right)$$

where,

$$\sum_{i=1}^{T} \pi_i c_{ai} = \sum_{a=1}^{m}\left(\sum_{i=1}^{T} \pi_i \overline{c}_{ai}\right)$$

EQUILIBRIUM

An Isolated Market

In case of a single market, equilibrium is characterised by an accounting price p_i and implied relative price $\pi_i = p_i/p_T$ such that $c_i^d = \overline{c}_i$ (demand equals fixed endowment) or equivalently $z_i = 0$ (excess demand equals zero). In the Walrasian model, movement toward equilibrium involves two facts:

(a) The accounting price of commodity i rises if there is excess demand and falls if there is excess supply. This is known as the Walrasian excess demand hypothesis. Thus,

$$dp_i = f_i(z_i),\ i = 1, 2, \ldots\ldots, T$$

$$f_i(0) = 0, \frac{df_i}{dz_i} > 0$$

If relative prices are considered then

$$d\pi_i = \frac{dp_i}{p_T} = \frac{f_i(z_i)}{p_T},\ i=1,2,\ldots\ldots\ldots, T-1$$

Here we see that the change in price is not across time, because each market is assumed to clear instantaneously at the same point in time.

(b) Offers to buy or sell at various relative prices are not binding unless markets clear. Only when the equilibrium price is obtained, contracts are then made final. This is known as the recontracting assumption.

Conditions for General Equilibrium

A set of T – 1 relative prices $(\pi_1^*, \ldots\ldots\ldots, \pi_{T-1}^*)$ and allocations $(c_{a1}^*, \ldots\ldots\ldots, c_{aT}^*)$ for individuals a, a = 1,......, m characterise the general equilibrium such that

$$c_{ai}^* = c_{ai}^d\left(\pi_1^*,......,\pi_{T-1}^*, \sum_{i=1}^{T}\pi_i\bar{c}_{ai}\right), i = 1,...., T; a = 1,....., m$$
...(4.1)

$$\Rightarrow c_i^* = \sum_{a=1}^{m} c_{ai}^* = \sum_{a=1}^{m} c_{ai}^d = c_i^d;$$

$$c_i^* = \bar{c}_i, i = 1,......, T \quad ...(4.2)$$

The equilibrium allocation must be optimal in that it must satisfy all demands for commodities at the specified set of prices, which is indicated by equation (4.1). Equation (4.2) indicates that such an allocation must be feasible, that is, sum to total resource endowment. Conditions (4.1) and (4.2) together imply a set of relative price such that excess demands are zero, or

$$c_i^d = \bar{c}_i, i = 1,........, T$$

The above statement of general equilibrium involves setting T excess demand equations equal to zero, but there are only T – 1 unknowns (relative prices). Walras solved this problem by showing that one of the equations, arbitrarily chosen, can be deduced from the other T – 1 equations. In other words, there are only T – 1 independent equations. The budget constraint for each individual is given by

$$\sum_{i=1}^{T}\pi_i c_{ai}^d - \sum_{i=1}^{T}\pi_i\bar{c}_{ai} = 0$$

Summing across all individuals, it must then be the case that

$$\sum_{a=1}^{m}\left(\sum_{i=1}^{T}\pi_i\bar{c}_{ai} - \sum_{i=1}^{T}\pi_i c_{ai}^d\right) = 0$$

Rearranging and substituting in c_i^d for $\sum_{a-1}^{m} c_{ai}^d$ and $\bar{c}_i$ for $\sum_{a-1}^{m}\bar{c}_{ai}$, we have

$$\sum_{i=1}^{T}\pi_i(c_{ai}^d - \bar{c}_{ai}) = 0$$

or, $$\sum_{i=1}^{T} \pi_i z_i = 0$$

The above expressions represent the Walras' law, which states that, the sum of the excess demands across all markets must be zero. The excess demand of each commodity is weighted by its relative price, so that all excess demands are in units of the numeraire. The above aggregate budget constraint is sometimes referred to as Say's law or Say's identity. If there is a distinction between the two, it is that Say's law explicitly excluded money as a 'market'. In this setting, one can understand how Say's conclusion that "supply creates its own demand" is arrived at in an economy composed of a single, aggregate commodity.

In this section we have considered that the endowments of the commodity good were bestowed on individuals each period. In the next section we are going to introduce production as the source of commodities.

A SIMPLE WALRASIAN MODEL WITH MONEY, FINANCIAL ASSETS, AND PRODUCTION

Now consider that at the start of each period, there exists a 'labour' market in which labour services are exchanged. Our new agents, denoted by 'firms,' hire the labour service provided by households. During the period, firms combine the labour services with an existing capital stock to produce output, which is sold in the output market net of output retained to replace capital used up during production. Revenues from the sale of output are distributed to 'households' in the form of wages during the period. At the end of the period, interest payments and dividends are made to households out of revenues. Each period agents also enter the output market to augment their capital stock, with such purchases financed by the issue of bonds and a new financial asset denoted by 'equity shares'.

Following are the assumptions of this model:

(a) The firms are initially endowed at time t with a capital stock $\overline{K}$ and a technology for transforming capital services from a capital stock and labour services into a single composite commodity. The technology is summarised by the production function $y_t = f(N_t, \overline{K})$, where $\overline{K}$ denotes the capital stock the firm inherits at time t, N_t denotes the employment of labour services arranged at time t for period t (from time t to time t + 1) and y_t denotes the constant rate of production of the commodity for period t (from time t to time t + 1). Similarly, for period i (i = t + 1, t + 2, ...), which runs from time i to time i + 1, output produced is given by $y_i = f(N_i, K_i)$.

(b) For output produced during period t (from time t to time t + 1), let p_t denotes its price when it is sold during the period up to and including time t + 1. Let p_{t+1} denote the price of output produced during period t + 1 that is sold beyond time t + 1 up to and including time t + 2, and so on. At time t, the price level associated with the prior period is denoted by $\overline{p}$.

(c) At the start of period t, agreements to exchange the N_t labour services during period t (from time t to t + 1) are entered into at the money wage rate denoted by w_t. Similarly, at the start of period t+1, N_{t+1} labour services are exchanged at the money wage rate w_{t+1}, and so on.

(d) Two types of financial assets—bonds and equity shares, are exchanged at the end of each period. Bonds yield a fixed money (coupon) payment z each future period in perpetuity. Now suppose $\overline{p}_b, p_{bt}$, and $p_{b,t+1}$ denote the money price of such bonds in markets at the end of periods t – 1, t, and t + 1, respectively; the gross interest rates over period t (from time t to time t + 1) and over period t + 1 (from time t + 1 to time t + 2) are then given by:

$$1+\overline{r}=(z+p_{bt})/\overline{p}_b$$

$$1+r_t=(z+p_{b,t+1})/p_{bt}$$

If $r_i = r_t$, i = t + 1, t + 2,......, then successive substitution for the price of bonds in future periods will result in the following expression for the price of bonds at time t:

$$\overline{p}_b=\frac{1}{1+\overline{r}}(z+p_{bt})=\frac{1}{1+\overline{r}}\left[z+\sum_{i=1}^{\infty}\frac{z}{(1+r_t)^i}\right]=\frac{1}{1+\overline{r}}\left(z+\frac{z}{r_t}\right),$$

where $p_{bt} = z/r_t$. $\overline{B}$ denotes the number of previously issued bonds outstanding at time t.

(e) Equity shares are the second type of financial asset exchanged at the end of each period. Let $\overline{s}$ denote the number of previously issued equity shares outstanding at time t. And let $\overline{p}_e$, p_{et}, and $p_{e,t+1}$ denote the money price of equity shares exchanged in markets at the end of periods t – 1, t, and t + 1, respectively. The gross (nominal)rate of return on equity shares over period t (from time t to time t + 1) and period t + 1 (from time t + 1 to time t + 2) is then given by

$$1+\overline{r}_e = \left[\left(p_t d_t/\overline{S}\right) + p_{et}\right]/\overline{p}_e$$

$$1+\overline{r}_{et} = \left[\left(p_{t+1} d_{t+1}/S_t\right) + p_{e,t+1}\right]/\overline{p}_{et}$$

where $p_t d_t$ and $p_{t+1} d_{t+1}$ denote total nominal dividend payments made at the end of periods t and t + 1 (at time t + 1 and time t + 2), respectively. S_t denotes the anticipated number of equity shares outstanding in the equity market at the end of period t.

(f) Households consider bonds and equity shares as perfect substitutes. Therefore, we can speak of a single "financial asset market" that incorporates both bonds and equity shares and determines a single "interest rate."

(g) There are incomplete markets. Let p_i^e, $i = t+1, t+2, \ldots\ldots$, denote the expectation formed in period t concerning the price of the consumption good over period *i*. Similarly, in period t we have p_{ei}^e, $i = t+1, \ldots\ldots$, and w_i^e, $i = t+1, \ldots\ldots$ Such expectations are assumed to be held with subjective certainty, allowing us to abstract from risk considerations for the moment.

(h) There are positive transaction costs to arranging exchanges of the consumption commodity during each period t. Money holdings serve to reduce the transaction costs of arranging exchanges during a period.

(i) It is prohibitively costly for individuals to directly store the 'composite' commodity for consumption in future periods. However, output not consumed during the period can be transformed into output in the subsequent periods through the augmentation of the capital stock, which permits higher rates of production of output in future periods.

(j) $y_t = f(N_t, \overline{K})$ represent the technology of the firm. y_t denotes the firm's planned (at time t) constant rate of output for the time period from time t to t + 1 to be sold during the period and at time t + 1, N_t denotes the firm's planned (at time t) rate of employment of labour during period (t, t + 1), with labour service purchased in the labour market at time t, and $\overline{K}$ denotes the firm's planned capital stock for period t. We take the capital stock for the current period, $\overline{K}$, as fixed at the individual firm level.

(k) The representative firm will choose the most preferred input combination, and implied output, given technology and prices.

At time t, the objective of the firm is to maximise the expected real market value of the $\overline{S}$ equity shares,

$$V_t = \frac{\overline{p}_e \overline{S}}{\overline{p}}$$

where $\overline{p}_e$ is the price of equity shares at the end of period t – 1.

The assumption that equity shares and bonds are perfect substitute means that the price of an equity share can be expressed as

$$\overline{p}_e = \left[(p_t d_t / \overline{S}) + p_{et}\right] / (1 + \overline{r})$$

where d_t denotes real dividends at the end of period t, so that $p_t d_t$ denotes nominal dividends, $\overline{S}$ denotes the number of equity shares outstanding at time t, p_{et} is the price of equity shares at the end of period t, and $\overline{r}$ denotes the interest rate over period t (i.e., from time t to t + 1).

Substituting in a similar expression for the price of equity shares in the next period, we obtain for an infinite horizon that

$$\overline{p}_e = [1/(1+\overline{r})]\left[(p_t d_t/\overline{S}) + \sum_{k=1}^{\infty}\left[(p_{t+k} d_{t+k})/S_{t+k-1}\right] \Big/ \prod_{j=1}^{k}(1+r_{t+j-1})\right]$$

The price of an equity share at the end of period t – 1 (at time t), $\overline{p}_e$, reflects the anticipated discounted future stream of nominal dividends per share.

Since $V_t = \overline{p}_e \overline{S}/\overline{p}$ is the real value of the firm, we can express the value of the firm as

$$V_t = \left[\overline{S}/\overline{p}(1+\overline{r})\right]\left[\left(p_t d_t/\overline{S}\right) + \sum_{k=1}^{\infty}\left[\left(p_{t+k}d_{t+k}\right)/S_{t+k-1}\right] \Big/ \prod_{j=1}^{k}\left(1+r_{t+j-1}\right)\right]$$

which means that the objective of the firm can be stated in terms of maximising the discounted stream of current and future dividends.

As we have by definition,

$$p_t = \overline{p}(1+\overline{\pi}),$$

$$p_{t+k} = \overline{p}(1+\overline{\pi})\left(\prod_{j=1}^{k}\left(1+r_{t+j-1}\right)\right), \; k = 1,2,3,\ldots..$$

where π_{t+j} denotes the rate of change in the price level between period t+j and t+j+1. Thus, we have

$$V_t = \left(\overline{S}/\overline{R}\right)\left[\left(d_t/\overline{S}\right) + \sum_{k=1}^{\infty}\left[d_{t+k}/S_{t+k-1}\right] \Big/ \prod_{j=1}^{k} R_{t+j-1}\right]$$

where $\overline{R} = (1+\overline{r})/(1+\overline{\pi})$ and $R_i = (1+r_i)/(1+\pi_i)$ denotes the real gross rate of interest for period i (from time i+1 to time i+2, i = t, t + 1,.....).

Now we will find an expression for the real dividends of the firm in each period. In general, we denote real dividends at the end of any period as the difference between a firm's total real revenue during the period and the total costs incurred during the period. Total revenue derives from the sale of output produced during the period. Also we can add revenues from a change in the number of equity shares outstanding or a change in the number of bonds outstanding at the end of the period. Total costs to the firm in any period include the agreed upon wage payments to the labour hired during the period, payments to replace depreciated capital, plus coupon payments at the end of the period to holders of previously issued bonds. Thus, the dividends of the firm can be given as

Dividends = revenue from sale of output – wages – interest payments + funds from change in outstanding bonds and stocks – costs to replace depreciated capital, add new capital, and capital and capital adjustment costs.

We can divide the above constraint into two separate constraints.

(a) *Firm's financing constraint*—it earmarks funds raised from the change in outstanding bonds and equity shares at the end of the period to pay for or 'finance' the installation of new capital stock during the period plus any capital adjustment costs.

(b) *Firm's distribution constraint*—it states that the revenues from the sale of output that exceed expenditure to meet wage payments, purchase of capital to replace that used up in the production process, and interest payments to bond holders at the end of the period, are distributed at the end of the period to households as dividends.

Thus, real dividend at the end of period t is given by:

$$d_t = y_t - (w_t/p_t)N_t - z\bar{B}/p_t - \delta\bar{K},$$

where,

y_t = output produced during period t,

w_t/p_t = real wage,

N_t = quantity of labour hired,

$z\bar{B}/p_t$ = real coupon payments at the end of the period on previously issued bonds, and

$\delta\bar{K}$ = purchases of capital during the prior period to replace that used up in the production process.

Real dividends for periods t + 1 and t + 2, paid at the end of each period are given by

$$d_{t+1} = y_{t+1} - (w_{t+1}/p_{t+1})N_{t+1} - zB_t/p_{t+1} - \delta K_{t+1}$$

$$d_{t+2} = y_{t+2} - (w_{t+2}/p_{t+2})N_{t+2} - zB_{t+1}/p_{t+2} - \delta K_{t+2}$$

The above definition of dividends is also termed as the "firm's distribution constraint". This constraint simply indicates that revenue from the sale of output net of that retained to replace capital used up in the production process is distributed to households either as wage payments, interest payments, or dividends. Thus, we have

$$d_t + (w_t/p_t)\,N_t + z\overline{B}/p_t = y_t - \delta\overline{K}$$

$$d_{t+1} + (w_{t+1}/p_{t+1})\,N_{t+1} + zB_t/p_{t+1} = y_{t+1} - \delta K_{t+1}$$

The changes in the firm's holdings of capital, as well as any associated adjustment costs, are financed by a change in outstanding equity shares and/ or bonds. This linking of funding for capital purchases to the issuing of equity shares and bonds denotes the "firm's financing constraint". For example, at the end of periods t + 1, t + 2, ..., we have the following financial constraints of the firm:

$$K_{t+1} - \overline{K} + \psi(I_{nt}) = \left[p_{et}\,(S_t - \overline{S}) + p_{bt}\,(B_t - \overline{B})\right]/p_t$$

$$K_{t+2} - K_{t+1} + \psi(I_{n,t+1}) = \left[p_{e,t+1}\,(S_{t+1} - S_t) + p_{b,t+1}\,(B_{t+1} - B_t)\right]/p_{t+1}$$

Where, $\psi(I_i)$ denotes the costs of installing new capital at rate I_i during period i (between time i and time i + 1), a cost that depends directly on the rate of net investment ($I_{ni} = K_{i+1} - K_i$) planned at time t to occur between time i and i + 1.

Since bonds and equity shares are perfect substitutes, we can rewrite the above firm's financing constraints in the following form:

$$I_{nt} + \psi(I_{nt}) = A_t - \overline{A}_t = \text{net } A_t$$

$$I_{n,t+1} + \psi(I_{n,t+1}) = A_{t+1} - \overline{A}_{t+1} = \text{net } A_{t+1}$$

where I_{ni} denotes net real investment (i.e. $K_{i+1} - K_i$), A_i denotes the real planned (at time t) value of total equity shares and bonds to be outstanding after the financial market at the end of period i, and $\overline{A}_i$ denotes the initial real value of equity shares and bonds for period i reflecting financing and capital decisions in prior periods but period i prices. For example,

$$A_t = [p_{et}S_t + p_{bt}B_t]/p_t \text{ and } \overline{A}_t = [p_{et}\overline{S} + p_{bt}\overline{B}]/p_t$$

$$A_{t+1} = [p_{e,t+1}S_{t+1} + p_{b,t+1}B_{t+1}]/p_{t+1} \text{ and}$$

$$\overline{A}_{t+1} = [p_{e,t+1}S_t + p_{b,t+1}B_t]/p_{t+1}$$

Here we note the following characteristic of the firm's financing constraints:

(a) Net capital purchases planned for period i to be installed between time i and time i + 1 are paid for at the end of period i when completely installed from the sale of financial assets at that time.

(b) The firms purchase the output of the composite good to augment the capital stock. That is, we have a 'one-sector' model in which the same good serves both households (for consumption) and firms (for investment). There is only a single commodity price.

(c) The firm financing constraint holds whether the firm finances capital with new bonds, new equity shares, or retained earnings.

An important aspect of the above financing constraint is that it incorporates potential adjustment costs to purchase of capital as captured by the terms $\psi(\cdot)$, which depend on I_{nt}, $I_{n,\,t+1}$,......, where I_{ni} denotes the planned (at time t) net rate of investment for period i. The total cost of capital purchases is thus the sum of

(a) the real payments (or receipts if negative) involved in the purchase (or sale if negative) of capital in the output market and

(b) potential real payments, denoted 'installation' or adjustment costs, associated with new capital acquisitions.

For period t, adjustment costs are given by $\psi(I_{nt})$, where I_{nt} denotes net investment between time t and t + 1. Gross investment for period t is given by $I_{nt} + \delta\bar{K}$. Thus, we can decompose gross investment over the period into the change in the capital stock, $K_{t+1} - \bar{K}$, which is termed "planned net investment," and the replacement of capital used up in the production process, $\delta\bar{K}$, which is termed 'depreciation'.

In general, adjustment costs over period t of length h are given by $h\psi(I_{nt}/h)$, where the limit of the term I_{nt}/h defines the rate of net investment. In continuous time the planned rate of investment would be defined by the rate of gross investment,

$$i_t = \lim_{h\to 0} \frac{I_t}{h} = \lim_{h\to 0} \frac{K_{t+h} - \bar{K} + h\delta\bar{K}}{h} = \dot{K}_t + \delta K_t$$

and the adjustment cost function in continuous time would be $\psi(i_{nt})$.

For the aggregate rate of gross investment to be defined by the above expression, K must equal $\bar{K}$. We will consider two approaches here.

(a) We assume zero adjustment costs, i.e. $\psi = 0$. This situation is referred as 'perfect malleability' which implies that the rate of investment may not be defined at the level of the individual firm. That is, if the existing capital stock were higher or lower than the planned level, investment would be infinitely positive or negative. However, it can be shown that with zero adjustment costs, the output market in a continuous-time model at a point in time is simply a 'capital market' and the expression $K_t = \bar{K}$ emerges as an equilibrium condition with respect to the capital market at time t. Here we can apply L'Hospital's rule to define the aggregate rate of investment in the continuous-time model with zero adjustment costs as:

$$i_t = \lim_{h\to 0} \frac{K_{t+h} - \bar{K}}{h} = \frac{\lim_{h\to 0} d(K_{t+h} - \bar{K})/dh}{\lim_{h\to 0} dh/dh} = \dot{K}$$

where i_t is rate of investment.

(b) In contrast to the case (a), one can assume adjustment costs that take the following form:

$$\psi(0) = 0$$

$$\psi(\beta) > 0, \text{ if } \beta > 0,\ \psi'' > 0, \text{ and } \lim_{\beta\to\infty} \psi(\beta) = \infty$$

$$\psi(\beta) < 0, \text{ if } \beta < 0$$

The above set of assumption reflects the presumption that adjustment costs increase at an increasing rate with the rate of change in capital, and that it is infinitely costly to change the capital stock arbitrarily fast. The result of such adjustment costs in both discrete-time analysis and continuous-time analysis is that at time t the firm chooses $K_t = \bar{K}$. At time t the firm views the inherited capital stock as optimal since it is prohibitively costly to change the capital stock at a point in time given such adjustment costs.

Firm's Optimisation Problem

At time t the firm makes plans with respect to current and future employment of labour (N_t, N_{t+1},......), the future employment of capital (K_{t+1}, K_{t+2},......), the stock of outstanding bonds (B_t, B_{t+1},......), and the stock of outstanding equity shares (S_t, S_{t+1},......) in order to maximise the real value of the previously issued equity shares outstanding at time t, with that real value given in general form by

$$V_t = (\bar{S}/\bar{R})\left[d_t/\bar{S} + \sum_{k=1}^{\infty}\left[d_{t+k}/S_{t+k-1}\right]\Big/\prod_{j=1}^{k}R_{t+j-1}\right]$$

In general, the firm's problem can be stated as:

$$\max\left(\bar{S}/\bar{R}\right)\left[d_t/\bar{S} + \sum_{k=1}^{\infty}\left[d_{t+k}/S_{t+k-1}\right]\Big/\prod_{j=1}^{k}R_{t+j-1}\right]$$

Subject to the financing constraints

$$-\left[K_{t+1} - \bar{K} + \psi(K_{t+1} - \bar{K})\right] + \left(p_{et}/p_t\right)\cdot\left[B_t - \bar{B}\right]$$

$$+\left(p_{bt}/p_t\right)\cdot(S_t - \bar{S}) = 0$$

$$-\left[K_{t+2} - K_{t+1} + \psi(K_{t+2} - K_{t+1})\right] + \left(p_{e,t+1}/p_{t+1}\right)\cdot$$

$$[B_{t+1} - B_t] + \left(p_{b,t+1}/p_{t+1}\right)\cdot\left(S_{t+1} - S_t\right) = 0$$

. . . .

and the distribution constraints

$$d_t = y_t - \left(w_t/p_t\right)N_t - z\bar{B}/p_t - \delta\bar{K}$$

$$d_{t+1} = y_{t+1} - \left(w_{t+1}/p_{t+1}\right) N_{t+1} - zB_t/p_{t+1} - \delta K_{t+1}$$

$$d_{t+2} = y_{t+2} - \left(w_{t+2}/p_{t+2}\right) N_{t+2} - zB_{t+1}/p_{t+2} - \delta K_{t+2}$$

$$\ldots\ldots\ldots\ldots\ldots\ldots\ldots\ldots\ldots\ldots\ldots$$

and given the production functions

$$y_t = f(N_t, \overline{K})$$

$$y_{t+1} = f(N_{t+1}, K_{t+1})$$

$$\ldots\ldots\ldots\ldots$$

for i = t, t+1, ...

In the above problem we see that at the start of any given period, the firm inherits a stock of capital, an outstanding stock of bonds, and an outstanding stock of equity shares. These variables are state variables. Each period the firm chooses a set of the 'control' variables—employment and investment. These choices, in conjunction with the production function, result in outcomes in terms of:

(a) a one-period return (dividends) at the end of the period, and

(b) a new set of 'state' variables—capital stock and stock of financial assets (equity shares and bonds)—inherited in the subsequent period.

The objective of the firm is additive in these one-period returns (dividends). To reformulate the problem facing the firm as a dynamic programming problem, we use the conventional notation of dynamic programming problems.

A set of 'control' variable each period is given as

$$z_t = \{N_t, I_{nt}\}$$

$$z_{t+1} = \{N_{t+1}, I_{n,t+1}\} \text{ etc.}$$

A set of 'state' variables each period is given as

$$x_t = \{\overline{K}, \overline{B}, \overline{S}\}$$

$$x_{t+1} = \{K_{t+1}, B_t, S_t\} \text{ etc.}$$

"Transition functions" link the choices, specifically the choice of net investment during the period, to the capital stock available at the start of the next period as well as the stock of financial assets outstanding in the subsequent period. Thus, the choice of the net investment rate, I_{nt}, during period t dictates K_{t+1} given $\bar{K}$, since

$$K_{t+1} = I_{nt} + \bar{K}$$

From the firm's financing constraint, we know that the choice of the investment rate also determines the real stock of financial assets as:

$$(p_{et}/p_t)[B_t - \bar{B}] + (p_{bt}/p_t)[S_t - \bar{S}] = I_{nt} + \psi(I_{nt})$$

A set of one-period return functions evaluated at the end of period t is given as

$$r_t(\bar{K}, \bar{B}, \bar{S}) = d_t$$

$$r_{t+1}(K_{t+1}, B_t, S_t) = \bar{S}\, d_{t+1}/S_t R_t$$

....

We cannot solve the above problem for a unique optimal number of bonds or equity shares to have outstanding each period because bonds and equity shares are perfect substitutes. In such situation, without any loss of generality, we may restrict our focus to either bond or equity share financing. Thus, we can hold constant either bonds (i.e., $B_i = \bar{B}$, $i = t, t + 1, \ldots$) or equity shares (i.e., $S_i = \bar{S}$, $i = t, t + 1, \ldots$).

Alternatively, we can combine the distribution and financing constraints into a single expression for dividends and hold constant both equity shares and bonds. In such situation, we have "retained earnings" financing of changes in the capital stock and there is a single state variable, the stock of capital. The problem facing the firm then can be given by the Bellman equation for period t given inherited capital stock $\bar{K}$ as

$$W(\bar{K}) = \max_{N_t, I_{nt}, K_{t+1}} \left\{ d_t + W(K_{t+1}) \right\}$$

subject to the transition function

$$K_{t+1} = I_{nt} + \bar{K}$$

and given the following definitions for real dividends and output for period t,

$$d_t = y_t - (w_t/p_t)N_t - \delta\bar{K} - z\bar{B}/p_t - I_{nt} - \psi(I_{nt})$$

$$y_t = f(N_t, \bar{K})$$

We can obtain the first-order conditions by substituting the above definitions for real dividends and output into the Bellman equation and substituting in the transition function. The first-order conditions are:

$$\frac{\partial f_t}{\partial N_t} - \frac{w_t}{p_t} = 0$$

$$-(1+\psi'_t) + \frac{dW(K_{t+1})}{dK_{t+1}} = 0, \text{ where } \psi'_t = \frac{d\psi(I_{nt})}{dI_{nt}}$$

The first part of the first-order conditions is the standard condition that labour is employed up to the point where the real marginal gain for an additional unit of labour in terms of the increase in output attained in the current period (i.e., the marginal product of labour, $\partial f_t/\partial N_t$), equals the real marginal cost as reflected by the real wage, w_t/p_t. And the second part indicates the optimal choice of investment.

Optimal Investment: Zero Adjustment Costs

Let us consider the Bellman equation for period t + 1. Initially we will focus on the case of zero adjustment costs (i.e., $\psi = 0$, implying that ψ' = 0, i = t, t + 1,.....). Given the inherited capital stock K_{t+1} for period t + 1 and a fixed stock of equity shares, the Bellman equation for period t + 1 is given as

$$W(K_{t+1}) = \max_{N_{t+1}, I_{n,t+1}, K_{t+2}} \left\{ d_{t+1}(R_t)^{-1} + W(K_{t+2}) \right\}$$

subject to the transition function

$$K_{t+2} = I_{n,t+1} + K_{t+1}$$

and the following definitions for real dividends and output for period t+1:

$$d_{t+1} = y_{t+1} - (w_{t+1}/p_{t+1})N_{t+1} - \delta K_{t+1} - zB_t/p_{t+1} - I_{n,t+1}$$

$$y_{t+1} = f(N_{t+1}, K_{t+1})$$

assuming retained earnings financing of capital changes and zero adjustment costs.

Thus, we have

$$\frac{dW(K_{t+1})}{dK_{t+1}} = \frac{1}{R_t}\left(\frac{\partial f_{t+1}}{\partial K_{t+1} - \delta}\right) + \frac{dW(K_{t+2})}{dK_{t+2}} \qquad ...(4.3)$$

Now we will use first-order conditions for the Bellman equation for period t + 1 to clarify the nature of $dW(K_{t+2})/dK_{t+2}$ in equation (4.3). In particular, the optimal choice of investment in period t + 1 satisfies

$$\frac{-1}{R_t} + \frac{dW(K_{t+2})}{dK_{t+2}} = 0 \qquad ...(4.4)$$

Substituting (4.4) in (4.3), we get the following expression for the effect of a change in the inherited capital stock on the value function for period t + 1 as

$$\frac{dW(K_{t+1})}{dK_{t+1}} = \frac{1}{R_t}\left(\frac{\partial f_{t+1}}{\partial K_{t+1} - \delta}\right) + \frac{1}{R_t} \qquad ...(4.5)$$

Substituting (4.5) into the second part of the first order condition and considering $\psi' = 0$, we thus have that the optimal choice of investment in period t satisfies:

$$-1 + \frac{1}{R_t}\left(\frac{\partial f_{t+1}}{\partial K_{t+1} - \delta}\right) + \frac{1}{R_t} = 0 \qquad ...(4.6)$$

The above expression can be rearranged to obtain

$$\frac{\partial f_{t+1}}{\partial K_{t+1}} = m_t - \delta \qquad ...(4.7)$$

where,

m_t = Fisher's expected real rate of interest, and

$m_t = R_t - 1$

or, $m_t = (r_t - \pi_t)/(1 + \pi_t)$

Thus, we see that each period the firm chooses labour and capital such that the marginal gain in the subsequent period in terms of increased output equals the real marginal cost. In case of capital, the marginal cost is the rate of depreciation plus the expected real rate of interest.

The firm pays for one unit of capital at price p_t over the period t. The firm could have instead used these funds to reduce the outstanding stock of bonds by p_t, the cost of this capital (reduced dividends) in nominal terms is $p_t(1+r_t)$. In real terms, the cost one period later is anticipated to be $p_t(1+r_t)/p_{t+1}$. After one period, $1-\delta$ of the capital remains, so that the sale of remaining capital after one period of use (or the reduced purchases of new capital) reaps a nominal return of $(1-\delta)p_{t+1}$ and real return $(1-\delta)$. Thus, the real rental cost of the unit of capital is

$$p_t(1+r_t)/p_{t+1} - (1-\delta) = (1+r_t)/(1+\pi_{t+1}) - 1 + \delta$$

$$= (r_t - \pi_t)/(1+\pi_t) + \delta$$

$$= m_t + \delta$$

In the case of zero adjustment costs, the optimal behaviour of firms in period t and t + 1 is given by the following demand functions for period t and t + 1:

$$N_t^d = N^d(w_t/p_t, \bar{K})$$

$$I_{nt}^d = I_n^d(m_t + \delta, w_{t+1}/p_{t+1}, \bar{K})$$

where,

$$I_{nt}^d = K_{t+1}^d - \bar{K}; \text{ and}$$

$$K_{t+1}^d = K_t^d(m_t + \delta, w_{t+1}/p_{t+1})$$

Here one point should be noted that the anticipated real wage next period affects I_{nt}^d since changes in the real wage affect the employment of labour and thus, assuming $\partial^2 f/\partial N\,\partial K$ does not equal zero, the marginal product of capital. Similarly, it can be explained why $\bar{K}$ enters as an argument in the labour demand function. Thus in our discussion we find that planned investment demand when there are zero adjustment costs simply depends on adjacent expected real user costs of capital and real wages which implies that with zero adjustment costs, capital demand is a function of the expected real user cost of capital and the real wage over the next period alone.

TOBIN'S Q AND THE ADJUSTMENT COSTS FOR CAPITAL

In this section, we will consider the choice of capital when there exist adjustment costs. As we have seen, in the case of retained earnings financing the problem facing the firm is given as

$$W(\bar{K}) = \max_{N_t, I_{nt}, K_{t+1}} \{d_t + W(K_{t+1})\} \qquad \text{...(4.8)}$$

subject to the transition function

$$K_{t+1} = I_{nt} + \bar{K} \qquad \text{...(4.9)}$$

and given the following definitions for real dividends and output for period t:

$$d_t = y_t - (w_t/p_t)\,N_t - \delta\bar{K} - z\bar{B}/p_t - I_{nt} - \psi(I_{nt})$$

$$y_t = f(N_t, \bar{K})$$

We get the first-order conditions by substituting the above definitions for real dividends and output into the Bellman equation and substituting in the transition function. The first-order conditions are:

$$\frac{\partial f_t}{\partial N_t} - \frac{w_t}{p_t} = 0 \qquad \text{...(4.10)}$$

$$-(1 + \psi'_t) + \frac{dW(K_{t+1})}{dK_{t+1}} = 0, \text{ where } \psi'_t = \frac{d\psi(I_{nt})}{dI_{nt}} \qquad \text{...(4.11)}$$

These conditions are similar to the conditions that we have obtained in the case of retained earnings financing.

The problem facing the firm in period t + 1, assuming retained earnings financing of capital changes, is given by

$$W(K_{t+1}) = \max_{N_{t+1}, I_{n,t+1}, K_{t+2}} \{d_{t+1}/R_t + W(K_{t+2})\} \qquad \text{...(4.12)}$$

subject to the transition function

$$K_{t+2} = I_{n,t+1} + K_{t+1}$$

and the conditions for real dividends and output for period t:

$$d_{t+1} = y_{t+1} - \left(w_{t+1}/p_{t+1}\right)N_{t+1} - \delta K_{t+1} - z\bar{B}/p_{t+1} - I_{n,t+1} - \psi(I_{n,t+1})$$

$$y_{t+1} = f(N_{t+1}, K_{t+1})$$

Substituting the conditions of real dividends and output into the Bellman equation for period t + 1 and then substituting in the transition function we get the first-order conditions as

$$\frac{\partial f_{t+1}}{\partial N_{t+1}} - \frac{w_{t+1}}{p_{t+1}} = 0 \qquad \text{...(4.13)}$$

$$-(1+\psi'_{t+1}) + \frac{dW(K_{t+2})}{dK_{t+2}} = 0, \text{ where } \psi'_{t+1} = \frac{d\psi(I_{n,t+1})}{dI_{n,t+1}} \qquad \text{...(4.14)}$$

Here one point should be noted that $dK_{t+2}/dI_{n,t+1} = 1$.

Thus, we have from our expression for the value function at time t + 1, $W(K_{t+1})$,

$$\frac{dW(K_{t+1})}{dK_{t+1}} = \frac{1}{R_t}\left(\frac{\partial f_{t+1}}{\partial K_{t+1} - \delta}\right) + \frac{dW(K_{t+2})}{dK_{t+2}} \qquad \text{...(4.15)}$$

Substituting (4.14) in (4.15), and then substituting the resulting expression for $dW(K_{t+1})/dK_{t+1}$ into the first-order condition for I_{nt} (equation (4.11)), we have

$$-(1+\psi'_t) + \frac{1}{R_t}\left(\frac{\partial f_{t+1}}{\partial K_{t+1} - \delta d}\right) + \frac{1+\psi'_{t+1}}{R_t} = 0 \qquad \text{...(4.16)}$$

Simplifying, equation (4.16) we get

$$\frac{\partial f_{t+1}}{\partial K_{t+1}} = m_t + \delta + (m_t + 1)\psi'_t - \psi'_{t+1} \qquad \text{...(4.17)}$$

where,

$$\psi'_t = \psi'(I^d_{nt}) \text{ and } \psi'_{t+1} = \psi'(I^d_{n,t+1})$$

The equation (4.17) shows that the choice of investment in period t is linked to the optimal choice of investment next period. Since, this holds for each period in the future, the choice of investment today is linked to investment decisions over all subsequent periods.

Now let us consider an identical real rate of return over time, then we have $R_i = R_t = 1+m$, $i = t+1, t+2,\ldots\ldots$, where $(1+m) = (1+r)/(1+\pi)$. We also assume that the firm has attained its optimal capital stock so that $K^d_{t+1} = \bar{K}$ and $I^d_{nt} = 0$. If we separate capital and labour in production function, then the assumption of an invariant real interest rate implies that I^d_{ni}, $i = t+1, t+2,\ldots\ldots$, equal zero as well. In such situation, ψ'_t and ψ'_{t+1} can be replaced by a common $\psi'(0) > 0$. Thus, the first-order condition can be written as

$$\partial f_{t+1}/\partial K_{t+1} - m - \delta = \psi'_m$$

Dividing by m and adding one to both sides, we have

$$Q = 1 + \left[\partial f_{t+1}/\partial K_{t+1} - m - \delta\right]/m = 1 + \psi' > 1 \quad \ldots(4.18)$$

where Q is called Tobin's marginal Q which represents the ratio of the market value of an additional unit of capital to its replacement cost.

Since, given adjustment costs, the market value of an additional unit of capital exceeds its replacement cost, so Tobin's marginal Q is greater than one. And investment demand planned over the coming period determines marginal adjustment costs $\psi'(I^d_{nt})$, therefore, investment can be written in terms of Tobin's Q. Since the optimal rate of investment is that rate for which Q – 1 is equal to the marginal cost of installation. Therefore, we can expressed the net investment demand as

$$I^d_{nt} = I^d_{nt}(Q-1)$$

$$\frac{dI^d_{nt}}{d(Q-1)} > 0$$

We should keep in mind that the Q theory of investment is not operational as long as Q is not observable.

Tobin's average Q is defined as the ratio of the total value of the firm's existing capital to its total replacement cost. For instance, for one sector model in which the cost of capital and output are identical we have

$$\text{Tobin's average } Q = \frac{V}{K}.$$

If the firm is a price-taker, production function is linearly homogenous in K and N, and if expectations of future real interest rates and real wages are static, then the marginal and average Q are identical.

If the real interest rate and real wage are invariant and the firm is at the optimal level of capital so that the capital stock is invariant over time, then, omitting time identifiers, we have

$$V = \sum_{k=1}^{\infty} d/R^k$$

where,

$$d = y - (w/p)N - \delta K, \text{ since } \psi(I_{nt}^d) = \psi(0) = 0$$

Thus, we have

$$V = [y - (w/p)N - \delta K]/m$$

here, we have considered m = R–1.

By Euler's theorem for a linear homogeneous production function and the marginal productivity condition for labour which reflects the price-taker assumption, the first two terms in the expression becomes $K(\partial f/\partial K)$. Dividing by K, we thus obtain

$$\text{Tobin's average } Q = V/K = [\partial f/\partial K - m - \delta]/m + 1$$

which is the same expression as that for Tobin's marginal Q.

Now we will bring the household into our macroeconomic model. Two agents inhibit our expanded macroeconomic model with production, firms and households. The decisions of household can be broken down into three types—consumption/saving, portfolio, and labour supply.

The consumption/saving decision states that the representative household must determine at time t the consumption purchases over each period at the implied rate $c_t, c_{t+1}, \ldots$. And the portfolio decision states that the individual must determine at time t the collection of assets to hold at the end of each period. In our model we consider three types of assets:

(a) Nominal money balances (M_i)—planned at time t to be held at the end of period i, i = t, t + 1, ...

(b) Nominal value of bonds ($p_{bi}B_i$)—planned at time t to be held at the end of period i, where B_i denotes the planned number of bonds held and p_{bi} denotes the money price of bonds at the end of period i; and

(c) Nominal value of equity shares ($p_{ei}S_i$)—planned at time t to be held at the end of period i; where p_{ei} denotes the money price of an equity shares at the end of period i and S_i denotes the number of equity shares planned at time t to be held at the end of period i.

We will consider bonds and equity shares as a single entity with respect to households' portfolio decisions because they are perfect substitutes. Let A_i denote the real holdings of financial assets planned at time t to be held at the end of period i, i = t, t + 1, ... Thus, for period t we have

$$A_t = [p_{et}S_t + p_{bt}B_t]/p_t$$

and so on. Excluding current dividend and interest payments, the real value of inherited financial assets at the end of period i reflecting portfolio decisions in the prior period will be denoted by $\bar{A}_i$, i = t, t + 1, ... For example,

$$\bar{A}_t = \left[p_{et}\bar{S} + p_{bt}\bar{B}\right]/p_t$$

$$\bar{A}_{t+1} = \left[p_{e,t+1}S_t + p_{b,t+1}B_t\right]/p_{t+1}$$

The Problem of the Household

We make following assumptions for the analysis of the household's problem.

(a) The representative household's preferences are described by the utility function

$$u(c_t, c_{t+1}, \ldots\ldots, M_t/p_t, M_{t+1}/p_{t+1}, \ldots\ldots, 1 - N_t, 1 - N_{t+1}, \ldots\ldots),$$

where,

c_i = household's planned rate of consumption during period i,

M_i = representative household's planned nominal holdings of money at the end of period i,

N_i = household's planned rate of supply of labour services during period i, and

$1 - N_i$ = planned rate of leisure during period i.

Here we have assumed that

$$\frac{\partial u}{\partial c_i} > 0$$

$$\frac{\partial u}{\partial (M_i/p_i)} > 0, \text{ and}$$

$$\frac{\partial u}{\partial (1 - N_i)} > 0, \quad i = t, t+1, \ldots..$$

The total utility for the representative household at time t with an infinite planning horizon is given by

$$\sum_{i=t}^{\infty} \beta^{i-t} \, u(c_i, M_i/p_i, 1 - N_i)$$

where β denotes the fixed personal or utility discount factor, with $0 < \beta < 1$.

(b) A rational individual will choose the most preferred sequence of consumption, money holdings, and labour supply from the set of feasible alternatives. The feasible set of consumption, money holdings, and leisure,

$$(c_t, c_{t+1}, \ldots., M_t/p_t, M_{t+1}/p_{t+1}, \ldots\ldots, 1 - N_t, 1 - N_{t+1}, \ldots.),$$

is defined by the set of equalities:

$$(w_t/p_t)N_t + z\bar{B}/p_t + \bar{A}_t + \bar{M}/p_t - [c_t + M_t/p_t + A_t] = 0$$

$$(w_{t+1}/p_{t+1})N_{t+1} + zB_t/p_{t+1} + \bar{A}_{t+1} + M_t/p_{t+1}$$
$$-[c_{t+1} + M_{t+1}/p_{t+1} + A_{t+1}] = 0$$

The sum of dividends, wage payments, and interest payments equals total output minus depreciation. For period t,

$$(w_t/p_t)N_t + d_t + z\overline{B}/p_t = y_t - \delta\overline{K}$$

and so on.

Now we can express the household problem in terms of a set of Bellman equations. Assuming perfect foresight, we thus have for period t (time t to t + 1):

$$W(\overline{x}_t) = \max_{c_t, N_t, M_t/p_t, x_{t+1}} \left[u(c_t, M_t/p_t, 1-N_t) + W(x_{t+1})\right]$$

subject to the transition function

$$x_{t+1} = R_t[\overline{x}_t + (w_t/p_t)N_t - c_t] - [R_t - R_{mt}]M_t/p_t$$

and given $\overline{x}_t$.

R_{mt} is the real gross rate of interest on money, that is, the gross real rate of return on money, and equals one divided by one plus the rate of inflation $(1/(1+\pi_t))$.

$\overline{x}_t$ is the total value in period t derived from the inherited holdings of money, bonds, and stocks and is given by

$$\overline{x}_t = d_t + z\overline{B}/p_t + \overline{A}_t + \overline{M}/p_t$$

where,

$$\overline{A}_t = [p_{et}\overline{S} + p_{bt}\overline{B}]/p_t$$

The difference between the total real value derived in period t from inherited bonds, stocks, and money balances plus real wage income, $\overline{x}_t + (w_t/p_t)N_t$, and consumption in period t, c_t, reflects the acquisition of bonds, equity shares, and money holdings at the end of period t by the representative household.

Let A_t denote the planned holdings of financial assets at the end of period t, we thus have from the household budget constraint,

$$A_t + M_t/p_t = \overline{x}_t + (w_t/p_t)N_t - c_t$$

where,

$$A_t = [p_{et}S_t + p_{bt}B_t]/p_t$$

Since, the gross real rate of return on financial assets, R_t, equals one plus the nominal interest rate divided by one plus the rate of inflation $((1+r_t)/(1+\pi_t))$. Therefore, in period t+1, the inherited real value of bonds, stocks, and money balances, including dividends and interest payments, is given by

$$x_{t+1} = R_t A_t + R_{mt} M_t / p_t$$

Substituting in the expression for A_t derived from the household budget constraint (i.e., $A_t = x_t + (w_t/p_t)\ Nt - c_t - M_t/p_t$) and rearranging, we obtain the transition function as

$$x_{t+1} = R_t \left[x_t + (w_t/p_t) N_t - c_t\right] - \left[R_t - R_{mt}\right] M_t/p_t$$

Substituting the transition function into Bellman's equation for period t, we have the following first-order conditions for c_t, N_t, and M_t/p_t assuming interior solutions (i.e., $c_t > 0$, $1 > N_t > 0$, and $M_t/P_t > 0$):

$$\partial u_t/\partial c_t - (\partial W(x_{t+1})/\partial x_{t+1}) R_t = 0 \quad \text{...(4.19)}$$

$$\partial u_t/\partial(1-N_t) + (\partial W(x_{t+1})/\partial x_{t+1}) R_t (w_t/p_t) = 0 \quad \text{...(4.20)}$$

$$\partial u_t/\partial(M_t/p_t) - (\partial W(x_{t+1})/\partial x_{t+1})(R_t - R_{mt}) = 0 \quad \text{...(4.21)}$$

The above conditions indicate that for period t we have from equations (4.19) and (4.20):

$$\frac{\partial u_t/\partial(1-N_t)}{\partial u_t/\partial c_t} = \frac{w_t}{p_t} \quad \text{...(4.22)}$$

The optimal choice of leisure is such that the marginal value of leisure in terms of consumption, that is, the marginal rate of substitution between leisure and consumption as given by

$$\frac{\partial u_t/\partial(1-N_t)}{\partial u_t/\partial c_t}$$

equals the marginal cost of leisure in terms of consumption forgone in the current period as given by the real wage w_t/p_t.

From (4.19) and (4.21) we have for period t:

$$\frac{\partial u_t/\partial(M_t/p_t)}{\partial u_t/\partial c_t} = (R_t)^{-1}(R_t - R_{mt})$$

The optimal choice of real money balances is such that the marginal rate of substitution between real money balances and consumption as given by

$$\frac{\partial u_t/\partial(M_t/p_t)}{\partial u_t/\partial c_t}$$

equals the marginal cost in terms of the present value of the loss in interest income in the subsequent period due to the holding of money balances instead of financial assets as given by the expression $(R_t)^{-1}(R_t - R_{mt})$.

$R_t - R_{mt}$ equals $(1+r_t)/(1+\pi_t) - 1/(1+\pi_t)$, which is simply $r_t/(1+\pi_t)$, or the anticipated nominal rate of interest. Given that $R_t = (1+r_t)/(1+\pi_t)$, we thus have that $(R_t)^{-1}(R_t - R_{mt}) = r_t/(1+r_t)$.

Now define $W(x_{t+1})$ as

$$W(x_{t+1}) = \max_{\substack{c_{t+1}, N_{t+1},\\ M_{t+1}/p_{t+1}, x_{t+2}}} \left[\beta u(c_{t+1}, M_{t+1}/p_{t+1}, 1 - N_{t+1}) + W(x_{t+2})\right]$$

where,

$$x_{t+2} = R_{t+1}\left[x_{t+1} + (w_{t+1}/p_{t+1})N_{t+1} - c_{t+1}\right]$$

$$- [R_{t+1} - R_{m,t+1}]\, M_{t+1}/p_{t+1}$$

given,

$$\bar{x}_{t+1} = d_{t+1} + zB_t/p_{t+1} + \bar{A}_{t+1} + M_t/p_{t+1}$$

$$\bar{A}_{t+1} = [p_{e,t+1}S_t + p_{b,t+1}B_t]/p_{t+1}$$

Now substituting the transition function into the Bellman equation for period t+1, we have the following first-order conditions for period t+1:

$$\beta\partial u_{t+1}/\partial c_{t+1} - (\partial W(x_{t+2})/\partial x_{t+2})R_{t+1} = 0 \qquad ...(4.23)$$

$$-\beta\partial u_{t+1}/\partial(1-N_{t+1}) + (\partial W(x_{t+2})/\partial x_{t+2})R_{t+1}(w_{t+1}/p_{t+1}) = 0 \qquad ...(4.24)$$

$$\beta\partial u_{t+1}/\partial(M_{t+1}/p_{t+1}) - (\partial W(x_{t+2})/\partial x_{t+2})(R_{t+1} - R_{m,t+1}) = 0 \qquad ...(4.25)$$

The above first-order conditions imply that the indirect effects of the change in x_{t+1} on $W(x_{t+1})$ through the effect of such a change on the choice of the optimal values of consumption, labour supply, and real money balances for period t+1 are zero. This is simply an application of the envelope theorem, which states that the change in the objective function adjusting the choice variables optimally is equal to the change in the objective function when one does not adjust the choice variables. Thus, along the transition function for x_{t+2} we get

$$\partial W(x_{t+1})/\partial x_{t+1} = \left(\partial W(c_{t+2})/\partial x_{t+2}\right)R_{t+1} \qquad ...(4.26)$$

Substituting equation (4.23) into (4.26), we get

$$\partial W(x_{t+1})/\partial x_{t+1} = \beta\,\partial u_{t+1}/\partial c_{t+1} \qquad ...(4.27)$$

Or, substituting (4.24) into (4.26), we have

$$\partial W(x_{t+1})/\partial x_{t+1} = \beta\left[\partial u_{t+1}/\partial(1 - N_{t+1})\right]p_{t+1}/w_{t+1} \qquad ...(4.28)$$

Combining equations (4.19) and (4.27) we get the solution for the optimal allocation of consumption between period t and period t+1 as

$$\frac{\partial u_t/\partial c_t}{\beta\partial u_{t+1}/\partial c_{t+1}} = R_t$$

Combining equations (4.21) and (4.27), we obtain the expression for the optimal portfolio choice of money as

$$\frac{\partial u_t/\partial(M_t/p_t)}{\beta\partial u_{t+1}/\partial c_{t+1}} = R_t - R_{mt}$$

Combining equations (4. 20) and (4.28), we obtain an expression for the optimal allocation of labour supply over time as

$$\frac{\partial u_t/\partial(1-N_t)}{\beta\partial u_{t+1}/\partial(1-N_{t+1})} = \frac{p_{t+1}}{w_{t+1}}\,R_t\,\frac{w_t}{p_t} \qquad ...(4.29)$$

Equation (4.22) indicates that at the optimal labour supply the household cannot be made better off by trading consumption for leisure within periods at the expected real wage for the period. Equation (4.29) indicates that at the optimum the household cannot be made better off by trading leisure across periods given the relevant real wages and the real interest rate.

Let us consider an increase in the real wage due to a rise in the money wage w_t. The increase in the net real wage means a steeper budget line, as the household's optimal leisure—consumption combination changes from $1-N_t^s$ and c_t^d to $(1-N_t^s)'$ and $(c_t^d)'$. An increase in the real wage has two conceptually distinct effects on the household's labour supply decision—an income effect and a substitution effect.

The income effect refers to the fact that an increase in the real wage makes the household better off because it leads to an increase in the household's feasible consumption set in the current period. The higher real wage means that the household, if it so desires, can increase both its leisure and consumption. Thus, the household is able to reach a higher indifference curve, which has associated with it a higher utility level. The substitution effect refers to the fact that the increase in the real wage makes an hour of leisure relatively more expensive in terms of consumption that must be forgone.

The substitution and income effects on leisure work in opposite directions. The substitution effect of the higher real wage causes leisure to fall and hours worked to rise, while the income effect causes leisure to rise and hours worked to fall. The net effect on leisure and hours worked depends on which effect dominates. If the substitution effect dominates, then a higher real wage results in a decrease in desired leisure and an increase in desired working hours. If the income effect dominates, the opposite is true and the individual's labour supply curve is 'backward bending' when plotted against the real wage.

Now consider a corner solution with respect to labour supply, in particular a household, denoted a, that has chosen not to participate in the labour market. For such household, let us consider the Bellman equation for period t and introduce explicitly the non-negativity constraint for labour supply, $N_t \geq 0$. Let μ_n denote the multiplier associated with this constraint, then the first-order conditions for household a's consumption and labour supply are

$$\partial u_{at}/\partial c_{at} - \left(\partial W(x_{a,t+1})/\partial x_{a,t+1}\right) R_t = 0$$

$$-\partial u_{at}/\partial(1-N_{at}) + \mu_n + \left(\partial W(x_{a,t+1})/\partial x_{a,t+1}\right) R_t w_t/p_t = 0$$

$$N_{at} \geq 0, \mu_n N_{at} = 0$$

Substituting the first equation into the second and rearranging we get

$$\frac{-\partial u_{at}/\partial(1-N_{at})}{\partial u_{at}/\partial c_{at}}=\frac{w_t}{p_t}+\frac{\mu_n}{\partial u_{at}/\partial c_{at}}$$

In case individuals not participating in the labour force, $\mu_n \geq 0$. The 'corner solution' is a case in which the marginal rate of substitution of leisure in terms of consumption is greater than the real wage. In other words, the absolute value of the indifference curve is equal to or greater than the absolute value of the budget line at the point where $N^s_{at}=0$. At the optimal choice, the corresponding indifference curve is more steeply sloped than the budget line. Even when all hours are devoted to leisure and none to work, the individual's marginal rate of substitution of leisure in terms of consumption still exceeds the real wage rate. In other words, the individual's valuation of leisure exceeds the market's valuation of leisure. As a result, individual a does not find it worthwhile to participate in the labour market.

The economy-wide labour supply response to an increase in the current real wage is a combination of an ambiguous effect on the labour supply of those currently working, but an unambiguous increase in the labour supply among those not working.

LABOUR MARKET INTERTEMPORAL SUBSTITUTION HYPOTHESIS

This hypothesis states that labour supply responds positively to transitory increase in real wages and increases in the real interest rate—a central hypothesis of modern, competitive models of the business cycle.

According to the intertemporal substitution hypothesis employment and work hours fluctuate cyclically because workers want to increase their leisure and non-market work during recessions when real wages are relatively low and reduce their leisure and non-market work during macroeconomic expansions when real wages are relatively high. Intertemporal substitution is the core of the labour market specification of empirical real business cycle models.

Now consider the equation (4.29) for the optimal allocation of labour supply over time. The view of labour supply embedded in equation (4.29) has life cycle as well as business cycle implications. With respect to life cycle implications, the theory predicts that workers will concentrate their labour supply in years of peak earnings, consuming leisure in larger than average amounts during childhood and old age. While with respect to the business cycle, it explains an apparent contradiction in the static theory of labour supply—the observed wage inelasticity of labour supply in the long run with short-run fluctuations in employment, which require an elastic labour supply if one takes a market clearing approach with respect to the labour market. It does so by introducing a distinction between a permanent change in the real wage and a temporary or transitory change in the real wage.

Suppose w^*/p^* represents the permanent or normal real wage, with the anticipated real wage next period equal to this value, such that

$$w_i/p_i = w^*/p^*, \qquad i = t+1, t+2, \ldots\ldots$$

Also, assume that

$$R_i = R^*, \qquad i = t, t+1, t+2, \ldots\ldots$$

In this case, equation (4.29) becomes

$$\frac{\partial u_t/\partial(1-N_t)}{\beta\partial u_{t+1}/\partial(1-N^*)} = R^* \frac{w_t/p_t}{w^*/p^*} \qquad \ldots(4.30)$$

where N* is the long-run supply of labour at normal wages.

Again assume that for the representative household, $\beta R^* = 1$. In this case, equation (4.30) becomes

$$\frac{\partial u_t/\partial(1-N_t)}{\partial u_{t+1}/\partial(1-N^*)} = \frac{w_t/p_t}{w^*/p^*} \qquad \ldots(4.31)$$

Equation (4.31) indicates that if the current real wage is higher than the normal real wage, then more labour is supplied than would be implied by the long-run labour supply function. Thus, this theory views suppliers of labour as reacting primarily to three variables:

(a) An anticipated 'normal' or 'permanent' real wage rate, which corresponds to the wage rate in the usual one-period analysis of the labour-leisure choice and has a negligible effect on labour supply;

(b) The deviation of the current real wage from this normal rate, which has a strong positive effect on labour supply;

(c) And the expected real rate of interest.

Here one point should be noted that the equation (4.29) does not explicitly identify the initial asset holdings as a variable that affects the relative choice of labour supply across periods. Similarly, the condition for the optimal choice of consumption across periods did not have the initial value of assets affecting the relative consumption purchases across periods.

Now let us consider the more general case in which agent a chooses not only consumption across time but also the portfolio of assets. That is, we will consider the following problem

$$\max_{\substack{c_{at},\ldots,c_{a,t+T} \\ x_{a,t+1},\ldots,x_{a,t+T+1} \\ M_{at}/p_t,\ldots,M_{a,t+T}/p_{t+T}}} \sum_{i=t}^{t+T} \beta^{i-t} u^a(c_{ai}, M_{ai}/p_i)$$

Subject to

$$-x_{a,t+1} + R_t[\bar{x}_{at} + \bar{c}_{at} - c_{at}] - [R_t - R_{mt}]M_{at}/p_t = 0$$

$$-x_{a,t+2} + R_{t+1}[\bar{x}_{a,t+1} + \bar{c}_{a,t+1} - c_{a,t+1}] - [R_{t+1} - R_{m,t+1}]M_{a,t+1}/p_{t+1} = 0$$

$$-x_{a,t+3} + R_{t+2}[\bar{x}_{a,t+2} + \bar{c}_{a,t+2} - c_{a,t+2}] - [R_{t+2} - R_{m,t+2}]M_{a,t+2}/p_{t+2} = 0$$

$$\cdots\cdots\cdots\cdots\cdots\cdots\cdots\cdots$$

$$-x_{a,t+T+1} + R_{t+T}[\bar{x}_{a,t+T} + \bar{c}_{a,t+T} - c_{a,t+T}] - [R_{t+T} - R_{m,t+T}] M_{a,t+T}/p_{t+T} = 0$$

$$x_{a,t+T+1} \geq 0$$

To simplify the problem we assume interior solutions, in this case not only with respect to the consumption good but also with respect to money holdings. Suppose that λ_i, i = t, ... + T, denote the Lagrange multipliers for the constraints linking the real asset holdings at the end of period i with their real value at the end of period i + 1, and let μ_T denote the multiplier for the nonnegativity condition that $x_{a,t+T+1} \geq 0$.

The first order conditions are

$$\partial L/\partial c_{ai} = \beta^{i-t} du_i^a/dc_{ai} - \lambda_i R_i = 0, \qquad i = t,\ldots.., t+T$$

$$\partial L/\partial(M_{ai}/p_i) = \beta^{i-t}\,\partial u_i^a/\partial(M_{ai}/p_i) - \lambda_i[R_i - R_{mi}] = 0, \qquad i = t,\ldots.., t+T$$

$$\partial L/\partial x_{a,i+1} = -\lambda_i + \lambda_{i+1}R_{i+1} = 0, \qquad i = t,\ldots.., t+T-1,$$

$$\partial L/\partial x_{a,t+T+1} = -\lambda_{t+T} + \mu_T = 0,$$

$$\partial L/\partial \lambda_i = -x_{a,i+1} + R_i(x_{ai} + \bar{c}_{ai} - c_{ai}) - [R_i - R_{mi}]M_{ai}/p_i = 0, \qquad i = t,\ldots.., t+T$$

$$\partial L/\partial \mu_T = x_{a,t+T+1} \geq 0,$$

$$\mu_T \partial L/\partial \mu_T = \mu_T x_{a,t+T+1} = 0$$

$$\lambda_i \geq 0, \qquad i = t,\ldots.., t+T$$

$$\mu_T \geq 0$$

where $u_i^a = u^a(c_{ai}, M_{ai}/p_i), i = t,\ldots\ldots,t+T$. To isolate the portfolio choice, consider the portfolio choice of money and bond holdings for a given level of current consumption. That is, let us look at the optimal choice of M_{ai}/p_i given that c_{ai} is held constant. From the second set of constants we have

$$\beta^{i-t}\,\partial u_i^a/\partial(M_{ai}/p_i) - \lambda_i[R_i - R_{mi}] = 0$$

Substituting the condition for the optimal choice of the total value of assets in that period, $\lambda_i = \lambda_{i+1}R_{i+1}$ we have

$$\beta^{i-t}\,\partial u_i^a/\partial(M_{ai}/p_i) - \lambda_{i+1}R_{i+1}[R_i - R_{mi}] = 0$$

Now substituting the condition for the optimal choice of consumption next period (i+1), as given by

$$\beta^{i-t+1}\,du_{i+1}^a/dc_{a,i+1} - \lambda_{i+1}R_{i+1} = 0$$

we have

$$\beta^{i-t}\,\partial u_i^a/\partial(M_{ai}/p_i) - \beta^{i-t+1}\left(du_{i+1}^a/dc_{a,i+1}\right)[R_i - R_{mi}] = 0$$

Rearranging gives

$$\frac{du_i^a/d(M_{ai}/p_i)}{\beta du_{i+1}^a/dc_{a,i+1}} = R_i - R_{mi}$$

As we know that the expected gross real return on bonds in period i, R_i, equals $(1+r_i)/(1+\pi_i)$, and that the expected gross real return on money, R_{mi}, equals $1/(1+\pi_i)$, the above expression can be written as

$$\frac{du_i^a/d(M_{ai}/p_i)}{\beta du_{i+1}^a/dc_{a,i+1}} = \frac{r_i}{1-\pi_i}$$

As the length of the period goes to zero, the expected rate of inflation term would vanish. This implies that the optimal division of assets between money and bonds depends primarily on the money interest rate alone. An increase in money holding with no change in current consumption means a reduction in bond holdings, and thus the loss of nominal interest income r_i, or real interest income $r_i/(1+\pi_i)$.

Agent a's demand functions at time t can be shown to be homogeneous of degree 0 in the current price level p_t, initial money balances $\bar{M}_a$, and initial bond holdings $\bar{B}_a$. In such type of economy, this is said to reflect the absence of money illusion. One critical reason for this is the assumption of unit elastic expectations with respect to future prices, so that changes in the current price level leave unchanged the expected rates of change in the price level in subsequent periods. Also the current and expected future money payments attached to bonds are being held constant, so that given the fixed money payments x on maturity, interest rates are unchanged. Alternatively, one could have money prices and the fixed future money payment attached to one-period bonds rise by the same proportion.

Thus, individual a's demand for the consumption good and real money balances at time t can be represented by

$$c_{at}^d = c_{at}^d(r_t, r_{t+1}, \ldots\ldots, r_{t+T-1}, \pi_t, \ldots\ldots, \pi_{t+T-1}, W_{at})$$

$$M_{at}^d/p_t = M_{at}^d/p_t(r_t, r_{t+1}, \ldots\ldots, r_{t+T-1}, \pi_t, \ldots\ldots, \pi_{t+T-1}, W_{at})$$

where $\overline{x}_{at}$ is the individual's real wealth at the end of period t, as given by

$$W_{at} = \overline{x}_{at} + \overline{c}_{at} + \sum_{j=t}^{t+T-1}\left[\prod_{i=t}^{j}(R_i)\right]^{-1}(\overline{c}_{aj+1})$$

From the budget constraint for period t, we know that the above two demand conditions imply a real demand for bonds of a similar form since

$$p_{bt}B_{at}^{d}/p_t = \overline{c}_{at} + \overline{x}_{at} - \left[c_{at}^{d} + M_{at}^{d}/p_t\right]$$

The above demand functions do not depend solely on wealth and the pattern of expected real rates of interest since, given the portfolio choice, a given pattern of expected real interest rates could alter demand depending on the underlying values of the money interest rate. Thus, individual a's excess demand function for the consumption good and money in period t are defined by

$$z_{at} = c_{at}^{d} - \overline{c}_{at}$$

$$z_{am} = M_{at}^{d}/p_t - \overline{M}_a/p_t, \text{ and}$$

$$z_{ab} = pb_t B_{at}^{d}/p_t$$

The real balance effect indicates the effect of a change in real balances $\left(\overline{M}_a/p_t\right)$ on individual demand for goods other than money. As before, there is a real balance effect that reflects a wealth effect. That is, a decrease in initial real balances leads to a reduction in real money demand, M_{at}^{d}/p_t, and a reduction in the real demand for bonds, $p_{bt}B_{at}^{d}/p_t$. There is also what might be referred to as a real indebtedness effect in that a change in price alters not only real money balances but also real initial debt. If $B_a >. 0$, an increase in p_t reduces wealth, while if $\overline{B}_a < 0$, an increase in p_t increases wealth.

Simple Determination of Income and Employment

5

In the previous chapters, we have discussed basic macroeconomic relationships and the definitional complexity of contemporary macroeconomic concepts—national income accounting, national income, national income identities, GDP, disposable personal income etc. In this chapter we begin our analysis of the reasons output and employment vary. The purpose of this chapter is to review the essential elements of the major approaches to macroeconomic theory and policy.

Before the 1930s there was no macroeconomics, i.e. the study of the overall economy rather than its constituent parts. It is with Keynes' General Theory that it begins, as well as the effort to deduce from the history of economic thought what were the implicit models of previous economic thinkers. The classical model is a logical extension of the combined thinking of a variety of economists prior to the 1930s and it draws from various models developed in price, distribution, and monetary theory. The classical model assumes that input and output markets are competitive and price and wages are flexible.

The so-called Classical School of economic thought begins with Adam Smith (1723-1790) and his *An Inquiry into the Wealth of Nations* in 1776 and runs through the last great Classical economist John Stuart Mill (1806-1873). In essence, the Classical School emerged as a response to the previous dominant school—the Mercantilists. The Mercantilists believed that wealth consists of money, or gold and silver, is a popular notion which naturally arise from the double function of money, as the instrument of commerce and as the measure of value. A rich country, in the same manner as a rich man, is supposed to be a country abounding in money. To increase the stock of money, in the form of gold and silver, Mercantilist rulers granted monopolies to friends and relatives in order to increase domestic production of goods and services and placed severe restrictions on the import of foreign goods and services. Such Crown grants of industrial privilege were a particular object of concern to Smith and all the Classical School that believed it was real factors of production combined with free markets as opposed to state-sponsored monopolies and free trade rather than import restrictions that would increase the wealth of a nation defined, in essence, as the productive capacity of the economy not the quantity of money it held. The Mercantilists and later the Bullionist view survived, however, to form the basis of what is now called the Monetarist model of the macroeconomics.

In short, Classical economics compared to Mercantilism:

(a) stressed the role of real as opposed to monetary factors in determining real outcomes like output and employment. Money was considered strictly a medium of exchange not a causal factor in economic growth; and

(b) stressed the role of the self-adjusting marketplace to ensure output and employment. Government has no role in ensuring adequate demand or employment other than essential infrastructures.

OUTPUT AND EMPLOYMENT IN THE CLASSICAL MODEL

The starting point for analysis of the classical engine is the production function:

$$Y = f(L, R, K, T) \qquad ...(5.1)$$

where,

Y = real output per period (real GNP),

L = number of man-hours of labour employed,

R = natural resources employed,

K = existing capital stock, and

T = level of technology.

For the short-run analysis, the level of technology, the existing capital stock, and natural resources are taken to be given. Hence, short-run variations in the level of output can be traced directly to variations in man-hours of labour employed in the production process.

Accordingly, in the short-run, all changes in Y depend upon changes in L. The relationship is shown in Fig. 5.1 and displays a quality that is in fact derived from the Neo-Classical School or Marginalists—diminishing marginal product.

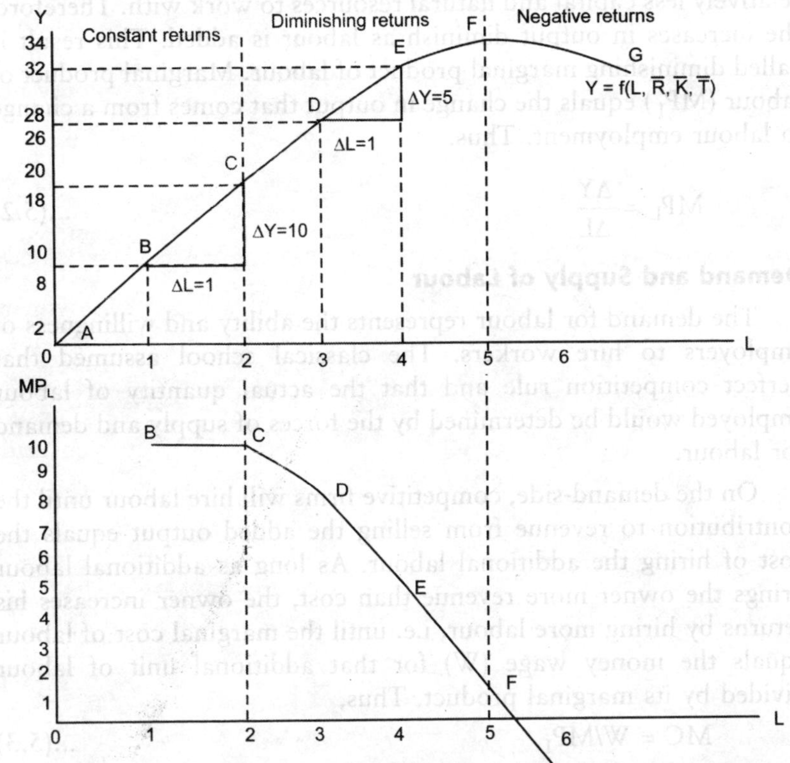

Fig. 5.1 : Production Function and Marginal Product of Labour Curves.

The classical production function shown by the Figure 5.1 displays some important characteristics:

(a) at low levels of L, the function is almost a straight line whose slope measures the increase in output for an increase in L. This section of the curve defines the 'constant returns to scale';

(b) as the level of L increases, however, the slope becomes more and more gentle reflecting 'diminishing marginal returns', i.e. output increases proportionately less than the increase in L; and,

(c) from the production function one can calculate a related curve—the marginal productivity of labour (MP_L).

The production function in the figure shows that output rises at a decreasing rate. The reason is that each additional worker has relatively less capital and natural resources to work with. Therefore, the increases in output diminish as labour is added. This result is called diminishing marginal product of labour. Marginal product of labour (MP_L) equals the change in output that comes from a change in labour employment. Thus,

$$MP_L = \frac{\Delta Y}{\Delta L} \qquad ...(5.2)$$

Demand and Supply of Labour

The demand for labour represents the ability and willingness of employers to hire workers. The classical school assumed that perfect competition rule and that the actual quantity of labour employed would be determined by the forces of supply and demand for labour.

On the demand-side, competitive firms will hire labour until the contribution to revenue from selling the added output equals the cost of hiring the additional labour. As long as additional labour brings the owner more revenue than cost, the owner increases his returns by hiring more labour, i.e. until the marginal cost of labour equals the money wage (W) for that additional unit of labour divided by its marginal product. Thus,

$$MC = W/MP_L \qquad ...(5.3)$$

Profit maximization, in the short-run would occur when the price for a unit of output equals MC, which in turn equals the money wage divided by the marginal productivity of the last unit of labour. Thus,

$$P = MC = W/MP_L$$

or, $$PM_L = W/P \qquad ...(5.4)$$

Equation (5.4) says that the amount of labour demanded at any real wage is equal to the marginal product of labour. Figure 5.2 illustrates the demand curve for labour.

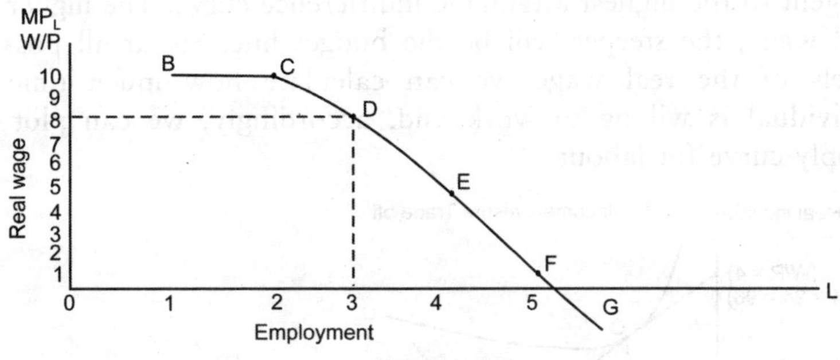

Fig. 5.2

The supply of labour represents the ability and willingness of workers to trade their leisure time for the income necessary to purchase goods and services. The workers allocate their time between work and leisure in order to maximise their utility. As real wages rise, the opportunity cost of not working rises. Utility is generated by real income earned through the disutility of work that can then be used to purchase marketable goods and services as well as leisure. There is therefore a trade-off between real income resulting from working and the pleasures or utility of leisure.

There are two effects on labour's choice between work and leisure. The substitution effect is the willingness to substitute work for the more expensive leisure. People work more as a result of higher wages. The income effect works in the opposite direction. With higher real wages, workers may wish to use their higher income to purchase leisure and work less. That is, workers may reach their desired standard of living with fewer hours of work and thus tend to supply less labour at higher wages. The classical model assumes that the substitution effect dominates for society as a whole, so that more labour is supplied at higher real wages.

Alternative levels of utility (U) can be plotted as a set of indifference or preference curve as shown in the Figure 5.3. In symbolic logic, we assume a utility function for workers U = f(W, l) where workers gain satisfaction through taste combinations of work or wages (W) and leisure (l). The slope of the indifference curve shows the trade off a worker is willing to make between work and leisure. In general, the higher the real wage, the more work will be chosen; the lower the real wage, the lower the amount of work supplied. A worker will maximise utility where the budget line is tangent to the highest attainable indifference curve. The higher the real wage, the steeper will be the budget line. So, at all possible levels of the real wage we can calculate how much time an individual is willing to work and, accordingly, we can plot the supply curve for labour.

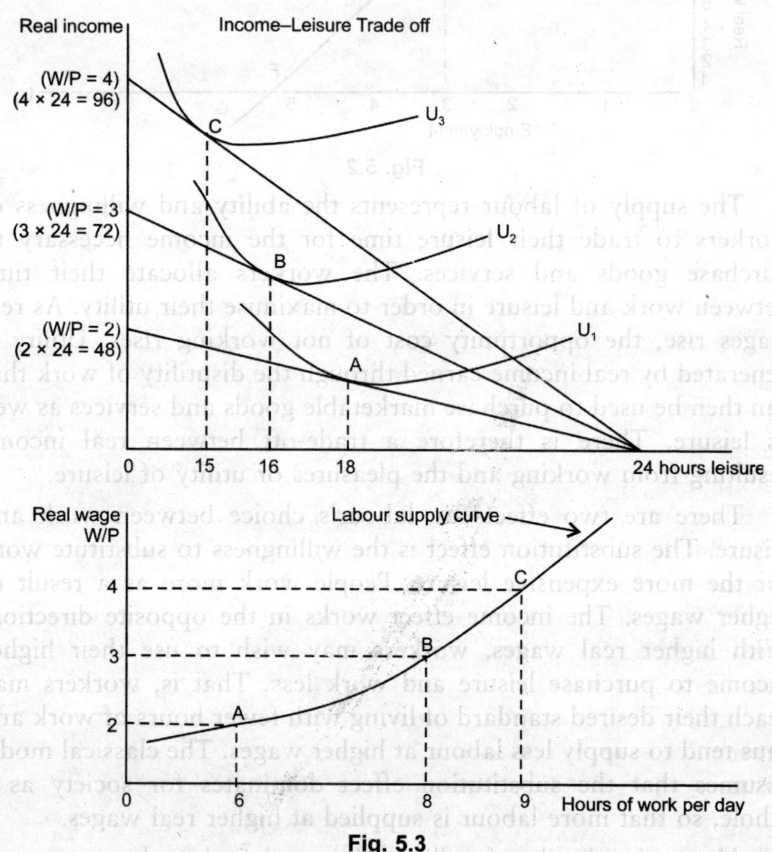

Fig. 5.3

Thus, from Figure 5.3 we see that the supply of labour is a positive function of the real wage, i.e., the higher the real wage, the higher the supply of labour.

The intersection of supply and demand determines the equilibrium real wage $(W/P)_E$ and equilibrium employment (L_E). Figure 5.4 describe this statement.

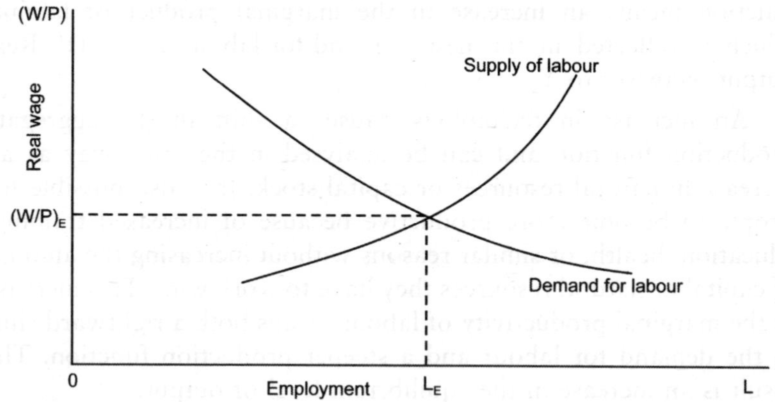

Fig. 5.4

Applying this employment level, L_E, to the production function in Fig. 5.1, we determine the short-run equilibrium level of output, Y_E.

If wages were free to adjust, there could be unemployment only during the transitions from a higher to a lower equilibrium level of employment. The transition time would be the length of time until workers accepted the necessity of a lower real wage. If wages were inflexible downward, then an increase in the supply of labour or a decrease in the demand for labour would cause unemployment, as would any setting of wages above the market clearing wages. In the classical model, the only source of unemployment is wage inflexibility, and the classicists did not expect wage inflexibility to occur in the absence of perverse government policy to maintain wages. They expected the economy to tend toward full employment without government stabilization policies being necessary.

In the classical model, the level of output can be increased by any of the following:

(a) by an increase in natural resources or capital;

(b) by an increase in the level of technology;

(c) by an increase in the marginal productivity of labour;

(d) by an increase in the available labour force.

Now consider the Figure 5.5. In this figure we see that an increase in natural resources to R′ and in capital goods to K′ raises the production function. The greater slope in the production function means an increase in the marginal product of labour, which is reflected in the new demand-for-labour curve D′. Real output increases to Y_2.

An increase in technology causes a shift in the aggregate production function and can be analysed in the same way as an increase in natural resources or capital stock. It is also possible for people to become more productive because of increased training, education, health, or similar reasons without increasing the amount of capital or natural resources they have to work with. This increase in the marginal productivity of labour means both a rightward shift in the demand for labour and a steeper production function. The result is an increase in the equilibrium level of output.

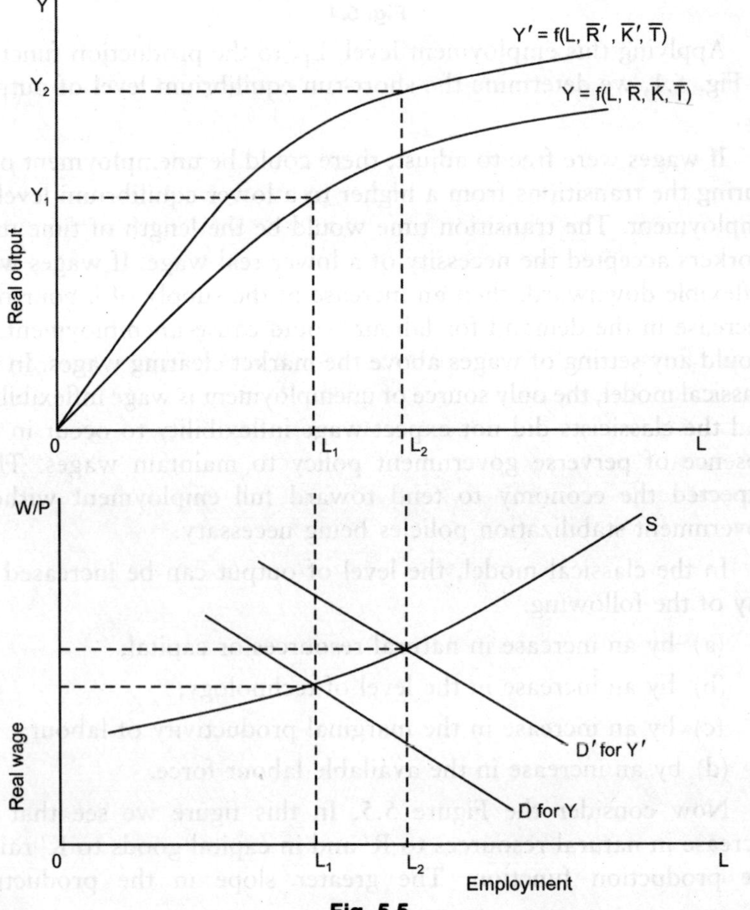

Fig. 5.5

An increase in the available labour force shifts the labour supply curve rightward. A larger supply of labour may result from a structural or demographic change, such as women entering the labour force, or from a higher population growth rate. Such an increase in labour supply results in a corresponding increase in employment and a fall in real wages. The increase in employment then translates into an increase in real output.

In the long run, when all factors can be varied, the level of employment is determined by everything that affects the marginal productivity of labour, such as education and training, and everything that affects the supply of labour, such as changing attitude toward women working outside the home. Output in the long run is a function of employment levels, natural resources, capital, and the level of technology.

OUTPUT, EMPLOYMENT, AND PRICE LEVEL RELATIONSHIPS IN THE CLASSICAL MODEL

The relationship between output and price level or aggregate supply can be determined by allowing the price level to vary and observing the effect on output and employment. The Figure 5.6 represents the derivation of aggregate supply for the classical model. Because output is determined purely by supply factors under the classical model, demand plays no role. Similarly factors like the quantity of money, level of government spending, and demand for investment goods are all demand factors that play no role in determining output in the classical model. Taxes that affect supply side factors will, however, affect output. Factors affecting the classical equilibrium include changes in technology, reduction of the price of raw materials as well as growth of the capital stock.

If we start with the original price level, P_1, in Panel (a), supply and demand for labour produce an equilibrium nominal wage of W_1 and employment of L_1. Using employment of L_1, Panel (b) shows that real output is Y_1. In Panel (d), real output, Y_1, and its corresponding price level, P_1, yield point A on the aggregate supply curve. When price level increases to P_2, employment remains the same. Therefore, real output remains the same in Panel (b). In Panel (d), the higher price level, P_2, corresponds to the same output, Y_1, as indicated by point B. Price changes do not affect aggregate output. Thus, we get a vertical supply curve.

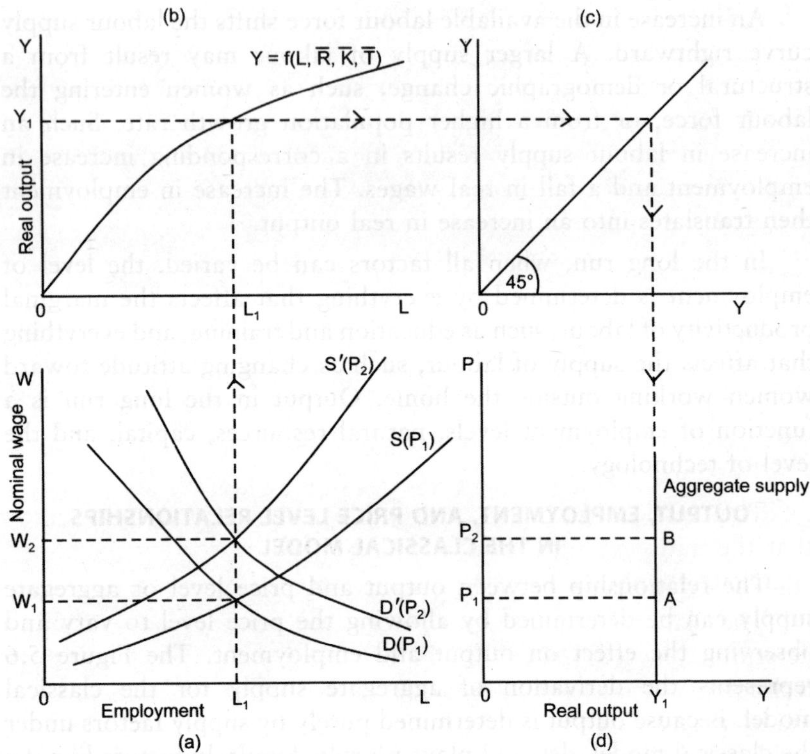

Fig. 5.6

The vertical aggregate supply curve of the classical model results from the following assumptions concerning labour markets:

(a) The supply and demand for labour are a function of the real wage.

(b) Everyone knows the actual price level and the nominal wage and therefore knows the real wage as well.

(c) Nominal wages are perfectly flexible in either direction. Wage flexibility means there are no impediments to wages changing in response to changes in the labour supply or demand.

(d) The vertical aggregate supply curve assumes price flexibility in the output market.

Implications of the vertical supply curve for economic policymakers are:

(a) In order to increase the level of output, aggregate supply must shift to the right which can be accomplished in the following ways: (i) an increase in technology, natural resources, or the stock of productive capital, and (ii) an increase in the marginal productivity of labour or an increase in the supply of labour.

The policy implication for government is that to gain an increase in output levels, appropriate policies must be designed to stimulate the changes as stated above.

(b) Policies, aimed at increasing output and employment by regulating or influencing the level of aggregate demand are doomed to failure. Shifts in the aggregate demand curve affect only the level of prices, leaving output and employment unchanged.

The classical model is a supply side model in that it stipulates that the nation's output can be increased only through increasing aggregate supply.

The classical model implies that output and employment are determined by real factors such as human capital, natural resources, technology, and capital. The role of government in the classical model may include promoting economic growth by establishing a stable political system and by limiting tax and regulatory obstacles to the growth of the productive inputs, but the classical model has no role for output stabilization policy. Decreases in output are temporary, self-correcting disequilibria. In fact, government spending cannot even increase aggregate demand, assuming the spending is not financed by increases in the money supply.

Thus, in our analysis we find that classical theory of employment is based on two fundamental postulates:

(a) The wage is equal to the marginal product of labour.

(b) The utility of the wage when a given volume of labour is employed is equal to the marginal disutility of that amount of employment.

This postulate is compatible with what may be called 'frictional' unemployment. For a realistic interpretation of it legitimately allows for various inexactnesses of adjustment that stand in the way of continuous full employment. For instance, unemployment due to a temporary want of balance between the relative quantities of specialised resources as a result of miscalculation or intermittent demand; or to time-lags consequent on unforeseen changes; or to the fact that the change-over from one employment to another cannot be effected without a certain delay, so that there will always exist in a non-static society a proportion of resources unemployed between jobs. In addition to 'frictional' unemployment, the postulate is also compatible with 'voluntary' unemployment due to the refusal or inability of a unit of labour, as a result of legislation or social practices or of combination for collective bargaining or of slow response to change or of mere human obstinacy, to accept a reward corresponding to the value of the product attributable to its marginal productivity. But these two categories of 'frictional' unemployment and 'voluntary' unemployment are comprehensive. The classical postulates do not admit of the possibility of the third category, which is defined as 'involuntary' unemployment.

The above stated two postulates of the classical theory determine the volume of employed resources. The first gives us the demand schedule for employment; the second gives us the supply schedule. The amount of employment is fixed at the point where the utility of the marginal product balances the disutility of the marginal employment. It would follow from this that there are only four possible means of increasing employment:

(a) an improvement in organisation or in foresight which diminishes 'frictional' unemployment;
(b) a decrease in the marginal disutility of labour, as expressed by the real wage for which additional labour is available, so as to diminish 'voluntary' unemployment;
(c) an increase in the marginal physical productivity of labour in the wage-goods industries;
(d) an increase in the price of non-wage-goods compared with, the price of wage-goods, associated with a shift in the expenditure of non-wage-earners from wage-goods to non-wage-goods.

There are two objections to the second postulate of the classical theory. The first relates to the actual behaviour of labour. A fall in real wages due to a rise in prices, with money-wages unaltered, does not, as a rule, cause the supply of available labour on offer at the current wage to fall below the amount actually employed prior to the rise of prices. All those who are now unemployed though willing to work at the current wage, will withdraw the offer of their labour in the event of even a small rise in the cost of living. But the other objection flows from our disputing the assumption that the general level of real wages is directly determined by the character of the wage bargain. In assuming that the wage bargain determines the real wage the classical school have slipt in an illicit assumption. There may be no method available to labour as a whole whereby it can bring the general level of money-wage into conformity with the marginal disutility of the current volume of employment. There may exist no expedient by which labour as a whole can reduce its real wage to a given figure by making revised money bargains with the entrepreneurs.

Having explained the basic concepts and methodological issues, we are now equipped to proceed to the analysis of our main issue: What determines the level of income, employment and output in a closed economy? Many of these ideas and concepts were first presented by a British economist John Maynard Keynes in his famous book *General Theory of Employment, Interest and Money* (1936). Some of the ideas which Keynes originally presented have undergone significant changes and modification as a result of continuous research on macro economics. However, one must concede that there was not much systematic thinking on these topics before Keynes and his contribution to this branch of economic science was so fundamental that modern macro economics is also known as Keynesian Economics.

The basic idea of Keynesian economics is very simple. Marshall taught that equilibrium quantity of any good in the market depends upon demand price and supply price of any commodity. The demand schedule is a schedule of different quantities of a good which shall be bought at different prices. These prices are known as demand price. The demand price is the price at which the buyers demand a particular good. Such a demand schedule is shown as the curve DD in Fig. 5.7. The supply schedule is a schedule of different quantities of same good which shall be supplied at different prices. The supply price of a good is the price at which the suppliers supply the good. The equilibrium quantity and prices are determined at a point where demand price becomes equal to supply price, i.e., quantity demanded of good is exactly equal to the quantity supplied. In Figure 5.7, this has been shown as $\overline{Y}$ and $\overline{P}$ where DD curve intersects SS curve. This diagram is also known as Marshallian cross. Keynes was a disciple of Marshall and he used basically the same idea to explain employment determination in the economy. Keynes argued that employment like all other goods also has demand price and a supply price.

Since, Keynes is concerned with the economy as a whole, and he wants to determine total employment in the economy, therefore, he speaks of aggregate demand price and aggregate supply price of employment.

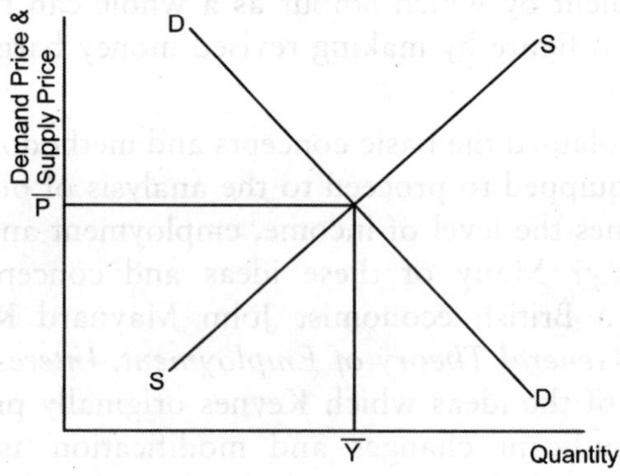

Fig. 5.7: Marshallian Cross showing Price and Output Determination of Good.

The aggregate demand schedule of the economy shows the amount of proceeds (income measured in Rupees) which all firms really expect to get if they can sell the output produced by different levels of employment.

The aggregate supply schedule shows what all firms in any economy must expect to receive from the sale of output produced by the same number of men.

Keynes thought that workers would not accept reductions in nominal wages even if the price level fell. This is due to the fact that

(a) workers would resist any downward change in their relative positions in the distribution of wages, and

(b) the piecemeal nature of wage determination would encourage workers' resistance to any wage reduction.

Let us examine the effect of downward wage inflexibility on aggregate supply. Although Keynes emphasised the importance of relative wages for the supply of labour, the conventional modelling technique is to assume that the supply of labour is a function of the real wage above the existing level of nominal wages, but that the nominal wage will not fall. This condition can be described by the Figure 5.8.

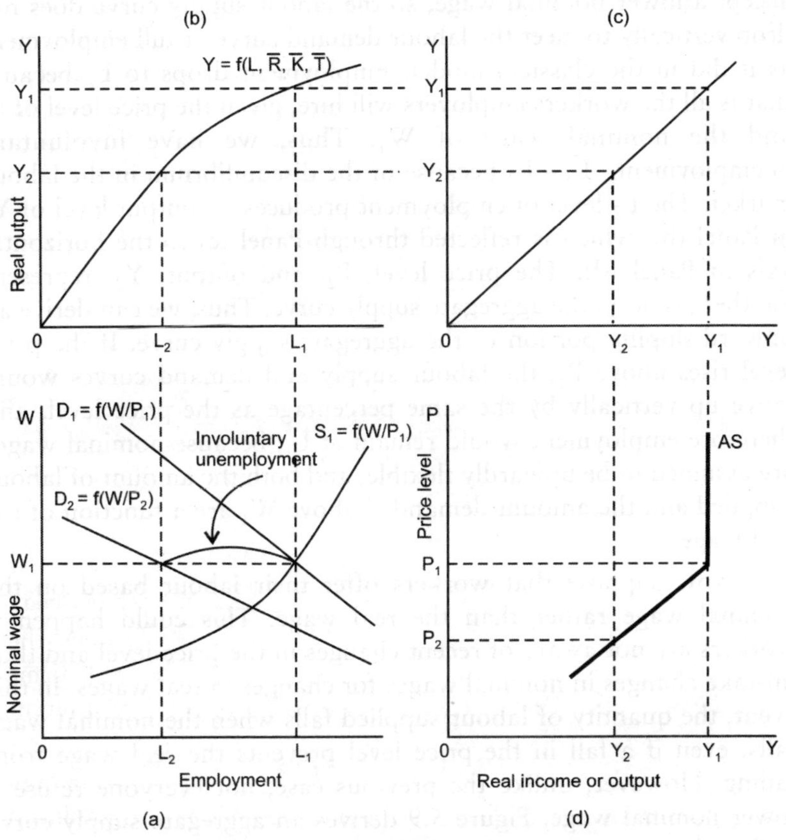

Fig. 5.8

Beginning in Panel (a) of the figure, note that initially the price level is at P_1. Labour supply, S_1, and demand, D_1, are in equilibrium with employment equal to L_1 and the nominal wage equal to W_1. An employment level of L_1 produces an output of Y_1 in Panel (b), which is reflected through Panel (c) to the horizontal axis in Panel (d). The price level of P_1 and output of Y_1 represents a point on the aggregate supply curve.

Now suppose that the price level falls to P_2. As we know that the amount of labour demanded is a function of the real wage, the lower price level means each nominal wage represents a higher real wage. Therefore, drawn against the nominal wage, the labour demand curve drops vertically so that for each level of employment the real wage is the same on D_2 as it was on D_1. Labour will not accept a lower nominal wage, so the labour supply curve does not drop vertically to meet the labour demand curve at full employment as it did in the classical model. Employment drops to L_2 because that is all the workers employers will hire, given the price level of P_2 and the nominal wage of W_1. Thus, we have involuntary unemployment, $L_1 - L_2$ because of the disequilibrium in the labour market. The L_2 level of employment produces an output level of Y_2 in Panel (b), which is reflected through Panel (c) to the horizontal axis in Panel (d). The price level, P_2, and output, Y_2, represent another point on the aggregate supply curve. Thus, we can derive an upward-sloping portion of the aggregate supply curve. If the price level rises above P_1, the labour supply and demand curves would move up vertically by the same percentage as the price level, and therefore employment would remain at L_1, because nominal wages are assumed to be upwardly flexible, and both the amount of labour supplied and the amount demanded above W_1 are a function of the real wage.

Now suppose that workers offer their labour based on the nominal wage rather than the real wage. This could happen if workers are not aware of recent changes in the price level and thus mistake changes in nominal wages for changes in real wages. In this event, the quantity of labour supplied falls when the nominal wage falls, even if a fall in the price level prevents the real wage from falling. However, unlike the previous case, not everyone refuse a lower nominal wage. Figure 5.9 derives an aggregate supply curve under the assumption that labour supply is a function of the nominal wage.

Comparing Fig. 5.8 and Fig. 5.9 we find that initial conditions are same in both the cases. Employment is L_1, output is Y_1, then the price level drops from P_1 to P_2. As discussed before, the labour demand curve drawn against the nominal wage must drop so that the real wage will be the same for each level of employment. The labour supply curve does not move because it is a function of the nominal wage. The result in Panel (a) is a new equilibrium employment L_2. Note that employment has fallen from L_1 to L_2, but the labour market clears. Those willing to work at the nominal wage W_2 have jobs. Nevertheless, if the people represented by $L_1 - L_2$ continue to search for jobs paying the wage W_1, they will be counted as unemployed. This type of unemployment is termed as voluntary unemployment since these people are unwilling to work at the going wage.

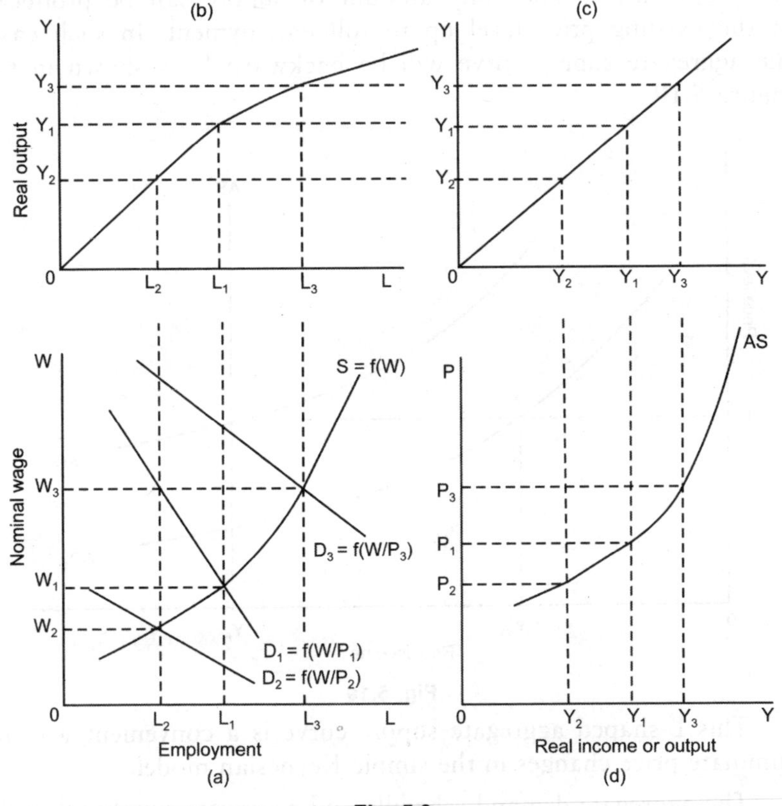

Fig. 5.9

When price level rises above P_1, the demand curve will shift up vertically in proportion to the change in the price level in order to maintain the correspondence between real wages and labour demand. That is, a higher price level makes each nominal wage represent a lower real wage, and the labour demand curve shifts rightward. However, workers do not recognise the rise in prices and mistakenly believe they have an opportunity to earn a higher real wage when the nominal wage rises. Therefore, supply of labour increases. Due to this the aggregate supply continues to slope upward even to the right of Y_1 in Panel (d).

Keynes postulated that the aggregate supply curve may be upward-sloping at output levels below full utilisation of resources under conditions of downward wage inflexibility. Suppose prices, as well as wages, are inflexible at output levels below full employment. Then any amount of supply can be produced at the existing price level up to full employment. In such case, the aggregate supply curve will be backward L as shown in the Figure 5.10.

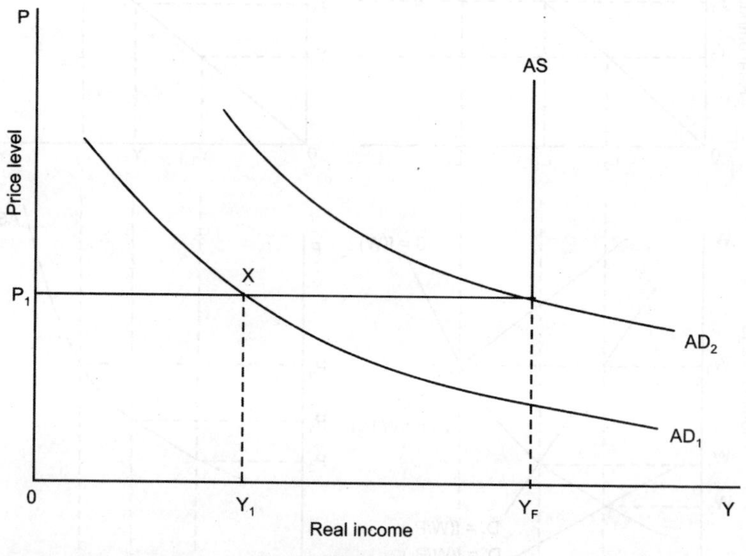

Fig. 5.10

This L-shaped aggregate supply curve is a convenient way to eliminate price changes in the simple Keynesian model.

The aggregate demand schedule and aggregate supply schedule are shown in Fig. 5.11 The Y-axis measures total receipts or income from the sale of output which is produced by a given level of employment. The X-axis measures the volume of employment. Each level of employment will have both, aggregate demand price and aggregate supply price. Aggregate demand price is a measure of revenue or (income) which all firms really expect to get. On the other hand, aggregate supply price is a measure of cost of employment in the economy (the proceed or receipts which all the firms must expect to spend in order to employ a certain number of people). Now let us consider point L_1. At this point of employment, aggregate demand price is greater than aggregate supply price. This means that employers (all firms) expect to get more than what they will spend to employ OL_1 people. In other words, the revenue obtained by OL_1 volume of employment exceeds the cost incurred upon it. Consequently, it is not only profitable to employ OL_1 volume of people, but also to expand it. Thus volume of employment will tend to move to the right hand side from OL_1. Now consider the point OL_2. At this point the aggregate supply price of employment is greater than its aggregate demand price which means that the cost of OL_2 amount of employment will be greater than the revenue or receipts which is expected to be obtained by the sale of output produced by this volume of employment. Consequently, it is not profitable for the firms to employ OL_2 people and employment will tend to move to the left hand side.

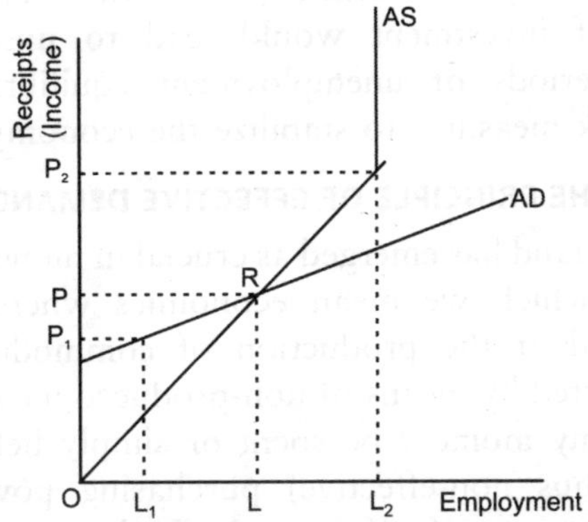

Fig. 5.11: Employment Determination in the Economy.

The equilibrium level of employment occurs where the aggregate demand curve intersects the aggregate supply curve, i.e., aggregate demand price of employment is exactly equal to its aggregate supply price. In Fig. 5.11 this is shown at the point R where OL people are employed and they produce OP amount of income. At this point of employment there will be no tendency among the employers either to expand the employment or to curtail it, simply because, the income they expect to get from this level of employment will be exactly to the cost they will be incurring upon it. Consequently, there will be no tendency either to cut back the employment or to increase it.

The aggregate demand is unstable in the Keynesian model. If planned saving out of full employment income exceeds planned investment, the economy will contract to an unemployment equilibrium. In the classical model, we have seen that the interest rate adjusts to make planned saving equal planned investment at full employment. Keynes did not believe that the interest rate mechanism would necessarily equate planned saving to planned investment at full employment. According to him

(a) saving and investment are done by different people;
(b) saving is primarily a function of income rather than the interest rate; and
(c) saving would not automatically become loanable funds used by business to invest.

In the simple Keynesian model, planned spending (aggregate demand) determines equilibrium income, and that equilibrium may not be at full employment. Thus, Keynes was very concerned that the volatility of investment would lead to unstable aggregate demand and periods of unemployment equilibrium unless the government took measures to stabilize the economy.

THE PRINCIPLE OF EFFECTIVE DEMAND

Effective demand has emerged as crucial in monetary production economies, by which we mean economies where the economic activity is aimed at the production of commodities, which are normally transacted by means of non-produced means of exchange, which may at any moment be spent or simply held as a store of abstract (and thus non-effective) purchasing power. In such a context, the relevance of effective demand increases even more, when the economic systems are moving in time with a high degree of technical change and ever flowing innovations. Perhaps, it is precisely because Keynes was kept by the events of his time, to deal with the short run, that his remarkable intuition was indeed able to perceive, but not explicitly to state the principle of effective demand.

In a given state of technique, resources and costs, the employment of a given volume of labour by an entrepreneur involves him in two kinds of expense:

(a) the amounts which he pays out to the factors of production (exclusive of other entrepreneurs) for their current services, which is called the factor cost of the employment; and

(b) the amounts he pays out to other entrepreneurs for what he has to purchase from them together with the sacrifice which he incurs by employing the equipment instead of leaving it idle, which is called the user cost of the employment.

The excess of the value of the resulting output over the sum of its factor cost and its user cost is the profit or the income of the entrepreneur. The factor cost is the same thing, looked at from the point of view of the entrepreneur, as what the factors of production regard as their income. Thus, the factor cost and the entrepreneur's profit make up, between them, what we shall define as the total income resulting from the employment given by the entrepreneur.

The entrepreneur's profit thus defined is the quantity, which he endeavours to maximise when he is deciding what amount of employment to offer. It is sometimes convenient, when we are looking at it from the entrepreneur's standpoint, to call the aggregate income (i.e. factor cost plus profit) resulting from a given amount of employment the proceeds of that employment. On the other hand, the aggregate supply price of the output of a given amount of employment is the expectation of proceeds that will just make it worth the while of the entrepreneurs to give that employment.

Thus, it follows that in a given situation of technique, resources and factor cost per unit of employment, the amount of employment, both in each individual firm and industry and in aggregate, depends on the amount of the proceeds that the entrepreneurs expect to receive from the corresponding output. Entrepreneurs will endeavour to fix the amount of employment at the level, which they expect to maximise the excess of the proceeds over the factor cost.

Let AS be the aggregate supply price of the output from employing L men, the relationship between AS and L being written as $AS = f(L)$, which is called the aggregate supply function. Similarly, let AD be proceeds that entrepreneurs expect to receive from the relationship between AD and L being written as $AD = f^*(L)$, which is called the aggregate demand function.

Now if for a given value of L the expected proceeds are greater than the aggregate supply price, i.e. if AD is greater than AS, there will be an incentive to entrepreneurs to increase employment beyond L and, if necessary, to raise costs by competing with one another for the factors of production, up to the value of L for which AS has become equal to AD. Thus, the volume of employment is given by the point of intersection between the aggregate demand function and the aggregate supply function; for it is at this point that the entrepreneurs' expectations of profits will be maximised. The value of AD at the point of the aggregate demand function, where it is intersected by the aggregate supply function, is called the effective demand. This is also known as the break-even point.

The principle of effective demand states that level of employment, given the aggregate supply, depends upon effective demand, which in turn depends upon aggregate demand. If effective demand is low, the level of employment will be low. If effective demand is higher, level of employment in the economy will be higher.

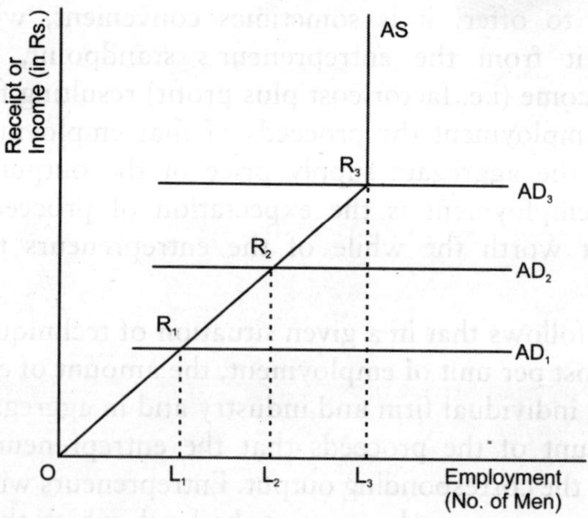

Fig. 5.12: Effective Demand Depends upon Level of Aggregate Demand.

This is shown in Fig. 5.12 in which X-axis measures employment and Y-axis measures receipts or income. As is the aggregate supply schedule about which we have already learnt. If aggregate demand is AD_1, then point of intersection of aggregate demand and aggregate supply is R_1 at which OL_1 employment is determined. However, if somehow the level of aggregate demand could be raised to AD_2, the point of effective demand will move to R_2 and employment will rise to OL_2. Similarly, if aggregate demand rises to AD_3, effective demand is at R_3 and OL_3 employment will result. Note that employment cannot rise above OL_3 aggregate supply curve becomes horizontal to vertical axis (we will discover it later why this is so) and further increase in the aggregate demand will not result in any increase in employment. Thus when level of employment is reached to OL_3 we say that full employment has been achieved.

Perhaps, it is precisely because Keynes was kept, by the events of his time, to deal with the short-run, that his remarkable intuition was indeed able to perceive, but not explicitly to state, the principle of effective demand. The critics of Keynes have concentrated almost exclusively on the controversial, but secondary, issues concerning how Keynes tried to construct his short-run aggregate supply function, the effect of which, would simply be to define a different point of effective demand. Insufficient attention has been paid, on the other hand, to the main point, where Keynesian model encompasses changes both in technology and in the composition of demand.

Following are the few characteristics of such a theoretical scheme, that are especially relevant to the problems:

(a) It concerns a monetary production economy and it gives a complete configuration of all economic variables, both at a given point of time and through time.

(b) It evinces a process of determination of production in which the principle of effective demand emerges in a pure way.

(c) It contains a macroeconomic condition for full employment in which the various components of the economic system appear to be constantly pushed away from automatically fulfilling Say's law (i.e. from full employment). And yet, the model shows the multiplicity of ways and the direction in which our actual institutions can aim at bringing the over all economic system back, towards the conditions of full employment.

(d) It thereby expresses the principle of effective demand in its full generality, not only at a static stage but also in a dynamic context, independently of the actual form taken by the market structure and thus of the institutional set-up of society.

Through this channel again, effective demand would be back on the scene. If, at the fundamental stage of operation of the dynamics of our economic systems, the evolution of technology and of demand composition are constantly pushing the economic system away from macroeconomic equilibrium (and thus away from full employment) the search becomes vital for appropriate countervailing institutional mechanisms. The important point to stress is that the achievement of the correct size of effective demand, at a given point of time, would solve the problem only temporarily. The structural character of economic dynamics makes it sure that no solution—even if perfectly satisfactory at a given point of time—would ever be a permanent, once-for-all, solution. For, in the following period of time, it would have to be re-considered, re-adapted, even re-placed by a solution. This is what makes so important to investigate and to grasp the true nature of Keynes's principle of effective demand, with reference to the long run.

Effective Demand is not Aggregate Demand

The Keynes's theory of effective demand is not the same as the theory of aggregate demand. The theory of effective demand is a theory about the factors that determine investment in a monetary production economy, while the theory of aggregate demand is a theory of boosting the various components of current expenditure (private or public) to secure some numerical measure of potential output. It must also be pointed out that what Keynes called the aggregate demand curve is not a curve of the current money expenditures as a function of current prices (i.e., the GDP curve in contemporary economic models). Rather, it is a curve of the expected future expenditures (or proceeds), which will validate the entrepreneurs' decision to produce and employ L number of people today. Increasing current expenditures may or may not improve those expectations, which means that pumping aggregate demand today is not guaranteed to improve the conditions that underpin the point of effective demand.

Unemployment for Keynes, in all cases (regardless of the phase in the business cycle), was a result of deficient effective demand, not deficient aggregate demand. But because there is only one point of effective demand consistent with full employment, to pin it down is no easy task. This point is given by the cross-section of the current supply price of output and the future demand price of output. In the short run, there is no swift way of reducing the supply price of output (i.e., the cost of production) other than by lowering wages, which would be counterproductive. This is because bidding down wages makes sure that the extra output will not be sold, even if it can be produced at a lower cost. In other words, lowering wages is likely to reduce total employment. For these reasons, and in rejection of Say's law, he argued that one must work on the demand side. To do this, policy can attempt to influence the independent factors that determine the level of employment—the marginal propensity to consume (MPC), the marginal efficiency of money (MEM), or the marginal efficiency of capital (MEC).

When total demand is deficient, policies can attempt to boost either private or public investment. Private investment can be encouraged by reducing the interest rate (i.e., the MEM), which, given the state of expectations, will reduce the cost of finance. Alternatively, one may attempt to change the MPC via income redistribution schemes towards those individuals with high propensities to consume and away from those who have high propensities to save. Finally, another way of moving the point of effective demand is to boost expected profitability from investment (i.e., the MEC), which could be done by increasing total current money expenditures in the economy, i.e., via aggregate demand. It is in recessions that the case is made for vigorous aggregate demand stimulus. Total current spending will help validate past expenditures undertaken by entrepreneurs and can help stabilise investment and the business cycle. There are many factors, that can affect the point of effective demand and boosting aggregate demand is but one option of influencing these factors. However, "plugging the gap," as it is discussed today, is not the leading method of Keynesian analysis; this is because, as the entire corpus of this work shows, while it is possible to move the point of effective demand, it is impossible to fix it at full employment.

THE CONCEPT OF FULL EMPLOYMENT

It is necessary to go back to the thirties to find the roots of the full employment concept. We may refer first to Pigou in his '*Theory of Unemployment*' (Pigou, 1933). Pigou did not refer to full employment but to employment only. As for the concept of unemployment he explicitly indicates that it is not so clear cut as that of employment and carefully mentions different elements that must be taken into account to explain finally that 'the quantity of unemployment is equal to the number of wage earners minus the quantity of employment' to end up redefining even this concept further relating it to the number of vacancies 'the quantity of unemployment prevailing at any time is equal to the number of would-be wage earners minus the quantity of labour demanded plus the number of unfilled vacancies'.

According to Keynesian definition of unemployment, men are involuntarily unemployed if, in the event of a small rise in the price of wage-goods relatively to the money-wage, both the aggregate supply of labour willing to work for the current money-wage and the aggregate demand for it at that wage would be greater than the existing volume of employment. It follows from this definition that the equality of the real wage to the marginal disutility of employment presupposed by the second postulate, realistically interpreted, corresponds to the absence of 'involuntary unemployment'. He refers to full employment as a situation in which aggregate employment is inelastic in response to an increase in its effective demand for its output. Full employment as a situation in which all those persons seeking work in a community are able to find suitable work fairly readily, with the consequence that a very high proportion of the working population is actually at work at any one time. To achieve this in practice, the number of unfilled vacancies must exceed the number of persons seeking work as in any locality, some vacancies may not be suitable for local applicants. For many business leaders full employment was thought in terms of labour market tightness, it was a level behind which on-the-job discipline and wages could be affected. Conversely for many politicians the objective of full employment was a means to get away from social unrest and gain some legitimacy for modernised post-war capitalism. Full employment was thus never given a precise definition.

According to Joan Robinson British writers have employed several definitions of 'full employment'. Initially Keynes, following Marshall, utilised a definition in terms of 'disutility of work'. Beveridge says that there is full employment when there exist more vacant jobs than unemployed workers. Other consider full employment the level of employment from which monetary wages start to rise.

One of the important aspects of the problem of unemployment is the statistical determination of who and how many are unemployed. Statistics start also from the consideration of full employment as the measure of equilibrium in the labour market. The measure of unemployment is the net result of the difference between two terms, but in fact, neither of them is easy to define and fix. The working population, labour supply—is considered as the people that are willing to work—either occupied or non-occupied but looking actively for a job (unemployed in its strict sense). Nevertheless the limits between labour, work and activity and inactivity are difficult to mark—when it is part of the working population the student or the housewife that would be willing to work provided that . . . ?, when is the family help looking for a wage job, the seasonal worker that does not look for work during the slack season, the unwilling part-time worker? Further, how to account for the number of potential workers, hidden labour supply or of discouraged workers, not to mention the self-employed people or the seekers of part-time tasks? Labour demand presents also a wide variety of types—from a person that needs a casual labourer or an enterprise that wishes to engage part-time or seasonal workers to an employer requiring hundreds of full time workers. The situations and corresponding categories are heterogeneous, the fluidity among many positions pretty high, but we try to measure homogenous numbers.

Although there are several ways to measure employment/ unemployment, the two most usual are the unemployed people registered at the employment offices and the labour forces sample surveys based on a substantial sample of people. The later is considered far more satisfactory than the former and usually utilised to measure employment and unemployment. The survey definitions used may be summarised as follows:

> The definitions of ILO/OECD consider several categories within total employment including all persons above a specified age who during a specified brief period, either one week or one day, were in the categories of paid employment-either at work, defined as persons who during the reference period performed some work for wage or salary, in cash or in kind or with a job but not at work or self-employment-performing work for profit or family gain again at work or not at work. However, the key thing in these definitions is

> that, for operational purposes, the notion of some work may be interpreted as work for at least one hour. That is, any person working for a wage or self-employed for more than an hour in a week or a day, according to countries, are considered within the total employment figure.

Unemployment is defined as the persons that during the reference period (day or week) are without work, currently available for work or seeking work, 'work' being defined as in the employment definition, that is, as at least one hour during the reference period. The ILO/OECD guidelines list a number of ways in which the criterion of 'seeking employment' can be satisfied. These include direct applications to employers, checking on work sites and placing or answering advertisements, in addition to what is in most countries the most common way of seeking work, namely registering at employment offices. They also provide with definitions of more difficult points such as discouraged workers, seasonal workers without work, sub employment, and others. All in all it accounts that persons working at least one hour during the reference period are considered as employed and that unemployed people are the persons not working even that minimum amount of time.

The difficulties of measurement increase if comparisons between countries and different periods are intended. Although it has been explained that the definitions commonly used are of an international character, due to the importance of institutional regulations in the labour market. The situation may be changed by legal norms making comparisons very difficult if not meaningless.

It is also easy to detect a clear ideological option in the traditional concept of full employment. No doubt related to the history of labour and the labour movement in the past and to the situation of many workers at present, most social leaders and especially trade union leaders maintain the traditional idea of full employment as their main aim in relation with the labour market. When they rightly criticise the conditions that labour market 'flexibility' creates and the deterioration of the standard of living of many workers that it causes, they tend to conclude that the traditional concept of full employment—permanent full time jobs—is the desiderata for the future. Flexibility imposed by capital favour temporal work, part-time contracting according to business interests, subcontracting, different forms of uncertain work and 'black' labour against stable employment (either full-time or part-time).

This preocupation increases yet due to the dominant view of the labour market with its clasical idea that 'rigidity of the labour market' and high wages are at the basis of the high unemployment and that only the increase in 'flexibility' and wage contention will lead to improve the employment situation (full employment is not even considered as an objective). It is well known that this idea is the basis of the legitimation of the present situation of the labour market and of an employment policy with disastrous consequences for the workers. Moreover, most people who do not seem to care much for unemployment tend to favour the view that any modality of paid activity may be considered as employment, what in fact provokes a contrary reaction on the part of people who suffer directly or care about unemployment. No surprise, then, that flexibility is considered very negative and its implementation rejected by the unions and other social agents.

At present social agents (mainly unions) generally tend to favour traditional full employment as the main objective of a healthy and fair labour market and the one that makes possible to have a life project as well as maintain the traditional culture of work as the main social and collective identity item. Nevertheless, many of them also recognise that the labour market is changing rapidly, that the whole concept of work and employment is in discussion and that adaptation to new realities imperative. They recognise that there are new forms of labour different from traditional permanent full time jobs that under some conditions may be considered as positive employment. However, as the labour market stands only a very small minority of workers really benefit of these new modalities and they have to go back to the traditional concept for the welfare of the workers. It is not a simple situation to manage.

The traditional concept and the main ideological options strenghten the view that a satisfactory employment situation requires some sort of permanent full time engagement of employers and workers at decent wages and rely to it the concept of full employment; on the other hand the statistical computation of what apparently reflects that phenomenon merely relies upon a very loose view of work based on an hour actitivy without any other conditions. Paradoxically the data collected in the later way is used unqualifiedly as if it reflected the former position.

The mainstream approach to unemployment is also driven by good intentions. The solution is to provide incentives for accelerated investment and growth (giving tax breaks and cutting interest rates) and to pump enough aggregate demand via tax cuts, unemployment insurance, or some other form of spending. The problem of unemployment is addressed by pushing the economy onto some new growth path, while preventing those who are left behind from drowning via income transfers. These are the contemporary aggregate demand policies. And while they are not policies that lack good intentions, Keynes would argue today that they are neither clever, nor driven by the stead fast intellectual conviction that full employment is a real possibility. So it is constructive to revisit Keynes's view of employment policy once again to see what role aggregate demand policies played in his analytical approach.

Although there is much disagreement on his theoretical contributions, there is a general agreement across the theoretical spectrum that boosting aggregate demand is the Keynesian solution for full employment. While aggregate demand has an important place in Keynes's analysis of the business cycle, filling the gap is not his method for fiscal policy. Rather, he had a targeted demand approach to full employment of a specific kind. He favored public employment schemes, generally in the form of public works, which were to be implemented both in recessions and in economies near full employment. To subscribe to such a plan, however, requires conviction of its advantages and cleverness in its execution. Keynes had both.

Because Keynes's theory is mistakenly referred to as "depression economics," public works are generally viewed as "depression solutions." General fiscal policy that fills the demand gap between actual and potential output dominates theory and policy. "Closing the gap," it will be argued here, is a backward way of thinking about full employment policy and is not the essence of the Keynesian contribution. What was truly innovative in Keynes's work was the principle of effective demand, which is quite distinct from what has become known as the theory of aggregate demand. Once we make this distinction, it becomes clear why Keynes did not speak of "fiscal policy" in general, but he spoke of public works.

Furthermore, for Keynes, the key measure of the desirability of public policies was their net employment-generation effect. Targeting demand via public works would be done irrespective of the stage of the business cycle; whether this targeting meant more public works or better distributed public works depended on the level of economic activity. This distinction is important in evaluating fiscal policy. Today's aggregate demand approach to full employment is not Keynes's solution. In addition, it is important to note that the Keynesian method is one of unemployment targeting, which is also distinct from what is known as industry targeting. The first question to ask is what role did output gap analysis have in Keynes's method. The standard textbook Keynesian model shows how fiscal stimuli close the gap between full employment output and current output. This could be done via increasing government spending, cutting taxes, or balancing the budget—policies that work through different multiplier effects. While rejecting the Keynesian analysis, the New Economic Consensus model and much of mainstream theory still use the gap method to argue in support of monetary or fiscal policy by stipulating various demand- or supply-side effects of each. While the policy recommendations across the theoretical spectrum diverge significantly, plugging the gap is a core economic concept that underpins them. This methodology is also embraced by many Post Keynesians.

It is easy to see how Keynes's own writings have encouraged such an interpretation. Keynes, after all, emphasized that his was a theory of aggregates and that he set out to explain the determination of output and employment as a whole. Largely overlooked is the fact that he also had a clear theory of pricing, which provided the micro foundations of his macro theory. He first stressed that an exogenous (or quasi-independent) marginal propensity to consume of less than one left a gap between consumption and income, meaning that firms' outlays on wages did not return back to them in the form of revenue from consumption. The withdrawal of purchasing power from saving undermined full employment and could be plugged by investment spending only under certain very special circumstances in a manner similar to that in classical theory. In general, however, Keynes argued that investment did not normally manage to do so, leaving the economy to operate below full employment. As he pointed out, "the evidence indicates that full, or even approximately full, employment is a rare and short-lived occurrence." So, he set out to understand the forces behind investment, which made it chronically ineffective in attaining or maintaining full employment. After spelling out these forces, he concluded that it was the job of public policy to "establish a closer approximation of full employment as nearly as is practicable." This conclusion has largely been interpreted to mean that if the demand gap is not filled by investment spending, it can be filled by government spending, but the type of fiscal policy that could do the job is left to interpretation. The key is to increase money expenditures sufficiently to produce full employment. Keynes, however, did not endorse just any fiscal policy and he specifically objected to those that aimed to stabilize consumption as policies for full employment. This would rule out contemporary unemployment insurance, which he did not believe would solve the unemployment problem; it would also exclude modern tax rebates, various consumption subsidies, and other transfer payments.

Keynes wanted to stabilize investment, but he also did not believe that stabilizing private investment could do the job. Boosting aggregate demand to encourage private investment had serious limitations, which were well understood by his contemporaries' limitations, which could easily be overcome by public investment.

To understand his approach to policy we need to examine:

(a) how effective demand differs from aggregate demand;
(b) why fixing the point of effective demand at full employment is not possible;
(c) how a policy of public works circumvents this problem, irrespective of the stages in the business cycle; and
(d) what role the method of "plugging the gap" plays in Keynes's analysis.

All of this has to be studied in the context of Keynes's steadfast intellectual conviction that the real problem, fundamental yet essentially simple, is to provide employment for every one. Full employment is an objective in recessions and in expansions, as well as in the long run. The long period of unemployment seems to have lead to a situation where the mere fact of being able to earn some money is considered as employment and statistically computed as such. Regardless of the level of earnings, the conditions of work, the stability of the job, the relationship of the work with the qualification of the person and so on and so forth. The question that sprouts unavoidably then is, employment, full employment for what? Is it not assumed that employment relates to obtaining through work the income necessary for the well being of the people? Employment must be conceived in relation to the objective to guarantee to each person a capacity of autonomous self-development. In order to fulfill this aim people need resources, material and cultural as well, a secure social environment, created by a combination of safety nets, and a social framework dominated by trusty relations. If employment embodies features that hardly imply well-being, are we inquiring about employment or about survival?

The Problem with Fixing Effective Demand at Full Employment

Working with the marginal efficiency of money to influence private investment in the face of depressed expectation, Keynes argued, may prove to be like "pushing on a string." This would make monetary policy futile, especially when interest rates are already very low. Secondly, boosting the marginal efficiency of capital (or profit expectations) also has its limitations because it is not under the direct control of policy.

Low rates of interest and an increase in total money expenditures can improve the profits outlook and entice entrepreneurs to redirect their money from financial assets to real production. Government spending can be thought of as filling "the cash boxes of private entrepreneurs", but how large an injection of liquidity is need to induce those investors to start employing is difficult to gauge. This is because while aggregate demand will increase the amount of liquid assets in the system, it may not be able to expediently shift individual preference away from holding them. Such would be the problems under a liquidity-trap scenario where money, as Keynes argued, becomes "a bottomless sink of purchasing power and there is no value for it at which demand for it is diverted into a demand for other things". The trouble with filling investor's cash boxes as a policy for full employment rests with the state of expectations, which may or may not improve fast enough with the provision of liquid financial assets.

In any event, it is during severe slumps that we find strongest support for broad aggregate demand management policies, because we can be reasonably sure that an increase in money expenditure would sooner or later increase employment. As Harrod put it: "In times of depression and unemployment it was desirable to encourage spending and lavishness." But even in recessions, any type of aggregate demand policy will not have equal employment creation effects; when swift reduction of unemployment is needed, targeted demand via public works would do the job. And Keynes always advocated large-scale public capital improvements in severe slumps.

Suppose, however, that we are in an expansion. Private spending and investment are strong and the economy is approaching full employment. In these circumstances, additional money expenditures will boost the MEC, but will not have the same employment-creation effects as in recessions. This is due to the structure of the economy. Near full employment, the MEC may be quite high, but aggregate demand will likely increase it further in those industries that have already been saturated and are producing at full capacity. This is because for Keynes, "effective demand spends itself, partly in affecting output and partly in affecting price", which will depend on the respective two elasticities. According to him some products take time to produce, so that it is practically impossible to increase the supply for them quickly. Thus, if additional demand is directed to them without notice, they will show low elasticity of employment.

Affecting the MEC near full employment via an increase in aggregate demand need not have the same employment-creation effects. In fact, it will likely produce inflationary pressures in those industries with low elasticity of employment. Because the structure of the economy distributes the increase in aggregate effective demand unevenly, a boost in total current expenditures will not be able to absorb the remaining (structurally) unemployed and will also push up prices in certain industries. The first problem with boosting aggregate demand in expansions is that it causes prices to rise before it produces full employment. The second problem is that near full employment it also creates more unequal income distribution between capital and labor, favoring the latter. Keynes argued if the increase in demand is directed to products with a relatively low elasticity of employment, a larger proportion of it will go to swell the incomes of entrepreneurs and a smaller proportion to swell the incomes of wage earners and other price cost factors.

For these reasons, to guarantee full employment in expansions, it is not more demand, but appropriately distributed demand, is needed. For the ways in which we suppose the increase in aggregate demand to be distributed between different commodities may considerably influence the volume of employment. If for example the increased demand is largely directed towards products, which have a high elasticity of employment, the aggregate increase in employment will be greater than if it is largely directed towards products, which have low elasticity of employment. In the same way, employment may fall off without there having been any change in aggregate demand, if the direction of demand is changed in favor of products having a relatively low elasticity of employment.

Thus, general aggregate demand helps in depressions, but to yield maximum employment creation, it is more effective to target it to the unemployed directly via public works. Close to full employment, an increase in aggregate demand brings inflationary and distributional problems because of the structure of production. As Keynes recognized, the closer we are to full employment, the more troublesome it becomes to secure a further given increase in employment via an increase in aggregate real income. We cannot conclude from this that the goal of full employment is abandoned once we approach it, as it is done by mainstream economists who define full employment as the noninflationary level of unemployment or the remaining frictional and structural unemployment.

For Keynes, even in expansions, the goal of full employment is still important. The problem to wrestle with is structural unemployment, which should "be treated as something to be handled forcibly and not something to be defeatist about." To deal with structural unemployment, government can redirect its public works to those "special areas" with the highest remaining unemployment. Keynes and the government had agreed that they could take "the contract to the men, rather than the men to the contract". These are the core reasons why fixing the point of effective demand at full employment is hard to do. These difficulties were well understood and developed by Keynes's associates and followers.

The Problem of Output Gap

Keynes did speak of a demand gap, however, but in the aggregate he emphasized the shortfall in the demand for labor, not the demand for output. In the deliberations about budgetary planning after the war, Keynes, in collaboration with Rick Stone, attempted to give guidance on budgetary expenditures needed to sustain full employment. All calculations were based on some assumptions of the number of employed and unemployed men and women. The goal was to outline a method of measuring current production as a function of employment, labor productivity, and factor prices. In other words, any output gap that needed to be plugged was measured in terms of number of unemployed that need to be hired.

For Keynes, the gap that needed closing was the labor demand gap, not an output gap as measured in current prices. In fact, he explicitly objected to the latter measure. Let's first look at the textbook method for solving unemployment by closing the output gap. This approach comes to us from various incarnations of Okun's law, which posit a statistical relationship between the rate of growth of output and unemployment. The law states that a 1 percent increase in unemployment would bring about approximately a 3 percent decline in GDP growth. This relationship has been flipped and used as a policy guide, suggesting that to reduce unemployment, the rate of growth in current output must be greater than the rate of growth in potential output. In other words, if policy manages to stimulate growth at a rate faster than the rate of growth of potential GDP, unemployment can be reduced and (possibly) even eliminated. This approach has given rise to broad-based, pro-growth policies. Note however that the original observation of Arthur Okun (the economist after whom the law is named) was that, when growth deviated by 1 percent from its long-term trend, unemployment fell by 0.3 percent. He cautioned that the relationship between growth and unemployment was very weak. Reversing his analysis, however, has given powerful ammunition to growth-at-all-cost policies. Because investment is the active component of growth, private-investment stimuli of various kinds (supply- or demand-side) have been the preferred policy option to close the output gap.

Accelerating growth would produce full employment, so long as the economy does not run into some inflationary barrier in the meantime. But, as Keynes had pointed out, price pressures in certain sectors tend to kick in before output reaches its full employment level. Modern policy often sacrifices the goal of full employment in the name of maintaining price stability, since the latter is considered to be more devastating to economic stability. Paradoxically, it is precisely this approach of closing the gap that advocates pro-investment, growth-at-all-cost aggregate demand policies that is generating the inflationary pressures. Consequently, the whole enterprise of achieving full employment is doomed to fail from the outset because of the inappropriate tools employed.

Keynes, too, was interested in closing the gap, but he measured it in labor units, which is one reason why he emphasized the primary employment effects of public works. Public investment is a direct approach to reducing unemployment. Add to that the secondary employment effects produced by the multiplier effect and we can estimate how much public-works spending is needed to close the labor demand gap. Whenever Keynes spoke of how much national income and expenditure are needed to maintain full employment, his "calculations are in terms of equivalent men and women, if they are unemployed". He did not talk about deficient demand of output, but of deficient demand of labor. This lends methodological support to the present argument that the Keynes's approach to full employment was one of targeted demand, whereby policy targets unemployment directly, and not some generalized level of output or economic activity.

Thus, instead of aiming for some level of growth, which may or may not bring full employment, the objective should be to target a clear and attainable goal of full employment directly. Okun's law, or any form of gap analysis that compares current output to some level of potential output, is a backward way of thinking about full employment. When the goal is growth via stimulating investment, policy tends to produce inflationary forces that, in turn, induce additional policy measures to fight inflation, which defeats the original purpose and automatically precludes the economy from reaching full employment (this is why potential output in mainstream theory is not consistent with zero involuntary unemployment, but is pegged at the noninflationary level of unemployment). Policies that target a particular rate of growth may be associated with many different levels of employment.

An alternative policy option is one that targets full employment and is associated with different levels of growth. This is not an argument for sacrificing growth in the name of full employment; it is an argument that growth and full employment are two different objectives, which may require different policies where one need not conflict with the other. One could also argue that what constitutes adequate growth will be difficult to ascertain before full employment has been attained. When full employment is achieved via a direct job creation, market forces aided by a careful institutional design of the public sector programs will determine the distribution of private and public employment, technique of production, productivity, and, therefore, growth. Keynes flatly rejected calculations of potential output. While acknowledging his support for the important work of Mr. Colin Clark (the father of British national statistics), Keynes vigorously critiqued his calculations of gross national income, which were often taken to give the potential rate of current consumption and investment measured at market prices. This method was unacceptable to Keynes because such estimates were impossible to produce over a period of time, since they would depend on the "technical considerations and the precise character of the plant in use." Such measures of potential output have useful meaning only over an "instantaneous or very brief period." Keynes saw no practical purpose for such estimates, since the economy was an evolving organism where the character of consumption and investment changed.

Potential output is even more misleading (Keynes calls it an 'impostor') as a concept for the long run. Such measures do not take into account that shifts in consumption and investment may involve loss of capital or labor when they only attempt to look at the market value of consumption or investment goods. In fact, changing the structure of production and diverting resources from one use to another is the key reason why potential output cannot be measured over the long run or over a year for that matter. Most importantly, the loss of labor from such a diversion needs to be treated separately, which is why Keynes's national output definition is in terms of manhours which might be worked.

Modern output gap analysis is wholly inconsistent with Keynes's method for producing full employment. Any attempt at integration of these approaches must either redefine potential output in terms of wage units or unemployment must be addressed directly and independently of the definition of potential output. Our income is only another name for what we produce when we are employed. Any meaningful Keynesian approach to filling the gap would be limited to plugging the labor demand gap. Keynes's method is also useful because potential output is not limited to hiring all those who are presently unemployed. For Keynes, expansion of output would depend on "greater intensity of work by the existing labor force and on the increase of the labor force from the ranks of the unemployed and from those not previously in the labor market". In other words, he has a more dynamic view of potential output that will fluctuate not just with the unemployed, but also with those that may be currently outside the labor market.

Filling the gap according to traditional aggregate demand management methods usually relies on stimulating investment and growth. It therefore attempts to manage the most unstable aspects of the economy and those that all but ensure a below full employment equilibrium. As experience has shown, filling the gap this way is an impossible thing to do due to the volatility of profit expectations, the associated inflationary and distributional problems near full employment, and the structure of production. Thereby pro-growth, pro-investment policies that attempt to push growth faster than the growth in potential output as a function of current prices is a wrongheaded approach for full employment. But so is attempting to pump enough government deficit spending. The only sense in which we can speak about plugging the gap is to speak of plugging the gap for labor, and for Keynes this was done directly via public works. To reinstate the link between fiscal policy and full employment it is necessary to understand and embrace Keynes's methodology of measuring output, something that has been emphasised little by Post Keynesians.

Expectation as Determinant of Output and Employment

The expectations, upon which business decisions depend, fall into two groups:

(a) The first type is concerned with the price which a manufacturer can expect to get for his 'finished' output at the time whenhe commits himself to starting the process which will produce it; out being 'finished' (from the point of view of the manufacturer) when it is ready to be used or to be sold to a second party. This is called short-term expectation.

(b) The second type is concerned with what the entrepreneur can hope to earn in the shape of future returns if he purchases (or, perhaps, manufactures) 'finished' output as an addition to his capital equpment. This is called long-term expectation.

Thus, the behaviour of each individual firm in deciding its daily output will be determined by its short-term expectations—expectations as to the cost of output on various possible scales and expectations as to the sale proceeds of this output; though, in the case of additions to capital equipment and even of sales to distributors, these short-term expectations will largely depend on the long-term expectations of other parties. It is upon these various expectations that the amount of employment, which the firms offer, will depend.

The actually realised results of the production and sale of output will only be relevant to employment insofar as they cause a modification of subsequent expectations. A change in expectations (whether short-term or long-term) will only produce its full effects on employment over a considerable period. The change in employment due to a change in expectations will not be the same on the second day after the change as on the first, or the same on the third day as on the second, and so on, even though there be no further change in expectations.

In the case of short-term expectations, changes in expectations are not sufficiently violent or rapid, when they are for the worse, to cause the abandonment of work on all the productive processes. In the case of long-term expectations, equipment, which will not be replaced, will continue to give employment until it is worn out; whilst when the change in long-term expectations is for the better, employment may be at a higher level at first, then it will be after there has been time to adjust the equipment to the new situation.

Let us consider the process of transition to a long-period position due to a change in expectation, which is not confused or interrupted by any further change in expectation. We will first suppose that the change is of such a character that the new long-period employment will be greater than the old. Now, as a rule, it will only be the rate of input which will be much affected at the beginning, that is to say, the volume of work on the earlier stages of new processes of production, whilst the output of consumption goods and the amount of employment on the later stages of processes which were started before the change will remain much the same as before. Insofar as there were stocks of partly finished goods, this conclusion may be modified; though it is likely to remain true that the initial increase in employment will be modest. As, however, the days pass by, employment will gradually increase. Moreover, it is easy to conceive of conditions, which will cause it to increase at some stage to a higher level than the new long-period employment. For the process of building up capital to satisfy the new state of expectation may lead to more employment and also to more current consumption than will occur when the long-period position has been reached.

Thus, the change in expectation may lead to a gradual increase in the level of employment, rising to a peak and then declining to the new long-period level. The same thing may occur even if the new long-period level is the same as the old, if the change represents a change in the direction of consumption, which renders certain existing processes and their equipment obsolete. If the new long-period employment is less than the old, the level of employment during the transition may fall for a time below what the new long-period level is going to be. Thus, a mere change in expectation is capable of producing an oscillation of the same kind of shape as a cyclical movement, in the course of working itself out.

It is evident from the above that the level of employment at any time depends, in a sense, not merely on the existing state of expectation but on the states of expectation which have existed over a certain past period. Nevertheless past expectations, which have not yet worked themselves out, are embodied in the today's capital equipment with reference to which the entrepreneur has to make today's decisions, and only influence his decisions insofar as they are so embodied. It follows, therefore, that, in spite of the above, today's employment can be correctly described as being governed by today's expectations taken in conjunction with today's capital equipment.

In the case of durable goods, the producer's short-term expectations are based on the current long-term expectations of the investor; and it is of the nature of long-term expectations that they cannot be checked at short intervals in the light of realised results.

VOLUNTARY, INVOLUNTARY AND FRICTIONAL UNEMPLOYMENT

It is very natural to refer to unemployment while discussing the determination of employment, simply because the presence of one is the absence of the other. If employment is low, it means unemployment is high and if employment is high it means unemployment is low. Keynes has classified unemployment into following three categories:

(a) Frictional unemployment

(b) Voluntary unemployment

(c) Involuntary unemployment

Let us understand every one of these three types of unemployment.

Frictional Unemployment. Frictional unemployment is that type of unemployment which may come into existence because of less than perfect functioning of the economy. The people may be unemployed for short periods when they change over from one job to another. They may be unemployed because the flow of information about the job situation and about the conditions in the job market may not be very smooth. They may also become unemployed for sometime if firms switch over from one technology to the other technology. Unemployment may also result from the streamlining of organizational set up of firms etc. All these are illustrations of frictional unemployment.

Voluntary Unemployment. Keynes defines voluntary unemployment in the following words:

> Voluntary unemployment (is) due to the refusal or inability of a unit of labour, as a result of legislation or social practices or of combination for collective bargaining or of slow response to change or of mere human obstinacy, to accept a reward corresponding to the value of the product attributable to its marginal productivity.[1]

Thus, according to Keynes, voluntary unemployment is the result of a single individual's action who for one reason or the other refuses to accept the current market wage rate (which is in fact equal to the value of his own marginal product). Keynes outlines the following main reasons for voluntary unemployment:

(a) Legislation

(b) Social customs

(c) Labour unions, and

(d) Slow response to change

Because of any above reason the individual does not accept the job and prefers to remain unemployed. This type of unemployment is called voluntary unemployment.

Involuntary Unemployment. Involuntary unemployment has been defined by Keynes in the following manner:

> Men are involuntarily unemployed if, in the event of a small rise in the price of wage-goods relatively to the money wage, both the aggregate supply of labour willing to work for the current money-wage and the aggregate demand for it at that wage would be greater than the existing volume of employment.[2]

Although the definition of involuntary unemployment given by Keynes appears to be cumbersome, the basic idea behind it is quite simple. Involuntary unemployment exists if people are willing to work at the going market wage rate but there are no jobs for them. In this situation, people are unemployed because of scarcity of jobs. They are unwillingly unemployed. That is why it is called involuntary unemployment. In order to understand this concept clearly, let us go back to Fig. 5.12. Given the aggregate supply, OL_3 amount of labour is available for employment. Since the level of aggregate demand is AD_1 only OL_1 persons are employed and $L_1 L_3$ persons are involuntarily unemployed. If the level of aggregate demand rises to AD_2 employment rises to OL_2 and involuntary unemployment is reduced to $L_2 L_3$. Similarly when the level of aggregate demand rises to AD_3, all the available labour is employed, i.e., full employment is achieved and involuntary unemployment is reduced to zero. Thus, following conclusions emerge out of the foregoing analysis:

(a) In situations of full employment involuntary unemployment is zero.

(b) Involuntary unemployment may be reduced or even eliminated by increasing the level of aggregate demand.

One must also mention that it is only involuntary unemployment which cannot exist with full employment. This is so because existence of full employment has been defined as absence of involuntary unemployment. Hence, their simultaneous occurrence would be contradiction in terms. However, frictional unemployment and voluntary unemployment may exist simultaneously with full employment. This implies that unemployment is not zero when economy achieves full employment. Some unemployment is tolerable even if the situation of full employment has been reached. How much is that 'some unemployment' which is consistent with full employment? Firstly, no magnitude of this type of unemployment may be given *a priori*. It is a question of empirical verification. For example, its has been estimated for the U.S.A. that magnitude of frictional and voluntary unemployment ranges between 4 percent and 5 percent per annum. Thus, if the American economy achieves 95 percent to 96 percent employment, it is regarded as full employment level. However, if the rate of unemployment reached to 10-12 percent, the U.S. economy is taken as recessionary and involuntary unemployment is said to be present. Secondly, the magnitude of frictional and voluntary unemployment would differ from country to country and from time to time. This is so because the magnitudes of frictional and voluntary unemployment depend upon technological conditions, progress of science and technology and its application to productive processes, social customs and conditions, legislative framework etc. which differ from society to society.

UNDEREMPLOYMENT EQUILIBRIUM

Let us go back again to Fig. 5.12 which shows that involuntary employment may persist if the level of aggregate demand is low. The point R_3 at which there is no involuntary unemployment is known as full employment equilibrium. However, the economy is also in equilibrium at the points R_1 and R_2 simply because the aggregate demand and aggregate supply are equal at these points. Despite the fact that economy is in equilibrium this cannot be concealed that significant involuntary unemployment may be present in the economy. That is the reason that these equilibrium points are designated as underemployment equilibrium. In terms of Fig. 5.12, the points R_1 and R_2 show the situations of underemployment equilibrium.

Keynes was the first economist to show the possibility of underemployment equilibrium. The economists before Keynes, whom he calls classical economists used to believe that underemployment equilibrium is not possible. The classical economists were of the opinion that full employment shall always be maintained and involuntary unemployment cannot occur. This conclusion was based upon certain assumption about the labour market which shall be taken up later. At this moment, it is sufficient to know that classical economists assumed a vertical aggregate supply function which has been shown in Fig. 5.13(b). Employment as shown on the X-axis and Y-axis shows receipts or income. The point N_F shows full employment. Since the aggregate supply curve is vertical, therefore economy would always operate at the full employment level and the increases in the aggregate demand will not succeed in increasing the level of employment. In contrast to the classical aggregate supply function, Keynesian aggregate supply function has been depicted in Fig. 5.13(a). As you can see the aggregate supply function begins at the origin which means that employment can become zero in special circumstances. Thereafter, output or income rises with the increases in employment. As N_F full employment is reached and aggregate supply curve becomes vertical, which is similar to the classical aggregate supply function shown in Fig. 5.13(b).

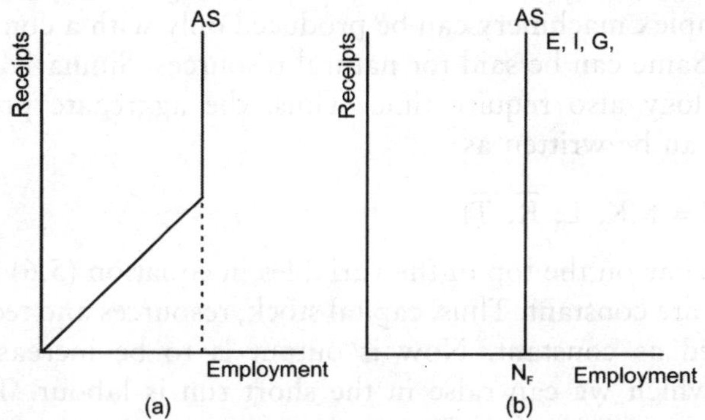

Fig. 5.13: Keynesian and Classical Aggregate Supply Functions.

WHY AGGREGATE SUPPLY IS NOT CONSIDERED?

We have seen that the level of employment depends on the aggregate demand and aggregate supply schedules. We have also shown that the level of aggregate demand shall determine the level of effective demand if the aggregate supply is given. Let us examine in this section how far the assumption of given aggregate supply is justified.

The aggregate supply function of an economy depends upon the physical conditions of production. It depends upon the amounts of capital stock, natural resources, technology, etc. It also depends upon the productivity of men, machines and natural resources. In other words, the aggregate supply depends upon aggregate production function of the economy which is given below:

$$Y = f(K, L, R, T) \qquad ...(5.5)$$

where,

Y = flow of output per period,

K = flow of machine services per period,

L = flow of labour services per period,

R = flow of services of natural resources, and

T = Some appropriate index of technology.

If we want increases in output then we must increase either one or all or some of these variables. Now let us consider what variables we can increase in the short run (meaning thereby a short period of time such as a year). The capital stock cannot be increased within a reasonable short period of time. Capital constitutes of building, roads, bridges, machines, etc. It takes time to produce these things. Some complex machinery can be produced only with a considerable time lag. Same can be said for natural resources. Similarly, changes in technology also require time. Thus, the aggregate production function can be written as

$$Y = f(\overline{K}, L, \overline{R}, \overline{T}) \qquad ...(5.6)$$

where the bar on the top of the variables in equation (5.6) indicates that these are constant. Thus, capital stock, resources and technology are treated as constant. Now if output is to be increased, only variable which we can raise in the short run is labour. Thus, the short run production function can be written as

$$Y = f(L) \qquad ...(5.7)$$

which means that income or output depends upon labour employed. By increasing the level of employment, the level of income and output can be raised. One may ask, "If capital and natural resources are constant, then how employment could be raised? After all labour works with the help of machine and materials?" This is a very legitimate question and this is also true that labour works with machines and materials. The clue to answer of this question lies in the fact that what do we mean by capital is constant. $\overline{K}$, $\overline{R}$, and $\overline{T}$ in equation (5.6) mean that their available supply is constant and cannot be increased. However, it does not say anything about how much of available supply is utilised. Whenever there is involuntary unemployment (remember that employment can be increased only in situations when involuntary unemployment is present) capital and other resources are also unemployed. The reason for this is that labour always works with some amount of machines and materials. Consequently, in the event of general unemployment of labour, the utilization of other resources is also at a very low level. This situation is known as excess capacity. When excess capacity is present, shortage (or scarcity) of capital is no problem. The total output can be increased only by increasing employment of labour because capital is already there working at less than its full capacity.

Thus, the essential thing about Keynesian economics is that it is essentially concerned with short run and its logical formulations and deductions are applicable only to the cases when excess capacity exists particularly in the machine building industries. In the presence of excess capacity, it is reasonable to assume that aggregate supply is given and aggregate demand shall determine the level of employment. Thus, in the following pages we shall evoke the assumption of given aggregate supply and concentrate our analysis on aggregate demands, its determinant and their role in the determination of income and employment in an economy.

COMPONENTS OF AGGREGATE DEMAND

In the last chapter, we have learnt that aggregate demand will determine the level of income and employment if aggregate supply is given. For reasons explained above we have also assumed the aggregate supply to be given. Now, let us proceed to find out the determinants of aggregate demand which in turn will determine the level of income and employment in the economy. To keep the analysis simple, let us make the following assumptions:

(a) That there is no government. The government neither imposes a tax nor incurs any expenditure.

(b) That there is no foreign trade sector in the economy.

With these two assumptions, aggregate demand can be decomposed into the following components:

(a) *Consumption demand*. A part of income may be demanded by the individuals so that they could buy the goods and services they need. From expenditure point of view, this is called personal consumption expenditure. Thus, the expenditure on food, clothing, shelter, books, entertainment, transport, etc. constitutes consumption expenditure.

(b) *Investment demand*. In order to produce the goods and services for consumption, one needs to make investment. One has to buy machines, raw materials, lands and buildings etc. so that the process of production may be carried out. This type of expenditure which helps production to rise is called investment expenditure.

Thus, we have the following macro-economic equation:

$$Y = C + I \quad \text{...(5.8)}$$

where,

Y = Income,

C = Consumption expenditure, and

I = Investment expenditure.

The right hand side of equation (5.8) represents total expenditure and the left hand side represents income. On the one hand, this equation states that consumption demand and investment demand are the two components of aggregate demand and on the other hand, it tells that total expenditure (aggregate demand) and aggregate supply must be equal. Thus, equation (5.8) can be taken as an identity as well as an equilibrium condition.

GOVERNMENT IN THE SIMPLE KEYNESIAN MODEL

Firms produce goods because people have decided to buy them. Aggregate demand theory starts by examining people's decisions to buy goods, or their spending decisions. Many factors influence spending. If a personal tax cut occurs, then the demand for consumption goods by households will rise. If interest rates rise because of a change in monetary policy, then investment demand from firms is likely to fall. If there is a cut in defence spending, then government demand will fall. By adding up the spending demands of the various sectors of the economy we obtain an estimate of aggregate spending. But a crucial next step is to see if this aggregate spending is consistent with the income that the public is basing its spending decisions on. Because total spending is an aggregation of demand in all sectors of the economy, we refer to the total as aggregate demand.

Government spending (G) for goods and services is a part of aggregate demand. Therefore, aggregate demand (planned spending) in three-sector model is given by

$$Y = C + I + G$$

Government spending does not include transfer payments, which are payments for which no current product or service is required. Such transfer payments are used by the recipients to buy goods and services and thus are reflected in household consumption (C) rather than government spending (G). The government affects aggregate demand indirectly through its transfer payments and taxing policy.

With the addition of transfer payments and taxes, the income available to the households for consumption or saving, called real disposable personal income, (Y_D), will differ from real income, (Y). Disposable income (Y_D) equals income (Y) plus transfer payments (TR) minus taxes (T).

$$Y_D = Y + TR - T \quad ...(5.9)$$

Consumption function shows consumption consisting of an autonomous part, $\bar{C}$, and a portion related to disposable income, cY_D as

$$C = \bar{C} + cY_D \quad ...(5.10)$$

From (5.9) and (5.10) we have

$$C = \bar{C} + cY + cTR - cT \quad ...(5.11)$$

The saving function is given as

$$S_P = \bar{S} + sY_D = -\bar{C} + (1 - c)Y_D \quad ...(5.12)$$

Substituting equation (5.9) for Y_D in equation (5.12), we have

$$S_P = -\bar{C} + (1 - c)Y + (1 - c)TR - (1 - c)T \quad ...(5.13)$$

In the above equations, subscript P denotes the private saving.

The consumption function and aggregate demand for the three-sector model, where investment, government spending, transfer payments, and taxes are all assumed to be autonomous to income changes can be represented by the Figure 5.14.

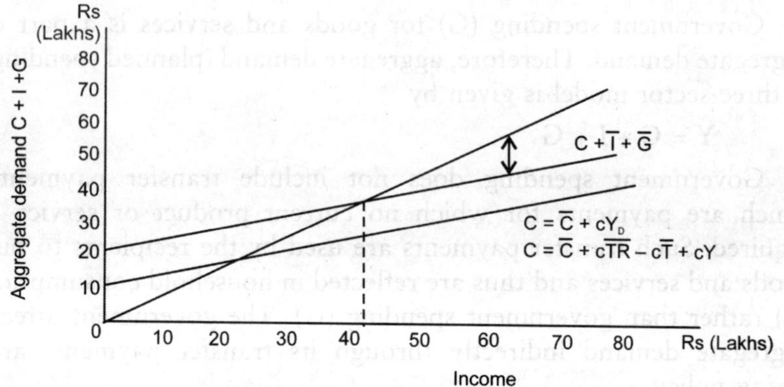

Fig. 5.14

At equilibrium, aggregate demand must equal output (income).

$$Y = C + I + G$$

The simplest Keynesian model assumes that everything except consumption is autonomous in order to focus on the basic argument for government stabilization policy. Therefore, we have

$$I = \overline{I}$$
$$G = \overline{G}$$
$$C = \overline{C} + cY_D$$
$$Y_D = Y + TR - T$$
$$TR = \overline{TR}$$
$$T = \overline{T}$$

Consumption in terms of income rather than disposable income is given by

$$C = \overline{C} + cY + c\overline{TR} - c\overline{T}$$

If transfers and taxes are unrelated to income, then the autonomous portion of consumption becomes $\overline{C} + c\overline{TR} - c\overline{T}$ rather than just $\overline{C}$. Substituting for C, I, and G in aggregate demand we have

$$AD = \overline{C} + cY + c\overline{TR} - c\overline{T} + \overline{I} + \overline{G} \quad ...(5.14)$$

Let $\bar{A}$ be autonomous spending, then we have

$$\bar{A} = \bar{C} + c\overline{TR} - c\bar{T} + \bar{I} + \bar{G} \qquad ...(5.15)$$

Now,

$$AD = \bar{A} + cY \qquad ...(5.16)$$

In equilibrium,

$$AD = Y$$

Using equation (5.16) for AD, we have

$$\bar{A} + cY = Y$$

or, $$Y_e = \frac{1}{1-c}\bar{A} \qquad ...(5.17)$$

Equation (5.17) implies that any change in autonomous spending can be multiplied by 1/(1 – c) to obtain the change in equilibrium income.

$$\Delta Y_e = \frac{1}{1-c}\Delta\bar{A}$$

Let Y_{e_1} describes the initial equilibrium in Figure 5.14. Here we have used the following assumed values:

marginal propensity to consume,	$c = 1/2$
transfer payments,	$\overline{TR} = 10$
taxes,	$\bar{T} = 15$
government spending,	$\bar{G} = 5$
investment,	$\bar{I} = 5$
autonomous consumption,	$\bar{C} = 12.5$

$$\bar{C} + c\overline{TR} - c\bar{T} = 12.5 + (1/2)(50) - (1/2)(15) = 30$$

Aggregate demand is given by

$$AD = C + I + G = [\bar{C} + c\overline{TR} - c\bar{T} + cY] + \bar{I} + \bar{G}$$

Autonomous demand is given by

$$\bar{A} = \bar{C} + c\overline{TR} - c\bar{T} + \bar{I} + \bar{G}$$
$$= 12.5 + (1/2)(10) - (1/2)(15) + 5 + 5 = 20$$

Aggregate demand is

$$AD = \bar{A} + cY = 20 + (1/2)Y$$

In equilibrium, aggregate demand must equal income.

$$\bar{A} + cY = Y$$

or,

$$Y_{e_1} = \frac{1}{1-c}\bar{A} = \frac{1}{1-(1/2)}(20) = 40$$

Where, 1/(1 – c) is the autonomous spending multiplier.

Now suppose that the full employment income is at Y_F = Rs. 50 lakhs. What can the government do to achieve full employment? There is a Rs 5 lakhs deficiency in aggregate demand, which, if added, would be multiplied by 1/(1–1/2) or by 2 to yield the extra Rs. 10 lakhs of income necessary to raise equilibrium income from Rs 40 lakhs to Rs. 50 lakhs. Solving equation (5.14) for aggregate demand using output (y) of 50 we have

$$AD = \bar{C} + c\overline{TR} - c\bar{T} + cY + \bar{I} + \bar{G}$$
$$= 12.5 + (1/2)(5) - (1/2)(15) + (1/2)(50) + 5 + 5 = 45$$

Since, Y_F = Rs.50, and AD = 45, the deficiency in aggregate demand is $Y_F - AD$, which equals 5. How can we eliminate the full employment gap in aggregate demand? The government could increase government spending by Rs. 5 lakhs, or it could increase transfer payments by Rs. 10 lacks (which would increase consumption by Rs. 5 lacks according to the consumption function in equation (5.11)), or it could reduce taxes by Rs. 10 lakhs (which would also increase consumption by Rs. 5 lakhs according to equation (5.11)). When increased government spending of Rs 5 lakhs is assumed to raise aggregate demand by Rs. 5, we are assuming that the government spending does not replace private spending. That is not necessarily the case. For example, government transportation may replace private transportation, and school lunch subsidies mostly replace private consumption. One of the key assumptions in the simple Keynesian model is that government spending does not replace private spending. Under this assumption, the transfer payments or taxes would have to be changed more than government spending to have the same effect on aggregate demand. The reason is that every rupee of government spending is assumed to increase aggregate demand, but transfer payments or taxes change income to households, who then spend according to the marginal propensity to consume. The change in aggregate demand is $c\Delta\overline{TR}$ or $-c\Delta\overline{T}$. If we consider directly about the effect of change in taxes on equilibrium income, we apply the autonomous spending multiplier to the autonomous change in consumption of $-c\Delta\overline{T}$.

$$\Delta Y_e = \left(\frac{1}{1-c}\right)(-c\Delta\overline{T}) \qquad ...(5.18)$$

or,

$$\Delta Y_e = \frac{-c}{1-c}(\Delta\overline{T})$$

Therefore, the tax multiplier is – C/(1 – C).

EXPORTS AND IMPORTS IN THE SIMPLE KEYNESIAN MODEL

In this section, we will consider the effects of introducing exports and imports into the simple Keynesian model. Our focus is on the roles of imports and exports in determining equilibrium income. We know that GNP or GDP (Y) consists of consumption, investment, and government expenditure plus net exports. Net exports are exports minus imports. In the open economy, the condition for equilibrium output is given by

$$Y = C + I + G + X - Z \qquad ...(5.19)$$

where,

X = exports, and

Z = imports.

Exports are the foreign demand for domestic output and therefore belong in aggregate demand. Also, since imports are included in C, I, and G but are not demands for domestic goods, we must subtract them out of aggregate demand.

We take investment and government spending as exogenous—an autonomous expenditure components. Consumption is given by the function

$$C = \overline{C} + cY_D \qquad ...(5.20)$$

For simplicity, we assume that imports consist solely of consumption goods. The demand for imports is assumed to depend on income and to have an autonomous component.

$$Z = u + vY, \quad u > 0, \quad 0 < v < 1 \qquad ...(5.21)$$

where,

u = the autonomous component of imports, and

v = the marginal propensity to import.

The foreign demand for imports will depend on the level of foreign income, being determined by an import demand function. Therefore, foreign income and hence, the demand for exports are considered exogenous. The additional variables that influence exports and imports are the relative price levels in the two countries and the level of the exchange rate. These variables will determine the relative costs of the two countries' products to citizens of either country. However, here we are assuming that price levels and the exchange rate are fixed.

With imports given by equation (5.21) and exports assumed to be exogenous, we can compute equilibrium income from equation (5.19) as follows:

$$Y = C + I + G + X - Z$$

$$= \bar{C} + cY + I + G + X - u - vY$$

$$Y - cY + vY = \bar{C} + I + G + X - u$$

$$(1 - c + v)Y = \bar{C} + I + G + X - u$$

$$\bar{Y} = \frac{1}{1 - c + v}(\bar{C} + I + G + X - u) \qquad ...(5.22)$$

Now we will examine the effects of allowing for foreign trade in the model by comparing equation (5.22) with the equivalent expression for equilibrium income from the closed economy model (5.17). This expression, omitting the tax variable (T), can be written as

$$\bar{Y} = \frac{1}{1 - c}(\bar{C} + I + G) \qquad ...(5.23)$$

In both equations (5.22) and (5.23) equilibrium income is expressed as the product of two terms, the autonomous expenditure multiplier and the level of autonomous expenditures.

Now let us take first the autonomous expenditure multiplier, $1/(1 - c + v)$ in equation (5.22) as opposed to $1/(1 - c)$ in equation (5.23) for the closed economy model. Since v, the marginal propensity to import is greater than zero, the multiplier in (5.22), $1/(1 - c + v)$ will be smaller than the multiplier in (5.23), $1/(1 - c)$. It implies that the more open an economy is to foreign trade (the higher is v), the lower will be the autonomous expenditure multiplier.

The autonomous expenditure multiplier gives the change in equilibrium income per unit change in autonomous expenditure. It follows, therefore, that the more open an economy is, the smaller will be the response of income to aggregate demand shocks such as changes in government spending or autonomous changes in investment demand. A change in autonomous expenditures—a change in government spending, for example—will have a direct effect on income and an induced effect on consumption with a further effect on income. The higher the value of v, the larger the proportion of this induced effect on consumption that will be a change in demand for foreign, not domestic, consumer goods. Consequently, the induced effect on demand for domestic goods and hence, on domestic income will be smaller. The increase in imports per unit of income constitutes an additional leakage from the circular flow of domestic income at each round of the multiplier process and reduces the value of the autonomous expenditure multiplier.

Now we will consider the second term in the expression for equilibrium income in the open economy case (equation 5.22), the level of autonomous expenditures. In addition to the elements for a closed economy, autonomous expenditures for the open economy include the level of exports and the autonomous component of imports. Autonomous components of aggregate demand are those that are not directly determined by income. Rather, shifts in the components of autonomous expenditures affect the level of aggregate demand for a given level of income and result in changes in equilibrium income. Thus, changes in the level exports and autonomous changes in import demand are additional shocks that will change equilibrium income.

Now once again consider the equation (5.22) for computing the multiplier effects of changes in X and u.

$$\frac{\Delta\bar{Y}}{\Delta X} = \frac{1}{1 - c + v} \quad ...(5.24)$$

$$\frac{\Delta\bar{Y}}{\Delta u} = \frac{-1}{1 - c + v} \quad ...(5.25)$$

An increase in the demand for our exports is an increase in aggregate demand for domestically produced output and will increase equilibrium income just as would an increase in government spending or an autonomous increase in investment, which can be given by

$$\frac{\Delta\bar{Y}}{\Delta G} = \frac{\Delta\bar{Y}}{\Delta I} = \frac{1}{1 - c + v} \quad ...(5.26)$$

On the other hand, an autonomous increase in import demand, an increase in u, is seen to cause a decline in equilibrium income. An autonomous increase in import demand represents a shift from demand for domestic goods to demand for foreign goods. As such, the autonomous increase in import demand is a decline in demand for domestic output and causes equilibrium income to decline.

CONSUMPTION FUNCTION

The idea behind the theory of consumption function is very simple. The largest component of total spending is consumption spending, which is the spending by households for food, clothing, automobiles, education, and all the other goods and services that consumers buy. As such, it is one of the main determinants of an economy's aggregate demand (that is, the sum of all planned expenditures in the economy). Have you ever thought upon what factor your consumption depends? For any student of economics and for an intelligent layman as well, the answer would be obvious—disposable income! Disposable income is your take-home pay, the amount you have left after taxes have been deducted. Because we do not consider government sector in this section, no taxes are collected, which means that disposable income will equal total income, or GDP. For both individual households and society as a whole, a positive relationship exists between the amount of disposable income and the amount of consumption spending.

The relationship between disposable income and consumption spending is called the consumption function. A consumption function shows the amounts that households plan to spend at different levels of disposable income. Thus, consumption function specifies a certain relationship between two aggregate economic variables—consumption and income. It states that consumption is an increasing function of income, i.e., the consumption will tend to rise as income rises.

A large amount of material has therefore been written regarding the consumption function; many macroeconomics policies rely on an ability to influence the aggregate demand in an economy without directly increasing government expenditure. The most famous paper is J. M. Keynes' *General Theory of Employment, Interest and Money*, published in 1936, during the Great Depression. Although the work covered many areas of economic theory, the most relevant idea here was that the major (and perhaps only) influence on personal consumption was an individual's income. Keynes' theories centre on the equation

$$C = a + bY \qquad \text{...(5.27)}$$

which shows that the consumption level is influenced by an autonomous variable (a), and a constant fraction of income (bY). Keynes theorised that the autonomous variable would always be positive, and the multiple of income would be between one and zero, varying according to the individuals in the economy.

In Figure 5.15 income is measured along the horizontal axis and consumption expenditure along the vertical axis.

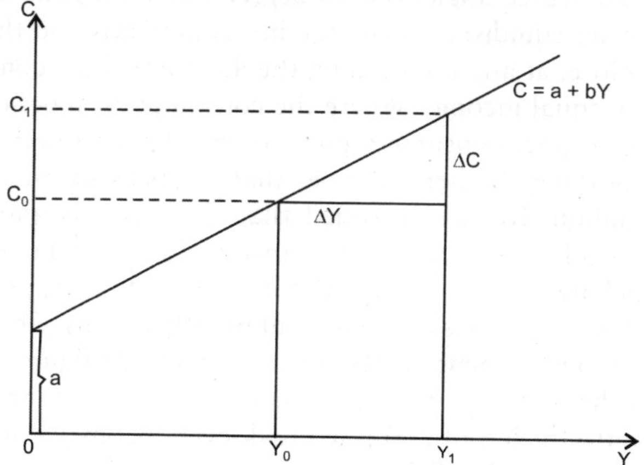

Fig. 5.15: A General Linear Consumption Function.

The consumption function described in equation (5.27) is called a linear consumption function because it is depicted in the form of a line. In Fig. 5.15, a is the intercept and b is the slope of line.

The data on the income and consumption expenditure of a hypothetical economy is presented in Table 5.1. In column (1) income is given and column (2) gives consumption expenditure. The ratio of consumption expenditure to income (C/Y) is given in column (3). This ratio is known as average propensity to consume. Not that average propensity to consume is declining as income rises. The reason for declining average propensity to consume (APC) is that consumption rises more slowly than income.

Table 5.1: Consumption Function of a Hypothetical Economy

Y	C	C/Y	ΔC	ΔY	ΔC/ΔY
100	125	1.25	-	-	-
200	200	1.00	75	100	0.75
300	275	0.90	75	100	0.75
400	350	0.87	75	100	0.75
500	425	0.85	75	100	0.75

Figure 5.16 plots the consumption function depicted in the above table.

The consumption function slopes upward and to the right because consumption spending increases with income. We determine the income level where every rupee is spent by using the 45-degree line drawn in the diagram. Because the vertical and horizontal axes meet at a 90-degree angle, the 45-degree line represents a series of points that are equidistant from the horizontal axis and the vertical axis. Therefore, at any point along the 45-degree line, consumption expenditure equal income. Where the consumption function crosses the 45-degree line, consumers plan to spend everything they earn and save nothing. In our example that happens at an income of Rs. 200 million. Keynes reasoned that there is a certain level of consumption that is necessary for an individual to stay alive; this would typically consist of expenditure on food, heat, and shelter, although in certain cases it would contain other items. This amount, the autonomous element a, (Rs. 75 million in our figure 5.16), can be seen as the intercept with the Y-axis. At this point, and, indeed, at any pointto the left of 200 (the break-even income), consumption is above income, and individuals must use money from savings (that is, they must dissave) to pay for the deficit. At 200 consumption exactly equals income, and there is no saving or dissaving, while above this level of income (to the right) the individual will save any surplus income not consumed.

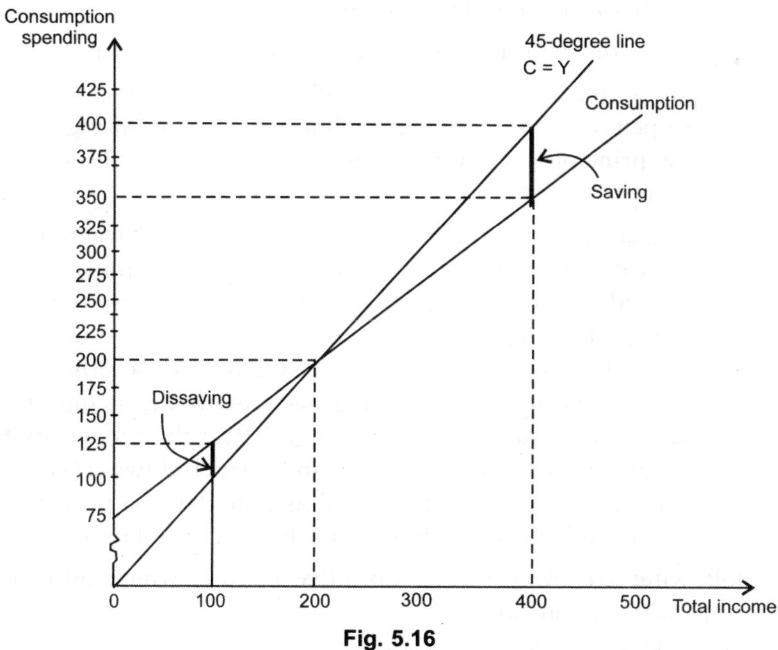

Fig. 5.16

At income less than Rs. 200 million, there is dissaving, or negative saving. When income is Rs. 100 million, consumers plan to dissave Rs. 25 million. The distance between the 45-degree line and the consumption function gets wider as income increases because the amount of saving increases with income.

According to Fig. 5.16, when income is Rs.100 million, households desire to spend Rs. 125 million. At that income, they are dissaving Rs. 25 million; that is, they are dipping into their savings accounts or borrowing to help finance some minimum standard of living. Higher levels of income involve more consumption spending and more saving or less dissaving. In our example Rs. 200 million represents the income level at which every rupee earned is spent; there is neither saving nor dissaving. At higher incomes, households wish to save a portion of their income. For instance, at an income of Rs. 400 million, households plan to save Rs. 50 million.

MARGINAL PROPENSITY TO CONSUME

Marginal propensity to consume is the change in consumption from a given change in income. The amount that an individual spends on consumption depends:

(a) partly on the amount of its income,
(b) partly on the other objective attendant circumstances, and
(c) partly on the subjective needs and the psychological propensities and habits of the individuals composing it and the principles on which the income is divided between them.

The subjective factors include those psychological characteristics of human nature and those social practices and institutions, which, though not inalterable, are unlikely to undergo a material change over a short period of time except in abnormal or revolutionary circumstances. In comparing one social system with another of a different type, it is necessary to take account of the manners in which changes in the subjective factors may affect the propensity to consume. But, in general, we shall in what follows take the subjective factors as given; and we shall assume that the propensity to consume depends only on changes in the objective factors.

Following are the principle objective factors, which influence the propensity to consume:

(a) a change in the wage unit,
(b) a change in the difference between income and net income,
(c) windfall changes in capital-values not allowed for in calculating net income,
(d) changes in the rate of time discounting—in the ratio of exchange between present goods and future goods,
(e) change in fiscal policy, and
(f) change in expectations of the relation between the present and the future level of income.

Thus, in a given situation the propensity to consume may be considered a fairly stable function, provided that we have eliminated changes in the wage unit in terms of money. Windfall changes in capital values will be capable of changing the propensity to consume, and substantial changes in the rate of interest and in fiscal policy may make some difference; but the other objective factors which might affect it, whilst they must not be overlooked, are not likely to be important in ordinary circumstances. The fact that, given the general economic situation, the expenditure on consumption in terms of the wage unit depends in the main, on the volume of output and employment is the justification for summing up the other factors in the portmanteau function "propensity to consume". For whilst the other factors are capable of varying, the aggregate income measured in terms of the wage unit is, as a rule, the principal variable upon which the consumption-constituent of the aggregate demand function will depend. Thus, the propensity to consume is a fairly stable function so that, as a rule, the amount of aggregate consumption mainly depends on the amount of aggregate income (both measured in terms of wage-units), changes in the propensity itself being treated as a secondary influence.

A decline in income due to a decline in the level of employment may even cause consumption to exceed income not only by some individuals and institution using up the financial reserves which they have accumulated in better times, but also by the Government, which will be liable to run into a budgetary deficit or will provide unemployment relief out of borrowed money. Thus, when employment falls to a low level, aggregate consumption will decline by a smaller amount than that by which real income has declined, by reason both of the habitual behaviour of individuals and also of the probable policy of governments; which is the explanation why a new position of equilibrium can usually be reached within a modest range of fluctuation. Otherwise, a fall in employment and income, once started, might proceed to extreme lengths.

Now we shall discuss the second category of factors which affect the amount of consumption out of a given income, namely, those subjective and social incentives which determine how much is spent, given the aggregate of income in terms of wage units and given the relevant objective factors which we have already discussed. The following are the main subjective characters, which affect the marginal propensity to consume of an individual:

(a) to build up a reserve against unforeseen contingencies,

(b) to provide for an anticipated future relation between the income and the needs of the individual different from that which exists in the present, as, for example, in relation to old age, family education, or the maintenance of dependents,

(c) to enjoy interest and appreciation, i.e. because a larger real consumption at a later date is preferred to a smaller immediate consumption,

(d) to enjoy a gradually increasing expenditure, since it gratifies a common instinct to look forward to a gradually improving standard of life rather than the contrary, even though the capacity for enjoyment may be diminishing,

(e) to enjoy a sense of independence and the power to do things, though without a clear idea or definite intention of specific action,

(f) to secure a *masse de manoeuvre* to carry out speculative or business projects,

(g) to bequeath a fortune, and

(h) to satisfy pure miserliness, i.e. unreasonable but insistent inhibitions against acts of expenditure as such.

Apart from the savings accumulated by individuals, there is also the large amount of income, varying perhaps from one-third to two-thirds of the total accumulation in a modern industrial community, which is withheld by Central and local government, by Institutions and by Business Corporations, for the following motives:

(a) *The motive of enterprise*: To secure resources to carry out further capital investment without incurring debt or raising further capital on the market.

(b) *The motive of liquidity:* To secure liquid resources to meet emergencies, difficulties and depressions.

(c) *The motive of improvement*: To secure a gradually increasing income, which, incidentally, will protect the management from criticism, since increasing income due to accumulation is seldom distinguished from increasing income due to efficiency.

(d) The motive of financial prudence and the anxiety to be "on the right side" by making a financial provision in excess of user and supplementary cost, so as to discharge debt and write off the cost of assets ahead of, rather than behind, the actual rate of wastages and obsolescence, the strength of this motive mainly depending on the quantity and character of the capital equipment and the rate of technical change.

Corresponding to these motives which favour the withholding of a part of income from consumption, there are also operative at times motive which lead to an excess of consumption over income. Several of the motives towards positive saving catalogued above as affecting individuals have their intended counterpart in negative saving at a later date, as, for example, with saving to provide for family needs or old age.

Since the main background of subjective and social incentives changes slowly, whilst the short-period influence of changes in the rate of interest and the other objective factors is often of secondary importance, we are left with the conclusion that short-period changes in consumption largely depends on changes in the rate at which income is being earned and not on changes in the propensity to consume out of a given income.

From the above discussion we see that the way households react to change in income depends on their marginal propensity to consume (MPC). The MPC is the fraction of each additional earned rupee that households spend on consumption, or the change in consumption spending divided by the change in income:

$$\text{Marginal propensity to consume (MPC)} = \frac{\text{Change in consumption spending}}{\text{Change in Income}}$$

or, $\text{MPC} = dC/dY$

In our example of a hypothetical economy in the previous section, we find that when income is 100 million, consumption is 125 million and when income rises to 200 million, consumption has also risen to 200 million. Thus, the change in consumption is 75 million while the change in income is 100 million. Therefore, marginal propensity to consume (MPC) is

$$\text{MPC} = 75/100 = 0.75$$

We can relate the marginal propensity to consume to the consumption function easily if we know that the slope of any line is the vertical change divided by the horizontal change. The slope of the consumption function is the change in the consumption spending divided by the change in income, which is precisely how we define the marginal propensity to consume. In other words, the slope of the consumption function is equal to the economy's MPC. If the

MPC in our example were higher the slope of the consumption function would be steeper; if the MPC were lower, the consumption function would be flatter.

The consumption function depicted in Figure 5.16 has the following equation.

$$C = 75 + 0.75\,Y \quad ...(5.28)$$

where 75 is intercept term and slope is 0.75. Thus, from Figure 5.16 we see that MPC and slope of the consumption function are the same. In other words, the slope of the consumption represents MPC. Comparing equation (5.27) and equation (5.28) we find that a = 75 and b = 0.75. Thus, b represents the slope as well as MPC. This can be shown as follows.

Let,

Y_0 = initial level of income,

Y_1 = new level of income,

C_0 = initial level of consumption,

C_1 = new level of consumption,

dY = change in income, and

dC = change in consumption.

Now the two consumption equations can be written as

$$C_0 = a + bY_0 \quad ...(5.29)$$

$$C_1 = a + bY_1 \quad ...(5.30)$$

Subtracting equation (5.29) from equation (5.30), we get

$$C_1 - C_0 = a + bY_1 - a - bY_0$$

$$C_1 - C_0 = b(Y_1 - Y_0) \quad ...(5.31)$$

Dividing equation (5.31) by $(Y_1 - Y_0)$, we get

$$\frac{C_1 - C_0}{Y_1 - Y_0} = \frac{b(Y_1 - Y_0)}{(Y_1 - Y_0)}$$

$$\frac{C_1 - C_0}{Y_1 - Y_0} = \frac{dC}{dY} = b \quad ...(5.32)$$

Equation (5.32) shows that b is marginal propensity to consume as well as slope.

Keynes propounded a psychological law of consumption, which says that if there is a given increase in income then the resulting increase in consumption would be less than the original increase in income. The meaning of this 'law' is that the MPC would be always greater than zero and its value would always be between the range zero and unity.

Using the diagram it is quite easy to see why the MPC cannot be greater (or even equal to) one—if this was the case, and the autonomous level of consumption was strictly greater than zero, the two level would never cross and the individual would be in a permanent state of dissaving. It was further theorised that, as this analysis concerned independent individuals, it would be followed by an entire economy, which consists of such individuals. Although the MPC would be different for each person, the average figure would still be constant. This enabled Keynes to predict how an economy would react to change in national income, and how this may be beneficial in policy making.

Following the publication of Keynes' *General Theory*, a great deal of work was carried out to either prove or disprove the ideas contained within it. The data used for the analysis did indeed roughly follow Keynes' theories, but it was noted that the long-term data (average over five years) gave different results to those concerning only short periods of time. It was noted that, as the data became more long term, the autonomous constant tended to zero, and the MPC tended to one.

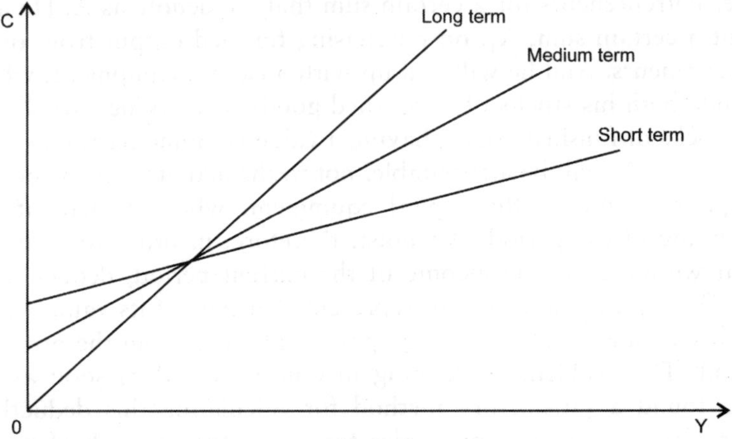

Fig. 5.17

Now, the discussion about consumption can be summarised as follows:

(a) MPC is constant;

(b) MPC is greater than zero ($b > 0$);

(c) The value of MPC is always between zero and unity, ($0 < b < 1$);

(d) The APC is greater than MPC (APC > b). This can be shown as follows:

$$C = a + bY$$

$$APC = \frac{C}{Y} = \frac{a}{Y} + b > b$$

$$APC > MPC.$$

(e) APC declines as income rises but MPC remains constant. The reason is that a/Y declines with increase in income but b is constant. Therefore, a/Y + b declines as income rises.

SAVING FUNCTION

Saving means the excess of income over expenditure on consumption. Thus, any doubts about the meaning of saving must arise from doubts about the meaning either of income or of consumption. Therefore, before defining saving function, we shall consider income.

An entrepreneur will sold his finished output to consumers or to other entrepreneurs for a certain sum that we denote as A. He also spent a certain sum, A_1, on purchasing finished output from other entrepreneurs. And he will end up with a capital equipment, which include both his stocks of unfinished goods or working capital and his stocks of finished goods, having a value G. Some part, however, of $A + G - A_1$ will be attributable, not to the activities of the period in question, but to the capital equipment, which he had at the beginning of the period. We must, therefore, in order to arrive at what we mean by the income of the current period, deduct from $A + G - A_1$ a certain sum, to represent that part of its value which has been contributed by the equipment inherited from the previous period. The problem of defining income is solved as soon as we have found a satisfactory method for calculating this deduction. There are two possible principles for calculating it, each of which has a certain significance—one of them in connection with production, and the other in connection with consumption.

The actual value G of the capital equipment at the end of the period is the net result of the entrepreneur, on the one hand, having maintained and improved it during the period, both by purchases from other entrepreneurs and by work done upon it by himself, and, on the other hand, having exhausted or depreciated it through using it to produce output. If he had decided not to use it to produce output, there is, nevertheless, a certain optimum sum which it would have paid him to spend on maintaining and improving it. Let us suppose that, in this event, he would have spent M′ on its maintenance and improvement, and that, having had this spent on it, it would have been worth G′ at the end of the period. That is to say, G′ – M′ is the maximum net value which might have been conserved from the previous period, if it had not been used to produce A. The excess of this potential value of the equipment over $G - A_1$ is the measure of what has been sacrificed to produce A. let this quantity be

$$(G' - M') - (G - A_1),$$

which measures the sacrifice of value involved in the production of A, the user cost of A. Let us write the user cost as U. The amount paid out by the entrepreneur to the other factors of production in return for their services, which from their point of view is their income, which is called the factor cost of A. The sum of the factor cost F and the user cost U is called the prime cost of the output A.

Now we can define the income of the entrepreneur as being the excess of the value of his finished output sold during the period over his prime cost. The entrepreneur's income is taken as being equal to the quantity, depending on his scale of production, which he endeavours to maximise, i.e., to his gross profit in the ordinary sense of this term. Since the income of the rest of the community is equal to the entrepreneur's factor cost, aggregate income is equal to A – U. Income, thus defined, is a completely unambiguous quantity.

Furthermore, the effective demand is simply the aggregate income (or proceeds) which the entrepreneurs expect to receive, inclusive of the incomes, which they will hand on to other factors of production, from the amount of current employment which they decide to give. The aggregate demand function relates various hypothetical quantities of employment to the proceeds, which their outputs are expected to yield; and the effective demand is the point on the aggregate demand function, which becomes effective because, taken in conjunction with the conditions of supply, it corresponds to the level of employment, which maximises the entrepreneur's expectation of profit.

We turn, next, to the second of the principles referred to above. We have dealt so far with that part of the change in the value of the capital equipment at the end of the period as compared with its value at the beginning which is due to the voluntary decisions of the entrepreneur in seeking to maximise his profit. But there may, in addition, be an involuntary loss (or gain) in the value of his capital equipment, occurring for reasons beyond his control and irrespective of his current decisions, on account of a change in market values, wastage by obsolescence or the mere passage of time, or destruction by catastrophe such as war or earthquake. Now some part of these involuntary losses, while they are unavoidable, are not unexpected; such as losses through the lapse of time irrespective of use, and also normal obsolescence which, as Professor Pigou expresses it, "is sufficiently regular to be foreseen, if not in detail, at least in the large", including, we may add, those losses to the community as a whole which are sufficiently regular to be commonly regarded as 'insurable risks'.

For the moment ignore the fact that the amount of the expected loss depends on when the expectation is assumed to be framed, and let us call the depreciation of the equipment, which is involuntary but not unexpected, i.e., the excess of the expected depreciation over the user cost, the supplementary cost, which we shall call V. It is, hardly necessary to point out that this definition is not the same as Marshall's definition of supplementary cost, though the underlying idea, namely, of dealing with that part of the expected depreciation that does not enter into prime cost, in similar. In reckoning, therefore, the net income and the net profit of the entrepreneur it is usual to deduct the estimated amount of the supplementary cost from his income and gross profit as defined above. For the psychological effect on the entrepreneur, when he is considering what he is free to spend and to save, of the supplementary cost is virtually the same as though it came off his gross profit. In his capacity as a producer deciding whether or not to use the equipment, prime cost and gross profit, as defined above, are the significant concepts. But in his capacity as a consumer the amount of the supplementary cost works on his mind in the same way as if it were a part of the prime cost. Hence we shall not only come nearest to common usage but will also arrive at a concept which is relevant to the amount of consumption, if, in defining aggregate net income, we deduct the supplementary cost as well as the user cost, so that aggregate net income is equal to A – U – V.

There remains the change in the value of the equipment, due to unforeseen changes in market values, exceptional obsolescence or destruction by catastrophe, which is both involuntary and in a broad sense unforeseen. The causal significance of net income lies in the psychological influence of the magnitude of V on the amount of current consumption, since net income is what we suppose the ordinary man to reckon his available income to be when he is deciding how much to spend on current consumption.

Net income, based on an equivocal criterion, which different authorities might interpret differently, is not perfectly clear-cut. Professor Hayek, for example, has suggested that an individual owner of capital goods might aim at keeping the income he derives from his possession constant, so that he would not feel himself free to spend his income on consumption until he had set aside sufficient to offset any tendency of his investment-income to decline for whatever reason. If such an individual exists; but, obviously, no theoretical objection can be raised against this deduction as providing a possible psychological criterion of net income. But when Professor Hayek infers that the concepts of saving and investment suffer from a corresponding vagueness, he is only right if he means net saving and net investment. The saving and the investment, which are relevant to the theory of employment, are clear of this defect, and are capable of objective definition, as we have shown above.

Thus, it is a mistake to put all the emphasis on net income, which is only relevant to decisions concerning consumption, and is, moreover, only separated from various other factors affecting consumption by a narrow line; and to overlook the concept of income proper, which is the concept relevant to decisions concerning current production and is quite unambiguous.

Whenever income accrues to a person, he may put it to any of the two uses:

(a) A part of the total income, he will consume. This is known as consumption expenditure.

(b) The rest, which he does not consume, is saved. This is called saving.

From this point of view income is to be either consumed or is to be saved. Thus, compared to equation (5.5) we have another macroeconomic relationship:

$$Y = C + S \qquad \text{...(5.33)}$$

where,

Y = Income,

C = Consumption expenditure, and

S = Savings.

Since, we have defined saving as income not consumed, equation (5.33) can be modified as:

$$S = Y - C, \qquad \text{...(5.34)}$$

Equation (5.34) tells that saving is a residual. The income, which is left after consumption, is saving. Since consumption is a function of income, saving must also be a function of income and is represented by

$$S = f(Y) \qquad \text{...(5.35)}$$

Depending on the analysis, the actual functional form of the equation can be linear, with a constant slope, or curvilinear, with a changing slope. The most common form is linear, such as the one presented here:

$$S = c + dY \qquad \text{...(5.36)}$$

The two key parameters that characterise the saving function are slope and intercept. The slope of the saving function (d) measures the change in saving resulting from a change in income. If income changes by Rs. 1, then saving changes by Rs. d. This slope is generally assumed and empirically documented to be greater than zero, but less than one ($0 < d < 1$). It is conceptually identified as induced saving and the marginal propensity to save. And the intercept of the saving function (c) measures the amount of saving undertaken if income is zero. If income is zero, then saving is Rs. c.

The intercept is generally assumed and empirically documented to be negative ($c < 0$). It is conceptually identified as autonomous saving.

It is often useful to state the saving function using parameters for the consumption function. The saving function can be obtained if we deduct consumption function from income.

$$S = Y - (a + bY)$$

$$S = -a + (1 - b)Y \qquad ...(5.37)$$

Comparing equations (5.36) and (5.37) we find that the intercept is – a rather than c and the slope is (1 – b) rather than d. This alternative specification shows the connection between the saving function and the consumption function. The intercept of the saving function (–a) is the negative of the intercept of the consumption function (a). The slope of the saving function (1 – b) is one minus the slope of the consumption function (b), meaning that the sum of the marginal propensity to consume (b) and the marginal propensity to save (1 – b) is equal to one, which is just another way of saying that a portion of additional income is consumed and the rest is saved.

The saving function described in equation (5.37) has been drawn in Figure 5.18 in which income is measured on horizontal axis and saving has been measured on the vertical axis. This saving function has been derived from the consumption function described in Figure 5.15. Its intercept is – a which is negative and its slope is (1 – b). There two magnitudes really depend upon magnitudes of consumption function; a is numerically the same but its sign is different and (1 – b) obviously depends upon b.

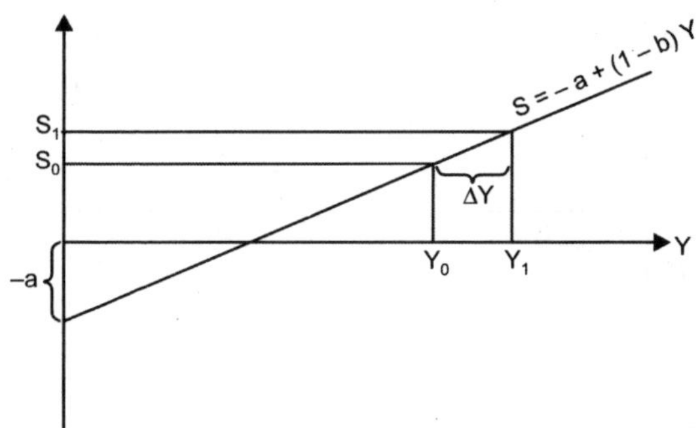

Fig. 5.18: A General Linear Saving Function.

The income and consumption data presented in Table 5.1 can be used to generate the saving function. This has been done in Table 5.2. Columns (1) and (2) which provide data upon income and consumption are taken from Table 5.1. Column (3) gives the total savings of our hypothetical economy. Notice that saving is negative when income is too low. When income is 200 consumption and income become equal. This is zero saving point. Sometimes, it is referred as break-even point also. After this level of income, saving become positive and increase steadily with the increases in income. The saving function which is implicit in the Table 5.2 has been depicted in Figure 5.19. This saving function has the following line.

$$S = -75 + 0.25\ Y \qquad \text{...(5.38)}$$

Table 5.2: Saving Function of a Hypothetical Economy

Y	Y	S = Y – C	S/Y	ΔS	ΔY	ΔS/ΔY
(1)	(2)	(3)	(4)	(5)	(6)	(7)
100	125	–25	–0.25	—	—	0
200	200	0	0	25	100	0.25
300	275	25	0.08	25	100	0.25
400	350	50	0.12	25	100	0.25
500	425	75	0.15	25	100	0.25

Let us recall that consumption function based upon the same data and represented in equation (5.28) was C = 75 + 0.75 Y. Notice that intercept of saving function is same but only sign has changed, i.e., it has become negative from positive. The slope of saving function is 0.25 which we obtain if we subtract the slope of consumption function (0.75) from unity.

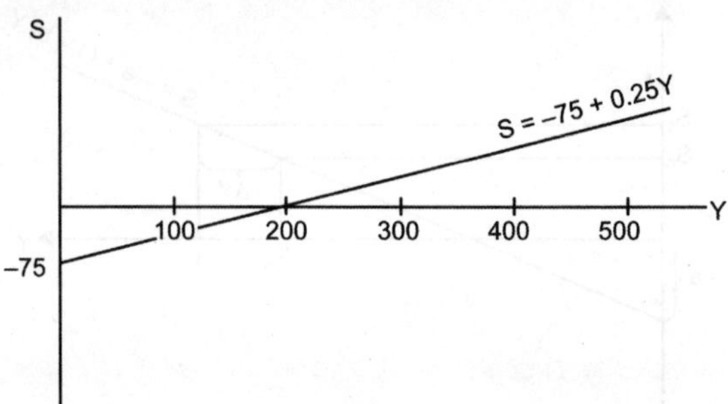

Fig. 5.19: Saving Function of Hypothetical Economy.

The concepts of average propensity to save (APS) and marginal propensity to save (MPS) are also similar to those of APC and MPC in case of consumption function.

$$\text{Average propensity to save} = \frac{\text{Saving}}{\text{Income}}$$

$$APS = \frac{S}{Y} \qquad \text{...(5.39)}$$

In case of linear saving function APS is given by

$$S = -a + (1 - b)\,Y$$

$$APS = \frac{S}{Y} = -\frac{a}{Y} + (1 - b) \qquad \text{...(5.40)}$$

Notice that average propensity to save tends to increase as income rises. This is so because the first term of the expression on right hand side in equation (5.40) tends to rise while (1 – b) remains constant.

The marginal propensity to save, like marginal propensity to consume, is the change in saving due to a given change in income.

$$\text{Marginal propensity to save} = \frac{\text{Change in saving}}{\text{Change in income}}$$

$$MPS = \frac{\Delta S}{\Delta Y} \qquad \text{...(5.41)}$$

In case of linear saving function MPS can be calculated as follows:

Let,

Y_0 = original level of income,

Y_1 = new level of income,

S_0 = original level of saving,

S_1 = new level of saving,

$Y_1 - Y_0 = \Delta Y$ = change in income, and

$S_1 - S_0 = \Delta S$ = change in saving.

But,

$$S_1 = -a + (1 - b)\,Y_1$$

$$S_0 = -a + (1 - b)\,Y_0$$

Therefore,

$$S_1 - S_0 = - a + (1 - b)\, Y_1 - [- a + (1 - b)\, Y_0]$$

or, $$S_1 - S_0 = - a + (1 - b)\, Y_1 - (1 - b)\, Y_0 + a$$

or, $$S_1 - S_0 = (1 - b)\, Y_1 - (1 - b)\, Y_0$$

or, $$S_1 - S_0 = (1 - b)\, (Y_1 - Y_0) \qquad ...(5.42)$$

Dividing (5.42) on both sides by $Y_1 - Y_0$

We get

$$\frac{S_1 - S_0}{Y_1 - Y_0} = \frac{(1-b)\,(Y_1 - Y_0)}{(Y_1 - Y_0)}$$

Thus,

$$\frac{S_1 - S_0}{Y_1 - Y_0} = \frac{\Delta S}{\Delta Y} = (1-b) \qquad ...(5.43)$$

Thus, it is shown that (1 – b) is the marginal propensity to save which is also the slope of linear saving function.

The saving function captures the relation between saving and income. However, income is not the only factor influencing saving. Now consider the following saving function:

$$S = f(Y, O_F), \qquad ...(5.44)$$

where, O_F is specified as other factors affecting saving. These other factors are more commonly referred to as consumption expenditures determinants because the primarily influence consumption, but also subsequent affect saving. Some of the more notable consumption saving determinants are consumer confidence, interest rates, and wealth.

Consumer confidence is the general optimism or pessimism, the household sector has about the state of the economy. More optimism means more consumption, and thus less saving. Interest rates affect the cost of borrowing the funds used to purchase durable goods. Higher interest rates mean less consumption and thus more saving. Wealth is the financial and physical assets owned by the household sector. More financial wealth means more consumption and less saving, while more physical assets mean less consumption and more saving. These determinants cause saving to change even though income does not change. Or another way of stating this, determinants cause saving to change at every level of income. For a linear saving function, this change is reflected by a change in the intercept term (– a). For a saving line, the change is seen as an upward or downward shift.

The discussion about the saving function can be summarized as follows:

(a) MPS is constant,

(b) MPS is greater than zero i.e., $(1 - b) > 0$,

(c) The value of MPS is always between zero and unity, i.e., $0 < (1 - b) < 1$,

(d) The MPS is greater than APS. This is easy to see. APS is $-\frac{a}{Y} + (1-b)$ while MPS is $(1 - b)$, obviously

$$(1-b) > \left[-\frac{a}{Y} + (1-b)\right]$$

(e) The APS declines as income rises but MPS remains constant.

RELATIONSHIP BETWEEN PROPENSITY TO CONSUME AND PROPENSITY TO SAVE

The propensity to save and propensity to consume are related with each other in a special way. It shall be useful to keep the following two theorems in mind.

(a) The sum of APC and APS is always unity. This can be shown as follows

We know that:

$$Y = C + S$$

Dividing both sides of above equation by Y we have

$$\left.\begin{aligned} \frac{Y}{Y} &= \frac{C}{Y} + \frac{S}{Y} \\ 1 &= \frac{C}{Y} + \frac{S}{Y} \end{aligned}\right\}$$

or, $$APS + APC = 1 \qquad ...(5.45)$$

(b) The sum of marginal propensity to consume and marginal propensity to save is also unity. This can be shown as follows:

We know that

$$C + S = Y.$$

The same relation can be written for changes in consumption, savings, and income.

$$\Delta C + \Delta S = \Delta Y$$

Dividing the above equation by ΔY on both sides, we get

$$\left.\begin{aligned}\frac{\Delta C}{\Delta Y} + \frac{\Delta S}{\Delta Y} &= \frac{\Delta Y}{\Delta Y} \\ \frac{\Delta C}{\Delta Y} + \frac{\Delta S}{\Delta Y} &= 1\end{aligned}\right\}$$

$$MPC + MPS = 1 \qquad \text{...(5.46)}$$

DETERMINATION OF EQUILIBRIUM LEVEL OF INCOME

Now we have equipped ourselves to understand the process of income determination in a simple economy. The process of income determination is shown in Figure 5.20. In the construction of this diagram the thick break line is very fundamental. It is 45° line and its function is to divide the diagram into two equal parts. The advantage to this device is that we can turn the axes with the help of 45° line and the entries on horizontal axis can be read on the vertical axis. In Figure 5.20 income (aggregate supply) is measured on the horizontal axis and consumption and investment (components of aggregate demand) are measured on the vertical axis. Thus the 45° line has been labelled Y = C + I because at all points along this line aggregate demand (C + I) equals aggregate supply. That is the reason why some economists have dubbed it as a suppressed aggregate supply line.

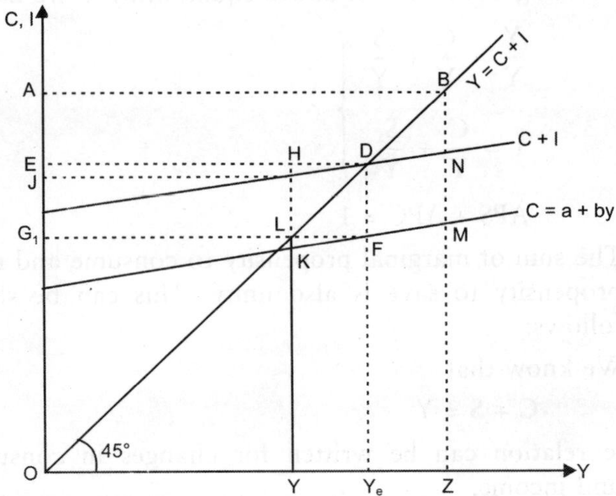

Fig. 5.20: Determination of Equilibrium Level of Income.

The line C is a consumption function which was described in this chapter earlier. The C-Line intersects the 45° line at the point L. Before the point L, consumption exceeds income. Therefore, savings would be negative. This level of consumption cannot be sustained as consumption is more and income is less. Consequently income has to rise. At the point L consumption and income are equal. So this is the break-even point. Beyond the point L, consumption is below income, therefore, positive savings must result.

The next line in the diagram is C + I line or the aggregate demand line. The vertical distance between the aggregate demand line and C-line is investment. Note that the amount of investment is the same at all levels of income. When the income is OY, KY is the consumption expenditure and HK is investment expenditure. When income is Y_e, consumption expenditure is F Y_e and investment is DF. Similarly, when income is OZ, consumption is MZ and investment is NM. It can be seen through the diagram that amount of investment is the same, at all levels of income as HK = DF = NM. It would mean that amount of investment does not depend upon income. Such type of investment is said to be exogenous.

Note that aggregate demand line intersects 45° line at the point D. Before D, aggregate demand is more than aggregate supply. This situation prevails when the level of income is OY. This income level cannot be sustained and income would tend to rise. Suppose that income rises to OZ. At this level MZ is consumption expenditure and NM is the investment expenditure. The total amount of aggregate demand is NZ which falls short of aggregate supply which is BZ. At this level of income, excess capacity appears in the economy and the magnitude of excess capacity is BN. In fact, to sustain OZ amount of income, BM amount of investment must be made. But the actual amount of investment is only NM. Thus, income would tend to fall unless it reaches OY_e.

The only sustainable level of income is at the point D where C + I line intersects 45° line. At this point aggregate demand and aggregate supply would be equal. Consequently, the equilibrium level of income is Y_e. The equilibrium level of consumption is FY_e and equilibrium level of investment is DF. This is equilibrium level because at this level of income there would be no inherent tendency for income either to rise or to fall.

A Numerical Example

Let us apply the above theory to the case of our hypothetical economy for which the consumption function is C = 50 + 0.75Y. The process of income determination in a hypothetical economy has been shown in Figure 5.21. Income has been shown on the horizontal axis and consumption and investment expenditures have been shown on the vertical axis. The 45° line showing Y = C + I has also been drawn. Then consumption function (C = 50 + 0.75 Y) is plotted. It intersects the 45° line when the level of income is 200. At this level of income, consumption expenditure is also 200. Thus, before the income level of 200 is achieved C-line is above the 45° line and after that it is below the 45° line.

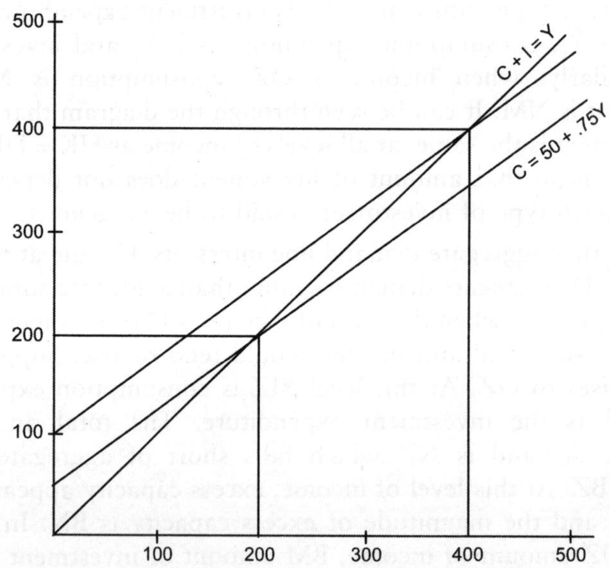

Fig. 5.21: Income Determination in a Hypothetical Economy

It is assumed that an autonomous investment of 50 takes place in our hypothetical economy irrespective of level of income. Thus, 50 is measured on the vertical axis on the top of the point when consumption function begins. From this Point, a line parallel to the C-line is drawn. This is the aggregate demand line of our hypothetical eeonomy. Since, C + I line is parallel to C-line, the distance between two lines is the same at all points. This assumes that level of investment is 50 irrespective of level of income. The equilibrium level of income is determined where C + I line intersects 45° line. If we draw a perpendicular from the point of intersection on the horizontal axis, it falls upon where the level of income is 400. Thus, equilibrium level of income is 400. The equilibrium level of income can also be found with the help of a little mathematics. We have the macro economic relations:

$$Y = C + \bar{I} \qquad ...(5.47)$$

and

$$C = a + bY \qquad ...(5.48)$$

Substituting the equation (5.48) into (5.47) we get

$$Y = a + bY + \bar{I} \qquad ...(5.49)$$

$\bar{I}$ in equation (5.49) indicates that investment is given exogenously. Collecting the terms which contain Y on the left hand side, (5.42) can be rewritten as

$$Y - bY = a + \bar{I}$$

$$Y(1 - b) = a + \bar{I}$$

$$Y = \frac{1}{1-b}(a + \bar{I}) \qquad ...(5.50)$$

Equation (5.50) gives the equilibrium level of income for a simple economy. If the amount of exogenous investment (I), and intercept and slope of the consumption function (a and b) are given, equilibrium level of income can be calculated.

In the example of our hypothetical economy the following values are given

$$a = 50$$

$$b = 0.75$$

$$I = 50$$

Thus equilibrium level of income would be

$$Y = \frac{1}{1-0.75}(50+50)$$

$$= \frac{1}{0.25}(100)$$

$$= 400$$

Note that equilibrium level of income obtained through this method is exactly the same as obtained through graphical method. The equilibrium level of consumption can be calculated easily by substituting the solution obtained in equation (5.50) into consumption function given in the equation (5.48).

$$C = a + b\left\{\frac{1}{1-b}(a+\bar{I})\right\} \qquad ...(5.51)$$

In case of our example

$$\begin{aligned} C &= 50 + 0.75\ (400) \\ &= 50 + 300.0 \\ &= 350.0 \end{aligned}$$

Thus, equilibrium level of consumption obtained through this method is also the same as obtained through graphical method.

NOTES

1. John Maynard Keynes: *General Theory of Employment, Interest and Money* (1936), Harbinger edition, p. 6.
2. Keynes, *op. cit.* p. 6.

6 Saving, Investment, and Multipliers

In the previous chapter we have defined saving as the excess of income over what is spent on consumption. Any deviation from this meaning of saving would be very inconvenient and misleading. Nor is there any important difference of opinion as to what is meant by expenditure on consumption. Thus, the differences of usage arise either out of the definition of investment or out of that of income. Let us consider investment first.

In general, usage it is common to mean by investment, the purchase of an asset, old or new, by an individual or a corporation. Sometimes, the term might be restricted to the purchase of an asset on the Stock Exchange. Here we consider just as readily of investing, for example, in a house, or in a machine, or in a stock of finished or unfinished goods; and, broadly speaking, new investment, as distinguished from reinvestment, means the purchase of a capital asset of any kind out of income. If we reckon the sale of an investment as being negative, i.e. disinvestment, exchanges of old investments necessarily cancel out.

We have to adjust for the creation and discharge of debts (including changes in the quantity of credit or money); but since for the community as a whole the increase or decrease of the aggregate creditor position is always exactly equal to the increase or decrease of the aggregate debtor position, this complication also cancels out when we are dealing with aggregate investment.

Investment, thus defined, includes, therefore, the increment of capital equipment, whether it consists of fixed capital, working capital or liquid capital; and the significant differences of definition (apart from the distinction between investment and net investment) are due to the exclusion from investment of one or more of these categories. Some economists give great importance to changes in liquid capital, i.e. to undesigned increments (or decrements) in the stock of unsold goods, have suggested a possible definition of investment from which such changes are excluded. In this case an excess of saving over investment would be the same thing as an undesigned increment in the stock of unsold goods, i.e. as an increase of liquid capital.

It seems probable that capital formation and capital consumption, as used by the Austrian school of economists, are not identical with either investment or disinvestment as defined above or with net investment and disinvestment.

Now we come to the divergence between saving and investment which are due to a special definition of income and hence of the excess of income over consumption. Here our definition of income differs from our previous definition by reckoning as the income of entrepreneurs not their actually realised profits but their normal profit. Thus, by an excess of saving over investment, we meant that the scale of output was such that entrepreneurs were earning a less than normal profit from their ownership of the capital equipment; and by an increased excess of saving over investment we meant that a decline was taking place in the actual profits, so that they would be under a motive to contract output. The volume of employment and consequently of output and real income is fixed by the entrepreneur under the motive of seeking to maximise its present and prospective profits (the allowance for user cost being determined by his view as to the use of equipment which will maximise his return from it over its whole life); whilst the volume of employment which will maximise his profit depends on the aggregate demand function given by his expectations of the sum of the proceeds resulting from consumption and investment respectively on various hypotheses. The concept of changes in the excess of investment over saving, as defined in Treatise on Money, was a way of handling changes in profit, though Keynes did not in that book distinguish clearly between expected and realised results. He there argued that change in the excess of investment over saving was the motive force governing changes in the volume of output.

The expectation of an increased excess of investment over saving, given the former volume of em ployment and output, will induce entrepreneurs to increase the volume of employment and output. The significance of these arguments lies in its attempt to show that the volume of employment is determined by the estimates of effective demand made by the entrepreneurs, an expected increase of investment relatively to saving as defined in Treatise on Money, being a criterion of an increase in effective demand.

D.H. Robertson has defined today's income as being equal to yesterday's consumption plus investment, so that today's saving is equal to yesterday's investment plus the excess of yesterday's consumption over today's consumption. On this definition, saving can exceed investment, namely, by the excess of yesterday's income over today's income. Thus, when Robertson says that there is an excess of saving over investment, he means literally the same thing as Keynes when he say that income is falling, and the excess of saving in his sense is exactly equal to the decline of income in Keynesian sense. If it were true that current expectations were always determined by yesterday's realised results, today's effective demand would be equal to yesterday's income. Thus, Robertson's method might be regarded as an alternative attempt to Keynesian (being, perhaps, a first approximation to it) to make the same distinction, so vital for causal analysis, that Keynes had tried to make by the contrast between effective demand and income.

The prevalence of the idea that saving and investment, taken in their straightforward sense, can differ from one another, is to be explained by an optical illusion due to regarding an individual depositor's relation to his bank as being a one-sided transaction, instead of seeing it as the two-sided transaction, which it actually is. It is supposed that a depositor and his bank can somehow contrive between them to perform an operation by which savings can disappear into the banking system so that they are lost to investment, or, contrariwise, that the banking system can make it possible for investment to occur, to which no saving corresponds. But no one can save without acquiring an asset, whether it be cash or a debt or capital goods; and no one can acquire an asset which he did not previously possess, unless either an asset of equal value is newly produced or someone else parts with an asset of that value which he previously had.

In the first alternative there is a corresponding new investment; in the second alternative someone else must be dis-saving an equal sum. For his loss of wealth must be due to his consumption exceeding his income, and not to a loss on capital account through a change in the value of a capital asset, since it is not a case of his suffering a loss of value which his asset formerly had; he is duly receiving the current value of his asset and yet is not relating this value in wealth of any form, i.e. he must be spending it on current consumption in excess of current income. Moreover, if it is the banking system, which parts with an asset, someone must be parting with cash. It implies that the aggregate saving of the first individual and of others taken together must necessarily be equal to the amount of current new investment.

The creation of credit by the banking system allows investment to take place to which 'no genuine saving' corresponds can only be the result of isolating one of the consequences of the increased bank credit to the exclusion of the others. If the grant of a bank credit to an entrepreneur additional to the credits already existing allows him to make an addition to current investment, which would not have occurred otherwise, incomes will necessarily be increased and at a rate which will normally exceed the rate of increased investment. Moreover, except in conditions of full employment, there will be an increase of real income as well as of money-income. The public will exercise a free choice as to the portion in which they divide their increase of income between saving and spending; and it is impossible that the intention of the entrepreneur who has borrowed in order to increase investment can become effective at a faster rate than the public decide to increase their savings. Moreover, the savings, which result from this decision, are just as genuine as any other savings.

An unexpected increase of investment in a particular direction may cause an irregularity in the rate of aggregate saving and investment, which would not have occurred if it has been sufficiently foreseen. The grant of the bank-credit will set up three tendencies:

(a) for output to increase,

(b) for the marginal product to rise in value in terms of the wage unit, and

(c) for the wage unit to rise in terms of money.

These tendencies may affect the distribution of real income between different groups. But, these tendencies are characteristic of a state of increasing output as such, and will occur just as much if the increase in output has been initiated otherwise than by an increase in bank credit.

Thus, the old fashioned view that saving always involves investment, though incomplete and misleading, is formally sounder than the newfangled view that there can be saving without investment or investment without genuine saving. The error lies in proceeding to the plausible inference that, when an individual saves, he will increase aggregate investment by an equal amount. It is true, that, when an individual saves he increases his own wealth. But the conclusion that he also increases aggregate wealth fails to allow for the possibility that an act of individual saving may react on someone else's savings and hence on someone else's wealth. The reconciliation of the identity between saving and investment with the apparent 'free-will' of the individual to save what he chooses irrespective of what he or others may be investing, essentially depends on saving being, like spending, a two sided affair. For although the amount of his own saving is unlikely to have any significant influence on his own income, the reactions of the amount of his consumption on the incomes of others makes it impossible for all individuals simultaneously to save any given sums. Every such attempt to save more by reducing consumption will so affect incomes that the attempt necessarily defeats itself. It is, of course, just as impossible for the community as a whole to save less than the amount of current investment, since the attempt to do so will necessarily raise incomes to a level at which the sums which individuals choose to save add up to a figure exactly equal to the amount of investment.

EQUALITY OF SAVING AND INVESTMENT

It has already been shown that equilibrium income is determined at the point where aggregate demand and aggregate supply are equal. However, the equilibrium condition can be stated in an another alternative way: Equilibrium level of income will be determined where saving and investment are equal. The equality of saving and investment can be easily seen. Saving depends on income, i.e., Saving is a positive function of income. Income is, however, the aggregation of consumption and investment. That is the expenditure side of income determination is summarised in the equation

$$Y = C + I \qquad \text{...(6.1)}$$

and income received approach is summarized in the following equation:

$$Y = C + S \quad ...(6.2)$$

Since the left hand sides of equations (6.1) and (6.2) are equal the right hand side must also be equated.

Thus,

$$C + S = C + I \quad ...(6.3)$$

After eliminating C from the both side of equation (6.3), we get

$$S = I \quad ...(6.4)$$

Equation (6.4) says that if income and expenditure in the economy have to be equal, saving and investment must also be equal.

The equality of saving and investment is an intricate and most puzzling aspect of income determination. Hence, one must be very careful in understanding this concept which occupies a fundamental position in the theory of income determination. Most of the time this confusion is the result of a failure of making a distinction between identity and equilibrium conditions. $Y = C + I$ and, $Y = C + S$, which have been written above as equations (6.1) and (6.2) are identities. An identity is a relation which is true by definition. Thus total expenditure is composed of consumption expenditure and investment expenditure. It is so, because it is defined that way. If the situation demanded, it could have been defined in any other way. Thus another identity would have been written. On the other hand, an equilibrium condition states a relation, which is not true by definition but becomes true when certain conditions are fulfilled, i.e., it becomes true when equilibrium is achieved.

In the national income accounting identity, saving refers to cash income saved and investment refers to expenditure on real capital goods. The identity derives from the fact that any expenditure on investment must be financed by saving somewhere in the system, and any income saved must be invested somewhere in the system. The financial system operates as the intermediary by channelling savings into investment. It is important also to realise that the identity is between both planned and unplanned savings and investment. For example, if a firm purchase a stock of goods it intends to sell, but is unable to do so, then this would be counted an unplanned inventory investment.

Suppose that a constant proportional income tax rate t, and that a constant average proportion of pre-tax income c, is consumed, and a constant average proportion of pre-tax income $s = 1 - c - t$ is saved (so that $c + s + t = 1$)), and let G be government expenditure on all goods and I be private investment expenditure. The national income accounting identity can then be expressed as

$$C + I + G = cY + I + G = Y$$

or,

$$cY + I + G = Y(c + s + t) \qquad ...(6.5)$$

The government budget surplus B is given as

$$B = tY - G \qquad ...(6.6)$$

Combining equation (6.5) and equation (6.6) we have

$$I = sY + B \qquad ...(6.7)$$

This identity tells us that private sector investment is equal to private saving plus government saving. A budget surplus implies government saving because the government is raising more in tax revenue that it is spending. The government must be using this surplus to pay off debt, so it is buying bonds and other assets from the private sector. The money it is giving to the private sector to purchase back this government debt (or build up government asset holdings), is being either consumed or invested. Since we have assumed that consumption is a constant proportion of income/output, private sector consumption will not increase despite the increase in government saving provided the economy remains at potential output so that Y remains unchanged after the tightening of the budget.

An improvement in the government budget surplus therefore implies an increase in private sector investment, if private sector consumption, savings and overall output remain unchanged. This is obvious when we consider from the perspective of aggregate supply that the only way to make room for more I at full employment when C is fixed so that $\overline{Y} = \overline{C} + \overline{I} + \overline{G}$ is to make G smaller and thus improve the government budget surplus.

Note that if Y is below potential output $\overline{Y}$ then, given a particular government spending level (fixed G) and saving rate, investment $I = sY + B$ must be below potential investment $\overline{I} = s\overline{Y} + \overline{B}$

(higher output will also improve the government budget position by increasing tax revenues). It is therefore not the case by identity that actual savings and investment equal potential savings and investment. It is also, as we have seen, not the case by identity that desired savings equal desired investment. We do not have to be at the intersection of the demand and supply curves for saving for the identity to apply; we can be anywhere on the diagram because actual saving always equals actual investment, even when the market is in disequilibrium. To say that the equality of saving and investment is an equilibrium condition implies more than that actual (planned and unplanned) savings equal actual (planned and unplanned) investment. It refers to a microeconomic equilibrium in the sense that interest rates have brought savings and investment into lines so that desired savings equal desired investment. The equality between desired savings and investment is a property of the equilibrium in terms of the Keynesian multiplier model. However, when output is away from its potential value, the interpretation of the equilibrium of the Keynesian multiplier model must be that some markets in the economy are distorted from their competitive equilibria, leading to inefficiencies in many different markets.

The interpretation of $\bar{Y}$ in the Keynesian neo-classical synthesis model is the level of output, which would pertain if the labour market were in equilibrium. In this special case, then, the quality of savings and investment is part of a general equilibrium in the microeconomic sense. However, when output is away from its potential level, the equality of savings and investment is only a partial equilibrium in the microeconomic sense. If there is 'excess' unemployment then savings and investment must be away from their true general equilibrium levels.

The relationship described in equation (6.4) is an identity as well as an equilibrium condition. However, it does not play a significant role in income determination, as an identity but as an equilibrium condition. To understand the dual role of saving and investment, let us first understand the concepts of desired and realised magnitudes of savings and investment.

DESIRED AND REALISED SAVING AND INVESTMENT

To begin with let us state that we must distinguish between four concepts: desired saving, desired investment, realised saving, and realised investment. Thus, both saving and investment have two set of magnitudes—desired and realised. Let us also state that desired is used here in the same meaning as expected or anticipated. Similarly, realised means actual. Some writers prefer to use the term *ex-ante* for desired and *ex-post* for realised or actual. Thus, we must always remember that

ex-ante = desired = expected = anticipated = intended, and
ex-post = realised = actual

It may also be clear just by the choice and nature of words that desired magnitude of some variable points to the future and realised to the past. Thus, by realised saving, we mean the level or amount which was actually saved in a given period. Similarly, realised investment refers to the amount which was actually invested.

In an accounting sense, saving and investment are always equal. Income which is received but not consumed, is saved and invested. Thus, net investment and saving are equal to each other. This is an identity which refers only to realised saving and realised investment.

$$S^R = I^R \qquad \text{...(6.8)}$$

However, the equality between the desired saving and desired investment is not so easily achieved.

$$S^d = I^d \qquad \text{...(6.9)}$$

Equation (6.9) is an equilibrium condition. There is no reason why desired saving and desired investment would always be equal. On the other hand, it is more likely that there would be discrepancy between desired saving and desired investment. The desired level of saving is the amount which the individuals would like to save at any level of income. Similarly, desired level of investment is the amount which the investors would like to invest under some given condition. It is not difficult to see that the groups of savers (individuals who save) and investors (individuals and firms who invest) are not the same in a modern economy.

Saving is done mostly by the households depending upon their level of income. They do not know how much investors are planning to invest in the next periods. Similarly, investors are also not aware that what amount of saving would be forthcoming in the next period and be available for investment. They have to take their investment decisions about the next period right here and now. Hence the investment decisions are not dependent upon savings. Thus, the discrepancy between desired saving and desired investment is in the logic of things. The equality between ex-ante saving and investment shall not come automatically. However, if the system works in a certain manner this equality may be achieved. That is why the equality of desired saving and desired investment is taken as an equilibrium condition as described in equation (6.9).

To understand its working, let us assume that net investment takes the form of changes in inventories. (Inventory means stock of goods for sale.) If desired saving is greater than desired investment then actual investment will be greater than desired investment. This is because desired savings will instantaneously be translated into actual saving. Since actual saving and actual investment are always equal, the actual investment will be greater than desired savings. Symbolically, this can be shown as follows:

$$S^d > I^d$$

$$I^a > I^d$$

$$I^a = S^a$$

$$I^a > S^d$$

$$I^u = I^d - I^a \qquad ...(6.10)$$

where I^u is the unintended investment, which is the difference between actual investment and desired investment.

This is obvious from equation (6.10) that when actual investment becomes equal to desired investment, the unintended investment is zero. Similarly, when desired investment exceeds actual investment, then unintended investment is negative. Thus, in a situation where desired saving is greater than desired investment, the goods will not be sold and investors would like to cut down the production in order to meet this situation. Consequently, income would decline. Since saving is function of income, desired saving will also decline with the decline in income to the extent that desired saving and investment become equal and unintended investment becomes zero.

If the level of desired saving is less than desired investment, there would be a deficiency of inventories. It means that there is demand for more goods by the households and entrepreneurs are not keeping up the supply with the demand. This will encourage the entrepreneurs to increase the production which will raise the level of income. The desired saving will also rise with rising income to the extent that desired investment and desired saving become equal.

Thus, the equilibrium condition of income determination can be stated either in terms of equality of aggregate demand and aggregate supply or equality of desired saving and investment.

AN ALTERNATIVE TREATMENT OF INCOME DETERMINATION

The process of equality between the desired saying and desired investment described above can also be used to illustrate income determination. In Figure 6.1 income has been measured along the horizontal axis. It is assumed, as before, that level of investment is given exogenously and is constant with the level of income. In terms of Figure 6.1, OG amount is invested irrespective of level of income. Note that this is also the level of desired investment. Since it remains constant, it has been depicted in the figure as a line parallel to the horizontal axis. The saving function S is given by the line $S = -a + (1 - b)Y$, where $-a$ is the intercept and $(1 - b)$ is the slope of saving function. When income is Y_1, desired level of saving $AY_1 = OB$ is less than desired level of investment which is OG. Thus, unintended investment is negative. At this stage, inventories are deficient and there is unsatisfied demand. In other words, aggregate demand is more than aggregate supply. Consequently, production would expand and income would rise. Thus, we move along the horizontal axis from left to the right. With increase in income, saving also rises and we move along the saving function S from the point D and onwards. As we reach the income level OY_2, the desired level of saving is OC but desired level of investment is

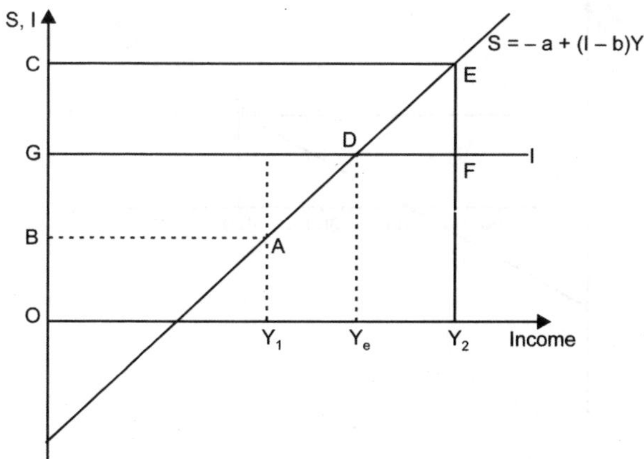

Fig. 6.1: Income Determination by Equality of Saving and Investment.

only OG. Now desired saving exceeds desired investment. Thus unintended investment takes place and its magnitude is equal to EF or GC. The inventories would be piled up. Consequently, entrepreneurs would begin reducing production. Thus OY_2 level of income cannot be sustained and income would start falling.

The equilibrium level of income would be determined at the point D where the income level is OY_e. At this level of income, desired saving is OC and desired investment is also OC. Both are equal. The amount of unintended investment is zero at this level of income. Consequently, there would be no tendency in the aggregate demand to change and thus equilibrium would be established.

The aggregate demand and aggregate supply approach and saving investment approach would give the same solution to equilibrium income determination.

This can be easily seen with the help of example of our hypothetical economy. This has been done in the Figure 6.2. The saving function of our hypothetical economy is S = –50 + 0.25 *Y* where –50 is the intercept and 0.25 is the slope. The level of investment is 50 which remains constant at all levels of income. At income levels less than 400 desired saving is less than desired investment as the saving line is below investment line. So income would tend to rise at income levels lower than 400. At income levels higher than 400 desired saving exceeds desired investment as saving line is above the investment line. Thus, income would tend to

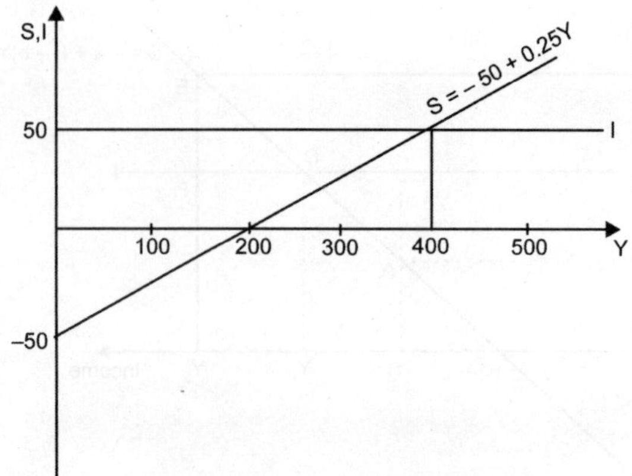

Fig. 6.2: Alternative Approach to Income Determination in a Hypothetical Economy.

decline for the reasons mentioned above. The equilibrium level of income is determined when income is 400. At this level of income, saving line intersects investment line. This is the equilibrium level of income because desired saving and desired investment become equal here.

The same process of income determination is depicted in Table 6.1 when income is 100, saving is –25 and desired investment is 50. When income rises to 200, saving is zero and desired investment is 50. Since desired saving is much less the desired investment, unintended investment is negative.

Table 6.1: Saving Investment and Income Determination in a Hypothetical Economy

Y	S	I	Unintended Investments
100	–25	50	–75
200	0	50	–50
300	25	50	–25
400	50	50	0
500	75	50	25

Aggregate demand is more than aggregate supply and income keeps on rising. If income rises to 500, saving rises to 75 but desired investment is 50 only. Hence the amount of unintended investment occurring at this level of income would be 25. There will be unsold stocks of goods. Consequently, equilibrium level of income would be determined at 400 where desired saving and desired investment both are 50 and unintended investment would be zero.

CHANGES IN INVESTMENT

It has been assumed so far that investment is exogenous. We still retain that assumption, but allow for exogenous changes in the level of investment. Such exogenous changes in investment may occur due to discovery of some new technique of production, a new market or a new product. The entrepreneurs would like to take the advantage of new production possibilities and enhance their exogenous investment. Let us assume that this is a permanent change in net investment. Initially, this will cause a disequilibrium as desired investment would exceed actual investment which in turn is equal to desired saving and investment. The inventories held by producers fall below the desired level as the households maintain their old levels of consumption. Thus, to raise the inventories up to the desired levels, entrepreneurs increase their production which increase in income. The desired savings also rise because of increase in income and once again equilibrium between desired saving and desired investment is achieved.

The changes in investment and its impact upon aggregate demand are shown in Figure 6.3. As before, income is shown on the horizontal axis and consumption and investment expenditure on the vertical axis. The C-line represents consumption function which has the break-even point at the point A where it intersects 45° line. The old aggregate demand line is shown by C + I line which intersects 45° line at the point B. The original equilibrium level of income is determined at this point. The vertical distance between C-line and C + I line shows the original level of investment.

Now, let us suppose that exogenous investment changes and there is an increase in investment. This is shown as the vertical distance between C + I + ΔI line and C + I line where ΔI is the change in investment. The increased level of investment pushes the aggregate demand line upward (i.e. aggregate demand is increased). The new aggregate demand line is depicted whereas C + I + ΔI line which intersects the 45° line at C. As it has been said before that 45° line represents a suppressed aggregate supply line, aggregate demand and aggregate supply are again equal at the point C and new equilibrium level of income Y_1 is determined at this point. The difference between Y_1 and Y_0 is ΔY, the increase in income as a result of change in investment, ΔI.

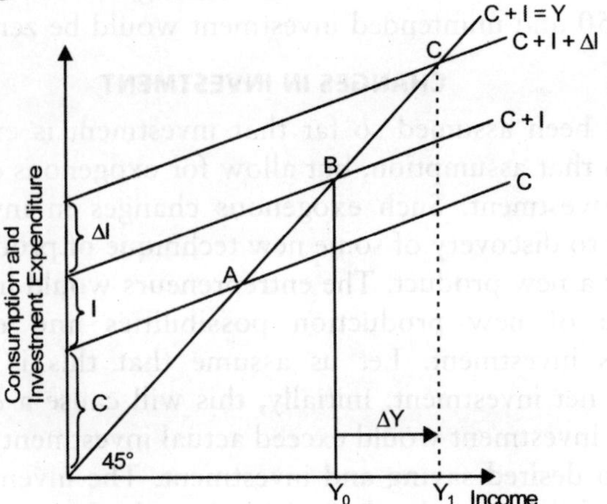

Fig. 6.3: The Effect of a Change in Investment upon Aggregate Demand.

It should be kept in mind that increase in investment can cause income to rise only in case aggregate supply function is Keynesian. Only in this case, an underemployment equilibrium exists and idle resources are available. These idle resources are put to use with the new investment and more income is generated. This is illustrated in Figure 6.4 in which income is measured along the horizontal axis and price level is measured along the vertical axis. Aggregate supply function is represented by the curve AS. As full employment income Y is achieved aggregate supply curve becomes perfectly inelastic with respect to price level. When aggregate demand is at the level AD_0, income is Y_0. When there is a given increase in exogenous investment the AD curve shifts to the right. New level of aggregate demand is AD_1 and new level of income is Y_1.

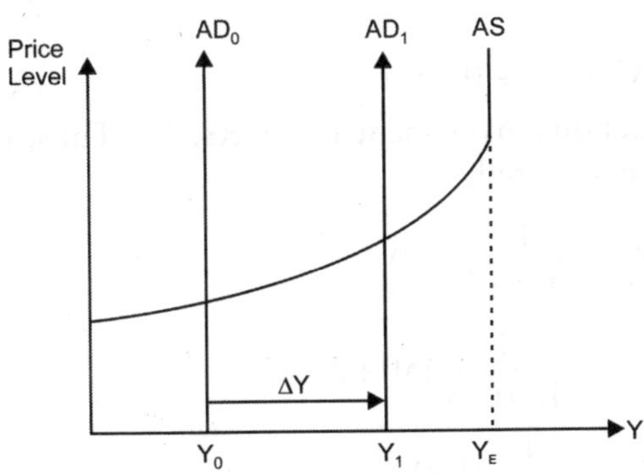

Fig. 6.4: Change in Aggregate Demand.

The new level of equilibrium can be determined algebraically also. We have new level of aggregate demand

$$Y_1 = C + I + \Delta I \qquad \text{...(6.11)}$$

where,

ΔI = increase in investment.

The consumption will now be a function of new level of income,

$$C = a + bY_1 \qquad \text{...(6.12)}$$

Substituting equation (6.12) into equation (6.11) we get

$$Y_1 = a + bY_1 + I + \Delta I$$

$$Y_1 - bY_1 = a + I + \Delta I$$

$$(1 - b)\, Y_1 = a + I + \Delta I$$

$$Y_1 = \frac{1}{1-b}(a + I + \Delta I) \qquad \text{...(6.13)}$$

Y_1 is new equilibrium level of income. Let us recall that original level of equilibrium is

$$Y_0 = \frac{1}{1-b}(a+I) \qquad ...(6.14)$$

The change in income will be

$$Y_1 - Y_0 = \frac{1}{1-b}(a + I + \Delta I) - \frac{1}{1-b}(a + I)$$

$$\Delta Y = \frac{1}{1-b}(\Delta I) \qquad ...(6.15)$$

A NUMERICAL EXAMPLE

In case of our hypothetical economy, the consumption function was

$$C = 50 + 0.75\ Y$$

and the exogenous investment I was Rs. 50. Thus, original level of income was calculated.

$$Y_0 = \frac{1}{1-b}(a+I)$$

$$Y_0 = \frac{1}{1-0.75}(50+50)$$

$$Y_0 = \frac{1}{0.25}(100)$$

$$Y_0 = 400$$

Let us now assume that investment rises by Rs. 25. Thus, new level of equilibrium income would be

$$Y_1 = \frac{1}{1-b}(a+I+\Delta I)$$

$$= \frac{1}{1-0.75}(50+50+25)$$

$$= \frac{1}{0.25}(125)$$

$$= 500.$$

Thus, change in income is Rs. 100 when investment rises by Rs. 25.

MULTIPLIER PRINCIPLE

The conception of the multiplier was first introduced into economic theory by R.F. Kahn in his article on "The Relation of Home Investment to Unemployment" (*Economic Journal*, June 1931). His argument in this article depends on the fundamental notion that, if the propensity to consume in various hypothetical circumstances is (together with certain other conditions) taken as given and we conceive the monetary or other public authority to take steps to stimulate or to retard investment, the change in the amount of employment will be a function of the net change in the amount of investment; and it aimed at laying down general principles by which to estimate the actual quantitative relationship between an increment of net investment and the increment of aggregate employment which will be associated with it.

The cumulatively reinforcing induced interaction between consumption, production, factor payments, and income that amplifies autonomous changes in investment, government spending, exports, taxes, or other shocks to the macroeconomy. The multiplier principle is so named because relatively small autonomous changes generate relatively larger, or multiple, induced changes in aggregate production. This principle is commonly represented by a multiplier, which is a specific number with a value greater than one.

The essence of the multiplier principle is that relatively small changes in autonomous expenditures or other shocks cause relatively large overall changes in aggregate production and income. The multiplier principle works because a change in autonomous expenditures triggers a change in aggregate production, factor payments, and income, which then induces changes in other expenditures, especially consumption. These induced expenditures cause further changes in aggregate production, factor payments, and income, which induce further changes in expenditures. The process is cumulative and reinforcing.

The multiplier principle is a direct implication of Keynesian economics. The key to the multiplier principle is induced expenditures, which depend on aggregate production and income, especially induced consumption expenditures. Induced consumption expenditure, as capture by the marginal propensity to consume, are the cornerstone of Keynesian economics.

Assumptions of the Multiplier Theory

The concept of multiplier is based on the following assumptions:

(a) The new higher level of investment is maintained long enough for the completion of the adjustment process.

(b) There is no induced investment, *i.e.* the accelerator is inoperative.

(c) There is no change in the marginal propensity to consume during the adjustment process.

(d) The output of consumer goods is responsive to effective demand for these.

Let us briefly discuss each of these assumptions one by one.

If the rate of investment suffers a decline before the completion of the adjustment process, income would experience a downturn before it could touch the equilibrium level corresponding to the rate of investment attained as a result of the stimulating increment of investment. Investment must, therefore, be maintained at the higher level long enough to attain the increment of income suggested by the multiplier.

The initial (autonomous) increment of investment and the resultant multiplication of income are very likely to have induced effects on investment owing to a number of reasons:

(a) Increase in demand for consumer goods would require an increase in output that would involve induced investment first in working capital and later in fixed capital. And according to the acceleration principle such induced increase in investment would be more than proportionate to the increase in output which induced it.

(b) The improved business outlook, and the prospect of a rise in the price of capital goods, may induce businessmen to carry out overdue replacement and renewal of plant. Further, businessmen may start enlarging their stock in anticipation of larger turnover and higher prices. Both these developments would increase the rate of investment.

(c) If the initial autonomous investment takes the form of an accelerated programme of public investment, it may involve unbalanced budgets and a growing public debt. This might adversely affect confidence and thus discourage private investment.

(d) The expansionary process generated by the initial autonomous investment may lead to a rise in the interest rates. If the banking system is unable to expand credit adequately, the increase in the transaction demand for money resulting from a higher level of income may reduce the amount available for satisfying the liquidity demand for money and thus raise the rate of interest. A rise in the rate of interest would tend to discourage private investment. The rate of interest, however, can also move in the reverse direction. If the expansionary process causes price rises, which are expected to continue, the liquidity demand for money might decrease leading to a decline in the interest rate. Similar would be the result if the banking section responds to expansion by new credit creation that more than offsets the increase in the transactions demand for money. The decline in the rate of interest might encourage private investment.

(e) The assumption of an absence of induced changes in investment is still more untenable in an open economy. In an open economy, part of the additional income may be spent on additional imports. If there is no induced increase in exports, the induced increase in imports will represent a corresponding decline in net foreign investment. The original increment of investment would be offset to the extent of this decline; in other words, the multiplicand will be reduced by this amount. But it is very likely that there would be some induced increase in exports also. Decline in the net foreign investment of the country undertaking the initial increment of investment means an equivalent increase in the net foreign investment of other countries. This sets into operation the multiplier process into those countries. The resulting higher levels of economic activity and income in these countries are likely to increase their imports from the first country. The initial increment of investment in a given country is thus offset, in relation to the multiplier effect, only to the extent of the excess of induced increase of imports over the increase of exports. Thus, when the original increment of investment induces changes in private domestic investment or net foreign investment, such changes must be taken into account in determining the total effect of the former on income.

The assumption of unchanged marginal propensity to consume may also not hold good in actual practice. Because of differences in the distribution of income, the marginal propensity to consume differs from person to person and from class to class. Thus, the marginal propensity to consume of the community as a whole depends, *inter alia*, on the distribution of national income. It would, therefore, remain unchanged only if the multiplication of income leaves unchanged the pattern of the income distribution. However, it is seldom true in actual practice, particularly when the changes in investment and income involved are large.

The multiplier is the ratio of increase in real income to the stimulating increase in the real investment. It can be greater than unity only if the increase in money investment associated with the increment of real investment stimulates, in response to the chain reaction of increased consumer spending thus generated, larger output of consumer goods. In case, the output of consumer goods does not respond to increase in the effective demand for it, the multiplier effect will just be dissipated in inflationary price changes.

The following are likely in a modern community to be the factors, which are most important not to overlook in the multiplier process.

(a) The method of financing the policy and the increased working cash, required by the increased employment and the associated rise of prices, may have the effect of increasing the rate of interest and so retarding investment in other directions, unless the monetary authority takes steps to the contrary; whilst, at the same time, the increased cost of capital goods will reduce their marginal efficiency to the private investor, and this will require an actual fall in the rate of interest to offset it.

(b) With the confused psychology that often prevails, the Government programme may, though its effect on 'confidence', increase liquidity preference or diminish the marginal efficiency of capital, which, again, may retard other investment unless measures are taken to offset it.

(c) In an open system with foreign trade relations, some part of the multiplier of the increased investment will accrue to the benefit of employment in foreign countries, since a proportion of the increased consumption will diminish our own country's favourable foreign balance; so that, if we consider only the effect on domestic employment as distinct from world employment, we must diminish the full figure of the multiplier. On the other hand, our own country may recover a portion of this leakage through favourable repercussions due to the action of the multiplier in the foreign country in increasing its economic activity.

If we consider a change of substantial amount, we have to allow for a progressive change in the marginal propensity to consume, as the position of the margin is gradually shifted; and hence in the multiplier. The marginal propensity to consume is not constant for all levels of employment, and it is probable that there will be a tendency for it to diminish as employment increases. When real income increases, the community will wish to consume a gradually diminishing proportion of it.

The increase of employment will tend, owing to the effect of diminishing returns in the short period, to increase the proportion of aggregate income, which accrues to the entrepreneurs, whose individual marginal propensity to consume is probably less than the average for the community as a whole. In the second place, unemployment is likely to be associated with negative saving in certain quarters, private or public, because the unemployment may be living either on the savings of themselves and their friends or on public relief which is partly financed out of loans; with the result that re-employment will gradually diminish these particular acts of negative saving and reduce, therefore, the marginal propensity to consume more rapidly than would have occurred from an equal increase in the country's real income accruing in different circumstances. In any case, the multiplier is likely to be greater for a small net increment of investment than for a large increment; so that, where substantial changes are in view, we must be guided by the average value of the multiplier based on the average marginal propensity to consume over the range in question.

It is, however, to the general principle of the multiplier to which we have to look for an explanation of how fluctuations in the amount of investment, which are a comparatively small proportion of the national income, are capable of generating fluctuations in aggregate employment and income so much greater in amplitude than themselves.

The multiplier principle is best illustrated using the circular flow model of the economy. The circular flow is a model of the continuous production, factor payment, income, and expenditure interaction among the four major sectors (household, business, government, and foreign), that takes place through the three aggregate macroeconomic markets (product, resource, and financial). The circular flow is likely to experience several additional rounds of aggregate production, factor payments, income, and consumption expenditures. Each subsequently round, however, is smaller than the previous round, meaning that the process eventually winds down to infinitely small values. But with each round, additional aggregate production is generated.

Calculation of Multipliers

To understand how multipliers are calculated, we have to know the meaning of direct, indirect and induced effects of the multiplier.

(a) Direct effects are those occurring to the firm that exports additional goods or services.

(b) Indirect effects occur to industries in the backward linked industries that supply the exporting firm.

(c) Induced effects result from households spending some of the additional income they receive in the local area.

To illustrate the three effects, we shall consider an example of Atlantic Publishers and Distributors.

The company got an order from books sellers for additional books worth Rs. 10 million. Because of new orders, the company must add workers and spend additional money for transportation services, utilities and other production needs. Atlantic's expenditure for the additional production inputs used in manufacturing the books sellers order are referred to as 'direct effects'. Direct effects are production changes required to produce the product.

Atlantic's additional spending triggers a series of chain reactions, or spin-off effects. Logging companies and businesses, which supply Atlantic with raw materials and services, must increase their production to meet Atlantic's needs. Likewise, the increase in sales of Atlantic's suppliers generates more business for the firms that supply them. These effects are referred to as 'indirect effects' and occur in the backward linked industries. Indirect effects result from production changes in industries that supply the firm where the changes was initiated.

Each rupee of employee income earned in the direct and indirect activities triggers an additional chain of spending. This spin-off effect is referred to as an 'induced effect', which is sometimes called the consumption effect. The worker hired by Atlantic to fill the order for books sellers earn new income as do the new workers hired to supply Atlantic's increased needs. Induced effects occur as households spend some of their additional income on goods and services in the local community. The increased production of Atlantic generates additional income, some of which is spent on goods and services within the community, thus increasing the multiplier effect.

A multiplier is a simple ratio. Most multipliers are calculated as

$$\text{Multiplier} = \frac{\text{Total change}}{\text{Initial change}}$$

We often read or hear about Type I and Type II multipliers. This is economic jargon for identifying which effects are included when calculating the multiplier. Type I multipliers include the direct and indirect effects. The indirect effects are those associated with changes in the backward linked industries due to an increase in demand from the directly affected industry. Therefore, Type I multipliers are calculated as follows:

$$\text{Type I Multiplier} = \frac{(\text{Direct} + \text{Indirect Effects})}{\text{Direct Effects}}$$

A Type III multiplier (sometimes referred to as Type II) includes the direct, indirect and induced effects. It includes the effect on the backward linked industries as well as the induced or consumption effect. Type III multipliers are similar to Type II multipliers, except the method of calculating the induced effects are different. Type III multipliers are calculated as follows:

$$\text{Type III Multiplier} = \frac{(\text{Direct} + \text{Indirect} + \text{Induced Effects})}{\text{Direct Effects}}$$

Economic multipliers provide estimates of the total impact resulting from an initial change in economic output (final demand). The higher the multiplier, the greater the effect on the local economy.

Investment Multiplier

Simple multipliers are those, which involve but one marginal relationship. The most important of them are the investment multiplier and the consumption multiplier. The first has gained great prominence on account of its introduction by Keynes; and the second is a symmetric counterpart of the first.

Keynes was concerned to focus on domestic investment as a critical macro-economic variable. Investment is what drives the economy, and where entrepreneurs judge that future aggregate demand will weaken, they will hesitate to invest. Thus, entrepreneurial expectations about aggregate demand work through investment and become a self-fulfilling prophecy. In consequence, the economy can remain 'stuck' at less than full employment.

Let C be the rate of consumption, I the rate of investment, and Y the national income per unit of time. Therefore, we have

Consumption function, $C = C(Y)$

Marginal propensity to consume, $C' = C'(Y)$

Investment function, $I = I(Y)$

Marginal propensity to invest, $I' = I'(Y)$

From the relation $Y = C + I$, we have

$$\frac{dC}{dY} + \frac{dI}{dY} = 1$$

When, if I is a free variable and $C = C(Y)$,

$$\frac{dY}{dI} = \frac{1}{1 - C'} \qquad \text{...(6.16)}$$

And, if C is a free variable and $I = I(Y)$,

$$\frac{dY}{dC} = \frac{1}{1 - I'} \qquad \text{...(6.17)}$$

Equation (6.16) gives the investment multiplier, which is equal to the reciprocal of the marginal propensity to save; and equation (6.17) gives the consumption multiplier, which is equal to the marginal reluctance to invest.

These two multipliers can also be obtained, by the Kahn-Clark method, as sums of infinite geometric progression, namely

$$\frac{dY}{dI} = 1 + C' + (C')^2 + \dots \dots \qquad \dots(6.18)$$

and

$$\frac{dY}{dC} = 1 + I' + (I')^2 + \dots \dots \qquad \dots(6.19)$$

If $|C'| < 1$ or $|I'| < 1$, these sums are equal to the expressions (6.16) and (6.17), respectively. The first condition is implied in the well-established empirical fact $0 < C' < 1$; the second condition holds when the system is stable. The stability condition of the system is $C' + I' < 1$, which, given $0 < C' < 1$, implies $0 < I' < 1$.

The interpretation of the consumption multiplier is similar to that of the investment multiplier. The consumption multiplier indicates the marginal effect upon national income of an increase in the rate of consumption in the same way as the investment multiplier indicates the marginal effect upon national income of an increase in the rate of investment. Thus,

$$dY = \frac{1}{1 - C'} dI$$

and

$$dY = \frac{1}{1 - I'} dC$$

the multiplicand dI or dC, respectively, indicates the total increment in the rate of investment or in the rate of consumption in the economy. As a rule, any initial autonomous increment in investment leads to (positive or negative) additional investments, which are induced by the increase in national income resulting from the increase in consumption generated by the initial investment. In a similar way, any autonomous increment in consumption leads to induced additional consumption, due to the increase in national income resulting from the increase in investment generated by the initial increase in consumption. The multiplicands dI and dC have to be interpreted as representing not the initial increment in I or C, but the total increment, which includes all induced increments, in addition to the initial one. This imposes a serious limitation upon the practical application of the multipliers given by equation (6.16) and equation (6.17).

The same limitation of multiplier arises with regard to the effect upon national income of an initial increment in government consumption expenditure (e.g. for relief, or for the armed forces). The multiplicand dC includes, in addition to the increase in the government's expenditure, all the induced increases in private consumption. Unless the latter are already known, dC cannot be calculated and the multiplier formula $\frac{1}{1-I'}$ is of no practical use.

The difficulty mentioned above can, however, be overcome by means of an extension of the multiplier technique, which leads to multipliers which involve two or more marginal relationships. Such multipliers will be called compound multipliers.

Compound multipliers: Let dI_0 be an initial autonomous increment in the rate of investment. This implies an equal increase in the national income and leads to induced consumption equal to $C'dI_0$ and to induced investment equal to $I'dI_0$. The result is an induced increase in income $(C' + I')\, dI_0$, which, in turn, leads to a further induced increase in income $(C' + I')\,(C' + I')\, dI_0$. The total increase in national income is thus,

$$dY = [1 + (C' + I') + (C' + I')^2 + \dots \dots]dI_0$$

and the compound investment multiplier is

$$\frac{dY}{dI_0} = \frac{1}{(1-(C'+I')}, \text{ provided } |C' + I'| < 1. \qquad \dots(6.20)$$

An initial autonomous increment dC_0 in the rate of consumption implies an equal increase in the national income and leads, through induced investment and consumption, to further increments in income $(C' + I')dC_0$, $(C' + I')\,(C' + I')\, dC_0$, etc. Thus, we have

$$dY = [1 + (C' + I') + (C' + I')^2 + \dots]dC_0$$

and, if $|C' + I'| < 1$, the compound consumption multiplier is

$$\frac{dY}{dC_0} = \frac{1}{1-(C'+I')} \qquad \dots(6.21)$$

In equation (6.20) and equation (6.21), dI_0 and dC_0 are the autonomous increment in investment or consumption, respectively. These multipliers measure the marginal effect of such an autonomous increment upon the national income and can thus be used for the problems mentioned in the preceding section, for which the simple multiplier formula proved inadequate. Induced investment and consumption are not included in the multiplicands dI_0 and dC_0, but are taken care of by the multiplier formula.

The argument about the alleged negative effect of government spending upon national income can be stated correctly in the form of the statement that the multiplier is negative, if the multiplier meant is the compound multiplier represented by equation (6.20) and equation (6.21). Such a multiplier can be negative, indeed, if the marginal propensity to invest is negative and outweighs the effect of the positive marginal propensity to consume. Such a situation, however, is incompatible with the stability condition of the system. In order that the multiplier be negative, we must have $(1 - (C' + I')) < 0$, while the stability condition requires $(1 - (C' + I')) > 0$. Thus, only in unstable systems can the compound multiplier represented by equation (6.20) or equation (6.21) be negative. In this case, it cannot be finite either, because the convergence condition $|C' + I'| < 1$ is not satisfied in an unstable system.

From equation (6.20) and equation (6.21) we obtain

$$\frac{dY}{dI_0} = \frac{dY}{dC_0} \qquad ...(6.22)$$

i.e., the compound investment multiplier and the compound consumption multiplier are identical. Thus, any given autonomous increment in expenditure has exactly the same effect upon national income, irrespective of whether the expenditure is for investment or for consumption. The identity of the two multipliers suggests combining them into one simple multiplier expressing the marginal relationship between national income and spending. For this we consider $E' = E'(Y) = C' + I'$ as the marginal propensity to spend, and equation (6.20) and equation (6.21) turn into

$$\frac{dY}{dE} = \frac{1}{1 - E'} \qquad ...(6.23)$$

This may be called the spending multiplier. dE is the autonomous increment in the rate of spending. The denominator $1 - E'$ is the marginal reluctance to spend (propensity to hoard). The stability condition can be expressed in the form $1 - E' > 0$, i.e., the reluctance to spend is an increasing function of national income.

A comparison of equation (6.23) with equation (6.16) and (6.17) gives the relation between the simple investment multiplier and the simple consumption multiplier.

Value of the multiplier: We can find out the value of multiplier if we know the value of either marginal propensity to consume (MPC) or marginal propensity to save (MPS).

If MPC = 1/3, we calculate the value of multiplier as shown below:

Multiplier, $$K = \frac{1}{1 - MPC} = \frac{1}{1 - \frac{1}{3}} = \frac{1}{\frac{2}{3}} = \frac{3}{2}$$

The various values of multiplier corresponding to different values of MPC can be worked out as follows:

MPC	0	1/3	1/2	3/4	4/5	9/10	1
Multiplier (K)	1	3/2	2	4	5	10	∞

Employment Multiplier

The significance and potential of any industry can be observed by looking at two important indicators—the output multiplier and the employment multiplier. The output multiplier can be defined as the total increase in output for every unit increase in final demand of a particular sector. The employment multiplier is specified as man-years of additional employment created for a unitary increase in the output of the sector. Both these measures spell out the backward linkages with other sectors of the economy in terms of output and employment effects.

Communities often wish to know the number of jobs that will be created as a result of a new economic activity. The employment multiplier measures the total change in employment resulting from an initial change in employment of an industry. The additional employment in the new activity multiplied by the employment multiplier for the industry provides an estimate of the total new jobs created in the area of study (i.e., country, state or region).

The employment multiplier is the ratio of increase in total employment (N) to the increase in primary employment (N_2) in the same way in which income multiplier is the ratio of increase in income to the increase in primary investment. Thus, the expression for the increase in employment, $\Delta N = K\Delta N_2$, is similar to the expression for increase in income, $\Delta Y = K\Delta I$, where K is the multiplier. Prof. Kahn believed that an initial increase in employment leads to a very large increase in total employment. The discussions on public works recognize that besides the original 'primary' employment in the public works, there will be 'secondary' employment resulting from public works.

The 'secondary' employment is that which occurs in consumption goods industries as a result of the primary employment in investment goods industries. Suppose, for illustration, that 4 lakh people are employed for construction of a canal. The newly employed people would demand more consumer goods, which means greater demand for consumer goods industries. This will lead to additional employment in such industries. The additional workers employed in consumer goods industries would have additional income, part of which will again be spent on consumer goods; this would give a further fillip to secondary employment. Through the repetition of this process, the final total increase in employment would be much greater than the initial increase in employment, which gives rise to the total increase in employment. If the magnitude of the multiplier is 4, an initial employment of 4 lakh workers will result in a total employment of 16 lakh workers.

Prof. Hansen believes that we do not do great violence to the fact if we take employment multiplier (K′) to be equal to investment multiplier (K), though we have no reason to presume them to be equal to each other. To simplify the analysis, we take them identical for practical purposes, particularly in the short period.

Backward Operation of Multiplier

The process of income propagation through multiplier works not only in the forward direction but also in the backward direction depending upon the direction of the initial change in investment. Assuming the marginal propensity to consume equal to 3/4, a decline in investment by Rs. 100 for instance, will result in decline in national income by Rs. 400. The higher the MPC, the larger the value of the multiplier and hence the greater would be the cumulative decline in income. The same, as we have already seen, is true in case of a movement of income in the forward direction. Thus, economies with a higher marginal propensity to consume would be subjected to greater jerks and shocks as a result of changes in investment. The underdeveloped countries in which an overwhelming majority of people live from hand to mouth provide examples of such economies.

DERIVATION OF MULTIPLIER: ALTERNATIVE TECHNIQUE

The multiplier can be derived in the following way.

For equilibrium level of income we can write

$$Y = C + I \quad \text{...(6.24)}$$

Rewriting the equation (6.24) due to changes in the variables i.e., changes in income followed by changes in investment, we can write

$$\Delta Y = \Delta C + \Delta I \quad \text{...(6.25)}$$

In simple Keynesian model of income determination, changes in consumption are function of changes in income considering change in investment as autonomous or independent.

Consumption function,

$$C = a + bY \quad \text{...(6.26)}$$

Where a is a constant term, b is marginal propensity to consume (MPC) assuming as constant. Hence, change in consumption is a function of change in income.

Therefore,

$$\Delta C = b\,\Delta Y \quad \text{...(6.27)}$$

Substituting (6.27) into (6.25), we get

$$\Delta Y = b\,\Delta Y + \Delta I$$

or, $$\Delta Y (1 - b) = \Delta I$$

or, $$\Delta Y = \frac{\Delta I}{(1 - b)}$$

or, $$\frac{\Delta Y}{\Delta I} = \frac{1}{1 - b}$$

or, $$K = \frac{1}{1 - b}$$

or, $$K = \frac{1}{1 - MPC} = \frac{I}{MPS}$$

where $K = \frac{\Delta Y}{\Delta I}$ is the multiplier which is the ratio of change in income and change in investment; b = MPC and MPC + MPS = 1.

This is the same formula of multiplier obtained above. We mention that the value of multiplier $\frac{\Delta Y}{\Delta Y}$ remains same as long as marginal propensity to consume remains the same.

LEAKAGES AND LIMITATIONS OF THE MULTIPLIER

We have seen that whole of the newly created income is not spent and a part of it is saved. Income which is not spent for consumption is known as 'Leakage' in the cumulative income stream. The leakage limits the extent of the total increase in national income. If there were no leakage, that is, if the marginal propensity to consume were one, a small increase in investment would lead to full employment and inflation would start beyond that. But because of leakage, in actual practice, the successive increases in income resulting from a certain initial investment diminish at each stage and, therefore, the final total increase in income is a finite amount. The leakage can take several forms, important of which are stated below:

Debt Cancellation: A part of the income received by people may be used for paying off old debts to banks and individuals, who may, in turn, fail to spend. To this extent, the consumption is not stimulated and the value of the multiplier is correspondingly reduced.

Imports: If imports exceed exports, part of the increased income resulting from increased investment will go abroad and would not, therefore, be available for expenditure within the country. This is particularly true in the short period. In the long period, increased income in foreign countries will increase their demand for exports of the importing country and will thus have favourable effects on the income of the latter country; this effect will, however, not materialise or materialise only partially if imports are restricted in the former countries.

Price Inflation: So long as there exist unemployed productive resources, an increase in investment has expansionary effects, but once the full employment or near full employment level is reached, increase in investment will go to rise in prices and to the cost of the factors of production because at this level factors of production become scarce and the consumer goods industries and investment goods industries outbid each other for obtaining the scarce resources. Thus a part of the increased income is dissipated in a rise in prices instead of expanding consumption, income and employment.

Hoarding: Hoarding and the tendency of the people to hold idle cash balances form another leakage. If the people have high liquidity preference and a tendency to hold cash balances, their expenditure on consumption would be less which would lower the magnitude of the multiplier.

Purchase of Stocks and Securities: A part of the newly created income may be used for buying old stocks and securities instead of being spent on increased consumption. Such financial investments diminish the magnitude of the multiplier because increased incomes instead of being spent on consumption, are spent on nominal (not real) investment.

Taxation: A part of increment in income received as a result of increase in investment is also used for payment of taxes. This part of income does not appear in the successive rounds of consumption expenditure in the multiplier process. This is an important leakage. But if the Government spends the money equal to the taxation, it would not have any adverse effect on the increase in income and investment and thus there would be no leakage in the multiplier process. It is not necessary that all the money raised through taxation is spent by the Government.

Saving: An important leakage in the process of income propagation is saving. If the MPC were equal to 1, i.e., if the entire increment in income were to be spent by people on buying consumer goods, then even a single increase in investment would go on creating additional increment in income till the stage of full employment is reached in the economy. But the MPC is seldom equal to 1. In actual practice, the people do not spend the entire increment in income on consumer goods. On the contrary, they save a part of it. The saved portion of the increased income thus comes out of the income-stream, limiting the value of the multiplier. Thus, the higher the propensity to save of the people, the lower shall be the value of the multiplier.

Full Employment Situation: The multiplier principle does not work in case of full employment. When resources of the country (capital and labour) are fully or near fully employed, further production will not be possible. Therefore, additional investment will only lead to inflation, not to the generation of additional real income.

Accumulation of the Idle Cash Deposits: A part of the increased income may be saved in the form of idle bank deposits, which cannot affect the consumption function in the upward direction.

Non-availability of Consumer Goods and Services: Another limitation of multiplier arises due to the lack of adequate and instant supply of consumer goods and services. The multiplier theory assumes an instant and matching supply of consumer goods and services. But, in general, the supply of goods does not follow instantly the rise in demand. There is always a time lag. During the lag period, newly earned income creates additional demand for goods and services, which build, in turn, demand pressure that pushes the prices of consumer goods up, leading to inflation. Inflation eats a part of consumption expenditure. This reduces the real consumer expenditure, which constrains the multiplier effect.

Corporation Saving: This affects the marginal propensity to consume of the people. It has inevitable repercussion on the value of the multiplier. Likewise, undistributed profits of business corporations also represent a leakage because they are not available to the shareholders for being spent on consumer goods.

It is because of these leakages that the process of income propagation runs out soon. If there were no such leakages from the income stream, then the process of income propagation would go on and on till there was full employment and even inflation. To the extent that these leakages from the income-stream can be plugged, the initial increase in investment would have greater multiplier effects on the process of income generation.

The multiplier is based on certain assumptions. It will operate to the full extent only if these assumptions are actually realised in practice. Following are the main limitations of the multiplier:

(a) *Availability of consumer goods:* The process of income generation is subject to the availability of consumer goods. If the consumer goods are available in adequate quantity, the multiplier will continue to work and new incomes propagate. If there is a scarcity of consumer goods, the income recipients will not be able to spend as much on consumer goods as they would desire. The MPC will fall and consequently the multiplier declines.

(b) *Maintenance of investment:* In order to achieve the full value of the multiplier, it is necessary that the various increments in investment are repeated at regular intervals. In case it is not done, it will not be possible to raise the income to the multiplier level.

(c) *Net increase in investment:* In order to realise the full value of the multiplier, it is also essential that there should be a net increase in investment in the economy. What it implies is that an act of investment in one sector should not be offset by an act of disinvestment in some other sector of the economy. If this happens, there shall be no net increase in investment and the working of the multiplier shall be inevitable hindered.

(d) *No investment from induced consumption:* In order to realise the actual value of the multiplier, it is assumed that there are no effects of induced consumption on investment. It is assumed that the accelerator does not operate and that the investment increases only by the original amount. In case, the accelerator is allowed to operate and the effects of induced consumption or investment are also taken into account, then the value of the multiplier would be far greater and would also be achieved at an earlier stage in the process of income propagation.

(e) *No change in the MPC:* In order to achieve the actual value of the multiplier, it is also necessary to assume that there will be no change in the marginal propensity to consume during the process of income generation. The multiplier depends upon the MPC. If the MPC undergoes a change due to some unforeseen causes, the value of the multiplier will also change.

(f) *Existence of closed economy:* In order to realise the full value of the multiplier, it is also necessary to assume the existence of a closed economy in the country in question. In case, the country concerned has trade relation with other countries, it is possible for the multiplier to have a value either more or less than its real value.

(g) *No time-lag between successive expenditure on consumption:* In order to realise the full value of the multiplier, it is assumed that there are no time lags between the receipt of income and the spending of it. What it implies is that the consumers should immediately spend the income as soon as they receive it. But, as we know, this does not always happen in real life. There is always a time lag between the receipt of income and the spending of it, though this time lag may be of short duration.

(h) *Existence of less than full employment:* So long as there is involuntary unemployment or less than full employment in the economy, income, output and employment will continue to expand on account of the operation of the multiplier. But the moment full employment stage is reached, income, output and employment will stop increasing, howsoever high the MPC may be.

MULTIPLIER NOT NECESSARILY ASSOCIATED WITH INCREMENT OF INVESTMENT

Throughout the above analysis we have referred to 'investment' outlays the initiator of the process of income propagation. In fact, the initial outlay need not be on investment. The multiplier becomes operative whenever an outlay involves injection of purchasing power into the income stream from outside irrespective of the nature of the outlay, i.e., irrespective of the fact whether such outlay is on public or private investment or on consumption. What is required is total expenditure in excess of the current flow of income irrespective of the nature of expenditure.

STATIC NATURE OF KEYNES' CONCEPT OF MULTIPLIER

Keynes' theory of investment multiplier has been criticised on the ground that is static in nature and has no connection with the dynamic process of income generation. It does not tell us what happens in between the initial increase in investment and the final increase in income. We do not know how and by what stages of time intervals the final increase in the total income is reached. Keynes' concept of multiplier shows the process of income expansion from one point of equilibrium to another and that too under static assumptions. No idea is given of the actual sequence of events and no time-lags are involved. The whole process of income propagation is automatic, unhampered by time or other factors. Post-Keynesians have pointed out that the value of the multiplier is affected by the fact that the particular doses of investment take time to exert their full influence in raising income. Because of the existence of time-lags, it takes longer time to reach the final position and the income rises at a rate slower than that at which it would have risen in the absence of time-lags. Keynes appears to have thought that the effect to such lags would be unimportant. He, however, was not unaware of the existence of time-lags. He, in fact, discusses, though briefly, three concepts of multiplier viz. (1) the logical theory of multiplier assuming no time-lags, (2) the period analysis concept of the multiplier based on the assumption of time-lags, and (3) 'comparative statics' timeless concept of multiplier in which the transition process or the path is skipped over completely.

DYNAMIC MULTIPLIER

If there is an economically significant time-lag between an initial investment expenditure and its reappearance as income, different equations expressing lagged consumption and investment must replace static equations so that the discrete steps involved in the multiplier process may be traced. We may build a simple dynamic system involving a consumption lag but no investment lag such as

$$C_t = a\,(Y_{t-1} - Y_0) + C_0 \qquad \text{...(6.28)}$$

$$I_t = \bar{I} \qquad \text{...(6.29)}$$

$$Y_t = C_t + I_t \qquad \text{...(6.30)}$$

$$= a\,(Y_{t-1} - Y_0) + C_0 + I_t \qquad \text{...(6.31)}$$

where C_t stands for consumption at time t, a for the marginal propensity to consumer, Y_{t-1} for income in the previous period. Y_0 for income in the initial period, C_0 for consumption in the initial period, I_t for investment at time t, and I for constant autonomous investment.

The essential point to notice about the general multiplier equation (6.31) is that consumption is lagged, that is, it is dependent on the income of the preceding period over and above some arbitrary initial income.

Multiplier Sequence: Given the marginal propensity to consume and the investment multiplicand, national income will be found to grow exponentially although usually in dwindling series. The geometric progression of income involved can be shown in the following general system of equation:

$$Y_1 = \Delta I$$

$$Y_2 = \Delta\bar{I} + c\Delta\bar{I} = (1 + c)\Delta\bar{I}$$

$$Y_3 = \Delta\bar{I} + \Delta c\bar{I} + c^2\Delta\bar{I} = (1 + c + c^2)\Delta\bar{I}$$

$$Y_n = \Delta\bar{I} + c\Delta\bar{I} + c^2\Delta\bar{I} + \ldots\ldots + c^{n-1}\Delta\bar{I}$$

$$= (1 + c + c^2 + \ldots\ldots. + c^{n-1})\Delta I$$

Here Y_1, Y_2 and so forth are the national income of the first multiplier period, that of the second period etc. that is $Y = Y_t$ and $t = 1, 2, \ldots.n$. $\Delta\bar{I}$ is the investment multiplicand consider occurring once; c is the marginal propensity to consume governing the multiplier. The nth term of the above progression or the final sum of all the terms of the sequence will be found equal to the multiplier times the initial increment of autonomous investment:

$$Y_n = \sum_{1}^{\infty} \frac{1 - c^{n-1}}{1 - c} \Delta\bar{I} = k\Delta\bar{I} = \Delta y$$

if $n = \infty$, as in the static multiplier theory.

Assuming $\bar{I} = 10$, $c = ½$ and $n = \infty$, the above system of equations can be made more explicit:

$$y_1 = \bar{I}\Delta = 10$$

$$y_2 = \bar{I}\Delta + \tfrac{1}{2}\Delta\bar{I} = 10 + (0.5)\,10 = 15$$

$$y_3 = \left[1 + \tfrac{1}{2} + \left(\tfrac{1}{2}\right)^2\right]\Delta\bar{I} = (1 + 0.5 + 0.25)10 = 17.5$$

$$y_n = \left[1 + \tfrac{1}{2} + \left(\tfrac{1}{2}\right)^2 + \ldots\ldots\ldots\left(\tfrac{1}{2}\right)^{n-1}\right]\Delta\bar{I}$$

$$= (1 + 0.5 + 0.25 + \ldots\ldots\ldots.)\ 10 = 20$$

$$= \frac{1}{1 - c}\Delta\bar{I} = k\Delta\bar{I} = 2 \times 10 = 20$$

The ultimate result in the *n*th period, that is, 20, is what we must expect since the marginal propensity to consume is assumed to be $\frac{1}{2}$ so as to give a multiplier coefficient of 2, given an additional autonomous investment of 10. Of greater analytical importance, though, is that the above sequence shows the cumulative increases of income above the base period, step by step, until a final total of 20 is reached.

Dynamic Process of Income Propagation: Let us now analyse the dynamic process of successive changes in income in terms of the Fig. 6.5.

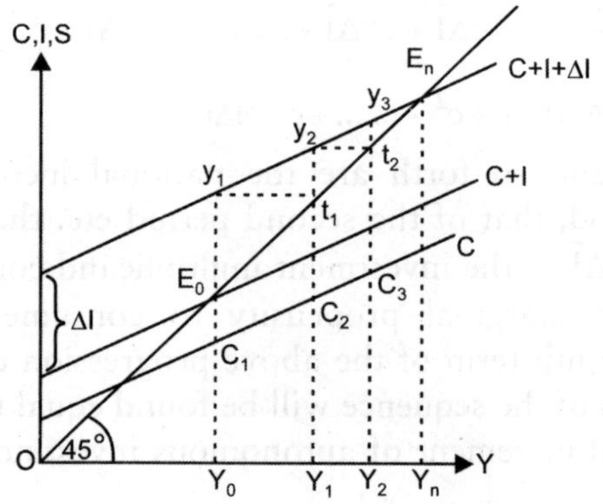

Fig. 6.5: Dynamic Multiplier

We assume that consumption depends on the income of the preceding period, $C = C_t = a\,Y_{t-1}$ where a is the marginal propensity to consume and also that investment is a function of income and an autonomous constant $I = I_t$. In diagram 6.5, consumption, investment, and savings are measured along the vertical axis and income is measured along the horizontal axis—all magnitudes being in real terms. The C curve relates consumption to the income of the preceding period had has a constant slope of 0.5. The original investment schedule is the vertical distance between the C curve and the C + I curve, while the new investment schedule is that between the C curve and the C + I + ΔI curve, which gives a constant level of investment equal to ΔI. Savings out of previous income are measured by the vertical distance between the 45° line and the C curve. The system is initial settled at a equilibrium point E_0, where savings and investment are equal

$$(E_0C_1 = E_0C_1)$$

In period 0, before the change, consumption is C_1Y_0 and income OY_0 or E_0Y_0, thus leaving E_0C_1 both as saving and investment. Now investment increases by $\Delta\bar{I}$ from period 0 to period 1 and stays at this level. What is the effect of this? Consumption remains unchanged because consumers have not yet had an opportunity to adjust themselves to change. Similarly, intended savings remain unchanged. This means that investment exceeds intended savings by an amount equal to the increment of investment, or by y_1E_0. This excess of investment over intended savings for period 1 (equal to actual saving for period 0) account for the unexpected increment of income from period 0 to period 1.

In period 1 there is an equal horizontal change, Y_1t_1 ($=Y_0\,Y_1$), for the vertical change of y_1E_0. In other words, income increases over OY_0 by the amount of excess investment in period 1 after the injection of $\Delta\bar{I}$. The total income received in period 1 is therefore OY_1($= OY_0 + Y_0Y_1$). What would happen to saving investment relation in this period? Investment is again $I + \Delta\bar{I}$ or Y_2C_2 and savings corresponding to previous income OY_0 are t_1C_2, thus making intended savings fall short of investment by Y_2t_1 ($=y_2C_2 - t_1C_2$). This excess investment is what causes income to increase from period 1 to the next, that is, by Y_1Y_2 ($=y_2t_2 - y_2t_1$).

Though consumption increases from C_1Y_0 to C_1Y_1 corresponding to the increased total income of OY_1, this extra consumption amounts to half of extra income Y_0Y_1. Similarly, savings increases by half of extra income Y_0Y_1. This explains why intended savings in period 1 fall short of investment. As such income expands by an amount equal to the above excess of investment over intended savings, or by y_2t_1, which amount is equal to the horizontal change of y_2t_2. It is thus that period 2 is ushered in and total income received is OY_2. But investment in this period still exceeds savings by y_3t_2 ($=y_3C_3 - t_2C_3$), since intended savings corresponding to previous income OY_1 amount to t_2C_3, which amount is y_3t_2 short of a total investment of y_3C_3 (constant $I + \Delta\bar{I}$). This excess of investment over intended savings in period 2 leads to an increase in income from period 2 to period 3.

The gap between intended savings and intended investment (the vertical distance between the $C + I + \Delta\bar{I}$ curve and the 45° line) becomes smaller and smaller, and the increment of income which it produces, until the gap is completely wiped out. The constant stream of new investment has developed its full effect, and aggregate income has reached the stationary higher level of Y_n in the nth period. The system has become stable at the new and higher equilibrium point E_n. Income has reached there via E_0, y_1, t_1, y_2, t_2, Y_3,......E_n. The multiplier has done its job, for it has caused income to expand to cause intended savings to expand up to the new level of investment, that is where $S_n = \bar{I}_n$. Thus in the nth period the savings gap (the vertical distance between the 45° vertical line and the C curve at Y_n) exactly equals the sum of old investment plus new investment (the vertical distance between the $C + I + \Delta\bar{I}$ curve and the C curve at Y_n).

CRITICISM OF MULTIPLIER

Keynes' concept of multiplier has been severely criticised by many economists. In his famous article "Mr. Keynes' Theory of the Multiplier: A Methodological Criticism" published in 1936, Haberler criticised Keynes' concept of multiplier as being a mere tautology, i.e., defining something as necessarily true and then proclaiming as a discovery the 'truth' of the relationship made inevitable by definition. Keynes defines multiplier (K) as below:

$$K \text{ (Multiplier)} = \frac{\Delta Y}{\Delta I}$$

We have already seen earlier that the above equation can also be written as:

$$K = \frac{1}{1 - MPC} \text{ or } \frac{1}{MPS}$$

The above equation like other identity equations (i.e. MV = PT or I = S) tells us nothing. It does not throw any light on the behaviour pattern of MPC over time or during transition from one equilibrium position to another. It is not subject to a verifiable behaviour pattern and as such is simply a tautology. If the concept of multiplier is to be used for estimating increase in national income during a specified period, it must be possible to advance reasonable hypothesis in regard to the behaviour of MPC or MPS over time; if this is not possible, the concept of multiplier will be of no use. Multiplier is a mere deduction as $K = \frac{1}{MPS}$ and MPS is not something independent which can be obtained independently of multiplier and then itself determining multiplier and through it determines income which would be created. In order to find out the value of the multiplier (K), we first find out how much income has been created and then divide it by investment. We have deducted that multiplier (K) is equal to $\frac{1}{MPS}$. We have found the magnitude of the marginal propensity to save and thus the size of the multiplier simply by finding what has actually happened and then using what has actually happened to predict what would happen. It is not surprising that in the investment (ΔI), times (X) the multiplier $\left(\frac{1}{1-MPS}\right)$ or $\left(\frac{\Delta Y}{\Delta I}\right)$ change should be equal to change in total income (ΔY). In other words, it does not make much to say that

$$\Delta I \times \frac{\Delta Y}{\Delta I} = \Delta Y$$

It is always true and there is no need to demonstrate it. If Keynes' concept of multiplier is to be freed from the criticism of being tautological, we must assume short-run normal behaviour pattern of MPC and MPS.

Prof. A.G. Hart considers the concept of multiplier a useless 'fifth wheel'. The concept has also been criticised severely by Prof. Henry Hazlitt. He refers to it as "a strange concept about which some Keynesians make more fuss than about anything else in the Keynesian system." He dubs it as a 'myth' and asks "What reason is there to suppose that there is any such thing as the multiplier?" He points out that "there is never any precise, predeterminable or mechanical relationship between social income, consumption, investment and extend of employment." It is, therefore, just "a worthless toy", the type of thing made depressingly familiar by monetary cranks. Further the concept of multiplier rests on an assumption which is very unrealistic, namely, that there already exists unemployment in the economy. There is no reason why Keynes should assume that substantial unemployment is the 'general situation' and 'full employment' is only a ;special situation'. Another fallacy pointed out by Hazlitt in Keynes concept of multiplier is the assumption that the entire fraction of a community's income that is not consumed' is 'hoarded' and that no part of this 'unconsumed income is 'invested'. The 'propensity to consume' determines the multiplier only on the assumption that what is not spent on consumption is not spent on anything at all, or is hoarded, and not invested. But this is inconsistent with what Keynes had said earlier that savings and investment were not only equal but also identical; savings and investment can be equal only if what is not spent on consumption is invested. The acceptance of the concept of multiplier, however, gives rise to the problem of inequality between savings and investment.

To cite Prof. Hutt, "The practical harm brought by thinking along investment multiplier lines has been that it has caused investment (expenditure in the process of net accumulation) to be regarded as a causal factor and not, as it ought to be regarded, as the result of thrift which recovery normally includes." He further states, "But the intellectual harm has been indirectly even more serious. The conventional multiplier apparatus is rubbish. It should be expunged from the text books, its place being, taken by an exposition of the dynamic implications of the Say's Law".

In the words of Brooman, "Keynes' multiplier.....is a static concept. It gives little insight into the process by which the economy tries to achieve a new equilibrium. The process by which output adjusts itself to a new level of demand is assumed to take place instantaneously or at least so quickly that none of the parameters of the system has time to change—consumers' preferences remain unchanged, the distribution of income as before and so on. In real life, it is very unlikely that this would hold good."

Prof. Stigler considers multiplier to be "the fuzziest part of his (Keynes) theory". According to him, "The concept (of multiplier) often seems like nothing but a cheap jack way of getting some thing for nothing and appears to carry with it a spurious numerical accuracy."

Keynes' concept of multiplier concentrates exclusively on consumption. It would be more realistic to speak of "marginal propensity to spend" rather than "marginal propensity to consume" and then to consider the impact of an initial increase in investment not only on consumption but also on investment. Further, in a dynamic economy, the "marginal propensity to spend"—even if we use that term for the "marginal propensity to consume"—is not likely to remain constant. To cite Gordon, "Thus, it is not likely that in a dynamic world we shall be able to predict with much accuracy the multiplying effect over the cycle of a given increase in private investment or public spending."[1]

The Keynesian concept of multiplier assumes a linear relation between aggregate consumption and aggregate income. Lawrence Klein, however, points out that empirical studies regarding behaviour of aggregate consumption in relation to aggregate income show that the actual trends in spending have a much more complicated relationship which may be of a non-linear type. Further, consumption is not the function of only income and the marginal propensity to consume does not remain constant.

IMPORTANCE OF THE MULTIPLIER THEORY

The main justification for public investment or a programme of public works as an anti-depression measure lies in the multiplier theory. The multiplier being greater than unity, income increases by several times the increment of investment. In a deep depression when profitability might have sunk very low only public investment, being autonomous of the profit motive, might provide the key to a substantial and steady injection of new purchasing power for adequate multiplication of income.

Public investment can be directed more easily to those sectors of the economy where, the leakages from the income stream being small, the multiplier effect of the new injection of purchasing power on income and employment is the greatest. For example, if the new investment is directed to industries with a high ratio of wages to total cost, or to areas or sectors of the economy with the highest incidence of unemployment and only to a smaller extent to raise wages and prices, the stimulus to employment and income will be relatively large.

Owing to the multiplier effect, the cost of an employment motivated public works programme to the government, as distinguished from the community, may be very limited. For the increased expenditure of the government may be substantially compensated by larger revenue receipts that a higher level of income brings in and by the smaller needs of expenditure on the unemployed. As such the government may undertake investment considered not worthwhile by the private entrepreneur. The latter may, however, be provided with an equally strong incentive to undertake such investment if the government grants him a subsidy equal to the increase in revenue receipts, and the saving on doles to the unemployed, that will result from it.

A knowledge of the concept of multiplier is very helpful in understanding the causes of the business cycle and also for its forecasting and control.

NOTE

1. R.A. Gordon, *Business Fluctuations*, pp. 118-19.

Government Expenditure, Taxation, and Theory of Income Determination

7

GOVERNMENT AND SIMPLE INCOME DETERMINATION MODEL

In the previous chapters, we have presented a model of income determination which was based upon following assumptions:

(a) There was no government expenditure and the government did not impose any taxes either.

(b) There is no foreign trade in the economy.

(c) All investment was assumed to be exogenously given.

(d) The level of retained profit is zero.

Now, we relax our first assumption and incorporate the actions of the government into our analysis. All other assumptions are still retained. We may relax them one by one as we introduce new variables into our simple model of income determination. This method of analysis is known as the technique of successive approximation.

Currently, the government has become a force in the social and economic spheres to reckon with. There was a time, about two hundred years ago, when a limited role was assigned to the government. Under the influence of philosophies of individualism and liberalism, it was thought that the government which rules the least is the best. Translated in terms of economic principles, it was summed up in the philosophy of *laissez faire* which meant that the economy must be left alone. The government should not intervene in the economic system. It must confine its activities to have minimum or three activities *viz.*, administration, defence and judicial services. However, you must recognise that, under the modern conditions, government will have to intervene into economy to a large extent even if it confines itself to the provision of administration, defence and justices and restricts its role in other spheres and sectors, keeping in line with the liberal tradition. Let us take, for example, the case of defence which has been one of the most traditional though most important functions of the governments. In the modern times, a country requires not only a large military force but army, navy, and air force having a large number of guns, tanks, artillery, bombs, air crafts, bomber aeroplanes, war ships, anti aircraft guns, submarines, missiles, and rockets etc. To manufacture these, governments would require a large supply of iron and steel, engineering goods, electric appliances, computers, etc. This means that government will have to intervene in the economy in a big way in order to perform even its traditional functions.

In the modern times, the functions of the governments have been enlarged to a great extent. The government ensures that all essential goods of consumption must be available in the market at reasonable prices. To attain this objective sometimes, governments have to resort to price controls and undertake the direct distribution of goods. The governments spend huge sums of money on education, health care, and social welfare schemes. They have to run public administration and organise the judicial services in order to preserve law and order in the society. In the developed countries, the governments give unemployment bonus to unemployed. Thus, the range of governmental functions have been diversified. To fulfil these objective functions, governments sometime also undertake production of certain selected goods. For example, in our own country there is a sizable and significant public sector which produces not only utilities such as telephone, telegraph, postal services and transport but manufactures such basic goods as iron and steel and consumer goods such as bread and soft drinks. However, not all capitalist governments undertake the production of goods and services themselves. Mostly, they buy it from the private sector. The private sector produces goods and services and government sector generates demand for it. Therefore, the government expenditure should be taken as a component of aggregate demand of economy.

To meet its expenditure, the government imposes a number of taxes. A tax is nothing but a leakage from the circular flow of income. If the government would not have imposed the tax, the income would have remained available with the private individuals and the expenditure flow would have been strengthened. Hence a tax is a leakage from the flow in the same sense as saving is a leakage. But saving is invested and thus investment represents an injunction into the flow. Similarly, the revenue collected by the government through taxes is spent in the form of public expenditure and represents an injunction into the circular flow of income.

The modified system of income determination comprises of the following five equations:

$$Y = C + I + G \quad ...(7.1)$$

$$C = a + bY_d \quad ...(7.2)$$

$$I = \overline{I} \quad ...(7.3)$$

$$G = \overline{G} \quad ...(7.4)$$

$$T = \overline{T} \quad ...(7.5)$$

where,

Y = income,

C = consumption expenditure,

G = government expenditure,

I = investment expenditure,

T = total taxes, and

Y_d = disposable income.

The equation (7.1) is an identity which defines the components of aggregate demand. According to this equation there are three components of aggregate demands—consumption expenditure, investment expenditure, and government expenditure. The equation (7.2) describes a consumption function and states that consumption expenditure is a linear function of disposable income. The equations (7.3), (7.4) and (7.5) describe that investment expenditure, government expenditure and taxes are given exogeneously.

The above system of equation can be solved if we add another identity defining disposable income.

$$Y_d = Y - T \quad ...(7.6)$$

The equation (7.6) states that disposable income is that part of income which is left with the individuals after paying the taxes which are due to the government.

Substituting equation (7.3) and (7.4) into equation (7.1) we get:

$$Y = C + \overline{I} + \overline{G} \quad ...(7.7)$$

Let us once again recall that a bar upon a variable means that related magnitude is given exogeneously. Substituting equation (7.2) into the equation (7.7) we get

$$Y = a + bY_d + \bar{I} + \bar{G} \qquad ...(7.8)$$

Also, substitute equation (7.6) into (7.8) and get

$$Y = a + b\,(Y - T) + \bar{I} + \bar{G} \qquad ...(7.9)$$

which can be simplified as

$$Y = a + bY - b\bar{T} + \bar{I} + \bar{G} \qquad ...(7.10)$$

collecting terms on the left hand side we can write

$$Y - Yb = a - b\bar{T} + \bar{I} + \bar{G} \qquad ...(7.11)$$

$$Y\,(1 - b) = a - b\bar{T} + \bar{I} + \bar{G} \qquad ...(7.12)$$

$$Y = \frac{1}{1-b}\left[a - b\bar{T} + \bar{I} + \bar{G}\right] \qquad ...(7.13)$$

The equation (7.13) gives the equilibrium level of income after incorporating government expenditure and taxes when both of these are given exogenously.

The level of government expenditure may not be constant over time. Like all other economic magnitudes, government expenditure is also subject to change. It may rise or fall. One may wonder what impact it will have upon aggregate economic activity. If the government expenditure rises then aggregate economic activity is likely to rise or fall or is not affected by at all? Since we have agreed to use income as a measure of aggregate economic activity, we shall investigate the impact of a change in the level of government expenditure upon the level of income of an economy.

Let us suppose that level of government expenditure rises. Since government expenditure is now taken as a component of aggregate demand, aggregate demand itself would rise as a result of an increase in government expenditure. Given aggregate supply, an increase in aggregate demand will cause income to rise. Thus the net result of an increase in government expenditure would be an increase in the level of income. However, the verbal argument shall not be able to show that how much increase in government expenditure will lead to how much increase in income. We can do so by resorting to the equation (7.13). Let us assume that level of government expenditure rises from G to ΔG while all other magnitudes remain constant. Then, the equilibrium level of income would be

$$Y + \Delta Y = \frac{1}{1-b}(a - b\overline{T} + \overline{I} + \overline{G} + \Delta G) \qquad ...(7.14)$$

The equation (7.14) defines the new level of income. The resultant increase in income can be calculated if we substract the old level of income from new level of income. Thus, by subtracting equation (7.13) from the equation (7.14) we get

$$Y + \Delta Y - Y = \frac{1}{1-b}(a - b\overline{T} + \overline{I} + \overline{G} + \overline{\Delta G}) - \frac{1}{1-b}(a - b\overline{T} + \overline{I} + \overline{G}) \qquad ...(7.15)$$

$$\Delta Y = \frac{1}{1-b}\Delta G \qquad ...(7.16)$$

The equation (7.16) states that if government expenditure rises by ΔG then income would increase $\frac{1}{1-b}$ times; where b is the marginal propensity to consume.

Dividing Equation (7.16) by ΔG on the both sides we get:

$$\frac{\Delta Y}{\Delta G} = \frac{1}{1-b} \qquad ...(7.17)$$

The relation described in the equation (7.17) is known as government expenditure multiplier. It is also the inverse of marginal propensity to save. We know that marginal propensity to consume is always positive and less than unity ($0 < b < 1$) and so is marginal propensity to save ($0 < 1 - b < 1$). Therefore, the government expenditure multiplier shall never be zero unless marginal propensity to consume is unity. Since, marginal propensity to save cannot be one by definition, multiplier cannot be zero. Similarly, multiplier cannot be equal to unity because marginal propensity to save cannot be zero. Consequently, the value of government expenditure multiplier shall always be positive and greater than one.

You shall also notice that conceptually government expenditure multiplier described in equation (7.17) is the same as investment multiplier discussed earlier and obtained in equation (7.16). They differ only in explanation and interpretation, otherwise, both are identical.

A GRAPHIC EXAMPLE

The above analysis of impact of a change in the government expenditure can also be explained with the help of familiar Keynesian Cross diagram depicted in the Figure 7.1. The horizontal axis measures income and vertical axis measures consumption expenditure, investment expenditure and government expenditure. C—line is the consumption function. The vertical distance from any point on this line to any point on the horizonal axis gives the amount of consumption expenditure at that level of income. The next line is C + I line which includes consumption and investment expenditure both. The vertical distance between C—line and C + I line gives the amount of investment. Since the amount of investment is constant (or invariant) with respect to income the C + I line has been drawn parallel to the C—line. This is so because all investment is assumed to be given exogenously at this point. The vertical distance between C—line and C + I line is the investment. The next line which is above C + I line is C + I + G line and includes consumption expenditures, investment expenditure and government expenditure. It is the original aggregate demand line. We already know that 45° line is nothing but an aggregate supply line. Equilibrium level of income is determined where aggregate demand and aggregate supply are equal. This is the point C in the Figure 7.1. We draw a perpendicular from the point C on the horizontal axis. This perpendicular cuts the horizontal axis at the point Y_0, hence

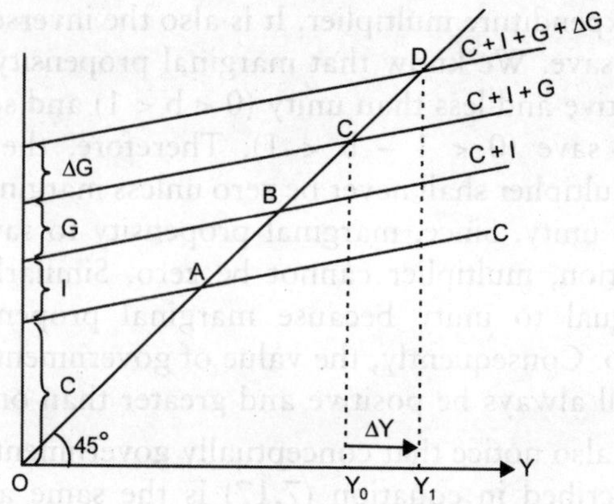

Fig. 7.1: The Government Expenditure Multiplier.

OY_0 level of equilibrium income is achieved. Let us suppose now that government expenditure rises from G to ΔG. Consequently, aggregate demand rises and aggregate demand line is further pushed up from C + I + G line to C + I + G + ΔG line which shows the new level of aggregate demand. The vertical distance between lines C + I + G and C + I gives the amount of government expenditure. Similarly, the vertical distance between C + I + G + ΔG lines and C + I + G line gives the change in public expenditure. Both of these lines run parallel to each other because public expenditure is also given exogenously and does not depend upon the level of income. The new line C + I + G + ΔG cuts the 45° at the point D. This is the point where new level of aggregate demand and aggregate supply become equal. So new level of equilibrium income is determined at this point. If we drop a perpendicular from the point D upon the horizontal axis, it cuts it at the point Y_1 and OY_1 level of income is determined. The difference between OY_0 and OY_1 is ΔY. The ratio of ΔY and ΔG is the government expenditure multiplier which tells us how much the income would rise if there is a given increase in public expenditure.

LUMP SUM TAX MULTIPLIER

The above treatment of public expenditure is based upon the assumption that public expenditure is autonomous, i.e., it does not depend upon the level of income. If the amount of tax is independent of level of income, it is called the lump sum tax. Its amount in money terms may be fixed. For example, the original level of tax was 10 crores rupees. It may be increased to 12 crores rupees. This is an increase in the lump sum tax. The lump sum tax multiplier helps us to find out the impact of a given change in the lump sum tax upon the level of income. It can be calculated as follows:

The original level of Equilibrium given by the equation (7.13) can be written in case of variable tax rate as

$$Y = \frac{1}{1-b}\left(a - bT + \bar{I} + \bar{G}\right) \qquad \text{...(7.18)}$$

Let us assume now that lump sum tax rises from T to ΔT. The change in income as a result of this change would be given by the following equation:

$$Y + \Delta Y = \frac{1}{1-b}\,[a - b(T + \Delta T) + \bar{I} + \bar{G}] \qquad \text{...(7.19)}$$

which can be simplified as

$$Y + \Delta Y = \frac{1}{1-b}(a - bT - b\Delta T + \bar{I} + \bar{G}) \qquad ...(7.20)$$

Subtracting (7.18) from (7.20), we get

$$Y + \Delta Y - Y = \frac{1}{1-b}\left[a - bT - b\Delta T + \bar{I} + \bar{G}\right] - \frac{1}{1-b}\left[a - bT + \bar{I} + \bar{G}\right] \qquad ...(7.21)$$

$$\Delta Y = \frac{1}{1-b}[-b\Delta T]$$

or,

$$\Delta Y = \frac{-b\Delta T}{1-b} \qquad ...(7.22)$$

If we divide both sides of equation (7.22) by ΔT we get the lump-sum tax multiplier

$$\frac{\Delta Y}{\Delta T} = \frac{-b}{1-b} \qquad ...(7.23)$$

Let us first note that sign of lump sum tax multiplier is negative which means that an increase in the amount of taxes would tend to reduce the income while an increase in public expenditure tends to raise income. The reason for this is that a tax, being a transfer of income from private individuals to the government lowers consumption. The reduction in consumption expenditure by a given amount of tax is MPC × tax. For example, if MPC is b and tax rises by the amount ΔT then reduction in consumption would be

$$\Delta C = -b\Delta T \qquad ...(7.24)$$

Also notice that expression on the right hand side of equation (7.24) appears as the numerator of the lump sum tax multiplier given in equation (7.23). Another point which must be carefully noted is that absolute value of tax multiple is less than the government expenditure multiplier. Thus, an increase in government spending, matched by an equal increase in taxation, results in an over-all increase in aggregate demand.

BALANCED BUDGET MULTIPLIER

The government budget is balanced if the government expenditure is exactly equal to tax-revenue. A balanced budget is not neutral to increase in income. Instead, a balanced budget tends to increase the level of aggregate demand and thus increase income because the absolute value of government expenditure multiplier is more than the absolute value of tax multiplier. In other words, the expansionary effect of public expenditure is stronger than contractionary effect of taxes. Therefore, even if the amounts of public expenditure and tax are exactly equal, the net effect will be that of expansion. We can show it as follows:

Let us assume $\Delta G = \Delta T = \Delta E$

where E is the equal change in the government expenditure and taxes. Increase in aggregate demand caused by public expenditure will be

$$\Delta Y_G = \frac{\Delta E}{1-b} \qquad \text{...(7.25)}$$

where,

ΔY_G = increase in aggregate demand caused by government expenditure.

An equal increase in taxes will tend to lower aggregate demand. Making use of lump sum tax multiplier given in equation (7.24), the reduction in aggregate demand can be written as

$$\Delta Y_T = \frac{-b\Delta E}{1-b} \qquad \text{...(7.26)}$$

where Y_T = reduction in aggregate demand caused by equal taxes.

The over all change in aggregate demand caused by a balanced budget will be the algebraic sum of increases and decreases caused be public expenditure and taxes respectively. Hence, the net effect will be

$$\Delta Y = \Delta Y_G + \Delta Y_T = \frac{\Delta E}{1-b} - \frac{b\Delta E}{1-b} \qquad \text{...(7.27)}$$

$$= \frac{\Delta E - b\Delta E}{1-b}$$

$$= \frac{\Delta E\ (1-b)}{1-b}$$

$$\therefore \quad \Delta Y = \Delta E \qquad ...(7.28)$$

Dividing equation (7.28) by ΔE we get

$$\frac{\Delta Y}{\Delta E} = 1 \qquad (7.29)$$

which is balanced budget multiplier.

The balanced budget multiplier can be worked out in another way also.

The effect of public expenditure is

$$\Delta Y_G = \frac{\Delta G}{1-b} \qquad ...(7.30)$$

The effect of tax is

$$\Delta Y_T = \frac{-b\ \Delta T}{1-b} \qquad ...(7.31)$$

The net effect is given by

$$\Delta Y = \Delta Y_G + \Delta Y_T$$

$$\text{or,} \quad \Delta Y = \frac{\Delta G}{1-b} - \frac{b\Delta T}{1-b} \qquad ...(7.32)$$

Since balanced budget implies ΔG = ΔT.

Substitute ΔG for ΔT and we get

$$\Delta Y = \frac{\Delta G}{1-b} - \frac{b\ \Delta G}{1-b} \qquad ...(7.33)$$

$$\Delta Y = \frac{\Delta G(1-b)}{1-b} \qquad ...(7.34)$$

$$\Delta Y = \Delta G \qquad ...(7.35)$$

Dividing equation (7.35) by ΔG we get

$$\frac{\Delta Y}{\Delta G} = \frac{\Delta G}{\Delta G} = 1 \qquad ...(7.36)$$

Equation (7.36) also describes the balanced budget multiplier which is the same as in equation (7.29). It is also interesting to note that the sum of public expenditure and tax multiplier is also unity.

$$\frac{1}{1-b} - \frac{b}{1-b} = 1 \qquad ...(7.37)$$

We have seen above that balanced budget multiplier is always equal to unity. On the one hand, it shows that balanced budget is not neutral to income. An equal increase in the level of taxes does not completely offsets the expansionary effects of public expenditure, though it is capable of retarding them to a great extent. Even then, balanced budget would be able to generate an increase in the aggregate demand equal to its own size. On the other hand, its significance lies in realizing the fact that in case of a balanced budget, most relevant variable to look at, is, its own size. It becomes important at what level the budget is balanced. Obviously, the effects of a budget balanced at Rs. 500 crores will be different from a budget which is balanced at Rs. 5,000 crores. The former will generate an income of Rs. 500 crores and the latter will generate an income of Rs. 5,000 crores. In the classical period, balanced budget was often favoured by economists on the ground that a balanced budget does not interfere with the functioning of private economy. The above analysis exposes the fallacy of classical economists and shows that it is not so.

TAX RATE MULTIPLIER

If you ponder a little, you shall discover that, in the ultimate analysis, all taxes are paid out of income. Hence, it is not reasonable to treat taxes as autonomous, or exogenously given. The tax revenue very much depends upon the level of income. If income is high, government will get more tax revenue. If income is low, the tax revenue would decline. If the taxes are made a function of income, the system of income determination could be written as follows:

$$Y = C + I + G \qquad ...(7.38)$$

$$C = a + bY_d \qquad ...(7.39)$$

$$I = \overline{I} \qquad ...(7.40)$$

$$G = \overline{G} \qquad ...(7.41)$$

$$Y_d = Y - T \qquad ...(7.42)$$

$$T = h + tY \qquad ...(7.43)$$

The equation (7.38) is an identity defining the various components of aggregate demand. Equation (7.39) shows that consumption expenditure is a linear function of disposable income. Investment and government expenditure are assumed to be exogenously given as shown in equations (7.40) and (7.41) respectively. An identity in equation (7.42) defines disposable income. You shall recall that equations (7.38) to (7.42) have appeared before also. The tax function is specified by equation (7.43). It is a behavioural equation because it shows the behaviour of a variable namely taxes.

The tax function specified in equation (7.43) is linear. Its intercept is h and its slope is t. The average rate of taxes can be calculated if we divide both sides of equation (7.43) by Y.

$$\frac{T}{Y} = \frac{h}{Y} + t \qquad ...(7.44)$$

The marginal tax rate can be calculated by differentiating T with respect to Y.

$$\frac{dT}{dY} = t \qquad ...(7.45)$$

The income-tax function can also be depicted in the form of a diagram as shown in the Fig. 7.2. Income is measured on the horizontal axis and taxes are measured on the vertical axis. The tax function is depicted in the form of a line BT. OB is the intercept of tax function while CY_1 is the amount of tax at the level of income OY_1. Hence the average rate of tax is CY_1/OY_1. When the level of income is OY_2, the amount of tax is DY_2, hence the average rate of

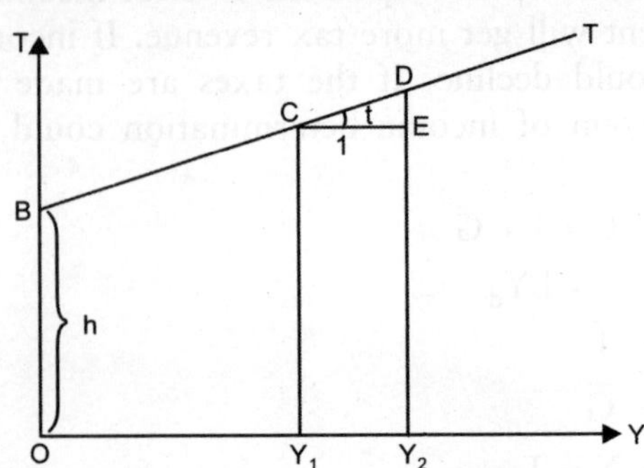

Fig. 7.2: Income-tax Function.

tax is DY_2/OY_2. You shall notice the average rate of tax declines as income increases. This can be seen from equation (7.44) also and T/Y declines as income increases because h/Y declines with the increases in income. The slope of the line BT is

$$\frac{DE}{CE} = \frac{DE}{Y_1Y_2}$$

But $\quad DE = t$ and let $Y_1Y_2 = 1$

Therefore, $$\frac{DE}{CE} = \frac{DE}{Y_1Y_2} = \frac{t}{1} = t$$

Thus, the slope of the line BT is t which is also the marginal rate of tax. Total amount of tax can be changed either by changing the vertical intercept (h) or slope (t) or both.

Then equilibrium level of income in the presence of tax function can be calculated in the following manner.

Substituting equation (7.39) into equation (7.38) we get

$$Y = a + bY_d + \bar{I} + \bar{G} \qquad ...(7.46)$$

Also substitute equation (7.42) into equation (7.46)

$$Y = a + b\,(Y - T) + \bar{I} + \bar{G} \qquad ...(7.47)$$

Also substitute equation (7.43) defining income tax function into above equation

$$Y = a + b\,[Y - (h + tY)] + \bar{I} + \bar{G} \qquad ...(7.48)$$

which can be simplified as,

$$Y = a + bY - bh - btY + \bar{I} + \bar{G} \qquad ...(7.49)$$

Collecting terms on the left hand side,

$$Y - bY + btY = a - bh + \bar{I} + \bar{G} \qquad ...(7.50)$$

or, $$Y - bY(1 - t) = a - bh + \bar{I} + \bar{G} \qquad ...(7.51)$$

or, $$Y\,[1 - b\,(1 - t)] = a - bh + \bar{I} + \bar{G} \qquad ...(7.52)$$

or, $$Y = \frac{1}{1 - b\,(1 - t)}\left[a - bh + \bar{I} + \bar{G}\right] \qquad ...(7.53)$$

which is equilibrium level of income. Notice that $\frac{1}{1-b(1-t)} < \frac{1}{1-b}$. Therefore, given the amounts of investment expenditure and public expenditure, more income will be generated if no tax is imposed, and if income tax is imposed, the amount of generated income will be comparatively low. This can be understood with the following example.

Let the behavioural equations be

$$C = 50 + 0.75\,Y$$

$$T = 15 + 0.20\,Y$$

and we have

$$\overline{G} = 50$$

$$\overline{I} = 50$$

then

$$a = 50$$

$$b = 0.75$$

$$h = 15$$

$$t = 0.20$$

If no income tax is imposed, equilibrium income is given by

$$Y = \frac{1}{1-b}(a + \overline{I} + \overline{G})$$

$$= \frac{1}{1-0.75}(50+50+50)$$

$$= \frac{1}{0.25}(150)$$

$$= 600$$

In case of income tax, equilibrium income is given by

$$Y = \frac{1}{[1-b(1-t)]}\left[a - bh + \overline{I} + \overline{G}\right]$$

$$Y = \frac{1}{[1-0.75(1-0.2)]}[50-(.75)(15)+50+50]$$

$$= \frac{1}{(1-0.75\times0.8)}\times 138.75 = \frac{1}{0.4}\times 138.75$$

$$= 346.875$$

The tax rate multiplier can be computed from equation (7.53) which can also be written as

$$Y = [a - bh + \bar{I} + \bar{G}]\,[1 - b\,(1 - t)]^{-1} \qquad ...(7.54)$$

Differentiating the above equation with respect to t we get

$$\frac{dY}{dt} = -b\left[a - bh + \bar{I} + \bar{G}\right][1 - b\,(1 - t)]^{-2} \qquad ...(7.55)$$

or,

$$\frac{dY}{dt} = \frac{-b\left[a - bh + \bar{I} + \bar{G}\right]}{[1 - b\,(1 - t)]\,[1 - b\,(1 - t)]} \qquad ...(7.56)$$

which can be rewritten as

$$\frac{dY}{dt} = \frac{-bY}{[1 - b\,(1 - t)]} \qquad ...(7.57)$$

which is the tax rate multiplier. Note that tax rate multiplier has a negative sign suggesting that income will be lowered if the tax rate is increased, and t is a function of income.

BUILT-IN STABILISER

Tax rate multiplier is sometimes referred as built-in stabilizer simply because it is a function of income. Built-instability results because income would decline if there is a decline in investment. Since taxes are a function of income, they automatically fall with the decline in income. The fall in taxes increases the magnitude of disposable income. This sets in motion the operation of tax rate multiplier which operates in the opposite direction to investment multiplier. Thus, in a situation of contracting investment expenditure when income is declining, taxes fall. This expands disposable income and increases consumption expenditure and aggregate demand, which in its turn would raise income. Similarly, in a situation of expanding investment expenditure, when income is increasing, taxes increase. This contracts disposable income and cuts the consumption expenditure and aggregate demand, which in its turn would lower income. Thus, tax rate multiplier tends to stabilise the economy both in the situations of recession and inflation. That is why it is known as built-in stabiliser.

Thus, we can summarize the above discussions in the following propositions:

(a) The change in government expenditure or the change in the amount of taxes affects aggregate demand.

(b) The balanced budget is not neutral. It is likely to increase the level of aggregate demand and income.

(c) The value of balanced budget multiplier is one.

(d) A greater increase (or decrease) in Y can be achieved if ΔG is not matched by ΔT.

(e) Taxes which are a function of income work as built-in stabiliser.

TRANSFER PAYMENT

Transfer payment is a special type of government expenditure. The government sometimes incurs certain expenditure which do not benefit the whole society (e.g. defence) nor do they are designed to provide some service (e.g. railways). Instead, they are designed to benefit some specific group of population. The examples of such expenditure may include unemployment bonus which benefits only those who are unemployed, old age pensions which are given only to those persons who have achieved a ripe old age and are not capable of earning their livelihood, educational scholarship given to meritorious poor students, and assistance towards health care etc. All these are welfare activities and the government carries them out because the society considers them to be good. Nevertheless, there are some important economic implications of such actions. Firstly, we must recognize that government is acting as a redistributive agent. These expenditures are incurred out of the tax revenue which the government collects from the private individuals. Thus, it is doing nothing more than this that it is collecting the money from some people and giving it to some other people. In other words, it is transferring the income from one segment of population to another segment. That is why it is called transfer payment. Secondly, we must see that transfer payments are mainly used for consumption purposes.

Incorporating the transfer payments following model of income determination could be worked out.

$$Y = C + I + G \quad ...(7.58)$$

$$C = a + b\,(Y - T + R) \quad ...(7.59)$$

$$I = \bar{I} \quad ...(7.60)$$

$$G = \bar{G} \quad ...(7.61)$$

$$T = \bar{T} \quad ...(7.62)$$

$$R = \bar{R} \quad ...(7.63)$$

In the above system of equations R is used to represent transfer payments. Equation (7.58) represents the components of aggregate demand. Equation (7.60) through equation (7.63) tell that investment, government expenditure, taxes, and transfer payments are assumed to be given exogenously. The consumption function described in equation (7.59) undergoes significant change in this model. Now, the disposable income does not constitute only of income minus taxes. The amount of transfer payment is added to it because this part of government expenditure is also available for consumption by private individual. Hence, it is very much component of disposable income and equation (7.59) takes account of this fact. Let us now solve this system of equation to determine the equilibrium level of income:

Substituting equations (7.62) and (7.63) into (7.59) we get

$$C = a + b\,(Y - \bar{T} + \bar{R}) \quad ...(7.64)$$

Also substitute equations (7.64), (7.60) and (7.61) into (7.58) to get

$$Y = a + b\,(Y - \bar{T} + \bar{R}) + \bar{I} + \bar{G} \quad ...(7.65)$$

and simplify

$$Y = a + bY - b\bar{T} + b\bar{R} + \bar{I} + \bar{G} \quad ...(7.66)$$

Collecting terms we can write

$$Y - bY = a - b\bar{T} + b\bar{R} + \bar{I} + \bar{G} \quad ...(7.67)$$

or, $$Y\,(1—b) = a - b\bar{T} + b\bar{R} + \bar{I} + \bar{G} \quad ...(7.68)$$

or, $$Y = \frac{1}{1-b}\left[a - b\bar{T} + b\bar{R} + \bar{I} + \bar{G}\right] \quad ...(7.69)$$

which is the equilibrium level of income. Suppose that transfer payment R rises to ΔR while all other magnitudes remain the same. Then, the new level of income could be written as

$$Y + \Delta Y = \frac{1}{1-b}\left[a - b\overline{T} + b\overline{R} + b\Delta R + \overline{I} + \overline{G}\right] \quad ...(7.70)$$

Subtracting (7.69) from (7.70) we get

$$\Delta Y = \frac{1}{1-b}\, b\Delta R \quad ...(7.71)$$

Dividing both sides of equation (7.71) by ΔR, we get

$$\frac{\Delta Y}{\Delta R} = \frac{b}{1-b} \quad ...(7.72)$$

which is nothing but transfer payment multiplier. On comparing this multiplier with the government expenditure multiplier, you shall discover that transfer payment multiplier is smaller than government expenditure multiplier.

$$\frac{b}{1-b} < \frac{1}{1-b} \quad ...(7.73)$$

This can easily be seen by taking some numbers. Let b = 0.75 then

$$\frac{1}{1-b} = \frac{1}{1-0.75} = 4$$

But,

$$\frac{b}{1-b} = \frac{0.75}{1-0.75} = 3$$

which shows that transfer payment multiplier is less than the government expenditure multiplier. Thus, we can also say that ΔY due to government expenditure will be more than the ΔY due to an increase in transfer payment, provided that the absolute amount of government expenditure and transfer payment is the same.

$$\frac{\Delta G}{1-b} > \frac{b\Delta R}{1-b} \text{ if } \Delta G = \Delta R \quad ...(7.74)$$

Now, let us suppose that transfer payment is financed by an increase of equal amount in tax. Then $\Delta T = \Delta R$. Notice that transfer payment multiplier and lump sum multiplier will operate in this case in opposite direction. The lump sum tax multiplier would tend to reduce income (hence, its sign will be negative) while the transfer payment multiplier will tend to raise the level of income. The net effect will be the algebraic sum of these two opposite magnitudes.

$$\Delta Y = \frac{-b\Delta T}{1-b} + \frac{b\Delta R}{1-b} \qquad \text{...(7.75)}$$

$$\text{Total change in } Y = \left\{\begin{array}{l}\text{Reduction in income}\\ \text{due to increase in}\\ \text{lump sum tax.}\end{array}\right\} + \left\{\begin{array}{l}\text{Increase in income due}\\ \text{to increase in transfer}\\ \text{payment.}\end{array}\right\}$$

Since the increase in transfer payment is exactly equal to increase in lump sum tax, put $\Delta R = \Delta T$ in the expression given in equation (7.75).

Thus, we have

$$\Delta Y = \frac{-b\Delta T + b\Delta T}{1-b} \qquad \text{...(7.76)}$$

$$\Delta Y = 0$$

which means that, an equal increase in taxes and transfer payment will completely neutralize each other and there shall be no consequent increase in income. Let us note carefully that this result is based upon two crucial assumptions: (i) that tax involved is a lump sum tax, (ii) that marginal propensity to consume is constant and is same for all classes. If either of the two assumptions is relaxed, the above result shall no longer hold. It is usually found that poor people have a higher MPC and rich people have a lower MPC. If richer section of population is taxed, and poorer people are given transfer payment, it may have as expansionary effect upon income generation even though the absolute magnitudes of taxes and transfer payment may be exactly equal.

Consumption Function

8

PSYCHOLOGICAL LAW OF CONSUMPTION

Keynes' Psychological Law of Consumption is of basic importance in the analysis of income, output and employment. This law is a statement of common experience that with an increase in income, consumption also increases but not to the extent of the increase in income. Keynes states, "The psychology of the community is such that when aggregate real income is increased, aggregate consumption is increased, but not so much as income."[1] To cite Keynes again, "The fundamental psychological law, upon which we are entitled to depend with great confidence both *a priori* from our knowledge of human nature and from the detailed facts of experience, is that men are disposed, as a rule and on the average, to increase their consumption as their income increases, but not by as much the increase in their income."[2] This law is known as 'Propensity to Consume' or 'Consumption Function.'

This law consists of three related propositions. The first proposition is that when aggregate income increases, consumption expenditure also increases but by a somewhat smaller amount. This is because as a person's income increases, his more and more wants get satisfied and, therefore, lesser and lesser amounts are spent out of subsequent increases in income. The second proposition is that when income increases, extra income is divided in some proportion between spending and saving. This follows from the first proposition because what is not spent is saved. The third proposition is that with the increase in income, both spending and saving go up. It is very unlikely that an increase in income will lead either to less spending or less saving than before. It would seldom happen that a person decreases his consumption or his saving with an increase in his income. Normally, he would spend more and also save more than before.

Keynes' Psychological Law of Consumption is based on three assumptions: Firstly, it is assumed that habits of people regarding spending do not change or that the propensity to consume remains the same. Normally, the propensity to consume is more or less stable and does remain unchanged. This assumption implies that, only income changes whereas other variables like income distribution, price movements, growth of population etc. remain more or less unchanged. The second assumption is that the conditions remain normal, that is, there is no hyper-inflation or war or any other such abnormal condition. The third assumption is that of the existence of a capitalistic *laissez faire* economy. The law may not hold good in an economy where the state interferes with consumption or productive enterprise. The government, for instance, may not permit an increase in consumption with an increase in income. The above assumptions are more or less realistic in a short period and under normal conditions. Keynes' Psychological Law of Consumption is, therefore, a rough approximation to the actual macro behaviour of free consumers and it is true that normally consumption increases with an increase in income but to the extent of the increase in income.

IMPLICATIONS OF KEYNES' PSYCHOLOGICAL LAW

Most of the economists agree with Prof. Hansen's view that Keynes' most notable contribution was his consumption function. Keynes' formulation of the consumption function is considered to be an epoch-making contribution to the tools of economic analysis. This is obvious from the implications of Keynes' psychological law mentioned below.

Vital Importance of Investment: One of the most important implications of Keynes' psychological law of consumption is that it brings about the crucial importance of investment if we are to attain an increasing level of income and employment. The law tells us that with every increase in income, the gap between income and consumption widens; and if the increasing income is to be maintained, more and more investment must be forthcoming to fill up this widening gap; if adequate investment is not forthcoming, there would appear a shortage of effective demand and as a result the economy would slip down. Thus the law highlights the vital importance of investment.

General over-production: The law tells us that there can occur a general over-production and unemployment. Since the marginal propensity to consume is less than unity, with an increase in income, consumption would tend to lag behind income, which would result in over-production and unemployment.

Repudiation of Say's Law: With the help of his psychological law of consumption, Keynes repudiates Say's law of market which states that every supply creates its own demand. Since the marginal propensity to consume is less than unity, all that is produced (supplied) is not automatically spent (demanded). The supply fails to create its own demand and as such there results a glut of products in the market.

Need for Government Intervention: Since the entire income earned is not automatically spent, there is no automatic and self-adjusting mechanism to ensure maintenance of a circular flow of income and expenditure. The *laissez faire* policy will, therefore, fail to deliver the goods and the state will have to intervene actively to ensure that aggregate effective demand does not fall short of aggregate supply.

Over-saving Gap: Since the increase in consumption expenditure does not keep pace with the increase in income, there arises the danger of an over-saving gap. This danger is more for rich countries than for poor countries.

Decline in MEC: As a result of the propensity to consume remaining unchanged or failing to rise with an increase in income, the expected rate of profitability or the marginal efficiency of capital may tend to decline. Decline in the marginal efficiency of capital can be prevented only by increasing consumption with an increase in income because ultimately the decisions to undertake investment are guided by the volume of consumption.

Income Propagation: Keynes' psychological law of consumption also explains the slow nature of income propagation. Since the marginal propensity to consume is less than unity, injection of increasing purchasing power into the income stream leads to smaller and smaller successive increments to income.

Underemployment Equilibrium: Equilibrium would be attained at full employment only if investment demand happens to be equal to the gap between aggregate income corresponding to full employment and aggregate consumption expenditure out of that income. But Keynes believed that the typical investment demand would not be adequate to fill the gap between the amount of income corresponding to full employment and the consumption demand out of that income, and, as such, the aggregate demand and supply schedules would interact at a point of less than full employment.

Secular Stagnation: With the increase in income, since consumption cannot be easily increased and investment demand becomes weaker and weaker, the economy may sooner or later reach a stage where it may not be able to provide outlets for its growing savings which is necessary for maintaining full employment. This stage is known as 'secular stagnation'. Such a situation could be avoided if the consumption function were not stable.

Turning Points of Trade Cycle: Keynes' psychological law of consumption is very helpful in explaining the turning points of the trade cycle. Before the publication of Keynes' General Theory there were several theories of trade cycle but none could offer a satisfactory explanation of turning points of the trade cycle. Keynes explained turning points of the trade cycle with the help of his stable consumption function. When the business cycle reaches the highest point of prosperity, income has increased, but marginal propensity of consume being less than unity, consumption does not increase correspondingly and the result is the downward start of the cycle. Similarly, when the business cycle reaches the lowest point, income has declined very low, but since people do not reduce their consumption to the full extent of decline in income, the upward phase of the cycle starts.

CONSUMPTION FUNCTION

The consumption function or the marginal propensity to consume is the relationship between income (Y) and consumption (C) and can be represented as C = f(Y). At various level of income, there will be corresponding levels of consumption. A schedule of consumer expenditure at various levels of income is called the schedule of propensity to consume.

Average and Marginal Propensities to Consume

The relationship between income and consumption is measured by the average and the marginal propensities to consume. The average propensity to consume is a relationship between total consumption and total income in a given time period while the marginal propensity to consume is the incremental change in consumption as a result of a given increment in income. In other words, average propensity to consume is the rate of consumption to income while the marginal propensity to consume is the ratio of change in consumption to the change in income. Thus,

$$APC = \frac{C}{Y}$$

$$MPC = \frac{\Delta C}{\Delta Y}$$

where ΔC is incremental change in consumption and ΔY is incremental change in income.

The normal relation between income and consumption is that when income rises, consumption also rises, but to an extent smaller than the rise in income. In other words, the ratio of an increase in consumption to an increase in income is always less than one. In technical terms, the marginal propensity to consume is less than unity.

The following table explains the relation between average propensity to consume (APC) and the marginal propensity to consume (MPC).

Income (Rs.)	Consumption (Rs.)	APC	MPC
1000	800	0.80	–
1100	870	0.79	0.7
1200	920	0.76	0.5
1300	950	0.73	0.3
1400	970	0.69	0.2

In Fig. 8.1, the function is represented by the curve CC. When the income is OL, the consumers desire to spend ON. If the income rises to OM, the expenditure increases to OP. The consumers would spend OC even when their income is zero. In other words, at zero income, instead of starving the people draw on past savings, sell property or borrow so as to buy consumer goods. The fact that CC is a straight line implies that as income rises, consumers' demand increases by an amount which always bears the same proportion to the increase in income, whatever the size of the increase and whatever the original level of income. In fact, the consumption function can take a number of shapes. Two more shapes are shown in Figs. 8.2 and 8.3. In Fig. 8.2, OC is a straight line starting from the origin, which implies that the consumers spend more with a rise in income but always spend the same proportion of income. The broken line marked Y = C indicates the position OC would take if the consumers spend whole of their income. The fact that OC slopes less steeply than the broken line means that the proportion of income consumed is always less than 100%. The curve $C_1C_2C_3$ in Fig. 8.3 shows a third shape of the consumption function. Even when the income is zero, the consumers incur a minimum expenditure of OC_1. This level of expenditure remains unchanged till the income does not rise above OY_1. At higher levels of income, consumption rises with a rise in income but by less than the increase in income. The diminishing slope of the curve between C_2 and C_3 shows that the proportion of income consumed falls progressively with a rise in income. APC at any point on the income-consumption curve is the slope of the line drawn from the point to the origin. MPC at any point on the income consumption curve is represented by the slope of the tangent to the income-consumption curve at that point.

Figures 8.1, 8.2, and 8.3 are based on the assumption that other things remain unchanged. If income is not the main determinant of consumers' expenditure, its influence may be submerged under those of other stronger forces. If interest rates, for instance, are a much more powerful determinant of consumers expenditure than income, it would be necessary to show a separate consumption

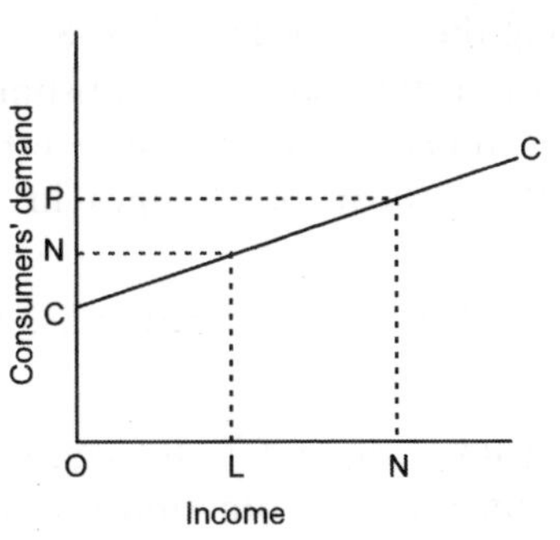

Fig. 8.1.

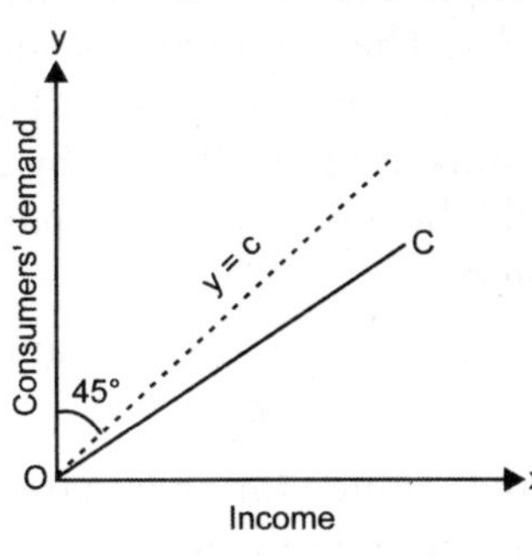

Fig. 8.2.

curve for each possible level of rate of interest. Instead of a single curve, like CC in Fig. 8.1, there would be a whole family of curves. In such a case the assumption of 'other things remain unchanged' would not be justified and as such the consumption function would not have much meaning; the direct relationship between interest rates and consumption would assume priority as an object of investment. The consumption function would be meaningful and useful only if it can be shown that income is, if not the sole determinant of consumers' demand, the most important of all the factors which influence it.

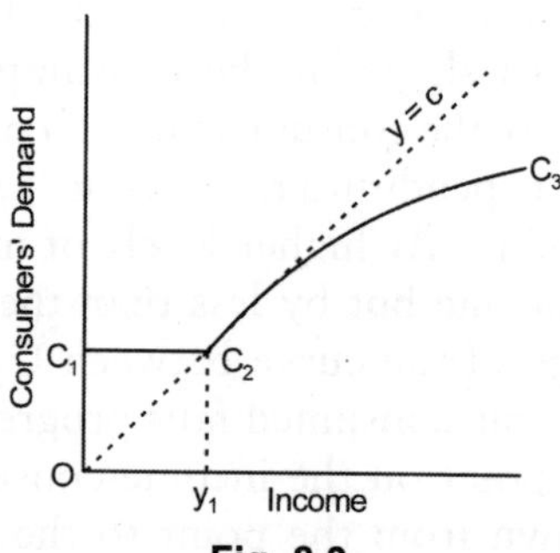

Fig. 8.3.

The relationship is normally expressed in terms of real income and real consumption. Consumers may respond differently to a rise in income, depending upon whether or not it is accompanied by a rise in the price level. If a simultaneous doubling of both incomes and prices leads consumers to double their expenditure and a doubling of income at unchanged prices leads them to raise expenditure by only 80 per cent, it would not be possible to represent the two situations by a single curve CC as shown in Fig. 8.1. The amounts measured along the axes of Figs. 8.1, 8.2 and 8.3 are at constant prices. This does not mean that the consumers' decisions are not affected by changes in prices but that these effects should be investigated separately from those of changes in real income.

Algebraically the consumption function can be written as:

$$C = C(Y_d)$$

where C stands for aggregate real consumption and Y_d for aggregate real disposable income. In case the consumption function is linear,

$$C = C_0 + bY_d$$

where b is the marginal propensity to consume and C_0 is the level of consumption at zero disposable income.

RELATIONSHIP BETWEEN APC AND MPC

Diagrammatic

With the increase in income, APC as well as MPC decline but the decline in MPC is more than that in APC. MPC is higher in poor countries than in rich countries. This is because in rich countries most of the essential wants of people have already been satisfied and, therefore, a major portion of the additional income is saved. In contrast, in poor countries people have many unsatisfied wants and as such a major portion of the additional income is spent for satisfying these wants. As pointed out by Prof. Hansen, sometimes MPC and APC in developed countries assume a constant ratio and become the cause of flattening of the consumption curve resulting in a shortage of effective demand and consequently leading to poverty amidst potential plenty.

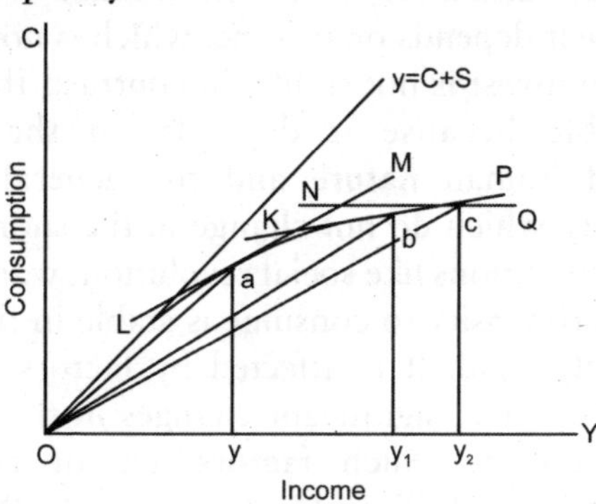

Fig. 8.4.

In the above figure, the curve OQ represents the consumption function. The APC at any point on this curve is shown by the slope of the straight line from this point to the origin. It would be seen that the slope of Oa is steeper than that of Ob, which means that the average propensity to consume is higher when income is Oy than when income is Oy_1. The MPC at any point on the curve OQ is shown by the slope of the tangent at that point on the curve. The slope of the tangent (or MPC) is greater when income is smaller (say Oy) than when it is larger (say Oy_2); in other words, LM is steeper than KP. It would also be seen from the diagram that when income increases from Oy to Oy_2, the decline in MPC (i.e. slope of KP) is greater than that in APC (i.e. slope of OC).

SAVING CURVE

Since income not consumed is income saved, the saving-income relation can be obtained from income-consumption relation. Savings at various levels of income can be obtained by subtraction consumption at those levels of income from the income. Since MPC + MPS = 1, MPS = 1 – MPC or 1 – dc/dy. Thus, if we know the marginal propensity to consume, we can obtain the marginal propensity to save by subtracting the marginal propensity to consume from one.

FACTORS DETERMINING CONSUMPTION FUNCTION

A clear distinction must be made between two questions: (i) how much will be spent for consumption, given the propensity to consume? and (ii) how much will be spent for consumption out of a given income? In other words, distinction should be made between the amount of consumption and the propensity to consume, that is between an amount and a schedule. The amount of consumption is not stable because it depends on income, which is not stable because the inducement to invest is not stable. In contrast, the propensity to consume is stable because it depends on the psychological characteristics of human nature and the general structure and practices of society which do not change in the short period except under abnormal conditions like social revolution, war, hyperinflation etc. Though the propensity to consume is stable in the short period, it is not absolutely rigid. It is affected by factors like changes in government fiscal policy, significant changes in the rate of interest and capital values etc. Such factors are of two types, viz. (i) objective factors and (ii) subjective factors. We first discuss objective factors.

Distribution of Income: This is an important factor determining the propensity to consume. Normally, the average and marginal propensities to consume of the poor people are higher than those of the rich. This is because the poor have a lot of unsatisfied wants and are likely to spend every additional unit of money that they obtain in satisfying those wants. In contrast, the rich have a high standard of living and relatively less urgent wants remain to be satisfied. Additional income in their case, therefore, is more likely to be saved than spent on consumption. Statistical studies show that a large portion of total saving is done by a relatively few high-income recipients and a small part of total saving is done by a large number of low-income recipients. Hence, the more equal the distribution of income, the higher will be the propensity to consume.

In a study of German time-series, Stachle[3] found that distribution of income was an important factor in determining aggregate consumption. The investigations using American "cross-section" data failed to find any significant relationship between income distribution and aggregate consumption.[4] These studies have led many economists to believe that policies aimed at reducing inequalities in the distribution of income will not be of significant help in raising the aggregate consumption.

Fiscal Policy: The fiscal policy of the government relating to taxation, expenditure and public debt appreciably affects the propensity to consume. A reduction in taxation will leave more post-tax incomes with people which would tend to increase their expenditure on consumption. In contrast, an increase in taxation will decrease consumption. A highly progressive tax system decreases inequalities in the distribution of income, which, as seen above, increases the propensity to consume.

Financial Policies of Corporations: If corporations and companies retain more reserves and distribute lesser profits in the form of dividends, the disposable incomes of the shareholders will be smaller. In contrast if more profits are distributed as dividends, more will be spent on consumption.

Changes in Expectations: If the consumers expect a shortage, or rise in price, of certain goods, they may rush to purchase such goods far in excess of their current needs. This would raise the consumption function. Such a thing often happens during war time. On the other hand, if the people expect a plenty of a decline in prices, of certain durable goods, they would tend to postpone purchases of such goods, which would lower the consumption function.

The consumption of a person is also influenced by expectations as to what his income will be in the future. If he expects an increase in income in future, he will tend to consume more than if he expects it to continue at its present level. If he takes a really long view, he will look ahead to prospective income during the rest of his working life, and try to adjust his consumption so that it is smoothed out over his life-span in the most satisfactory way.

Windfall Gains or Losses: Sudden and unexpected gains and losses in income affect consumption function. It is believed that the beneficiaries of windfall gains increase in their consumption above the normal level. The boom conditions during the late twenties in the U.S. economy created huge windfall gains which are believed to have raised the consumption function.

Liquid Assets: Changes in liquid assets of people affect their consumption. With an increase in their liquid assets (e.g. cash-balances, shares, securities etc.), the people have a tendency to increase their consumption. Increased liquidity caused by the method of financing World War II had an appreciable stimulating effect on consumption during the years following the war.

It is easier for a person to dis-save if his wealth is in liquid form. Such a person is not protected from the temptation to spend beyond his income by the inconvenience and possible embarrassment or loss involved in first having to cash a non-liquid asset. This factor, however, is not likely to be very important for, at least, two reasons. Firstly, it applies only to potential dis-savers and not to those who could reduce their current saving without having to cash assets. Secondly, the 'consumers' whose portfolios may be shifted in a more liquid direction by the central bank open market operations include, by and large, trust funds, pension plans, insurance companies, endowed institutions, and a relatively small number of wealthy persons in whose case dis-saving temptation is not much relevant.

Rate of Interest: It is not possible to say with certainty as to which way a change in the rate of interest will affect the consumption function. One possibility is that a higher reward for saving (i.e. a rise in the rate of interest) may stimulate savings and thereby decrease consumption. But some persons save with the objective of providing a fixed income for themselves in old age or for their dependents. With a rise in the rate of interest, such people can get the desired income from a smaller amount of savings and may therefore have a tendency to correspondingly increase their consumption. For the rich people saving is almost automatic and a little higher rate of interest will be no attraction for the poor. The classical economists believed that the savings would vary directly with the rate of interest. Keynes, however, considered the effect of variations in the rate of interest on savings as highly complex and uncertain. In his view "the short period influence of the interest rate on individual spending out of a given income is secondary and relatively unimportant, except perhaps, where usually large changes are in question."[5] It is in the long period that considerable changes in the rate of interest influence social habits affecting consumption function. Changes in the rate of interest have more influence on the purchase of consumable durables which are purchased on instalment basis. A rise in the rate of interest makes instalment buying more expensive and thereby tends to discourage consumption. Thus whether or not a rise in the interest rates lowers consumption function will depend on the relative strength of the opposing forces.

Duesenberry Hypothesis: Prof. Duesenberry had made two important observations on the factors affecting consumption function which are called 'Duesenberry Hypothesis'.[6] In his view, consumption expenditure of an individual is determined not only by his current income but also by his standard of living in the past. If income falls, the expenditure on consumption also falls but not to the same extent because people find it difficult to adjust their expenditure to the changed income. Secondly, he has suggested that an individual's consumption depends not only on the absolute amount of his income but also in its size relative to the incomes of others. His reaction to a change in income will differ according to whether or not others' incomes have changed by a similar amount: if they have, his consumption will change in the same proportion as his income; if they have not, his consumption will change in a smaller proportion. The consumption standards of low income groups are considerably influenced by the consumption standards of high income groups. The moment low income groups start using goods consumed by high income groups, the latter try to avoid consumption of such commodities and search for still better commodities. Such tendencies raise the consumption function.

Selling Effort: Those who advocate advertisement and other selling efforts as a means of increasing aggregate demand often overlook the fact that an increase in total consumer demand for one good or a class of goods may simply be at the cost of reduced demand for other goods. Nevertheless, given the level of income, an increase in selling effort may increase the total volume of consumer expenditure. But this factor has not been given much attention in the theory of aggregate demand because of three major reasons. In the first place, there is no independent measure of the volume of effective selling effort. Secondly, this volume probably does not fluctuate much in the short period. Thirdly, it has not been considered, at least, in the past, subject to social control.

Relative Prices: There is a tendency among economists to ignore the effect of changes in relative prices on the aggregate consumer demand in the belief that, like selling efforts, changes in relative prices increase demand for some products at the cost of that for other products. But, in fact, changes in relative prices can affect aggregate consumer demand. Much attention, however, has not been paid to this factor because there is no specific hypotheses as to whether this influence is important and in which direction it operates.

Volume of Wealth: The larger the wealth possessed by a person, the lower would be its marginal utility to him and as such the weaker would be the desire to add to future wealth by reducing current consumption.

Demographic Factors: Even at a given level of income, the consumption expenditure may differ widely from family to family. Such differences in consumption expenditure can partly be explained by "demographic factors" which include things like size of family, stage in the family 'life cycle', place of residence, occupation etc. Other things remaining unchanged, the large-size families would spend more than the short-sized families. Families with children college age would spend more than those with children of primary school age. Normally, the urban families have a tendency to spend more than the rural families. Farmers and small businessmen tend to spend less than the service people. Changes in demographic factors, however, occur over a long period and can, therefore, be ignored in the short-run analysis.

Terms of Consumer Credit: The terms of consumer credit exert an important influence on consumer purchases of durables and constitute possibly a strategic variable because of their susceptibility to social control, both through general monetary policy and through direct regulation. In recent years, there has been considerable increase in the volume of purchases of consumer durables financed by consumer credit and as such its cost and availability have assumed great importance.

It is generally recognised that the interest rate paid on instalment credit is not of so much importance as matters like the size of required down-payments, the length of the period over which the balance must be paid and the credit standards applied in judging request for credit expansion.

Permanent Income: A family's expenditure on consumption is determined not by its current income but by its permanent or normal income. Thus current changes in income do not affect consumption unless these changes also affect the household's belief as to what its normal income is likely to be. This approach provides an alternative explanation for the different behaviour of the long-run consumption functions. The apparent frequent shifting of the short-run consumption is to be explained largely by the fact the 'normal' income moves more slowly than current income and consumption is related mainly to the former. Over a long period, however, the trend in income, and consumption can be expected to rise more or less in proportion to such normal income.

Consumer Durables: The short-run instability of consumption expenditure in relation to income is considered to be concentrated in the area of consumer durables. The logic of the consumption function suggests that it is the current services rendered by durable goods which are desired in an amount related to current income. A small change in the desired level of current services of durable goods can lead to substantial changes in their rate of purchase. Large fluctuations in their purchases from year to year are quite consistent with only modest changes in the volume of current services rendered by consumers' stocks of durables because these stocks are the accumulation of a number of years' purchases. Thus factors affecting the timing of purchase of durable goods can significantly affect aggregate demand without involving any significant irregularity in the relationship between current consumption of the services of durable goods and income.

The purchases of durables are considerably influenced by the size of the existing stock of durable goods possessed by consumers and the age composition of this stock. The demand for durables, for instance, was very high in the post-war period because (i) during the war, consumer stocks of durables had either declined or had grown less in relation to consumer demand for their services on account of non-availability of durables and (ii) the stocks contained relatively old units. Similarly, in normal times if there are abnormally large sales of durables during a certain year, the sales may decline in the following years irrespective of the level of income or any other factor.

Though an important factor, the existing stock of durables is not the only factor influencing the volume of sales of durable goods. A recent study shows that the stock of automobiles on the road is an important variable for explaining new purchases of automobiles along with consumer incomes, relative prices of new and used cars and of cars relative to goods in general, and consumer credit terms.[7] Some other impair the significance of stocks by emphasizing style and performance changes, and consumers' comprehension and acceptance of them as important factors in the demand for durables. In other words, obsolescence can be as important as physical wearing out in creating a demand for new durable goods by people who already own them.[8]

Pigou Effect: Pigou effect says that the changes in the real value of liquid assets affect the consumption of the liquid asset holders. This is also known as 'Real value of money assets effect' or 'wealth effect'. A.C. Pigou proved first this effect in 1943. He showed that when money wages are cut, prices fall and then the value of money rises. As the value of money rises, the real value of assets increases. Such types of assets are stocks, shares, bank deposits, government securities, bonds, etc. whose values are fixed in monetary terms. The increase in the real value of these fixed assets will make the owners feel richer than before. As a result they will save less out of this present income and spend more on consumption. This will raise aggregate demand for output and thereby generate automatic full employment in the economy and the consumption function will shift upward. From the above discussion we observe that the Pigou effect is based on the following assumptions.

(a) There is flexible wage.

(b) There is flexible price.

(c) There is constant stock of money.

The Pigou effect can be shown in Figure 8.5.

In Figure 8.5(a), the economy is at y_1, level of income. As there is wage-price deflation. The consumption function shifts rightward from S_1 to S_2 and the level of income shifts from y_1 level to full employment level. Corresponding to y_1 and y_F in Figure 8.5(a) we get same y_1 and y_F in Figure 8.5(b). As explanation it is said that when the price falls from P_1 to P_2 with reduction in money wages, income increases from y_1 to the full employment level y_F and we get a downward sloping aggregate demand curve AD via consumption function.

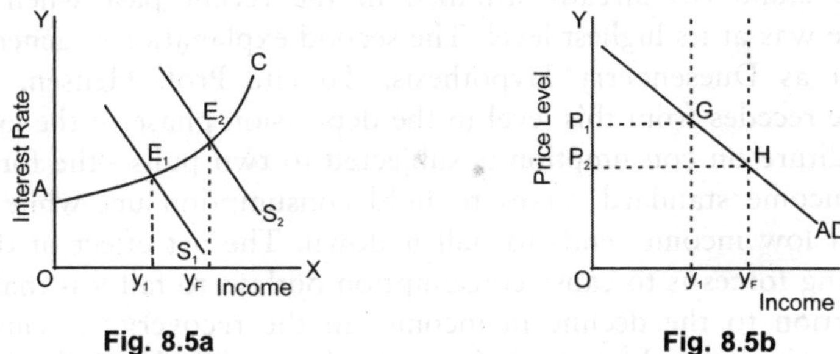

Fig. 8.5a

Fig. 8.5b

CYCLICAL AND SECULAR BEHAVIOUR OF CONSUMPTION FUNCTION

Keynes states that with an increase in income, the expenditure on consumption also increases but by less than the increase in income. Now the question arises: Does this relationship between income and consumption remain constant over time or is it subject to change? In other words, is there any difference between the cyclical and secular behaviour of the consumption function? In fact, Keynes did not make a clear-cut distinction between the cyclical (or short-period) and secular (or long-period) consumption function. But whatever he said about the consumption function certainly throws some light on this distinction.

Historical experience shows that during the up-swing of business cycle, when income rises, the expenditure on consumption does not rise in the same proportion. Similarly, during the down-swing of business cycle, when income declines, the expenditure on consumption does not decline in the same proportion. Thus the cyclical increase and decrease in consumption is less than in proportion to the increase and decrease in income. In other words, there is a lagged adjustment between income and consumption. In the short period, consumption does not get enough time to adjust itself to changes in income. The result is a flat consumption function curve representing the normal behaviour pattern of consumption. In other words, the consumption function or the propensity to consume remains more or less constant over a short period of time.

Keynes hinted at two major explanations for the consumption function being relatively flat. In the first place, consumption is basically determined by primary needs and, while a rise in real income will ultimately induce increase in consumption, the urge to change consumption. Secondly, consumption is basically determined by the standards already attained in the recent past when the income was at its highest level. The second explanation is generally known as Duesenberry Hypothesis. To cite Prof. Hensen, "As income recedes from this level in the depression phase of the cycle, expenditure on consumption is subjected to two pulls—the former high income standard serves to hold consumption up, while the current low income tends to pull it down. The net effect of these opposing forces is to cause consumption outlays to fall less than in proportion to the decline in income. In the recovery, as current income rises the depressant force weakens and the pull of the formerly achieved standard becomes increasingly ascendant."[9]

While cyclically consumption rises and declines less than in proportion to the rise and decline in national income, over a long period consumption has risen more or less in proportion to a rise in national income. To cite Hensen, "Even a little reflection on the course of economic history is enough to disclose the unmistakable fact that consumption has risen, broadly conceived, more or less in proportion to the spectacular growth in productivity which the last 150 years have witnessed."[10] Bowley and Stamp have observed vast shifts in consumption standards over a long period more or less in proportion to the rise in income.

Some economists, among whom particular mention may be made of Arthur Smithies[11] and James Tobin,[12] hold the view that the basic relationship between income and consumption is non-proportional. They, therefore, believe that the basis of income along the average propensity to consume should decline with a rise in the level of income in the long run. The time-series data relating to consumption and income, however, does not corroborate their hypothesis. They reconcile their position by stating that while the basic income-consumption relationship is of a non-proportional type, still the long-run data exhibits relationship of a proportional type because the basic non-proportional consumption function has undergone upward shifts as a consequence of factors other than income influencing the level of consumption. Among such other factors mention may be made of the following: (i) with an increase in accumulated wealth of households, the utility of further accumulation of wealth has declined and as such the households have tended to spend a larger portion of their incomes leading to an upward shift in the aggregate consumption function; (ii) since the propensity to consume of the urban people is higher than that of the rural people, the movement of population from rural to urban areas has shifted the consumption function upwards; (iii) the age composition of population has so changed that the ratio of old-age people to the total population has tended to rise and as these people consume but do not earn, the ratio of aggregate consumption to total consumption has risen and given an upward shift to the consumption function; (iv) the introduction of new consumer goods considered as 'essentials' by the typical household has also led to an upward shift in the consumption function.

GENERAL THEORIES OF CONSUMER SPENDING BEHAVIOUR

The household consumption expenditures account for approximately two thirds of gross national product (GNP) of a country. Present consumption and saving must add up to present disposable income. Therefore, any decision to consume more is simultaneously a decision to save less. An individual decision to save more in the present will enable greater consumption in the future. Personal consumption expenditure in the national income and product accounts are divided into three categories—durable goods, nondurable goods, and services. The purchases of a durable good results in an increase in the flow of consumable services, not only in the present but also in the future. Conceptually, we associate saving with the ability to increase consumption in the future. The personal consumption expenditure category of the national income and product accounts is not an exact measure of the concept of consumption used in most models of consumer behaviour. To measure the models' concept of consumption, we would need to combine a measure of each year's flow of services from the household's stock of durable goods with nondurable goods and services. The main reason that the national income and product accounts use purchases of durables rather than yearly flow of services from durable goods is that it is easier to gather accurate data on purchases.

In the late nineteenth century, theoretical explanations of consumer demand were derived from the neoclassical microeconomic analysis developed by Alfred Marshall in his Principles of Economics

[1890]. Neoclassical theory, however, was of limited use to market analysts because it took no account of the importance of interpersonal effects on consumer choice and could not offer an explanation of the increasingly strong influence of social factors, in particular the desire for status, on purchase decisions.

Marshall effectively ignored status-driven consumption in the first edition of Principles. He acknowledged "the unwholesome desire for wealth as a means of display" that was increasingly in evidence (particularly in the United States during the Gilded Age), and he condemned such expenditures, believing that they were rooted in personal vanity and created envy in others. However, there was no serious discussion of the economics of demand for status goods and, although recognizing the complexity of any consumption that was driven by social, rather than by utilitarian, considerations, the "special case" of interpersonal preference formation did not form part of Marshall's analysis.

Consumer behaviour theory, together with models derived from such theory, is intended to (a) identify consumer variables, (b) explain relationships between the variables, (c) develop operational definitions for the variables, and (d) specify cause-and-effect outcomes from variable interactions. In economic theory, consumer behaviour is addressed within the concepts of consumer preference and consumer surplus. Consumers' surplus is the excess amount of a consumer is willing to pay for a good, as opposed to doing without it, over the amount actually paid for the good. A consumers' surplus can exist only within the context of the concept of diminishing marginal utility. This concept holds that, at some point, consumption of additional incremental quantities of a good will yield successively smaller increase in utility. Thus, it is assumed that an individual will be willing to pay more for the first unit of consumption than for a unit consumed at some further along.

The economic theorists have come up with several alternative explanations of consumption function. The major landmarks in the theory of consumption function are—Absolute Income Hypothesis (Keynes, 1936), Relative Income Hypothesis (Duesenberry, 1948), Permanent Income Hypothesis (Friedman, 1957), and Life Cycle Hypothesis (Modigliani and Brumberg, 1954 and Ando and Modigliani, 1936). In what follows, we shall present a brief summary of each theory.

Absolute Income Hypothesis

Absolute Income Hypothesis (AIH) was proposed by John Maynard Keynes, and has been refined extensively during the 1960s and 1970s, notably by American economist James Tobin. The theory examines the relationship between income and consumption, and asserts that the individual's consumption depends on the individual's own current level of income as opposed to his income relative to other people's income or relative to past or future income. As income rises, the theory asserts, consumption will also rise but not necessarily at the same rate. Keynes advanced this hypothesis about consumption on the basis of "knowledge of human nature" and "detailed facts of experience."

The AIH is composed of the following postulates:

(a) Consumption is a stable function of income.

(b) The marginal propensity to consume is less in the short run than in the long run.

(c) In the long run, a smaller proportion of income will be consumed as income increases and hence marginal propensity to consume is less than average propensity to consume.

(d) Changes in the stock of wealth of households will directly affect their level of consumption.[13]

We can do no better than to look to Keynes' General Theory to find the support for these postulates. The first statement is borne out by the following quote from Keynes:

> "The fundamental psychological law upon which we are entitled to depend with great confidence both *a priori* from our knowledge of human nature and from the detailed facts of experience, is that *men are deposed*, as a rule and on the average, to increase their consumption as their income increases, but not by as much as the increase in their income. That is to say if C_w is the amount of consumption and Y_w is income (both measured in wage units), C_w has the same sign as Y_w, but is smaller in amount, i.e. $\frac{dC_w}{dY_w}$ is positive and less than unity."[14]

The above quotation from the general theory established that marginal propensity to consume is always positive and less than unity, $\left(0 < \frac{dC}{dY} < 1\right)$. By corollary, same limits could be established for marginal propensity to save. $\left(0 < \frac{dS}{dY} < 1\right)$. Main contention of the AIH which can be supported by the statements in *The General Theory* is this: Absolute changes in income are responsible for changes in saving, though the changes in savings are not proportional to changes in income. Keynes wrote in the general theory:

> "......it is also obvious that a higher absolute level of income will tend, as a rule, to widen the gap between income and consumption... These reasons will lead, as a rule, to a greater proportion of income as real income increases. But whether or not a greater proportion is saved, we take it as a fundamental psychological rule of any modern community that, when its real income is increased, it will not increase its consumption by an equal absolute amount, so that a greater *absolute* amount must be saved, unless a large and unusual change is occurring at the same time in other factors."[15]

Keynes was also prompt to recognise that a number of subjective factors were involved in the decision making process on savings. He listed eight different motives which lead individuals to save and refrain from spending the full amount of income.[16]

(i) *Motive of Precaution*: The individuals want to preserve a part of their current income to meet the unforeseen contingencies in the future.

(ii) *Motive of Foresight*: The individuals would like to provide for some anticipated needs which shall arise in future. These needs may be different from the present needs, or there may be no income when they arise. Hence, it is an act of foresight to save from the current income to satisfy these needs. The examples for such needs are family education, old age and maintenance of dependents etc.

(iii) *Motive of Calculation*: Individuals also like to save because they prefer larger consumption at a future date in comparison to a smaller consumption at present. Sometimes, individuals save to earn interest and keep their savings in the form of such commodities whose value is expected to appreciate, e.g., gold, real estate etc.

(iv) *Motive of Improvement*: Individuals enjoy a rising standard of living. Hence they prefer to save and invest so that they could get larger incomes to improve their standard of living.

(v) *Motive of Independence*: Individuals would like to retain some portion of their income because the possession of money in this form accords a sense of independence and confers upon them powers to do things of which they may not have a clear idea at the time of saving the income.

(vi) *Motive of Enterprise*: Some individuals save so that they can speculate or carry out certain business projects.

(vii) *Motive of Pride*: Individuals have a natural desire to bequeath some assets for their descendants. Hence, they save and accumulate wealth to satisfy this motive.

(viii) *Motive of Avarice*: Some people save just because they are miser and have some natural inhibitions against spending.

Keynes had also listed the comparable motives of consumption such as enjoyment, shortsightedness, generosity, miscalculation and extravagance. The economic research which followed the Keynesian revolution neglected these motives and was lacking in depth as far as the socio-psychological aspects of consumption and savings are concerned. Nevertheless, some of the motives indicated the direction which future research on the theory of consumption function might have taken. For example, the motives of improvement and significance of standard of living in saving behaviour becomes a cornerstone of the relative income hypothesis. The motives to bequeath a fortune to the descendants appears significantly in the life cycle formulations of saving behaviour. Keynes had also emphasized the importance of institutional and other social factors like education, population etc. as is evident in the following quotation from the general theory:

> "......the strength of all these motives will vary enormously according to the institutions and organization of the economic society which we presume, according to habits formed by race, education, convention, religion and current morals, according to present hopes and past experiences, according to the scale and technique of capital equipment, and according to the prevailing distribution of wealth and established standards of life."[17]

Keynes' theory as enunciated in the general theory and sketched above was not simplistic or one-sided. It emphasized the socio-cultural aspects as well as economic factors. Keynes' fundamental psychological law implied nothing more than that marginal propensity to consume was higher than the average propensity to consume. The early Keynesian writers ignored the qualifications Keynes had mentioned and adopted some simple version of the relationship between income and consumption. The simple 'Keynesian' formulation of consumption soon came into conflict with the observed facts. According to this version, the relationship between consumption and income (or between saving and income) is non-proportional and the relationship is postulated to be reversible in time. Though the earlier budget studies seem to confirm these conjectures, but the evidence from the time series data was found to be in conflict with the hypothesis. Firstly, if the relationship is claimed to be reversible then it must be possible to predict the future and past levels of consumption correctly. However, it was not possible to do so. The aggregate relation overestimates consumption if it is extrapolated back. Secondly, the empirical studies of saving done by Simon Kuznets and Goldsmith did not confirm the conjectures of hypothesis. Kuznets found that percentage of disposable income consumed had remained constant in the United States for a very long period (1867-1940) despite large growth in income. According to Kuznets estimates[18], the long run marginal propensity to consume ranged between 0.84 and 0.89 for different time periods between 1869-1940. The marginal propensity to consume in 1869-78 was 0.86, as well as for 1874-83. It was 0.85 for the year 1879-88 and declined a bit to 0.84 during 1889-98. For the period 1919-1928, he estimated the marginal propensity to consume to be 0.89. Raymond Goldsmith also calculated the long run marginal propensity to consume for the United States as 0.86

for the period 1897-1947 (excluding the such periods 1917-18 and 1942-45).[19] In this estimate Goldsmith used the consumption data which excluded the expenditure on consumer durables but included an estimate of the value of services rendered by the stock of durable goods.

The above findings have the following implications which are against the postulates of Absolute Income Hypothesis: (i) Intercept term does not exist in the saving function. (ii) The average propensity to consume and marginal propensity to consume do not decline with the increases in income as claimed by the AIH. Instead, they are constant. (iii) The marginal propensity to consume and average propensity to consume are equal to each other. The consumption function according to the AIH is

$$C = a + b\,Y \qquad ...(8.1)$$

where,

C = total consumption expenditure,

a = intercept term,

b = marginal propensity to consume,

Y = real income.

Thus, APC can be calculated as

$$\frac{C}{Y} = \frac{a}{Y} + b \qquad ...(8.2)$$

and MPC can be calculated as

$$\frac{dC}{dY} = b. \qquad ...(8.3)$$

It is obvious to see that

$$APC > MPC$$

The consumption function implied by the empirical studies of Kuznets and Goldsmith is

$$C = bY \qquad ...(8.4)$$

or, $$\frac{C}{Y} = b$$

Also, we have

$$\frac{dC}{dY} = b$$

Therefore $$\frac{C}{Y} = \frac{dC}{dY} \text{ or APC = MPC.}$$

In other words, the consumption and income are proportional to each other and are not non-proportional as the AIH would have us believed. Moreover, the AIH also lacked the sound theoretical foundation. It did not investigate the relationship between consumption, saving, income and wealth. Once the role of saving in creating wealth was recognized, it would be imperative to include all these variables within a single theoretical model. In fact, all these variables interact with each other. Accumulated savings are nothing but additions to wealth which generate income, which in its own turn is used either for further consumption or to increase the level of savings, and so on. This phenomenon necessarily involves a temporal dimension which was not taken into account in the AIH formulation. Further theoretical breakthrough were required to do this.

On an empirical level, the researchers tried to resolve the conflicts between theoretical postulates and observed constancy of saving ratios and its proportionality with income by bringing in new explanatory variables into consumption function. Consumption of the previous year, possession of liquid assets by the households, interest rates, real assets, urbanization, population and its age composition were such variables which were used as independent variables in a regression of consumption upon income. Since most of these studies were empirical in nature, theoretical connections between these variables and saving behaviour were not very specific.

Economists seeking to explain fluctuations in aggregate demand must provide a convincing explanation of the causes of fluctuations in consumption expenditures because they appear to imply large fluctuations in aggregate demand. The absolute income hypothesis represents a simple attempt to provide such an explanation. Equation 8.1 can be rewritten as

$$C_t = a + bY_{dt} = a + b\,(1 - t)Y \qquad \text{...(8.5)}$$

which says that planned real consumption expenditure is a linear function of current real household disposable income. Since we assume that consumers are always able to carry out their current consumption plans, this is also an expression for actual consumption expenditure. While this formulation has the advantage of simplicity and it suffers from the compelling disadvantage that it does not seem to provide a convincing explanation of the facts. This problem can be overcome by transforming the AIH equation into growth-rate form, and to compare predictions derived from this version of the AIH with patterns observed in the data. We take logarithms of both sides and exploit the fact that the derivative of the logarithm of a variable is its percentage rate of change. Thus, logarithmic differentiation gives

$$\frac{1}{C_t}\frac{dC_t}{dt} = \frac{bY_{dt}}{a + bY_{dt}}\frac{1}{Y_{dt}}\frac{dY_{dt}}{dt} \qquad \text{...(8.6)}$$

or,

$$\hat{C}_t = \gamma_t \hat{Y}_{dt} \qquad \text{...(8.7)}$$

where,

$$\gamma_t = \frac{bY_{dt}}{a + bY_{dt}}\frac{1}{Y_{dt}}$$

Here, the 'hat' over a variable denotes the percentage rate of change, and γ_t is a positive fraction, probably quite close to (but less than) one. The AIH assumes that a and b are constants, so that γ_t will be reasonably fixed as well, although it will get closer to one as Y_{dt} increases over time. It is a prediction of this model of consumption that growth rates of consumption and income should be almost the same, the difference between the two depending on the value of γ_t.

Intertemporal Choice

Intertemporal choices, decision in which the timing of costs and benefits are spread out over time, are both common and important. How much schooling to obtain, whom to marry, whether to have children, how much to save for retirement, how to invest, whether to buy a house, and if so which house to buy—all these vital decision have strong intertemporal components. As examples of individual decision-making, intertemporal choices are also interesting because the relevant economic theory makes unusually testable predictions. In many contexts, economic theories of individual behaviour are untestable because the predictions are too vague. Almost any choice, no matter how bizarre, can be rationalised by finding some utility function, for which the choice represents an optimal solution. In contrast, for decisions involving choices between time streams of money (receipts and payments), economic theory makes a precise and testable prediction, namely that (at the margin) people should discount money streams at the after tax market rate of interest.

In order to focus attention on consumption over time, we will usually consider examples where there is only one consumer good, but this good can be consumed in either of two time periods. We will be using two tricks—(a) one trick is to treat consumption in period 1 and consumption in period 2 as two distinct commodities. If you make period 1 consumption the numeraire, then the price of period 2 consumption is the amount of period 1 consumption that you have to give up to get an extra unit of period 2 consumption. This price turns out to be 1/(1 + r), where r is the interest rate. (b) The second is the way you treat income in the two different periods. Suppose that a consumer has an income of y_1 in period 1 and y_2 in period 2 and that there is no inflation. The total amount of period 1 consumption that this consumer could buy, if he borrowed as much money as he could possibly repay in period 2, is $y_1 + \frac{y_2}{1+r}$

Thus, the consumer can borrow or lend any monetary amount at a constant real rate of interest. There are no taxes. The consumer's budget equation for choosing consumption in two periods is

$$c_1 + \frac{c_2}{1+r} = y_1 + \frac{y_2}{1+r} \qquad ...(8.8)$$

Budget constraint represented by equation (8.8) looks just like the standard budget constraint, where the price of good 1 is 1, the price of good 2 is 1/(1 + r), and income is $y_1 + \frac{y_2}{1+r}$. Therefore, if we are given a consumer's utility function, the interest rate, and the consumer's income in each period, we can find his demand for consumption in periods 1 and 2. Having solved for consumption in each period, we can also find saving, since the consumer's saving is just the difference between his period 1 income and his period 1 consumption.

Equation (8.8) can be represented as in the Figure 8.6.

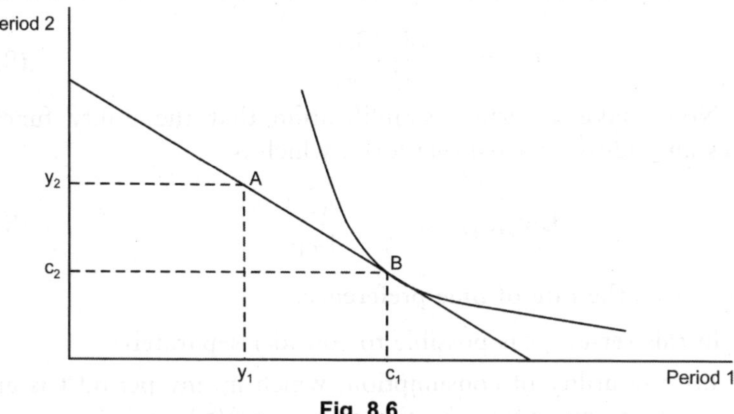

Fig. 8.6

Future income and consumption are represented on the vertical axis, and current income and consumption on the horizontal. In the Fig. 8.6, the point A with co-ordinates (y_2, y_1) will be on the budget constraint. At this point, consumer is neither borrowing nor lending. The slope of the line through A is – (1 + r), where r is the interest rate. The intercept on the horizontal axis is a measure of wealth, given by the present value of income, or $w = y_1 + y_2/(1 + r)$. For a given value of w, the equation of the line can be written as

$$y_2 = (1 + r)\, w - (1 + r)y_1 \qquad \text{...(8.9)}$$

Now suppose that the consumer wants to consume more than his income in period 1 and the consumption bundle can be represented as a single Hicksian composite consumption good, c. Point B in Fig. 8.6 indicates that present expenditure c_1 exceeds income y_1. This is financed by borrowing at interest rate r in period 1, and repaying the amount $(c_1 - y_1)(1 + r)$ in period 2.

Thus, the choice of consumption pattern for the consumer is obtained as the consumption stream (c_1, c_2), which maximises intertemporal utility $U(c_1, c_2)$. The slope of the utility curve is given by

$$dU = \frac{\partial U}{\partial c_1} dc_1 + \frac{\partial U}{\partial c_2} dc_2 = 0 \qquad \text{...(8.10)}$$

$$\frac{dc_2}{dc_1} = -\frac{\partial U / \partial c_1}{\partial U / \partial c_2} \qquad \text{...(8.11)}$$

The equilibrium point is found where the slope of the budget constraint is equal to the slope of the indifference curve, that is

$$-(1+r) = -\frac{\partial U / \partial c_1}{\partial U / \partial c_2} \qquad ...(8.12)$$

Now make a further simplification that the utility function takes an additively separable form, which is

$$U(c_1, c_2) = u(c_2) + \frac{u(c_2)}{1+\rho} \qquad ...(8.13)$$

where ρ is the rate of time preference.

In this set-up, it is possible to consider separately:

(a) the utility of consumption, which in any period t is given from the same sub-utility function $u(c_t)$, and

(b) the consumer's present valuation of that utility, which is just the future utility discounted by the rate of time preference.

In this case, the equilibrium condition is given by

$$-(1+r) = \frac{-(1+\rho)du / dc_1}{du / dc_2} \qquad ...(8.14)$$

If we take into account the fact that the budget constraint must be satisfied, the equilibrium conditions can be given as

$$u'(c_1) = u'(c_2)\frac{1+r}{1+\rho}$$

and
$$c_1 + \frac{c_2}{1+r} = y_1 + \frac{y_2}{1+r} \qquad ...(8.15)$$

Now suppose that the consumer lives for a long time, for convenience taken to be an infinite number of periods. In this case, the problem of the consumer is to choose a consumption stream to maximise the present valuation of the utility of the consumption stream. In other words, choose (c_t, c_{t+1}, c_{t+2}, ...) to maximise

$$U_1 = \frac{u(c_1)}{(1+\rho)} + \frac{u(c_2)}{(1+\rho)^2} + \frac{u(c_3)}{(1+\rho)^3} + ...$$

$$= \sum_{j=1}^{\infty} \{(1+\rho)^{-j} u(c_{t+j-1})\} \qquad ...(8.16)$$

Here, we assume that the consumer makes decisions at the beginning of the period, and receives income and undertakes consumption at the end of the period. We also assume that there is no uncertainty, and that the interest rate is constant. The consumer has to satisfy a budget constraint of the form

$$\sum_{j=1}^{\infty}\{(1+r)^{-j} c_{t+j-1}\} = \sum_{j=1}^{\infty}\{(1+r)^{-j} y_{t+j-1}\} \qquad ...(8.17)$$

Equation (8.17) states that the present value of consumption must equal the present value of income. The optimisation of utility subject to the budget constraint implies that in equilibrium

$$u'(c_t) = u'(c_{t+1})\frac{(1+r)}{(1+\rho)} \qquad ...(8.18)$$

Now let us explain the condition represented by equation (8.15). The first part of the equation (8.15) reflects the degree to which the consumer would prefer to consume today rather than tomorrow, and the rate of interest, which is the rate at which consumer can borrow and lend in the market. If the rate of time preference and the rate of interest are equal, it follows that $u'(c_1) = u'(c_2)$ so that $c_1 = c_2$, and consumption is constant over time. Conversely, if the rate of time preference is greater than the rate of interest, the consumer can be thought of as being relatively impatient. In terms of equation (8.15) this implies that $u'(c_1) < u'(c_2)$ and in each period the marginal utility of consumption is decreasing, it follows that $c_1 > c_2$.

Relative Income Hypothesis

James Duesenberry's formulation of Relative Income Hypothesis (RIH) was one of the earliest attempts to resolve the differences between the predictions based upon the AIH and observed phenomena. It has two parts—the first is that people's consumption is influenced by their relative position in the distribution of income and the second is that consumption is influenced by the comparison of their income to their own previous peak income. Unlike the AIH, Duesenberry regards the consumption function as a reversible function. He begins with a critique of Keynesian consumption function which is based upon the assumptions (i) that every individual's consumption behaviour is independent of that of every other individual, and (ii) that consumption relations are reversible in time.[20] He builds his model around the following four assumptions:

(a) Physical needs and social culture require the consumption of certain goods.

(b) Each of the needs, whether physical or cultural, may be satisfied by a number of goods which are qualitatively different.

(c) Some of these goods are regarded superior and some as inferior.

(d) There is some scale of ranking of these goods which might be used for any specific purpose.[21]

Duesenberry argues that there is some basic drive to secure a higher standard of living in the western societies leading to higher consumption. "In a fundamental sense the basic source of the drive toward higher consumption is to be found in the character of our culture."[22] He argues that introduction of new articles of consumption and the "demonstration effect" lead an individual to break his equilibrium and induce him to increase his expenditure on consumption. Duesenberry explains the demonstration effect in the following manner:

> ".........people believe that the consumption of high quality goods for any purpose is desirable and important. If they habitually use one set of goods, they can be made dissatisfied with them by a demonstration of the superiority of others. But more knowledge of the existence of superior goods is not a very effective habit breaker. Frequent contact with them may be. In this field it is not only true that "what you don't know won't hurt you" but that what you do know does hurt you."[23]

Through the operation of "demonstration effect" Duesenberry does away with the assumption of independent utilities which is implict in the AIH and introduce 'interdependence' in the utility function.[24] The utility function used by Duesenberry is

$$u_i = f_i\,(C_{i1}/R_1,\ C_{i2}/R_2,\ \ldots\ C_{in}/R_n,\ A_{i1}/R_1,\ \ldots A_{in}/R_n)$$

where,

u_i = utility function if ith individual.

$C_{i1} \ldots C_{in}$ = Consumption of n goods by the individual i.

$A_{i1} \ldots A_{in}$ = Values of n assets owned by the individual i.

$R_i = \Sigma a_{ij}$ C, a weighted average of consumption expenditure of other individuals; a_{ij} is the weight applied to consumption of jth individual by ith individuals.

Using the above utility function Duesenberry formulated the RIH which has been summarized in the following propositions:

(a) In periods of steadily rising income the aggregate saving ratio tends to be independent of income.

(b) The saving ratio will be affected by changes in interest rate, income expectations, the distribution of income, the rate of growth of income, and the ago distribution of population.

(c) On balance, changes in these variables have not been sufficiently large to have had much effects on the saving ratio.

(d) Over the trade cycle the saving ratio is dependent on the ratio of current income to previous peak income.[25]

The aggregate saving function deduced by the RIH is

$$\frac{S_t}{Y_t} = b\left(\frac{Yb}{Y_j}\right) + a \qquad ...(8.19)$$

where S_t = current saving, Y_t = current income. Y_j = previous peak income in case of time-series data. In case of cross-section data Y_j is income of other country or group.[26] A negative coefficient of b in the above equation would confirm the RIH. Thus, RIH was one of several attempts to reconcile the apparent inconsistencies of the AIH and to assert that consumers may not adjust their consumption (and hence savings) immediately and completely to the current level of income.

Let us consider the following model.

We will consider a small economy that faces a given world interest rate, r and a discrete and infinite time horizon with t = 0,1, 2,3,……, ∞. Every period, economy produces a composite good that may be consumed or invested. Output, Y, is produced combining physical capital, K and labour, 1 – L. The production function, f(K, 1 – L), is homogenous of degree one and satisfies the usual Inada conditions.

Since markets are competitive, factors are paid their marginal products and therefore,

$$w_t = f\left(\frac{K_t}{1-L_t}\right) - \left(\frac{K_t}{1-L_t}\right) f'\left(\frac{K_t}{1-L_t}\right) \qquad ...(8.20)$$

$$r_t = f'\left(\frac{K_t}{1-L_t}\right) - \delta \qquad ...(8.21)$$

where f denotes the production function in intensive form and capital is assumed to depreciate at the exponential rate δ.

Since we have assumed an open and small economy, facing a constant world rate of interest, r, the domestic capital labour ratio is pinned down by equation (8.21) with $r_t = r$. The degree of capital intensity, in turn, pins down the domestic wage rate at w. Any changes in labour supply are accommodated by capital flows so that the domestic wage and the interest rate remain constant at w and r respectively. Let us denote the gross return to capital by R = 1 + r.

Now consider that the individuals live for two periods—youth and old-age. At the end of his youth, each individual gives birth to a single offspring and therefore at any point in time there are two generations alive. Each generation is composed of n individuals, indexed by i = 1, 2, 3, ..., n.

Within a generation, individuals differ only in their initial levels of wealth left by their parents. The distribution of wealth in period t is represented by a cumulative distribution function $G_t(b)$. The initial distribution function $G_0(b)$ is given. Consider the i-th individual born in period t. In the initial period of his life, he is endowed with one unit of time that he allocates between leisure, l_t^i, and work. His labour income, $w(1 - l_t^i)$, together with his inherited wealth, b_t^i, is divided between current consumption, c_t^i, and saving, s_t^i. His first period budget constraint is given by

$$w(1 - l_t^i) + b_t^i = c_t^i + s_t^i \qquad ...(8.22)$$

In the second period, the individual is retired and his only source of income comes from the return on the savings he made when young, Rs_t^i. He allocates this income between old-age consumption, d^i_{t+1}, and inherits, b^i_{t+1}. Hence, the old-age budget constraint of the individual will be

$$Rs^i_t = d^i_{t+1} + b^i_{t+1} \qquad ...(8.23)$$

The following life-cycle utility function describes the preferences of an individual born in period t.

$$U_t\left(\hat{c}^i_t, l^i_t, d^i_{t+1}, b^i_{t+1}\right) = u\left(\hat{c}^i_t\right) + v\left(l^i_t\right) + \beta\left[u\left(\hat{d}^i_{t+1}\right) + \phi\left(b^i_{t+1}\right)\right] \qquad ...(8.24)$$

where, $0 < \beta < 1$ is the subjective discount factor. The three subutility functions, u(.), v(.) and ϕ(.), are assumed to be increasing, concave and to satisfy the standard Inada conditions.

As we have assumed that the satisfaction derived from consumption does not depend on the absolute level of consumption itself but rather in how it compares to the consumption of some reference group, therefore we adopt an additive specification for relative consumption; $\hat{c}^i_t = c^i_t - \gamma \hat{g}^i_t$ and $\hat{d}^i_{t+1} = d^i_{t+1} - \gamma \bar{o}^i_{t+1}$, where $\bar{g}^i_t$ and $\bar{o}^i_{t+1}$ are the average consumption levels of the reference group of the i-th individual when young and old respectively and $0 < \gamma < 1$ is a measure of the relatively concerns.

Since, all young households share the same reference group and therefore the reference level of consumption is given by

$$\bar{g}^i_t = \bar{c}_t = \frac{1}{n}\sum_{j=1}^{n} c^j_t \qquad ...(8.25)$$

and similarly all old households share the same reference group, with the reference level of consumption being,

$$\bar{o}^i_{t+1} = \bar{d}_{t+1} = \frac{1}{n}\sum_{j=1}^{n} d^j_{t+1} \qquad ...(8.26)$$

The i-th individual of the generation born in period t takes as given his inherited wealth, factor prices, and the choices of the other members of his generation, and chooses the amount of time devoted to work, $(1 - l^i_t)$, his level of saving, s^i_t, and the second-period consumption, d^i_{t+1}, to maximise his utility function

$$u(w(1-l^i_t) + b^i_t - s^i_t - \gamma\bar{c}_t) + v(l^i_t) + \beta[u(d^i_{t+1} - \gamma\bar{d}^i_{t+1}) + \phi(Rs^i_t - d^i_{t+1})]$$

The solution to this problem is characterised by the following optimality conditions,

$$u'(c^i_t - \gamma\bar{c}_t) = \beta R\phi'(Rs^i_t - d^i_{t+1}) \quad ...(8.27)$$

$$u'(c^i_t - \gamma\bar{c}_t)w = v'(l^i_t) \quad ...(8.28)$$

$$u'(d^i_{t+1} - \gamma\bar{d}_{t+1}) = \phi'(b^i_{t+1}) \quad ...(8.29)$$

An increase in the consumption of the reference group increases the marginal utility of consumption leading to a reduction in saving and leisure. Equations (8.27) - (8.29) together with the budget constraints, (8.22) and (8.23), implicitly define the optimal choices of leisure, saving and bequests as functions of the relative income of the individual. Equation (8.24) can be rewritten in logarithmic form as

$$U_t\,(\hat{c}^i_t, l^i_t, d^i_{t+1}, (b^i_{t+1}) = \ln(c^i_t - \gamma\bar{c}_t) + \mu\ln(l^i_t) + \beta\left[\ln(d^i_{t+1} - \gamma\bar{d}_{t+1}) + \alpha\ln(b^i_{t+1})\right] \quad ...(8.30)$$

where, $\mu > 0$ and $\alpha > 0$ denote the importance of leisure and bequest motives respectively.

Given the level of saving, s^i_t, an old individual at time t+1 chooses d^i_{t+1} and b^i_{t+1} to maximise

$$V = \ln(d^i_{t+1} - \gamma\bar{d}_{t+1}) + \alpha\ln(b^i_{t+1}) \quad ...(8.31)$$

subject to equation (8.23). The solution to the problem (8.31) is

$$d^i_{t+1} = \frac{1}{1+\alpha}(Rs^i_t + \alpha\gamma\bar{d}_{t+1}) \quad ...(8.32)$$

$$b^i_{t+1} = \frac{\alpha}{1+\alpha}(Rs^i_t - \gamma\bar{d}_{t+1}) \quad ...(8.33)$$

and therefore

$$V(Rs^i_t) = (1+\alpha)\ln(Rs^i_t - \gamma\bar{d}_{t+1}) + \ln\left(\frac{1}{1+\alpha}\right) + \alpha\ln\left(\frac{\alpha}{1+\alpha}\right) \quad ...(8.34)$$

The young individual at time t then chooses c_t^i, l_t^i, and s_t^i to maximise

$$\ln\left(c_t^i - \gamma\bar{c}_t\right) + \mu\ln\left(l_t^i\right) + \beta v(Rs_t^i) \quad ...(8.35)$$

subject to the equation (8.22). The necessary conditions for equation (8.35) are

$$wl_t^i = \mu(c_t^i - \gamma\bar{c}_t) \quad ...(8.36)$$

$$s_t^i = \beta(1+\alpha)(c_t^i - \gamma\bar{c}_t) + \frac{\gamma\bar{d}_{t+1}}{R} \quad ...(8.37)$$

From equations (8.22), (8.36) and (8.37), we have

$$c_t^i(1+\mu+(1+\alpha)\beta) = w + b_t^i - \frac{\gamma\bar{d}_{t+1}}{R} + (\mu+(1+\alpha)\beta)\gamma\bar{c}_t \quad ...(8.38)$$

Since household inherits the average bequest $\bar{b}_t$, equation (8.38) can be rewritten as

$$\bar{c}_t[1+(\mu+(1+\alpha)\beta)(1-\gamma)] = w + \bar{b}_t - \frac{\gamma\bar{d}_{t+1}}{R} \quad ...(8.39)$$

From equations (8.32) and (8.33) we have

$$\bar{d}_{t+1} = \frac{1}{1+(1-\gamma)\alpha}R\bar{s}_t \quad ...(8.40)$$

$$\bar{b}_{t+1} = \frac{(1-\gamma)\alpha}{1+(1-\gamma)\alpha}R\bar{s}_t \quad ...(8.41)$$

Substituting equation (8.40) into equation (8.37), we have

$$\bar{c}_t = \frac{1}{\beta[1+(1-\gamma)\alpha]}\bar{s}_t \quad ...(8.42)$$

The level of saving of the average individual born in period t can be obtained by substituting equations (8.40) and (8.42) into equation (8.39),

$$\bar{s}_t = \beta[1+(1-\gamma)\alpha]\chi(w+\bar{b}_t) = \beta[1+(1-\gamma)\alpha]\chi\tilde{\bar{y}}_t \quad ...(8.43)$$

where,

$$\chi = \frac{1}{1+(\mu+\alpha\beta)(1-\gamma)+\beta},$$

$$\tilde{\bar{y}}_t = w+\bar{b}_t.$$

$\tilde{\bar{y}}_t$ is the potential lifetime income of the average individual of the generation born at time t, i.e. the lifetime income of the agent that inherits the average bequest if all of his time endowed is devoted to work. Saving is just a constant fraction, $0 < \beta[1+(1-\gamma)\alpha]\chi < 1$, of this measure of lifetime income.

From equations (8.36), (8.39), (8.40), (8.41) and (8.43) we have

$$\bar{c}_t = \chi\tilde{\bar{y}}_t \quad \text{...(8.44)}$$

$$\bar{l}_t = \frac{\mu(1-\gamma)\chi\tilde{\bar{y}}_t}{w} \quad \text{...(8.45)}$$

$$\bar{d}_{t+1} = R\beta\,\chi\tilde{\bar{y}}_t \quad \text{...(8.46)}$$

$$\bar{b}_{t+1} = (1-\gamma)\alpha R\beta\chi\tilde{\bar{y}}_t \quad \text{...(8.47)}$$

We assume, $\frac{\bar{b}_t}{w} < \frac{1+\beta+\alpha\beta(1-\gamma)}{\mu(1-\gamma)}$, so that the constant $\bar{l}_t \le 1$ is satisfied with strict inequality.

Using the result of the average household, the behaviour of the i-th individual of the same generation can be characterised by substituting equation (8.44) and (8.46) into (8.38) to reach first period consumption for the i-th individual as

$$c_t^i = \frac{1}{1+\mu+(1+\alpha)\beta}\left\{\tilde{y}_t^i + (\beta\alpha+\mu)\gamma\chi\tilde{\bar{y}}_t\right\} \quad \text{...(8.48)}$$

The level of saving can be determined by combining equation (8.48) with (8.37) and (8.46) as

$$s_t^i = \frac{(1+\alpha)\beta}{1+\mu+(1+\alpha)\beta}\left\{\tilde{y}_t^i - \left(\frac{\alpha-\mu}{1+\alpha}\right)\gamma\chi\tilde{\bar{y}}_t\right\} \quad \text{...(8.49)}$$

where, $\tilde{y}_t^i = w + b_t^i$ is the potential lifetime income of the i-th household of the generation born at time t. In the equation (8.49) we see that the individual saving is a linear function of individual and average income.

Now we can solve for the remaining optimal choices as functions of individual and average potential lifetime income as

$$d_{t+1}^{i} = \frac{R\beta}{1+\mu+(1+\alpha)\beta}\left\{\tilde{y}_t^i + (\beta\alpha+\mu)\gamma\chi\bar{\tilde{y}}_t\right\} \quad ...(8.50)$$

$$l_t^i = \frac{\mu}{w(1+\mu+(1+\alpha)\beta)}\left\{\tilde{y}_t^i - (1+\beta)\,\gamma\chi\bar{\tilde{y}}_t\right\} \quad ...(8.51)$$

$$b_{t+1}^{i} = \frac{\alpha R\beta}{1+\mu+(1+\alpha)\beta}\left\{\tilde{y}_t^i - (1+\beta)\,\gamma\chi\bar{\tilde{y}}_t\right\} \quad ...(8.52)$$

Consumption of the i-th households, represented by equation (8.48) and (8.50), consists two components:

(a) The increase in the household's potential lifetime income.

(b) The influence of interpersonal comparisons and increases in the potential lifetime income of his reference group.

As a result, leisure and bequests depend on relative, rather than absolute income. When individual satisfaction depends on consumption comparisons across households, as a growing body of empirical evidence suggests, the relevant variable driving the saving and labour supply choices is the comparison between individual's potential lifetime income and the potential lifetime income of his reference group.

Duesenberry's RIH is criticised on the following issues.

(a) The RIH assumes a proportional increase in consumption with increase in income.

(b) This hypothesis assumes a direct relationship between consumption and income. But this may not happen every time.

(c) This hypothesis assumes consumers' behaviour fully irreversible. But consumers' behaviour is slowly irreversible over time.

(d) This hypothesis does not take into account other factors which influence consumers' expenditure such as asset holdings, urbanisation, age composition, the appearance of new consumer goods, etc.

(e) The RIH assumes that consumers' preferences are interdependent and the consumer expenditure is related to his consumption pattern. But it is not always true.

The Permanent Income Hypothesis

Friedman's permanent income hypothesis (PIH) is considered somewhat like a breakthrough which has opened up new vistas of research on saving and consumption function.[27] The permanent income hypothesis (PIH) of Friedman is based on three fundamental tenets.

(a) Friedman postulated that each household has some conception of his future expected income which is considered to be stable. This he calls permanent income. The actual income of the household (that is what is usually referred as income and termed by Friedman as measured income) may or may not coincide with the permanent income. The deviations between the measured income and permanent income are called the transitory income which may be either positive or negative. Thus, we have the following identity:

$$Y_m = Y_p + Y_{tr} \qquad ...(8.53)$$

which says that measured income is composed of permanent income and transitory income. The permanent income, according to Friedman, reflects "the effects of those factors that the unit regards as determining its capital value of wealth: the non-human wealth it owns, the personal attributes of earner in the unit such as their training, ability, personality, the attributes of the economic activity of the earners and so on. It is analogous to the 'expected' value of a probability distribution.[28] Transitory component of income, on the other hand reflects the effects of 'chance' or 'accidental' factors which cause the measured income to rise or fall temporarily. For example, a person gets some extra income by winning a lottery ticket, or some windfall such as some unexpected rise in the prices of shares etc. The income earned through such windfall gains is purely temporary and the consumer recognises it to be such. So he will not base his consumption upon such transitory income as he would have to cut down his consumption as soon as the temporary effect disappears completely. Thus, it is more likely that consumer shall base his consumption (and therefore savings) upon what he regards his permanent income.

Like income, measured consumption is also viewed as being composed of two elements—permanent consumption and transitory consumption:

$$C_m = C_p + C_{tr} \quad ...(8.54)$$

Permanent income at a particular period is the product of two factors: w, the wealth of the consumer, which is estimated at discounted present value of a stream of future expected receipts and the rate, r at which these expected receipts are discounted.

Mathematically, $w = \sum_{t=1}^{n} \frac{y_t}{(1+r)^t} \quad t = 1, 2, \ldots, n.$

Therefore,

$$w = \frac{y_1}{1+r} + \frac{y_2}{(1+r)^2} + \ldots + \frac{y_{n-1}}{(1+r)^{n-1}} + \frac{y_n}{(1+r)^n} \quad ...(8.55)$$

For simple formulation,

Let $y_1 = y_2 = y_3 = \ldots = y_{n-1} = y_n = y$

$$\therefore w = \frac{y}{1+r} + \frac{y}{(1+r)^2} + \ldots + \frac{y}{(1+r)^{n-1}} + \frac{y}{(1+r)^n}$$

$$= \frac{y}{1+r}\left\{1 + \frac{1}{(1+r)} + \frac{1}{(1+r)^2} + \ldots + \frac{1}{(1+r)^{n-1}}\right\}$$

$$= \frac{y}{1+r}.1.\frac{1-\left(\frac{1}{1+r}\right)^n}{1-\frac{1}{1+r}} \quad \because n \to \infty$$

$$= \frac{y}{1+r} \cdot \frac{1}{1-\frac{1}{1+r}} \quad \therefore \left(\frac{1}{1+r}\right)^n \to 0 \text{ as } r > 1$$

$$= \frac{y}{1+r} \cdot \frac{(1+r)}{r}$$

$$\therefore w = \frac{y}{r} \quad ...(8.56)$$

Here y means permanent income.

Therefore, $y_p = rw$

(b) Permanent consumption is a multiple, K of the permanent income. That is,

$$C_P = Ky_p \qquad [0 < K \leq 1] \qquad \text{...(8.57)}$$

where K depends on i, w, u, i.e.,

$$K = f(i, w, u)$$

where, i = rate of interest, w = the ratio of human to non-human (physical) capital, and u = catch all variable. Hence, $C_P = Ky_p$ postulates a proportional relationship between permanent consumption and permanent income. The factor of proportionality is K.

(c) Transitory income and permanent income, transitory consumption and permanent consumption, transitory consumption and transitory income are assumed to be uncorrelated.

That is, $$r(y_{tr}, y_p) = r(C_{tr}, C_P) = r(C_{tr}, y_{tr}) = 0 \qquad \text{...(8.58)}$$

where, r = coefficient of correlation.

As a result a consumer unit is assumed to be determined its standard of living on the basis of expected returns from its resources over its life time. This expected returns are assumed to be constant from time to time, though in actual practice, some fluctuation would result over time. Actual consumption and income deviate from the planned of permanent levels to the extent that transitory factors enter in.

From an empirical point of view this is a very difficult hypothesis to test but from the analytical point of view this is a very rich hypothesis. Under this hypothesis, the slope of the observed consumption function, $C = a + by$ can be shown to be equivalent to $b = KP_y$, where P_y is the ratio of variances of the permanent component of income (y_p) to the total income (y), i.e.,

$$P_y = \frac{\Sigma(y_p - \overline{y}_p)^2}{\Sigma(y - \overline{y})^2} \qquad \text{...(8.59)}$$

Since K is constant by assumption. This means that fluctuation in the slope of the measured income reflects the fluctuation in the permanent component of income.

The above version is regarded as a stricter version of PIH as it requires that marginal propensity to consume out of transitory income to be zero. However, several studies have reported positive but significantly different from zero marginal propensity to consume out of transitory income.[29] A rather mild version of PIH allows for marginal propensity to consume out of transitory income to be positive but it still requires that it must be less than the MPC out of permanent income.

The basic problem in the estimation of K is that being a 'theoretical construct' Y_p itself is unknown. In order to know K, it is imperative to estimate Y_p. For time-series data, permanent income can be viewed as a weighted average of present and past incomes. Friedman has given the following formula for estimation on permanent income.[30]

$$Y_p(T) = \beta \int_{T=t}^{\infty} e^{(\beta-\alpha)(t-T)}\, y_t\, dt \qquad ...(8.60)$$

where,

β = coefficient of adjustment between measured income and permanent income.

α = Growth rate of income.

T = Present time period.

t = Index of time period.

y_t = Measured income at the time t.

The discrete analogue of the above formula is

$$Y_p(T) = \beta\left[Y_t + e^{(\beta-\alpha)}Y_{t-1} + e^{(\beta-\alpha)2}Y_{t-2} + ... + e^{T(\beta-\alpha)}Y_{t-T}\right] \qquad ...(8.61)$$

The weights decline continuously. This means that higher weights are attached to present and more recent incomes and relatively lower weights are given to incomes of past periods.

The inverse of β is regarded as consumer's horizon, which is defined as the period required by the consumer to dichotomize the nature of abrupt and random changes. Friedman points out that the span of time which shall be relevant for calculation of permanent income depends upon the magnitude of β. If it is large, the discrepancy between measured income and expected income is removed at a rapid rate and the time span is shorter.[31] Conversely, a larger time span is required if β is small and thus rate of adjustment is low. For the United States, Friedman estimated the value of β to be 0.4 and the consumer horizon as 2½ years.[32] Williamson, in his study of saving function for a number of Asian countries also used a three year horizon.[33] Friend and Taubman also used three year horizon for pooled data from 22 developed and less developed countries.[34] The same practice was followed by Gupta in his study of per capita household saving in India.[35] Apparently it seems that these researchers have used a three year horizon simply because Friedman calculated the consumer horizon for close to three years in the United States. There is no reason why consumer horizon in developing countries which are so different not only in social and economic structures but also in behaviour pattern, has to be the same as in the advanced countries.

As pointed out earlier the forceful presentation of the PIH has been responsible for opening new vistas of research on consumption function. There has been a flood of research studies which have presented mixed types of evidences, sometimes supporting and sometimes rejecting the PIH. The distribution of National Service Life Insurance in 1950 in the United States and restitution payment by Germany to Israel made it possible to test the PIH directly. On the basis of American data Bodkin argued that there is no significant difference between the marginal propensity to consume out of permanent income and marginal propensity to consume out of transitory income while he treated the payment of dividend as transitory income.[36] Thus Bodkin's finding did not provide any evidence in favour of the PIH. On the other hand, on the basis of Israeli experience, treating the restitute payment as transitory income, Kreinin presented evidence in support of the PIH.[37] Kreinin's results shows that there is a significant difference between the marginal propensities to consume out of permanent and transitory income, though the correlation between consumption and transitory income is not zero as claimed by the strict version of the hypothesis. Thus, it seems that strict version of the PIH postulating a zero marginal propensity to consume out of transitory income is not tenable. However, one could concede the PIH claim that marginal propensities to consume permanent and transitory income are significantly different from each other. Holbrook and Stafford have tried a general formulation of the PIH using three year panel data of a sample of United States families.[38] They distinguish five different types of income viz. husband's income, wife's income and other member's income, transfer income, mixed capital and labor income, and other income. They have concluded that marginal propensity to consume was significantly different in each case. Thus, the essence of PIH seems to be that (i) savings are proportional to income and (ii) propensities to consume for different types of income are different.

Friedman's PIH has been criticised on following grounds.

(a) PIH assumes that the coefficient of correlation between transitory component of consumption and transitory component of income is zero. This is not real. The natural behaviour of consumers is very much contrary. Suppose, a person who has gained a profit does not deposit the entire amount in the bank but spends a whole or part of it in his current consumption. Similary a person who has faced a loss does reduce or postpone his current consumption.

(b) This hypothesis assumes that the APC of all families, whether they are rich or poor, is the same in the long run. But it is not practical. The consumption of the poor is higher relatively to their incomes while the saving of the rich is higher relatively to their incomes. Even consumption differs among the persons with same level of permanent income.

(c) This hypothesis cannot make distinction between human and non-human wealth.

(d) In this hypothesis, the concept of measured income creates confusion by bringing permanent and transitory components of income. Again, permanent and transitory components of consumption also create confusion.

The Life Cycle Hypothesis

The life cycle hypothesis (LCH) presents a well-defined linkage between the consumption plans of an individual and his income and income expectations as he passes from childhood, through the work participating years, into retirement and eventual disease. It was developed by American economist Irving Fisher and English economist Roy Harrod, before later being extended by Japanese economist Albert Ando and Italian-born economist Franco Modigliani.[39]

The main building block of life cycle models is saving decision, i.e., the division of income between consumption and saving. The saving decision is driven by preferences between present and future consumption. Given the income stream, the household receives over time, the sequence of optimal consumption and saving decisions over the entire life can be computed. The life cycle hypothesis assumes that people try to maximise their utility by developing an optimal consumption pattern over their lifetimes. The consumption path is constrained by the resources available to them. The present value of planned consumption must equal the present value of income plus the initial wealth. The LCH assumes that people smooth their consumption spending over their lifetimes by dissaving in their pre-working years and retirement years, while saving during most of their working years. This has been shown in Fig. 8.7.

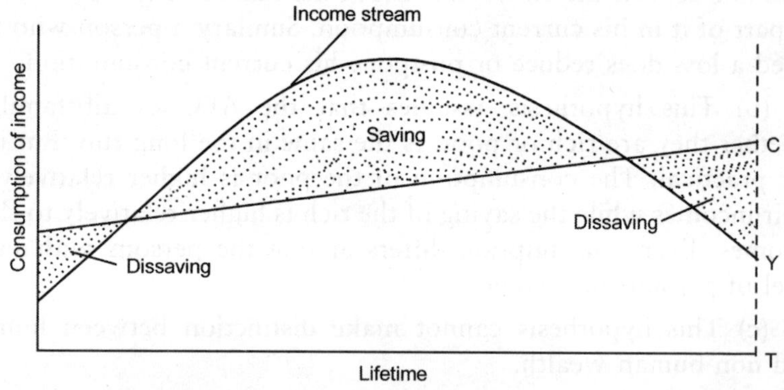

Fig. 8.7

In Fig. 8.7 consumption has been shown as rising gradually over the life cycle. The typical shape of the income profile over the life cycle starts with low income during the early years of the working life, then income increases until a peak is reached before retirement, while pension income during retirement is substantially lower. To make up for the lower income during retirement and to avoid a sharp drop in utility at the point of retirement, individuals will save some fraction of their income during their working life and dissave during retirement. This results in a hump-shaped savings profile over the life cycle—the main prediction of the life cycle theory.

The life cycle theory assumes that individuals try to maximise the utility deriving from their entire life cycle consumption. Therefore, consumption must be continuous, even if income through the life cycle is discontinuous; and saving is primarily done to finance consumption during the retirement period. For the pre-1950 economist, microeconomic profile of consumption and saving has, according to Modigliani, a number of macroeconomic implications:

(a) the saving rate of a country is entirely independent of its per capita income;
(b) different national saving rates are consistent with an identical individual life cycle behaviour;
(c) between countries with identical individual behaviour, the aggregate saving rate will be higher the higher the long-run growth rate of the economy. It will be zero for zero growth;
(d) the wealth-income ratio is a decreasing function of the growth rate, thus being largest at zero growth;
(e) an economy can accumulate a very substantial stock of wealth relative to income even if no wealth is passed on by bequests;
(f) the main parameter that controls the wealth-income ratio and the saving rate for given growth is the prevailing length of retirement.

The key, which rendered the multi-period analysis tractable under subjective certainty, was the specification that the lifetime utility function be homothetic—this permitted planned consumption for each future period to be written as a function of expected wealth as seen at the planning date, the functional parameters being in no way dependent upon wealth, but upon age and tastes. According to Modigliani, the life cycle hypothesis is based on the following assumptions:

(a) income is constant until retirement, zero thereafter;
(b) zero interest rate;
(c) constant consumption over the life cycle;
(d) absence of bequests.

It has been assumed that individuals derive utility only from present and future consumption and from the assets which he wants to bequeath. It is noteworthy that individual's utility function depends upon his own consumption. This utility function is maximized subject to the resources available to him. The resources of an individual are sum total of his current and discounted future earnings over his lifetime and his current net worth. Thus, an individual's consumption is given as follows:

$$C_T = f(V_t, t, T), \qquad T = t, 1 + t, \ldots\ldots\ldots\ldots\ldots\ldots\ldots, L$$

$$V_t = \sum_{T=1}^{N} \frac{Y_t}{(1+r)^{T+1-t}} + a_t \qquad \ldots(8.62)$$

C_T = Consumption,

T = index of time,

r = discount rate,

N = earning span,

t = Present age,

L = Life span,

Y = Income, and

a_t = asset at time t.

Thus, an individual's consumption is a function of his current income and future income (which in fact depends upon the rate of return on capital) with parameters depending upon age. The individual consumption function obtained above is then aggregated to get community's consumption function.

The LCH also implies that proportion of income saved is essentially independent of income. Thus, proportionality hypothesis of the RIH and PIH is confirmed while AIH is rejected. Furthermore, LCH maintains that proportion of income saved would depend upon the age-composition of the saver and his earning span. Thus, it brings age composition and family size as determinant of saving behaviour. Yotopoulos and Nugent have very cogently summarized the LCH position on this issue:

> "The life cycle hypothesis is cast in terms of an individual household member, with each member's consumption flow equalized through life. Savings, however, are measured per family and saving ratios are expressed as a proportion of income. Family incomes are observed to follow roughly parabolic paths over the earning span, rising sharply to a peak in the 35-54 age range and declining thereafter. Family size is also correlated with household age, reaching a peak at ages 35-44 and declining thereafter as children establish their own households. As a result of these two

forces, income per household member reaches a low at ages 35-44 and rises thereafter. After considering the age-of-household correlates of income and family size, equalization of consumption per household member would predict that average savings as a proportion of family income are high in the age group 45-64 and low in the age group 25-44 and at retirement."[40]

There have not been several attempts to test the LCH for developing countries, with two notable exceptions. Landsberger applied the LCH type model to Isreal.[41] He estimated the linear consumption function which discriminates between different age-groups of head of households. He took family consumption, family current income, windfall income and the age of the head of family as key variables. Regression equations were estimated for four age groups and for two types of consumption (consumer durables and non-durables) for two time periods. Landsberger wanted to investigate whether marginal propensity to consume changes with age. His results indicated that marginal propensity to consume increased with age for five out of the eight pairs. These were the only pairs for which the estimated parameters were statistically significant.

Kelley and Williamson have made an attempt to test the applicability of LCH formulation to Indonesia. They had cross-section data of 490 families collected through a sample survey in Jogjakarta region in Indonesia. Kelley and Williamson regressed per capita household saving against per capita household income for five household age groups, using the following equation:

$$\frac{S_h}{N} = a + \frac{bY_d}{N} \qquad \ldots(8.63)$$

where,

S_h = household saving,

Y_d = disposable income, and

N = Family size.

Statistically significant results were obtained for all but the 40-49 age group; estimated values of b the youngest group (20-29) to 0.599 for the oldest group (60-69). For the rural households they estimated marginal propensity to save increased from 0.133 in the age group 20-29 to 0.75 in the age group 60-69. Thus LCH formulation was considered to be confirmed by the data.[42]

The life cycle hypothesis has been criticised on the following reasons.

(a) The consumers, generally, do not always make plan for their expenditure on consumption over their life time. They stress more concentration on present consumption rather than on future consumption.

(b) This hypothesis pre-supposes that consumption is directly related to the assets possessed by the individual. Consumption increases with the increase in asset holding and vice versa.

(c) Consumption also depends upon individual's attitude towards life. Two persons having same income and assets may not consume same, i.e. one may consume more than the other.

(d) The life cycle theory assumes that each household, in making consumption decision, has at all times a definite and conscious vision, which they hold with enough certainty that it would be worthwhile to use this vision as a basis for rational planning of consumption decisions. However, these assumptions are unrealistic in the real world.

(e) It fails to recognise the presence of liquidity constraints. Even if a household or individual possessed a concrete vision of future income, there is little opportunity in real world capital markets for borrowing for any long period on the basis of this expected future income. As a result, consumption may be much more responsive to changes in current income, whether temporary or not, than would be predicted on the basis of the life cycle hypothesis.

(f) Bequests play an important role in determining saving, rather than life cycle motive, which emphasizes saving to finance consumption in retirement.

Policy Implication of the life cycle hypothesis

The life cycle hypothesis is a great framework to think about the policy implications, for instance about the effect on national saving of taxes, expenditures and government debt, or about the effect on individual and national saving when people must contribute to funded or unfunded pension plans.

Fiscal Policy: The key element in the Keynesian analysis of the multiplier effects of changes in investment or fiscal policy variables is the response of consumption to current income. According to the life cycle hypothesis, consumption is determined primarily by expected lifetime income and wealth. A change in current income has little influence on consumer behaviour. In the empirical work of Ando and Modigliani, expected future income is assumed to be proportional to current income. If this is correct, we would expect a strong response of consumption to current income, since changes in current income cause proportional changes in expected lifetime income as well. Ando and Modigliani's estimate of the consumption function implies that the MPC out of current labour income is 0.72. This value is high enough to be consistent with the earlier Keynesian multiplier analysis and to imply strong effects for changes in taxes and government spending. In other empirical work by Modigliani, expected lifetime income is assumed instead to depend on a weighted average of the past 12 quarters' income levels. With this assumption as well, the response of consumption to income was strong enough to produce results consistent with earlier Keynesian analysis. The life cycle hypothesis does not therefore seem to imply an essential modification of the general Keynesian multiplier or fiscal policy analysis.

Life cycle hypothesis suggests that expenditures financed by deficit tend to be paid by future generations; those financed by taxes are paid by current generations. National debt is therefore a burden; it reduces the stock of private capital, which in turn reduces the flow of output, if capital is productive. Modigliani provided the first test of this proposition using aggregate US wealth data.

Later Barro demonstrated that if agents have altruistic bequest motives, they behave as if they have infinite lives, and that models with altruistic consumers have sharply different implications concerning the relation between fiscal policy and national saving. Private saving being controlled by life cycle consideration, should be independent of the government budget stance, and therefore private wealth should be independent of national debt. It follows that the national debt tends to crowd out an equal amount of private capital at a social cost equal to the return on the lost capital, which is approximately equal to the government interest bill. This conclusion stands in sharp contrast to that advocated by the so-called Ricardian equivalence proposition, which holds that whenever the government runs a deficit, the private sector will save more in order to offset the unfavourable effect of the deficit on future generations.

The quantitative effect of deficits on saving depends on the length of the average planning horizon. If the horizon is infinite, as effectively postulated by proponents of the debt neutrality proposition, than taxes matter not at all, for given expenditure. This implies that budget deficits have no effect on national saving, and the same would be true of any transfer, including payment of interest on national debt. By contrast, if the planning horizon is of the order of the length of remaining life as postulated by the LCH, then the effect of deficit on national saving will be large.

Monetary Policy: The life cycle hypothesis implies that monetary policy may have important direct effects on consumption as well as investment. According to LCH, household wealth is one of the main determinants of consumption. Monetary policy affects household wealth and therefore consumption. Monetary policy actions affect wealth both directly by changing the quantity of money that is a component of household net wealth and by affecting interest rates and consequently the market value of other assets, such as government and private bonds and corporate equities. An increase in the interest rate resulting from a tight money policy will cause bond prices to fall and, hence, households to suffer capital losses on bonds. A decline in interest rates resulting from an expansionary monetary policy will cause bond prices to rise, with resulting capital gains on bonds. Equity prices would also be expected to move inversely with interest rates. Equities pay streams of dividends, and with higher market interest rates, the price investors will be willing to pay for an equity with a given dividend flow will fall.

Hence, the tight money policies reduce wealth and consumption, whereas expansionary policies have the opposite effects. Empirical work by Modigliani indicates that monetary policy effects on consumption are a large component of the overall effects of monetary policy. Tight money policies results in larger down payment requirements and stricter credit standards for consumer credit and increase the severity of the liquidity constraint facing many households. Expansionary monetary policies make credit more available and reduce liquidity constraints.

Social Security and the Age Profile of Saving and Wealth: According to life cycle hypothesis, pension wealth should be counted as part of individuals' resources, and argued forcefully that the transition to a social security regime would affect discretionary saving. In fact, if the LCH is correct in asserting that total saving is controlled by a target accumulation to support retirement, one might conclude that social security and discretionary wealth (or saving) should largely offset each other. This offset is the substitution effect pension saving crowding out discretionary saving. However, this effect might be well below one-for-one because of the induced retirement effect—the provision of social security pension facilitates earlier, longer retirement, which in turn tends to raise target wealth and saving. Modigliani took this point very seriously, and contributed to the debate providing international evidence that saving rates were higher in countries with less generous pensions, controlling for the expected length of retirement.

The presence of mandatory pension arrangements is also important in understanding to what extent people accumulate and deaccumulate wealth over the life cycle. A unique implication of LCH vis-à-vis the infinite horizon permanent income hypothesis or models in which people save mainly for precautionary purposes is a hump-shape age-wealth profile. Yet, if one looks at the microeconomic evidence on household saving rates by age, dissaving by the elderly is seldom observed.

Modigliani's point to address this criticism is that most evidence on age-saving and age-wealth profiles is based on a concept of disposable income that does not take into account the role of mandated saving through pension systems. Indeed, conventional disposable income treats pension contributions as taxes, and pension benefits as transfers. Since contributions entitle the payer to receive a pension after retirement, they should be regarded as a component of life cycle saving and hence added back to income. On the other hand, pension benefits accruing to the retired do not represent income produced, but rather a drawing from the pension wealth accumulated up to retirement. The greater the amount of mandatory saving, the greater is the difference between earned income and disposable income. Where mandatory contributions are sizable (as in all developed economies), large swings in total life cycle saving are almost completely eliminated if one uses the conventional definition of disposable income and saving. One could even imagine a situation in which mandatory contributions exactly equal the saving that people would have chosen otherwise. In countries where pension wealth is a major component of total wealth, the path of discretionary saving is a very poor indicator of saving targeted for retirement. In our application, we construct two measures of income. Conventional disposable income is obtained directly from the respondent. Earned income is computed adding the mandated contribution to social security—taken as an approximation to mandated saving through public pensions—and subtracting pensions from disposable income.

Recent developments in theory and practice

For a theory, that is so central to economic analysis, and that has been worked on by so many people, the life cycle hypothesis has aged well. And although the ways in which the theory is used have changed, the hypothesis continues to provide the framework in which economists think about intertemporal issues at both the individual and economy-wide levels. Over the last decade, new work had continued to modify and to challenge, both theoretically and empirically. We are still far from the sort of integration that Modigliani and Brumberg so successfully produced half a century ago, but there are results and ideas that are not easily reconciled with the life cycle theory as Modigliani thought about it.

Emphasizing that the young and old coexist at any time, overlapping generation models (of which Modigliani and Brumberg are now seen to be a special case) have been fruitful in depicting the equilibrium pattern of growth in an economy over time, in bringing into sharp relief the role of interest rates, and in weighing the welfare contribution of security and private market saving schemes. They have also sharpened up the treatment of bequests, both anticipated and accidental. They have lent themselves to simulation studies but have not proved rewarding for tests against empirical data. Also, models of dynamic labor supply have been developed in a life cycle hypothesis framework.

One issue is whether cross-country and long-term within-country differences in saving rates are really attributable to differences in growth rates. The long-run decline in the private saving rate cannot be blamed on demographic changes, nor on the productivity slowdown. The aggregate decline comes from a decline in saving rates for all age groups, not from a redistribution of lifetime income from young to old. The cross-country correlation between saving and growth has been analyzed in an important and imaginative paper by Christopher Carroll and Summers (1989) who start from the fact that, in more rapidly growing economies, the young are relatively much richer than the old. If the life cycle hypothesis is correct, even in part, the age profile of consumption should be relatively higher for the young than the old in more rapidly growing economies, so that higher growth should rotate the crosssectional age-profile of consumption clockwise. This does not appear to be the case. If we plot average consumption against age for a range of economies, the graphs are essentially on top of one another, with little evidence of tipping. This finding is consistent with the failure to find much life cycle saving in the household survey data, and certainly not enough to drive the growth to saving mechanism. Yet the test does not depend on the shaky information on household saving from the surveys, relying only on the much more robustly measured age-profile of consumption. Perhaps the causation runs, not from growth to the saving rate, but from the saving rate to growth, something that is consistent with standard models of economic growth if transitions to equilibrium are very slow, and given that national rates of investment are closely correlated with national rates of saving. While there is currently broad agreement on the existence of a correlation between saving and growth, there is no consensus on its causes.

The relationship between saving and the age-structure of the population is also a current topic of debate. Cross-country regressions regularly find that aggregate saving rates are lower when the population share of the elderly is high and when the population share of children is high, predictions that are in accord with the life-cycle theory if saving takes place in middle age when earnings are high, after the child-rearing ages, but prior to retirement. Such regressions have strong negative predictions for currently high saving countries whose populations are aging, particularly countries in South and East Asia. Yet, once again, the microeconomic evidence on the age-profiles of saving is not consistent with the large effects that are estimated from the cross-country regressions. The cross-country analysis also seems to be fragile to econometric technique, with results quite sensitive to plausible changes in statistical specification.

Another challenge to the life cycle hypothesis has come from thinking about uncertainty, something that Modigliani recognized as an unresolved issue from the earliest days. But he argued that the main effect of uncertainty would be to generate a demand for precautionary saving—a motive that had been recognized at least as early as Keynes—and that, except perhaps among the very young, the accumulated assets of life cycle savers could serve a double purpose, not only for retirement, but as a buffer against unexpected emergencies. So, he doubted that uncertainty would change the picture much. Theoretical results by Robert Merton (1969) provided further support; Merton showed that if risk is confined to financial assets, the basic rule for life cycle consumers of setting consumption proportional to assets, remains true when utility maximization was replaced by expected utility maximization. Of course, that leaves a hole in the argument—earnings themselves are uncertain—and that hole turns out to be important, at least in some cases.

Work on precautionary saving, particularly by Carroll (1997), has shown that people with uncertain future earnings who are sufficiently prudent will never borrow, if there is the possibility, however remote, that they will not earn enough to be able to repay their debts. If such people expect their earnings to grow over time, they will nevertheless keep their consumption within their current incomes, thus inducing a close articulation, or "tracking," between consumption and income. In this case, although people are maximizing their expected lifetime utility, as postulated by the life cycle theory under uncertainty, their consumption is effectively constrained by their current incomes. Such behavior is directly contrary to one of the central insights of the Modigliani model, that the profile of consumption can be detached from the profile of income, and much more like the pre-Modigliani and Keynesian accounts of saving. Very much the same result can be obtained in a theoretical model in which people want to borrow but cannot. People can save to smooth out their consumption, but they cannot have consumption greater than their income, except when they already have some assets in the bank.

In these extreme precautionary or "liquidity constrained" accounts of saving, consumption is smoothed, not over the whole life cycle, but over much shorted periods of a few years at a time. In the literature, this is often referred to as "high frequency" smoothing of income, as opposed to the "low frequency" or "life cycle frequency" smoothing that was postulated by Modigliani and Brumberg. These results are not inconsistent with Modigliani's argument about precautionary saving for (possibly the majority of) consumers who, under the original life cycle model, wish to save, not borrow. These will be people who are sufficiently patient so as to be happy to postpone their consumption, or who do not expect much income growth in the future. Indeed, it is possible to reconcile the traditional and the new view by noting that it is the youngest families who are likely to want to borrow, but either cannot or are too prudent to do so, and are therefore more or less constrained by their current earnings, while those in middle-age behave in the traditional lifecycle way.

Recent applications and extensions have related to the rapid development of social security and its effects on private savings, and variation of dates of retirement on the one hand and effects of switch from income or capital taxes to consumption taxes on the other. The social security studies have necessitated the use of more carefully defined wealth and income figures. The empirical research on the life cycle hypothesis has raised questions as to the adequacy of the life cycle model without much more attention to bequest issues or allowance for uncertainty as to date of death. In part, it is argued that the life cycle may apply to a large section of the population but the big savers and even the lowest earners may obey different criteria. Repeatedly in well-defined samples, though not in all, the decline in wealth with age was not significant; in more finely grouped data, it even rises with age.

The Life Cycle Version of the Relative Income Hypothesis

Duesenberry (1949), building on work by Brady and Friedman (1947), proposes the relative income hypothesis to rationalise the well-established differences between cross-sectional and time series properties of consumption. On the one hand, a wealth of budget studies shows a saving ratio that increases with income. On the other hand, Kuznets (1942) time series data presents a trendless saving ratio. Duesenberry (1949) postulates an individual consumptionfunction that depends on the current income of other people. Under this hypothesis, the cross-sectional positive correlation between saving ratios and income levels results from relative consumption concerns. The long run constancy of the aggregate saving rate arise because the effects of relatively concerns cancel out in the aggregation. The relative income hypothesis was replaced by Friedman's permanent income hypothesis as the dominant paradigm for understanding consumption behaviour. According to this view, consumption is driven by permanent income; as a result, saving is proportional to lifetime resources. This view explains the positive correlation between saving and income in cross-section data by transitory deviations from permanent income. In the aggregate, most transitory components cancel out, leading to the close relation between consumption and income observed in time series data. Despite the theoretical dominance of the permanent income hypothesis, recent empirical works finds important deviations from its basic predictions. Positional concerns lead households to choose levels of consumption and working hours above the welfare-maximizing levels. Our framework, in which consumption externalities interact with income inequality, allows for a more systematic exploration of the differential impact of relative consumption across the income distribution.

Since consumption and bequests are normal goods, their levels increase with income, although according to the standard version of the permanent income hypothesis their rates should be a constant fraction of lifetime resources. In order to illustrate our permanent income version of the relative income hypothesis it is convenient to define (actual) lifetime income as,

$$y_t^i = w(1-l_t^i) + b_t^i$$

$$= \frac{1+(1+\alpha)\beta}{1+\mu+(1+\alpha)\beta}(w+b_t^i) + \frac{\mu(1+\beta)\gamma\chi}{1+\mu+(1+\alpha)\beta}(w+\bar{b}_t) \quad ...(8.64)$$

The saving and bequest rates out of lifetime income are the ratio of (8.49) and (8.52) to (8.64) respectively. Differentiating these ratios with respect to wealth, measured by the initial bequest, we have the following comparative static results,

$$\frac{\partial(s_t^i / y_t^i)}{\partial b_t^i} = \frac{\beta\alpha\gamma\chi\bar{\tilde{y}}_t}{(1+\mu+(1+\alpha)\beta)(y_t^i)^2} > 0 \quad ...(8.65)$$

$$\frac{\partial(b^i_{t+1}/y^i_t)}{\partial b^i_t} = \alpha R(1+\beta)\frac{\partial(s^i_t/y^i_t)}{\partial b^i_t}$$

$$= \frac{\beta\alpha R(1+\beta)\gamma\chi\tilde{\bar{y}}_t}{(1+\mu+(1+\alpha)\beta)(y^i_t)^2} > 0 \qquad ...(8.66)$$

Finally, differentiating (8.51) with respect to wealth we have

$$\frac{\partial l^i_t}{\partial b^i_t} = \frac{\mu}{w(1+\mu+(1+\alpha)\beta)} > 0 \qquad (8.67)$$

In the absence of interpersonal comparisons, $\gamma = 0$; the saving rate is proportional to lifetime income and, as in the permanent income hypothesis, independent of the lifetime resources. Once we allow for consumption externalities, $\gamma > 0$; the saving rate increases with lifetime income. Poor households save a smaller proportion of their income and transfer a lower fraction of their wealth in the form of bequests than richer households do. This happens despite the fact that poor households work longer hours than their richer neighbors do. These results are consistent with abundant anecdotal evidence on the living conditions of low-income households.

Also, note that Duesenberry dealt with one additional empirical regularity of consumption data—consumption is more stable than income at high frequencies. He explained the rigidity of consumption by appealing to habit formation. In an intertemporal set up with forward-looking agents, this rigidity is a natural result of consumption smoothing, as in the permanent income hypothesis.

Implications of LCH and PIH Models

Keynes' model of an MPC between zero and one was at odds with time series evidence showing a roughly constant ratio of aggregate consumption to aggregate income despite persistent growth in the latter. This issue was addressed by the life cycle hypothesis (LCH) and the permanent income hypothesis (PIH). Virtually all economists since then have accepted the basic idea of both the LCH and the PIH, namely that households are forward-looking—they are concerned about future as well as current consumption and they take account of expected future income as well as current income.

LCH and PIH both attempt to look into the future. In the LCH model, people must estimate their lifetime labour income, while in PIH model people must be able to distiguish temporary from permanent changes in income in order to estimate their lifetime permanent incomes. Temporary income changes can be smoothed out by assuming that permanent income is a weighted average of present and past income, with the weights adding to 1 and declining as we go further back in time. Let us consider the following example:

$$Y_T^P = 0.4Y_T + 0.3Y_{T-1} + 0.2Y_{T-2} + 0.1Y_{T-3} \quad ...(8.68)$$

Equation (8.68) shows that our estimate of permanent income is based on past experiences, with stronger weights given to more recent experience.

People update their calaulations of permanent income by some fraction of how their actual income differs from the previous period's estimate of permanent income. Thus,

$$Y_T^P = Y_{T-1}^P + \delta(Y_T - Y_{T-1}^P) \quad ...(8.69)$$

where,

Y_T^P = current estimate of permanent income;

Y_{T-1}^P = previous period's estimate of permanent income;

Y_T = current income; and

δ = ranges from zero to 1.

This procedure is called adaptive expectations because people adapt their previous estimates according to current information. If current income, Y_T, equals the previous period's estimate of permanent income, Y_{T-1}^P, then the current estimate of permanent income, Y_T^P, is not changed from the previous estimates, Y_{T-1}^P.

The adaptive expectations model is criticised because it assumes that estimates of future income are made entirely on the basis of present and past income.

Rearranging terms of equations (8.69) we have

$$Y_T^P = \delta Y_T + (1-\delta) Y_{T-1}^P \quad ...(8.70)$$

Since the formula holds for the previous period, we know that

$$Y^P_{T-1} = \delta Y_{T-1} + (1-\delta) Y^P_{T-2} \quad ...(8.71)$$

Substituting equation (8.71) for Y^P_{T-1} in equation (8.70), we obtain

$$Y^P_T = \delta Y_T + (1-\delta)\left\{\delta Y_{T-1} + (1-\delta) Y^P_{T-2}\right\} \quad ...(8.72)$$

Also, we have

$$Y^P_{T-2} = \delta Y_{T-2} + (1-\delta) Y^P_{T-3} \quad ...(8.73)$$

Substituting equation (8.73) for Y^P_{T-2} in equation (8.72), we have

$$Y^P_T = \delta Y_T + (1-\delta)\left\{\delta Y_{T-1} + (1-\delta)(\delta Y_{T-2} + (1-\delta) Y^P_{T-3})\right\}$$

Continuing this process, we get

$$Y^P_T = \delta Y_T + \delta(1-\delta) Y_{T-1} + \delta(1-\delta)^2 Y_{T-2} + ... + \delta(1-\delta)^n Y_{T-n} \quad ...(8.74)$$

In some cases, future income estimates is made not on the basis of past and present income, but on knowledge of how income is determined within the society. For example, an engineering student from an IIT will have a strong expectation that his income will rise upon graduation.

One implication of the LCH and PIH models is that the MPC is lower out of temporary, as opposed to permanent change in income. If people are trying to smooth their consumption paths then individuals with more volatile incomes, such as farmers, artists, and brokers, should have lower marginal propensities to consume. Budget studies show that they do. These people realise that if they spend most of their extra income in a good season, it will be difficult to retain their standard of living during a bad season. Nationally, a lower MPC out of temporary changes in income means that consumption will not be reduced in proportion to the decrease in income during a recession. People will resist reducing their lifestyle because of the temporary change in income. The ratio of saving to disposable income should fall.

A lower MPC out of temporary changes in income is important because it means that the multiplier to random demand shocks is less than the simple Keynesian model would imply. That is, the economy may be more naturally stable than the Keynesian model implies. It also means that tax changes, which were known to be temporary, would have little effect on consumption because consumption is related to lifetime income.

A person might want to consume according to the life cycle or permanent income hypothesis but be unable to consume in low-income times because of liquidity constraints. Someone who is certain that his income would rise in the future, and thus desires to borrow against that future income might be blocked from borrowing because potential lenders do not share his conviction. Such a person would be more sensitive to current income, because an increase in current income would remove the liquidity constraint and enable him to consume, as he desires.

Another implication of the LCH and PIH models is that changes in wealth affect current consumption. Both the LCH and PIH models include wealth as a determinant of consumption. In the LCH model a reduction in wealth would force increased saving (reduced present consumption) in order to protect the later years' consumption path by rebuilding wealth. In the PIH model, a reduction in wealth lowers permanent income and thus consumption. Household wealth takes the form of real estate, stocks, bonds, money, and other real or financial assets. The importance of wealth to consumption is the reason for concern that debt financing of government outlays will reduce saving. If people view their government bonds as wealth, without an offsetting future tax liability, debt creation increases current consumption and reduces saving.

One of the implications of the LCH and PIH models is that consumer confidence affects consumption. Consumer confidence influences the estimates of future income necessary for calculating lifetime income flows or permanent income.

Another implication of the LCH and PIH models is that interest rates affect consumption. Interest rates enter the consumption-saving decision in three ways—(a) by substitution effect, (b) by income effect, and (c) by wealth valuation effect. The substitution effect from higher interest rates means that because future consumption is less expensive, people save more in order to substitute future consumption for present consumption. This means a steeper consumption path with less consumption in the beginning and more at the end.

The income effect means that with higher interest rates a given amount of saving will produce more consumption later. If people are saving for their retirement, less saving would produce the same retirement level of consumption.

A wealth valuation effect occurs because the value of existing wealth that produces a flow of income is reduced by increases in interest rates. Wealth is evaluated by what it will return. The wealth effect reinforces the substitution effect because an increase in interest rates reduces the value of wealth, which reduces current consumption.

Since people save in order to increase future consumption, saving is sensitive to the real after-tax interest rate expected over the relevant time horizons. When we include inflationary expectations and taxes on interest income, market interest rates are not real interest rates. The real after-tax interest rate expected is the market interest rate minus both the inflationary expectation and a correction for the effect of taxes on interest income. Saving is a function of the expected real after-tax interest rate because that is the only part of the market interest rate that increases future buying power.

NOTES

1. J.M. Keynes, *The General Theory of Employment, Interest and Money*, (London, 1936), p. 27.
2. *Ibid.*, p. 96.
3. H. Stachle, "Short Period Variations in the Distribution of Income", *Review of Economics Statistics,* 1937, pp. 133-43.
4. H. Lubell, "Effects of Income Redistribution on Consumers' Expenditure," *American Economic Review*, 1947, pp. 157-70 and Marschak, "Personal and Collective Budget Functions", *Review of Economics Statistics*, 1939, pp. 161-70.
5. J.M. Keynes, *The General Theory of Employment, Interest and Money* (London, 1936), p. 94.
6. J.S. Duesenberry, *Income Saving and the Theory of Consumer Behaviour* (1949).
7. D.B. Suits, "The Demand for New Automobiles in the United States,

1929-1956", *Review of Economics Statistics* (August, 1958), pp. 273-80.

8. E. Mueller, "The Desire for Innovations in Household Goods" in L.H. Clark (ed.). *Consumer Behaviour, Research on Consumer Reaction* (Harper Bros., 1958).
9. A.H. Hensen, *A Guide to Keynes* (New York, 1953), p. 81.
10. *Ibid.*, p. 78.
11. Arthur Smithies, "Forecasting Postwar Demand", *Economica* (January 1956).
12. James Tobin, "Relative Income, Absolute Income, and Saving" in *Money Trade and Economic Growth* (Macmillan, 1951).
13. F.R. Glahe, *Macro Economics—Theory and Policy,* Harcourt Brece Jovanovich, New York (1973), pp. 64-65.
14. J.M. Keynes, *The General Theory of Employment, Interest and Money* (1936) Harbinger edition, New York, p. 96.
15. J.M. Keynes, *Ibid.*, p. 97.
16. J.M. Keynes, *Ibid.*, pp. 107-108.
17. J.M. Keynes, *Ibid.*, p. 109.
18. Simon Kuznets, *Uses of National Income in Peace and War* (National Bureau of Economic Research), New York, 1942.
19. Raymond, W. Goldsmith, *A Study of Saving in the United States, Vol. III* (Princeton University Press) for the National Bureau of Economic Research: Princeton, N.J. 1956.
20. *Ibid.*, p. 1.
21. *Ibid.*, p. 22.
22. *Ibid.*, p. 26.
23. *Ibid.*, p. 27.
24. *Ibid.*, pp. 34-39.
25. *Ibid.*, p. 111.
26. D.B. Suits, "The Determinants of Consumer Expenditure: A Review of Present Knowledge", in D.B. Suits (ed.) *Impact of Monetary Policy,* Englewood Cliffs, N.J. Prentice Hall, p. 39.
27. M. Friedman, *A Theory of Consumption Function* (1957), Indian Edition, Oxford & IBH Publishing House, New Delhi, 1970.
28. *Ibid.*, p. 21.
29. J.G. Williamson, "Personal Savings in Developing Nations: An Intertemporal cross-section from Asia." *Economic Record*, 44, (June 1968) pp. 198-210. Also see I. Friend and P. Taubman "The

Aggregate Propensity to Save: Some Comparison and their Application to International Data" *Review of Economics and Statistics*, 48, (May 1948) pp. 113-123.

30. M. Friedman, *op. cit.*, p. 144.
31. *Ibid.*, p. 144.
32. *Ibid.*, p. 147.
33. J.G. Williamson, *op. cit.*
34. I. Friend and P. Taubman, *op. cit.*
35. K.L. Gupta, "Personal Savings in Developing Nations: Further Evidence" *American Economic Review* 46, June 1970, pp. 243-49.
36. R.G. Bodkin, "Windfall Income and Consumption" *American Economic Review* 49, (September 1959), pp. 602-614.
37. M.E. Kreinin, "Windfall Income and Consumption" *American Economic Review* 51 (June, 1961) pp. 388-390.
38. R. Holbrook and F. Stafford. "The Propensity to Consume Separate Type of Income: A Generalized Permanent Income Hypothesis." *Econometrica* 39 (January, 1971), pp. 1-21.
39. F. Modigliani & R. Brumberg, "Utility Analysis and the Consumption Function: An Interpretation of Cross-section Data" in K.K. Kurihara (ed.) *Post-Keynesian Economics*, London. (1955) Allen and Unwin, pp. 338-436. A. Ando and F. Modigliani "The Life Cycle Hypothesis of Savings : Aggregate Implications and Tests", *American Economic Review*, Vol. 53 (1963), pp. 54-82; E. Modigliani and A. Ando "Test of Life Cycle Hypothesis of Saving" *Bulletin of Oxford University Institute of Economics and Statistics*, Vol. 19 (May 1957), pp. 99-124.
40. P.A. Yotopoulos and J.B. Nugent, *Economics of Development: Empirical Investigations* (1976) Harper & Row, New York, pp. 177-178.
41. M. Landsberger "The Life Cycle Hypothesis: A Reinterpretation and Empirical Test", *American Economic Review* (March 1970), pp. 175-88.
42. A.C. Kelly and J.G. Williamson, "Household Saving Behaviour in the Developing Economics: The Indonesian Case," *Economic Development and Cultural Changes*, Vol. 16, No. 3 (April 1968), pp. 385-403.

Marginal Efficiency of Capital

9

The word 'efficiency' in the term "marginal efficiency of capital" represents the earning power, or rate of return over cost or profitability, of a capital asset. The marginal efficiency of a particular type of capital asset is the highest rate of return over cost expected from an additional, or marginal unit of that asset. The marginal efficiency of capital in general is the highest rate of return over cost expected from producing an additional, or marginal unit of the most profitable of all types of capital assets. Any available investment opportunity would be utilised so long as the expected rate of return over cost exceeds the rate of interest. Since the marginal efficiency of capital refers to the expected rate, rather than the current rate, of profit, it is liable to great fluctuations in the short run.

While deciding to make investment, the businessmen compare the expected rates of net return over the entire life of the capital asset with its supply price or the "replacement cost". If the former exceeds the latter the businessman will make investment, otherwise not. The prospective yield of a capital asset is what a businessman expects to obtain from selling the output resulting from that asset. These yields are in the form of a flow of money income over a period of time. If the total expected life of the new capital asset is divided into a series of periods, say years, the annual return may be referred to as a series of annuities represented by Q_1, Q_2, Q_3 where subscripts refer to the years of the respective annuities. If the values of Q's are estimated and if the cost of production of the asset which yields these returns is known, comparison of the expected returns with the cost gives the rate or ratio known as the marginal efficiency of capital. In other words, marginal efficiency of capital refers to the rate of discount at which the prospective yield of an asset is discounted so as to make it just equal to the supply price of the asset. Keynes[1] states, "More precisely, I define marginal efficiency of capital as being equal to the rate of discount which would make the present value of the series of annuities given by the return expected from the capital asset during its life just equal to its supply price." This definition can be expressed as below:

Supply price = Discounted Prospective Yields

$$C_R = \frac{Q_1}{1+r} + \frac{Q_2}{(1+r)^2} + \frac{Q_3}{(1+r)^3} + \ldots + \frac{Q_n}{(1+r)^n}$$

where C_R represents the supply price or replacement cost of the new capital asset; Q's indicate the prospective yields in the various years 1, 2, 3,...,n; and r stands for the rate of discount which will make the present value of the series of annual returns just equal to the supply price of the capital asset. Let us illustrate this with the help of a numerical example. Suppose the prospective annual yields from the use of the new capital asset having a life of only three years are as follows:

First year	Second year	Third year
Rs. 150	Rs. 100	Rs. 50

Further suppose the current supply price or the replacement cost of the capital asset is Rs. 264.30. Now, 8 percent would be the unique rate of discount which will equate the sum of the discount values of the prospective annual yields to the current supply price of the capital asset because

$$\text{Rs. } 264.30 = \frac{\text{Rs. } 150}{1.08} + \frac{\text{Rs. } 100}{(1.08)^2} + \frac{\text{Rs. } 50}{(1.08)^3}$$

In actual practice, it is very difficult to correctly estimate the expected return from a capital asset over its life time. Not only that, it is difficult to precisely estimate even the life of the capital asset. At best we can perhaps do not better than just guess "An estimate of what an investment will earn in five, ten or twenty years hence is based largely on guess work, on animal spirits, on adapting estimates to the average estimate, which in turn, is based on uninformed guesses."[2] Further the values of the Q's are not necessarily equal in all years, as assumed in our algebraic formulation stated above, except in a static society. In a dynamic world it is only by the rates accident that may one of them would turn out to be identical with some other.

If 8 percent is the highest rate of return expected on any newly produced capital asset, it is the marginal efficiency of a capital in general. Since the marginal efficiency of capital is expressed as a certain percent per year, it can be directly compared with the rate of interest. In the above example, if the rate of interest on money is less than 8 percent, it would be more profitable to construct the new capital asset in question than to lend money at interest or to buy an old capital asset of that type. People who can obtain money at less than 8 percent would make a profit by borrowing and constructing such assets. The market value of an asset which promises to yield Rs. 150 at the end of one year, Rs. 100 at the end of second year and Rs. 50 at the end of third year would be greater than Rs. 264.30, if the rate of interest is less than 8 percent. If the market rate of interest, for example, is 5 percent, the capital asset in question will have a present value of

$$\frac{\text{Rs. }150}{1.05} + \frac{\text{Rs. }100}{(1.05)^2} + \frac{\text{Rs. }50}{(1.05)^3} = 276.70$$

This is what Kenyes calls the demand price, in contrast with the supply price, of a capital asset. The demand price of any asset is defined as the sum of the expected future yields discounted at the current rate of interest. In contrast, the supply price is the sum of prospective yields discounted by the marginal efficiency of capital.

The greater would be the demand price, the lower the rate of interest at which it is discounted. The lower the rate of interest, therefore, the larger will be the number of capital assets for which the demand price will exceed the supply price and the higher will be the rate of investment in new capital assets.

The market value of a capital asset cannot, however, be determined from a knowledge of the marginal efficiency of capital. Nor can the rate of interest be deducted from the marginal efficiency of capital. Before the present market value of an asset can be worked out, the rate of interest must be determined independently from a knowledge of the quantity of money and the state of liquidity preference. The rate of interest as well as the marginal efficiency of capital must be known before the volume of investment can be determined. These two rates are determined independently of one another. The marginal efficiency of capital is determined by the supply price and the prospective yields of assets while the rate of interest depends upon the schedule of liquidity preference and the quantity of money in circulation. There is a sense, however, in which the marginal efficiency of capital adjusts to the rate of interest rather than the other way round. Changes in the quantum of investment directly affect the marginal efficiency of capital but not the rate of interest, and it is changes in the quantum of investment which bring the two rates to equality.

INVESTMENT DEMAND SCHEDULE

The different marginal efficiencies of capital at different levels of investment in a certain type of capital asset during a particular period can be represented in the form of a schedule. A curve representing such a schedule would take the shape of an ordinary demand curve slanting down towards right which indicates that as the investment in a certain type of capital asset during a particular period increases, its marginal efficiency decline. Keynes mentions two reasons for this:

> If there is an increased investment in any given type of capital during any period of time, the marginal efficiency of that type of capital will diminish as the investment in it is increased, partly because the prospective yield will fall as the supply of that type of capital is increased and partly because, as a rule, pressure on the facilities for producing that type of capital will cause its supply price to increase;....[3]

An aggregate of demand schedules for all different types of capital would give us a schedule relating the rate of aggregate investment to the corresponding marginal efficiency of capital in general which is also known as the investment demand schedule.

The position and shape of the investment demand schedule is of great importance in determining the volume of employment because it shows the extent to which the amount of investment will vary in response to changes in the rate of interest. The greater the elasticity of the schedule of the marginal efficiency of capital, the larger will be the increase in investment in response to a given decline in the rate of interest. Similarly, the smaller the elasticity of the marginal efficiency of capital, the smaller will be the increase in investment in response to a given decline in the rate of interest. The position and shape of the investment demand schedule depends upon many complex factors which are subject to different estimation by each entrepreneur and to frequent revision. It is, however, not impossible to draw an approximate schedule of the marginal efficiency for particular industries and for the economy as a whole at any given time. Experience shows that the schedule of the marginal efficiency of capital has a tendency to be less elastic rather than being more elastic. The variations in the rate of interest, therefore, do not much affect the flow of new investment. Much more important in this respect are the dynamic forces of growth and technological progress.

INVESTMENT

Marginal Efficiency of Capital and Rate of Interest

Income and employment in the Keynesian world are determined by mainly two factors: Consumption and Investment. By investment Keynes means new investment. When price of shares, capital, stocks, etc. are rising, original investment may show a higher monetary value—this should not be taken as additional investment. To the classical economist, investment is determined by two factors: marginal productivity of capital (MPC) and interest rate.

MPC is the actual marginal yield of investment. But Keynes is rightly of the view that the actual yield of investment takes place only when investment has been made and it has started yielding productivity. So MPC cannot determine factor of investment. The investment decision is based not on actual yield of investment but on the expected yield and the market rate of interest.

Keynes is right from the beginning of the view that expectation plays a major role in the case of investment decision. Based upon expectation, he modifies the classical conception that determines investment demand. In place of MPC, marginal efficiency of capital (MEC) is substituted. The MEC is the ratio of the expected yields or returns from an income-yielding capital asset to the supply price or replacement cost of this capital asset.

Keynes defines, "The MEC as being equal to that rate of discount which would make the present value of the series of annuities given by the returns expected from the capital asset during its life just equal to its supply price." Supply price may be determined by the following formula:

$$C_R = \frac{Q_1}{1+r} + \frac{Q_2}{(1+r)^2} + \frac{Q_3}{(1+r)^3} + \dots + \frac{Q_n}{(1+r)^n}$$

Where $Q_1, Q_2, Q_3, \dots, Q_n$ are series of prospective or expected annual returns or prospective yields, C_R is supply price or replacement cost, i.e. C_R indicates the price which the seller of the machine wants to charge as price by selling the machine. r is the rate of discount which will equate the present value of the prospective annual returns to the cost of capital goods. In other words, r is the marginal efficiency of capital (Keynes) or the rate of returns over cost (Fisher).

Let us now introduce the concept of demand price of investment. Let V stands for the value of capital goods or demand price, i be the market rate of interest.

Then, $$V = \frac{Q_1}{1+i} + \frac{Q_2}{(1+i)^2} + \frac{Q_3}{(1+i)^3} + \dots + \frac{Q_n}{(1+i)^n}$$

Keynes compares MEC, r with the market rate of interest, i to find out whether a particular investment is profitable or not.

In order to make investment profitable we have to get $V > C_R$ which shows $i < r$. On the other hand, if $i > r$, $V < C_R$ making investment unprofitable. In other words, given the objective of profit maximisation, an investor will increase the amount of investment so long as MEC > the current rate of interest. So, equilibrium amount of investment will be determined at the point where the MEC equals the rate of interest ($r = i$) indicating the equality between the demand price and the supply price of capital ($C_R = V$). Therefore, as long as the MEC is greater than the rate of interest the investor will invest till the MEC and rate of interest get equalised. In order to understand the relationship between the MEC and the rate of interest, a table given below is discussed.

MEC (%)	Rate of Interest (%)	Effect on Investment
5	4	Favourable
4	4	Neutral
3	4	unfavourable

In the first case, MEC > rate of interest implies that the effect of investment is favourable and the investor will go for new investment. In the second case, MEC = rate of interest shows that the effect of investment would be neutral. In this case the investors will not go for new investment. In the third case, MEC < rate of interest depicts that the effect of investment is unfavourable and the investors would clearly suffer loss if they go for new investment.

According to Keynes, MEC and the amount of new investment are inversely related. There are two main reasons for such inverse relationship: (i) As the amount of new investment increases, the 'prospective yields' from this capital decrease. Because as the production increases with increased investment, the product prices may be decreased. (ii) As the input price increases due to increased demand for investment, the prospective yields from the capital asset decline. Besides these two factors, there is another important factor which makes inverse relationship between the MEC and investment. The MEC or the expected rate of yield is based on subjective calculation, but the rate of interest is the actual cost of borrowing fund. Hence, greater the amount of investment, the greater may be amount of loss if things do not happen in accordance with expectation. Therefore, the investor has to take risk for increasing investment. As investment increases, the risk would also increase. This increasing risk will make the MEC fall. The relationship between investment and rate of interest is shown in Figure 9.1.

In this figure it is seen that when investment in capital asset is equal to OI_1, MEC is r_1. When the investment is increased to OI_2, MEC is r_2. Likewise, when investment rises to OI_3, MEC is r_3. That is, as investment increases, MEC decreases. Hence, inducement to invest depends upon the MEC and the rate of interest. Now what will be the equilibrium level of investment when the rate of interest and MEC curve are given. In this figure, both rate of interest and MEC are shown along the Y-axis.

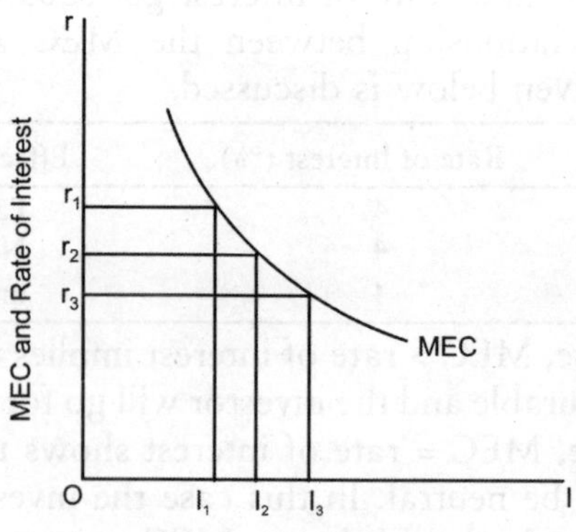

Fig. 9.1: Investment

The equilibrium level of investment will be established at the point where MEC equals to the current rate of interest. Thus, if the rate of interest is r_1, then I_1 investment will be undertaken. Hence, at OI_1 level of investment MEC is equal to the rate of interest. If the rate of interest falls to r_2, investment will rise to I_2 since at OI_2 level of investment the new rate of interest is equal to MEC. Thus, MEC curve shows the demand for investment at various rates of interest. Hence MEC curve represents the investment demand curve.

Evaluating a New Investment

A firm will carry out an investment in a new proposal if the total benefits accruing to the firm from the project are likely to exceed its total cost. In this regard, benefits are represented by cash inflows to the firm resulting from implementation of the project. An investment in a new equipment is made considering the net new revenues from increased production or the cost saving available due to technological superiority of the new equipment over existing equipment as the source of the cash inflows expected from such investment.

One another factor to be considered in evaluating the benefits and costs of an investment in new equipment is the effect of taxes. Taxes affect investment in the equipment in several ways.

(a) Additional earnings derived from the equipment are subject to the corporate income tax, which results in reduced net cash inflows.

(b) Non-cash expenses such as depreciation allowances become relevant to the evaluation process if they affect the amount of taxes that must be paid.

(c) The tax laws may be structured and periodically changed to provide special inducement to capital formation.

Let consider an example. We want to evaluate the total cash benefits accruing to a firm from the purchase of a new printer. The printer has a total cost of Rs. 50,000 and is expected to result in cost savings of Rs. 16,000 per year for the next five years. The firm is in the 50 percent marginal tax bracket and uses straight-line depreciation. The life of the printer is five years.

In this condition, we see that the annual cash benefit received by the firm from the new printer will be the annual cost saving minus additional taxes paid.

Let,

CF_T = total cash benefit in year T,

E_T = earning before depreciation and taxes available in year T,

D_T = depreciation allowance in year T, and

r = tax rate.

Then,

$$
\begin{aligned}
CF_T &= E_T - \text{taxes paid in year T} \\
&= E_T - r(E_T - D_T) \\
&= E_T - rE_T + rD_T \\
&= E_T(1 - r) + rD_T
\end{aligned}
$$

The above expression shows that the annual cash benefits to a firm from an investment in new equipment are equal to the after-tax cash increase resulting from the new equipment plus the tax shield provided by depreciation.

In our example,

$$
\begin{aligned}
E_T &= 16{,}000 \\
D_T &= 10{,}000 \\
r &= 0.5
\end{aligned}
$$

Thus, we have

$$
\begin{aligned}
CF_T &= 16{,}000(1 - 0.5) + 0.5(10{,}000) \\
&= 8{,}000 + 5{,}000 \\
&= 13{,}000.
\end{aligned}
$$

Now the total cash benefit in five years = 13,000 × 5 = Rs. 65,000, which is Rs. 15,000 more than the investment.

Marginal Efficiency of Investment (MEI) vs. Marginal Efficiency of Capital (MEC)

The MEI curve represents the interest elasticity of demand for investment (or capital goods), or in other words, how responsive investment is to a change in interest rates. Interest rates represent the cost of borrowing. Theoretically, the lower the rate of interest, the cheaper it is for firms to finance investment, and the more profitable the investment will be. Hence, the level of investment will rise.

Keynes, however, suggested that investment is in fact relatively unresponsive to changes in interest rates, particularly at the extreme ends of the Trade Cycle. During a recession, businessmen are generally pessimistic about the future outlook and there is also likely to be excessive unused productive capacity, which prevents a fall in interest rates from stimulating investment. On the other hand, during a boom, their optimism may cause them to disregard high interest rates. Hence, MEI is more likely to look like the relatively inelastic MEI_1 than the relatively elastic MEI_2.

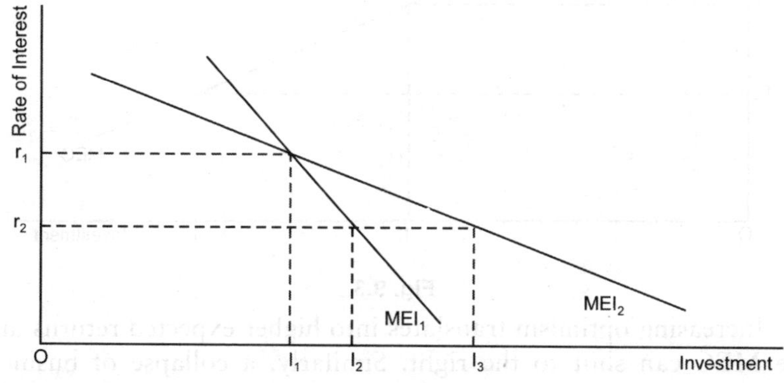

Fig. 9.2

Keynes instead emphasised the importance of expectations (entrepreneurship mood), which is affected by the state of the market for their product (which is in turn determined by factors like political stability, cost of production, conducive business climate etc). The expected rate of returns from investment is measured by Marginal Efficiency of Capital (MEC).

MEC is a downward sloping curve because, as the firm invests more, MEC will fall due to diminishing returns (i.e. the first few projects invested in tend to give a higher rate of returns, with subsequent projects yielding lower and lower returns).

The decision to invest is determined by a comparison of MEC and the opportunity cost of the investment (i.e. interest rate). As long as the MEC is greater than interest rates, firms will invest more (i.e. the project is regarded as worthwhile). It will stop in vesting when the MEC = i/r. Hence, as seen in the above diagram, if interest rates fall from r_1 to r_2, projects with lower expected returns, seen previously as unprofitable, will now appear viable, and so, more investment will occur. This increases investment from I_1 to I_2.

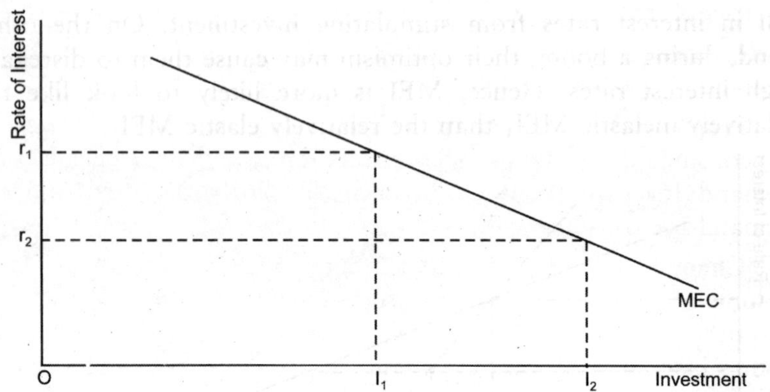

Fig. 9.3

Increasing optimism translates into higher expected returns and the MEC can shift to the right. Similarly, a collapse of business confidence causes a downward revision of future returns and the MEC curve shifts to the left.

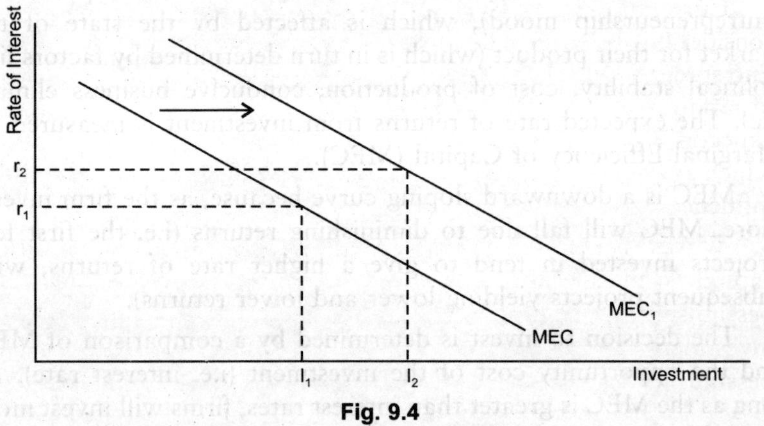

Fig. 9.4

Hence, it can be seen above that a rise in interest rates may not dampen investment if, at the same time, MEC has increased.

SHORT-RUN FACTORS AFFECTING MEC

The marginal efficiency of capital is influenced by a number of short-run as well as long-run factors. Among the former type of factors, the important are mentioned below:

Nature of Demand, Prices and Costs: A businessman's expectations about the rate of return from any given investment will decline if costs are expected to rise, or if prices and demand are likely to fall in the future. In contrast, MEC, will rise if the entrepreneurs expect a decline in costs, rise in prices, increase in demand or a combination of these.

Propensity to Consume: Short-run upward shifts in the propensity to consume have favourable effects on the MEC because the demand for capital goods is, at least, partly derived from the demand for consumer goods.

Changes in Liquid Assets: An entrepreneur possessing a large volume of liquid assets and of different types is in a more favourable position to take advantage of any investment opportunity that comes his way. On the other hand, if his assets are not liquid, he will find it difficult to undertake new investment for exploiting such an opportunity.

Changes in Income: The marginal efficiency of capital is influenced by sudden changes in income caused by windfall profits or losses, tax concessions or levies. It will be affected favourably by a rise in income and unfavourably by a decline in income.

Current State of Expenditure: The business expectations are considerably influenced by the prevailing rate of return on investment. Entrepreneurs often invest on the assumption that the current state of affairs will continue indefinitely. It is not possible to base expectations and hence investment on the future course of events which are so uncertain. Current expectations thus have an important influence on investment.

Waves of Optimism and Pessimism: The marginal efficiency of capital is considerably influenced by the waves of optimism and pessimism. During periods of optimism, rates of return on future investment are unduly over-estimated while during periods of pessimism they are badly underestimated.

LONG-RUN INFLUENCES ON MEC

Following may be mentioned among the important factors which influence the marginal efficiency of capital in the long run.

Population: A high rate of population growth stimulates investments because the basic requirements of a growing population require larger investments in fields like public utility services, residential buildings and consumer goods industries particularly those producing necessaries of life.

Techniques of Production: Introduction of new techniques of production, particularly those of a capital-intensive nature and those which lower the cost of production, give rise to huge investments. Great technical progress in the manufacture of steel, cars, rubber, glass, textiles, electrical goods etc. has substantially expanded the market for these goods which has resulted in large amount of investment.

Supply of Capital Equipment: The effects of population growth, expansion of territories and markets and improvements in the techniques of production, depend upon the existing supply of capital equipment. To the extent the existing plant and machinery are adequate to meet the increased demand resulting from the above mentioned factors, the new or induced investment will not occur. In contrast, if there exists no unutilised capacity, such factors would lead to an increase in investment.

EXPECTATION AND MARGINAL EFFICIENCY OF CAPITAL

The marginal efficiency of capital, as we have seen, depends upon the supply price or costs and the prospective yield or return. The prospective yield is the most important factor responsible for the unstable nature of the marginal efficiency of capital. The expectations of prospective yield are based partly on the existing events which can be more or less ascertained and partly on future facts which cannot be anticipated with confidence. It is because of the uncertain events on which the prospective yields primarily depend that the marginal efficiency of capital is so unstable. The unstable economic behaviour under capitalism is mainly attributable to the unstable nature of prospective yields from capital assets. The investment decisions are governed by expected yields and not by actual yields.

A prospective yield is what an entrepreneur expects to obtain from selling the output of his capital assets. In regard to the yields of assets, there are two types of expectations viz. (a) short-term expectations and (b) long-term expectations. Short-term expectations relate to sales proceeds from the output of existing plant. In such expectations, the size of the plant is assumed to be fixed and only the output from it is variable. The long-term expectations, in contrast, relate to sales proceeds from variations in the size of the plant or from the installation of an entirely new plant. In the long-term expectations, the size of the plant as well as the amount of output from it are variable.

Short-Term Expectations

Short-term expectations are more stable than the long-term expectations because the realised results of the recent past are a relatively safe guide to what will happen in the near future. In contrast, the past experience cannot serve as a sufficiently reliable guide to what will happen in the distant future. In case of short-term expectations, there is a high degree of continuity because most of the conditions which affect current output remain more or less the same from day to day, from week to week, and from month to month. In the absence of definite evidence for expecting a change, the most recent events may be expected, to continue in the near future. Short-term expectations can be checked in the light of realised results. Since realised results are a fairly good guide to the near future, it is not very unsafe to substitute them for expectations pertaining to the near future. The short-term expectations are relatively stable and, therefore, are unable to explain fluctuations in investment.

Long-Term Expectations

Long-term expectations regarding future yields, in contrast to short-term expectations, are highly unstable and, therefore, more important in explaining the fluctuations in aggregate investment and aggregate employment in the economic system. While it may be safe to assume that the economic activity next day or next week or next month will be more or less what it was during the previous day, or previous week, or previous month, experience warns us against assuming that the next three or four years will be like the past three or four years because the realised results of the past are not a reliable guide for the future.

There are, however, some factors affecting long-term considerations which do not depend upon uncertain things. Decisions to invest are partly based on facts regarding the existing stock of capital assets. The decision to build a new cotton textile mill, for instance, partly depends upon the existing total production capacity which is a fact and can be ascertained without much difficulty. Similarly, the power of the existing capacity to cope up with the existing demand at the prevailing prices are data of a more or less definite nature. But as we try to look into the distant future, the horizon becomes more clouded. The probable life and maintenance of the plant cannot be accurately predicted. Still less predictable are factors like possible changes in technology in the cotton textile industry which would govern the rate of obsolescence of the contemplated plant. There prevails uncertainty in regard to factors like level of effective demand twelve or fourteen years hence, the amount of new competition, the prices which would prevail from year to year, the possibility of war, the size of the export market, changes in tax burdens, conditions in the labour market, political climate in future years which will influence the extent of social control over industry etc. There is no probability calculus upon which to base scientific judgments in regard to such factors. The distant future can never be seen clearly. This is particularly so when entrepreneurial decisions are made by a large number of private entrepreneurs whose decisions are uncoordinated. The extremely uncertain conditions under which long-term expectations are formed result in great instability in the economic system. Long-terrn expectations are subject to sudden revisions. Periods of feverish investment activity tends to be followed by periods of extreme pessimism and depression in which investment in durable capital assets declines to very low levels. To quote Keynes:

> The outstanding fact is the extreme precariousness of the basis of knowledge on which our estimates of protective yield have to be made. Our knowledge of the factors which will govern the yield of an investment some years hence is usually very slight and often negligible. If we speak frankly, we have to admit that our basis of knowledge for estimating the yield ten years hence of railway, a copper mine, a textile factory, the goodwill of a patent medicine, an Atlantic liner, a building in the City of London amounts to little and sometimes to nothing or even five years hence. In fact, those who seriously attempt to make any such estimate are often so much in the minority that their behaviour does not govern the market.[4]

CRITICISM OF MEC

Keynes' concept of marginal efficiency of capital has been severely criticised on a number of counts. Saulnier points out that marginal efficiency of capital cannot be used as an analytical tool without presupposing a whole structure of distribution theory which enables us to distinguish between and evaluate the contributions of different productive factors.[5] Keynes did not pay adequate attention to this conceptual difficulty. Further, Keynes assumes the existence of perfect competition in the market and does not consider the qualifications necessary for an imperfectly competitive market. Moreover, Keynes' analysis of investment function is related to the rate of interest and the marginal efficiency of capital because he assumed that wages are equal to the marginal productivity of labour. But if this assumption is dropped the wage rate becomes a more important element in the theory.

Keynes' concept refers to the marginal efficiency of capital as a whole. Saulnier believes, however, that the most illuminating data for economic analysis are those relating to the expected returns on capital investment in different sectors of the economy. This has special significance in a market characterised by imperfect competition.[6]

Saulnier further points out that the Keynesian analysis does not contain an adequate explanation regarding the determination of the shape of the aggregate investment demand schedule. It does not explain variations in the productivity of capital with consideration of certain problems involved therein, such as: how will the MEC change if all other factors, besides the quantity of capital, are held constant? How will the MEC vary if, along with the variation of the quantity of capital, the labour is increasing in quantity and improving in quality, if new and more productive natural resource are being opened up, and if improved techniques of production are being introduced? Further, the Keynesian analysis does not discuss the 'economies' or 'diseconomies' which are likely to influence the shape of the investment demand schedule.[7] Saulnier concludes that Keynes' analysis is not complete, nor it provides a satisfactory explanation of the factors which determine the productivity of capital.

Prof. Hazlitt points out that Keynes uses the term 'marginal efficiency of capital' in so many different senses that it is difficult, if not impossible, to keep track of them. He fails to stick to any fixed meaning of the term and plays fast and loose with it. The ambiguities and bad reasoning that Keynes fell into could have been avoided if he had dropped this term altogether and used instead anyone of half dozen different terms then in use. Among the terms then in use like the marginal productivity, yield or utility or efficiency of capital, Keynes uses the vaguest among them, that is, efficiency of capital.

Keynes fails to recognise that interest rate is no less influenced by expectations than the marginal efficiency of capital. In other words, Keynes includes the marginal efficiency of capital in the realm of dynamic economics and the rate of interest in the realm of static economics. There is no justification for this assumption, nor does it correspond to real economic facts. Acceptance of this assumption would imply that entrepreneurs are influenced by their expectations but the lenders are not influenced by those, for which there is no justification.

CONTROL OF FLUCTUATIONS IN INVESTMENT

The precarious nature of long-term expectations, as we have seen, leads to so great instability in the marginal efficiency of capital as cannot be counteracted by any practical change in the rate of interest. This leads to violent fluctuations in private investment. Keynes, therefore, felt that it would not be safe to leave entire investment in the hands of private entrepreneurs who are guided by the marginal efficiency of capital or the expected rate of profit. The state, which is in a better position than private enterprise to calculate long-term needs in terms of general social advantage, should shoulder greater responsibility for directly organising investment. In other words, Keynes believed in the 'socialisation' of investment to control fluctuations in the marginal efficiency of capital. Keynes, however, was never in favour of complete nationalisation of investment. What he advocated, in fact, was just supplementing private investment with public investment.

NOTES

1. J.M. Keynes, *The General Theory of Employment, Interest and Money* (New York, 1936), p. 135.
2. Seymour E. Harris, "Ten Years After: What Remains of the *General Theory*" in Seymour E. Harris (Ed.), *The New Economics* (London, 1948), p. 50.
3. J.M. Keynes, *The General Theory of Employment, Interest and Money* (London, 1936), p. 136.

4. J.M. Keynes, *The General Theory of Employment, Interest and Money* (London, 1936), pp. 149-50.
5. R.J. Saulnier, *Contemporary Monetary Theory* (New York, 1947), pp. 340-41.
6. *Ibid.*, p. 341.
7. *Ibid.*, p. 342.

Rate of Interest

10

The marginal efficiency of capital may be said to govern the terms on which loanable funds are demanded for the purpose of new investment, while the rate of interest governs the terms on which funds are being currently supplied. Rate of interest, in turn, depends on the interaction of the schedule of the marginal efficiency of capital with the psychological propensity to save. However, in reality, these two factors cannot determine the rate of interest.

The psychological time-preferences of an individual require two distinct sets of decisions to carry them out completely. The first is concerned with that aspect of time-preference (known as propensity to consume) which determines for each individual how much of his income he will consume and how much he will reserve in some form of command over future consumption. The second is in what form he will hold the command over future consumption, which he has reserved, whether out of his current income or from previous savings. Does he want to hold it in the form of immediate liquid command or deferred command, for a specified or indefinite period, leaving it to future market conditions? In other words, what is the degree of his liquidity preference?

It should be noted that the rate of interest cannot be a return to saving or waiting. For example, if a man hoards his savings in cash, he earns no interest though he saves just as much as before. However, our definition of the rate of interest tells us that the rate of interest is the reward for parting with liquidity for a specified period. The rate of interest is nothing more than the inverse proportion between a sum of money and what can be obtained for parting with control over the money in exchange for a debt for a stated period. The rate of interest is not the 'price' which brings into equilibrium the demand for resources to invest with the readiness to abstain from present consumption. It is the 'price' which equilibrates the desire to hold wealth in the form of cash, which implies that if the rate of interest were lower, i.e., if the reward for parting with cash were diminished, the aggregate amount of cash which the public would wish to hold, would exceed the available supply, and that if the rate of interest were raised, there would be a surplus of cash which no one would be willing to hold. If this is correct, the quantity of money is the other factor, which, in conjunction with liquidity-preference, determines the actual rate of interest in given circumstances. Liquidity-preference is a potentiality or functional tendency, which fixes the quantity of money which the public will hold when the rate of interest is given. If r is the rate of interest, M the quantity of money and L the function of liquidity-preference, we have

$$M = L(r)$$

Why such a thing as liquidity-preference exists? There is a necessary condition failing which the existence of a liquidity-preference for money as a means of holding wealth could not exist. The necessary condition is the existence of uncertainty as to the future of the rate of interest. If the rate of interest ruling at all future times could be foreseen with certainty, all future rates could be inferred from the present rates of interest for debts of different maturities, which would be adjusted to the knowledge of future rates. If the current rate of interest is positive for debts of every maturity, it must always be more advantageous to purchase a debt than to hold cash as a store of wealth. If a need for liquid cash may conceivably arise before the expiry of stipulated time, there is a risk of a loss being incurred in purchasing a long-term debt and subsequently turning it into cash, as compared with holding cash. The actuarial profit or mathematical expectation of gain calculated in accordance with the existing probabilities must be sufficient to compensate for the risk of disappointment. There is, moreover, a further ground for liquidity-preference which results from the existence of uncertainty as to the future of the rate of interest, provided that there is an organised market for dealing in debts. Different people will estimate the prospects differently and anyone who differs from the predominant opinion as expressed in market quotations may have a good reason for keeping liquid resources in order to profit, if he is right, from its turning out in due course.

This is closely analogous to what we have already discussed in connection with the marginal efficiency of capital. Just as we found that the marginal efficiency of capital is fixed, not by the 'best' opinion, but by the market valuation as determined by mass psychology, so also expectations as to the future of the rate of interest as fixed by mass psychology, have their reactions on liquidity-preference; but with this addition that the individual, who believes that future rates of interest will be above the rates assumed by the market, has a reason for keeping actual liquid cash, whilst the individual who differs from the market in the other direction will have a motive for borrowing money for short periods in order to purchase debts of longer term. The market price will be fixed at the point at which the sales of the 'bears' and the purchases of the 'bulls' are balanced.

A first approximation to the concept of liquidity-preference is the concept of hoarding. If we were to substitute "propensity to hoard" for "hoarding", it would be equivalent. For the decision to hoard is not taken absolutely or without regard to the advantages offered for parting with liquidity—it results from a balancing of advantages, and we have, therefore, to know what lies in the other scale. Moreover, it is impossible for the actual amount of hoarding to change because of decisions on the part of the public, so long as we mean by "hoarding" the actual holding of cash. The amount of hoarding must be equal to the quantity of money and the quantity of money is not determined by the public. All that the propensity of the public towards hoarding can achieve is to determine the rate of interest at which the aggregate desire to hoard becomes equal to the available cash. The habit of overlooking the relation of the rate of interest to hoarding may be a part of the explanation why interest has been usually regarded as the reward of not spending, whereas in fact it is, the reward of not hoarding.

Thus, rate of interest is one of the important determinants of investment and hence of income, output and employment. It is one of the weapons in the hands of central banking authorities to fight problems of inflation, deflation and business fluctuations. It has also considerable influence on the rate of capital formation and hence on the rate of economic growth. A proper understanding of how the rate of interest is determined is, therefore, of vital importance.

THEORIES OF INTEREST

The important theories explaining the determination of the rate of interest are: (a) Classical or Real Theory, (b) Loanable Funds or Neo-classical Theory, and (c) Liquidity Preference or Keynesian Theory. All these theories attempt to explain the determination of the rate of interest through the equilibrium between the forces of demand and supply. In other words, in all these theories, rate of interest is the mechanism which brings about an equilibrium between demand and supply. The difference among these theories lies in the answer to the question: demand for what and supply of what? According to the Classical Theory, the rate of interest is determined by the demand for and supply of savings. Loanable Funds Theory states that the rate of interest is determined by the demand for and supply of loanable funds. In addition to current savings loanable funds also consist of dishoarding, bank credit and disinvestment. Keynesian Theory of Interest explains the determination of the rate of interest through the equilibrium between demand for money (i.e. liquidity preference) and the supply of money. Let us briefly examine these theories one by one.

Classical Theory

The theory of rate of interest as propounded by classical economists like Ricardo, Marshall and Pigou is known as the classical theory of the rate of interest. Cassel, Walras, Carver, Taussig and Prof. Knight also subscribed to this theory. According to this theory, the rate of interest is determined by the demand for saving to invest in capital goods and the supply of savings under free and perfect competition.

The demand for savings arises from those who desire to invest, that is, to purchase or make new capital goods. Capital goods are demanded because they are helpful in the production of consumption goods or, in other words, because they have a revenue productivity like other factors. Since capital is scarce, it is subject to alternative uses and is first put to the most productive use. As the amount of capital increases, additional units of capital are put to less productive uses. In other words, as the amount of capital increases, its marginal productivity tends to decline. An individual producer will push his investment of capital up to the point where the marginal productivity of capital equals the prevailing rate of interest. Thus the producers would use more capital at lower rates of interest and less capital at higher rates of interest. The demand curve for capital, therefore, slopes down towards the right.

The supply of capital depends upon a number of psychological and institutional factors which are generally grouped under "will to save" and "power to save". Those who make savings available have to postpone consumption of a part of their income. In other words, saving involves an element of waiting. But people prefer present enjoyment of goods and services to future enjoyment of those. If people are to be persuaded to save money and lend it to entrepreneurs, therefore, they must be offered some interest as reward. In other words, to make people to overcome their time preference, inducement must be offered in the form of interest. The larger the savings people make, the larger the consumption they will have to postpone, the greater must be the rate of interest they will ask to make such a postponement worthwhile. Thus to induce people to save more, a higher rate of interest must be offered. A higher rate of interest will also have to be paid if savings are to come from those persons whose rates of time-preference are relatively more strongly weighed in favour of present satisfactions. The supply curve of capital will, therefore, slope upward to the right.

Senior stated the theory in terms of abstinence. Saving was an act of abstaining from consumption. Since to abstain was painful, it was essential to reward people for this act. The idea of abstinence was, however, widely criticised on the ground that it suggested positive discomfort while the rich people, who are the main source of capital, save without the least inconvenience. To avoid this criticism, Marshall and Cassel explained the theory in terms of waiting. Bohm Bawerk and Irving Fisher developed the premium theory of interest. According to them, because people prefer present goods to future goods, there is a premium on present goods.

The demand for capital is identical with the investment demand function while the supply of capital is identical with the saving supply function. Thus, in the classical theory, an investment function is a downward sloping function of the rate of interest, i.e., investment increases with fall in interest rate and a saving function which is an upward rising function of the rate of interest, i.e. saving increases with rise in the rate of interest. The rate of interest, at which saving and investment is equal, is called natural rate of interest or the real rate of interest or the equilibrium rate of interest. In the classical theory, we get a saving function,

$S + f(r)$, and $\frac{dS}{dr} > 0$ and an investment function, $I = g(r)$ and $\frac{dI}{dr} < 0$. The equilibrium condition requires, $S = I$. There are three unknowns (S, I and r) in these three equations. We can find out the values of these three unknowns solving these three equations. The classical theory of interest rate can be explained with the help of following diagram (Fig. 10.1). In this diagram, we plot saving and investment along the X-axis and the rate of interest along the Y-axis. The saving supply curve SS is a positively sloping, i.e. upward rising curve while the investment demand curve II is negatively, i.e. downward sloping curve. They intersect at point M where the rate of interest is O r_0 and the saving supply equals to investment demand. O r_0 is the natural rate of interest or the equilibrium rate of interest, which will come to stay in the capital market. The market rate of interest is regarded as fluctuating around this long-run equilibrium rate of interest.

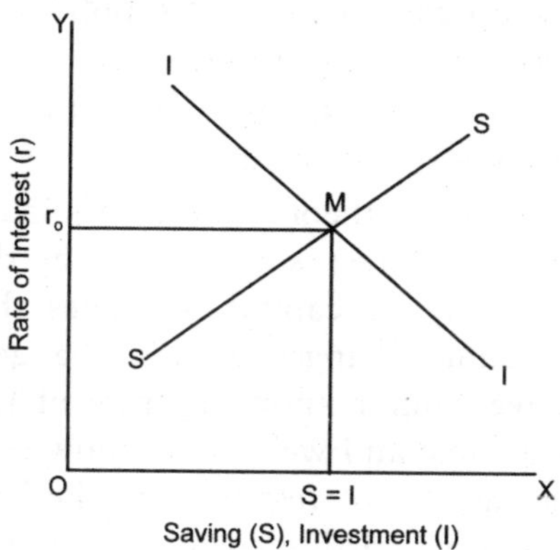

Fig. 10.1

The classical theory of the rate of interest has three important features. First, it is a purely flow theory, because saving and investment variables which determine the rate of interest are the flow quantities as distinct from the stock quantities per period of time.

Secondly, both saving and investment are the real variables as distinct from the monetary variables. The rate of interest is a real phenomenon. It is not determined by the quantity of money in circulation. Money acts only as a mediating agent. Any change in the money supply in the economy is neutralised by equi-proportionate change in prices keeping the real quantity of money unchanged. Consequently, if the money supply changes, the rate of interest remains unaffected.

Thirdly, if the equilibrium between saving and investment is disturbed due to a shift in one of the functions, it is re-established through changes in the rate of interest without affecting any other variable. Hence, this theory is self-contained and is not connected with the monetary sector in the economy.

Criticism of Classical Theory of Interest Rate: The classical theory of interest was sharply criticised by Keynes on a number of grounds. In the first place, this theory neglects changes in the level of income and assumes it to be constant. Keynes calls this theory as a special theory of interest because it is based on the assumption of a fixed level of income corresponding to a fixed level of employment (full employment). By ignoring changes in the level of income, it views the rate of interest as the factor which brings about an equality between the demand for and supply of investible funds. Keynes, in contrast, asserts that the equality between savings and investment is brought about not by changes in the rate of interest but by changes in the level of income.

Secondly, the classical theory is indeterminate. According to this theory, the rate of interest is determined by the intersection of demand for and supply of capital schedules. But according to Keynes, saving schedule changes with a change in the level of income. As such, we cannot know the rate of interest unless we know the level of income and we cannot know the level of income until we know the rate of interest because the level of investment and hence that of income partly depends on the rate of interest.

Thirdly, the classical theory assumes full employment of all productive resources. According to Keynes, so long as there are unemployed productive resources in the economy, there is no need to reward people to abstain from consumption so as to release resources for employment for the production of capital goods. The obvious way would be to utilise idle resources rather than withdrawing already employed resources. The emergence of the rate of interest, therefore, has to be explained by something other than the theory of 'waiting' or 'abstinence' or 'time-preference'. According to Keynes, interest is a payment for the use of money and is determined by the demand for and supply of money.

Fourthly, the classical theory neglects the important role played by the quantity of money, created money and bank credit, in the determination of the rate of interest. Though less important in 18th and 19th centuries, the role of banking and created money in the determination of the rate of interest has assumed great importance in modern times. Money is no more neutral and does not act simply as a veil as assumed by the classicals. In Keynes' analysis, money plays an active role in influencing the rate of interest.

Fifthly, the classical theory assumes both investment and savings to be interest-elastic. Statistical investigations, however, show that both of them are not very responsive to changes in the rate of interest. In fact, the relation between the two, if any, is rather indirect and weak.

Sixthly, the classical theory, unlike moot partial analyses of the kind, does not even give the first approximation provided by a statement like 'The price of shoes is determined by the supply and demand for shoes.'[1] In the case of shoes, such a simplification from the Walrasian formulation of general equilibrium is permissible because an increase in the demand for shoes does not normally have a very important effect on the supply of shoes. In contrast, such a relative independence does not hold good in case of savings. When there is an increase in the demand for savings, say because businessmen want to borrow money in order to spend it, there is likely to result from this an increase in the supply of savings. The additional spending will lead to an increase in income, part of which will be saved and offered on the loan market. The part of these incomes that is not saved but spent will increase incomes still further and part of these further additions to income will be saved and offered on the loan market. Such induced increases in the supply of savings may partly or wholly offset the effects of the increase in the demand for savings. Similarly, if there is a decrease in the supply of saving because some lenders decide to spend their money instead of lending it, this would increase the amount of money in the hands of those from whom the purchases are made which may directly or indirectly increase the supply of savings; alternatively, the money spent by the erstwhile lenders may flow into the hands of erstwhile borrowers who will decrease their demand for loans.

Finally, the classical theory assumes that the demand for funds is for purposes of investment and would vary inversely with the rate of interest. Keynes, however, shows that this may not be true. The investors, for instance, would be prepared to borrow and invest more even at a higher rate of interest if the expected rate of profit is still higher. Similarly, the investors may noι come forward to borrow even at very low rates of interest if the expected rates of profit are still lower.

Neo-classical or Loanable Funds Theory

This theory was first formulated by the Swedish economist, K. Wicksell. Other Swedish economists who refined his ideas include G. Myrdal, Lindahl and B. Ohlin. In England, D.H. Robertson developed this theory. According to this theory, interest is the price paid for the use of loanable funds. It asserts that the rate of interest is determined by the demand for and supply of loanable funds. The supply of loanable funds comes from four basic sources namely savings, dishoarding, bank credit and investment.

Savings: Savings by individuals or households constitute the most important sources of loanable funds. The savings are visualised in two ways. Firstly, as *ex-ante* savings, that is, savings planned by individuals at the beginning of a period in the hope of expected incomes and anticipated expenditures on consumption. Secondly, in the Robertsonian sense, that is, the difference between the income of the preceding period and the consumption of the present period. In either case, the volume of savings varies at different rates of interest. At a given level of income, the larger would be the savings, the higher is the rate of interest and *vice versa*.

Like individuals and households, business concerns also do saving. A part of the profits of the business concerns is distributed as dividend. The remaining undistributed profits constitute business or corporate savings. Such savings partly depend upon the current rate of interest. A higher rate of interest would stimulate business savings as a substitute for borrowing from the loan market. But the business savings are often invested by the firms themselves and therefore, most of them do not constitute loanable funds.

Dishoarding: This is another source of loanable funds. People may dishoard money from their hoardings of previous periods and make it available as loanable funds. A higher rate of interest will stimulate people to dishoard money. At lower rates of interest people will have a tendency to hold on to money.

Banking Credit: Banks are a third source of loanable funds. By creating credit, banks advance loans to business concerns. The new money created by the banks adds to the supply of loanable funds. By contracting their credit; they can also reduce the supply of loanable funds. Normally, other things remaining the same, the banks will have a tendency to lend more money at higher rates of interest and *vice versa*.

Disinvestment: It takes place when due to structural changes or unsuccessful venture the existing stock of capital equipment is allowed to wear out without being replaced or when the inventories are permitted to deplete below the level of the previous period. When this happens, a part of the revenue from the sale of the products instead of going into capital replacement, flows into the market for loanable funds. A higher rate of interest encourages disinvestment. When the rate of interest is high, some of the capital equipment may not produce a marginal revenue product equal to this rate of interest. The firm may allow such capital equipment to run down and bring the depreciation funds into the market for loanable funds.

Demand for Loanable Funds: Loanable funds are demanded mainly for three purposes viz. (1) investment, (2) consumption, and (3) hoarding.

Investment: A major portion of the demand for loanable funds comes from business concerns which borrow funds for purchasing or making new capital goods or for building up inventories. The price of loanable funds needed for purchasing capital goods is obviously the rate of interest. It would be profitable for businessmen to demand loanable funds up to the point at which the expected net rate of return on capital goods equals the rate of interest. The business concerns will have a tendency to purchase larger amounts of capital goods at a lower rate of interest. The demand for loanable funds for investment purposes, therefore, is interest-elastic and slopes downwards to the right.

Consumption: The second major demand for loanable funds comes from people who want to borrow funds for consumption purposes. People demand loanable funds when they desire to spend more than their current incomes and cash resources. Normally, loans for consumption are demanded for buying durable goods like automobiles, radios, refrigerators etc. A lower rate of interest will stimulate demand for loanable funds for consumption purposes and *vice versa*.

Hoarding: The third demand for loanable funds comes from those who want to hold idle cash balances for satisfying their liquidity preference. At higher rate of interest, people will have a tendency to hold lesser amounts of cash balances because the loss involved in holding cash balances will be greater. Similarly, at lower rates of interest, people will hold more money because it will not involve much loss.

Equilibrium between Total Demand for and Supply of Loanable Funds: The rate of interest is determined by equilibrium between total demand for and total supply of loanable funds. In Figure 10.2 the rate of interest is determined by the interaction of the demand for loanable funds curve DL and supply of loanable funds curve SL.

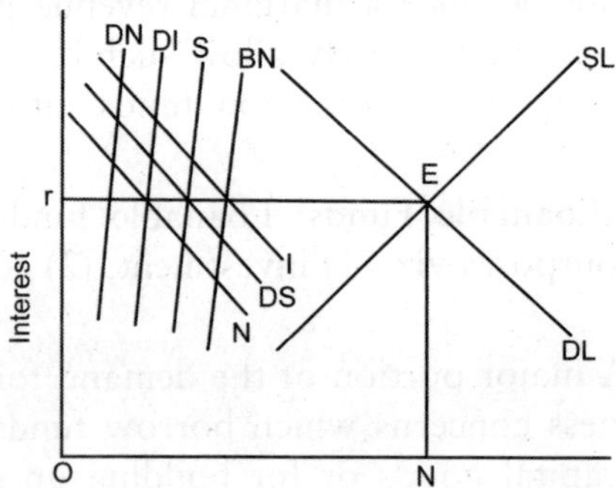

Fig. 10.2: Demand or Supply of Loanable Funds

The total supply curve of loanable funds SL is obtained by a lateral summation of the curves of saving (S), dishoarding (DH), bank money (BM) and disinvestment (DI). The aggregate loanable funds supply curve SL slopes upwards to the right showing a larger supply of the loanable funds at higher rates of interest. Similarly, the demand curve for loanable funds DL is obtained by a horizontal summation of the curves of investment (I), consumption (DS) and hoarding (H). The aggregate loanable fund demand curve DL slopes downwards to the right showing that the demand for loanable funds increases with a decline in the rate of interest.

DL and SL curves intersect at point E and thus determine the equilibrium rate of interest Or. At the equilibrium rate of interest Or, the supply of and demand for loanable funds are equal to ON. At any other interest rate either the demand for loanable funds will exceed the supply of loanable funds or the supply of loanable funds will exceed the demand for loanable funds and as a result the rate of interest will change until it reaches the level Or where the demand for and supply of loanable funds are equal.

It may be pointed out that at the equilibrium rate of interest where aggregate demand for and supply of loanable funds are equal, planned savings and investment may not be equal, as is evident from figure 10.2. In this figure, at the equilibrium rate of interest Or, the savings equal rA and investment equals rB. Investment rB is greater than savings rA. An excess of investment over saving will lead to an increase in income. The increase in income will shift saving curve S and the aggregate supply curve SL towards right. This shift in the savings curve S and loanable funds supply curve SL will lead to a change in the rate of interest. Thus the rate of interest as determined by the demand for and supply of loanable funds will not be a stable one if the savings and investment are not equal at that rate of interest and as such the interest rate will have a tendency to change. A stable equilibrium rate of interest will be attained only where the aggregate supply and demand curves of loanable funds determine the equilibrium rate of interest at which there also exists an equality between savings and investment.

We have explained above the various components of demand for and supply of loanable funds. It would be seen that saving (S) on supply side and dissaving (DS) on the demand side, dishoarding (DH) on supply side and hoarding (H) on the demand side and investment (I) on demand side and disinvestment (DI) on supply side are forces opposing each other. As these forces operate in the loanable funds market, it is their net effect which determines the market rate of interest. We can present the condition for an equilibrium rate of interest in a better and simplified manner if we use the concepts of net savings (i.e. savings minus dissavings), net hoarding (i.e. hoarding minus dishoarding) and net investment (i.e. investment minus disinvestment). This is shown below.

The equilibrium rate of interest is that at which the demand for loanable funds equals the supply of loanable funds. Writing the individual components on the demand and supply side in terms of symbols, the equilibrium rate of interest is determined when

$$S + DH + BM + DI = I + DS + H$$

In order to obtain net magnitudes we shift DS to the left side and DH and DI to the right side. The condition thus becomes

$$(S - DS) + BM = (I - DI) + (H - DH)$$

Or Net savings + Bank money = Net Investment + Net Hoarding.

Thus we find that the condition for equilibrium rate of interest is that the supply of net savings and bank money should be equal to the demand for net investment and net hoarding.

The classical theory did not take into consideration the importance of monetary factors like cash, credit, hoarding etc. It did not pay heed to the fact that the demand for money also arises from a desire to hoard. The non-classical theory, in contrast, considers monetary as well as non-monetary factors which have a bearing on the rate of interest.

Criticism of Loanable Funds Theory: Most of the criticisms made against the classical theory apply to loanable funds theory also. In fact, there is not such difference between the two theories. The major difference lies in the meaning of saving. In the classical theory, savings mean saving out of current income while in the loanable funds theory, savings refer to savings out of the income of the previous period. In the loanable funds theory, loanable funds consist of savings out of the income of the previous period plus borrowed bank deposits plus activated idle balances.

NATURAL AND MARKET RATE OF INTEREST

According to classical economists, natural rate of interest is that rate at which the demand for and supply of savings are in equilibrium. The market rate of interest will always correspond to this equilibrium rate of interest. The argument put forward in favour of the identity between the market and natural rates of interest is as follows: If the market rate of interest is higher than the natural or equilibrium rate of interest, supply of savings would exceed the demand of savings at that rate of interest. As a result of this, it would decline to the level of the natural rate of interest.

Similarly, if at any time, the market rate of interest declines below the natural rate, the demand of savings would exceed the supply of savings, which would raise the market rate of interest to the level of the natural rate of interest.

Thus the classical theory did not conceive the possibility of the existence of a divergence between the market rate of interest and the natural rate of interest. This analysis was the direct outcome of a view which allowed money only a passive role. The classicists firmly believed that the introduction of money did not alter the real process of production and distribution. It simply increased the efficiency of a barter economy.

In the classical theory savings were the only source of the whole supply of loanable funds. The classicists failed to recognise the fact that created money, by increasing the supply of loanable funds, could independently affect real economic progress by lowering the rate of interest. Knut Wicksell (1851-1926) attacked the classical approach and recognised the positive role of credit or bank loans in influencing the market rate and making it different from the so-called natural rate of interest. In his book *Interest and Prices* published in 1889, Wicksell analysed the differences which could occur between the natural rate of interest and the market rate of interest.

While the classicists considered any divergence between the natural rate and the market rate of interest to be of a fortuitous nature, Wickell argued that the divergence between the two was not of a fortuitous nature but owing to the intervention of the banks which by creating or destroying money cause the supply of loanable funds to deviate from the amount of real savings offered for investment in a barter economy. The creation of money by banks adds to the total supply of funds available for investors and as a result the market rate of interest is pushed below the natural rate of interest. In such a situation total investment will be in excess of total saving and the working of the famous Say's Law will be inhibited. Aggregate demand will exceed aggregate supply because a part of the aggregate demand which is financed by credit expansion has not made its own contribution to the supply of commodities: this will result in a rise in prices. Conversely, a restriction of credit by the banks will raise the market rate of interest above the natural rate of interest. Investment will fall short of the supply of saving. As a result, aggregate demand will fall short of aggregate supply and prices will decline.

Liquidity Preference Theory

Keynes put forward "Liquidity Preference Theory" of interest. According to this theory, the rate of interest is determined by the demand for and supply of money. Keynes' theory based on liquidity preference is known as *monetary* theory of interest as against the classical real theory of the rate of interest. Keynes' theory is called *monetary* theory because money plays an important role in it. Further, the rate of interest can be influenced or controlled by the central monetary authority through variations in the supply of money.

To Keynes, money is not only a medium of exchange but also a store of value. He laid more emphasis on the latter function of money. People desire to hold cash because it gives them a ready command over goods and services. People and business firms want to hold cash to meet day-to-day requirements, to provide against unforeseen contingencies and to earn from the future fluctuations of prices of bonds and securities. Thus those who have surplus money can either keep it in the form of ready cash or they may invest it in fixed income yielding assets like bonds and securities on which they earn a rate of interest, or they may purchase stocks on which they earn a rate of interest, dividend, or they may invest it in immovable property like houses on which they get rent. The desire to hold money as a store of wealth measures the extent of our distrust of our own calculation about the future. People do not want to hold all their wealth in interest-bearing assets because they are less liquid than cash and because their value is not fixed and varies from month to month, from week to week and from day to day. In view of this, it is rational to hoard money than to lend it. Interest is the reward which must be paid to overcome the liquidity.

The rate of interest depends on the strength of the liquidity preference in relation to the total quantity of money available to satisfy the desire for liquidity. The stronger the liquidity preference, the higher would be the rate of interest; and the greater the quantity of money, the lower would be the rate of interest. The rate of interest, like any other price, would be established at a level at which the demand for and supply of money are in equilibrium. An increase in the desire of the public to hold money may be met either by an increase in the price paid (rate of interest) or by an increase in the supply of money. Since the public cannot increase the supply of money, the direct result of an increase in its desire for money will not be to increase the quantity available but to increase the premium paid to those who give up their cash holdings. If the rate of interest did not rise with an increase in liquidity preference, the total quantity of money that public could desire to hold at the existing rate of interest would exceed the available supply. Similarly, if the rate of interest did not decline with a fall in liquidity preference, there would be surplus cash which no one would like to hold. In this manner, if the rate of interest tends to be too high or too low, an adjustment would take place equating the demand with the available supply. If the monetary authority agrees to expand the supply of money in proportion to the increase in liquidity preference, there would be no rise in the rate of interest.

According to Keynes, the demand for money or the desire to hold liquid cash arises out of three main motives viz. (a) the transanction motive, (b) the precautionary motive, and (c) the speculative motive. We discuss below these three motives in a little more details.

Transactions Motive: Money balances are held for the purpose of making transactions. Since the typical person is paid once a month or once a week and makes disbursements throughout the period, he must maintain some idle balance for transactions. A person who gets salary of y rupees at the beginning of the month makes consumption expenditures of c rupees at a uniform rate throughout the month will normally maintain a bank balance which averages one-half of his monthly expenditures i.e. $\frac{c}{2}$ rupees. If his income rises by Δy rupees, his consumption expenditure will rise by $b\Delta y$ rupees (assuming that his marginal propensity to consume is b) so that the average balance he must keep in his account will be $\frac{c + b\Delta y}{2}$. If the price level doubles, the amount he must maintain in his account will double. Thus the size of the cash balances depends upon the size of income, the frequency of income receipts and the frequency of income expenditure. If everybody received income in cash and simultaneously paid his expenses in cash, there would be no need to hold cash balances for transaction purposes. The greater is the length of interval between pay days, the larger will be the need for holding cash balances. Other things remaining the same, a person receiving monthly salary will require larger cash balances as compared with a person receiving daily wages.

It is quite possible that the transactions demand for money may depend not only on the level of income, frequency of income receipts and the frequency of income expenditure, but also, to some extent, on the rate of interest. Suppose that an individual plans to spend all his income at a uniform rate throughout the month. Of the y rupees which he receives at the beginning of the month, three-quarters will be idle for the first week (assuming that each month consists of four weeks); one-half of the balance will be idle for the first two weeks; and one-quarter will be idle for the first three weeks. He may, therefore, use these idle funds for purchasing an earning asset. At the beginning of the month he may use three-quarters of his income for purchasing bonds. At the end of the first week he requires some additional cash for transactions and therefore cashes in one-third of his bond holdings for expenditure during the second week. At the end of the second week he cashes in another one-third of his original bond purchases to spend during the third week; at the end of the third week he cashes in the remaining bonds. Instead of going into the bond market four times, he may go lesser times or more times. The more often he goes into the bond market, the less will be his average idle bank balance.

What governs the decision as to how many times to go into the market during the month? Since there is some cost of making each transaction, there is a definite disadvantage in going into the market which must be balanced against the desirability of holding earning assets as opposed to idle funds. Let us find out the optimum number of transactions. Let i be the rate of interest, n the number of transactions per income expenditure period, B the value of bond holdings, a the cost per transaction, c the transaction balance at the beginning of the month, and P the profit. Supposing that the cost of transactions depends only on the number of transactions and not on the size of the transactions, we have

$$C = na$$

At the beginning of the month, an individual will buy $\frac{(n-1)c}{n}$ bonds. Each $\frac{1}{n}$ days he sells $\frac{c}{n}$ bonds so that average bond holdings are

$$\overline{B} = \frac{(n-1)c}{2n}$$

Since the interest earnings on this average balance are $\frac{(n-1)ci}{2n}$, the total profit must be

$$P = \frac{(n-1)ci}{2n} - na$$

The optimum number of transactions is the value of n which makes P maximum. Accordingly,

$$\frac{dP}{dn} = \frac{2ci}{4n^2} - a = 0$$

So that

$$n = \sqrt{\frac{ci}{2a}}$$

Thus the optimum number of transactions depends on the rate of interest, the transactions cost, and the size of the beginning balance. It should be noted that when the rate of interest rises, the optimum number of transactions rises; this means that the transactions demand for money declines as the rate of interest rises.

Business firms, like individuals, also need to hold cash balances to bridge the gap between outlays for expenses and the receipt of cash from sales of finished products. As in the case of individuals, the longer is the interval, the larger will be the required size of balances. The business motive for holding cash will be stronger with an increase in the business activity. Payments from one entrepreneur to another will vary with the number of stages through which goods pass on their way to final completion, that is, the degree of integration in the economy as a whole. Other things remaining unchanged, an increase in integration will diminish the demand for money. Since factors like degree of business integration change slowly, fluctuations in the level of business activity are the only major factor responsible for changes in the demand for cash for transactions in the short run.

Precautionary Motive: Individuals, households and business firms normally have a tendency to hold more money than that required for transaction purposes. They hold more money because they want to take proper precautions against unforeseen future contingencies like sickness, unemployment, accidents; fire, old age etc. While going for shopping, an individual generally takes more money than just the amount he thinks will be needed for planned purposes. Plans may change, or opportunities may arise to make especially advantageous purchases if they are transacted on the spot without delay. The business firms require ready cash to meet contingent liabilities or to avail of unforeseen opportunities to make advantageous purchases. The amount of money held for precautionary motive varies widely with individuals and business firms according to their degree of financial conservatism, the nature of their enterprise, their access to the credit market, and the state of development of organized markets for conversion of earning assets like securities and stocks into cash. The demand for money for precautionary motive also depends upon income and the general level of business activity. Keynes takes the transactions and precautionary demand for money together because both are determined by the level of income.

Though the precautionary demand is probably quite closely related to the level of money income, as in the case of transaction demand, however, there may be some relation between the precautionary demand and the rate of interest. An increase in interest rates may make the purchase of earning assets so tempting that people may be willing to assume a slightly greater risk in the form of a lower precautionary balance in return for the added interest earnings.

Speculative Motive: The speculative motive relates to the desire to hold one's resources in liquid form with a view to take advantage of market movements. The object is to obtain profit from knowing better than the market what the future may bring forth. The speculative demand for money arises on account of the uncertainty regarding the future rate of interest. The individual investors are not sure of the terms and conditions on which the bonds owned by them can be converted into cash. If a particular individual, for instance, expects a decline in the prices of bonds, he would like to hold cash to take advantage of the situation when the prices actually decline. In this way, individuals safeguard themselves against possible losses. Similarly, if an individual expects a rise in the prices of bonds, he would buy bonds in anticipation of a rise in their prices. Thus the speculative motive for holding cash derives from a desire to keep one's resources in liquid form in readiness to take advantage of a turn in the market and to avoid a possible loss from holding securities in a falling market. This is known as the speculative demand for money. If there is no uncertainty about the future rate of interest, the rates at which debts of varying maturities can be converted into money at any future date would also be known with certainty. In such a situation, it would always be advantageous to own interest-bearing securities than possessing cash yielding no income and as such there would be no basis for liquidity preference for the speculative motive. This explains why the classical theory, resting upon static assumptions, attached no importance to the demand for money for speculative motive. It is here that Keynes' theory differs in a fundamental sense from the classical theory of interest. It is the speculative demand for money which introduces a dynamic clement in the analysis of the general price level and the volume of employment through a relationship between the current and prospective rates of interest and the profitability of investment. If the total quantity of money remains unchanged, speculative transactions affect output and employment by changing the rates of interest.

The size of the balances held for speculative motive varies inversely with the rate of interest. The speculative demand for money is less at a higher rate of interest and more at a lower rate of interest. What is the logic behind this proposition? When the rate of interest is low, security prices are high. As such, a large outlay would yièld only a small amount of return. In such a situation, purchase of bonds is not very attractive. Further, if in the past the rate of interest was high but has since fallen to a lower level below which it is not expected to go, the balance of expectations will be in favour of a future rise in the rate. If the rate of interest rises, those holding bonds would suffer a loss. If the people expect that the rate of interest will rise, they would prefer liquidity, because this would enable them a better bargain at a later date.

The above argument has been criticised on the ground that it implies an all-or-none kind of behaviour. If the interest earnings of a bond exceed the expected capital loss, it will be profitable to invest all one's funds in bonds. In contrast, if the expected capital loss is in excess of the interest earnings, no bond will be held. As such the moment, the critical point is reached where the scales tip in favour of bonds, there would be expected a conversion of cash into bonds on a large scale. Keynes' explanation for the fact that this wholesale conversion does not take place was based on the assumption that different people have different expectations in regard to the future. This view, however, is open to the criticism that, if the low rate of interest persists long enough, it will begin to be considered as permanent so that expectations will converge, the fear of capital loss will vanish and the speculative demand for money will vanish.

If the above theory is open to criticism, is there anything to the idea that there is speculative demand for money which has an inverse relation with the rate of interest? Data for the United States economy certainly suggest that there is, for when short-term-paper rates are plotted against average idle deposits, a strong inverse relationship emerges.[2] Is there an alternative explanation? To state the argument of the economists who hold that there is, we must prepare the ground by abandoning the notion that there is only one kind of security, and recognise instead that there is in reality a wide range of securities varying in diverse ways in respect of extent of risk, rate of interest, and date of maturity. Since the investors are not likely to want to keep all their eggs in one basket, they will instead diversify their portfolios and hold some of several different kinds of assets.[3] The portfolios would also include some money which, although earns no interest, has the advantage of a high liquidity premium.

For the sake of simplification, suppose that there are only two kinds of bonds—long-term and short-term and assume that an individual's portfolio consists of some long-term bonds and some short-term bonds and some cash. If the rate of interest rises, the earnings which are lost by holding cash become greater. Some of the investor's risk aversion will be long-term bonds for short-term bonds and some short-term bonds for cash. If the interest rates decline, the income on long-term bonds no longer compensates for the risk, while the loss of interest on account of holding cash and short-term bonds becomes relatively smaller. As such, with the decline in interest rates investors will have a tendency to adjust their portfolios in the direction of increased liquidity.

The above form of liquidity preference argument is free from dependence on one-sided expectation of the future and difficult to justify assumption that expectations will not ultimately converge. It depends on the simple principle of not putting all one's eggs in one basket and thus appeals to the commonsense and every day experience.

If the total supply of money is represented by M, we may denote that part of M held for transactions and precautionary motives as M_1 and that part held for speculative motive as M_2 so that $M = M_1+M_2$. The demand for money for transactions and precautionary motives is virtually interest-inelastic except when the rate of interest is very high. Since the demand for money for these motives depends upon income, it may be expressed as $M_1 = f(Y)$ or $M_1 = L_1(Y)$. In contrast, the money held for speculative motive is very sensitive to changes in the rate of interest. It may, therefore, be expressed as $M_2 = f(r)$ or $M_2 = L_2, (r)$ where r stands for the rate of interest. The equation $M = M_1 + M_2$ may be written as $M = L_1(Y) + L_2(r)$. Thus we find that, given the supply of money (M), the rate of interest is determined by the liquidity preference $(M_1 + M_2)$ and only that rate of interest will prevail in actual practice which brings about an equilibrium between the demand for liquidity and the supply of money. It may, however, be mentioned that though interest is related to the speculative motive only, the other two motives cannot be ignored because money held for one motive is a perfect substitute for money held under another motive.

In addition to the three motives mentioned by Keynes, the modern writers have mentioned three more motives which impel people to hold their assets in the form of money. These three motives are briefly described below:

Deflationary Motive. The deflationary motive for holding money appears when there is a general tendency towards a decline in prices. During periods of declining prices, both consumers and producers have a tendency to postpone their purchases expecting to buy cheaper at a later date. Thus, instead of buying goods, the people have a tendency to hold money. The deflationary motive for holding money is based on the speculative anticipation of people in regard to a decline in prices of goods and services. In a sense, this is also a speculative motive. But Keynes considers speculative motive for holding money in a narrower sense to mean speculation about future prices of only claims (bills, securities, bonds, shares etc.) while deflationary motive refers to speculation about future prices of goods and services.

Business Expansion Motive. The business-expansion motive for holding money refers to the tendency on the part of the business concerns to accumulate and hold money in order to finance their expansion plans. In recent years most of the companies have a tendency to depend on their own funds for expanding business in view of certain advantages involved in it. Similarly, the individuals have a tendency to accumulate and hold money to finance their purchases of expensive consumer durable goods like a refrigerator or television set. The business expansion motive is distinct from the transaction motive because the latter is used in narrower sense of current transactions.

Convenience Motive. The convenience motive refers to the fact that money is the most convenient way of keeping one's savings. If a person wants to keep his savings in the form of certain assets (like bonds, securities, furniture, house, precious metals), he has to undergo the inconvenience of going to the market, finding out the different goods available, searching the cheapest sources of supply of goods, making a choice between different assets available, and so forth and so on. The convenience motive for holding money is particularly important for people having small amounts of savings.

Since income (Y) partly depends on the rate of interest (r), changes either in r or M will affect the other indirectly. This relationship is important for monetary policy during periods of expanding output. If an increase in income or output is not accompanied by an increase in the total quantity of money (M), the increase in M_1 will take place by a transfer of funds from M_2. A decline in the amount of money available for speculative motive will push the rate of interest upwards which would have adverse effects on investment and hence on income. This rise in the rate of interest, which tends to inhibit expansion, can be offset by an increase in the total quantity of money (M) so that the increase in funds needed to meet the growing transactions demand will not be met at the expense of money needed to satisfy the speculative motive (M_2). Here the banking authority is required to act in such a way as will not permit a shortage of money to lead to a premature brake on expanding income and employment.

SUPPLY OF MONEY

Having analysed the demand for money, we now turn to the supply of money. The supply of money is different from the supply of a commodity. In case of a commodity, the supply is a *flow* over time. The commodity is being continuously produced. But in case of money, the supply is a *stock*. Money, unlike a commodity, is not being continuously produced and consumed. The supply of money, like the demand for money, is the supply of money to hold. Unless money is held by someone, it cannot exist. Thus the supply of money is the existing stock of money, all of which is held by someone or the other. An increase in the supply of money means not an increase in the sale of money by those who possess it, but an increase in the stock of money.

Unlike the demand for money, the supply of money is completely amenable to the state control because it is determined by the government and the central bank of the country. In his analysis of the rate of interest, Keynes assumes the quantity of money to be constant. In a short-period analysis, he considers this assumption to be quite reasonable.

The total supply of money consists of metallic coins, paper money and bank deposits. The first two constituents are completely under the control of the central bank which is generally a government-owned institution. In highly capitalist economies, bank deposits form the largest source of the total supply money. If money is defined as the perfectly liquid asset, the presumption would be against including saving and time deposits because the banks have a right to demand a certain number of days' notice for converting such deposits into legal money. Keynes, however, includes time deposits into money. Lending and borrowing activities of the banking system form the most important factor responsible for changes in the supply of money.

In Fig. 10.3, LP is the curve of liquidity preference for speculative motive. Curve LP shows the demand for money for speculative motive. It slopes downward to the right showing that at higher rates of interest, the demand for speculative motive is less and conversely. OM is the initial quantity of money available for satisfying liquidity preference for speculative motive. Or is the equilibrium rate of interest because at this rate the amount of money demanded (OM) is equal to its supply (OM). Now let us suppose that the supply of money is increased from OM to OM′ through open market operations. When the supply of money is increased to OM′ the rate of interest would decline to Or′ because the increased supply of money becomes equal to the speculative demand for money at Or′ rate of interest. Similarly, if the supply of money is decreased, there would occur a rise in the rate of interest.

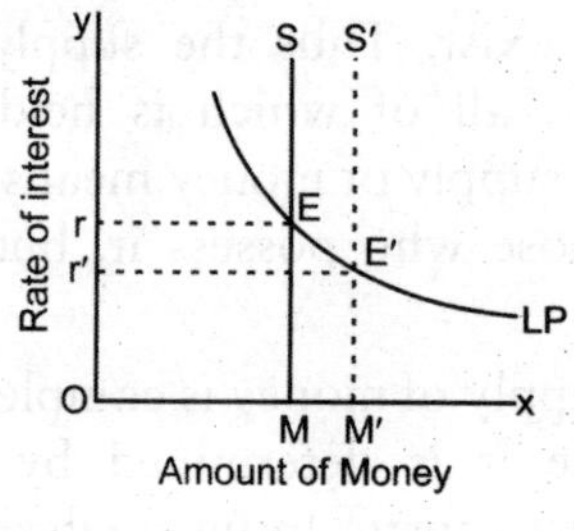

Fig. 10.3

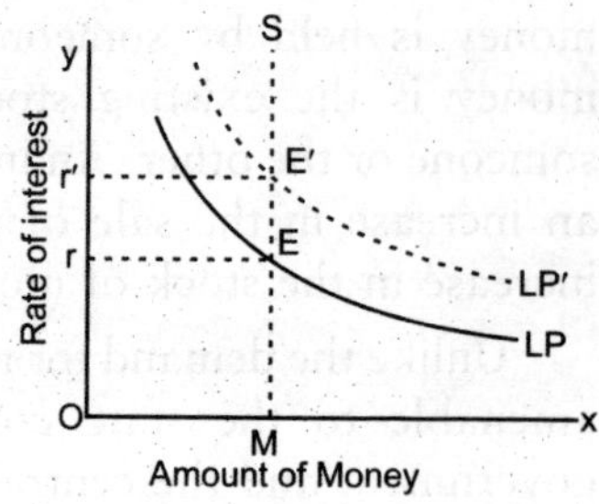

Fig. 10.4

In Fig. 10.4, assuming that the supply of money remains unchanged, if the liquidity preference curve rises from LP to LP′ the rate of interest would rise from Or to Or′ because the increased speculative demand for money is equal to the supply of money at Or′ rate of interest. Conversely, if the liquidity preference curve declines, there would occur a decline in the rate of interest.

IMPLICATIONS OF LIQUIDITY PREFERENCE THEORY

Interest Rate and Supply of Money: In the Keynesian analysis, the monetary authority is expected to stimulate employment by following a cheap money policy or, in other words, by lowering the rate of interest through an expansion in the supply of money. The logic behind easy monetary policy is that an expansion in the supply of money, other things remaining unchanged, will increase the money available for speculative motive (M_2) which would lead to a decline in the rate of interest. A fall in the rate of interest stimulates investment which leads to a multiple increase in income and employment. With the increase in income, the amount of money required for transactions (M_1) increases so that the total increase in money (M) is divided in some way between M_1 and M_2. The effectiveness of money stimulation depends upon the extent of decline in the rate of interest in response to an increase in M_2 (i.e. upon the elasticity of L_2 function), responsiveness of investment to a decline in the rate of interest (i.e. the elasticity of the schedule of the marginal efficiency of capital), and the magnitude of increase in income resulting from a certain increase in investment (i.e. the size of the investment multiplier).

Such a policy of monetary management, however, has serious limitations. An increase in the quantity of money will not lower the rate of interest if the liquidity preference is increasing faster than the quantity of money. Similarly, a decline in the rate of interest will not expand investment and employment if the marginal efficiency of capital is declining faster than the rate of interest. Thus in a severe depression when the liquidity preference is high and the expectations of entrepreneurs for profitable investment are low, monetary policy may fail to lift the economy out of depression.

Long-term Vs. Short-term Rate of Interest: Although we speak of the rate of interest without mentioning the period of maturity of the debt, this does not mean that there is only one rate of interest prevailing in the market. We adopt this practice only for simplifying the analysis. In the real money market, there exists a complex of rates of interest differing among themselves depending upon debts of varying maturities. The rate of interest on daily loans will be different from the rates of interest on weekly, monthly or yearly loans. Similarly, debts of longer maturity like four, seven or twelve years, will bear different rates of interest. To overcome the difficulties involved in talking of a number of rates of interest, a distinction is made between the short-term rate of interest paid on bank loans and the long-term rate of interest paid on bonds and securities. Since the speculative demand for money over a short period changes very violently, the short-term rate of interest is subject to greater violations than the long-term rate of interest. The long-term rate of interest is comparatively stable because over a long period, expectations of a conflicting nature cancel themselves out leaving very little influence on the rate of interest.

It is much easier to lower the short-term than the long-term rate of interest. The major obstacle to a decline in interest rates is the expectation that they may rise later to such an extent as makes it worthwhile to hold cash in anticipation of buying on more favourable terms at a later date. If the banking authority launches a large-scale open-market policy to lower the interest rates, it is natural to assume that this policy would probably be pursued for some time. There would be hardly any reason to expect a rise in the rate of interest in the near future and, therefore, there would be little incentive to remain liquid with a view to buying later on more favourable terms. Further, commitments to debts on short-terms would not involve substantial losses even if expectations turn out to be wrong. The securities may be held for a short-time until maturity when they are redeemed at face value.

It is more difficult to lower the long-term rate of interest and it tends to become increasingly resistant to further reductions at every step on its downward path. At some level, say about 2 percent, no further reductions may be possible. The loss from a rise in the interest rate from 2 to 3 percent, for instance, is much greater than that from 4 to 5 percent because the loss in capital value is greater and also because the interest income is less at the lower level.

The increasing risk of loss at lower rates of interest is reflected in the liquidity-preference schedule by a flattening out of the liquidity curve. The flattening of the curve indicates a growing elasticity of the liquidity-preference function which means a point will be reached below which it is very difficult to lower the rate of interest any further. Keynes suggested that at about 2 percent, the liquidity curve may become horizontal, indicating perfect elasticity, and meaning that no further reduction in the rate of interest can be brought about through a mere expansion in the quantity of money. At this rate of interest, the demand for money is absolute in the sense that everyone prefers to hold money rather than long-term securities yielding a return of 2 percent or less. A second reason for the liquidity preference curve becoming perfectly elastic at a certain minimum rate of interest is that this minimum rate of interest may not be adequate to compensate for the incidental out-lays and inconveniences involved in purchasing bonds. A third reason is that people may no longer expect any further fall in the interest rate and may expect it to rise in future. They, therefore, prefer to hold cash rather than bonds, securities and other earning assets yielding that minimum rate of interest or less than that. Thus, owing to the reasons mentioned above, the liquidity preference curve becomes perfectly elastic at a certain minimum rate of interest indicating that no further reduction in the interest rate can be attained merely by increasing the quantity of money.

Inverse Relationship between Rate of Interest and Bond Prices: There is a definite inverse relationship between interest rates and bond prices. In other words, when interest rates rise, bond prices fall, and when interest rates decline, bond prices rise. Changes in the prices of bonds in the organised securities markets reflect themselves in change in the liquidity preference of the people. A decline in liquidity preference is reflected in an increased desire on the part of people to buy bonds at current prices leading to a rise in the prices of bonds and a decline in the rate of interest. Similarly, an upward shift in the liquidity preference curve is reflected in an increased desire on the part of people to sell bonds in order to obtain more cash which leads to a decline in bond prices and a rise in the interest rate.

CRITICISM OF KEYNES' THEORY OF INTEREST

Keynes' theory of interest, like the classical theory, is indeterminate. The liquidity preference curve itself shifts up and down with changes in the level of income. The liquidity preference for transactions and precautionary motives cannot be known until we know the level of income. Thus we cannot know the liquidity preference curve and hence the rate of interest without knowing the level of income. The Keynesian theory tells us only the various schedules of liquidity preference at various levels of income and not what the rate of interest would be. To quote Hansen:

> In the Keynesian case the supply and demand for money schedule cannot give the income; in the classical case the demand and supply schedules for saving offer no solution until income is known. Precisely the same is true of loanable find theory. Keynes' criticism of the classical and loanable fund theories applies equally to his own theory.[4]

Prof. Hazlitt has pointed out that rate of interest is not purely a monetary phenomenon. Real forces like productivity of capital, thriftiness or time preference or savings also play an important role in the determination of rate of interest. While the classical economists were wrong in ignoring monetary factors, Keynes erred on the other side by ignoring real factors. In fact, as Wicksell has rightly pointed out, the theory of interest should take into consideration both money and real factors.

Keynes' theory of interest is self-contradictory. "For if a man is holding his funds in the form of time deposits or short-term treasury bills, he is being paid interest on them; therefore, he is getting interest and 'liquidity' too. What becomes, then, of Keynes' theory that interest is the reward for parting with liquidity."[5]

Keynes' theory goes contrary to the facts that it presumes to explain. If Keynes' theory were correct, the short-term interest rate would be the highest at the bottom of a depression when owing to declining prices, people's preference of liquidity is the strongest and lowest at the peak of the boom when due to all-round confidence the liquidity preference of the people is the weakest. But in actual practice, the interest rates are the lowest at the bottom of the depression and highest at the peak of the boom.

The rate of interest is not independent of the demand for investment funds as believed by Keynes. The amount of cash balances the businessmen will hold is considerably influenced by their demand for finance for investment purposes. The rate of interest, therefore, is not independent of the marginal efficiency of capital.

The distinction between liquidity and illiquidity is not so simple as assumed by Keynes. In fact, there are different degrees of liquidity and a complex system of rates of interest depending on the differences in the degree of liquidity. Keynes unnecessarily simplifies his theory by completely ignoring the time element and making distinction only between liquidity and illiquidity. In actual practice, we find that the rates of interest are different on daily, weekly, monthly, yearly and long-term loans.

Keynes' theory of liquidity preference is too narrow as an explanation of the rate of interest. In actual practice liquidity (or desire for money) arises on account of many factors and not only on account of motives mentioned by Keynes. It, for instance, also arises for investment. Further, the rate of interest influences and is in turn influenced by other important factors like the rate of saving, propensity to consume and the marginal efficiency of capital, which are neglected by the liquidity preference theory.

Keynes' ignores savings and explains interest as a reward for parting with liquidity. In actual practice, there can be no liquidity without saving. Prof. Jacob Viner pertinently remarks, "...without saving there can be no liquidity to surrender.... The rate of interest is the return for saving without liquidity."[6]

Prof. Patinkin points out that "Unfortunately, Keynes' analysis is repeatedly marred by a confusion.....between his basic proposition that the amount of money demanded is inversely dependent upon the rate of interest and the completely different proposition that the equilibrium rate of interest is inversely dependent upon the amount of money. His discussion of liquidity preference in the *General Theory* shifts uninhibitedly from one proposition to the other with never an indication that they are in any way not identical. More specifically, there is never a recognition that...the first of these propositions describes an individual-experiment and the second a market-experiment, and that the truth of the first need not imply the truth of the second."[7]

Prof. Patinkin further points that "Keynesian monetary theory never permits the speculative demand to absorb an increased supply of money except at a lower rate of interest. It never allows for the fact, provided the price level rises, such an absorption may take place even at an unchanged rate. Nor can this omission be explained as itself proving that the analysis of the *General Theory* proceeds on the assumption of absolute price rigidity. For there are passages in this work in which Keynes explicitly assumes the wage or price level to rise, in which he explains how this rise affects the transactions and precautionary demands, and in which he overlooks the fact that it may also affect the speculative demand."[8]

Moreover, "Keynes should have taken account of the fact that shifts in liquidity preference can, in principle, also affect the demand for commodities...in such a case, the rate of interest need not be affected."[9]

Despite all that has been said above the fact remains that Keynes' theory of interest is an improvement over the classical theory in that by introducing the dynamic concept of role of money namely 'as a link between the present and the future' and the consequent speculative demand for money, Keynes emphasizes how uncertainty and expectations exert an important influence on the levels of income and employment through the rate of interest.[10]

LIQUIDITY PREFERENCE VS. LOANABLE FUNDS

There has been an unnecessary controversy as to the choice between liquidity preference and loanable fund theories of the rate of interest. The advocates of the loanable funds theory claim that this theory is broader in scope and allows for more influences on the rate of interest than does the liquidity preference theory. An increase in consumption, for instance, decreases savings and thereby leads to a rise in the rate of interest. Similarly, a rise in the marginal efficiency of capital increases the demand for funds for investment and thereby leads to a rise in the rate of interest. The liquidity preference theory, in contrast, restricts the influences on the rate of interest to the demand for and supply of money for hoarding. The advocates of loanable funds theory admit that hoarding plays an important part in influencing the rate of interest but assert that this is not the only influence. On the supply side, while the liquidity preference theory is confined to the supply of money as determined by the monetary authority, the loanable funds theory includes not only bank money but also voluntary savings and dishoarded wealth. By linking the rate of interest with liquidity preference, quantity of credit, saving and investment, the loanable funds theory views the problem in a more practical way for it explains why market rate of interest is, and can be, different from the natural rate of interest.

The advocates of the liquidity preference, on the other hand, contend that this theory is an integral part of the analysis of the working of the economic system as a whole while the loanable funds theory is an exercise in partial equilibrium analysis and can hence be a square peg in a round whole in the general determinate system.

The liquidity preference theory runs in terms of stocks, *i.e.*, supply of money in the short-run and demand for it in the short-run varying with the expectations of future interest rates while the loanable funds theory runs in terms of flows, *i.e.*, so much supply of loanable funds and so much demand for loanable funds per period of time. Many economists believe that the theory of the rate of interest should be in terms of stocks rather than flows.

> Scitovszky has pointed out that in ordinary supply and demand analysis, price is the allocating mechanism between two flows... But in the case in which stocks are significant and are dependent upon price, he claimed that the equation of supply-demand flows may not lead to the correct result.... It is certainly obvious that money and earning assets are commodities which possess very large stocks. We know that interest is earned on existing stocks of assets as well as on the current flows. Interest is not the allocating mechanism between the supply and demand for credit flows rather the allocating mechanism between the holding of stocks of earning and non-earning assets.[11]

The advocates of the liquidity preference theory contend that the rate of interest is a monetary phenomenon and has to be separated from the productivity of capital. In the words of Klein:

> In essence, the Keynesian contribution was to point out that people can make two distinct types of decisions. They may decide upon saving or consuming their incomes, and they may decide upon holding idle cash or non-liquid securities. Each decision requires an economic calculation. In the former case, individuals decide on the basis of their incomes how much they want to spend on consumption and at the same time how much they want to save. In the latter case, they may decide on the basis of alternative rates of return (*i.e.*, interest rates) whether they want to hoard their historically accumulated saving in the form of cash or securities. The distinction between these two sets of decisions clearly calls for a liquidity preference theory of interest.[12]

The liquidity preference theory not only brings forth the important role of money but integrates money into the theory of output and employment for the economy as a whole.

STOCKS AND FLOWS

Keynesian theory runs in terms of stocks, i.e., the supply of money in the short-run and demand for it in the short-run varying with the expectations of future interest rates, while the classical and neo-classical theories run in terms of flows, i.e., so much supply of savings or loanable funds and so much demand for savings or loanable funds per period of time. Many economists hold the view that the theory of interest should be in terms of stocks rather than flows T. de Scitovszky[13] points out that in ordinary supply-and-demand analysis, price is the allocating mechanism between two flows, and that this approach is appropriate when dealing with commodities for which there do not exist large stocks or for which the stocks are independent of the price. But in the case in which stocks are significant and are dependent upon price, he holds that the equation of supply-demand flows may not lead to the proper result. For illustration, suppose that current production and consumption flows for some good are in equilibrium at the current market price and that this price is also an equilibrium point for the supply and demand for stocks. If now the demand for the consumer goods changes, the establishment of a new price at which the two flows will be in equilibrium will be hindered by the adjustment of stocks to the new price. If the change in demand takes the form of a decline in consumer's desires for the good, price will tend to fall in order to bring the flow schedules into equilibrium. But then the holders of stocks may desire to increase their holdings at the lower price. Thus the stockholder behaviour may counteract the flow adjustment and can prevent it from taking place. If one or more of these interest rates on alternative assets rise, the demand for cash as a proportion of total assets declines, and *vice versa*.

A change in the interest rate of any money substitute affects not only the demand for money but also the demand for all other assets related to the money substitute. To put it in a general form, the demand for any asset, including money, is a function of not just one interest rate but of many interest rates. This means that a change in the supply of any asset, including money, will change not just one interest rate but many. Further, a change in the interest rate on any asset affects not only the demand for that asset but the demand for all related assets, of which money may be one. Thus the interest rate on any asset is determined not by the supply of that asset alone, but by the supplies of all related assets.

RECONCILIATION OF TWO THEORIES

The modern economists are of the view that the controversy in regard to the choice between the two theories is unnecessary and uncalled for. Economists like Hicks, Lerner and Fellner have made attempts to reconcile the two theories. They believe that the two theories are more or less similar and can be used to express the same thing. In the classical loanable funds theory, an excess of demand for loanable funds over their supply leads to a rise in the rate of interest. Similarly, in the liquidity preference theory an increase in investment leads to more use of cash for transaction purposes which, other things remaining unchanged, means less cash available for speculative purpose which results in the rise in the rate of interest. In the same way, an increase in consumption means more cash for transaction purposes which, other things remaining same, means less cash available for speculative purpose and hence a rise in the rate of interest. Thus the liquidity preference approach as well as the loanable funds approach lead to the same results. Prof. Hamberg remarks:

> In view of the interchangeability of the two approaches to the explanation of the interest, it is a matter of complete indifference and personal choice, which one of the two approaches is used. Because of the similarities too, it is probably best to say that Keynes did not forge nearly as a new theory of rate of interest as he and others at first thought. Rather, his great emphasis of the influence of hoarding on the rate of interest constituted an invaluable addition to the theory of interest as it had been developed by the loanable fund theorists who incorporated much of Keynes' ideas into their theory to make it more complete.[14]

In fact, both the theories considered individually are indeterminate. A determinate theory can, of course, be obtained by a synthesis of the two theories. In the words of Hansen, "The neo-classical (loanable fund) formulation and the Keynesian formulation, *taken together,*[15] do supply us with an adequate theory of the rate of interest."[16] Such a synthesis is given below:

The loanable funds formulation gives us a family of loanable fund schedules (or saving schedule in the Keynesian-Pigovian sense) at various levels of income. These together with the investment-demand schedule give us the Hicksian IS curve. In other words, the loanable funds formulation can tell us what the various levels of income will be (given the investment-demand schedule and a family of loanable fund schedules) at different rates of interest. But it does not tell us what the rate of interest will be. From the Keynesian formulation we get a family of liquidity preference schedules at various levels of income. These, together with the supply of money determined by the monetary authority, give us the Hicksian L curve (which Hansen prefers to call the LM curve). The LM curve tells us what the various rates of interest will be (given the quantity of money and the family of liquidity preference curves) at different levels of income. But the liquidity schedule alone cannot tell us what the rate of interest will be.

Derivation of IS curve is shown in figure 10.5(a). With the rise in income, the savings curve shifts to the right and the rate of interest which equalises savings and investment declines. In figure 10.5(b), income (Y) is measured along X-axis and the corresponding rates of interest determined by the equality of savings and investment are plotted. Thus when income is Y_2, the relevant saving curve is S_2Y_2 and the corresponding rate of interest equalising savings and investment is r_4. Similarly, for other levels of income, the IS curve slopes downward for with a rise in income, the rate of interest declines.

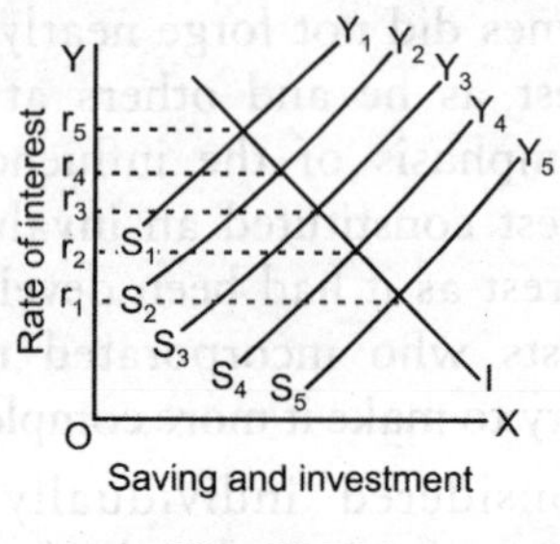

Fig. 10.5(*a*)

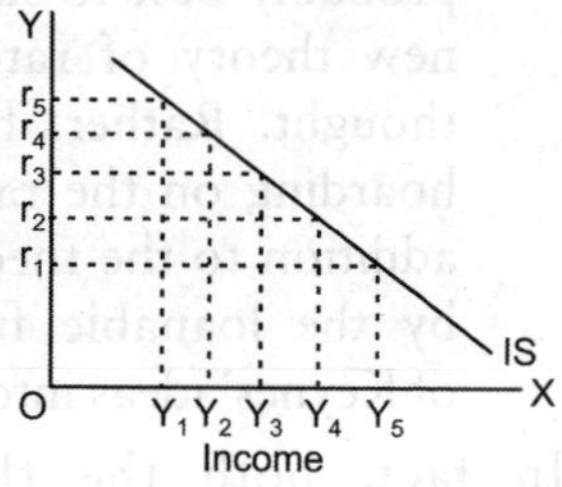

Fig. 10.5(*b*)

From Keynesian theory we obtain a family of liquidity preference curves at various income levels. These, together with the supply of money fixed by the monetary authority, give us the Hicksian LM curve (Figure 10.6).

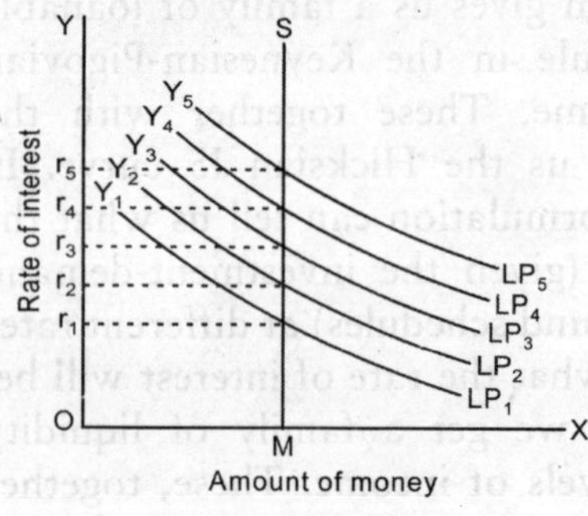

Fig. 10.6(*a*)

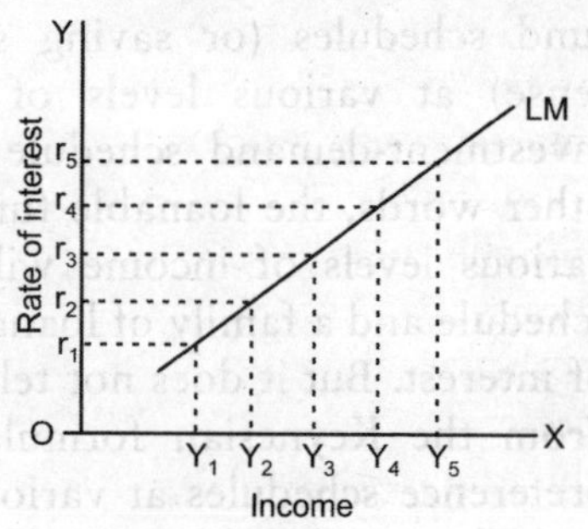

Fig. 10.6(*b*)

The LM curve tells us what the various rates of interest will be (given the quantity of money and the family of liquidity preference curves) at different levels of income. In figure 10.6(a) we have derived the LM curve from a family of liquidity preference curves. With the increase in income, liquidity preference curve shifts upward and as such the rate of interest which equates supply of money with demand for money rises. In figure 10.6(b) we measure income on the X-axis and plot the income levels corresponding to the various interest rates given at those income levels by the quantity of demand for and supply of money in figure 10.6(a).

The IS and LM curves are schedules relating the two variables, (i) income, and (ii) rate of interest. Income and the rate of interest are therefore determined together at the point of intersection of these two curves, that is E in figure 10.7. The equilibrium rate of interest thus determined is Or_3 and the level of income, determined is OY_3. At this point, income and rate of interest are related to each other in a way that (i) investment and savings are in equilibrium and (ii) the demand for money is in equilibrium with the supply of money.

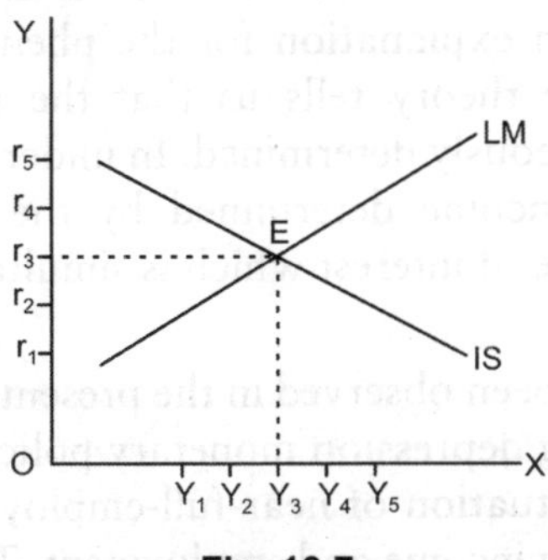

Fig. 10.7

Thus a determinate theory of interest is based on the synthesis of the two theories, or in other words, in a determinate theory, interest along with income is determined by four important forces: (i) marginal efficiency of capital, (ii) propensity to consume (save), (iii) the liquidity preference schedule, and (iv) the total supply of money. We see, therefore, that according to Hicks and Hansen, both monetary and real factors (i.e. productivity, thrift, liquidity preference and supply of money) play part in the determination of the rate of interest.

The Keynesian analysis, viewed as a whole, involved all of these. In this sense Keynes, unlike the neo-classicals, did have a determinate theory of interest. But Keynes never combined all the elements together to form an integrated theory of interest. He failed to explicitly point out that liquidity preference combined with the quantity of money can give us only LM curve and not the rate of interest. It was Hicks who utilised the Keynesian tools and presented a complete picture combining productivity, thrift, liquidity preference and supply of money.

EVALUATION OF HICKS-HANSEN DETERMINATE THEORY

The Hicks-Hansen determinate theory of the rate of interest is a useful integration of the classical and Keynes' theories of interest. Further it has been used to explain several policy muddles which neither classical nor Keynesian theory could explain. Two important examples are cited below:

Firstly, it is observed that in underdeveloped countries the rate of interest is low in spite of the fact that the need and demand for capital are high. The classical theory can not explain this phenomenon. The liquidity preference of people in these countries is also high but the rate of interest is low. Thus the Keynesian analysis also fails to offer an explanation for the phenomenon. The Hicks Hansen determinate theory tells us that the rate of interest and income are simultaneously determined. In underdeveloped countries, since the level of income determined by the real and monetary forces is low, the rate of interest which is simultaneously determined is also low.

Secondly, it has been observed in the present developed capitalist countries that during depression monetary policy alone fails to raise income while in a situation of near-full-employment it is successful in appreciably raising income and employment. This can be explained with the help of IS-LM diagram.

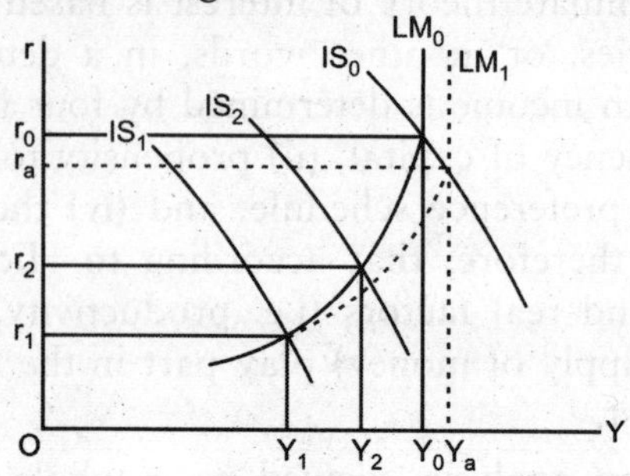

Fig. 10.8

In figure 10.8, the IS_0 curve which is relatively interest-elastic interesects LM_0 curve which is relatively interest-inelastic. At the point of intersection, the interest rate r_0 and income Y_0 are mutually determined.

Suppose that income at Y_0 is short of the full employment income. In order to increase income to full employment level, the monetary authority increases the supply of money so that LM_0 is shifted to LM_1. This leads to a decline in the interest rate to r_a and rise in income Y_a. This means boom conditions because Y_0 already represents a high level of employment (though not full employment). Thus it is obvious that if the IS curve is interest-elastic and the LM curve is interest-inelastic, an increase in the quantity of money will have an-expansionary effect and the monetary policy would succeed.

Now take the case of intersection of IS curve which is relatively interest-inelastic with LM_0 curve which is highly interest-elastic. In this case it is clear that income and employment cannot be raised by increasing the quantity of money, or in other words, monetary policy fails. In order to raise the level of income from Y_1 to Y_2 it is essential to shift the IS_1 curve to IS_2 and this would be possible only when the MEC schedule rises or when the consumption function is shifted upwards.

Under these circumstances the monetary policy fails and it is only the fiscal policy which can raise the MEC schedule and investment. This type of situation does arise in advanced countries which have large quantities of capital and hence a low marginal efficiency of capital and the low rate of interest under such conditions fails to induce new investment. The investment function I_1 being interest-inelastic, the IS curve would also have a tendency to be interest-inelastic. Investment outlets would, therefore, have to wait for an upward shift in the marginal efficiency of capital brought by factors like technological innovations, inventions of new products, development or regional resources, urban development, housing construction, rural electrification etc. which would shift IS_1 curve to IS_2.

Now let us consider the point of intersection of IS_2 curve which is relatively interest-inelastic and the LM_0 curve. In this case an increase in the quantity of money would shift the LM_0 curve to LM_1, which would lower the interest rate but increase income only to a small extent. The three cases described above represent near full-employment, underemployment and depression respectively.

But economists like Don Patinkin and Milton Friedman have criticised Hicks-Hansen formulation. They have pointed out that it is too simplified to be of any practical use. They hold the view that division of the economy into only two sectors—real and monetary—is an oversimplified presentation of the problem. They have suggested a general equilibrium analysis approach for determining the rate of interest and income. According to them, rate of interest is only one of prices which acts on and reacts to changes in the prices of all the commodities and services in the economy. In short, they prefer an integrated approach to the determination of not only income and rate of interest but of prices also.

REAL VERSUS MONETARY THEORIES OF INTEREST

The classical theories of interest concentrate on 'real forces' like productivity and thrift. The important role played by the monetary authorities in recent times and the existence of unemployment have considerably undermined the impact of real forces contemplated in these theories. As a result, the monetary theories of interest have assumed more importance. Today the popular theory of interest is either a liquidity preference theory, according to which the money rate of interest is determined by the demand for and supply of the stock of bonds, or a loanable funds theory, according to which the money rate of interest is determined by the demand for and supply of a flow of securities.

It is sometimes believed that there exists a conflict between the real and monetary theories of interest. According to real theories, interest is the yield of capital and a reward for foregoing present consumption. According to monetary theories, interest is the price of money and reward for parting with liquidity. Keynes himself believed that there exists a conflict between the real and monetary theories of interest when he remarked that interest is not a reward for waiting but a reward for not hoarding money.

In fact, the rate of interest is influenced by real as well as monetary forces. General equilibrium analysis shows that the rate of interest operates simultaneously, as D.H. Robertson has remarked, on "the threefold margin" of consumption decisions, investment decisions, and asset-portfolio decisions. In other words, interest simultaneously rewards waiting, reflects the pure yield of capital, and compensates for parting with liquidity. In actual practice, the rate of interest is influenced to some extent by all the elements expressed in the equation of Walras-Hicks general equilibrium. The loanable funds theory or the liquidity preference theory, therefore, represent only a form of partial equilibrium analysis of the determinants of the rate of interest. Determination of rate of interest can be properly viewed only by considering the rate of interest to be determined in a general equilibrium system.

PORTFOLIO BALANCE THEORY

This theory was developed independently but simultaneously by James Tobin, Gurley and Shaw, and others in the 1950s and early 1960s. The theory is a natural and logical extension of the theory of liquidity preference. Like the liquidity preference theory, the portfolio balance theory focusses attention on interest rates as being that which explains the demand for money and that which is directly and primarily affected by a change in the supply of money. But, unlike liquidity preference, portfolio balance theory does not assume that securities and other non-monetary assets are such perfect substitutes for each other that there is only one rate of interest. Instead it maintains that there are as many different interest rates as there are imperfect substitutes among earning assets. According to it relative interest rates on differentiated assets depend on the relative supplies of the assets.

Portfolio balance is basically a theory of asset choice. It is concerned with how individuals and the community allocate their holdings among alternative assets. It is a theory of the demand for assets, with the demand for each asset being measured as a proportion of total assets. To the extent money is an asset, portfolio balance is partly a theory of the demand for money.

The theory states that the demand for any asset, considered as a proportion of total assets, varies directly with its own interest rate and inversely with interest rates on substitute assets.[17] The demand for money varies directly with its own implicit rate of interest, and it varies inversely with interest rates on other assets.

Portfolio Balance under Static Expectations

In this section, we will discuss the portfolio balance model under static expectations, i.e., the expected rate of depreciation is zero. We will discuss risk and return in general and show how an investor's portfolio choice affected by risk and uncertainty. We also show why it could be optimal to diversify the portfolio, i.e., to include different assets in the portfolio in order to reduce the risk of the portfolio.

Even if domestic and foreign assets are very similar in most respects, there may be differences in risk caused by differences in liquidity, tax treatment, default risk, political risk, inflation risk, exchange control risk and exchange rate risks. It may also be the case that business cycles are not perfectly synchronised such that the rate of return on domestic and foreign assets are not synchronised implying that investors can hedge against capital losses by diversifying their portfolios. In other words, the risk associated with holding domestic and foreign bonds differs and an investor requires a higher expected rate of return on bonds that are more risky to compensate for the additional risk. There could exist a time varying risk premium on the foreign exchange market. For a risk premium to exist, the following three conditions must be satisfied:

(a) Domestic and foreign bonds are risky assets but the risk differs such that, for example, domestic bonds are relatively risky compared to foreign bonds. If they are equally risky and we assume perfect capital mobility, they are perfect substitutes. Therefore, we have to assume that the risk of holding domestic and foreign bonds differs.

(b) Agents are risk averse, i.e., investors accept risk if they expect a higher return on their investment. If investors were not risk averse, they would not require a higher rate of return on relatively risky bonds.

(c) There must be a difference between the risk-minimizing portfolio and the actual portfolio. The risk minimising portfolio is a theoretical portfolio that would minimise the risks facing the investors. Since, the amount of domestic and foreign bonds are given by the issuing authorities it may be the case that investors cannot hold this portfolio. If they cannot hold the risk minimising portfolio, then investors require a risk premium to compensate for the additional risk of the actual portfolio.

If all these three conditions are fulfilled, there must be a risk premium, which compensates investors for the higher risk exposure. The risk premium can be both positive and negative. If the expected return on domestic bonds is higher compared to the expected return on foreign bonds, then the risk premium is positive. If the expected return on domestic bonds is higher than the expected return on foreign bonds, then domestic bonds are more risky than foreign bonds and the risk premium is positive. Similarly, if the expected return on domestic bonds is lower than the expected return on foreign bonds, foreign bonds are more risky and the risk premium is negative.

Risk is defined as the variance of capital gains or losses. If gains and losses are expected to cancel in the long-run, then the expected value of the gain is zero. A riskless asset has a very small variance, i.e., there is a very small chance that the capital loss differs from zero. A risky asset has a high probability of a capital loss and therefore a high variance. A riskless asset such as money has a zero variance and consequently there is no chance of a capital loss. An investor, who can invest in two assets, money and bonds, will shift the portfolio in the direction of more bonds and less money if the interest rate rises. A higher return on bonds compensate for the higher risk, it overcomes the investor's risk aversion. A lower interest rate will shift the portfolio in the direction of more money and fewer bonds.

Let us consider two examples of portfolio choice, one with one riskfree and one risky asset, and the other with two risky assets. Also, assume that there are two available assets, money which is riskless and pays no return and bonds which yields a return of i percent. Let α denotes the share of the investor's portfolio, invested in bonds. In equilibrium, the portfolio consists of α_0 percent bonds and $1-\alpha_0$ percent money. The rate of return on the portfolio is given by

$$r = \alpha(g+i), \qquad \text{...(10.1)}$$

where, g is the capital gain.

The expected value of the rate of return on the portfolio is given by

$$E[r] = E[\alpha(g+i)]\alpha i \qquad \text{...(10.2)}$$

Here, we have assumed that E[g] = 0. The rate of return on the portfolio is equal to the percent of the wealth invested in bonds times the interest rate.

The variance of the rate of return on the portfolio is given by

$$E[r - E[r]]^2 = \sigma_r^2 = \alpha^2 \sigma_g^2 \qquad ...(10.3)$$

implying that the risk of the portfolio is equal to the percent of the wealth invested in bonds times the standard deviation of capital gains. That is,

$$\sigma_r = \alpha\sigma_g \qquad ...(10.4)$$

Let, us consider Fig. (10.9).

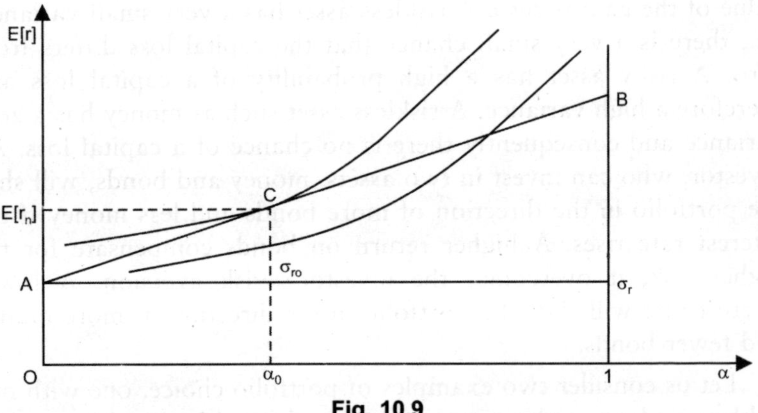

Fig. 10.9

In Fig. (10.9), AB is the opportunity line showing the relationship between expected return and riskiness of the portfolio. To obtain the opportunity line we take the ratio of the expected return on the portfolio and the standard deviation of the return on the portfolio, i.e.,

$$E[r] = \frac{i}{\sigma_g}\sigma_r \qquad ...(10.5)$$

The slope of the opportunity line is given by i/σ_g, which implies that a higher interest rate will lead to a steeper slope. At point A, $\alpha = 0$, and at this point the investor earns no return on the portfolio and at point B, $\alpha = 1$ and the investor earns a maximum return at the price of maximum risk.

If the investor is risk averse, risk and return are imperfect substitutes, there will be a set of indifference curves reflecting expected utility. In the above figure, the investor settles for point C where the slope of the opportunity line is equal to the slope of the indifference curve. In this way we can find α_0, the share of wealth invested in bonds.

Now consider the case of two risky assets—domestic bonds and foreign bonds. Suppose α be the percentage of the portfolio invested in foreign bonds. The rate of return on the portfolio is then given as

$$r = (1-\alpha)(g+i) + \alpha(g^* + i^*) \qquad ...(10.6)$$

implying that the expected return is

$$E[r] = (1-\alpha)i + \alpha i^* \qquad ...(10.7)$$

where, we have assumed that the expected value of the capital gain or loss is zero for both assets.

The variance of the rate of return on the portfolio is

$$\sigma_r^2 = E[r - E[r]] = (1-\alpha)^2 \sigma_g^2 + \alpha^2 \sigma_{g^*}^2 + 2\alpha(1-\alpha)\sigma_{g.g^*} \qquad ...(10.8)$$

where, $\sigma_{g.g^*}$ is the covariance between capital losses in domestic and foreign bonds.

The riskiness of the portfolio is dependent on the riskiness of the two types of bonds and the covariance of the capital loss between domestic and foreign bonds.

If the two risky assets are negatively correlated, capital loss on one asset tends to be offset by a capital gain on the other asset. Thus, the riskiness of the portfolio is reduced. Empirical evidence also suggests that the covariance between domestic and foreign assets is generally lower than the covariance between different domestic assets. This implies that international diversification is likely to reduce the riskiness of portfolios. Note that if domestic and foreign bonds are riskless, it follows that the riskiness of our portfolio is zero and the two assets are perfect substitutes. If the two assets are independently equally risky, $\sigma_g = \sigma_{g^*}$, then the riskiness of the portfolio will be less than the riskiness of domestic bonds if the covariance between capital losses of the two assets is negative. This further implies that international diversification makes sense even if interest rates are the same in both countries and the independent riskiness of the two assets is the same.

Finally, if the wealth of the investor is increased, then the investor will increase the demand for all assets. If, for example, there is an increase in wealth in the form of additional bonds, the investor will convert some of the bonds into money. Similarly, if there is an increase in wealth in the form of additional money, some money will be used to buy more bonds. Thus, a rise in the interest rate leads to greater risk taking and by diversifying the portfolio, the riskiness of the portfolio can be rduced.

Let us now assume that expectations are static, i.e., we assume that the expected rate of depreciation is zero and both domestic prices and output are fixed. The model economy we study is a small open economy such that the rest of the world can be taken as given and there is no reaction from the rest of the world.

We shall consider three assets—money (M), domestic bonds (B), denominated in domestic currency, and foreign bonds (F), denominated in foreign currency. We assume a fixed net supply of domestic bonds which is the sum of bond holdings of households and bond holdings of the monetary authority, i.e.,

$$\bar{B} = B_p + B_a \qquad ...(10.9)$$

where,

B_p = bonds held by the public, and

B_a = bonds held by monetary authority.

Similarly, foreign bonds are held by the public and the monetary authority and is represented as

$$F = F_p + F_a \qquad ...(10.10)$$

However, the holdings of foreign assets can increase or decrease over time via the current account surplus or deficit. The current account deficit, thus, reflects the accumulation of foreign assets and is defined as the partial derivatives of foreign bond holdings of the public with respect to time. Thus,

$$CA_d = \frac{\partial F}{\partial t} = \dot{F} = T + i^*(F_p + F_a) \qquad ...(10.11)$$

where,

T = trade balance, and

$i^*(F_p + F_a)$ = interest rate receipt from net holdings of foreign assets.

The trade balance is a function of the real exchange rate and domestic income,

$$T = T(S/P, Y), \quad \text{where } \frac{\partial T}{\partial S} > 0, \ \frac{\partial T}{\partial Y} < 0 \qquad ...(10.12)$$

where,

S = exchange rate, and

P = price level.

The monetary base is defined as the sum of domestic and foreign bond holdings of the monetary authority, i.e.,

$$M = B_a + SF_a \qquad ...(10.13)$$

Here one point should be noted that the foreign bonds are denominated in the foreign currency implying that we have to multiply with the exchange rate to convert the value of foreign bonds into the domestic currency.

The following identity gives the total national wealth of the economy.

$$\begin{aligned} W &= M + B_p + SF_p \\ &= B_a + SF_a + B_p + SF_p \\ &= \bar{B} + SF \qquad ...(10.14) \end{aligned}$$

Money demand is a function of the interest rate, expected change in the exchange rate, output, and financial wealth, i.e.,

$$M = m(i, E[\dot{S}], Y, W) \qquad ...(10.15)$$

where,

$$\frac{\partial m}{\partial i} < 0, \ \frac{\partial m}{\partial E[\dot{S}]} < 0, \ \frac{\partial m}{\partial Y} > 0, \text{ and } \frac{\partial m}{\partial W} > 0.$$

The demand for money is inversely realted to the interest rate and the expected change in the exchange rate and positively related to domestic income and wealth. The demand for domestic bonds is also a function of the same variables as the demand for money, i.e.,

$$B_p = b(i, E[\dot{S}], Y, W) \qquad ...(10.16)$$

where,

$$\frac{\partial b}{\partial i} > 0, \ \frac{\partial b}{\partial E[\dot{S}]} < 0, \ \frac{\partial b}{\partial Y} < 0, \text{ and } \frac{\partial b}{\partial W} > 0.$$

Thus, the demand for domestic bonds is invesely related to the expected change in the exchange rate and domestic income and positively related to the interest rate and financial wealth. Finally, the demand for foreign bonds is given by

$$SF_p = f(i, E[\dot{S}], Y, W) \qquad ...(10.17)$$

where,

$$\frac{\partial f}{\partial i} < 0,\ \frac{\partial f}{\partial E[\dot{S}]} > 0,\ \frac{\partial f}{\partial Y} < 0, \text{ and } \frac{\partial f}{\partial W} > 0.$$

The demand for foreign bonds is inversely related to the domestic interest rate and domestic income and positively related to the expected change in the exchange rate and financial wealth.

Now take the total differential of wealth indentity with respect to financial wealth W.

$$dW - \frac{\partial m}{\partial w} dW - \frac{\partial b}{\partial w} dW - \frac{\partial f}{\partial w} dW = 0$$

or, $$\frac{\partial m}{\partial w} + \frac{\partial b}{\partial w} + \frac{\partial f}{\partial w} = 1 \qquad ...(10.18)$$

This relation is implied since an increase in wealth can be held as either money, domestic bonds or foreign bonds. The change in the demand for the three assets must sum to one. This relation is known as the balance sheet constraint and is an identity.

Taking the total diferential of the wealth identity with respect to the interest rate and the expected change in the exchange rate, we have

$$\frac{\partial m}{\partial i} + \frac{\partial b}{\partial i} + \frac{\partial f}{\partial i} = 0 \qquad ...(10.19)$$

and $$\frac{\partial m}{\partial E[\dot{S}]} + \frac{\partial b}{\partial E[\dot{S}]} + \frac{\partial f}{\partial E[\dot{S}]} = 0 \qquad ...(10.20)$$

Also, $\frac{\partial m}{\partial i} < 0, \frac{\partial b}{\partial i} > 0, \frac{\partial f}{\partial i} < 0,$ and $\frac{\partial m}{\partial E[\dot{S}]} < 0, \frac{\partial b}{\partial E[\dot{S}]} < 0, \frac{\partial f}{\partial E[\dot{S}]} > 0$

If the interest rate rises, the investor adjusts its portfolio. Given the signs of the partial derivatives, the investor increases domestic bond holdings, decreases money, and foreign bond holdings. The second condition depicts the adjustment in portfolio due to expected change in exchange rate.

Now we will find a relationship between exchange rates and interest rates where the three asset markets are in equilibrium. Taking the total differential of the wealth equation with respect to i, W and S under the assumption that $dE[\dot{S}] = 0$, we have

$$dW = F_p d_S \qquad ...(10.21)$$

$$0 = \frac{\partial m}{\partial i} di + \frac{\partial m}{\partial w} dW \qquad ...(10.22)$$

$$0 = \frac{\partial b}{\partial i} di + \frac{\partial b}{\partial w} dW \qquad ...(10.23)$$

$$F_p dS = \frac{\partial f}{\partial i} di + \frac{\partial f}{\partial w} dW \qquad ...(10.24)$$

Inserting equation (10.21) into equation (10.22) we can find the money market schedule (all combinations of the interest rate and the exchange rate where the money market is in equilibrium).

$$di \frac{\partial m}{\partial i} = -\frac{\partial m}{\partial w} F_p \, dS \qquad ...(10.25)$$

Equation (10.25) implies the slope of the money market schedule as

$$\frac{dS}{di} = -\frac{\partial m / \partial i}{(\partial m / \partial w)F_p} > 0 \qquad ...(10.26)$$

since, $\frac{\partial m}{\partial i} < 0$ and $\frac{\partial m}{\partial w} > 0$.

Inserting equation (10.21) into (10.23), we can find the domestic bond schedule (all combinations of the interest rate and the exchange rate where the market for domestic bonds is in equilibrium) as

$$\frac{db}{di} di = -\frac{\partial b}{\partial w} F_p \, dS \qquad ...(10.27)$$

Equation (10.27) implies

$$\frac{dS}{di} = -\frac{\partial b / \partial i}{(\partial b / \partial w)F_p} < 0 \qquad ...(10.28)$$

since, $\frac{\partial b}{\partial i} > 0$ and $\frac{\partial b}{\partial w} > 0$.

Inserting equation (10.21) into (10.24), we can find the foreign bonds schedule (all combinations of the interest rate and the exchange rate where the market for foreign bonds is in equilibrium) as

$$F_p\, dS = \frac{\partial f}{\partial i}\, di + \frac{\partial f}{\partial w}\, F_p dS \qquad ...(10.29)$$

Equation (10.29) implies

$$\frac{dS}{di} = \frac{\partial f / \partial i}{\left(1 - \frac{\partial f}{\partial w}\right) F_p} < 0 \qquad ...(10.30)$$

Since, $\frac{\partial f}{\partial i} < 0$ and $\frac{\partial f}{\partial w} > 0$.

Now we will plot all the three schedules in the exchange rate-interest rate plane as shown in Fig. (10.10).

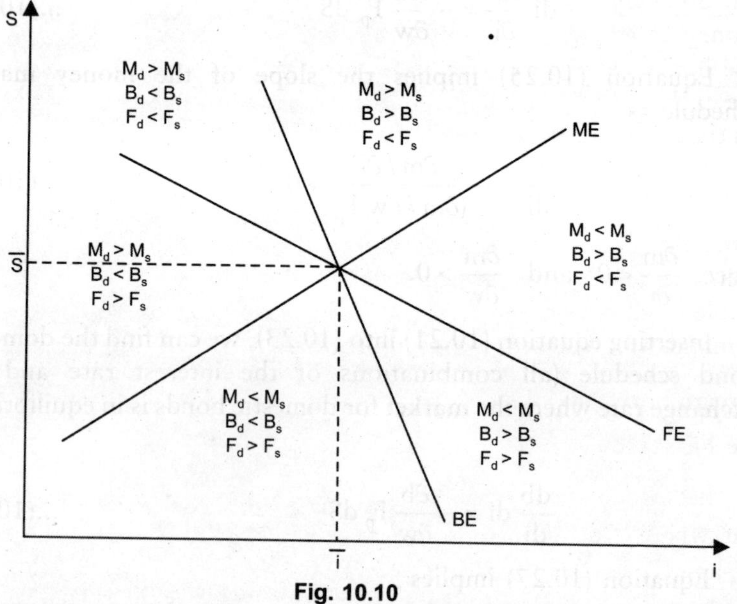

Fig. 10.10

The portfolio balance model is in equilibrium when all the three markets are in equilibrium—where the three schedules intersect.

The ME schedule is upward sloping and describes equilibrium in the domestic money market. The explanation is that a depreciation of the exchange rate (an increase in S) leads to an increase in the domestic investor's wealth (foreign assets are worth more after the depreciation). The increase in wealth leads to an increase in the demand for money. Since the money supply is fixed, the increase in the money demand can only be offset by an increase in the interest rate.

The BE schedule is downward sloping since a depreciation that raises the demand for domestic bonds increases the price of bonds leading to a fall in the interest rate which will reduce the demand for domestic bonds. A depreciation must then be offset by a fall in the interest rate.

Finally, the FE schedule depicting equilibrium on the market for foreign bonds is also downward sloping. The reason for this is that a depreciation of the exchange rate leads to an increased demand for domestic bonds and therefore investors are inclined to sell money and foreign bonds to buy domestic bonds. Alternatively, a rise in the interest rate makes domestic bonds more attractive and the exchange rate must depreciate in order to maintain equilibrium on the market for foreign bonds, i.e., to increase the value of foreign bonds measured in the domestic currency.

In the Fig. 10.10, the BE schedule is steeper than the FE schedule. The reason for this is that if this would not be the case, then the portfolio balance model is unstable. In order to have a stable model, we assume that changes in the interest rate affects the demand for domestic bonds more than it affects the demand for foreign bonds $\left|\frac{\partial f}{\partial i}\right| < \left|\frac{\partial b}{\partial i}\right|$, such that the BE schedule is steeper than the FE schedule.

Let us consider a point where the exchange rate is equal to $\bar{S}$, but where the interest rate is above its equilibrium value. If the exchange rate is fixed and the interest rate is above $\bar{i}$, then the demand for money must be lower than at equilibrium, there is excess supply of money. This implies that all points above the ME schedule, there is excess demand of money and all points below the ME schedule correspond to excess supply.

If the interest rate is above its equilibrium level indicating lower prices on domestic bonds and therefore greater demand for domestic bonds, there is excess demand for bonds above the BE schedule and excess supply of domestic bonds below the BE schedule.

At the same combination of interest rate and exchange rate, the demand for foreign bonds must decrease since a higher interest rate increases the demand for domestic bonds, a fall in the demand for money and the demand for foreign bonds. Therefore, above the FE schedule there is excess supply of foreign bonds. Alternatively, assume that the interest rate is at its equilibrium value $\bar{I}$. If the exchange rate is below its equilibrium value $S < \bar{S}$, (the exchange rate has appreciated), there is excess demand for foreign bonds which will drive up the exchange rate S, i.e., depreciate the currency so that equilibrium on the foreign exchange market is restored.

The money market schedule will shift up to the left if there is excess supply of money, the domestic bond schedule will shift up to the right if there is excess supply of domestic bonds and the foreign bond schedule will shift down to the left if there is excess supply of foreign bonds.

Monetary and Fiscal Policies

In this section, we will consider the short-run effects of monetary and fiscal policies on domestic interest rate and the exchange rate. Let consider the monetary policy first.

We will study three different operations on the foreign exchange market and the domestic money market—(a) open market operation, (b) non-sterilized foreign exchange operation, and (c) sterilized foreign exchange market intervention.

Suppose the monetary authority increases the private sectors holdings of money, i.e., they increase the money supply. To create more money in the economy, the monetary authority purchases domestic bonds from the public and sell money. This results in the increase in M and decrease in B, whereas W remains unchanged. In other words

$$dM = -dB_p = dB_a \qquad ...(10.31)$$

Now, consider the Fig. 10.11.

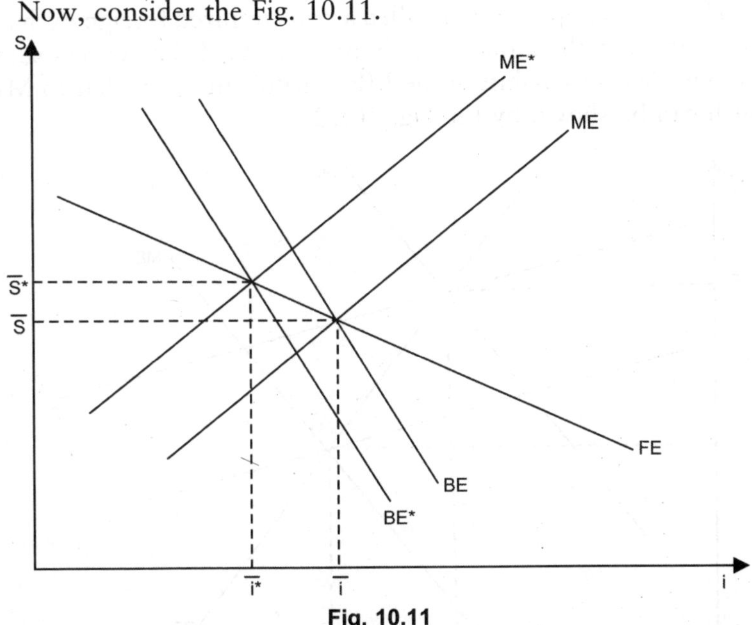

Fig. 10.11

At full equilibrium level, the interest rate is equal to $\overline{I}$ and the exchange rate is $\overline{S}$.

The monetary authority sells money and buys domestic bonds. This will drive up the demand for domestic bonds and therefore lead to an increase in bond prices implying that the interest rate must fall. The BE schedule must therefore shift down to the left to BE*. The excess supply of money in the portfolios that the public hold will increase the demand for both domestic and foreign bonds, which results in a fall in the interest rate and a depreciation of the exchange rate.

The ME schedule will shift up to the left to ME*. The FE schedule is unchanged because the open market operation involves only a swap of money for domestic bonds. In short, the open market operation leads to an increase in the demand for domestic bonds and excess supply of money. The total effect from this open market operation is that the interest rate falls from $\overline{i}$ to $\overline{i}'$ and the exchange rate depreciates from $\overline{S}$ to $\overline{S}'$.

Now suppose that the monetary authority buys foreign bonds from the private sector and sells money. In such case

$$dM = -SdF_p = SdF_a \qquad ...(10.32)$$

This market operation is called a non-sterilized foreign exchange operation since the money supply has increased. The excess supply of money leads to a shift in the ME schedule up to the left to ME*, which can be shown by the Fig. 10.12.

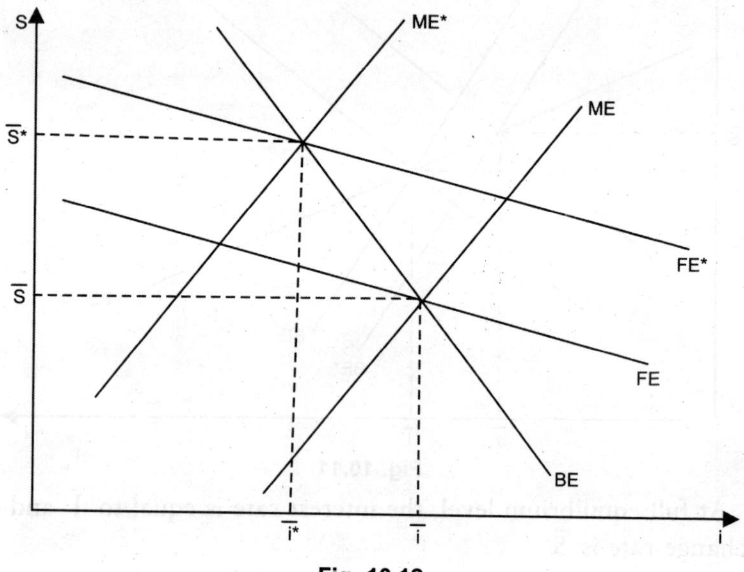

Fig. 10.12

For a given interest rate, the money supply has increased and there is excess supply of money and excess demand for foreign bonds. The FE schedule shifts up to the right such that the exchange rate depreciates and the interest rate falls. The shortage of foreign bonds in the portfolios requires the exchange rate to depreciate which in turn tends to increase the domestic currency value of investor's remaining holdings of foreign bonds. The fall in the interest rate is required to encourage investors to hold money. The BE schedule is unchanged since the monetary authority swaps money for foreign bonds. The main effects compared to the case when the monetary authority buys domestic bonds are the same in the short-run, the interest rate must fall, and the exchange rate must depreciate.

Now we will combine the two markets discussed in the preceding paragraph. Suppose the monetary authority buys foreign bonds from the public in the first stage and then in the second stage they sell domestic bonds to the public such that the money supply is unchanged. This implies that

$$dM = -SdF_p$$

and $$-dM = dB_p \tag{10.33}$$

Hence, $$-SdFp = dB_p$$

Thus, the sterilized foreign exchange operation only affects the currency positions in private portfolios, which change from foreign bonds to domestic bonds.

We have considered full equilibrium model with interest rate $\bar{i}$ and the exchange rate $\bar{S}$ depicted by the Fig. 10.13.

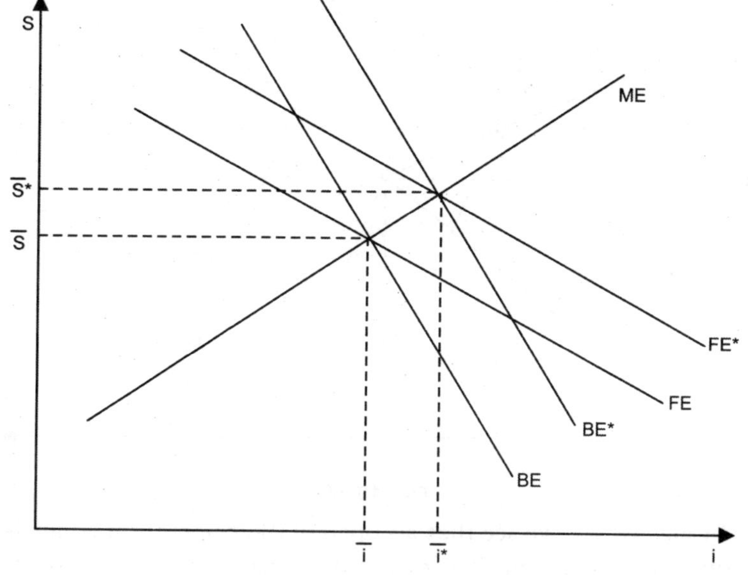

Fig. 10.13

Since the money supply is unchanged, the ME schedule is unaffected. There is excess demand for foreign bonds, which will lead to a shift up to the right from FE to FE*. The excess supply of domestic bonds causes a shift in the BE schedule up to the right to BE*. The net effect is a higher domestic interest rate and a depreciated currency. The currency depreciates because there is excess demand for foreign bonds requiring exchange rate depreciation to restore equilibrium. The excess supply of domestic bonds leads to a fall in bond prices and thus a rise in the interest rate. If the two assets are perfect substitutes, a swap of domestic for foreign bonds is an exchange of identical assets that cannot have any effect whatsoever on interest rates and exchange rates.

The open market operation and the non-sterilized foreign exchange operation lead to similar effects, a lower interest rate, and a depreciated currency. From a practical point of view it would be interesting to contrast these effects, i.e., to answer the question whether the implied effects are identical in size. We contrast the effects of the three different market operations in Fig. 10.14.

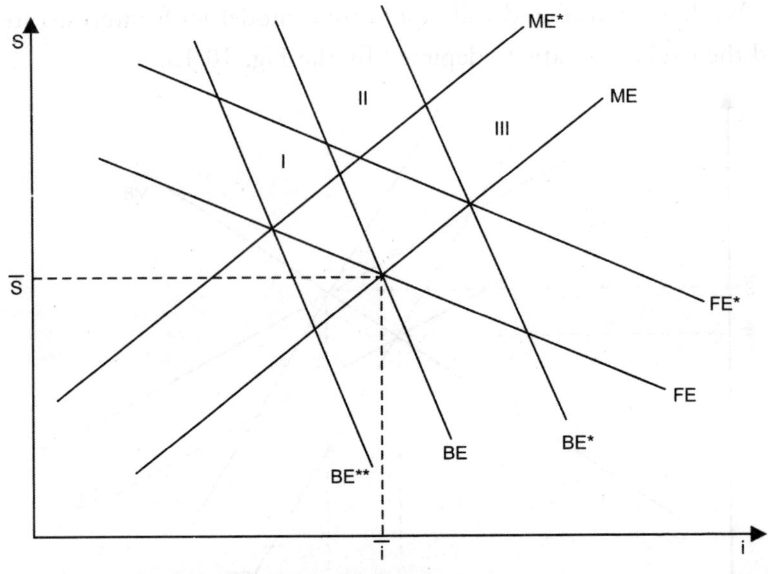

Fig. 10.14

In Fig. 10.14, we see that an open market operation (I) leads to a strong effect on the interest rate and a weak effect on the exchange rate whereas we obtain opposite predictions for a non-sterilized foreign exchange operation (II). The reason for this difference is that an open market operation creates a greater shortage of domestic bonds by creating a greater excess demand for domestic bonds, which can only be offset by a large fall in the interest rate. The stronger effect on the exchange rate from a non-sterilized foreign exchange operation stems from the fact that this operation creates a greater excess demand for foreign bonds, which can only be satisfied by a stronger depreciation of the exchange rate. A sterilized foreign exchange operation (III) also leads to a depreciated currency but the interest rate rises. The reason for this is that this operation creates an excess supply of domestic bonds leading to lower bond prices and therefore a higher interest rate.

Now assume that for some reason, foreign bonds become more risky compared to domestic bonds. Because of this change in risk, there will be a decreased demand for foreign bonds and an increased demand for domestic bonds. This implies that both the BE and the FE schedules shift, the ME schedule is unaffected since the supply of money is unchanged. This has been shown in Fig. 10.15.

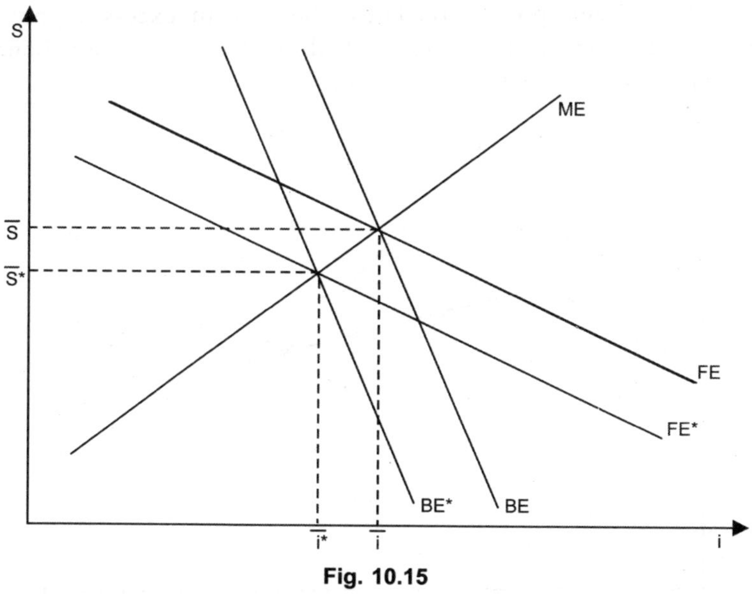

Fig. 10.15

The fall in the demand for foreign bonds induces a shift of the FE schedule down to the left and the increased demand for domestic bonds also leads to a shift down to left of the BE schedule. In the new equilibrium, the interest rate is lower and the exchange rate has appreciated. The decreased demand for foreign bonds induces an appreciation of the exchange rate whereas the increased demand for domestic bonds leads to higher bond prices and therefore lower interest rate.

Now we will consider the changes in various asset supplies on the equilibrium interest rate and exchange rate by considering the effects of fiscal policies.

Government can finance an increase in government expenditures by two ways—(a) borrowing from central bank; in this case both M and W increase by the amount of the deficit or the change in government expenditures; and (b) alternatively, borrowing from the public by selling bonds; in this case B and W increase by the amount of the deficit.

Borrowing from the central bank is called money financing, meaning that the central bank prints money. This implies that M and W increase by the amount of the government deficit. The rise in wealth increases the demand for both B and F as wealth holders try to rebalance their portfolios. Thus, there is an excess supply of money and excess demand for both domestic and foreign bonds. This can be shown by the Fig. 10.16.

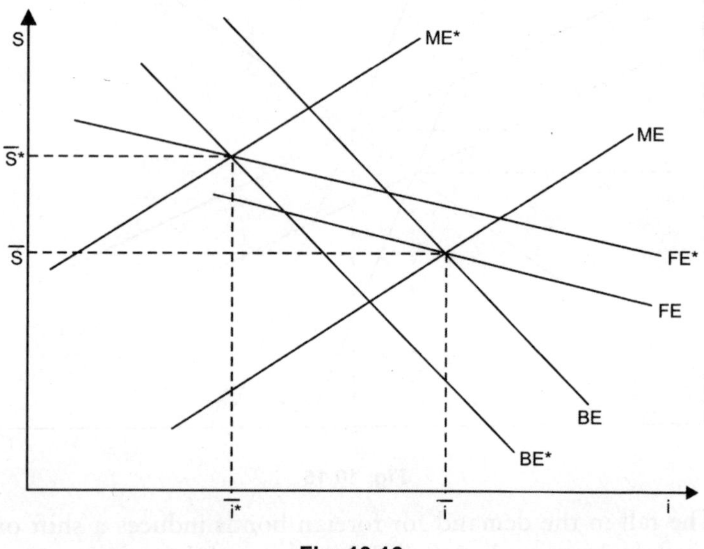

Fig. 10.16

In Fig. 10.16, we see that there is a upward shift in ME curve since there is an excess supply of money. Due to increase in wealth, there is excess demand for both domestic and foreign bonds. At the initial exchange rate there is excess demand for domestic bonds which drives up the price of bonds and thereby lower the interest rate. The BE curve, therefore, shifts down to the left to BE*. At the same time, there is excess demand for foreign bonds implying that a higher exchange rate is needed to eliminate the excess demand. The FE schedule shifts up to the right to FE*. There is a new full equilibrium, where the exchange rate is higher, and a lower interest rate. A budget deficit financed by printing money lowers the interest rate and leads to a depreciated currency.

The alternative for the government to finance a budget deficit is to borrow from the public. The government sells bonds to the private sector implying that both B and W increase by the same amount as the government deficit. The increase in total wealth raises the demand for foreign bonds. Therefore, a bond financed government deficit leads to excess supply of domestic bonds, excess demand for money, and excess demand for foreign bonds. Let us consider Fig. 10.17.

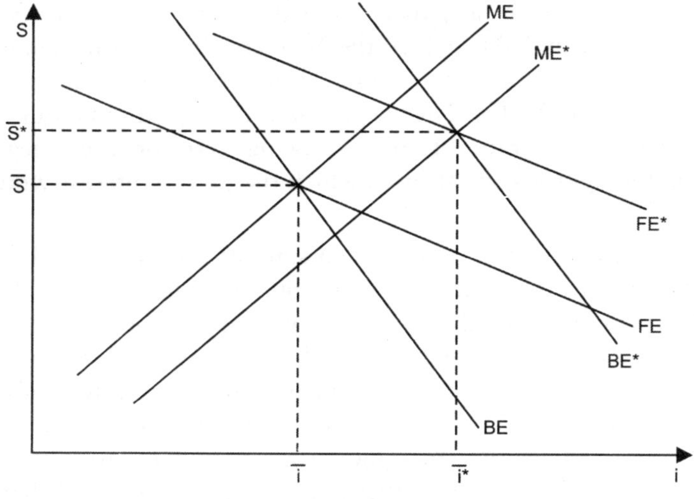

Fig. 10.17

Due to the excess demand for foreign bonds, the FE curve will shift up to the right to FE*. The increase in the supply of domestic bonds creating an excess supply of domestic bonds leads to lower bond prices and therefore a higher interest rate. The BE curve therefore shifts up to the right to BE*. Finally, there is excess demand for money leading to a shift in the ME curve down to the right to ME*. The total effect is a depreciated currency and a high interest rate.

Suppose there is a large shift in ME and BE curves, i.e., the effects from interest rate on money demand and the demand for domestic bonds are large. There is a large downward shift in the ME curve to ME* and a large shift up to the right in the BE curve.

There is a new long-run equilibrium where the exchange rate appreciates and where there is a large increase in the interest rate. Thus, the effect on the exchange rate is ambiguous. If domestic and foreign bonds are close substitutes, then any rise in the interest rate will produce a substitution from foreign bonds to domestic bonds. In this case, the substitution effect will dominate over the wealth effect and the price of foreign exchange will decline, i.e., the currency will appreciate. If the wealth effect dominates over the substitution effect, the currency will depreciate.

NEGATIVE RATE OF INTEREST

The early theorists upheld the possibility of a negative rate of interest. Foxwell in a paper entitled '*Some Social Aspects of Banking*' read in 1886 before the Bankers' Institution imagined a situation in which the rate of interest may become negative. Irving Fisher, in his book '*The Theory of Interest*', argued in favour of the possibility of the rate of interest being zero or even negative. Marshall imagines a situation in which the rate of interest would be negative.[18]

> We can therefore imagine a state of things in which stored up wealth could be put to but little use in which many persons wanted to make provision for their future while but few of those who wanted to borrow goods were able to offer good security for returning them or equivalent goods at a future date. In such a state of things the postponement of, and waiting for enjoyments would be an action that incurred a penalty rather than reaped a reward: by handing over his means to another to be taken care of a person could only expect to get a sure promise of something less and not of something more than that which he lent: the rate of interest would be negative.

Mill also conceived the possibility of an extremely low rate of interest owing to capital accumulation resulting from economic development.

In the real world, however, there is no possibility of the rate of interest becoming negative. So long as the demand for capital exceeds its supply, rate of the interest will always be positive. Some people hold the opinion that incomes in advanced countries are rising so fast that a stage may be reached when people's capacity to save increases so much that the supply of capital exceeds the demand for it. But in the real world, it is highly improbable that this stage will ever be reached. Actual experience shows that with the rise in income the demand for capital has not lagged behind its supply. The demand for capital has been rising quite fast as a result of factors like fast increase in population—at least in developing countries—increase in wants and change in tastes, innovations, development programmes of developing countries etc. On the supply side also, a positive rate of interest is necessary to induce people to forego their present consumption and save in order to provide funds to meet the demand for capital.

Keynes ruled out the possibility of reducing the rate of interest to zero even by a vast supply of money by the monetary authority. He held the view that there is a low positive rate of interest at which the liquidity preference curve becomes infinitely elastic, or in other words, becomes parallel to the horizontal axes. At a low positive rate of interest, there is what Keynes calls a 'liquidity trap'; or in other words, the demand of people for money is insatiable at this rate of interest. Even if the monetary authority goes on putting huge quantities of money in circulation, the rate of interest will not decline below a certain positive rate because at this rate people simply go on absorbing the additional money in their money balances. The monetary experience during the great depression corroborates the view held by Keynes.

Moreover, so long as capital remains productive, the rate of interest would remain positive and with economic progress the productivity of capital will increase rather than decrease. According to Prof. J.K. Metha the very phrase "negative rate of interest is an example of a curious contradiction in terms. Interest is the earning of capital. Capital, being a factor of production, is necessarily productive. Interest is, therefore, invariably positive."[19]

It may, however, be pointed out that although the money rate of interest cannot become zero or negative, the real rate of interest can and has in fact been negative during periods of rapidly rising prices.

For illustration, in 2002, the Federal Funds Rate was lower than the rate of inflation, resulting in a real interest rate that was, technically, negative. An example of a negative interest rate in the literal sense is a private placement with institutional investors of debt-plus-warrants, a security called "Squarz" of Berkshire Hathaway Corporation, controlled by Warren Buffett. Goldman Sachs, which designed the structure in mid-2002, called it the "first ever negative-coupon security." Taking advantage of low market interest rates and high stock market volatility, Berkshire would pay about 3 percent a year on the bonds being issued. But the investor would also receive a warrant allowing the purchase of Berkshire stock and to keep the warrant alive, investors would have to pay a higher rate, perhaps 3.75 percent, at the same time Berkshire made the interest payments. The net effect was a negative interest rate.

CO-EXISTENCE OF INFLATION AND HIGH INTEREST RATES

Inflation is a situation characterised by an excessive quantity of money in circulation. A high rate of interest existing side by side with an excessive quantity of money in circulation appears to be a state of inconsistency. Apparently, this appears to contradict the law of supply which states that, other things remaining unchanged, an increase in the supply of a commodity leads to a decline in its price. In fact, inflation and high interest rates can exist side by side without involving any contradiction and this would be obvious if the assumption of "other things remaining unchanged" is removed.

The rate of interest is determined not only by the supply of money but by both the demand for and supply of money. If increase in the demand for money is greater than that in the supply of money, the rate of interest would rise in spite of an increase in the quantity of money in circulation. During inflation rising prices increase the marginal efficiency of capital and thus stimulate investment. Keeping in view rising profits, the entrepreneurs do not mind borrowing at higher rates of i nterest.

During inflationary periods, the demand for money for speculative motive also rises very fast. Rising prices eliminate the risks of speculation and as such the entrepreneurs do not mind borrowing even at higher rates of interest to take advantage of the highly favourable conditions.

LOW INTEREST RATES IN UNDERDEVELOPED COUNTRIES

The underdeveloped countries are characterised by a shortage of capital. The existence of low interest rates in such countries appears to be quite paradoxical. The basic reason for low interest rates in underdeveloped countries is that, although the supply of capital is scarce, the demand for capital is not much. The shortage of demand for capital is explained by a low marginal efficiency of capital in these countries. The marginal efficiency of capital is low because of the small size of the market and lack of external economies like means of transportation and communication, power, supply of water, banking facilities, trained labour etc. Another reason for shortage of demand for capital is the availability of cheap labour in these countries. It is more profitable to make greater use of cheap labour than of scarce capital.

NOTES

1. Abba P. Lerner, "Interest Theory—Supply and Demand for Loans or Supply and Demand for Cash," in Seymour E. Harris (ed.), *The New Economics* (London, 1960), p. 656.
2. J. Tobin, "Liquidity Preference and Monetary Policy", *Review of Economics and Statistics*, 1947, pp. 124-31.
3. J. Tobin, "Liquidity Preferernce as *Behavior towards Risk*", *Review of Economic Studies*, 1958, pp. 65-86.
4. Alvin H. Hansen, *A Guide to Keynes* (New York, 1953), p. 141.
5. Henry Hazlitt, *The Failure of the "New Economics"* (New York, 1959), p. 193.
6. Jacob Viner, *Quarterly Journal of Economics*, (1936-37), p. 157.
7. Don Patinkin, *Money, Interest and Prices* (Tokyo, 1966), p. 372.
8. *Ibid.*, pp. 373-74.
9. *Ibid.*, p. 375.
10. Kenneth K. Kurihara, *Introduction to Keynesian Dynamics* (London, 1956), p. 72.
11. Lawrence R. Klein, *The Keynesian Revolution* (London, 1952), p. 123.
12. *Ibid.*
13. T. de Scitovszky, "A Study of Interest and Capital" *Economica New Series*, Vol. VII, 1940, p. 293.
14. D. Hamberg, *Business Cycles*, pp. 182-83.
15. Italics in original.

16. Alvin H. Hansen, *A Guide to Keynes* (New York, 1953), p. 143.
17. Interest rates are here defined in a broad general sense to include rates of return, yields, and other percentage measures of benefits received. In this sense, all assets have interest rates.
18. Alfred Marshall, *Principles*, Reprint 8th Edn., pp. 192-93.
19. J.K. Mehta, *Studies in Advanced Economic Theory*, p. 24.

IS-LM Analysis of Demand

11

In simple Keynesian model, equilibrium income is determined by the equality of planned saving and planned investment, because the interest rate is assumed to be constant, thus determining a single value for planned investm

ent. If we allow the interest rate to vary, we find that investment is an inverse function of the interest rate. Since investment is a component of aggregate spending, a higher interest rate reduces aggregate spending. Therefore, a variable interest rate means the loss of a unique equilibrium in the product market. We need a model with two equations in order to simultaneously determine a unique equilibrium income and interest rate. Such a model was developed by John Hicks as an extension of Keynes's work. It was the IS-LM model, which came out of the Econometric Conference held in Oxford during September 1936.

John Hicks constructed the IS-LM model (originally LL, not LM) as an interpretation of the General Theory of Keynes. He later presented it in "Mr. Keynes and the Classics: A Suggested Interpretation." He found some similarities between his model and the General Theory. Keynes based his theory on a period, which includes a past in which nothing could be done to alter the future. The future period is unknown, thus based on expectations. The core of the General Theory is based on Keynes effective demand theory, which also forms an essential part of the IS-LM model. Effective demand manifests itself in the spending of income. For income to increase, employment must increase, thus consumption increases, but at a lesser rate than income. Consumption and investment is equal, which means that employment cannot increase without investment. The downward sloping IS cure clearly indicates that an increase in investment leads to an increase in employment.

To explain how short-run fluctuations in aggregate demand affect output in an economy in which both real and monetary factors are taken into account, we use IS-LM model, where the IS and LM nomenclature is used to describe respectively, the real and monetary components of the model. The real part of the economy deals with the demand and supply decisions of households, firms and the government. Households, for instance, supply labour services and demand goods and services. They also save for future consumption. In each case the household is concerned with real variables or, in other words, with quantities. This is most obviously the case with the supply of labour and the demand for goods and services—the number of hours worked, a supermarket trolley of groceries, an appointment with the dentist all involve real quantities. So too is the decision to save, since it is a decision to defer real consumption to a later date. Borrowing and lending are the outcome of decisions about real goods and services which are either consumed, in the case of household saving, or provided, in the case of investment, at various points of time. Saving involves the deferral of consumption. Investment in real capital results in flow of goods and services in the future. The letters I and S stand for investment and saving, reflecting the origins of the IS curve in the real sector of the economy. On the other hand, the monetary sector deals with the demand for, and supply of, money. It involves with nominal variables, since the price level is defined in terms of money. Since the letters, L and M stand for the demand for and the supply of money, the LM curve is a representation of monetary equilibrium.

Despite similarities, there are two fundamental differences between the General Theory and the IS-LM model. The IS-LM model is a perfect competition model in which all the prices is flexible. Keynes however made use of price rigidity in his model. Keynes assumptions of money wage and price rigidity led to the Neo-classical Synthesis. Another feature of the General Theory concerns the length of the period. Keynes used a short-term period, assumed to be a year, while Hicks used an ultra short period called a week. Victoria Chick used a quarter as a suitable period in her analysis of the IS-LM model. She pointed out that investment component is fixed at the beginning of the quarter through interest rate as determined by the liquidity preference and long-term expectations.

The IS-LM model is constructed from an Investment Savings schedule and the demand for money (L) and supply of money (M) schedules. Hicks made use of two parameters to derive his schedule called the IS schedule. He determined the price of the one parameter in terms of another. For instance, the price of A in terms of C and B in terms of C. If A and B are equilibrates, the third (A and B) equilibrates. Keynes also used two parameters. He used income (Y) in terms of wage units and the rate of interest (r). He made investment to be dependent on the interest rate and savings to be dependent on income. For each rate of interest, there is a corresponding level of income at which savings equals investment. Therefore, there is no excess demand in the goods market. Hicks expressed this relation between income and interest rates as the IS curve.

According to the General Theory, the level of income also depends on the desire to consume. If consumption rises with income, but the marginal propensity to consume is less than unity, the saving must rise with income. Another feature of Keynes theory is that of savings been equal to investment. An increase in income results in increase savings, which results in a decrease in the interest rate. Saving and investment are equal and the locus of these equilibrium points represents the downward sloping IS curve.

Liquidity preference theory or demand for money is another characteristic of the General theory. The money market equilibrium requires the demand for money and the supply of money to be equal. It therefore also depends on the relationship between interest rates and the level of income. The demand for money can be analysed on the motives for people to hold money. Keynes identified three motives namely the transaction, precautionary and speculative motive. The transaction motive depends positively on the level of income. An increase in the level of income thus will increase the demand for active balances (transaction and precautionary motive). The demand for idle balances (speculative motive) depends upon the function of interest rates based on expectations of future interest rate.

The locus of combinations between income and interest rates is the LM curve, which equilibrates the money market. The point where the IS curve and the LM curve intersects is the point where the interest rate and the level of income is consistent with the equilibrium. The slope of the IS-LM curves is essential in the sense that monetary and fiscal policy is dependent on it. In some cases these policies looses its potency in the sense that no matter how much money supply is increased, the interest rate refuses to fall. This extreme case is called the liquidity trap of which Keynes only accepts as a possibility. This case is also based on the expectations in the fall in interest rates to a level where any increase in the money stock will lead to idle balances, which will make the liquidity preferences absolute. While the Neo-classical Synthesis differ from the IS-LM model in the sense that consumption is not determined by income alone, but also through wealth effects as introduced by Pigou. Like the IS-LM curve, a fall in price will shift both the LM and IS curve rightwards as it is presented in the wealth effects of Pigou. The increase in the real value of money leads to an increase in wealth, thus increasing consumption that is equal to investment. Monetary policy, together with price and wage flexibility can restore the economy to full employment, but the adjustment process might be to slow, and can be speeded through fiscal policy. The acceptance of this view forms the basis of the Neo-classical Synthesis.

An essential part of the General Theory is the effective demand theory, in terms of which aggregate supply is equal to aggregate demand. According to Say's law, "supply creates its own demand." In terms of a monetary economy, it will mean that the value of things sold is equal to the value of things bought. The introduction of money as a medium of exchange, however, does not necessarily agree with this notion, because income won't be necessarily entirely been spent on purchases, and even if so, it will only cover recovery costs and not large profits. This notion strengthens the IS-LM model in the sense that the part of the money not been spent will either be invested or saved.

The effective demand theory can be divided into an endogenous and exogenous component. The endogenous component reflects production and the exogenous component the capital expenditure such as investments. It is necessary for the exogenous component to be introduced into the theory, because its aggregate demand can be a function of aggregate supply, thus not necessarily equal. The difference between the level of output and the endogenous demand (propensity to consume) forms the exogenous components.

An increase in the exogenous demand will lead to an increase in production, thus causing an increase in endogenous demand. An increase in labour and capital will not automatically cause production to increase, unless exogenous demand increases. In a capitalist economy, the increase in output will induce growth in actual output, if exogenous demand increases at the same time. Therefore, it can be argued that full employment requires deliberate demand management. The intersection of the IS-LM curve occurs below full employment. Through monetary and fiscal policy (deliberate demand management), the IS-LM curve can be adjusted to increase at full employment.

When we look at the appropriateness of the IS-LM model, it can be said that the savings supply the loanable funds, which in turn is available for investments or capital incurred. Thus, it can be said that savings equal investment as Keynes conceived. Furthermore, the supply and demand for savings is brought to equality through changes in income and employment, not the interest rate (price of savings). This support Keynes views that income and savings are interrelated. However, he neglects the effect of interest rates on savings; instead, he introduced the liquidity preference theory to show the effects of the interest rate.

The critics of Keynesian economics used the notion that interest rates does not generate capital expenditure to equal full employment savings in order to vindicate their view that involuntary employment does not exist. This is also the argument for the liquidity trap, which led to the Neo-classical Synthesis. Keynes believed that real wages have an adverse effect on employment. This is only plausible when assumed that the lower the real wages, the higher the employments, thus real wages are in excess of marginal disutility of labour. Friedman later associated an increase in employment as inflationary and temporary of nature. Weitzman argued that in an effort to increase output, the equilibrium trade off between real wages and employment will tend to make wage adjustment mechanisms ineffective. Price flexibility therefore cannot make the necessary adjustment to maintain full employment. The IS-LM curve will therefore intersect below full employment level, as perceived by Keynes.

The fact that the IS-LM curve intersects below the level of output associated with full employment leads us to believe that Keynes proposes disequilibrium economics. His rejection of the second postulate of the classical theory, which in effect emulates market clearing, caused Davidson to believe he reputes the axiom of gross substitution. According to the axiom substitution effects discards or counters negative income consequences. The rejection of gross substitution leads to some excess-demand function to path from downward sloping, which contradicts the IS-LM model. Keynes argued that the elasticity of substitution as a property of money is zero, thus questioning the relevance of money within a monetary economy and in essence rejecting the general equilibrium. Hahn makes it clear that it is impossible to use labour to produce money. The IS-LM model thus will be in equilibrium below the level of full employment, strengthening Keynes view of disequilibrium economics.

Keynes also adopted a close economy, thus ignoring the effects of the international market on the level of employment. This means no mobility of labour, and viewed foreign trade to be irrelevant to the problem of unemployment. However, the introduction of foreign investment could be used to adjust shortages of domestic investment where an economy suffers from insufficient investment resulting in an increase in production to the level of full employment. However, an increase in interest rates in an effort to attract foreign investment can lead to domestic investments to be less attractive. The export component is regarded to be exogenous with regard to demand. Exports and not export surplus is an important factor that could determine the level of employment depending on the kind of economy and the region from which it emanates. The IS-LM model was constructed from the components of a close economy; thus, it can be said that exports and imports were neglected in the early stages.

THE IS CURVE: PRODUCT MARKET EQUILIBRIUM

Derivation of the IS Curve

The IS curve shows all the combinations of the interest rate r and income Y that satisfy the income identity, the consumption function, the investment function, and the net export function. In other words, it is the set of points for which spending balance occurs, i.e., the product market is in equilibrium.

The condition for equilibrium in the product market is given as

$$Y = C + I + G \qquad ...(11.1)$$

An equivalent statement of this equilibrium condition can be written as

$$I + G = S + T \qquad ...(11.2)$$

where,

Y = income,

C = consumption,

I = investment,

G = government spending,

S = saving, and

T = taxes.

Now, let us consider a simple case where we neglect the government sector, i.e., G and T are zero. This implies that

$$I(r) = S(Y) \qquad ...(11.3)$$

Equation (11.3) shows the dependence of investment on the interest rate and of saving on the level of income. Thus, IS curve is constructed to find combinations of the interest rate and level of income that equate investment with saving.

We will use the Keynesian cross to derive the IS curve and to derive the Keynesian cross we consider the determinants of planned expenditure, which is the amount households, firms, and the government plan to spend on goods and services.

Let us consider a closed economy, so that net exports are zero. In such an economy, planned expenditure is given by

$$E = C + I + G \qquad ...(11.4)$$

and consumption function is given by

$$C = C\,(Y - T) \qquad ...(11.5)$$

Equation (11.5) states that consumption depends on disposable income (Y – T), where T is the tax. Here, we also assume that planned investment, government expenditure and taxes are fixed, i.e.,

$$I = \bar{I}, \;\; G = \bar{G}, \;\text{ and }\; T = \bar{T}$$

Using above conditions, equation (11.4) can be written as

$$E = C(Y - \bar{T}) + \bar{I} + \bar{G} \qquad ...(11.6)$$

The economy is in equilibrium when actual expenditure equals planned expenditure, i.e.,

Actual expenditure (Y) = Planned expenditure (E)

The 45-degree line in Fig. (11.1) shows the points, where the above condition holds.

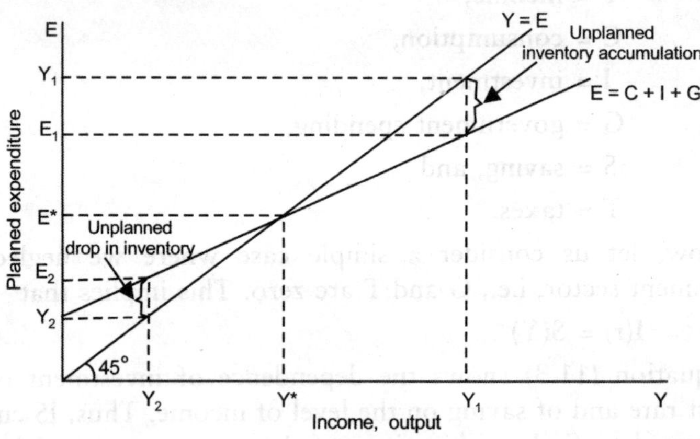

Fig. 11.1

The equilibrium of the economy is at point (Y*, E*), where the planned expenditure function crosses the 45-degree line. The economy gets to the equilibrium position through the adjustment process, where inventories play an important role. Unplanned changes in inventories induce firms to change production levels, which in turn changes income and expenditure.

If firms are producing at level Y_1, then planned expenditure E_1 falls short of production, so that firms accumulate inventories. This inventory accumulation induces firms to reduce production. Similarly, if firms are producing at level Y_2, then planned expenditure E_2 exceeds production, so that firms run down their inventories. This fall in inventories induces firms to raise production.

Thus, the Keynesian cross shows how income Y is determined for given levels of planned investment I and fiscal policy G and T. This model can be used to show how income changes when one of these exogenous variables changes.

We can use the investment function and the Keynesian cross diagram to determine how income changes when the interest rate changes. Because investment is inversely related to the interest rate, an increase in the interest rate from r_1 to r_2 reduces the quantity of investment from I_1 to I_2. The reduction in planned investment, in turn, shifts the expenditure function downward. The shift in the expenditure function leads to a lower level of income. Hence, an increase in the interest rate lowers income. The IS curve summarizes the relationship between the interest rate and the level of income that results from the investment function and the Keynesian cross.

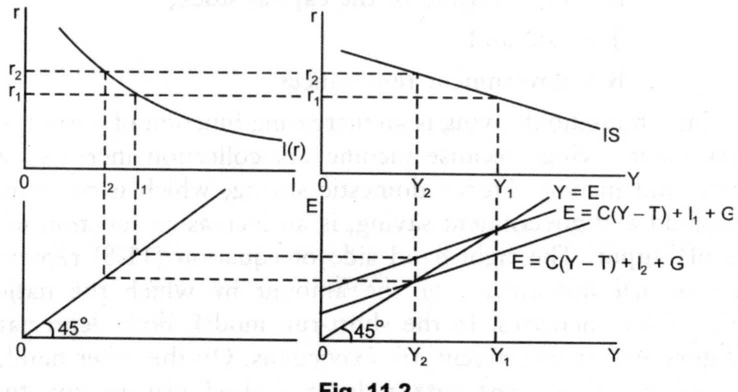

Fig. 11.2

At interest rates r_1 and r_2, investment levels will be I_1 and I_2. To generate equilibrium in the product market, levels of income must be at Y_1 and Y_2 respectively. Therefore, interest rate income combinations (r_1, Y_1) and (r_2, Y_2) are equilibrium points along the IS schedule which slopes downward to the right.

Let us consider the second method of derivation of the IS curve. The market for goods and service is in equilibrium when the desired supply of goods and services is equal to the demand, more explicitly,

$$Y^s = Y^d = C^d + I^d + GC^d + GI^d \qquad ...(11.7)$$

where,

Y^S = supply of goods and services,

Y^d = demand of goods and services,

C^d = household consumption,

I^d = household and firms investment,

GC^d = government consumption expenditures, and

GI^d = government investment expenditure.

Since, the IS curve reflects goods market equilibrium, it is not necessary to carry forward the demand and supply superscripts. Thus, we have

$$(Y + R - D - T - C) + (T - GC - R) = (I + GI - D) \quad ...(11.8)$$

$\Rightarrow$ Private saving + government saving = net investment

where,

D = depreciation of the capital stock,

T = tax, and

R = government remittances

Since, household saving is an increasing function of output, so is government saving, because income tax collection increases with output and income. Hence domestic saving, which is the sum of household and government saving, is an increasing function of the rate of output. The right-hand side of equation (11.8) represents domestic net investment, or the amount by which the nation's capital stock increases. In the short-run model, both depreciation and government investment are exogenous. On the other hand, an increase in the interest rate reduces desired private investment expenditures. Hence, domestic net investment is a decreasing function of the interest rate. The left-hand panel of Fig. 11.3 depicts the domestic saving and investment functions together. Domestic net investment is shown as the downward-sloping line. Domestic saving is a vertical line because it is invariant to the interest rate. Increase in output and income shift the savings function to the right, while decreases shift it to the left.

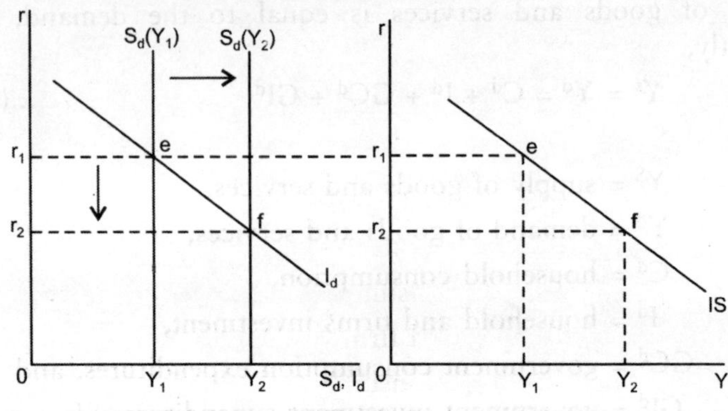

Fig. 11.3

The left-hand panel is used to derive the IS curve. Point e, at (r_1, Y_1) represents a position where planned saving and investment are equal. Hence, e must be a point on the IS curve in the right-hand panel of the Fig. 11.3. An increase from Y_1 to Y_2 shifts the saving function to the right, requiring a fall in the interest rate to r_2 to restore a balance between planned saving and investment. Point f represents a new equilibrium in both panels of the diagram. Continuing in this way, we can trace out the IS curve.

A completely general approach, which does not rely on explicit functions for consumption and investment, is to start from the general functional expression underlying equation (11.8),

$$S_d (Y; \alpha_C, GC) = I_d (r; \alpha_I, GI) \qquad ...(11.9)$$

The left-hand side of the equation (11.9) says that domestic saving is a function of a number of variables. Y, which appears before the semicolon, is an endogenous variable, while the variables and parameters following the semicolon are exogenous determinants of saving. For instance, an increase in initial wealth reduces the flow of household saving because it increases the shift parameter α, and reduces planned household saving. Hence domestic saving falls. An increase in government consumption also reduces domestic saving. The endogenous variables are those whose equilibrium values are obtained as part of the overall solution to the model, while the exogenous variables and parameters are those, which are taken as given. Thus, α_C is an exogenous shift parameter. All its determinants are exogenous to the model, and changes in the value of α_C shift the savings function. Moreover, the right-hand side of equation (11.9) has a similar interpretation. The endogenous determinant of domestic investment is r; the exogenous variables is government investment and the shift parameter is α_I. Taking the differential of equation (11.9) we have

$$\frac{\partial S_d}{\partial Y} dY + \frac{\partial S_d}{\partial \alpha_C} d\alpha_C + \frac{\partial S_d}{\partial GC} dGC = \frac{\partial I_d}{\partial r} dr + \frac{\partial I_d}{\partial \alpha_I} d\alpha_I + \frac{\partial I_d}{\partial GI} dGI \qquad ...(11.10)$$

The slope of the IS curve is obtained by setting the changes in the exogenous variables and shift parameters to zero, and solving for $\frac{dr}{dY}$.

$$d\alpha_C = dGC = dGI = d\alpha_I = 0 \qquad ...(11.11)$$

$$\frac{\partial S_d}{\partial Y} dY = \frac{\partial I_d}{\partial r} dr$$

$$\frac{dr}{dY} = \frac{\partial S_d / \partial Y}{\partial I_d / \partial r} \qquad ...(11.12)$$

The vertical shifts in the IS curve are obtained by setting dY to zero and allowing one of the exogenous variables or shift parameters to changes. For example, suppose there is a change in initial wealth, resulting in a change in α_C. Then the vertical shift in the IS curve is given by

$$\frac{\partial S_d}{\partial \alpha_C} d\alpha_C = \frac{\partial I_d}{\partial r} dr$$

$$\Rightarrow \frac{dr}{d\alpha_C} = \frac{\partial S_d / \partial \alpha_C}{\partial I_d / \partial r} \qquad ...(11.13)$$

As we know that an increase in α reduces planned household saving so that $\frac{\partial S_d}{\partial \alpha_C} < 0$, which together with $\frac{\partial I_d}{\partial r} < 0$ implies that $\frac{dr}{d\alpha_C} > 0$. Thus, IS curve shifts upwards in r, Y space.

The IS curve can also be derived using the specific linear expressions for the consumption and investment functions. Using the equations for the consumption and investment in the goods-market equilibrium condition, we get

$$Y^S = C^d + I^d + GC^d + GI^d$$

or, $$Y = \{\alpha_C + \beta(1-\tau)Y\} + \{\alpha_I - \mu r\} + GC + GI \qquad ...(11.14)$$

where,

$$C^d = \{\alpha_C + \beta(1-\tau)Y\},$$

$$I^d = \{\alpha_I - \mu r\}$$

Rearranging equation (11.14), we get

$$r = \frac{\alpha_C + \alpha_I + GC + GI}{\mu} - \frac{1-\beta(1-\tau)}{\mu}Y$$

$$= \alpha_{IS} - \frac{1-\beta(1-\tau)}{\mu}Y \qquad \text{...(11.15)}$$

where,

$$\alpha_{IS} = \frac{\alpha_C + \alpha_I + GC + GI}{\mu}$$

Equation (11.15) is the equation of IS curve having vertical intercept of α_{IS}. As in the diagrammatic derivation, equation (11.15) shows that the interest rate for which the goods market is in equilibrium decreases as the rate of output increases.

Differentiating equation (11.15), we have

$$\frac{dr}{dY} = -\frac{1-\beta(1-\tau)}{\mu} \qquad \text{...(11.16)}$$

Comparing equations (11.12) and (11.16) taking the numerator first, we have

$$1-\beta(1-\tau) = \frac{\partial S}{\partial Y} + \frac{\partial GS}{\partial Y} = (1-\tau)(1-\beta) + \tau = \frac{\partial S_d}{\partial Y}$$

Comparison of the denominators gives

$$\frac{\partial I_d}{\partial r} = -\mu$$

Hence, equations (11.12) and (11.16) are exactly equivalent.

Thus, in each case the IS curve is a locus of r, Y pairs for which the goods market is in equilibrium. In order to maintain equilibrium, an increase in planned output Y^s must be associated with a reduction in the interest rate if the equilibrium condition, $Y^s = Y^d$, is to be maintained. Here one point should be noted that IS curve is not a casual relationship. Its graph is not to be read as saying that changes in the interest rate cause changes in the equilibrium level of output, because r is itself an endogenous variables in the model, and the interaction of asset markets and the goods market jointly determine interest rates and output.

Slope of the IS curve: From equation (11.15) we find that the IS curve will be steeper the greater the marginal propensity to save and the smaller the interest sensitivity of investment. If the marginal propensity to save is larger, the saving will shift more with income. This will necessitate a greater increase in investment to maintain equality with saving. Greater investment would be possible only if interest rates fell further. Let us depict this in the Fig. 11.4.

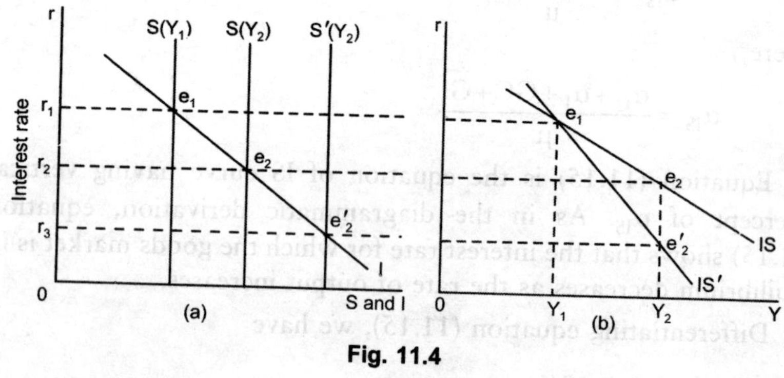

Fig. 11.4

Fig. 11.4 illustrates the effect of the increase in the marginal propensity to save on the slope of the IS curve. For a given increase in income, the amount saved becomes greater as the marginal propensity to save increases. S′ represents a higher marginal propensity to save than S. To bring investment equal to the greater saving, S′, the interest rate must fall to r_1, producing the steeper IS′ curve depicted in panel (b).

Now we will look the effect of the interest sensitivity of investment on the slope of the IS curve. Consider the Fig. 11.5.

In Fig. 11.5, the investment function, I, is more interest-sensitive than I′, i.e., a fall in interest rate stimulates more investment along I than along I′. Saving is assumed to be a function of income, not interest rates. At income level Y_1 and interest rate r_1, we have planned saving equal to planned investment on either investment function. As income rises to Y_2, the amount of planned saving rises. In order to stimulate the additional investment necessary to sustain the higher income, the interest rate must fall. The less interest-sensitive investment is, the more the interest rate has to drop to stimulate the necessary increase in investment. The interest rate must drop to r_3 along the less interest-sensitive investment schedule, I′, but only to r_2 along I in order to induce enough investment to meet saving out of income Y_2. The corresponding interest rates and incomes that produce equality between planned saving and investment for each investment function are graphed in panel (b) of Fig. 11.5. The lower interest rate necessary to bring equilibrium with the less interest-sensitive I′ produces the steeper IS′ curve. Thus, the smaller the interest sensitivity of investment, the steeper the IS curve.

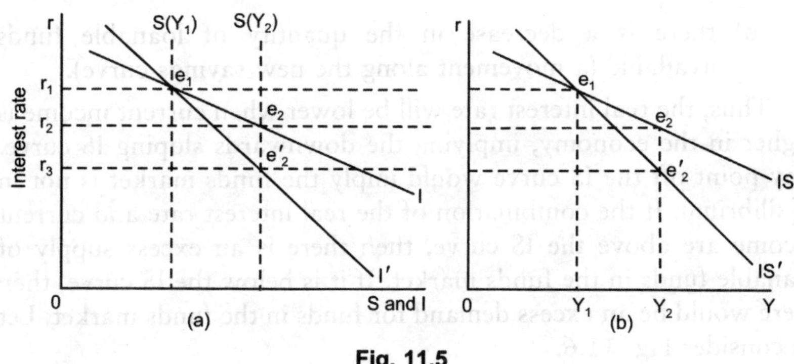

Fig. 11.5

Loanable-Fund Interpretation of the IS Curve

The IS curve is a curve describing combinations of income and real interest rates where the funds market is in equilibrium. Along the IS curve, we will have net national savings equal to investment so that

$$Y - C - G = I$$

or,
$$S = I.$$

National saving represents the supply of loanable funds, and investment represents the demand for these funds.

Substituting the consumption function for C and the investment function for I, we have

$$Y - C(Y - T) - G = I(r) \qquad ...(11.17)$$

The left-hand side of the equation (11.17) states that the supply of loanable funds depends on income and fiscal policy. The right-hand side states that the demand for loanable funds depends on the interest rate. The interest rate adjusts to equilibrate the supply and demand for loans.

When people have more income, there is a larger supply of loanable funds available. An increase in current income would shift the savings curve out, implying that there would initially be an excess supply of loanable funds in the funds market. In order for the loanable funds market to reach a new equilibrium, the interest rate must fall so that

(a) there is an increase in the demand for loanable funds (a movement along the investment curve as it becomes cheaper to borrow) and

(b) there is a decrease in the quantity of loanable funds available (a movement along the new savings curve).

Thus, the real interest rate will be lower when current income is higher in the economy, implying the downwards sloping IS curve. Any point off the IS curve would imply the funds market is not in equilibrium. If the combination of the real interest rate and current income are above the IS curve, then there is an excess supply of loanable funds in the funds market. If it is below the IS curve, then there would be an excess demand for funds in the funds market. Let us consider Fig. 11.6.

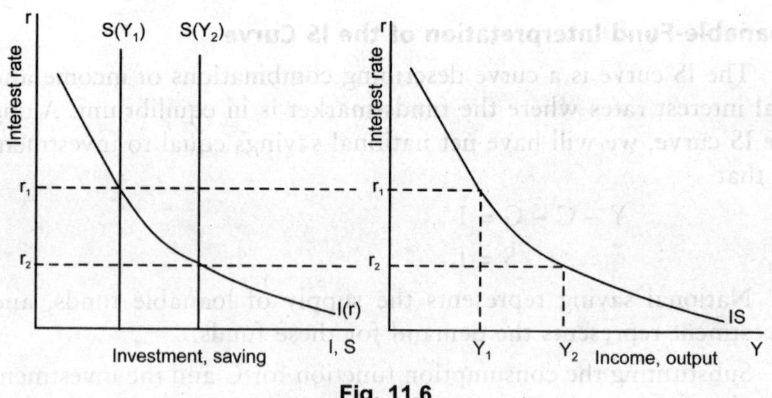

Fig. 11.6

When income rises from Y_1 to Y_2, national saving increases. Consumption rises by less than income, because the marginal propensity to consume is less than one. The increased supply of loanable funds drives down the interest rate from r_1 to r_2. The IS curve summarizes this relationship—higher income implies higher saving, which in turn implies a lower equilibrium interest rate. For this reason, the IS curve slope downward.

If there is an increase in savings, keeping current income fixed, the real interest rate will fall because there is a large supply of loanable funds available. Since current income is assumed to stay the same and the new interest rate is lower, this implies that the new IS curve must lie below the initial curve, the entire IS curve will shift back.

If firms want to undertake more investment, this implies there will be a higher demand for loanable funds in the funds market. Since current income is kept at the same level, this implies that the real interest rate must rise in order for the supply and demand for loanable funds to be equal. Since the new interest rate is higher while current income is assumed to remain constant, this implies that the new IS curve must lie above the initial curve, the entire IS curve will shift out.

The IS curve does not determine either income Y or the interest rate r. Instead, the IS curve is a relationship between Y and r arising in the market for goods and services or, equivalently, the market for loanable funds.

Shifts in IS Curve

Anything, excluding interest rates and income, that affects saving or investment will shift the IS curve. Here we drop the assumption that government expenditures and taxes are zero. With the government sector in the model, the condition for product market equilibrium is given by

$$I(r) + G = S(Y - T) + T \qquad \text{...(11.18)}$$

From the equilibrium condition (11.18), it can be seen that a change in either the level of government spending (G) or the level of taxes (T) will disturb an initial product market equilibrium position—this will be a shift in the IS curve.

Changes in Government Expenditure: When government expenditure increases from an initial level G_0 to a higher level G_1, the shift in the IS curve can be depicted by Fig. 11.7.

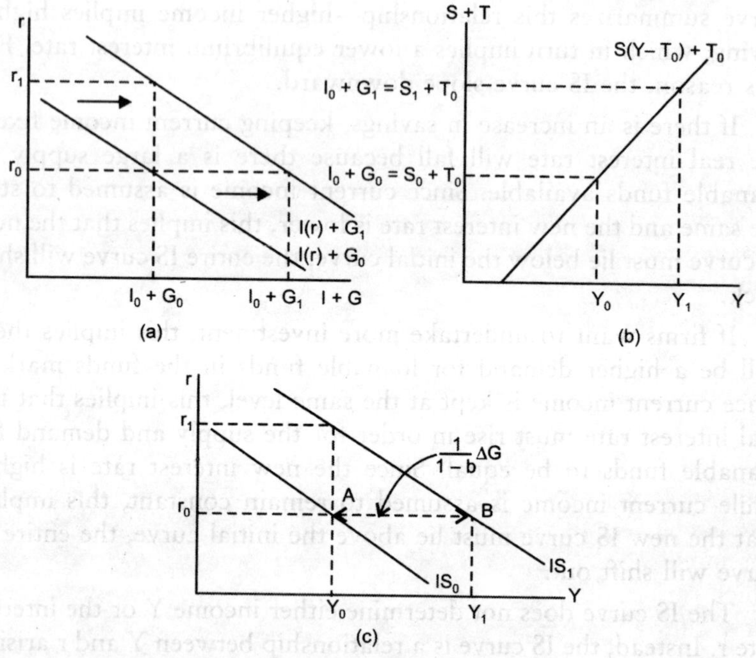

Fig. 11.7

At interest rate r_0, an increase in government spending increases the total of investment plus government spending from $I_0 + G_0$ to $I_0 + G_1$ in Panel (a). To maintain the condition $I + G = S + T$, with a fixed level of taxes, saving must rises from S_0 to S_1, which requires income to be Y_1 instead of Y_0 in Panel (b). At interest rate r_0, the equilibrium point in the product market is point B instead of point A. An increase in government spending shifts the IS schedule to the right from IS_0 to IS_1 in Panel (c).

Now the question is, how much the IS curve shifts to the right, the horizontal distance from A to B in Panel (c). For each one-unit increase in government expenditure with taxes assumed unchanged, to restore equilibrium at a given interest rate in the product market saving must be higher by one unit. So the question of the amount of the horizontal shift in the IS curve is that of the amount of the increase in income required to generate new saving equal to the increase in government spending. The increase in saving per unit increase in income is given by the MPS equal to $(1 - b)$, the required increase in income will be $\Delta G(1/(1-b))$, which is the horizontal shift in the IS curve. Thus, at interest rate r_0,

$$\Delta G = \Delta S = (1-b)\Delta Y$$

$$\Delta Y = \frac{1}{1-b}\Delta G \quad ...(11.19)$$

Equation (11.19) gives the amount of the horizontal shift in the IS schedule. The amount of the horizontal shift in the IS curve per unit increase in G is (1/(1 – b)), the autonomous expenditure multiplier.

Increase Investment: If firms want to undertake more investment, this implies there will be a higher demand for loanable funds in the funds market. Since current income is kept at the same level, this implies that the real interest rate must rise in order for the supply and demand for loanable funds to be equal. Since the new interest rate is higher while current income is assumed to remain constant, this implies that the new IS curve must lie above the initial curve, which results in the shift of the entire IS curve out. This shift in IS curve can be shown as in Fig. 11.8.

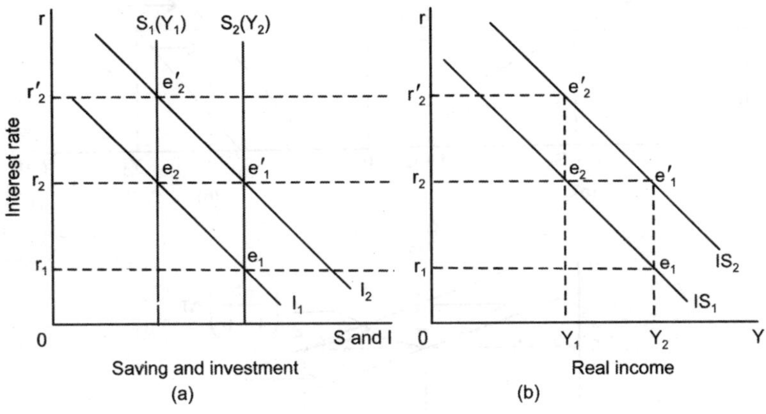

Fig. 11.8

Panel (a) of Fig. 11.8 shows that an increase in the investment function from I_1 to I_2 means that interest rates must rise to choke off greater investment and/or income must rise to bring saving up to a higher investment. For each given interest rate, equality of saving and investment occurs at a higher income, which shifts the IS curve rightward in Panel (b).

Changes in Taxes: The effect on the position of the IS curve of a tax increase from T_0 to T_1 is depicted in Fig. 11.9. For each one rupee increase in taxes at a given income level, taxes are higher by one rupee and saving is less by (1 – b) rupee. An increase of one rupee in taxes lowers disposable income by one rupee and reduces saving by the MPS (1 – b). Since for a given income level the decline in saving is less than the increase in taxes, an increase in taxes will shift the S + T schedule upward. In Panel (b), an increase in taxes from T_0 to T_1 shifts the schedule from $[S(Y - T_0) + T_0]$ to $[S(Y - T_1) + T_1]$.

At interest rate r_0, we can find the level of government expenditures plus investment along the I(r) + G schedule at $I_0 + G_0$. Equilibrium in the product market requires an equal amount of saving plus taxes. At T_0, the equilibrium level of saving plus taxes is $S_0 + T_0$, and this requires income to be at Y_0. This combination of (r_0, Y_0) is a point on the initial IS curve IS_0, represented by the point A in Panel (c).

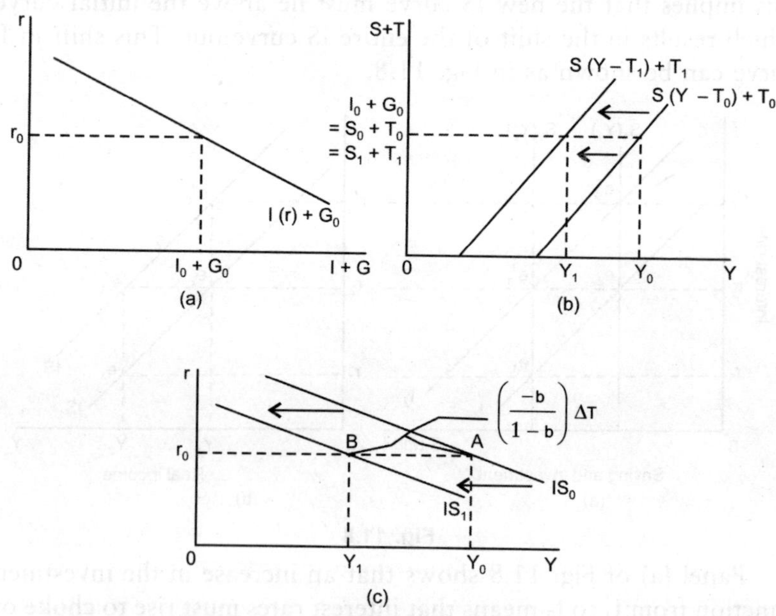

Fig. 11.9

With the higher level of taxes, for saving plus taxes to be unchanged, saving and therefore income must be lower. The new level of income required for product market equilibrium is given by Y_1 in Panel (b). The corresponding point on the new IS curve is point B in Panel (c). Thus, the increase in taxes shifts the IS curve to the left.

For a given rate of interest, a tax change does not affect the left-hand side of the equilibrium condition for the product market given by equation (11.18); investment and government spending are unchanged. So for equilibrium at the same interest rate, the right-hand side must also be unchanged; saving plus taxes must be unchanged. This requires that the increase in taxes be exactly balanced by a decline in saving, i.e.,

$$\Delta S + \Delta T = 0 \qquad ...(11.20)$$

The change in saving is expressed as

$$\Delta S = (1 - b)\,\Delta(Y - T) = (1 - b)\,\Delta Y - (1 - b)\,\Delta T \qquad ...(11.21)$$

From (11.20) and (11.21) we have

$$(1 - b)\,\Delta Y - (1 - b)\,\Delta T + \Delta T = 0$$

$$(1 - b)\,\Delta Y - \Delta T + b\Delta T + \Delta T = 0$$

$$(1 - b)\,\Delta Y + b\Delta T = 0$$

$$\Delta Y = \frac{-b}{1-b}\,\Delta T \qquad ...(11.22)$$

From equation (11.22) we see that the amount by which the IS curve shifts to the left for one unit increase in taxes, $-b/(1 - b)$, is just equal to the tax multiplier of simple Keynesian model.

Change in Savings: If the savings curve shifts out, for any reason, the IS curve shifts back. If there is an increase in savings, keeping current income fixed, the real interest rate will fall because there is a larger supply of loanable funds available. Since current income is assumed to stay the same and the new interest rate is lower, this implies that the new IS curve must lie below the initial curve. Thus, the entire IS curve will shift back.

Change in Aggregate Demand: If the IS curve shifts out, the aggregate demand curve will shift out. For instance, suppose that businesses expect future economic conditions to improve. As a result of the optimistic view of future business conditions, firms will want to have more investment today. This causes the investment curve to shift out, implying that there will be an increase in the demand for loanable funds in the funds market. Keeping current income fixed, this means that the IS curve will shift up (out). With the shift of the IS curve out, the funds market would be in equilibrium at the higher interest rate and current level of income.

THE LM CURVE: MONEY MARKET EQUILIBRIUM

The LM curve shows all combinations of the interest rate r and income Y that satisfy the money demand relationship for a fixed level of the money supply and for a predetermined value of the price level.

According to Keynes, the demand for real money balances (liquidity preferences, measured in wage-units) is a function of income (because of the transactions motive for holding money) and the interest rate (because of the speculative motive). Tobin was dissatisfied with Keynes's treatment of both transactions and speculative motives. He did not consider that Keynes had explained why people hold money and near-money even though other marketable assets have higher yields, or why the demand for money and near-money is empirically observed to vary inversely with those yields. As Tobin interpreted Keynes, Keynes assumed that an agent must hold the same expectation of short-term returns on all assets the agent chooses to hold. Otherwise, the agent would wish to shift his portfolio entirely out of the lower-yielding assets into the highest-yielding asset. Money and low-yield short securities are thus held by those agents who expect capital losses on long-term bonds (because of an increase in interest rates) sufficient that their expected net short-term yields on bonds would be not higher than on money and near-money.

A reduction in current interest rates could induce expectations of a future rise in interest rates, but clearly, if Keynes's speculators had, individually or in aggregate, unbiased expectations, there would be no justification for a liquidity preference function with negative sensitivity to the current rate of interest. Tobin reformulated the demand for money as an asset, Keynes's speculative motive for holding money, as the behaviour of risk-averse investors to risk (as distinct from fundamental Keynesian uncertainty). Investors have preferences over the distribution of returns to their overall portfolios, rather than individual assets. Money and highly liquid short-term securities, such as treasury bills (near-money), differ from other assets not only in expected return (zero nominal return on narrowly-defined money, lower nominal returns on treasury bills and interest-bearing bank deposits than on the other assets) but also in risk (with money as a risk-less asset in nominal terms, or, allowing for changes in the purchasing power of money, a less risky asset in real terms). While Keynes's liquidity preference theory implied that each agent would own only one asset, Tobin's investors would hold a mix of money and other assets.

The treatment of money in Tobin as one of many assets, each having a distribution of returns with some particular mean and variance, was the basis of the "general equilibrium approach to the monetary theory" of Tobin, in which a vector of market-clearing asset prices (and hence asset returns) is determined by the whole range of asset supplies and demands, providing a channel through which open-market operations changing the relative supplies of money and bonds affect the cost of capital.

Keynes's presentation of the transaction motive for holding money offered no reason for an inverse relation between money demand and interest, and simply posited a direct relation between liquidity preference and income, with no derivation of how much money should be held for a given rate of spending. Independently of each other, Baumol and Tobin derived the transactions demand for money from the need to use money as means of payment and the existence of transactions costs of converting funds from interest-bearing assets into money.

Now we will discuss how changes in the interest rate affect the quantity of money demanded. That is, other things remaining the same, what is the shape of the demand for money function drawn against interest rates? Higher interest rates make it relatively more attractive to hold bonds and earn the interest. Lower interest rates make bonds relatively less attractive because the convenience of holding money is less costly in terms of the smaller interest rate forgone to hold the completely liquid asset, money. Liquidity refers to the ease with which assets can be turned into money. If there are conversion fees and possible changes in value, an asset is not very liquid. Money is definitely the most liquid asset. Therefore, the demand for money can be called liquidity preference. Keynes gave additional reasons for the inverse relationship of the quantity of money demanded and interest rates. He added an asset demand for money, which is inversely related to interest rates, to the classical transactions demand for money, which is dependent on income.

Following Keynes, Fig. 11.10 shows the demand for money for a given income level as an inverse function of the interest rate.

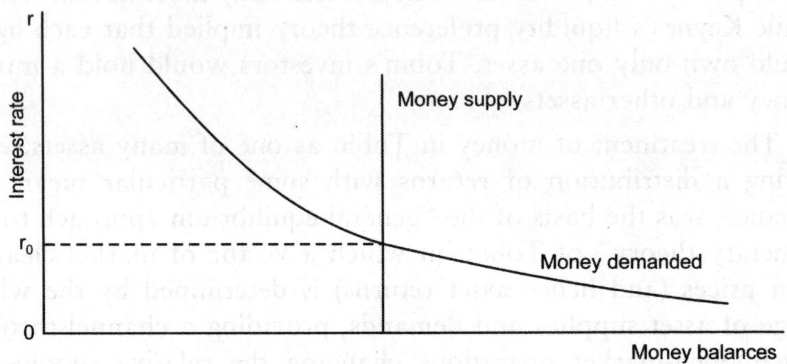

Fig. 11.10

The vertical money supply curve in Fig. 11.10 assumes that the money supply is a fixed amount determined by the monetary authority. Given the level of income, the interest rate is determined by the intersection of the supply and demand for money. The demand for real money balance is given by

$$\frac{M^d}{P} = L(r) \qquad \text{...(11.23)}$$

or,

$$L = \bar{L} + kY - hr \qquad \text{...(11.24)}$$

where,

$L = \frac{M^d}{p} =$ real demand for money,

$\bar{L} =$ autonomous real money demand, which for simplicity can be assumed to be zero,

$k =$ sensitivity of real money demand to change in income,

$Y =$ income,

$h =$ sensitivity of real money demand to changes in interest rates, and

$r =$ rate of interest.

Derivation of the LM Curve

The LM curve represents possible combinations of interest rates and income for which the demand for money and the supply of money are equal. Thus, the LM schedule can be derived straightway from the money market equilibrium condition

$$M^S = M^d$$

where, demand for money consists of transaction demand for money (M_t), and speculative demand for money (M_{sp}).

$$\begin{aligned} M^d &= M_t + M_{sp} \\ &= kY + L(r) \qquad \text{...(11.25)} \end{aligned}$$

Thus, the money market equilibrium condition can be written as

$$M^s = M^d = kY + L(r) \qquad \text{...(11.26)}$$

Equation (11.26) gives the LM function, which can be used to derive the LM curve.

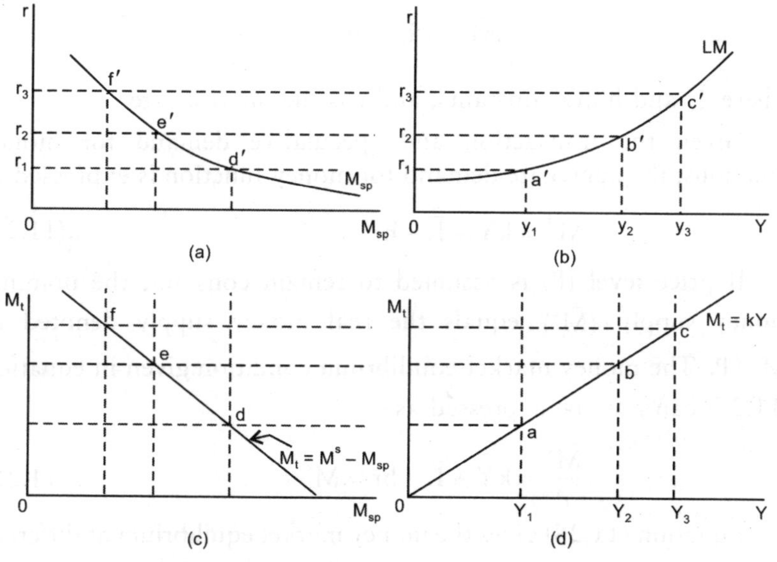

Fig. 11.11

Panel (d) shows the derivation of demand curve for transaction money at different levels of income (Y), interest rate (r) and speculative cash balance. The relationship between M_t and Y is given by a function $M_t = kY$.

Let us start from point a in Panel (d). From 'a' we get a point 'd' in panel (c) and 'd″ in Panel (a). Finally we get a point 'a″ in Panel (b). Similarly, we get points 'b″ and 'c″ in Panel (b). Joining points 'a″, 'b″ and 'c″ we get the LM curve, which gives the equilibrium value of r and Y in the money market.

Algebracially we can derive the LM curve from the money market equilibrium condition

$$M^d = \bar{M}^s$$

where,

$\bar{M}^s$ = fixed money supply.

In the Keynesian system, the speculative demand function produces a curvilinear schedule with a part made of straight horizontal line, that is, the part showing liquidity trap. For simplicity, we assume a straight-line demand function for speculative demand for money as

$$M_{sp} = \bar{L} - hr$$

where $\bar{L}$ and h are constants, and r is the interest rate.

Given the transaction and speculative demand for money functions, the aggregate demand for money function is expressed as

$$M^d = kY + \bar{L} - hr \qquad ...(11.27)$$

If price level (P) is assumed to remain constant, the nominal money supply ($\bar{M}^s$) equals the real money supply denoted as $\bar{M}^s / P$. The money market equilibrium condition given in equation (11.27) can now be expressed as

$$\frac{\bar{M}^s}{P} = kY + \bar{L} - hr = \bar{M}^s \qquad ...(11.28)$$

Equation (11.28) gives the money market equilibrium at different levels of income and the rate of interest. From this equation is derived the LM schedule. By manipulating equation (11.28), we get the LM function as

$$Y = \frac{1}{k}(\bar{M}^s - \bar{L} + hr) \qquad ...(11.29)$$

Equation (11.29) gives the LM function, which can be used to derive the LM curve.

If $\bar{L} = 0$, equation (11.28) can be written as

$$\frac{\bar{M}^s}{P} = kY - hr$$

$$r = \frac{k}{h}Y - \frac{\bar{M}^s}{hP} \quad \text{...(11.30)}$$

Slope of the LM Curve: The LM curve slopes upward. The reason for this is that an increase in the interest rate r reduces the demand for money. But the money supply is fixed. Hence, income must adjust to bring money demand back up. A rise in income is what is required. A rise in income will increase the demand for money and offset the decline in money demand brought about by the rise in the interest rate. In sum, the increase in the interest rate is associated with an increase in income. Thus the LM curve is upward-sloping. Assuming a vertical supply of money schedule, the slope of the LM curve becomes greater as the effect of income on the demand for money (k) becomes stronger and as the interest sensitivity of money demand (h) lessens. From equation (11.30), we find the slope of the LM curve to be k/h.

Consider an increase in income, ΔY, from Y to Y_1. The income-induced increase in money demand as a result of this change will equal $k\Delta Y$, where k is the parameter giving the increase in money demand (for transaction purposes) per unit increase in income from equation (11.28). The interest rate will have to rise by enough to offset this income-induced increase in money demand. The higher the value of k, the larger the increase in money demand per unit increase in income, and, hence, the larger upward adjustment in the interest rate required to restore total money demand to the level of the fixed money stock. The higher the value of k is, the steeper will be the LM curve.

For a given income-induced increase in money demand, the amount by which the interest rate has to rise to restore total money demand to the value of the fixed money stock depends on how elastic money demand is with respect to changes in the rate of interest. In equation (11.28) the interest elasticity of money demand depends on the value of h, which determines the amount of the change in money demand for a given change in the interest rate ($-h = \Delta M^d / \Delta r$). This relationship between the interest elasticity of money demand and the slope of the LM curve is shown in Fig. 11.12.

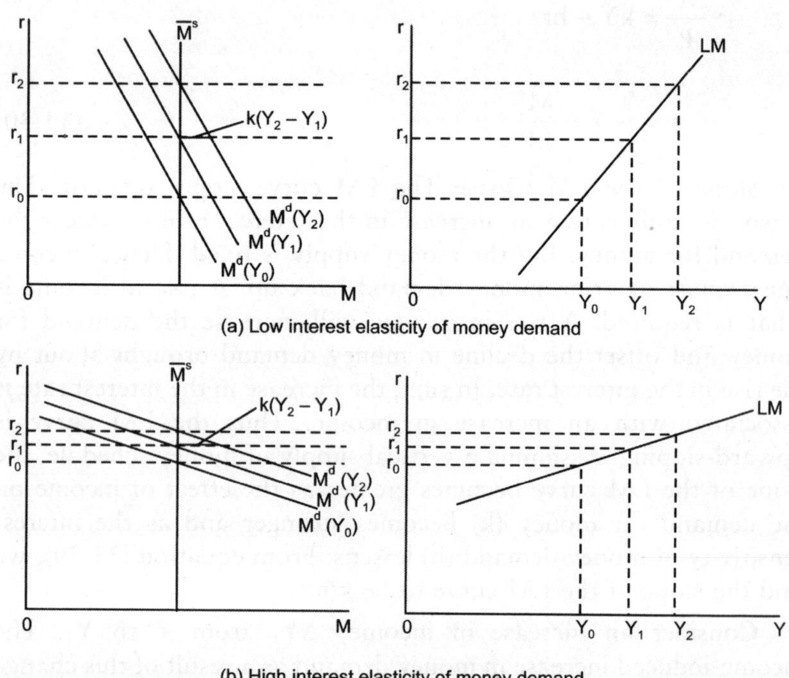

(a) Low interest elasticity of money demand

(b) High interest elasticity of money demand

Fig. 11.12

Panel (a) of the Fig. 11.12 illustrates the case of a low interest elasticity of money demand. The money demand curve is steep, reflecting the fact that large changes in the interest rate will not change the level of money demand by very much. Increase in income from Y_0 to Y_1 and then to Y_2 will shift the money demand schedule to the right in Panel (a) of Fig. 11.12, from $M^d(Y_0)$ to $M^d(Y_1)$, then to $M^d(Y_2)$. These increases in income cause increases in the transaction demand for money equal to $k(Y_1 - Y_0)$ and $k(Y_2 - Y_1)$, respectively. Since a given increase in the interest rate will not reduce money demand by much, the interest rate will have to rise by a large amount to reduce money demand back to the fixed $\overline{M}^s$ level. Due to this fact, the LM curve is steep in Panel (a) of the Fig. 11.12.

In Panel (b) of the Fig. 11.12, highly interest-elastic money demand condition has been considered. Here the money demand curve is quite flat. A small drop in the interest rate increases money demand significantly. Here again the money demand curve shifts to the right as income increases from Y_0 to Y_1, then to Y_2. The graph is constructed such that the increase in income and the value of k from equation (11.28) are the same as in Panel (a) of the Fig. 11.12. Thus, the income-induced increase in money demand is the same in Panel (a) and Panel (b) of the Fig. 11.12. In Panel (b), the interest rate must rise by a relatively small amount to restore equilibrium in the money market. As a consequence, the LM curve in Panel (b) is relatively flat. If money demand is highly responsive to change in the interest rate, a relatively small rise in the interest rate will offset the income-induced increase in transaction balances as income rises from Y_0 to Y_1, then to Y_2.

There are two special cases concerning the slope of the LM curve that are worth noting. First, if the demand for money is perfectly interest elastic, the LM curve will be horizontal, as only a small increase in interest rates would be required to restore money market equilibrium following an increase in income. Alternatively, if the demand for money is perfectly inelastic, the LM curve will be vertical. Given that money demand is insensitive to interest rate changes, an infinte increase will be needed. These two cases are displayed in Fig. 11.13.

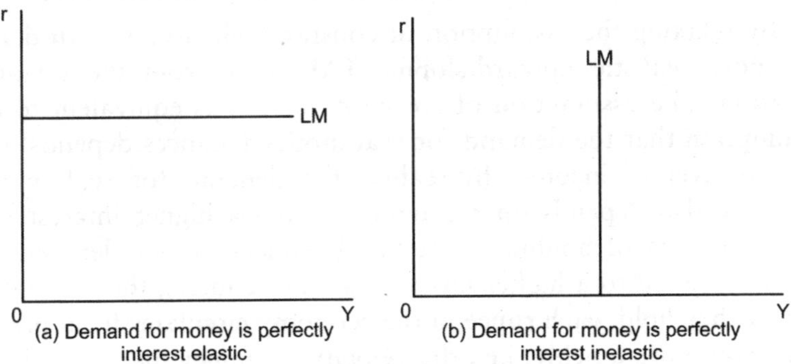

Fig. 11.13

The steepness of the LM curve depends on two factors:

(a) k, the responsiveness of the demand for money to the income level. If k is large, the higher will be the responsiveness of demand for money to income and, the steeper would be the LM curve.

(b) h, the responsiveness of the demand for money to the rate of interest,

(i) If h is close to zero, the demand for money is insensitive to the interest rate. Thus, the LM curve will be nearly vertical.

(ii) If h is small, the demand for money is not very sensitive to the interest rate. Thus, the LM curve will be very steep.

(iii) If h is large, the demand for money is very sensitive to the interest rate. Thus, the LM curve will be close to horizontal. In that case, to maintain the equilibrium in the money market, a small change in the rate of interest must be accompained by a large change in the income level.

Quantity-Equation Interpretation of the LM Curve

The quantity equation is given as

$$MV = PY$$

where, V is constant. This assumption implies that, for any given price level, the supply of money alone determines the level of income. Because this level of income does not depend on the interest rate, the quantity theory is equivalent to a vertical LM curve.

By relaxing the assumption of constant velocity, we can derive the more realistic upward-sloping LM curve from the quantity equation. The assumption of constant velocity is equivalent to the assumption that the demand for real money balances depends only on the level of income. In reality, the demand for real money balances also depends on the interest rate—a higher interest rate raises the cost of holding money and reduces money demand. As people respond to a higher interest rate by reducing the amount of money they hold, each rupee in the economy circulates from person to person more quickly, i.e., the velocity of money increases. Thus, we have

$$MV(r) = PY \qquad ...(11.31)$$

In equation (11.31), the velocity function V(r) indicates that velocity is positively related to the interest rate. This form of the quantity equation yields an LM curve that slopes upward. Because an increase in the interest rates raises the velocity of money, it raises the level of income for any given money supply and price level. The LM curve expresses this positive relationship between the interest rate and income.

Equation (11.31) also shows why changes in the money supply shift the LM curve. For any given interest rate and price level, an increase in the money supply raises the level of income. Thus, increases in the money supply shift the LM curve to the right, and decreases in the money supply shift the LM curve to the left.

The quantity equation merely provides another way to express the theory behind the LM curve. This interpretation of the LM curve is substantively the same as that provided by the theory of liquidity preference. In both the cases, we find that the LM curve represents a positive relationship between income and the interest rate. Here one point should be noted that the LM curve by itself does not determine either income Y or the interest rate r, it is only a relationship between these two endogenous variables.

Shifts in LM Curve

Anything, excluding interest rates and income that are reflected as movements along the LM curve, which affects the demand for money will shift the LM curve. Changes in the money supply, changes in the price level or changes in exogenous money demand will shift the LM curve.

In order to determine the position of LM curve two factors are considered—exogenously fixed money stock and the money demand function. The money stock is assumed to be a policy variable, and when we consider an increase in the money stock, for example, we mean a policy action changing the setting of this policy instrument to a new level. A shift in money demand function means a change in the amount of money demanded for given levels of the interest rate and income, what Keynes called a shift in liquidity preference.

Factors causing the LM curve to shift out

Increase in the money supply: Suppose Reserve Bank follows an expansionary monetary policy. All else equal, money supply increases relative to money demand—excess supply of money. Fig. 11.14 illustrates the effects of an increase in the money stock from M_0^s to M_1^s.

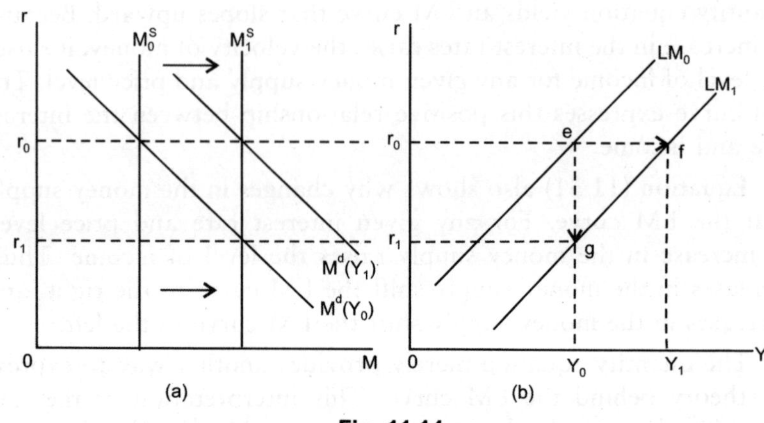

Fig. 11.14

Initially, with money supply M_0^s, the interest rate r_0 will be an equilibrium rate when income is at Y_0 in panel (a) of Fig. 11.14. This r_0, Y_0 combination is represented by point (e) on the LM curve, LM_0 in the panel (b) of the Fig. 11.14. If the money supply is increased to M_1^s, r_0 will be an equilibrium interest rate in the money market only with a higher income level Y_1. This r_0, Y_1 combination is represented by point (f) on the new LM curve, LM_1. The increase in the money supply shifts the LM curve to the right. Similarly, a decline in the money supply shifts the LM schedule upward and to the left.

Decrease in the price level: All else equal, money demand goes down relative to money supply resulting in excess supply of money. This will shift the LM curve to the right.

Exogenous negative shocks to money demand: (for example, use of plastic money). All else equal, money demand goes down relative to money supply resulting in excess supply of money. This will shift the LM curve to the right.

Factors causing the LM curve to shift in

Excess demand for money: Suppose that there is an increase in money demand for a given level of income and the interest rate. The effect of increased in money demand can be illustrated by Fig. 11.15.

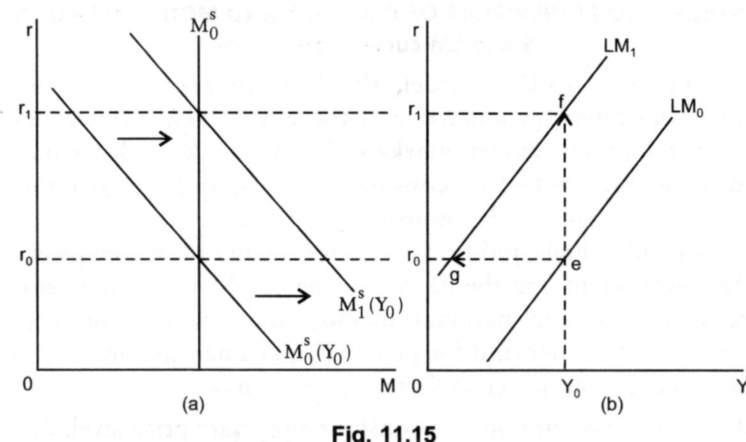

Fig. 11.15

Panel (a) of the Fig. 11.15 shows an initial equilibrium in the money market corresponding to income level Y_0. Initially, money demand is given by $M_0^d(Y_0)$. The equilibrium interest rate is r_0. Now we assume that the money demand function shifts to $M_1^d(Y_0)$, an increase in money demand for a given level of income. Note here that it is the function that shifts, from $M_0^d(Y_0)$ to $M_1^d(Y_0)$. At the unchanged level of income, Y_0, equilibrium in the money market requires an interest rate of r_1. The point on the new LM curve, LM_1 for a given level of income Y_0 will be above the old LM curve. This point is shown as point 'f' in panel (b). Maintaining equilibrium in the money market at r_0 after the shift in the money demand curve would require a fall in income to a level below Y_0, which would shift the schedule in panel (a) back down to the level of the original $M_0^d(Y_0)$ line. Thus the point on LM_1 at r_0 is to the left of LM_0. This point is shown as point 'g' in panel (b). Thus, a shift in the money demand function that increases the demand for money at a given level of both the interest rate and income shifts the LM curve upward and to the left.

Increase in price level: All else equal, money demand increases relative to money supply resulting excess demand for money. This will shifts the LM curve upward and to the left.

Exogenous positive shock to money demand: All else equal, money demand increases relative to money supply resulting excess demand for money. This will shifts the LM curve upward and to the left.

INTEGRATED EQUILIBRIUM OF PRODUCT AND MONEY MARKETS (IS and LM curves combined)

In the basic IS/LM model, the behaviour of the economic agents—consumers, producers, and the government—is reconciled by the product and money markets. The product market balances the demand for product by consumers, firms, and the government with national income. The money market balances the demand for money by individuals and firms with the supply of money provided by the government and the banks. In the equilibrium, all economic aggregates, including national income and the rate of interest adjust, so that the demand for product equals national income, and the demand for money equals the supply of money.

Under the assumption of a constant aggregate price level, IS/LM model determines real income and the interest rate. An unchanging aggregate price level means that any amount of goods and services demanded will be supplied at the existing price level. Therefore, when used as a real income-determining model, the underlying assumption of the IS/LM model is that aggregate supply is horizontal in the relevant range. To satisfy all five relationships of the model, the values of r and Y must be on both the IS curve and the LM curve, that is, at the intersection of the IS curve and the LM curve. The IS curve incorporates the theory of consumption, investment, and net exports and the income identity, while the LM curve incorporates the theory of money demand and money supply. The values of the interest rate and income that we are looking for are thus at the intersection of the LM curve and the IS curve. Once we have determined the levels of income Y and the interest rate r, we can determine consumption C, investment I, and net exports X. Consumption is obtained by putting the value of income into the consumption function, investment is obtained by putting the value of the interest rate into the investment function, and net exports are obtained by putting income and the interest rate into the net export function.

Having derived the IS and LM curves, we can now integrate the product and money market analyses to show the general equilibrium of the two sectors. Fig. 11.16 presents the IS and LM curves derived in Fig. 11.2 and Fig. 11.11 respectively. As noted earlier IS curve shows the equilibrium level of Y at different levels of r with the condition that I = S. Similarly, LM curve shows the equilibrium levels of Y at different levels of r with the condition that $M^d = M^s$.

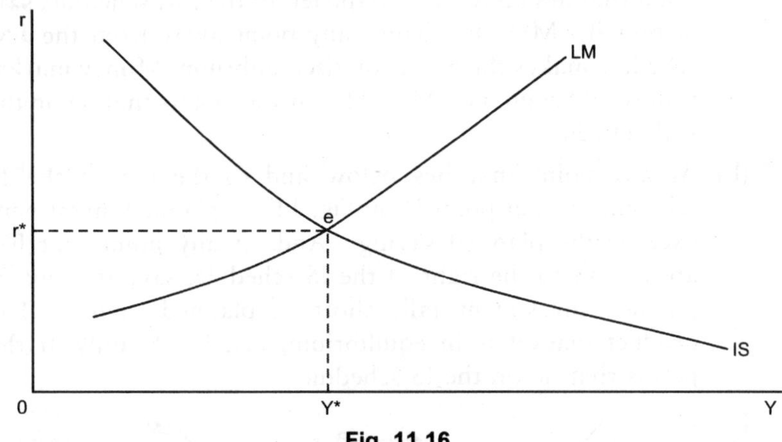

Fig. 11.16

As shown in Fig. 11.16, the IS and LM curves intersect at point e. Point e gives the unique combination of r and Y that satisfies the equilibrium conditions of both the product and the money markets. Point e is the only point that satisfies the 'double condition' of the general equilibrium, that is, I = S and $M^d = M^s$ at the same interest rate (r) and income (Y). Point e is, therefore, the point of general equilibrium. At point e, both product and money markets are in equilibrium. Thus, (r^*, Y^*) is the equilibrium pair of rate of interest and income at which both the product and money markets are in equilibrium.

At all other points, there is a divergence between the IS and LM curves. This divergence creates the condition of disequilibrium. There is no general equilibrium at any other point other than e. The system has, however, a tendency to converge to point e, the point of the general equilibrium.

The dynamics of adjustment: Let us now look into the adjustment process by which an economy moves from the state of disequilibrium to its equilibrium. The economy is in disequilibrium on any other portion than the point of intersection of the IS and LM schedule. In respect of disequilibrium analysis, two important principles need to be borne in mind for further analysis.

(a) At any point that lies below and to the right of the LM schedule, say, at point D in Fig. 11.17, $M^d > M^s$. And at any point that lies above and to the left of the LM schedule, say, at pint B, $M^s > M^d$. Thus, any point away from the LM schedule makes the points of disequilibrium. Money market is in equilibrium, i.e., $M^d = M^s$, only at points that lie on the LM schedule.

(b) At any point that lies below and to the left of the IS schedule, say, at point D, in Fig. 11.17, planned investment exceeds the planned savings. And, at any point that lies above and to the right of the IS schedule, say, at point B, planned investment falls short of planned savings. The product market is in equilibrium, i.e., I = S, only at the points that lie on the IS schedule.

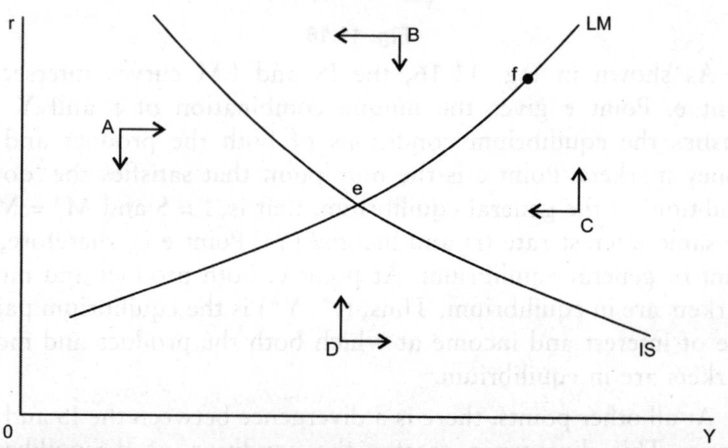

Fig. 11.17

Now consider the points above the LM schedule such as points A and B. At all points above the LM schedule, there will be an excess supply of money. At the level of income for either point A or B, the corresponding interest rate is too high for money market equilibrium. With an excess supply of money, there is downward pressure on the interest rate, as indicated by the downward-direction arrow. There is a tendency to move toward the LM schedule. Conversely, at points below the LM schedule, such as points C and D, there will be an excess demand for money, and consequently upward pressure on the interest rate.

To the right of the IS schedule, output will exceed aggregate demand or, analogously, saving plus taxes will exceed investment plus government spending. At the levels of the interest rate for either point B or C, the corresponding output level that will equate investment plus government spending to saving plus taxes, an output level given by the point along the IS curve, is below the actual output level. There is an excess supply of output, and therefore a downward pressure on output, as indicated by the arrows pointing to the left. Conversely, at points to the left of this IS schedule, such as points A and D, actual output is below the level that will clear the product market. There .s an excess demand for output, and there will be upward pressure on output, as indicated by the rightward-directed arrows at these points.

Also, the points on one schedule but on the other are also disequilibrium points relative to one of the two markets. Consider a point 'f' on the LM curve. The point 'f' is a point of equilibrium for the money market but a point of excess supply for the product market. Similarly, any point along the IS curve other than point e would result in disequilibrium in the money market. It is only at point e that both the money and product market are in equilibrium. There is no excess demand or supply in either the money or the product market, and therefore there is no pressure for the interest rate or output to change.

The Algebra of the IS/LM Model

In simple Keynesian model, private saving function shows private saving (S_p) as consisting of an autonomous part not affected by income or interest rates ($\bar{S}$) and a part that is equal to the marginal propensity to save (s) times disposable income (Y_D), i.e.,

$$S_p = \bar{S} + sY_D \quad ...(11.32)$$

Government saving (S_G) equals taxes collected (T) minus transfer payments ($\overline{TR}$) and government spending ($\bar{G}$), i.e.,

$$S_G = T - \overline{TR} - \bar{G} \quad ...(11.33)$$

The investment function is given as

$$I = \bar{I} - jr \quad ...(11.34)$$

Equation (11.34) ignores any income effect on investment and gives planned investment (I) as consisting of an autonomous portion, $\overline{I}$, and a negative relationship to the real interest rate (r).

To obtain equilibrium values of income and interest rates, planned saving must equal planned investment, i.e.,

$$S_P + S_G = I \quad ...(11.35)$$

or, $$\overline{S} + sY_D + T - \overline{TR} - \overline{G} = \overline{I} - jr \quad ...(11.36)$$

Disposable income is given by

$$Y_D = Y + \overline{TR} - T \quad ...(11.37)$$

Substituting equation (11.37) in equation (11.36) we have

$$\overline{S} + sY + s\overline{TR} - sT + T - \overline{TR} - \overline{G} = \overline{I} - jr \quad ...(11.38)$$

or, $$sY - sT + T = -\overline{S} - s\overline{TR} + \overline{TR} + \overline{G} + \overline{I} - jr$$

or, $$sY - sT + T = -\overline{S} + (1 - S)\,\overline{TR} + \overline{G} + \overline{I} - jr \quad ...(11.39)$$

Consumption function is represented as

$$C = \overline{C} + cY_D,$$

and saving function as

$$S = \overline{S} + sY_D$$

Since, the marginal propensity to consume (c) and the marginal propensity to save (s) add to 1, saving (S) plus consumption (C) must add to disposable income. This implies $-\overline{S}$ must equal $\overline{C}$.

Let us represent autonomous spending by $\overline{A}$ and

$$\overline{A} = \overline{C} + (1 - s)\,\overline{TR} + \overline{G} + \overline{I}$$

Substituting $\overline{A}$ for autonomous spending in equation (11.39) we have

$$sY - sT + T = \overline{A} - jr \quad ...(11.40)$$

Assume that taxes (T) are fraction of income and represented as

$$T = tY$$

Substituting for T in equation (11.40) we have

$$sY - stY + tY = \bar{A} - jr \qquad ...(11.41)$$

or,
$$(s - st + t)Y = \bar{A} - jr$$

or,
$$Y = \frac{\bar{A}}{s - st + t} - \frac{jr}{s - st + t} \qquad ...(11.42)$$

or,
$$Y = m\bar{A} - mjr \qquad ...(11.43)$$

where,

$$m = \frac{1}{s - st + t}$$

m is the ordinary multiplier for autonomous changes in the real goods and services market and is equivalent to $1/[1 - c(1 - t)]$.

Equation (11.43) shows the equilibrium in the real goods and services market by using Y for real income. Since prices are assumed to be constant in the income-determining IS/LM model, Y is used for nominal income, because for constant price levels, nominal and real income are identical.

Now we will consider the LM curve. The real demand for money is a function of real income and market interest rates (i). We are assuming no inflationary expectation, so the market interest rate (i) equals the real interest rate (r).

The demand for money is

$L = kY - hr$

The equilibrium condition in the money market is $M^s/P = L$. Therefore,

$$\frac{M^s}{P} = kY - hr \qquad ...(11.44)$$

or,
$$r = \frac{1}{h}\left(kY - \frac{M^s}{P}\right) \qquad ...(11.45)$$

Since, the interest rates must be the same in both markets for equilibrium, we can substitute this expression for interest in the money market equation for r in the real goods and services market equation.

$$Y = m\bar{A} - \frac{mj}{h}\left(kY - \frac{M^s}{P}\right)$$

or, $$Y = m\bar{A} - \frac{mjk}{h}Y + \frac{mj}{h}\cdot\frac{M^s}{P}$$

or, $$\left(1+\frac{mjk}{h}\right)Y = m\bar{A} + \frac{mj}{h}\cdot\frac{M^s}{p}$$

or, $$Y = \frac{m}{\left(1+\frac{mjk}{h}\right)}\bar{A} + \frac{mj}{\left(1+\frac{mjk}{h}\right)h}\cdot\frac{M^s}{P}$$

or, $$Y = \frac{hm}{h+mjk}\bar{A} + \frac{mj}{h+mjk}\cdot\frac{M^s}{P} \qquad ...(11.46)$$

Equation (11.46) shows that real income depends on autonomous spending ($\bar{A}$) and the real value of the money supply (M^s/P); and has two multipliers—fiscal policy multiplier {hm / (h + mjk)} and monetary policy multiplier, {mj / (h + mjk)}. Where, h measures the interest sensitivity of the demand for money. If the demand for money is insensitive to change in interest rates, then h approaches zero, and so does the fiscal multiplier. This describes the case of the nearly vertical LM curve where fiscal policy has little effect on real income. If h is large, the LM curve will be flatter.

The interest sensitivity of investment, j appears in the denominator. Larger j reduces the fiscal multiplier. The sensitivity of the real demand for money to real income is denoted by k. As the real income rises from the fiscal stimulus, more money will be demanded, which increases interest rates as people sell financial instruments. Whenever interest rates rise, investment falls according to j. Large k therefore also reduces the fiscal multiplier.

If the Keynesian multiplier, m is very small, the fiscal multiplier will approach zero. From equation (11.46) we see that the fiscal multiplier approach zero if m approaches zero, which can be denoted by a rightward movement of IS curve by mΔG.

The smaller the interest rate sensitivity of investment (j), the more vertical the IS curve and the smaller the effect on real income of increasing the money supply. A larger j means a flatter IS curve and the greater effect on real income of increase in the money supply.

The smaller k is, the greater the monetary multiplier. The smaller k is, the more real income must increase to make people willing to hold the increased money supply.

The smaller the interest sensitivity of the demand for money (h) is, the steeper the LM curve and the greater the expansion in real income from increases in the money supply.

Now consider that private saving also depends on real interest rates and investment on income. Then, we have

$$S_p = \overline{S} + sY_D + wr \qquad ...(11.47)$$

and $$I = \overline{I} + fY - jr \qquad ...(11.48)$$

where f is the marginal propensity to invest.

Government saving is given by

$$S_G = T - \overline{TR} - \overline{G} \qquad ...(11.49)$$

For equilibrium,

$$S_p + S_G = I \qquad ...(11.50)$$

or, $$\overline{S} + sY_D + wr + T - \overline{TR} - \overline{G} = \overline{I} + fY - jr \qquad ...(11.51)$$

Disposable income (Y_D) and taxes (T) are defined as

$$Y_D = Y + \overline{TR} - T$$

and $$T = tY$$

Substituting for Y_D and T in equation (11.51), we have

$$\overline{S} + sY + s\overline{TR} - stY + wr + tY - \overline{TR} - \overline{G} = \overline{I} + fY - jr \qquad ...(11.52)$$

Taking autonomous terms together, and considering $-\overline{S} = \overline{C}$, we have

$$\overline{A} = \overline{C} + (1 - s)\,\overline{TR} + \overline{G} + \overline{I}$$

Equation (11.52) becomes

$$sY - stY + tY - fY = \bar{A} - wr - jr \qquad ...(11.53)$$

or, $$(s - st + t - f)Y = \bar{A} - (w + j)r$$

or, $$Y = \frac{\bar{A}}{s - st + t - f} - \frac{(w + j)r}{s - st + t - f} \qquad ...(11.54)$$

or, $$Y = m'\bar{A} - m'(w + j)r \qquad ...(11.55)$$

where,

$$m' = \frac{1}{s - st + t - f}$$

The simple multiplier of autonomous spending is increased by the marginal propensity to invest (f) entering the denominator with a negative sign.

From the money market equilibrium, we have

$$r = \frac{1}{h}\left(kY - \frac{M^s}{P}\right)$$

Now, using r of the money market equilibrium into the real goods market equilibrium equation (11.55) we have

$$Y = m'\bar{A} - m'(w + j)\frac{1}{h}\left(kY - \frac{M^s}{P}\right)$$

or, $$hY = hm'\bar{A} - m'kY(w + j) + m'(w + j)\frac{M^s}{P}$$

or, $$hY + m'k(w + j)Y = hm'\bar{A} + m'(w + j)\frac{M^s}{P}$$

or, $$Y = \frac{hm'}{h + m'(j + w)k} \cdot \bar{A} + \frac{m'(w + j)}{h + m'(j + w)k} \cdot \frac{M^s}{P} \qquad ...(11.56)$$

The larger the multiplier (m′), the greater are both the fiscal and monetary multipliers. The interest sensitivity of the saving function (w) reduces the fiscal multiplier, $\{hm' / (h + m'(j + w)k)]$ and raises the monetary multiplier, $\{m'(j + w) / (h + m'(j + w)k)\}$.

Aggregate Demand Derived from IS/LM Model

The aggregate demand curve is a relationship between the price level and the level of national income. In this section we will use the IS/LM model to derive the aggregate demand curve. IS/LM model can be used to show that national income falls as the price level rises; the downward-sloping aggregate demand curve expresses this relationship.

By using the IS/LM model in isolation, one is assuming that prices are fixed, so that we can derive the implication of, say, higher government expenditure, on output and interest rates. But assuming that prices are fixed and output is flexible, is another way of saying that the aggregate supply curve is horizontal. This is one of the main assumptions underlying analysis with the IS/LM model. This is arguably a good enough approximation in the short run, but not in the medium or long run.

If the price level rises, the real value of any nominal money supply is reduced. Fig. 11.18 illustrates the impact of a changing price level. For any given money supply M, a higher price level P causes a lower supply of real money balances M/P. A lower supply of real money balances shift the LM curve upward, which raises the interest rate and lowers the equilibrium level of income.

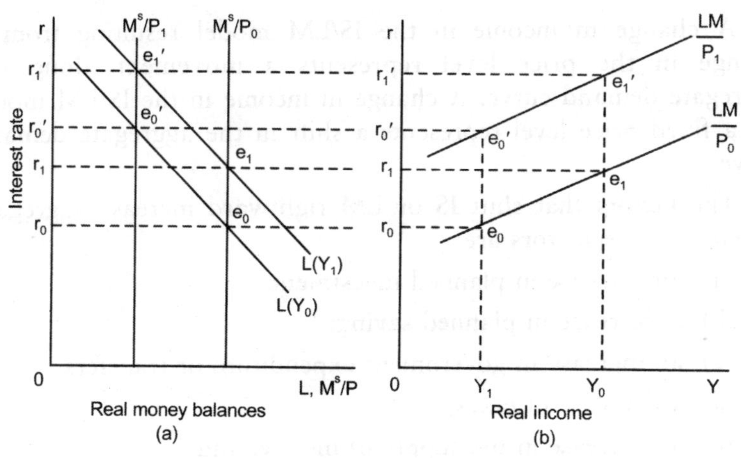

Fig. 11.18

In Fig. 11.18, we see that when the price level rises from P_0 to P_1, national income falls from Y_0 to Y_1. When the price level rises from P_0 to P_1 the real money supply shifts leftward in panel (a). At income level Y_0 and the original interest rate of r_0, the real money supply is now less than the real demand for money. People will sell financial assets until the interest rate rises to r_0'. At r_0' the amount of real balance demand has been reduced to equal the real supply. At each level of income a higher interest rate is necessary to bring equality in the real supply and demand for money. People would want to sell financial assets to get money balances. But with more people wanting to sell than buy, sellers would have to lower the price of financial assets, which means that the coupon paid would be a higher percentage of the price of the asset, i.e., interest rates are higher. Interest rates will continue to rise until the real demand for money equals the real supply at e_0.

If prices are variable, we have a family of LM curves representing equilibrium in the money market for different price levels. Then, there is no longer a unique equality of IS and LM, but rather one for every price level. Different possible equilibrium price levels mean different LM curves. Fig. 11.19 illustrates the derivation of aggregate demand curve from IS/LM model.

Panel (b) of Fig. 11.19 depicts the possible combinations of prices and real income that bring equilibrium in both the money and real goods and services markets.

A change in income in the IS/LM model resulting from a change in the price level represents a movement along the aggregate demand curve. A change in income in the IS/LM model for a fixed price level represents a shift in the aggregate demand curve.

The factors that shift IS or LM rightward increase aggregate demand. These factors are:

(a) an increase in planned investment;

(b) a decrease in planned saving;

(c) an increase in government expenditure or transfers;

(d) a decrease in taxes;

(e) an increase in the supply of money; and

(f) a decrease in the demand for money.

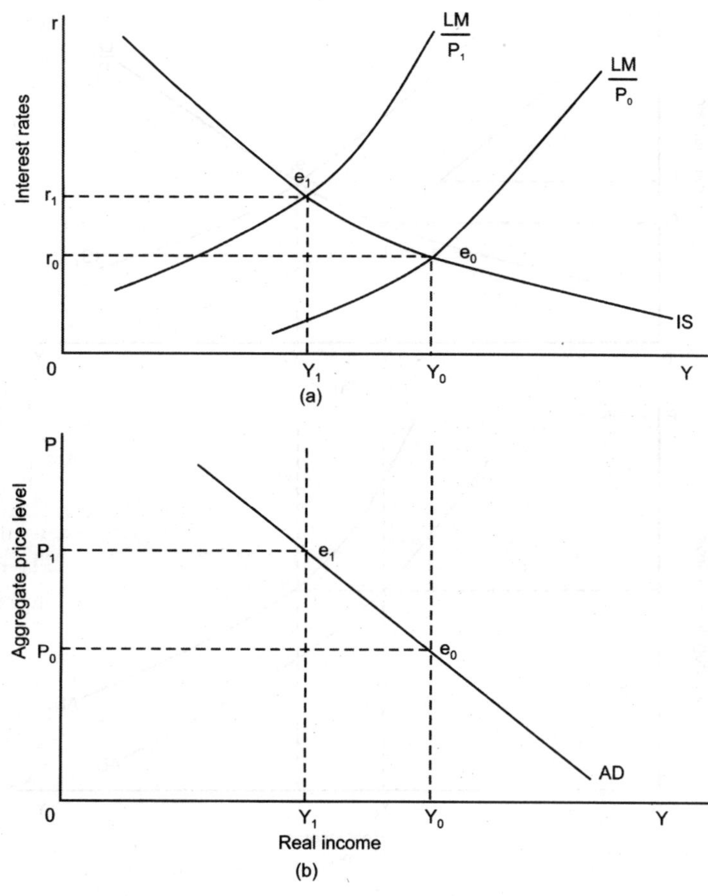

Fig. 11.19

Let us consider the case of an increase in government expenditure. Fig. 11.20 describes this situation.

An increase in government expenditure shifts IS curve rightward by the multiplier times the new amount of government spending. In the presence of an upward-sloping LM curve, aggregate demand does not move as far right as IS curve. Interest rate rises to a new equilibrium point e_1. Equilibrium points e_0 and e_1 both corresponds to the same price level 'P'. Therefore, e_0 and e_1 represents two different aggregate demand curves as shown in Panel (b).

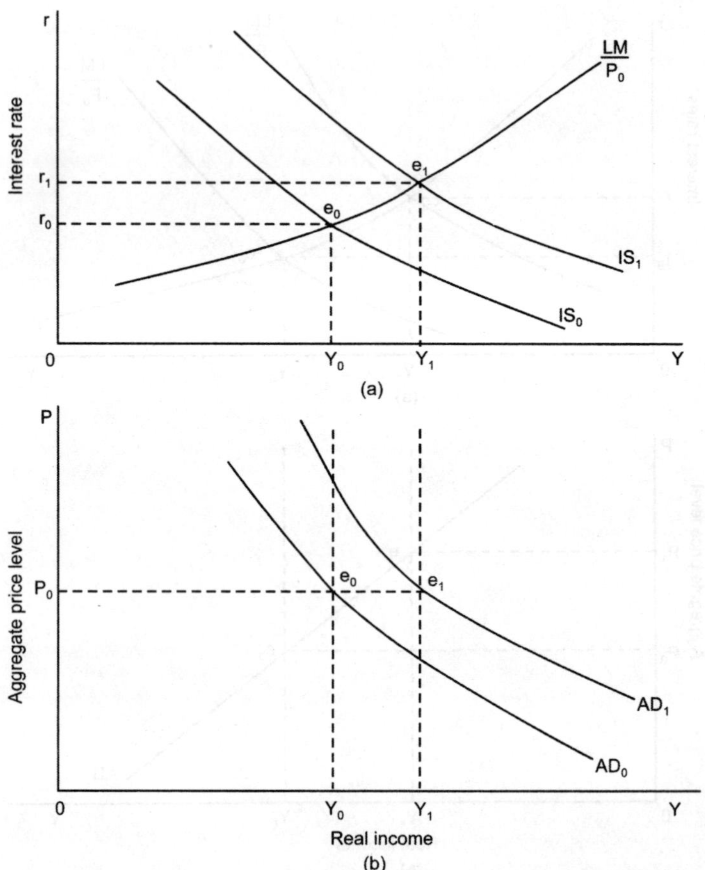

Fig. 11.20

The slope of the aggregate demand curve depends on the slope of the IS and LM curves. The steeper the IS curve and the flatter the LM curve, the steeper the aggregate demand curve will be. A steeper aggregate demand curve means that a given change in prices will be accompanied by a smaller change in real income.

Let us consider an increase in the price level. This can be represented by Fig. 11.21.

Increase in price level from P_0 to P_1 shifts the LM curve from $\frac{LM}{P_0}$ to $\frac{LM}{P_1}$. Real income must fall and/or interest rates must rise to make people satisfied with the lower real money supply. The steeper the IS curve, the more interest rates must rise to decrease investment and thus real income. The rising interest rate causes the amount of money demanded to fall. The equilibrium point moves from e_1 to e_1'. Thus, the aggregate demand curve AD′ is steeper because the rise in prices is accompanied by a smaller decrease in real income.

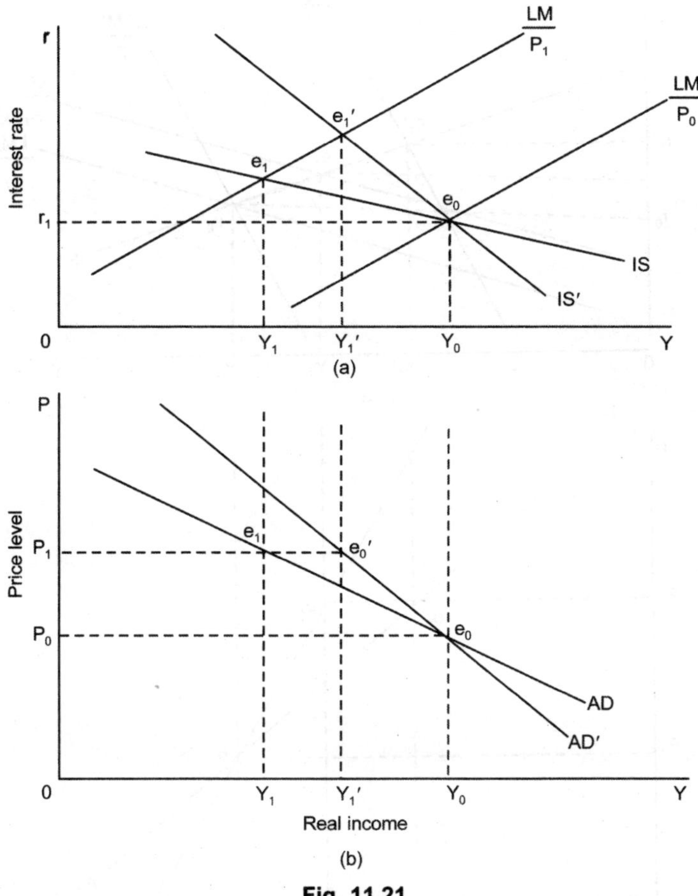

Fig. 11.21

The steeper LM curves yield a flatter aggregate demand curve. This can be shown by Fig. 11.22.

An increase in the price level shifts each LM curve leftward by the same amount. Real income must fall and/or interest rates must rise to make people satisfied with the lower real money supply. The steeper the LM curves, the more interest rates will have to rise and income fall in order for people to be satisfied with the reduced real money supply. The greater decrease in real income associated with the same increase in the price level from P_0 to P_1 yields the flatter aggregate demand curve, AD′ in panel (b) in Fig. 11.22.

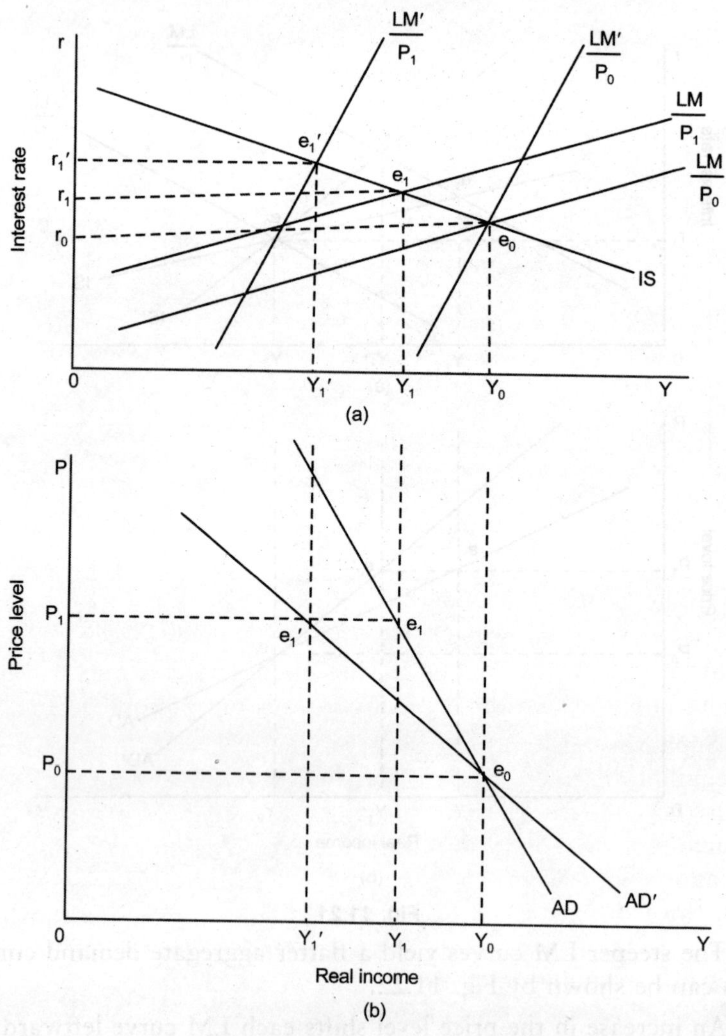

Fig. 11.22

COBWEB EQUILIBRIUM IN THE IS/LM MODEL

Let us consider that the market equilibrate in sequential order. First one market clears, and then another, then the first clears in response to changes from the second market, and so on. Such a process would result in a cobweb equilibrium. Consider the Fig. 11.23.

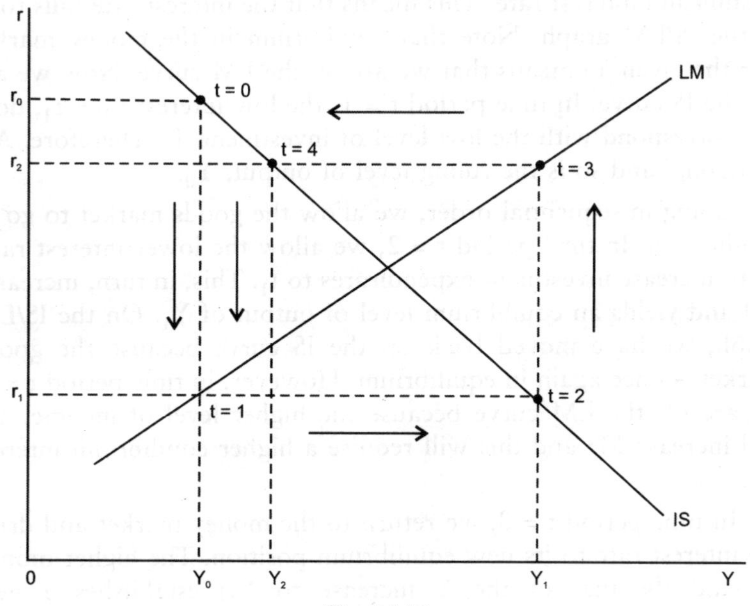

Fig. 11.23

At r_0 and Y_0 in Fig. 11.23, the interest rate is out of general equilibrium and that the level of output is out of equilibrium.

Suppose we assume that, the money market clears first, generating an equilibrium interest rate. The new level of investment (resulting from the changed r) leads to a new aggregate demand and we assume that the goods market then clears. The new Y will change M^d and new r will result. The new r will lead to a new investment and, through a changed aggregate demand, a new Y. Eventually, these r and Y will settle down at their general, or mutually compatible, equilibrium levels. This is given, of course, by the intersection of the IS and LM curves.

In time period zero, t = 0, there is disequilibrium. Clearly, being off the LM curve means that the money market is not in equilibrium.

The Cobweb Equilibration explanation that follows is based on the assumption that markets clear sequentially.

As mentioned above, we start at t = 0, with the interest rate above the equilibrium interest rate and the goods market in equilibrium for the given interest rate, r_0. In the next period, t = 1, suppose the bond market clears so that the interest rate equals the equilibrium interest rate. This means that the interest rate falls to r_1 in the IS/LM graph. Note that equilibrium in the money market (for the given Y) means that we are on the LM curve. Now we are off the IS curve. In time period t = 1, the low interest rate, r_1, does not correspond with the low level of investment, I_0. Therefore, AD is 'wrong' and so is the ruling level of output, Y_0.

Going in sequential order, we allow the goods market to go to equilibrium. In time period t = 2, we allow the lower interest rate, r_1, to increase investment expenditures to I_1. This, in turn, increases AD and yields an equilibrium level of output of Y_1. On the IS/LM graph, we have moved back on the IS curve because the goods market is once again in equilibrium. However, in time period t = 2, we are off the LM curve because the higher level of income, Y_1, will increase M^d and this will require a higher equilibrium interest rate.

In time period t = 3, we return to the money market and drive the interest rate to its new equilibrium position. The higher money demand (because of the Y increase to Y_1) establishes a new equilibrium interest rate of r_2 . In the IS/LM graph, we are now back on the LM curve because the money market is in equilibrium; but we are off the IS curve because the goods market is in disequilibrium—the higher interest rate at r_2 will change the level of investment which will change AD and Y.

In time period t = 4, we return to the goods market in order to allow the forces in the model to determine the equilibrium level of output. The higher interest rate, r_2 determines a lower level of investment, I_2, which leads, through AD, to lower equilibrium level of output, Y_2. In the IS/LM graph, the economy is now at r_2 and Y_1—in goods market equilibrium, but in money market disequilibrium. This process will continue, untill the economy reaches a state of rest at r_e and Y_e in time period t = n in Fig. 11.24.

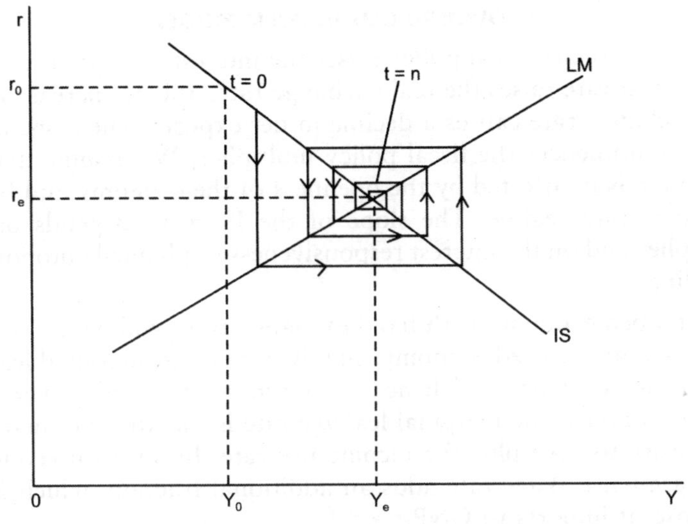

Fig. 11.24

The equilibrium path in Fig. 11.24 looks like a cobweb, hence the name "Cobweb equilibrium". The intersection of the IS and LM curves gives equilibrium solutions for r and Y because there are forces that drive these variables to equilibrium. Although the IS/LM Cobweb equilibrium process may be more difficult to understand than the micro supply and demand equilibrium process, it is conceptually identical.

However, the Cobweb equilibrium process is not widely accepted, because the most economists feel that the sequential market clearing assumption is incorrect. After all, there is no reason why the money and goods market must clear in alternating order. Furthermore, the model generates a pattern for the endogenous variables that is not observed. From an initial equilibrium, as shown in Fig. 11.23, an increase in the money supply in time period t = 0 would generate the following changes—a large decrease in r, while Y remained constant (in t = 1); then a large increase in Y, while r remained constant (in t = 2); then a large increase in r, while Y remained constant (in t = 3); then a large decrease in Y, while r remained constant (in t = 4); and so on. Such a pattern in r and Y is not empirically observed. Although not widely accepted, the Cobweb equilibrium process is a theoretical possibility. It helps to understand the IS/LM model and explain a possible rationale for why IS = LM generates the (r_e, Y_e) combination.

CROWDING OUT IN IS/LM MODEL

Expansionary fiscal policy raises the interest rate, an increase in the interest rate raises the real exchange rate, and an increase in the real exchange rate causes a decline in net exports. The slope of the IS curve influences the fiscal policy multiplier. We assume that the LM curve is unaffected by the openness of the economy and by the exchange rate regime. The slope of the IS curve depends on the multiplier and on the interest responsiveness of planned autonomous spending.

An open economy with fixed exchange rates will have a steeper IS curve than a closed economy, simply because its marginal leakage rate must be higher and hence its multiplier must be lower. In a closed economy, the marginal leakage rate is the after-tax marginal propensity to save plus the income tax rate. In an open economy, the marginal leakage rate adds an additional fraction, which is the response of imports to GNP.

The analysis of the crowding-out effect shows that a flat IS curve leads to a reduction in private spending in response to a higher interest rate. Thus, crowding out increases and the fiscal policy multiplier decreases. In an open economy with fixed exchange rates, however, the marginal leakage rate must be higher than in a closed economy, since there is an added leakage from the circular flow into imports. Hence, in an open economy with fixed exchange rates the IS curve is steeper, the crowding out effect is smaller, and the fiscal policy multiplier is larger than in a closed economy. This can be shown by the Fig. 11.25.

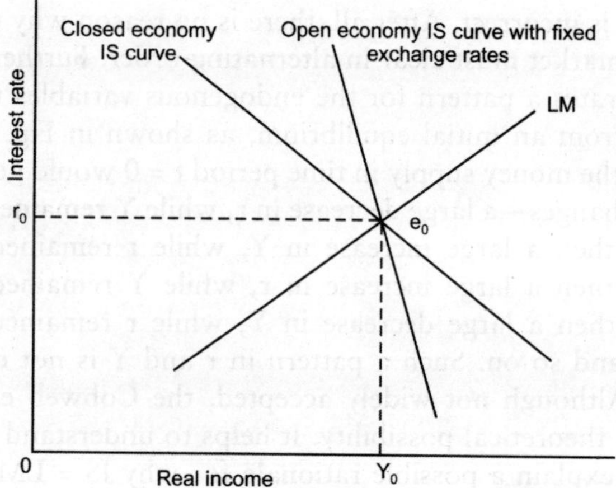

Fig. 11.25

However, the opposite effect occurs when an open economy shifts from a fixed exchange rate system to a flexible exchange rate system, as shown in Fig. 11.26.

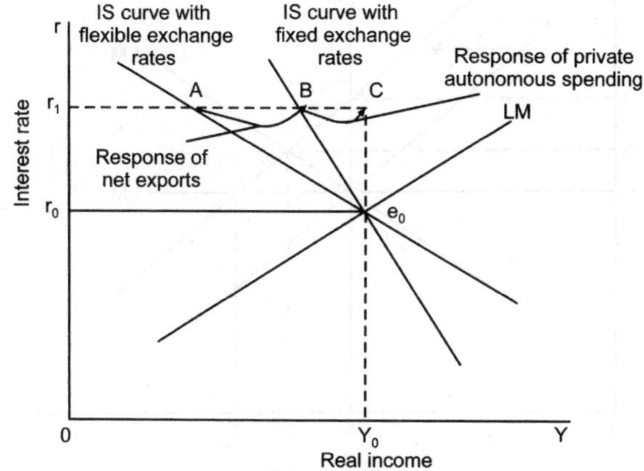

Fig. 11.26

We consider an assumed increase in interest rates and examine the crowding out effect along the new IS curve. The distance BC denotes the crowding out effect resulting from an increase in the interest rate from r_0 to r_1, with a fixed exchange rate. BC indicates the response of private autonomous spending to the higher interest rate. But with flexible exchange rates, higher interest rates also cause an appreciation of the foreign exchange rate and a reduction in net exports. This impact on net exports is shown by the distance between A and B.

Thus, a fiscal policy stimulus creates both a domestic and international crowding out effect in an open economy with flexible exchange rates. The international crowding out effect is the distance AB, the domestic effect is BC. Comparing the figures (11.25) and (11.26) we can find out whether the crowding out effect in the open economy with flexible exchange rates is larger or smaller than in the closed economy. The switch from fixed to flexible exchange rates has led to a flatter IS curve, a reduced fiscal policy multiplier, and an increased importance of the crowding out effect.

When the LM curve is less than perfectly elastic, expansionary fiscal policy will lead to some degree of financial "crowding out". In essence, the steeper the LM curve, the more crowding out will take place. Fig. 11.27 depicts what happens when a rightward shift in the IS curve takes place under different assumptions about the elasticity of the LM curve.

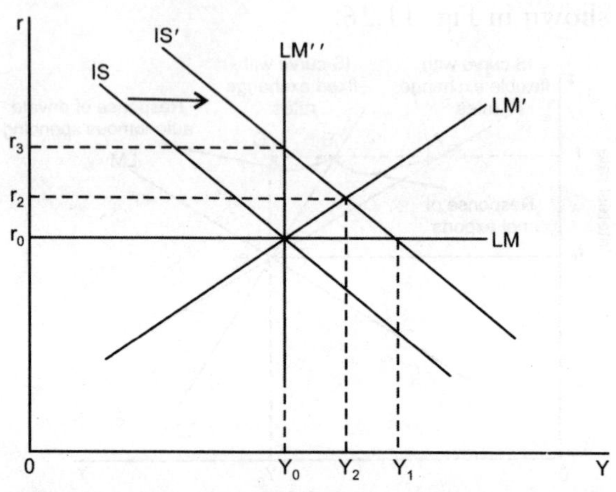

Fig. 11.27

Financial crowding out occurs where a rise in the interest rate leads to a reduction in private investment. How much crowding out occurs depends on the slope of the LM and IS curves.

Suppose that Government increases fiscal spending, as shown by a rightward shift from IS to IS′. If the LM curve is horizontal, no crowding out takes place and national income rises from Y_0 to Y_1. In the case of vertical LM curve (represented by LM″), there is full crowding out—fiscal policy is totally ineffective and national income does not rise. In the intermediate case (shown by LM′), national income will rise from Y_0 to Y_2 and there is 'partial' financial crowding out.

Increased fiscal spending, unless accompanied by a loosening of monetary policy, leads to a rise in interest rates. This rise causes private investment to contract. Thus, fiscal expansion by the public sector is offset by a contraction of investment in the private sector, an effect, which results in national income growing less than it would have had the rate of interest not risen. In general the steeper the LM curve, the more crowding out takes place. Crowding out will be strongest close to full-employment where the LM segment is steepest. Full crowding out (or a vertical LM curve) means that an increase in aggregate demand brought about by increased Government spending causes such a rise in the interest rate that private investment falls by an amount that exactly offsets the expansionary effect of the initial change in government expenditure.

Financial crowding out via the interest rate mechanism is only one potential form of crowding out. If foreign exchange is scarce or rationed and if private and public investment, more public spending might use up foreign exchange thus limiting its availability to the private sector, i.e., foreign exchange crowding out.

If an investment licensing system exists, more public investment might mean a reduction in the licences available to the private sector, i.e., administrative crowding out.

Full financial crowding out case seems unlikely to occur in practice. Whether increased fiscal expenditure leads to an interest rate rise depends on how it is financed. Even if increased Government expenditure is financed by borrowing from the non-bank public, rising domestic interest rates may serve to attract overseas capital. Full crowding out is unlikely because the private sector investment decision does not depend on the interest rate alone but on a variety of factors, crucially it depends on entrepreneurial expectations about the buoyancy of future demand.

Increased public spending, as Keynes argued, may serve to stimulate aggregate demand, raise incomes and improve the economic outlook in a manner leading entrepreneurs to invest more, not less. This is called the "crowding in" argument. The argument for "crowding in" gains greater force where public spending is directed at improving the economic and social infrastructure in a manner, which complements private investment, an argument put forward in the early economic development literature by such writers as Nurkse and Gershenkron. While there may be good reasons for limiting public spending, particularly where it is likely to contribute to inflation, the argument for strong "crowding out" is not terribly convincing. Policy makers often use the concept in contradictory ways. One example is that of the European Central Bank (ECB). The ECB currently argues—(a) that public spending must not be increased because it might lead to "crowding out"; and (b) that interest rates must remain high because of the danger of inflation.

POLICY ANALYSIS WITH IS/LM MODEL

In this section we shall use the IS/LM model to analyse the effects of various policy actions on the equilibrium levels of income and the interest rate. As we know from the previous section of this chapter that equilibrium levels of income and the interest rate are those given by the intersection of the IS and LM curves and the factors that change these equilibrium levels are those that shift either the IS or the LM curve. In this section, we shall consider how such shifts affect income and the interest rate when we consider the two schedules together. We also consider how the magnitude of the effects of different policies depends on the slopes of the IS and LM curves. The slopes of the IS/LM curves depend on various features of the economic system, the most important being the interest sensitivity of investment and of money demand.

Monetary policy in the IS/LM model refers to the alteration of the (nominal) money supply by the Reserve Bank. The money supply is regarded as exogenous and hence as directly controllable by the monetary authorities. Although the discussion of monetary policy is limited in the IS/LM framework, it nevertheless allows some basic exploration of the economic impact of an expanding or contracting money supply. Whereas fiscal policy is the management of the government's budget (which consists of inflows of tax revenue and outflows of expenditure) in order to affect the level and composition of aggregate demand in the economy.

In the 1950s the Keynesian idea of using monetary and fiscal policy instruments to influence aggregate demand gradually gained widespread acceptance by policy-makers in industrial economies. The reason was if the instruments of demand management (including government expenditure, tax rates, and the money supply) have predictable effects on the level of aggregate demand, then they can be used to offset fluctuations in demand originating in the private sector, and hence keep aggregate demand close to that required to induce the full employment level of output. If the behaviour of the economy is sufficiently predictable, it is possible to react in a discretionary way to private sector demand disturbances. In this context, fluctuations in private consumption and particularly investment were interpreted as disturbance, which could be offset by an active demand management policy.

Friedman argued instead that active demand management policies could be destabilising. His argument was not so much that the policy-maker could only influence the economy after some delay. It was, rather, that knowledge of the economy was so imprecise that demand management policy may actually destabilise the economy, rather than having its desired effect. For example, the authorities may observe that the economy is in a period with excess demand, and seek to exert a contractionary influence by using the instruments at their disposal. The problem is that, unless the size and timing of the effects of the policy instruments are known with a reasonable degree of precision, the authorities may end up contracting the economy just at the time when the inflationary period would have abated in any case. In this situation, policy only succeeds in deepening the contraction and making the fluctuations more extreme than they otherwise would have been.

When analysing policy issues, it is often necessary to distinguish between the impact of action taken by policy-makers and the effects of changes originating elsewhere in the economy. This distinction is the basis for the notion of a policy instrument, a variable under the direct control of the policy-maker. Authorities can control the real world counterparts to these variables. Let us consider taxes as an example. Total real net tax collections have a lump-sum component and an endogenous component, so it is clear that tax collections are not a policy instrument because changes in household disposable income result in changes in revenue even though the policy instruments, lump-sum taxes and marginal tax rate, are unchanged. Income tax law, for instance, applies a schedule of income tax rates to nominal incomes. This has the implication that, if nominal income changes by the same proportion as prices, real tax rates change because of the so-called 'tax creep' effect. Here one point should be considered that real tax collections change, not because of an intended change by policy-makers, but because of an endogenous reaction to endogenous variables in the system. Of course, tax creep does not arise in a model where prices are assumed to be fixed.

If the Reserve Bank operates monetary policy by controlling the money supply, then the instrument, which is directly under the control of the Reserve Bank, is the monetary base, since this comprises liabilities of the Reserve Bank. However, in an economy with private banks, the money supply comprises not only liabilities of the Reserve Bank, but also liabilities of the private banks. The money supply is only a policy instrument if, in response to changes in the monetary base, bank deposits changes in a perfectly predictable way.

Real Influences

Fiscal policy variables are one set of factors that shift the IS schedule and hence affect equilibrium income and the interest rate. Let consider an increase in government spending as one of the fiscal policy instruments. Fig. 11.28 depicts this situation.

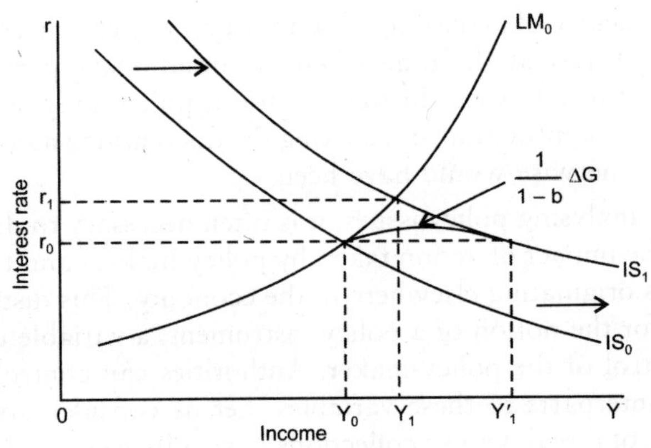

Fig. 11.28

The increase in government spending shifts the IS schedule out to the right. The equilibrium level of income rises, as does the equilibrium level of the interest rate. The force pushing up the level of income is the increase in aggregate demand both directly as government demand rises and then indirectly as a result of an income-induced increase in consumer expenditures. Here one point should be noticed that the LM schedule does not shift. At a given level of income, equilibrium in the money market, and therefore in the bond market, is undisturbed by the government spending change. It is the rise in income in response to the fiscal policy shift that necessitates the interest rate adjustment. As income increases, the transaction demand for money rises. The money stock is not changed, so the attempt to increase transactions balances requires a decline in the demand for bonds. It is this income-induced increase in money demand and decline in bond demand that causes the interest rate to rise. In the aggregate, the public cannot increase money holdings; the money stock is fixed. This will push up the interest rate, reducing the speculative demand for money and causing individuals to economise on the amount of transactions balances held for any level of income. At the new equilibrium the interest rate must rise sufficiently that net money demand is unchanged even though income is higher.

Now consider the effect of tax on the equilibrium level of income and interest rate. Let us consider an increase in tax rate. This will shift the IS curve to the left which can be depicted in Fig. 11.29.

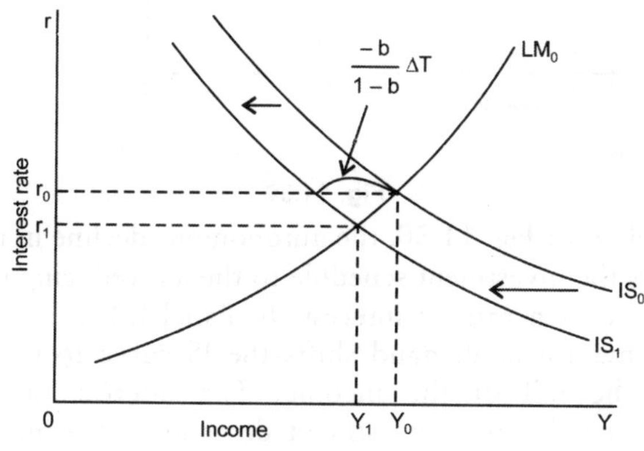

Fig. 11.29

In Fig. 11.29, we see, because of taxes, income and interest rate decline. Income declines as taxes rise because the tax increase lowers disposable income and causes consumption to decline. As income declines as a result of the tax increase, money demand declines and bond demand increases. This causes the interest rate to fall.

A decrease in taxes has just the opposite effects of the tax increase. The IS curve shift to the right, and both income and interest rate rise. Fiscal policy variables are not only the factors that can shift the IS curve. Any autonomous change in aggregate demand will have the effect. Let us consider the effect of an autonomous change in investment demand. By an autonomous change in investment demand, we mean a shift in the function giving the level of investment for each level of the interest rate. Such a change would occur if as a result of some exogenous event, the expected profitability of investment project changed. We will describe this condition in Fig. 11.30.

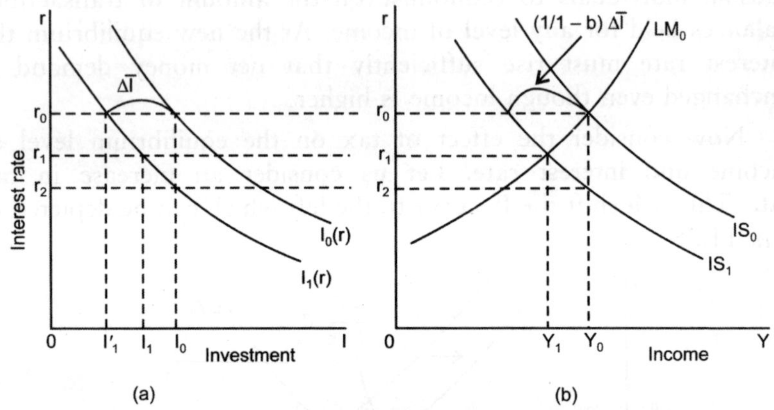

Fig. 11.30

In Panel (a) of Fig. 11.30, the autonomous decline in investment of $\Delta\bar{I}$ shifts the investment schedule to the left reducing the level of investment at each rate of interest. In Panel (b), the autonomous decline in investment demand shifts the IS curve to the left. This results in the fall of the income. The interest rate declines. Income declines because investment demand at the initial interest rate has fallen. As income falls, an income-induced decline in consumption spending also occurs. The interest rate decline is also income-induced, as was the case when we considered the interest rate effects of fiscal policy changes. The decline in income causes money demand to fall and bond demand to rise; consequently, the interest rate falls. Here one point should be noticed that the decline in the interest rate causes investment to return somewhat toward its initial level. At new equilibrium, investment demand is at I_1, having increased from I'_1 to I_1 as a result of the decline in the interest rate.

The IS/LM model includes the money market, while there is no such money market in the simple Keynesian model. When government-spending increases, the rate of interest must rise to maintain equilibrium in the money market. The increase in the interest rate will cause a decline in investment spending. The decline in investment spending will partially offset the increase in aggregate demand resulting from the increase in government spending.

Consequently, the increase in income will be less than that in the simple Keynesian model, where investment was taken as completely autonomous. By neglecting the necessary increase in the interest rate and consequent decline in investment that accompany an increase in government spending, the simple Keynesian model overstated the effect of an increase in government expenditure.

In the IS/LM curve version of the Keynesian model, the interest rate played a stabilising role such that a change in investment demand did not affect aggregate demand. The interest rate fell sufficiently to restore aggregate demand to its initial level. Whereas in the IS/LM model the interest rate adjustment is stabilizing but incomplete. For income to be unchanged with an autonomous decline in investment, the interest rate would have to fall to the level, where income would be at the original level along the new IS curve.

Measures of the Fiscal Surplus

The starting point for any measure of the demand management stance of fiscal policy must be a view of the process by which fiscal policy works. In other words, such a measure must be based on a model of some kind. In the IS/LM model, a natural definition of fiscal stimulus or contraction is provided by the degree to which changes in fiscal instruments shift the IS curve. Clearly, it is not the level but the changes in fiscal surplus, which is proposed as an indicator of fiscal stimulus.

The change in the fiscal surplus is not, of itself, a particularly good indicator of the shifts in the IS curve. The fiscal surplus is endogenous, so that changes in private sector demand, in addition to changes in fiscal instruments, have an influence on the actual value of fiscal surplus. Because shifts in the IS curve reflect exogenous changes, endogenous variations in fiscal surplus are clearly not a very useful indicator of fiscal stance. To avoid this 'endogeneity' problem, a common procedure has been to evaluate changes in fiscal surplus at a given level of output. This can be better illustrated with Fig. 11.31.

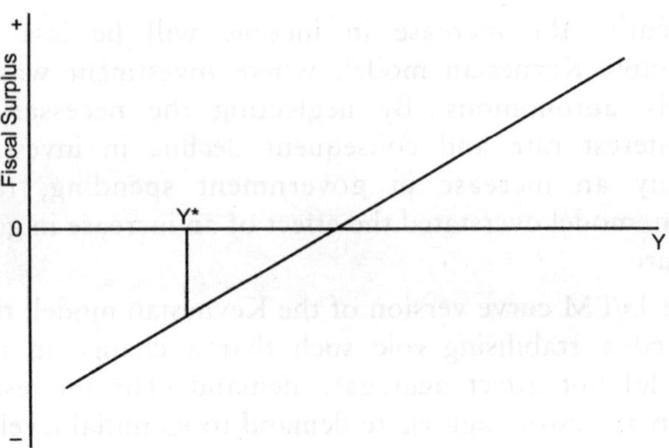

Fig. 11.31

The fiscal surplus line is upward sloping, reflecting increases in taxes, and reduction in welfare payments, as income increases. Let us consider Y* is some benchmark level of output. If changes in fiscal surplus are measured at this benchmark level, it allows the analyst to distinguish between changes in policy, which shift the fiscal surplus curve, from movements along the curve resulting from cyclical fluctuations in economic activity.

Benchmark output is taken to be a 'normal' or 'high employment' level. In the process of cyclical adjustment the main components of expenditures, transfers and tax receipts are adjusted to levels, which would have applied had output been at its normal level. This approach presumes that the analyst is able to establish a consistent measure of normal output and how it evolves over time.

In order to generate equal shifts in the IS curve, a cut in lump-sum taxes must be (1/MPC) times larger than an increase in government expenditure. Hence, a comparison between two fiscal impacts measures, as shown in Fig. 11.32, can be misleading.

The measure shown in Fig. 11.32 can be taken to indicate that the cyclically adjusted effect of the tax cut is larger than for the increase in government consumption. But these changes to fiscal instruments have the same short-run impact on aggregate demand. As the comparison between lump-sum taxes and government expenditures implies, each of the different instruments must be weighted (with the weight reflecting its initial impact on aggregate demand) before inferences can be drawn as to the effects of changes in the fiscal surplus.

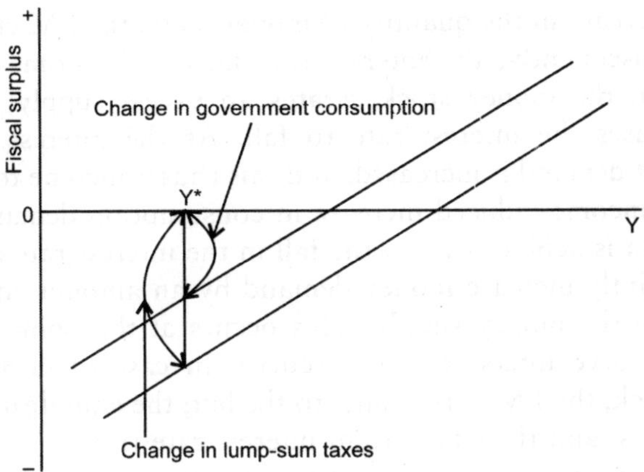

Fig. 11.32

A measure of fiscal impact must always be based on a model. So even after the adjustment indicated above, it is important to remember that these measures are only useful if the IS/LM model itself gives a reasonably accurate account of the way the economy behaves. In practice, both policy-makers and private-sector economists use more complex models to analyse the effects of policy. One important extension is to take into account open-economy aspects of the problem. The 'perfectly elastic supply' version of the IS/LM model also implies that variation in fiscal policy are not the only means by which policy can be used to influence aggregate demand.

Monetary Influences

Suppose the quantity of money supply increases. Fig. 11.33 illustrates the effects of an increase in the quantity of money.

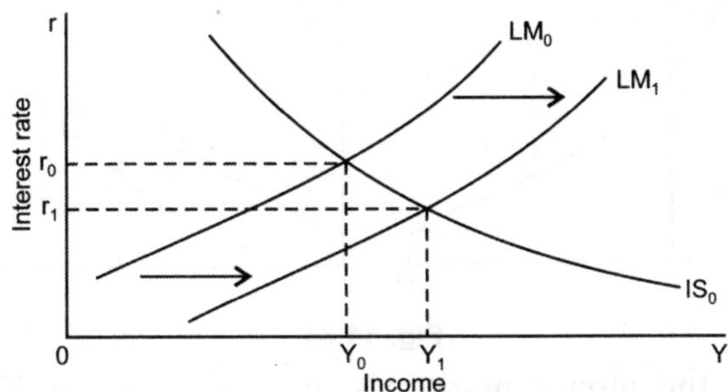

Fig. 11.33

An increase in the quantity of money shifts the LM curve to the right. Consequently, the interest rate falls and income rises. The increase in the money stock creates an excess supply of money, which causes the interest rate to fall. As the interest rate falls, investment demand is increased, and this causes income to rise, with a further income-induced increase in consumption demand. A new equilibrium is achieved when the fall in the interest rate and rise in income jointly increase money demand by an amount equal to the increase in the money supply. This occurs at the point where the new LM curve intersects the IS curve. In case of decline in the money stock, the LM curve shifts to the left; the equilibrium level of income falls; and the equilibrium interest rate rises.

A shift in the money demand function has also an effect on the LM curve. Let us consider an increase in money demand for given levels of income and the interest rate. Such a portfolio shift away from bonds into money will shift the LM curve to the left and the interest rate will rise. The higher interest rate will cause income to decline. An increase in money demand, in the sense of a shift in the function such that more money is demanded at a given level of income and interest rate, has the same effect as a decline in the money stock. Equilibrium income falls and the interest rate rises.

An open market transaction induces the private sector to change the composition of the assets it holds, a process known as portfolio substitution. Changes in the private sector asset portfolio are, in turn, reflected by a shift in the LM curve. Fig. 11.34 illustrates the process.

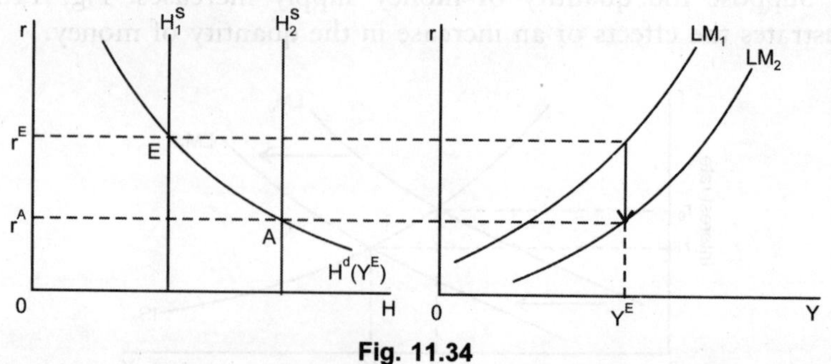

Fig. 11.34

Initially the money market is in equilibrium at Y^E, r^E. The money supply is given by H_1^s, and is equal to money demand. If Y^E

is a goods market equilibrium value, the bond market must also be in equilibrium by Walras's law. Now suppose that an open market operation bond purchase is made by the Reserve Bank, shifting the money supply schedule to the right. In order to execute the bond purchase, the Bank offers a higher bond price, so that the interest rate falls because of the inverse relation between the bond price and the interest rate. The interest rate at which asset market equilibrium is restored is r^A, and the LM curve shifts down so that at A asset markets are again in equilibrium. The amount of the downward shift of the LM curve depends on the size of the interest effect on the demand for money.

If the 'liquidity trap' situation applies, an expansion in the money supply is an ineffectual mechanism for demand expansion in the IS/LM model. Unless the interest rate can be made to fall, private-sector investment demand does not increase.[1] This reasoning underlay Keynes's advocacy of the use of fiscal rather than monetary policy as an instrument for demand expansion. But more usually, the short-run closed economy IS/LM model with static price expectations suggests that a monetary expansion can induce a fall in the interest rate and an expansion in demand.

The increase in income and reduction in the interest rate depend on all the relationships in the system. The ratio of the change in income to the change in the interest rate is determined by the slope of the IS curve, because the LM curve shifts down while the IS curve is unchanged. Fig. 11.35 provides a diagrammatic illustration.

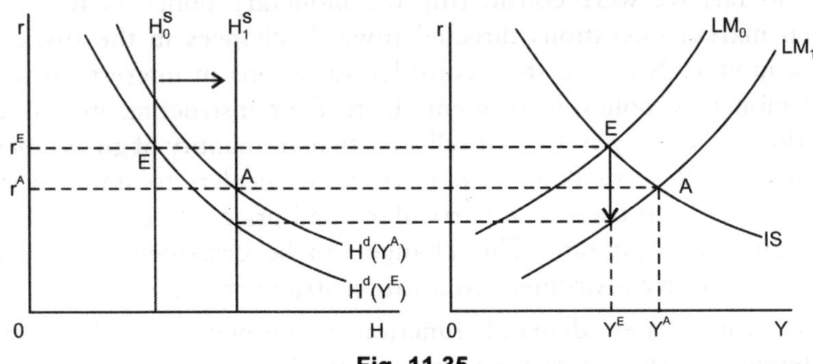

Fig. 11.35

The economy is initially in equilibrium represented by the point E in both panels of the Fig. 11.35. Monetary expansion shifts the money supply schedule to the right, and shifts the LM curve. Now, however, the fall in interest rate induces an increase in investment expenditure, which increases output. As income and expenditure increase, transaction demand for money by both households and firms increases, shifting the money demand curve to the right. Here we find that

(a) the greater the shift in the LM curve,
(b) the smaller the income effect on the demand for money, and
(c) the flatter the IS schedule, the larger is the expansionary effect of an open market bond purchase.

So long as the monetary expansion induces an increase in income, the result of the wealth effects is unambiguous—both income and wealth increase. The open market operation results in a substitution between money and bonds, and an increase in the capital stock. Private-sector wealth increases. The crucial issue here is whether, after various revisions to the IS/LM model, a monetary expansion can actually reduce the real interest rate. In small open economies with no restrictions of international borrowing and lending, the real interest rate is, in the long-run, strongly influenced by international markets. There must be some doubt as to whether domestic monetary policy influences investment through the real interest rate mechanism which plays a central role in the IS/LM model.

Monetary Instrument under Uncertainty

So far, we were considering the monetary policy in terms of open market operations directed towards changes in the stock of base money. Now we shall consider variations in interest rates as the monetary policy instrument. Instead of instructing its money market traders to purchase or sell a particular quantity of government bonds, the Reserve Bank now instructs its dealers to stand in the market ready to trade at a particular bond price, or equivalently, a particular interest rate. This change can be described as a move from a quantity instrument to a rate instrument.

If the money demand function is known, it makes little difference to the interest rate/money stock outcome when money supply or interest rate is chosen as the monetary instrument. Fig. 11.36 shows the consequences of a Reserve Bank decision to lower interest rates.

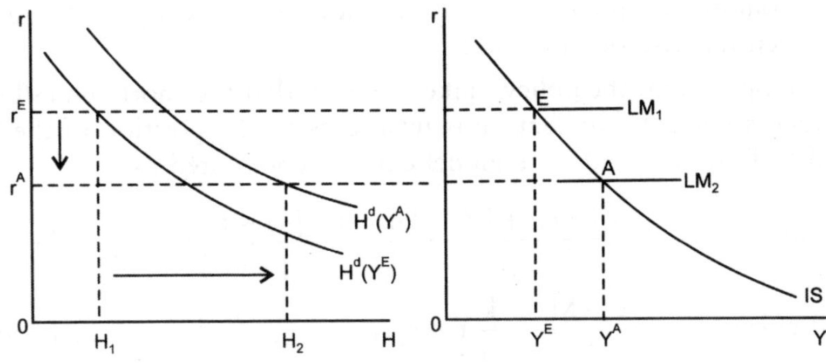

Fig. 11.36

Starting in equilibrium, the Reserve Bank announces that it stands ready to buy and sell bonds at the higher price, which corresponds to the lower nominal interest rate. In effect, trade in bonds at this price is combined with a decision to supply base money with perfect elasticity. The quantity of money demanded, then determines the money stock, which is willingly held at Y^E and the lower interest rate.

General equilibrium consequences of the lower interest rate (assuming static price expectations) are traced out in the right-hand panel of the Fig. 11.36. For given investors' expectations, a lower interest rate stimulates investment demand, increasing output and income. This process is reflected by a movement along the IS curve, from E to A. In turn higher income and hence transaction demand for money leads to an increase in the money stock from H_1 to H_2. Since the money supply is perfectly elastic, the Reserve Bank's monetary policy just involves choosing a point on the IS curve. The money stock is demand determined.

Now we shall develop two approaches to the choice between monetary policy instruments—(a) In the first, it is assumed that output supply is perfectly elastic, prices are fixed and price expectations are static. (b) In the second, we consider the alternative polar case, where the economy is at the natural rate of output, prices are flexible, and expectations are endogenous. Both are based on the closed economy IS/LM framework.

In a situation where policy-makers have complete certainty about the structure of the macroeconomy, there is little to choose between the use of an interest rate instrument and a base money instrument. However, in the case of uncertainty in the structure of the economy, economists have to face a lot of difficulty in choosing between macroeconomic models.

Suppose that the policy-maker believes that the short-run IS/LM model is correct, but that he is unsure as to the position of the IS and LM curves. Thus, the model can be represented as

$$\text{IS curve,} \quad r = \frac{\alpha_C + \alpha_I + GC + GI}{\mu} - \frac{1-\beta(1-\tau)}{\mu}Y + \varepsilon_{IS} \quad \text{...(11.57)}$$

$$\text{LM curve,} \quad r = \frac{\bar{L} - \bar{M}^S}{h} + \frac{k}{h}Y + \varepsilon_{LM} \quad \text{...(11.58)}$$

The disturbance terms (epsilon) in each of the equation reflect a limited amount of uncertainty. Here, the slopes of the IS and LM schedules are known for certain, but elements of the intercept term can vary in a random way. A positive value for ε_{IS} could reflect a positive disturbance to either α_C or α_I. For example, an unforeseen improvement in investors' expectations results in a positive value for the IS disturbance. Similarly, a negative value for ε_{LM} reflects a negative disturbance to the intercept in the money demand function.[2]

In an IS/LM diagram, a positive real disturbance shifts the IS curve upwards; a negative value for ε_{IS} shifts the IS curve downwards. Similarly, nominal disturbances shift the LM curve. The average value of the disturbance terms is zero, and in this sense the solid lines in Fig. 11.37 represent the expected position of the IS and LM curves. The dotted lines indicate IS and LM curves for particular values of the disturbances.

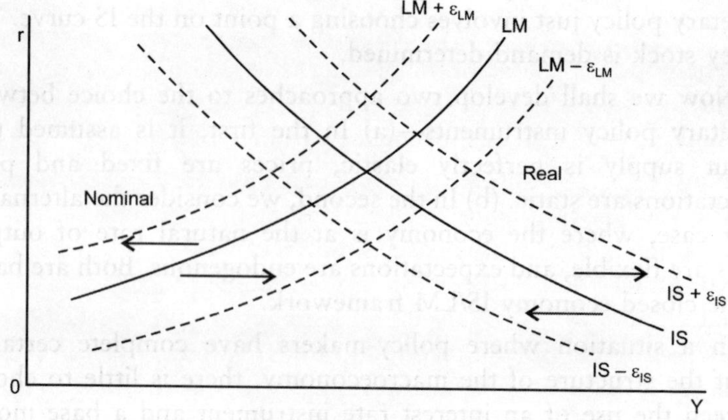

Fig. 11.37

Now suppose that nominal shocks are small relative to real shocks. This situation can be represented by Fig. 11.38. The dotted line in this figure lie close to the expected position of the LM curve, but there is a wide band of variation around the expected IS curve. If the Reserve Bank chooses an interest rate instrument, there are two possible outcomes for output, given by Y_1 and Y_2. In this situation, variation in money demand is irrelevant because base money is supplied elastically. If a base money instrument is chosen, the four outcomes are possible. For example, Y_5 corresponds to the simultaneous occurrence of both a negative real and nominal disturbance. The other three outcomes represent alternative combinations of disturbances.

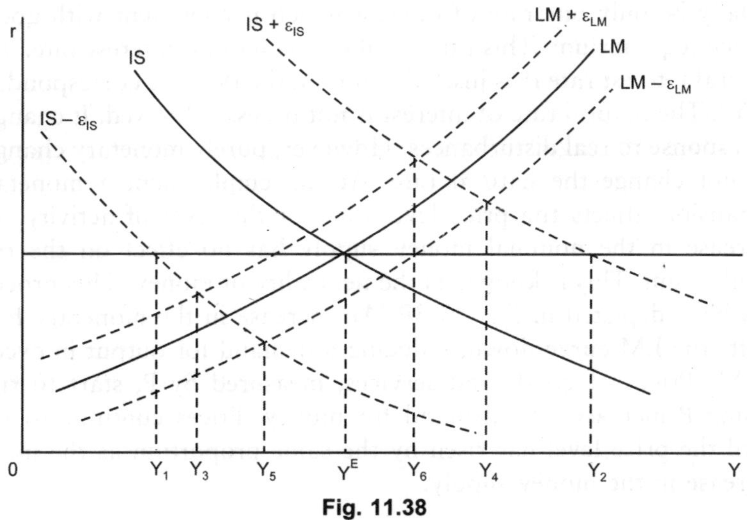

Fig. 11.38

The policy objective of the planner is to stabilise output, to keep output as close as possible to Y^E. The policy-maker prefers the instrument, which gives the smaller variance of output.

Now we shall consider the choice of monetary instruments in a situation where the economy is initially at full capacity output and prices are flexible. In this case, simply comparing the variance of output under alternative monetary instruments provides only a partial picture. We must also analyse policy from the point of view of the stability of the economy under alternative choices of policy rule. Explicit analysis of stability fills an important gap in comparative static experiments. A comparative static experiment comprises three parts—(a) first an initial equilibrium is described, (b) then a shock, which may be a change in a policy variable or an exogenous variable, is postulated, (c) finally, the new equilibrium is described.

The comparison between the new and old equilibria provides information regarding the effects of the shock on an economy of the type described by the model. This technique is very useful, but it relies on the assumption that the economy's adjustment process following the shock does in fact lead to a stable convergence to the new equilibrium.

Initially we shall consider a closed economy with static price expectations. If the economy is at full employment Y^n, there will usually be only one rate of interest which is consistent with goods market equilibrium. This rate is called the natural interest rate. The natural interest rate r^n is just the point on the IS curve corresponding to Y^n. The natural rate of interest is not necessarily fixed. It changes in response to real disturbances. However, purely monetary changes do not change the natural rate. At full employment a monetary expansion affects the price level but not the level of activity. An increase in the nominal money supply has no effect on the real equilibrium. This is known as the neutrality of money. This process has been depicted in Fig. 11.39. An increase in the monetary base shifts the LM curve down, inducing a demand for output in excess of Y^n. Prices of goods and services, measured by P, start to rise. Rising P increases the demand for money. Prices continue to rise until the price level has risen by the same proportion as the initial increase in the money supply.

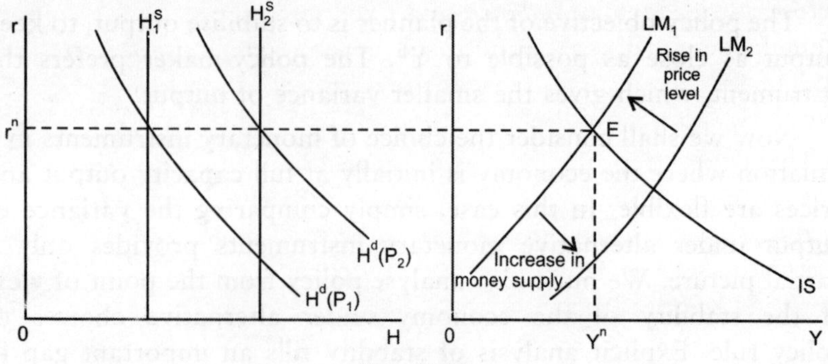

Fig. 11.39

Let us assume static price expectations, a closed economy and an initial full employment equilibrium. Now suppose that the propensity to save falls, so that the IS schedule shifts to the right. This implies an increase in the natural interest rate as shown in Fig. 11.40.

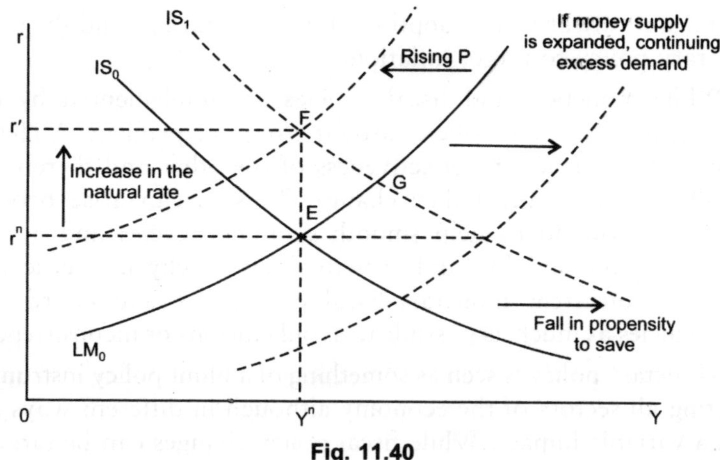

Fig. 11.40

If the monetary base is held fixed in nominal terms, the temporary equilibrium at G implies excess demand for goods, and the price level rises with consequent falls in the real money supply. The rising price level eventually leads to a restoration of equilibrium at F.

Now suppose that the Reserve Bank wishes to maintain the original interest rate. Since we have assumed static price expectations, it is not necessary to distinguish between the real and nominal interest rates. The maintenance of a fixed interest rate requires that nominal money supply be increased by more than the increase in prices in an attempt to increase the real money supply, and hence to drive the interest rate down.

The assumption of static price expectations can be sustained in the case of inflation because it implies that the private sector continually make forecasting errors. A better account is considering the situation where inflation expectations are formed adaptively.

EFFECTIVENESS OF MONETARY AND FISCAL POLICY

There has been a major shift within macroeconomic policy over the past two decades or so in terms of the relative importance given in both policy and theoretical terms to monetary policy and to fiscal policy with the former gaining considerably in importance, and the latter being rarely mentioned. Furthermore, the nature of monetary policy has shifted away from any attempt to control some monetary aggregate, and instead monetary policy has focused on the setting of interest rates as the key policy instrument. There has also been a general shift towards the adoption of inflation targets and the use of monetary policy to target inflation.

While monetary and fiscal policies are implemented by two different bodies, these policies are far from independent. A change in one will influence the effectiveness of the other and thereby the overall impact of any policy change. Tension can arise between what each will do to help smooth economic cycles and achieve macroeconomic stability and growth. That is why it is crucial to pursue a consistent monetary-fiscal policy mix and coordinates these policies as much as possible to avoid tensions or inconsistencies.

Monetary policy is seen as something of a blunt policy instrument affecting all sectors of the economy although in different ways and with a variable impact. While fiscal policy changes can be targeted to affect certain groups (e.g. increases in means-tested benefits for low income households, reductions in the rate of corporation tax for small-medium sized enterprises, investment allowances for businesses in certain regions).

While Keynesian in structure with its use of the IS and LM schedules, the Mundell-Fleming model carried a non-Keynesian lesson for a flexible exchange rate regime, that monetary policy is effective and fiscal policy is not. The reasoning goes as follows—with perfectly elastic capital flows, beginning from balanced trade and a position of less than full employment, an increase in the money supply increases output, which generates a trade deficit; the trade deficit is instantaneously eliminated by depreciation of the exchange rate, which via exports and imports generates the effective demand to bring an equilibrium in product and money markets. In contrast, an increase in government expenditure instantaneously places upward pressure on the domestic interest rate, which results in an appreciation of the currency to cancel the fiscal expansion.[3] While these two conclusions are based on the extreme assumption of perfect capital flows, it is typical to present them as the general lesson: fiscal policy is effective with a fixed exchange rate and ineffective with a flexible rate, and the opposite holds for monetary policy.[4]

Whether a fiscal policy actions are effective or not, we compare the effect of the policy action on income with the effect predicted by the simple Keynesian model. In moving the IS/LM curve model, we add a money market to the Keynesian system. By comparing the effect of fiscal policy in the IS/LM model with the effect in the simple Keynesian system, where fiscal policy variables are major determinants of income, we see how the addition of the money market modifies our previous result. The distance of the horizontal shift in the IS curve for a given fiscal policy action equals the effect on income in the simple Keynesian model. To evaluate the effectiveness of monetary policy, we compare the effect on income of the change in the money stock with the horizontal distance of the shift in the LM curve. The horizontal shift in the LM curve when the money stock changes, is equal to $\Delta M(1/c_1)$, where c_1 is the coefficient on income in the money demand function. The coefficient c_1 gives the amount of the increase in money demand per unit of income; therefore, $\Delta M(1/c_1)$ gives the increase in income that could occur for an increase in the money stock if all new money balances went to support increased transactions demand for money due to increased income. Now consider the Fig. 11.41.

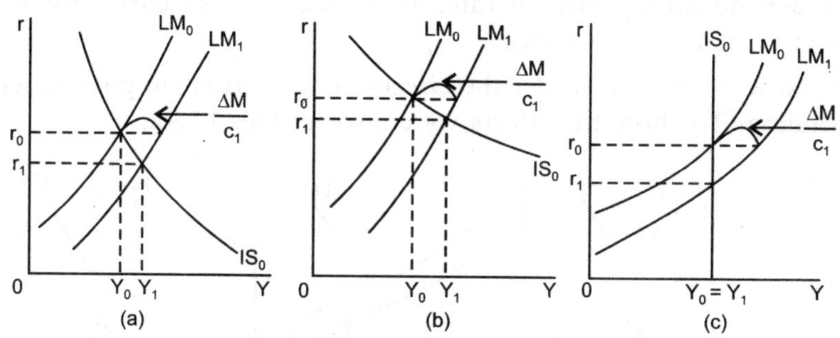

Fig. 11.41

In panel (a) of the Fig. 11.41, the IS curve is steep, reflecting a low interest elasticity of investment demand. In this case, monetary policy is relatively ineffective. Income rises very little because of the increase in the money stock. In panel (b), IS curve has been drawn much flatter, reflecting a higher interest elasticity of investment demand. In this case, income rises more than that of the previous case. Thus, the monetary policy becomes more effective when the IS curve is flatter. Within the IS/LM curve model, monetary policy affects income by lowering the interest rate and stimulating investment demand. If investment demand is little affected by interest rate changes, monetary policy will be ineffective. In panel (b), monetary policy has correspondingly greater effects due to the assumption of greater interest sensitivity.

The monetary policy is ineffective when the IS curve is steep, that is, when investment is interest-inelastic. Monetary policy is more effective the higher the interest elasticity of investment, and thus the flatter the IS curve.

The IS curve will be vertical if investment is completely insensitive to changes in the interest rate (interest elasticity equals zero). The effect of an increase in the money stock for this case has been shown in panel (c) of Fig. 11.41. If the IS curve is vertical, increasing the money stock simply shifts the LM curve down along the IS curve. The interest rate falls until money demand increases by enough to restore equilibrium in the money market, but income is unchanged. To increase income, the increase in the money stock and resulting fall in the interest rate must stimulate investment demand. When the IS curve is vertical, investment is not affected by monetary policy because, by assumption, investment demand does not depend on the interest rate. The steeper the IS curve, the less effective is monetary policy.

Now we shall consider the effects of an increase in government spending. To show the effects we construct Fig. 11.42.

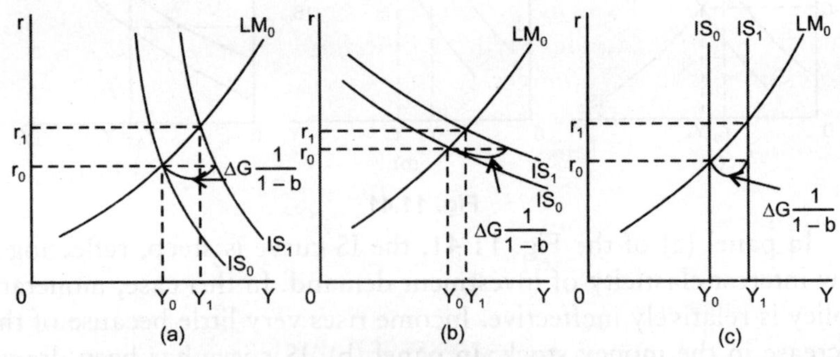

Fig. 11.42

In Fig. 11.42, the increase in government spending shifts the IS curve from IS_0 to IS_1. The horizontal distance of the shift in the curve, $\Delta G(1/(1-b))$ is the same in all the cases, meaning that the size of the policy action as well as the autonomous expenditure multiplier from the simple Keynesian model are equal in both the cases (a) and (b). Here we see that fiscal policy is much more effective where the IS curve is steep.

Interest inelastic investment leads to steep IS curve. The less sensitive investment is to the interest rate, the greater the effect of a given fiscal policy action is. As income increases following the rise in government spending, the interest rate must rise to keep the money market in equilibrium. This rise in the interest rate causes investment to decline, partially offsetting the expansionary effect of the government spending increase. It is this interest-rate-induced decline in investment that causes the income response in the IS/LM curve model to fall short of the response given by the multiplier from the simple Keynesian system; that is, income rises by less than the horizontal shift in the IS curve.

The effect of investment is referred to as "crowding out". One factor determining the importance of such crowding out of private investment is the slope of the IS curve. If investment is not very sensitive to change in the interest rate then the interest rate increase will cause only a slight drop in investment, and income will rise by almost the full amount of the horizontal shift in the IS curve. On the other hand, if the investment is highly interest sensitive then the rise in the interest rate will reduce investment substantially, and the increase in income will be reduced significantly relative to the prediction of the simple Keynesian model. In the case of vertical IS curve, investment is completely interest insensitive. The increase in government expenditure causes the interest rate to rise but this does not result in any decline in investment. Income increases by the full amount of the distance of the horizontal shift in the IS curve. In this case, due to crowding out of private investment the simple Keynesian model does not overstate the effects of fiscal policy.

A high interest elasticity of money demand causes the LM schedule to be relatively flat. At progressively lower values of the interest elasticity of money demand, the LM curve will become steeper. If money demand is completely insensitive to the interest rate, the LM curve will be vertical. Let us consider the Fig. 11.43.

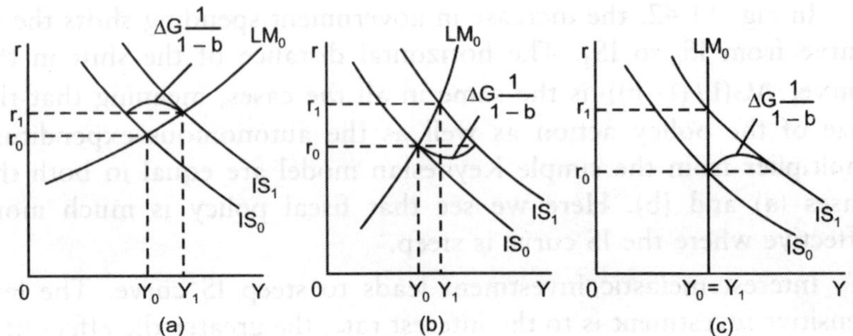

Fig. 11.43

In each panel the increase in government expenditure is assumed to shift the IS curve from IS_0 to IS_1. The slope of IS curve is assumed to be same in each panel of the figure. The size of the increase in government expenditure is also assumed to be the same in each case. From the figure, we find that the effect on income of this expansionary fiscal policy action is largest when the LM curve is relatively flat and less when the curve is relatively steep. In case of vertical LM curve, the increase in government expenditure has no effect on equilibrium income. Fiscal policy is seen to be most effective when the interest elasticity of money demand is high, making the LM curve relatively flat. The reason for this is that the increase in government spending causes income to rise and as income rises, the demand for transactions balance increases, and to re-equilibrate the money market with an unchanged stock of money requires a rise in the interest rate. The rise in the interest rate must lower the speculative demand for money and causes individuals and corporations to economise on the use of transaction balances. If money demand is highly sensitive to changes in the interest rate, only a small rise in the interest rate is required to restore equilibrium in the money market.

In Panel (a) of Fig. 11.43 we see that a small increase in the interest rate, other things being equal, leads to a small[5] decline in investment. With little crowding out of private investment, income rises by nearly the full amount of the horizontal shift in the IS curve. When money demand is relatively interest inelastic, a greater increase in the interest rate is required to re-equilibrate the money market as income rises. The larger increase in the interest rate leads to a larger decline in investment spending, offsetting more of the expansionary effect of the increase in government expenditure. Consequently, the increase in income for the steeper LM curve is a smaller proportion of the horizontal shift in the IS curve. In the case of complete inelastic money demand, only one level of income can be an equilibrium level—the level that generates transaction demand just equal to the fixed money stock. An increase in aggregate demand, caused by an increase in government spending, creates an upward pressure on income at a given interest rate. However, the attempt to increase income leads to an increased demand for transaction balances and causes the interest rate to rise.

Now consider the effects of an increase in the quantity of money for the LM curve. To describe this case consider Fig. 11.44.

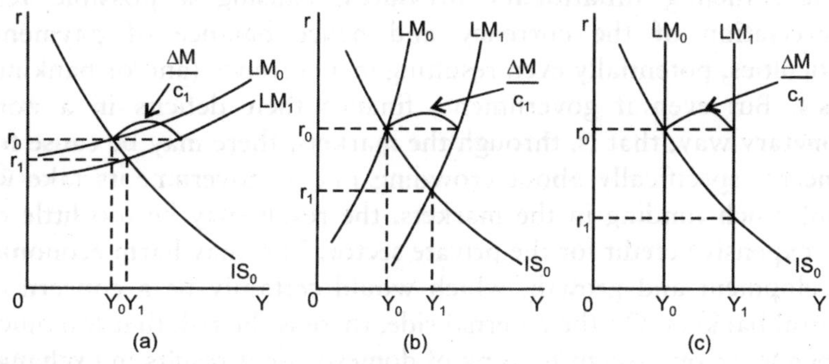

Fig. 11.44

In Fig. 11.44 we see that monetary policy is less effective in panel (a), where the LM curve is relatively flat reflecting high interest elasticity of money demand. The effect on income of the increase in the money stock is successively greater as we consider panel (b), where the interest elasticity of money demand is lower, and in panel (c), where the interest elasticity of money demand is zero and the LM curve is vertical. The reason for this can be explained as follows.

At the initial level of income and the interest rate the increase in the money stock will create an excess supply of money, causing the interest rate to fall. This fall in the interest rate will stimulate investment and, hence, income. The interest rate must decline to a point where the lower interest rate and higher income level have increased money demand by an amount equal to the increase in the money supply. In each part of Fig. 11.44, an increase in the money stock shifts the LM curve to the right from LM_0 to LM_1. Monetary policy is least effective in panel (a), where the LM curve is relatively flat; more effective in panel (b), where the LM curve is steeper; and most effective in panel (c), where the LM curve is vertical.

How does fiscal policy affect monetary policy? There are both direct and indirect channels. Starting with the first category, there are a number of ways in which fiscal policy may impinge on monetary policy. First and foremost, an expansionary fiscal policy may result in excessive fiscal deficits, which may create a strong temptation for governments to resort to the printing press (i.e., monetary financing by the central bank) to finance the deficits. An expansionary fiscal policy, then, leads to an expansionary monetary policy, fueling inflationary pressures, causing a possible real appreciation of the currency and hence balance of payments difficulties, potentially even resulting in a currency (and/or banking) crisis. But even if governments finance their deficits in a non-monetary way, that is, through the markets, there may be cause for concern, specifically about crowding out: if governments take up (too) much funding in the markets, the result may be too little or too expensive credit for the private sector. This may harm economic development and growth, which would certainly be a concern of central bankers. On the external side, there is the risk that too much dependence on foreign funding of domestic debt results in exchange rate and/or balance-of-payments risks, which again would be worrying to central banks.

There is another, more direct channel of fiscal policy affecting central bankers and that is the impact of indirect taxes on the price level and thus on inflation. If governments feel forced to resort to substantial increases in indirect taxes—sales taxes, value added taxes—rather than taxes on various forms of income, this will have a direct impact on prices. The key concern here is that an increase in one leads to a wage price spiral and therefore permanent (higher) inflation and inflationary expectations.

In addition to these direct relationships between fiscal and monetary policy, there is the more indirect channel through expectations. Perceptions and expectations of large and on-going budget deficits and resulting large borrowing requirements may trigger a lack of confidence in the economic prospects. This may become a risk to the stability in financial markets. Such a lack of confidence in the sustainability of the financial position of the government may become a potential destabilizing factor on bond and foreign exchange markets, eventually even leading to the collapse of the monetary regime.

NOTES

1. If money is counted as part of private-sector wealth, the wealth effect may increase consumption demand in the following period. The Keynesian view is that these wealth effects are small.
2. In a more general model with a private banking system, disturbance to the LM schedule also arise from changes in bank lending and deposit taking behaviour.
3. Peter B. Kenen gives the following summary:

   Fiscal and monetary policy under a flexible exchange rate

   - with perfect capital mobility, the effectiveness of monetary policy is maximised, but fiscal policy is deprived of any effect on the domestic economy;
   - as capital mobility falls, the effectiveness of monetary policy diminishes, but its effect on income is always larger than the effect obtained with a pegged exchange rate and complete sterilization;
   - as capital mobility falls, the effectiveness of fiscal policy grows, and its effect on income can be larger than the effect obtained with a pegged exchange rate and complete sterilisation.

   Dunn and Mutti provide one of the most complete discussions, considering fiscal expansion with flexible exchange rates for the three possible cases in the Mundell-Fleming model: perfect capital mobility (fiscal policy completely ineffective); when the balance of payments schedule is flatter than the LM schedule (currency appreciates, partially effective); and when the balance of payments schedule is steeper than the LM schedule (currency depreciates, with fiscal policy more effective).
4. For the sake of simplicity, the theoretical discussion assumes a clean float; accordingly, it is assumed that the exchange rate moves sufficiently to maintain equilibrium in the payments accounts. These assumptions permit rather clear distinction between the workings of a flexible and fixed exchange rate system.
5. The primary "other thing" being held equal in this case is the amount by which a given increase in the interest rate will cause investment to decline—the interest elasticity of investment.

Saving-Investment Equality

12

Expansions and contractions in economic activity can be explained more specifically by savings-investment process. The concepts of saving and investment, and the differences between them have been used by writers, relying on their everyday meaning. Neither of these terms has been given precise definition. Subsequent inquiry by the Swedish or 'Stockholm School', which built on Wicksell's work, and by Denis Robertson and J.M. Keynes, made it apparent that it was important to define 'saving' and 'investment' when using them as part of analytical inquiry. In the overinvestment theories, the equality of S and I is associated with an equilibrium state. If I exceeds S (i.e., I > S) with this framework, the result is inflation; an excess of S over I (i.e., S > I) provides deflation. These concepts lent themselves well to expressing what was generally inferred to be happening during periods of propensity and depression. There remaining, however, the matter of how saving and investment should be defined if one is to be consistent in finding out differences between them.

The theory of saving-investment clearly indicates that interest rates cannot be depend upon to bring saving and investment into equality at full employment. Therefore, an increase in the real stock of money either through a general fall in the price-wage level or through monetary expansion cannot reduce chronic unemployment through its effect on interest rates. However, the basic conclusions of the saving-investment theory rest on the assumption that it is only through interest rates that saving and investment can be significantly affected by a change in the real stock of money.

A change in the real stock of money can be expected to have a direct effect on saving and investment. This is an effect quite apart from any effect that may result from changes in interest rates. It is an effect so potent that, in a sensitive-price economy, the only condition of adjustment would be one of full or optimum employment. Thus, the saving-investment theory does not depart sufficiently from the classical assumption to provide an explanation for continued unemployment. This challenge to the saving-investment theory rests on a partial but not complete repudiation of the role, which that theory assigns to interest rates. It is reasonable to accept Keynes's view that interest is, in part, a reward for surrendering liquidity, and that therefore interest hold the outstanding stock of money rather than make additional loans. However, Keynes goes further and claims that the rate of interest is the 'price' which equilibrates the desire to hold wealth in the form of cash with the available quantity of cash. If this were true, there would seem to be no reason to question the saving-investment theory. Actually, interest rates would seem to be only one of the factors that equilibrate the desire to hold wealth in the form of money with the outstanding stock of money. According to Hicks, the demand for money is a function not only of interest rates but also of income. The level of real money holdings is likely to affect both the desire to save and the desire to invest. The larger the real money holdings of the individual (the real value of other assets and income being the same) the greater his protection against the future and the larger the part of his income he can spend on consumption without a threat to his security. Likewise, the more liquid an enterprise, the more risks it can take. This means that saving and investment expenditure must also adjust so that the community is just and only just satisfied to hold the outstanding stock of money rather than make additional expenditures on consumption or capital goods. If this position were accepted, then both interest rates and the level of income would play a part in maintaining monetary adjustment. Interest rates would tend to adjust so that the community would rather hold money than make further loans and income would tend to adjust so that the community would rather hold money than spend at a greater rate on consumption or investment goods.

Two propositions set forth by Keynes regarding the relation between saving and investment are:

(a) saving is equal to investment and

(b) saving is determined by investment (i.e., saving results from investment).

In this chapter, we will deal the first proposition.

Income is always the sum of consumption expenditures and investment expenditures, i.e., $Y = C + I$, or $I = Y - C$.

Income is always either consumed or saved, i.e., $Y = C + S$, or $S = Y - C$.

Therefore, $I = S$.

The difficulty in this proposition is that an individual may save more or less than the amounts he invests; and that, moreover, the people who save are not the same as those who invest.

It should be understood at the outset that the statement $S = I$ necessarily depends on the definitions of S and I. The two magnitudes are equal on Keynes's definitions, but not necessarily on other definitions. One source of confusion is that, before writing the *General Theory*, Keynes himself had defined saving in such a way that S and I could be unequal. His argument in the *Treatise on Money (1930)*, had revolved around this inequality of S and I. In that work Keynes had defined S as including only saving out of factor incomes and normal profit, but excluding saving out of abnormal, or windfall, profits. Saving so defined does not equal investment, except in equalibrium, when there are no abnormal profits or losses. In the *General Theory* S is defined as including saving out of abnormal profit, or, in other words, saving is defined as saving out of aggregate income. On that definition S always equals I.

A second source of confusion is that people often think of S and I as pertaining to different income periods. The amount saved out of yesterday's income is not related to the amount invested today. If S and I are defined in this sense, the equality of S and I does not hold. In the so-called "period analysis," today's income (Y) is not consumed or saved until tomorrow. Today's consumption is made out of yesterday's Y. The part of yesterday's Y which is not consumed today is today's S. This S is independent of today's I and may be larger or smaller than today's I. Keynes did not use period analysis, but defined Y, C, I, and S as all pertaining to the same period. Only if viewed in this way is it true that $S = I$.

An analysis of the problem shows that the basic reason for the differences of opinion lies in the definitions adopted by different economists and not in any defects of logic. Those who quarrel with the definitions given by others do so mainly on the basis of the usefulness of the definitions put forth. We briefly discuss below the important definitions of saving and investment put forward by different economists.

(a) Keynes in his *General Theory of Employment, Interest and Money* defines S as the difference between income earned in a period and the consumption in the same period and I as the expenditure on investment in the same period (and therefore also the income earned in that period other than in the production of consumption goods). In this sense S is always equal to investment.

(b) Keynes in his *Treatise on Money* defines S_t as the difference between "normal" (instead of actual) income and consumption, and is as such less than the S of the *General Theory* by as much as 'normal' income is less than actual income; I_t is defined just like I in the *General Theory*. $I_t - S_t$ (which is the same as $S - S_t$), therefore, represents the excess of actual over 'normal' income—"abnormal profits."

(c) In Robertson's writings, S_r is defined as income earned yesterday (instead of today and therefore disposable today) minus today's consumption and is therefore less than *S* by as much as income earned yesterday is less than income earned today. I_r is defined in the same way as I. $I_r - S_r$ (which is the same as $S - S_r$), therefore, represents the excess of income earned today over income earned yesterday.

(d) The Swedish economists—Ohlin, Lundberg and particularly Myrdal-define S_e as *expected* or *ex-ante* saving and I_e as *expected* or *ex-ante* investment.

KEYNES IN GENERAL THEORY

Keynes, in the *General Theory* defines saving and investment in such a way that they are necessarily equal.

> Whilst, therefore, the amount of saving is an outcome of the collective behaviour of individual consumers and the amount of investment of the collective behaviour of individual entrepreneurs, these two amounts are necessarily equal, since each of them is equal to the value of current output, the current investment is equal to the value of that part of current output which is not consumed, and that

> saving is equal to the excess of income over consumption, ...the equality of saving and investment necessarily follows.[1]

To cite Keynes again, "...saving and investment have been so defined that they are necessarily equal in amount, being, for the community as a whole, merely different aspects of the same thing."

Keynes argues at times that saving and investment are not only always equal but "merely different aspects of the same thing". And yet he deplores saving while approving investment.

Equality between investment and saving is a consequence of changes in the level of income. If investment increases, then income will increase until the saving out of the higher income is equal to the increased investment; and if investment falls, income will fall until the saving out of the lower income is equal to the reduced investment. Hence, these concepts are geared to the fundamental idea of a shifting equilibrium as distinguished from a special, full-employment equilibrium in which investment equals saving only at full-employment.

Keynesian theory deals with the economic system as a whole, the terms investment, saving, and income mean aggregate or total national or social investment, saving, and income. Investment is the addition to the existing stock of real capital assets and additions to inventories. This use of the term is to be carefully distinguished from purely financial investment such as the purchase of a stock or bond in the securities market. No addition is made to real capital as a result of such a transaction and therefore no real investment occurs.

The exact line of demarcation between investment and consumption is not a matter of great importance so long as it is consistently maintained. Some expenditure such as those for food and clothing are clearly consumption. Others such as the building of factories and railroads clearly represent investment. Some items such as consumer's durable goods are not so easily classified. It is customary, for example, to regard outlays on housing construction as investment and outlays for automobiles as consumption, but this distinction is clearly one, which might be, and has been, a subject of debate.

Investment includes additions to inventories as well as to fixed capital. These additions may be either intentional or unintentional.

Intended increases are motivated by larger volume of sales or by anticipation of price changes or by other related factors, which are part of the ordinary planning activities of business enterprise. Unintended investment is the accumulation of unsold finished goods arising from unforeseen changes in the market. Some writers view the distinction between intended and unintended accumulations of inventories as of prime significance but for Keynes' general theory the difference is not important. Saving is defined as the excess of income over consumption expenditure. This definition applies to individual saving and to aggregate saving of the economic system. However, in dealing with the over all behaviour of the economic system, account must frequently be taken of factors which may be ignored when we are concerned only with the behaviour of the individual units in isolation. Saving is behaviour of this type. Although individual saving and community saving are both defined in the same terms, and although community saving is the net result of the saving of all individual units within the community, individual saving does not always result in community saving. Individual saving is not spending for consumption, and a failure to spend by one individual may reduce the income of others and hence impair their ability to save. Unless it is clearly understood that the kind of saving Keynes is talking about in the *General Theory* is aggregate or collective saving, the equality between investment and saving will be difficult to grasp. The fundamental fact about saving is that its volume depends upon income. At varying levels of national income, the community will want to save amounts, which are more or less stable and predictable at any given time. In other words, the propensity to save is stable. Investment, on the other hand, does not depend to any significant degree upon the size of the national income. Investment depends mainly on dynamic factors like growth of population, geographical expansion, and technological progress as these growth factors affect the profit expectations of entrepreneurs. Individuals save without any thought of building factories or otherwise making real investment. Entrepreneurs invest without ascertaining whether or not there has been an equivalent amount of saving. Despite the fact that investors and savers are, as a rule, two separate sets of persons who make their decisions freely and independently of one another, the net result of their collective behaviour is to invest and to save in the aggregate identical amounts during any given period. The clue to this equality is found in fluctuations in income. Whereas experience indicates that saving is stable, more or less predictable, and induced, investment is unstable, unpredictable, and autonomous.

Hence, in terms of the facts of experience, the behaviour of investors is a more dynamic factor than is the behaviour of savers. Investment rules the roost. Varying levels of income cannot be sustained unless the amounts of saving at these levels of income are offset by an equivalent volume of investment. If potential savings are not offset, the potential income corresponding to these savings cannot be realised. The equilibrium level of income is realised where saving out of income is just equal to the actual amount of investment.

One of the drawbacks, though perhaps not a very important one, of adopting Keynes' concepts is that it means departing from the ordinary usage. "It is an uncommon use of terms to say that a newly employed workman who receives his wage at the beginning of the week, and spends it entirely in the course of the week, 'saves' the money in the meantime, and that as soon as he spends the money it is 'saved' by the next recipient...and so on."[2] Further, the Keynesian concepts do not distinguish between investment which is financed out of inflationary credit or dishoarding and that financed out of the current supply of voluntary savings. Beyond doubt, it makes a lot of difference whether investment is financed from one source or the other; and the concepts which ignore this difference are not very useful. Moreover, Keynes' concepts are neither useful for the analysis of the cumulative process nor of any help in dealing with the problem of credit policy. The only advantage which these concepts appear to possess is that they avoid the necessity of defining the unit period which is the crucial problem in regard to other definitions.

KEYNES IN TREATISE

In the *Treatise*, Keynes had adopted a different definition of Y and, therefore, could maintain that S can be different from I. There all receipts do not form part of Y. Abnormal profits or losses are neither to be added to income nor are they to be subtracted from it. For this reason Keynes could state that when I rises, the only result is that total expenditure is more, so that profits (Q) rise. Since savings are coming out of normal income, the result is that I > S by an amount equal to additional investment or profits Q. Similarly, if investment falls, abnormal losses take place and lead to a situation where S > I. Keynes was excluding occurrence of abnormal profits or losses from the income accounts to show the effect of changing investment on prices. His main purpose was to find out the way prices of consumption goods and capital goods get determined and fluctuate with changing investment leading to abnormal profits or losses.

In the *Treatise*, Keynes defined investment as the 'value of unconsumed output'; savings was defined as 'income minus consumption.' The implication is that an excess of saving over investment is a state in which the economy experiences losses; analogously, by definition, an excess of investment over savings implies that the economy is experiencing profit. Profits and losses are defined in the *Treatise* as the amount by which actual entrepreneurial income exceeds or falls short of the level that induces entrepreneurs to alter aggregate output and employment. The main theme of the *Treatise* is the problem of price level stability, whereas the short-run problem of changes in output, employment, and income is the chief focus of *The General Theory of Employment, Interest and Money*. According to the schematic of the treaties, output is divided into what Keynes called available and non-available output. These categories correspond to consumption and capital goods output. Wage costs are the primary costs of production for both types of output. In order for the price level to be stable over time, wage earners, together with profit receivers, must save enough of their income to equal the value of the non-available output (i.e., investment) produced. In other words, if the price level is to be stable, saving (S) must equal investment (I). If this condition is not met (i.e., if S < I or S > I), the price level will change. This will create windfall gains or losses that will cause the balance between saving and investment to be restored. For example, if there are windfalls, more resources will be utilised in the investment sector. The accompanying increase in the price level increases profits while at the same time reducing real wages (i.e., there is a transfer of income to capitalist). Their higher savings propensities generate an increase in total savings until their level is equal to the new level of investment.

The definition of saving and investment that Keynes found useful in the *Treatise* for explaining price-level changes were discarded in his subsequent, and more famous, *General Theory of Employment, Money and Interest*. What is important here is to recognise that he fashioned definitions of savings and investment in the *Treaties* that were comparable with his emphasis on the critical role of entrepreneural decisions about investment as the chief determinant of the system. Furthermore, he emphassized that investment decisions do not automatically match decisions to save out of income. This point was to become as central to Keynes's later intellectual disputes with Classicism as his repudiation of the quantity theory of money. Thus, there is a common thread running between the Treatise and The General Theory, in which his focus shifts from the problem of explaining price-level stability to the problem of explaining the phenomenon of less-than-full employment.

The possibility of inequality of S and I in the *Treatise* was useful for Keynes because it could help in the explanation of fluctuations in prices. In his *General Theory*, on the other hand, the definitions adopted were of greater significance because there his purpose was not to discuss changes in prices but rather to eliminate them for finding out changes in real income and output.

ROBERTSON'S CONCEPTS

In Robertson's view, an equality between saving and investment can exist both at the top of the boom and at the bottom of the depression; and the same would be true of an equality between the money rate of interest and the natural rate if this is supposed to be identical with an equality between saving and investment.

Robertson in his famous article on "Saving and Hoarding" assumes that a man's disposable income is the income received not on that day but on the previous day. The day is a finite period in which our definition, unless otherwise stated, does not admit of a piece of money coming to do more than one job in a day. Savings on any one day is the difference between income paid out on the previous day and outlay on consumer's goods in the next day—the day in question. He defined today's income as being equal to yesterday's consumption plus investment, so that today's saving, in his sense, is equal to yesterday's investment plus the excess of yesterday's consumption over today's consumption. On this definition, saving can exceed investment by the excess of yesterday's income over today's income. Thus, when Mr Robertson says that there is an excess of saving over investment, he means literally the same thing as Keynes means when he says that income is falling, and the excess of saving in his sense is exactly equal to the decline of income in Keynesian sense. If it were true that current expectations were always determined by yesterday's realised results, today's effective demand would be equal to yesterday's income. Thus, Mr Robertson's method might be regarded as an alternative attempt to Keynesian (being, perhaps, a first approximation to it) to make the same distinction, so vital for causal analysis, that Keynes had tried to make by the contrast between effective demand and income.

Robertson's concepts can be used as instruments for analysing economic events over time, showing how the events of one period influence the events of the next. The relation between S and I at each moment tells us whether the system contains a tendency to an upswing or a downswing.

Since S and I may be equal in the depression, it is evident that their equality cannot provide a norm of monetary policy, at least not by itself. It can be used solely as an instrument of theoretical analysis, which is the only use to which Robertson himself puts it.

Dr. F.A. Lutz prefers the Robertsonian definitions to other definitions. He states, "In contradiction to Mr. Lerner's view, it is the contention of this article that the assumption of a time-lag between receipts and expenditure in Robertson's sense is closer to reality than the assumption of simultaneity between them and is necessary for the analysis of economic events over time."[3] To this Lerner replies that "Keynesian simultaneity between receipts and expenditure is implicit in the proposition that I = S only in the sense that there is no interval between the moment X receives a payment from Y and the moment when Y makes this same payment to X. Hence the question of time-lag is not there. Robertson's time-lag is quite different which is the time elapsing between the moment that X receives his income from Y and the moment when he spends this income on consumer goods purchased from Z. Simultaneity between such receipt and expenditure is impossible. However this kind of simultaneity has nowhere been assumed by Keynes. Thus criticism based on this reasoning must be based on a confusion between the two meanings of a time-lag between receipts and expenditures."

Dr. Lutz prefers Robertsonian definitions also because they are dynamic and they permit to speak of gap between S and I which provide a guide for credit policy. Replying to this argument, Dr. Klein states, "Both claims are confused. Robertson's definitions are dynamic only in the most trivial sense. They define observed aggregates at different points of time, but they give no functional relation to economic behaviour so that one can solve for each variable in the system as a function of time alone. Robertson did not realise the existence of a consumption schedule, a saving schedule or an investment schedule. He has set up a few lagged definitions but has presented no truly dynamical relations."[4] Further Lutz's interpretation of Robertson's I and S consists of one or all the elements: (i) abnormal profits, (ii) excess of income earned today over income earned yesterday, (iii) unexpected income, and (iv) unexpected depletions. None of these can tell us ambiguously whether economic activity is going up or down and cannot provide us any guide for credit policy.

Another argument advanced by Lutz against the Keynesian concepts is, "They do not allow us to distinguish between investment which is financed out of inflationary credit or dishoarding from investment which is financed out of the current supply of voluntary savings... and a terminology that conceals this difference hardly seems commendable". To this argument, Prof. Lerner replies, "If this means that the use of the Keynesian terminology prevents us from discussing the effects of increases in the amount of money or of diminutions in liquidity preference or increases in the marginal efficiency schedule of investment it clearly is incorrect."[5]

The final argument put forward by Lutz in favour of Robertsonian approach is that it appears more impressive because it purports to provide an explanation of fluctuations both in income as well as in prices. Further, by varying the time interval between different 'days' or by varying the lengths of the 'days' for different sectors of the economy, it may be possible to weave out intricate patterns in which the fluctuations in income and prices occur in an economy. But in actual practice, the Robertsonian analysis, just like the Keynesian analysis, is not of much help. Robertsonian analysis does not tell us why I should exceed S or *vice versa*. It does not tell us what should cause such a change and in what direction this change should be expected to take place in the next period. If it is maintained that changes in I and S in the next period will depend upon prices and incomes respectively, we have to find out the causal relationships between income and consumption and prices and investment decisions. In other words, we have to study the causes which determine investment and consumption decisions and that is what Keynes does in his *General Theory* and Keynes certainly does it more systematically and more successfully. Keynes' equality between S and I is not, therefore, meaningless. It has its own place and cannot be replaced by any substitute.

Prof. Lerner mentions the following reasons for criticism of equality between saving and investment by some writers.[6]

(a) They fail to recognise that all items involved are payments (or differences between payments) over a period of time and not amounts existing at some point of time. They represent flows which can be measured.

(b) They fail to understand that while every person is free to save either more or less than he invests, all persons considered together are not free because the total investments are equal to total savings.

(c) They fail to visualise expenditure as a flow with the flow of income during the same period.

(d) They fail to recognise that the equation does not mention equilibrium.

(e) They fail to realise that the proposition (S = I) is only an analytical phenomenon and does not represent the working in the real world.

To cite Prof. Hansen, "Clearly it is not a question of one definition being wrong and another being right... The only question is their usefulness. In period analysis, Robertsonian definitions are useful and indeed necessary. In time-rates-of-change analysis, the Keynesian definitions are appropriate." Now all the countries use Keynesian definitions for calculating national income because in national income measurements all variables must apply to the same period.

EX-ANTE AND *EX-POST* CONCEPTS

In the 1920s and early 1930s Ohlin, Myrdal, and Lindahl contributed to the further development of Wicksell's monetary theory by applying it to conditions of less than full employment and in their own way arrived at results partly anticipating and paralleling the income and employment analysis of Keynes's *General Theory*. The Stockholm school, as it came to be known, operated with the help of a new equilibrium concept, which like Keynes's aggregate equilibrium and unlike the conventional microeconomic equilibrium was no longer dfined in terms of a maximum position. The Stockholm school's "monetary equilibrium" referred to a situation characterised by equality of the natural and the loan rate of interest as well as by stability of the price level.

The Stockholm school fostered a dynamic period, or sequence, analysis of income determination, in which expectations figured prominently and which preferred to employ *ex-ante* and *ex-post* concepts rather than instantaneous adjustments. These concepts proved of great value in the later discussion of Keynes's *General Theory* when it came to the elucidation of the meaning of the equality of saving and investment, on which Keynes insisted.

Economists, such as Ohlin, Gunnar Myrdal of Stockholm school, developed an alternative set of definitions to those proposed by Keynes in *The Treatise on Money*. They distinguished between plans or expectations and the income, savings, and investment amounts that are actually realised. Magnitudes that are associated with plans are *ex-ante* manifestations. The businesses and households decide to save based on the incomes they expect. Entrepreneurs expect certain demands, interest rates, costs of production, and prices, and they formulate their investment plans based on these expectations. *Ex-ante* magnitudes for the economy as a whole represent the summing up of these expectations. According to this school of thoughts, there is no reason for planned saving and planned investment to be equal *ex-ante*. However, they will be equal *ex-post*.

An inequality between saving and investment *ex-ante* sets into motion a process that causes realised income to be different from expected income, realised saving to be different from planned saving, and actual new investment to differ from what was planned. Unexpected income, unexpected new investment, and unintentional new savings materialise. An excess of investment *ex-ante* over savings has a stimulating effect and is characteristic of the prosperity phase of the cycle. If savings exceed investment *ex-ante*, retailers find themselves with greater stocks than they expected or lower receipts. This generates a contraction, which brings about equality between saving and investment *ex-post*. No more can be saved than is compatible with realised income; the latter depends on entrepreneural decisions about investment.

In spite of different definitions of saving and investment, Keynes and economists, such as Ohlin, Gunnar Myrdal, are in agreement that—

(a) saving and investment reflect decisions made by two different criteria or two different persons; and
(b) entrepreneurial decisions about investment are the dominant factor in generating change, and their decisions with regard to saving and investment are un-coordinated, *ex-ante* investments are not likely to be equal to *ex-ante* savings.

In the *General Theory,* Keynes namely defined income as being identical to the value of current output and concluded that saving and investment are necessarily equal to each other. Nonetheless, the principle of effective demand to all appearances allows aggregate supply and demand to adjust to each other (on account of the definitions endorsed by Keynes, this amounts to allow saving and investment to adjust to each other), their equation being conditional upon the level of employment offered by firms. Then, the reference to *ex ante* and *ex post* analysis might be not only a convenience but also a necessity; it should reconcile the identity and the conditional equation of aggregate supply and demand. Current investment can exceed the current saving. This is possible where the excess investment that cannot be financed out of current saving is financed through newly created money or through dishoarding, *i.e.,* by drawing upon past savings. Similarly, current saving will exceed current investment if people increase their hoardings. The system is out of equilibrium almost always in the sense that *ex-ante* investment is out of tune with *ex-ante* savings.

The equilibrium level of income is reached when both the savers and investors are in equilibrium. The savers would be in equilibrium only when they succeed in actually saving that amount which they intend to save. The investors would be in equilibrium when the actual investment equals the investment intended by them. The double condition of equilibrium would, therefore, be satisfied when

(a) Intended Saving = Actual Saving
(b) Intended Investment = Actual Investment

Since saving is that part of the current product which is not consumed (S = Y – C) and investment is also equal to the part of current product not consumed (I = Y – C), it follows that the actual (ex-post) investment must be always equal to the actual (ex-post) saving. Thus by definition we have:

Actual Saving = Actual Investment

It does not, however, follow from the above that *ex-ante* (intended) investment and *ex-ante* (intended) saving must also always be equal. In equilibrium, of course, where the intended saving equals the actual saving and the intended investment is equal to the actual investment, it follows from the identity of actual saving and actual investment that:

ex-ante (intended) saving = *ex-ante* (intended) investment.

The process through which the two *ex-ante* quantities are ultimately brought into equilibrium position from one of disequilibrium at the beginning of the period operates through multiplier repercussions on income variable. If *ex-ante* investment exceeds *ex-ante* saving, the level of income would rise, which in turn would increase the volume of savings and the two would become equal in the equilibrium. Similarly, if savings are in excess of investment, the level of income would decline, which in turn would decrease the volume of savings and the two would become equal in the equilibrium. This is illustrated by diagram 12.1.

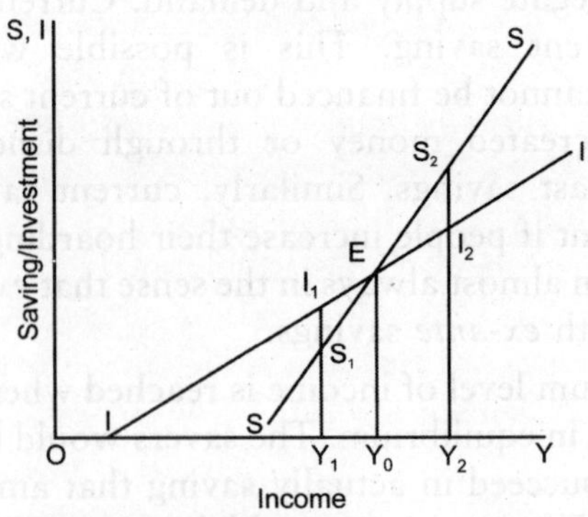

Fig. 12.1

SS represents the saving curve and II the investment curve. The two curves intersect each other at point E which gives the equilibrium level of income or OY_0. At the OY_1 level of income Y_1I_1 is the *ex-ante* investment and Y_1S_1 is the *ex-ante* saving, which is less than *ex-ante* investment. Since *ex-ante* investment is greater than *ex-ante* saving, the level of income must rise and reach OY_0 where *ex-ante* saving becomes equal to *ex-ante* investment. When the income is OY_2, the *ex-ante* saving Y_2S_2 exceeds the *ex-ante* investment Y_2I_2. Since *ex-ante* savings are larger than *ex-ante* investment, the level of income must decline and reach OY_0 level, where the *ex-ante* savings become equal to *ex-ante* investment.

How useful are these *ex-ante* concepts of savings and investment as the analytical tools which Myrdal intends them to be? In Myrdal's treatment saving and investment are calculated *ex-ante* for a unit-period the length of which is arbitrarily chosen. It is, however, obvious that we are not free to choose the unit-period arbitrarily. If the intention is to talk about plans being fixed in advance for a certain period or time, the period must be so chosen that no changes in plans occur within it. This is the definition of the unit period which Ohlin and Lundberg adopt. But this is significant only when applied to an individual enterprise; there is no such period for all entrepreneurs in the aggregate. The length as well as the timing of their individual planning period vary, so that plans are stopping and starting at every moment. Any attempt, therefore, to analyse the *ex-ante* concepts leads logically to the identification of the perioa with an extremely short "finite but indivisible" unit of time. This appears virtually abandonment of the *ex-ante* concepts in favour of Robertson's approach.

Let us assume, however, that even though the period has ultimately to be reduced to a very small unit of time, it is still sensible to speak of plans being made *ex-ante* for this period. What differences are there, then, between the *ex-ante* approach and Robertson's approach? In the first place, the *ex-ante* concepts relate to saving and investment which are planned in a moment of time to be executed over the succeeding period of time, while Robertson is looking at the process of saving and investment as it takes place during the period. This does not, however, mean that Robertson's terms include unintentional saving or dis-saving (profits or losses) and unintentional investment or dis-investment (accumulation or depletion of stocks), which may be made during the period. Unintentional saving (or dis-saving) is not included because Robertson does not add profits (or substract losses) made during the period to the disposable income of that period but carries them forward to the disposable income of the next period. Unintentional investment (or dis-investment) is not included because he abstracts from stocks, on which this item depends. If he were to include stocks, he would have to specifically define his investment as intended investment carried out during the period, so as to arrive at consistent results.

Secondly, it appears as if the magnitude of S according to the *ex-ante* calculations might differ from the magnitude of S according to Robertson's calculation for the reason that the *ex-ante* saving is conceived of as being determined on the basis of the income that people expect to receive in the forthcoming period, while Robertson's saving is made out of the income actually received in the preceding period. But the difference is illusory. From Robertson's point of view, it does not matter whether the saving which people decide to do in the forthcoming period is determined by them as some portion of the income received in the last period or as some portion of the income which they hope to receive in the forthcoming period. Robertson is not concerned with the factors which influence people's decisions as to the amount of saving they want to do, but only with the actual carrying out of their plans; and these plans can only be executed out of the amount of income already received.

Thirdly, the *ex-ante* concepts refer explicitly to expectations while Robertson's concepts do not. The results of applying the concepts, however, are the same in both cases. If, for example, *ex-ante* investment is greater than *ex-ante* saving, we have an expansion in the period to which the *ex-ante* plans relate. According to Robertson's concepts also, an excess of I over S shows an expansion for this period.

In the *General Theory* Keynes defined income as being identical to the value of current output and concluded that saving and investment are necessarily equal to each other. Nonetheless, the principle of effective demand to all appearances allows aggregate supply and demand to adjust to each other (on account of the definitions endorsed by Keynes, this amounts to allow saving and investment to adjust to each other), their equation being conditional upon the level of employment offered by firms. Then, the reference to *ex-ante* and *ex-post* analysis might be not only a convenience but also a necessity— it should reconcile the identity and the conditional equation of aggregate supply and demand.

Keynes's dismissal of *ex-ante* and *ex-post* analysis is not an oddity at all, it is in accordance with his theory of the effective demand and his rejection of the orthodox theory which considered employment as a variable determined within a comprehensive price system. The dismissal of *ex-ante* and *ex-post* analysis is coherent with the latter principle which, despite common interpreting, is not a process adjusting *ex-ante* supply and demand. Keynes further opposed to *ex-ante* and *ex-post* analysis with reference to his formulation of the 'finance motive'. This principle confirms the identity of saving and investment (and so the identity of supply and demand), which therefore cannot be subject to any adjustment process (neither *ex-ante* nor *ex-post*). This line of reasoning is puzzling however, since the principle of effective demand presupposes a possible discrepancy between aggregate supply and demand. The principle of effective demand is linked to a theory of income distribution where profits are a redistributed share of factor income, which is transferred to firms when prices exceed factor costs. So, the identity and the equilibrium condition are reconcilable, they relate to separate measurements of income and output, factor cost and prices.

In real economies, different production processes are simultaneously underway which take more or less time and overlap one another. Some productions started in a preceding period come to an end in the current period, while others are started during the current period which are still underway when it is over. Hence, it is difficult to refer to a definite time period relevant for computing aggregate results which could be traced back to aggregate expectations reckoned at some earlier date. Keynes confirmed the point in his 1937 lecture as, "When one is dealing with aggregates, aggregate effective demand at time A has no corresponding aggregate income at time B. All one can compare is the expected and actual income resulting to an entrepreneur from a particular decision."

A *priori*, Keynes's argument is simply grounded on a practical difficulty relating to the adapting of the *ex-ante* and *ex-post* analysis, which would be suitable at a microeconomic level, for the macroeconomic level. Since individual production processes are of different lengths and overlap one another, it would be arbitrary to divide time into *ex-ante* and *ex-post* phases for the economy as a whole. Otherwise, the principle of effective demand might be jeopardised as well.

To move on unambiguously from individual processes to production as a whole would require that all the processes be of the same length and start simultaneously, which is obviously unrealistic. How, then, could the principle of the aggregate effective demand be stated?

According to Keynes, the general public does not make *ex-ante* decisions with regard to saving. Thus, there are no distinct supply and demand forces available, which would be based on the behaviour of two different categories of agents, entrepreneurs and individuals, and which would adjust to each other and determine income. *Ex-ante* is solely the domain of entrepreneurs decisions, with the latter having to foresee what the demand will be (otherwise they would loose money). In other words, employment (and thence income) determination is in no way analogous to price determination. Actually, according to Keynes, there is a law governing the relation between (aggregate) supply and demand, but this law is *ex-post* and is dependent on investment and consumption (with the latter being *ex-post* variables). All what entrepreneurs can do is to take this law into account in order to make accurate expectations. Then, the principle of effective demand is not challenged by the overlapping of individual production processes and the related impossibility of dividing time into *ex-ante* and *ex-post* phases— the *ex-ante* and *ex-post* analysis is irrelevant to it anyway.

A brief reference to Myrdal's *Monetary Equilibrium* shows that the Swedish economist also dealt with the question of the unit of time, which he proposed to solve by reducing the actual time-dimension of macroeconomic variables such as income, saving and investment to a point of time. Some of these quantities refer directly to a point of time. That is true of 'capital value' as also of such quantities as demand and supply prices. Other terms – as e.g. 'income', 'revenue', 'return', 'expenses', 'savings', 'investments' – imply, however, a time period for which they are reckoned. However, in order to be unambiguous they must also refer to a point of time at which they are calculated.

Prices are quantities that directly refer to a point of time—they are determined at a point of time, after an *ex-ante* adjustment process has taken place. As for the macroeconomic quantities, Myrdal proposed to refer to the point of time at which they are calculated. Nonetheless, how are macroeconomic quantities determined? Myrdal further explained that *ex-ante* disparity and *ex-post* balance are made consistent through prices changes, which result from the behaviour of economic agents which is based on *ex-ante* anticipations—For these anticipations determine the behaviour of the economic subjects and consequently those changes in the whole price system which during a period actually occur as a result of the actions of individuals.

Thus, while comparing Keynes's approach to Myrdal's, we get confirmation of our interpretation. As is well-known, Keynes's principle of effective demand is concerned with entrepreneurs expectations. According to this principle, entrepreneurs are ready to offer the volume of employment for which the proceeds they "expect to receive from the employment of N men" meet "the expectations of proceeds which will just make it worth the while of (them) to give that employment." Keynes called this particular value of the expected proceeds 'the effective demand.' At first sight, we could argue that Keynes and Myrdal simply disagreed with respect to the emphasis to be put on entrepreneurs' expectations. According to Myrdal the expectations of the general public (who asks for goods) deserve as much attention as entrepreneurs' anticipations. However, both approaches are actually different from each other. Just as stated above, in Keynes's view there is no *ex-ante* adjustment process between supply and demand. Contrariwise, according to Myrdal, expectations of the economic subjects determine *ex-ante* supplies and demands whose adjustment determines the whole price system (and changes in it during a given period) and hence income, saving, consumption and investment. Thus, a clear cut line undoubtedly separates both approaches. According to Keynes, the sequence from entrepreneurs' expectations and decisions to income determination cannot be encapsulated in a global system of (simultaneous) equations. His dismissal of *ex-ante* and *ex-post* analysis helps us to understand this feature of his approach, which has been underestimated by Hicks when he initiated the IS-LM model and is still neglected by all those who limit Keynes's originality to adjusting quantities instead of prices. It is also, contrariwise, a justification to the well-known emphasis put by Post Keynesian literature onto (among other issues) the role of entrepreneurs expectations in a world of radical uncertainty (entrepreneurs make decisions which have to take into account decisions by consumers at a time when the latter have not yet made any decision) and historical time.

HANSEN'S APPROACH

Hansen has made an attempt to resolve the saving-investment controversy. To cite him "One source of confusion arose from the failure of his (Keynes') critics to realise that while investment and saving are always *equal*, they are not always in *equilibrium*. All this could have been avoided had Keynes made it clear from the outset that the *equality* of saving and investment does not mean that they are necessarily in *equilibrium*. He was realistic enough to see this, as is revealed again and again in different sections of his book. But he never explicitly stated it, doubtless because the matter had not been clearly, thought through."[7] He continues, "If the economy is in a moving equilibrium, so that the variables are always in a normal (desired) functional relationship to each other, then indeed saving and investment will not only be *equal* but will also be in equilibrium. But if the process of change involves a lagged adjustment of certain-variables, this will not be the case. If, for example, there is an expenditure lag (*i.e.* if consumers adjust their expenditures slowly to changes in income), then, until the lag has worked itself out, *actual* consumption will not be equal to *desired* consumption (and actual saving will not be equal to *desired* saving). Similarly, if there is an output lag, producers being slow to adjust to increases (or decreases) in sales, then unintended disinvestment (or investment) in inventory stocks will occur. Thus actual investment will diverge from desired (intended) investment. Under either of these conditions (expenditure lag or production lag) saving and investment, though *equal*, will not be in equilibrium. There can obviously be no *equilibrium* condition until the lags have been worked through. In equilibrium conditions (lags having been overcome) saving and investment are both *equal* and in equilibrium, and this is true whether the system is in moving or in stable equilibrium. But if the system is not in equilibrium, saving and investment, while still *equal* will not be in *equilibrium*."[8]

KLEIN'S APPROACH

Dr. Klein states, "The entire confusion in connection with the saving-investment controversy can be traced to a failure to distinguish between *schedules* and *observables*."[9] According to him there exists a functional relationship between S and Y on the one hand, and between I and Y on the other hand. Thus S and I schedules represent various amounts of S and I respectively corresponding to the various levels of national income. If these schedules showing relationship between income, S and I (independent of each other) are smooth curves, there would exist a unique level of income at which S and I calculated from their respective schedules are equal. This is S – I equality in the schedule sense. Observable S(I) refers to that particular level of S(I) calculated from the S(I) schedule from a knowledge of the unique equilibrium value of national income which equates S and I. Observable values refers to a single point while schedules are series of points along curves. The observed levels of S and I are those two values on the schedules corresponding to the observed level of income; all other values of S and I along schedules are not observed.

When Keynes said that S is always equal to I, he was referring to the observable. But when he said, "when investment changes, income must necessarily change in just that degree which is necessary to make the change in saving equal the change in investment,"[10] he was referring to the process of adjustment which achieves an equilibrium. As observable over time S and I are always equal but there can be a divergency between them at a virtual or unobserved level of income.

HAWTREY'S CONCEPTS

According to Hawtrey, equilibrium exists if active I is equal to active S. If active S exceeds active I, the result will be passive investment owing to unintentional accumulation of stocks or, assuming: that there are no stocks, passive dis-saving due to losses. Similarly, if active I exceeds active S, there will result passive disinvestment owing to depletion of stocks or passive saving in the form of profits. If a very long period is chosen, the passive savings which are made within the period can become active savings within the same period because those who possess passive savings may decide within this period whether to spend them or to save them "actively." The same is true of passive investment. If such a situation is to be avoided, there is no alternative but to take a very short period. In case a very short period is taken, we are back again at Robertson's concepts.

SAVING AND INVESTMENT EQUALITY (CLASSICAL POSITION)

Keynes was not the first person to visualise equality between saving and investment. Classical economists also talked of this equality. There are, however, important differences between Keynes and classicals. Firstly, according to classicals equality between saving and investment is brought about by the rate of interest. If savings exceed investment, the rate of interest declines. A decline in the rate of interest discourages savings and encourages investment and thus an equality is brought about between the two. Similarly, if investment exceeds savings, the rate of interest rises. A rise in the rate of interest stimulates savings and discourages investment and thus an equality is brought about between the two. In this way, changes in the rate of interest correct any disequilibrium that may arise between savings and investment. Secondly, the classicals believed that the equality between saving and investment is brought about at full employment level of income.

The classical position is defended by arguing that the investment function is really higher (or the saving function lower) than represented by the Keynesian, so that desired full employment savings and investment can be equated at a positive rate of interest. However, this is beside the point that the fundamental disagreement between Keynesian and classical economics lies in the former's denial of the automaticity of full employment posited by the latter. Hence, a successful restatement of the classical position must demonstrate the existence of some automatic mechanism, which will always bring about full employment. To argue that if the investment or saving function is at a certain level, full employment will be brought about is irrelevant; what must be shown is that there exist forces that will automatically bring the investment or saving functions to the required level. In other words, the issue at stake is not the possible, but the automatic, generation of full employment.

The contrast between Keynes' *General Theory* of interest and the special theory of interest of the classical school is analogous to the contrast between his general theory of employment and the special theory of employment of the classical school. Both distinctions between the general theory and a special theory arise from the difference between fluctuating levels of employment and income in contrast with the fixed level of full employment and a corresponding fixed level of income. By neglecting the all important changes in the level of income, the classical school is led into the error of viewing the rate of interest as the factor, which brings about the equality of saving and investment, that is, the equality of demand for investible funds and the supply of funds provided by saving. Thus, the rate of interest is determined by the point of interaction of the investment demand schedule and the supply schedule.

Keynes accepted the classical position of equality of saving and investment but attributes this equaltity to changes in the level of income rather than the rate of interest. Keynes also would agree with the classical theory that if the level of income is assumed to be given, the current rate of interest lies at the point of intersection of the investment-demand schedule and the schedule of saving which will be made at varying rates of interest out of that level of income. The classical error lies in assuming that the investment-demand schedule can change without causing the level of income to change.

From Keynes' theory, we know that a fall in the schedule of the marginal efficiency of capital will cause investment to fall. The fall in investment leads to a decrease in income, and out of the reduced income, less will be saved. Thus, it is inconsistent to assume that the investment-demand schedule can shift without at the same time causing a shift in the saving schedule. In order to find the saving schedule, which is relevant to the new investment schedule, the rate of interest must first be determined by introducing the state of liquidity preference and the quantity of money.

Keynes believed that the equality between saving and investment is brought about not by the rate of interest but by income. For instance, if investment exceeds savings, increased investment increases the aggregate income of the community to such a level that the increased saving out of increased income becomes equal to increased investment. Further, Keynes believes that saving and investment can be equal, in fact, normally are so, at less than full employment.

SAVING AND INVESTMENT (ACCOUNTING EQUALITY)

Accounting equality between saving and investment is also called logical identity. This is very similar to the identity between purchases and sales. Price is determined by demand and supply and at each price total amount sold is equal to total amount bought. This is so because every transaction has two aspects viz. buying and selling or income and expenditure. The identity between saving and investment holds true at all levels of income irrespective of the fact that saving and investment are done by different sets of people. Employment of labour at any time results in a certain amount of national output which, in turn, results in the creation of national income. This national output consists of (i) consumption goods and (ii) investment goods. In algebraic terms, $O = C + I$. Similarly, national income is divided between consumption expenditure and saving. In algebraic terms, $Y = C + S$. We know that by definition $O = Y$. From this it follows that $C + I = C + S$ or $I = S$. This equality between saving and investment can be expressed in another way also. Keynes defines savings as the difference between income and consumption i.e. $S = Y - C$. Further, investment is the difference between income and consumption, i.e., $I = Y - C$. Since $Y - C$ is common in both the equations $S = I$.

What is the economic significance of the accounting equality between S and I ? The answer is that it shows the condition that must be satisfied in order to reach the equilibrium level of income, that is, a condition characterised by the equality of planned saving and investment. The accounting equality between S and I implies that unless the economy as a whole is willing and able to invest at the same rate at which the general public is disposed to save, producers will have to contract or expand output and employment in order to maximise their expectation of profit or to minimise their expectation of loss until the economy gains a position of equilibrium. Further the accounting equality has the richer implication that the determinants of consumer and entrepreneurial behaviour must be investigated if the economy as a whole is temporarily in dislocation.

SAVING AND INVESTMENT (FUNCTIONAL EQUALITY)

The accounting equality between saving and investment is not of much use for analytical purposes. It throws no light on the casual factors that go to determine savings, investment, consumption and income. It also does not show the mechanism by which an equality is brought about. Accounting equality shows simply the statistical result of the behaviour of the national income or economic system during a given period. Functional equality, in contrast, shows the actual behaviour and the process of adjustment of saving and investment in the economy as a whole. In other words, it puts life into dead statistics.

Though savings and investment in the statistical sense are identically equal at all times and at any level of income, saving and investment in the schedule sense are equal only in equilibrium, or in other words, at the equilibrium level of income. In order to facilitate exposition we may compare the equilibrium of savings and investment with that of supply and demand. Just as there can be inequality between supply and demand except in equilibrium, so can there be inequality between saving and investment except in equilibrium. Just as supply and demand are brought into equilibrium by the equilibrating mechanism of price, so are saving and investment in the schedule sense equilibrated by the income mechanism. Supply and demand are equal only at the equilibrium price, that is, the price at which the quantity demanded is precisely the same as the quantity offered. If the demand exceeds supply, the price would rise to the equilibrium level and if the supply exceeds demand, the price would decline to the equilibrium level. The supply and demand would remain unequal until and unless they reach the equilibrium price.

Let us construct a dynamical model for the equilibrium of savings and investment. The three variables involved in this model are independent variable Y and dependent variables S and I. The rate of change of income is functionally related to savings and investment in such a manner that income must rise when investment exceeds savings and decline when savings exceed investment. Savings and investment are equal only at the equilibrium level of income, that is, an income, which is neither rising nor declining. Thus the equality between saving and investment is brought about through changes in the level of income.

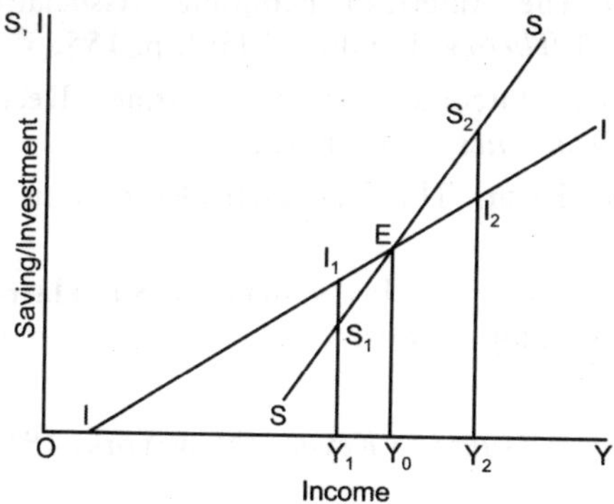

Fig. 12.2.

The diagram given above illustrates the equilibrium process of savings-investment adjustment. Both the saving and investment are along the vertical axis and income is measured along the horizontal axis. The savings function, S, intersects the investment function, I, from below, indicating that stable equilibrium is under study. The situation would be one of unstable equilibrium if the I curve intersects the S curve from below because in that case income would move away from the equilibrium level. If we start from income Y_2, investment is greater than savings by I_2S_2. This excess of investment over savings would cause the level of income to rise till it reaches the equilibrium level of income, at which savings and investment are equal. In contrast, if we start from an income Y_1, savings exceed investment by I_1S_1, which would cause the income to decline till it reaches the equilibrium level.

Thus, saving and investment in the schedule sense are brought into equality, over time, by the equilibrating mechanism of income. This way of looking at savings and investment is consistent with the common-sense view that, though decisions to save and decision to invest are made by different people and for different motives in the course of time these decisions get somehow reconciled through the "invisible hand" of *income*. This implies that income, while influencing savings and investment, may itself be influenced by them.

NOTES

1. J.M. Keynes, *The General Theory of Employment, Interest and Money* (London, 1936), p. 63.
2. Friedrich A. Lutz, "The outcome of the Saving-Investment Discussion", reprinted in The American Economic Association, *Readings in Business Cycle Theory* (London, 1950), p. 155.
3. F.A. Lutz, "The Outcome of Saving-Investment Decisions", *Quarterly Journal of Economics*, August, 1938.
4. Lawrence R. Klein, The Keynesian Revolution (London, 1952), pp. 116-17.
5. A.P. Lerner, "Saving and Investment" in S.E. Harris (ed.), *The New Economics* (London, 1960).
6. *Ibid.*, p. 633.
7. A.H. Hansen, *A Guide to Keynes* (New York, 1953), p. 59.
8. *Ibid.*, pp. 59-60.

9. Lawrence R. Klein, *The Keynesian Revolution* (London, 1956), p. 11.
10. J.M. Keynes, *The General Theory of Employment, Interest and Money* (London, 1936), p. 18.

Principle of Acceleration

13

The multiplier process postulates a cause-effect relationship from decreases in business investment to multiple decreases in output. Many business cycle theories have stated that often the cause-effect relationship runs the other way—from decreases in output to decreases in investment. The accelerator principle captures the idea that investment depends on output, in particular the growth of output, given the condition of a constant relationship between an economy's capital stock and output. This is another theory of investment. Put simply, the accelerator model suggests a positive relationship between investment and the rate of growth of demand or output. This principle assumes that there is a desired capital stock for a given level of output and interest rates. A rise in output or a fall in interest rates may prompt increased levels of investment as firms adjust to reach the new optimal capital stock level.

The accelerator principle is also known as "principle of accelerated or magnified derived demand" or "the relation". Though casually mentioned in the *General Theory*, the principle does not form an important part of the Keynes' analysis of income, output, employment and business fluctuations. The principle as stated by Aftalion, Carver, Bickerdike and others is much older than the concept of multiplier. However, it generally associated with the name of American economist John Maurice Clark who made this concept popular. This principle became more popular when it was found that this principle combined with the Keynesian consumption function could explain self-generating cyclical mechanism. This concept was further refined and developed by a number of economists such as Harrod, Samuelson, Hicks, Goodwin, Robertson, Haberler, Pigou, Ragnar Frisch, Fellner, Hansen, Kuznets, Hayek, Mathews, Klecki and Kaldor.

The accelerator model works on the basis of a fixed capital to output ratio which implies that in order to produce extra goods and services a business needs to adjust its investment to meet changes in demand. According to this principle, each level of output needs a specific amount of capital. Therefore, if output (and the capital required to procure the necessary machinery) is expected to rise, the amount of capital within an economy will also increase.

The accelerator principle is attractive because it can explain changes in investment, which do not run parrel to demand. With the help of the relation between capital stock and output ('naïve' accelerator), the highly different phases of investment activity can be explained, but that the individual annual observations follow another set of rules. Within the 'flexible' accelerator, the attempts that use only flow magnitudes do not represent a further development, but rather a counter-hypothesis of the original accelerator concept—flow magnitudes can explain medium-term variations only to a very small extent. This is contrary to the accelerator concept that explains considerable investment variations with the help of relatively small output variations. Attempts that explain investment variations through a connection between output and capital stock, expand the accelerator theory insofar as they take account of disequilibrium situations. The econometrically estimated equations give an excellent picture of short-term and medium-term investment activity. The economic interpretation of this equation shows, however, that in addition to the explicitly used variables (capital stock and output) other magnitudes contribute implicitly to these excellent results. The merit of the accelerator theory then is not to be seen in a complete "explanation" of investment behaviour, but rather in the fact that it shows highly variable investment demand for capacity purposes which again is dampened by other factors in such a way as to exhibit medium-term variations in capacity utilisation.

The problem to which the Keynesian theory was chiefly addressed was how to rescue an economy, which had got into a grave depression. In the light of *The General Theory* this problem seemed in principle tolerably easy to solve, and the various fiscal and monetary measures suggested are now universally familiar. Preoccupation with the problem of the slump and the excess capacity associated with it caused less attention to be paid to the more difficult problem of how to keep the economy in a boom situation once that had been attained. To approach this problem, we need a more explicit treatment of the factors affecting the marginal efficiency of capital than is provided in the General Theory—a need which the acceleration principle and related formulations intend to fill.

MEANING

While the multiplier shows the effect of investment on consumption (and hence on income), the accelerator shows the effect of a change in consumption on investment. An increase in demand for consumption goods will lead to an increase in demand for equipment required to produce these goods. Since the production of a given amount of final output normally requires an amount of capital several times larger than the output produced with it during any short period (say a year), an increase in demand for final goods will result in an additional demand for capital goods several times larger than the new final demand. The principle of acceleration thus states that an increase in demand for consumption goods results in several times larger increase in demand for capital goods. The accelerator measures the change in investment goods industries as a result of changes in consumption goods industries. When incomes are rising, investment rises even faster; when incomes cease rising and stabilize at some level, investment may drop off very sharply. The principle of acceleration is based on the theory that the demand for services of capital goods industries is derived from current consumption demand and states that a given increase in demand for consumption goods in the economy generally results in an accelerated or magnified demand for capital goods, the latter bringing a stimulus to the whole economy. The acceleration coefficient is the numerical value of the relation between an increase in income (ΔY) and the resulting increase in investment (ΔI) via increase in consumption (ΔC). If, for instance, an increase in consumption expenditure of Rs. 4 crores induces businessmen to increase their investment by Rs. 16 crores, the accelerator would be 16/4 = 4.

Retailers and wholesalers may increase their inventories if it is their custom to keep their inventories in a fixed proportion to the rate of sales. New orders will, in this case, increase by more than the increase in sales. A similar but often much stronger effect is to be expected when the increased demand relates to durable consumers' goods. Durable consumer goods are demanded because of the services they render. To enjoy the services of durable goods through their life-time, the durable goods have first to be produced. Thus, the increased demand for services leads to an accelerated demand for the goods which render these services. While the increase in income may be just enough to pay for the services which are rendered monthly or to make small payments on the instalment plan, the demand cannot be satisfied unless the durable consumers' goods are produced as a whole. The increased demand for services of durable consumers' goods (like furniture, automobiles, radio sets, television sets, refrigerators, houses) leads to an accelerated demand for the durable consumer goods themselves. The larger the difference between the sale price of the service (e.g. monthly rent) and the total cost of the durable goods (e.g. house) or the larger the number of instalments, the greater would be the magnification of an original change in demand and the greater the opportunity for new investments.

Sometimes, production of increased consumer goods resulting from a rise in their demand may not lead to an increase in the capital equipment producing these goods. The existing equipment may wear out on account of constant use with the result that the increased demand for consumer goods cannot be met. This actually happened in India during the Second World War. In the absence of induced investment, the increased demand for consumer goods levelled off and as such the accelerator did not operate during all these years.

The factual basis of the acceleration principle is the knowledge that fluctuations in output and employment in investment goods industries are greater than in consumption goods industries. The more capitalised the methods of production are, the greater would be the value of the accelerator. The accelerator, however, cannot and does not claim to be able to explain all types of fluctuations. The prices of raw materials, for instance, fluctuate more violently than the prices of investment goods because the supply of raw materials, particularly agricultural commodities, is much more inelastic in response to the changes in demand than is the supply of manufactured goods.

Acceleration principle simply says that the amount of investment expenditure in any period of time depends on the change in level of income in the period. If I_t is investment expenditure in period t, Y_t and Y_{t-1} are the income levels in period t and period t – 1 respectively. The change in the level of income is $(Y_t - Y_{t-1})$. The acceleration principle says that:

$$I_t = \beta (Y_t - Y_{t-1}), \text{ where } 0 < \beta < 1$$

Assumptions

The assumptions on which the acceleration principle is based can be enumerated as follows:

(a) The total capital stock of the economy is fully utilised.

(b) The firms increase their capital stock to meet the increase in the demand for their products.

(c) The capital-output ratio is fixed. The optimum stock of capital is some constant proportion of output.

(d) There is no ceilling on investment and the supply of capital goods is perfectly elastic.

(e) Capital goods are perfectly divisible.

(f) Capital stock is optimally adjusted in each period.

(g) The increase in the demand for output occurs autonomously and not with response to the increase in investment.

(h) There are either fixed coefficients of production or variable coefficients of production, production is subject to constant returns to scale.

(i) There is no change of input prices.

The amount of optimum capital stock depends on the amount of output produced. The optimum capital stock increases with the increase in output. If output increases more quickly, the greater will be the demand for additional capital stock. It means that additional capital stock depends on the additional output produced, i.e. ΔK is a function of ΔY. Here ΔK is investment, I. Hence, I is a function of ΔY. This relationship can be analysed with the help of the Fig. 13.1. Suppose, output, Y is a function of capital, K and labour, L.

In Fig. 13.1, horizontal axis represents capital while vertical axis represents labour. Y_0 and Y_1 represent isoquant showing fixed level of output produced from different combinations of capital and labour. We get optimum capital stock K_0 for output level Y_0 and optimum capital stock K_1 for output level Y_1. The optimum capital stock increases from K_0 to K_1 with the increase in output level from Y_0 to Y_1. That is, the change in the optimum capital stock depends on the change in the planned output level. This is the main reason behind the acceleration principle.

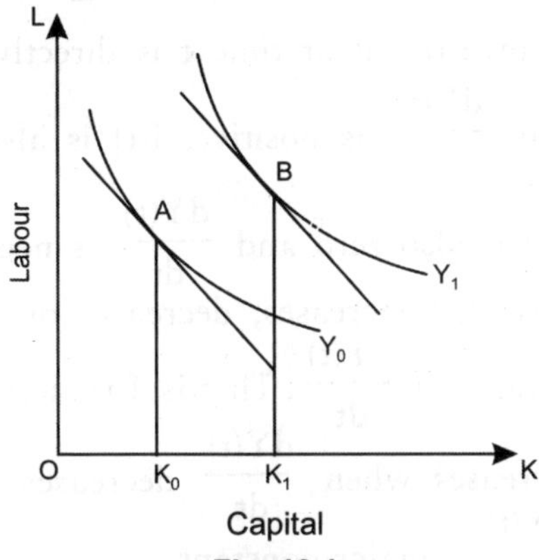

Fig. 13.1

It makes again two further implicit assumptions. (a) It assumes that the firms are always in equilibrium in using of inputs having no excess capacity. If there is excess capacity, the level of output can be increased without increasing the stock of capital. (b) The supply of capital goods is infinitely elastic so that adjustment is possible without lags. If the supply of capital goods is not perfectly elastic and if the capital goods require sometime to be produced investment increases only after a time lag.

Generally, we assume a linear relationship between I_t and $(Y_t - Y_{t-1})$, i.e. $I_t = \beta(Y_t - Y_{t-1})$ where β is called accelerator or the acceleration coefficient and also represents optimum capital-output ratio. If there is a fixed proportionality between capital and output,

then $\dfrac{K_t}{Y_t} = \beta$ or, $K_t = \beta Y_t$

Similarly, $K_{t-1} = \beta\, Y_{t-1}$

$\therefore\ K_t - K_{t-1} = \beta(Y_t - Y_{t-1})$

or, $I_t = \beta(Y_t - Y_{t-1})$

where change in capital stock is called investment. If we assume that K(t) and Y(t) are continuous functions of time (t), then the acceleration principle can be written as:

$$\frac{dK(t)}{dt} = \beta \cdot \frac{dY(t)}{dt}, \quad \text{i.e.} \quad I(t) = \beta \cdot \frac{dY(t)}{dt}$$

In this form, investment at time t is directly proportional to $\frac{dY(t)}{dt}$. So long as $\frac{dY(t)}{dt}$ is positive, I(t) is also positive, when $\frac{dY(t)}{dt}$ is zero, I(t) is also zero and $\frac{dY(t)}{dt}$ is negative, I(t) is also negative. Therefore, I(t) increases, decreases or remains constant depending on the value of $\frac{dY(t)}{dt}$. That is, I(t) increases when $\frac{dY(t)}{dt}$ increases, I(t) decreases when $\frac{dY(t)}{dt}$ decreases and I(t) remains constant when $\frac{dY(t)}{dt}$ remains constant.

Hence, investment depends not on the absolute level of income but to the rate of change in the level of income. Thus, total output increases, but we cannot say that investment increases, investment may decrease, because investment is not related with total output but related with the rate of growth of output. In the following diagram (Fig. 13.2) we can explain the relationship between output and investment.

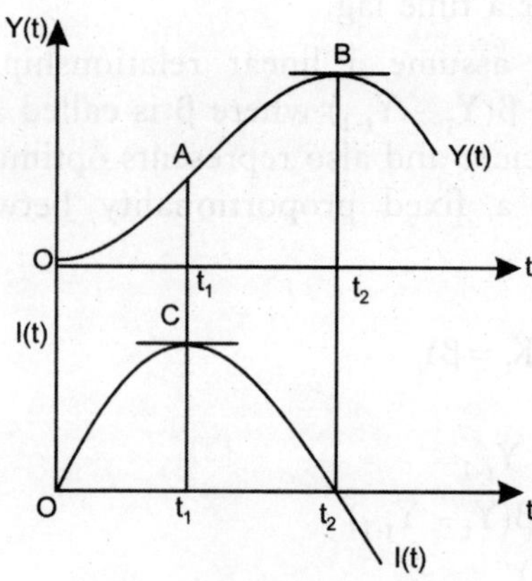

Fig. 13.2

In Fig. 13.2, as t increases, the rate of growth of income first increases, reaches its maximum and then decreases. The curve Y(t) is first convex from below and then concave. So long as Y(t) is convex $\frac{dY(t)}{dt}$ is rising. At point of inflexion A, $\frac{dY(t)}{dt}$ is maximum, when Y(t) is concave, $\frac{dY(t)}{dt}$ is decreasing. When Y(t) is maximum at point B, $\frac{dY(t)}{dt}$ = O and Y(t) is decreasing $\frac{dY(t)}{dt}$ is negative.

In the lower part of the diagram the I(t) curve is derived from the Y(t) curve from the upper part. How is it derived? It is shown below:

(a) Up to point A in the upper part of the diagram, $\frac{dY(t)}{dt}$ is increasing and hence I(t) is increasing up to point B in the lower part of the diagram both corresonding to the period t_1.

(b) At the point of inflexion, A, corresponding to the period t_1, $\frac{dY(t)}{dt}$ is maximum and I(t) is also maximum, at point C.

(c) Between A and B on Y(t) curve $\frac{dY(t)}{dt}$ is decreasing corresponding to the period between t_1 and t_2, hence I(t) is also decreasing.

(d) At point B on Y(t) corresponding to the period t_2, $\frac{dY(t)}{dt}$ is zero and hence I(t) is also zero.

(e) Beyond B on Y(t) corresponding to the period after t_2, $\frac{dY(t)}{dt}$ is negative and hence I(t) is also negative.

Therefore, I(t) depends not on Y(t) but on $\frac{dY(t)}{dt}$. I(t) increases when $\frac{dY(t)}{dt}$ increases. I(t) is maximum when $\frac{dY(t)}{dt}$ is maximum.

I(t) decreases when $\frac{dY(t)}{dt}$ decreases. I(t) is zero when $\frac{dY(t)}{dt}$ is zero. I(t) is negative when $\frac{dY(t)}{dt}$ is negative.

The implication of the above-discussed rigid model is that desired investment is proportional to changes in the level of output. It implies that net investment will be positive when output rises and will be negative when output falls. This model has been criticised on the following grounds:

(a) It does not allow for the substitution of labour for capital in order to increase output.

(b) It is not appropriate to a situation where excess productive capacity exists.

(c) Current investment spending is arguably not the result of current changes in output.

To come out of the above criticism, we shall consider the flexible accelerator model, which can accommodate lags in the adjustment of the capital stock to output changes by means of a partial adjustment technique. We know from the previous analysis,

$$I_t = K_t - K_{t-1} = \beta Y_t - K_{t-1}$$

If we add an adjustment factor, δ, the above equation can be written as

$$I_t = \delta(\beta Y_t - K_{t-1}), \text{ where } 0 < \delta < 1$$

The adjustment factor, δ, reflects the impact of current output changes (desired changes in the capital stock) on the current level of investment spending. If δ = 1, the flexible accelerator model would revert to the rigid accelerator model. If δ = 0, there would be no relationship between output changes and investment spending. The actual value of δ depends on the lag between capital appropriations and capital expenditures and may be influenced by cost of capital considerations. If the cost of capital is expected to fall, investment will be delayed. The size of δ also reflects the fact that current levels of investment spending may depend on previous output levels as well as the current output levels. If δ is constant, a higher K_{t-1} results in a lower level of investment spending given the current output level. It implies that idle capacity might have on reducing investment spending. Here we find that the accelerator model addresses two of the main criticisms of the rigid accelerator model, thereby preserving the accelerator principle as one of the tools for analysing and explaining the level of investment spending.

The flexible accelerator model can also be modified to allow for variations in the speed with which investment is undertaken to fill the gap between the desired and actual capital stock. This is a choice variable to the firm and may be influenced by credit conditions, including the level of the interest rate, tax considerations, and other variables. Other things being equal, less investment would be undertaken to eliminate discrepancies between the actual and desired capital stock when the interest rate was high than when the interest rate was low. Thus, the flexible accelerator model is not inconsistent with the assumption that investment is negatively related to the interest rate.

KEYNESIAN EXPENDITURE MULTIPLIER AND THE ACCELERATOR

The multiplier plays a key role in the Keynesian approach to business cycles. The interaction of the multiplier process and the accelerator explains why periods of economic expansion and contraction will tend to develop their own momentum. Following an initial increase in autonomous investment, the rise in income due to the multiplier process will be reinforced by an increase in new investment, via the accelerator, which will in turn have a further multiplier effect on income, and so on. Combining the so-called 'multiplier-accelerator model' with an analysis of 'ceilings' and 'floors' allows exponents of the Keynesian approach to account for both upper and lower turning points in the business cycle.

Using only autonomous investment, the multiplier effect is given as

$$\Delta Y = \frac{1}{1-c}\Delta I, \quad \text{where c is the MPC.}$$

The accelerator provides a theoretical justification for including income in the investment function. The inclusion of income in the investment function increases the size of the simple multiplier. We have

$$C = \overline{C} + cY, \qquad 0 < c < 1$$
$$I = \overline{I} + fY, \qquad 0 < f < 1$$

In equilibrium, income equals aggregate demand, i.e.,

$$Y = C + I$$

or, $Y = \bar{C} + cY + \bar{I} + fY$

or, $(1 - c - f)\,Y = \bar{C} + \bar{I}$

Thus, at equilibrium

$$Y_e = \frac{1}{(1 - c - f)}(\bar{C} + \bar{I})$$

Due to autonomous change in investment $(\Delta\bar{I})$, the change in equilibrium income is given by

$$\Delta Y_e = \frac{1}{(1 - c - f)}\Delta\bar{I}$$

From the above equation, we see that the presence of an accelerator reduces the denominator of the multiplier expression, which leads to increase in the value of the multiplier. Thus, an autonomous change in spending results in larger change in aggregate demand. This would imply greater output volatility as the economy reacts to autonomous changes in investment, which might occur because of innovation or business optimism or pessimism. In the case of volatile autonomous investment, a higher multiplier means a less stable private economy. If a countercyclical fiscal policy is pursued, the required adjustment in government spending is smaller due to larger multiplier.

In order to illustrate the difference between the process set in motion by appropriately chosen investments and that described by the Keynesian multiplier and the accelerator theory, we consider an example. According to the Keynesian theoretical model the government builds a road without worrying whether or not it is really useful, since the important thing is to set the multiplier in motion by any investment whatever—even by digging ditches in the sea. According to the second model, before deciding to build a road, the government examines all the other possible ways to invest the money available and builds the road only when an inquiry into the country's needs, related to the available means, shows that the building of the road is relatively the most advantageous investment for the national economy; among other things on account of other investments that it may stimulate, not as a result of increased demand for consumer goods but because the road will generate traffic, etc. At this point it becomes easier to understand the significance of the type of investment, which is linked to the concept that there are other and in practice often more important means that those of Keynesian multiplier theory by which an initial expenditure triggers a series of repercussions that multiply its effects.

No forecast of the effects of the investment can come out of the Kynesian multiplier. Such a forecast has to be based on a thorough study of the country's economy, the resources available, production costs, markets, export potential and so on. It is a matter that, in part, can be linked to today's sectoral multipliers and to a more detailed analysis of the real and nominal effects of the Keynesian multiplier itself, in which the scope for different sectors to respond to increased demand by expanding physical production are also considered.

Taken together, the multiplier and the accelerator give an explanation of both parts of total effective demand (consumption and investment) in terms of the same macro-economic variables. Keynes had explained why an economic system may fall into a depression. The principle of acceleration came also to explain how depressions can recur regularly. The introduction of changes in income immediately carried the investigation over to dynamic analysis. For, a change in income induces a larger change in investment (accelerator), and this change in investment generates an even larger change in income (multiplier). The analysis of this accelerator-multipler interaction has given rise to practically all modern theories of the trade cycle. These theories represent the culmination of the theory of effective demand.

MULTIPLIER AND ACCELERATOR DISTINGUISHED

Inspite of the formal symmetry of the multiplier and the accelerator relations, there are substantial differences between the two. The multiplier shows the effect of a change in investment on income and employment and the accelerator shows the effect of a change in consumption on investment. While the multiplier depends upon the propensity to consume, the accelerator depends upon the durability of the equipment. In other words, the former depends upon psychological factors while the later is dependent upon operational factors. In fact, accelerator is also psychological in its origin and content but becomes highly technical on operational plane.

When income is inserted as the argument of the consumption function, that is precisely what is meant. However, when a change of income is inserted as the argument of the investment function that is not really what is meant. Ideally, what should be inserted is the expected change in income. Since, expectations cannot be quantified, we must be content with using the past change in income as a proxy variable for the expected change in income. This places the two equations at two quite different levels of abstraction, the one concerning the accelerator relation being the more remote of the two. The difficulty here is that one cannot hope to consider this asymmetry by any mathematical formulation. The theorist must therefore be keenly aware, in evaluating the conclusions, that at the point of departure there is an investment function that has a weaker theoretical foundation than the consumption function.

The multiplier relation always remains formally the same, whether the system is in a situation of idle productive capacity or in a situation of full capacity utilization. The principle of acceleration, on the other hand, works at its best in a situation of full capacity utilization. When there is idle capacity, the principle may still be working but in an attenuated form, or in any case in a more complicated way. If the analysis of the interaction of the multiplier and the accelerator has taken the economic theory of effective demand to its peak, it has also clearly strained to the limits of its possibilities. For, as soon as economic investigation is carried over from the Keynesian short run to movements through time, and the capital stock can no longer be taken as given but is itself changing, then another side of the picture is bound to become relevant—the evolution through time of the physical possibilities of production.

The principle of the multiplier, as laid out by R.F. Kahn and J.M. Keynes is that if investment increases, there will be an increase in output as a result of a 'multiplier' relationship between equilibrium output and the autonomous components of spending. The principle of the accelerator, as laid out by Albert Aftalion and John Maurice Clark, was that investment decisions on the part of firms are at least in part dependent upon expectations of future increases in demand, which may, in turn, be extrapolated from any current or past increases in aggregate demand or output. Thus, the multiplier principle implies that investment increases output whereas the acceleration principle implies that increases in output will themselves induce increases in investment.

THE BUSINESS CYCLE AND THE MULTIPLIER-ACCELERATOR

The business cycle can be explained by combining the multiplier and the accelerator models. The business cycle passes through the following four steps:

(a) Government expenditure increases, and boosts consumer income.

(b) Consumer income raises aggregate output through the multiplier effect.

(c) Net investment increases through the acceleration process.

(d) The process starts to repeat itself.

We describe the process by assuming that the economy is tending toward full employment, real GNP is rising, and business sales are rising at an increasing rate. Because of the accelerator, this results in increased investment. And because of the multiplier, the increased investment increases real GNP by a multiple of itself. In other words, the accelerator and multiplier work together to expand the economy and move it faster toward full-employment output. Let us consider the Samuelson's linear multiplier-accelerator model of business cycle, which may be described by following equations.

$$Y_t = g_t + C_t + I_t$$
$$C_t = \alpha Y_{t-1}$$
$$I_t = \beta(C_t - C_{t-1})$$
$$g_t = 1$$

where,

Y_t = National income,

g_t = Government expenditure,

C_t = Consumption expenditure,

I_t = Induced private investment,

t = Time period, and

α and β = Constants.

The second order linear difference equation in output can be written as,

$$Y_t = 1 + \alpha (1 + \beta)Y_{t-1} - \alpha\beta Y_{t-2}$$

Thus, we see that there are various solution paths for national income to be derived from this model, depending on the values of the roots off the equation, or equivalently, the relationships between the parameters α and β. In general, a number of solution paths for a second order linear difference equations are possible. The various possible responses to a positive, unsustained, displacement to g_t at time t_0 are shown in Fig. 13.3.

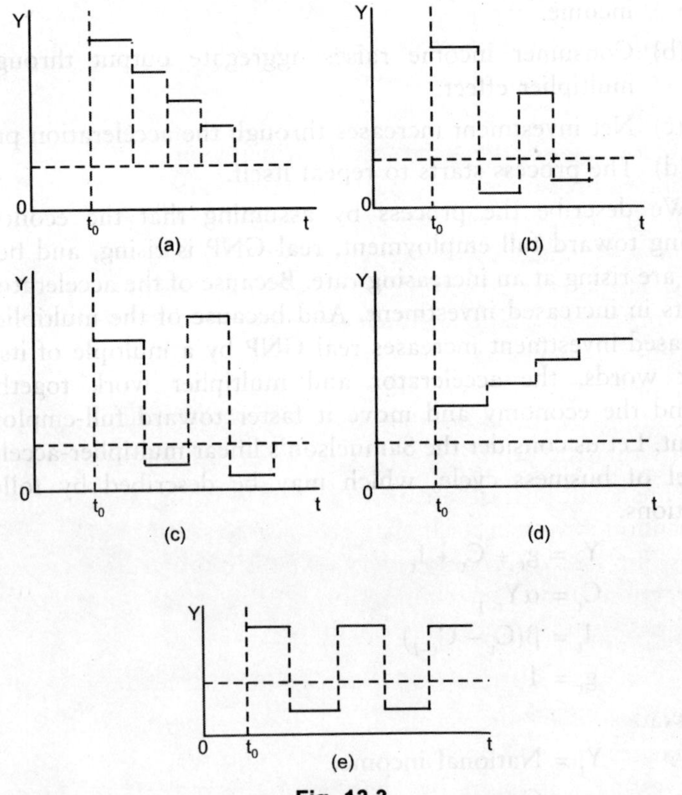

Fig. 13.3

Negative displacements result in similar solution paths, but with income starting below the original equilibrium following the shock so that, in Panel (d), income will decrease at an increasing rate. Sustained displacements to government expenditure will yield similar solution paths except that the respective solution paths will converge to, diverge from, or oscillate around, a new asymptotic equilibrium, which is $(1/1 - \alpha)$ times the constant level of government expenditure (Samuelson, 1939). In Panel (b), perfectly regular periodic fluctuations in g_t will result eventually in fluctuations of income of the same period.

At full employment, the growth rate in business sales slows down. Because of the accelerator, investment falls and because of the multiplier, there is a multiple decrease in real GNP. As real GNP falls, sales decrease further, leading to another round of cuts in investment. At some point, the economy will bottom out and the process is likely to repeat itself. The multiplier-accelerator theory of the business cycle holds that the boom naturally leads into the bust, and the bust naturally leads into the boom. The theory implies that the private sector itself contains the seeds of the business cycle.

According to the accelerator principle, rapid output growth stimulates investment. High investment in turn stimulates more output growth, and the process continues until the capacity of the economy is reached, at which point the economic growth rate slows. The slower growth in turn reduces investment spending and inventory accumulation, which tends to send the economy into a recession. The process then works in reverse until the trough is reached, and the economy then stabilizes and turns up again. A key implication of the multiplier-acceleratory theory of the business cycle is that the private economy is inherently unstable.

Thus, multiplier-accelerator theories look for mechanisms within the economic system itself that give rise to self-generating business cycles. In this approach, every expansion breeds recession and contraction, and every contraction breeds revival and expansion—in a quasi-regular, repeating chain.

CONCEPT OF INDUCED INVESTMENT

Traditionally, the accelerator refers to the investment induced by changes in consumption only; but it may also be viewed in terms of investment induced by changes in output as a whole which includes investment. Hicks, in fact, considers accelerator in the latter sense and rightly so. For the relation, he substitutes the investment co-efficient (v) defined as "the ratio of the induced investment to the changes in output which called it forth". The strength of the acceleration effect, if measured by the total amount of induced investment generated in a given period, would depend on the relevant change in output and the size of the investment co-efficient.

The above concept of 'induced' investment is based on the fundamental assumption that producers of capital goods as a whole adjust their investment programmes to the changing level of national income, considering the latter as the best single index of the profit outlook. The main justification for conceiving of 'induced' investment in terms of the marginal propensity to invest rather than in terms of the traditional acceleration coefficient lies in the fact that the former is a behavioural relation on a par with the marginal propensity to consume while the latter is a technological relation between the additional stock of capital equipment and the additional physical output. Thus, the marginal propensity to invest can have as large or small values as business confidence, profit expectations and financial prudence are assumed to influence investment policies in given conditions of technology. When, however, a change in the stock of capital (positive net investment) must be considered as an explicit variable, as in a long-run growth analysis, then induced investment must be conceived in terms of acceleration coefficient or the capital-output ratio. A corollary justification for viewing 'induced' investment from the point of view of the marginal propensity to invest lies in the advantage it affords for analysing the behaviour of gross investment and hence of GNP, irrespective of whether the stock of capital and hence production capacity are thereby increased or decreased (which latter changes are the concern mainly of growth economics).

FORMS OF INDUCED INVESTMENT

The total induced investment consists of induced investment in fixed capital, in working capital, and in inventories. Hicks defines working capital as "goods in process as well as such minimum stocks of materials and half-finished goods as are technically necessary in the production process". Inventories or what Hicks calls "liquid capital", is defined as "reserve stocks not technically necessary". Some minimum amount of liquid capital, consisting of reserve stocks of finished as well unfinished goods, would be necessary for conveniently carrying out production. Investment in the three forms, because of the differences in their nature, responds differently to changes in consumption or output. It is, therefore, necessary to study the response separately for the three forms.

Induced Investment in Fixed Capital

Strength of the acceleration effect: A change in output, by necessitating the adjustment of the capital stock to the new level of output induces investment in a given capital. The total amount of induced investment in a given period depends upon the relevant change (s) in output and the related Investment Coefficient (v). If it is assumed that the entire induced investment generated by a given change in output occurs in the period immediately following such change, induced investment in the nth period would be $v(Y_{n-1} - Y_{n-2})$ where Y_n is output in the nth period and v is the Investment Coefficient. If the induced investment effect of a given change in output extends over a number of periods, induced investment in the *n*th period would be

$$v_1(Y_{n-1} - Y_{n-2}) + v_2(Y_{n-2} - Y_{n-3}) + ... + v_p(Y_{n-p} - Y_{n-p-1})$$

where Y_n is output in the nth period, v_p is the induced investment which materializes p periods later as the result of a change in output of one unit in some particular period, and p is the number of periods following that in which the change in output occurs over which the induced investment effect of such change extends. On the same assumption the total induced investment generated by the change, in output in the nth period would be

$$(Y_n - Y_{n-1})\ (v_1 + v_2 + v_3 + ... + v_n)$$

In this case the Investment Coefficient v would be the sum total of the partial coefficients v_1, v_2, v_3, ...v_p.

The larger the v, the greater (in absolute amount) is the total induced investment generated by a given change in output. In case of positive induced investment generated by an increase in output, the strength of v depends on (a) the degree of capital intensity of the production techniques employed, (b) the existence of unused plant capacity relevant to the given increment of output, (c) the scope for the utilisation of capital-saving inventions in effecting replacement and renewals of plant, (d) the nature of the expected increase in the demand for output, and (e) the proportion of increase in output foreseen and provided for in previous capital outlays. The higher the ratio of capital to output (i.e. the capital intensity of production techniques), the large would obviously be v. The existence of unused plant capacity in the lines in which the increase in demand for output occurs makes the required increase in output possible without addition to the stock of fixed capital. The existence of relevant idle capacity, therefore, lowers v. If the rate of capital-saving invention, and that of depreciation and obsolescence of plant, are high enough, it may be possible to replace the capital stock falling due for replacement and renewal by one with a higher ratio of output to capital at a rate that would enable the required increase in output to be achieved without net addition to the total capital stock. The larger the scope for the rise in this way of the ratio of output to capital, the lower will be v. Increase in the demand for output induces net addition to the capital stock only if it is expected to last. In case the increase in demand for output is not expected to continue, the producers would have a tendency to meet the increased demand by utilising the existing plant capacity more intensively, in fact even at a rate higher than the optimum rate of utilization. Lastly, to the extent the increase in demand has been foreseen and investment outlay undertaken in anticipation of it, it would not, when it occurs, induce further investment.

Time-shape of induced investment: Having discussed the factors on which depends the strength of the acceleration effect, now we turn to the shape of induced investment through time. Let us start from a stationary state characterised by constant output, zero net investment and gross investment equal to the constant rate of depreciation. Let us now assume that a once-for-all increase in output, expected to be permanent, takes place. The capital stock will need to be adjusted to the new level of output; increase in output would thus induce positive net investment. Assume that the additional capital goods can be produced within a single 'period'. During the first period gross investment would rise above its previous level by the value of the additional capital goods, and since depreciation, being based on the previously existing stock of capital, would remain unchanged, net investment would also be equal to the same amount. In the next period, when the additional capital stock has already been acquired, gross investment will decline to the level prevailing under the initial stationary equilibrium. But now there is the extra depreciation on the new capital stock. As such the net investment will become negative by this amount. When the new capital goods are due for replacement, and if they are replaced in a single period, gross investment will once again rise to the level of the period during which they were first created. But because of the extra depreciation of the now larger capital-stock, net investment in this period will be lower than in that period by the amount of this extra depreciation. In the next period, gross investment will revert to the initial level and net investment become negative and so on. The first phase of positive net investment induced by the increase in output is called the 'initial hump' and the subsequently altering phase of negative and positive net investment the 'tail' of the 'stream' of a new investment induced by such increase in output.

In case the capital goods comprising the additional investment, and their replacements, have different lives, there will be a 'stream' of net investment corresponding to each part of the investment. Since the flows and ebbs of each stream (i.e., the alternating spans of positive and negative net investment) will occur at different times and be superimposed, fluctuations will be damped to the extent such ups and downs are mutually offset. Further damping will occur if actual life of each portion of equipment turns out to be different from its normal life. The more effective will be the damping, the longer is the period over which the initial investment spreads.

Now assume that the increase in output is not once-for-all but it is followed in latter periods by other increases in output, each inducing a fresh stream of net investment with the above time-shape. Since these streams begin at different periods of time, when added together, their flows and ebbs may mutually offset. A succession of increases in output may thus tend to damp fluctuations in net investment.

Induced Investment in Working Capital and Liquid Capital

Let us assume a once-for-all increase in the demand for output at a time when both working capital and liquid capital are fully adjusted to a previously constant level of output. On the assumption of continuous production, requiring outputs at all stages of the production process, the rate of investment1 in working capital will rise from the beginning to the end of the production process. After that it will decrease sharply to zero because then total working capital would have been adjusted to the higher level of output.

Investment in liquid capital will, however, respond differently to an increase in output. During the time taken by output to attain the higher level, increased demand will be met by drawing upon stocks. Thus the period of investment in working capital will be marked by disinvestment in liquid capital. The end of this period is characterised by the cessation both of investment in working capital and disinvestment in liquid capital so that taking the two together net investment falls to zero.

Unlike investment in fixed capital, there is no necessary asymmetry between rises and declines in output in their effects on investment in working and liquid capital. In the first phase following the decline in output, there is positive net investment in liquid capital and disinvestment in working capital. At the close of this period both positive investment in liquid capital and disinvestment in working capital ceases, leaving the total net investment zero.

Induced investment in fixed capital depends upon actual changes in output, for directly, in the Marshallian short period, business responds to changes in demand for output by varying the rate of utilisation of existing capacity. It is only the in-appropriateness of the existing stock of fixed capital for the new level of output that, in due course, causes this stock to be suitably adjusted. The induced investment in working and the liquid-capital occurs in response to changes in demand for output and precedes the actual change in output.

Total Induced Investment

The above analysis shows that investment responds typically to increases in demand for output in three phases. During the first phase, there is positive investment in working capital and disinvestment in stocks, both falling to zero at its close. During the second phase, there is positive investment in stocks (necessary to rebuild them after the withdrawals in the first phase and to adjust them to the new higher level of output). During the third phase, extending to the distant future, there are oscillations in net investment or owing to altering periods of negative and positive net investment in fixed capital represented by the 'tail' of the induced stream of investment in fixed capital.

Similarly, the decline in demand proceeds in three phases: during the first phase there is disinvestment in working capital and positive investment in stocks, both falling to zero at its close; during the second phase there will be disinvestment both in fixed capital and stocks; during the third phase there would be oscillations in net investment represented by the 'tail' of the induced stream of disinvestment in fixed capital. Though total net disinvestment in the second phase is comparable, for an equal change in demand, to the total net investment in response to increase in demand, yet the existence of a ceiling to the possible rate of disinvestment may cause it to be spread over a longer period. Since the initial trough in the second phase of investment's reaction to decline in demand might be flatter than the corresponding initial hump produced by investment's response to an equal increase in demand, oscillations in net investment in the third phase would be damped, and hence less important in the first phase. Lastly, while the induced investment streams produced by successive rises in demand that supervene upon one another can be superimposed, such superimposition may not be possible when successive declines in demand supervene upon one another, for rate of disinvestment already may have touched its ceiling. The supervening declines in demand would not then intensify but prolong disinvestment.

Table 13.1: Working of Accelerator

(Figures in crores of Rupees)

Period	*Output of final goods*	*Capital goods required*	*New capital goods required*	*Replacement*	*Total new capital goods required*
1	2	3	4	5	6 = 4 + 5
1	1,000	500	0	50	50
2	1,200	600	100	50	150
3	1,300	650	50	60	110
4	1,300	650	0	65	65
5	1,200	600	–50	65	15
6	1,100	550	–50	60	10
7	1,000	500	–50	55	5
8	900	450	–50	50	0

Table 13.1 explains the working of the acceleration principle. Let us suppose that production of final goods worth Rs. 2 requires capital goods worth Re. 1; the life of the capital goods is 10 years and 10 percent of them are accordingly replaced each year.

The first row in Table 13.1 shows the position in the first period. In the second period, output of final goods rises by Rs. 200 crores and the requirement of new capital goods by Rs. 100 crores (col. 4). The total amount of new capital goods required (col. 6) is Rs. 150 crores. Thus a 20 percent increase (from Rs. 1,000 crores to Rs. 1,200 crores) in output results in a 200 percent increase (from Rs. 50 crores to Rs. 150 crores) in capital goods. In the third period, the output of final goods rises, but only by Rs. 100 crores, over the preceding period. This requires an increase of Rs. 110 crores in the total new capital goods. Inspite of an 8 percent rise (from Rs. 1,200 crores to Rs. 1,300 crores) in output of final goods, there is a decline of 26.67 percent (from Rs. 150 crores to Rs. 110 crores) in capital goods industry. This is so because the absolute increase of Rs. 200 crores in the output of final goods has not been maintained. In the fourth period, the output of final goods remains unchanged at Rs. 1,300 crores. No new capital goods are required except for replacement. Production in the capital goods industry drops by 40.09 percent (from Rs. 110 crores to Rs. 65 crores). In the eighth period, the output of final goods declines by Rs. 100 crores and the capital goods industry collapses.

The above example leads to an important generalisation. When there is an absolute increase in the production of final goods, the rise in the capital goods industry is magnified. If the increase in the production goods is maintained, the capital goods industry will only manage to avoid a decline. As the increment in the final goods industry declines, the capital goods industry suffers an absolute decline and in greater proportion. Thus a depression can set in simply because consumption has stopped growing so rapidly. In other words, the depression can start even if the consumption has not dropped off absolutely but only levelled off at a high level. Any change in output of final goods causes a multiple change in the production of capital goods. This magnifying effect is the root cause of fluctuations in the capital goods industry. Thus the principle of acceleration provides a powerful explanation of the destabilising forces working in the economy during a trade cycle. This explanation teaches us a lesson that in order to keep the economy prosperous, mere standing still or running at a slow pace is not enough, we must run faster and faster to ward off the danger of a depression. "We have all heard of situations", says Samuelson, "where people have to keep running in order to standstill. In economic world, matters may be still worse: the system may have to keep running at an ever-faster pace in order to standstill."[1]

The strength of the accelerator primarily depends upon (i) the capital-output ratio or capital coefficient and (ii) the durability of the capital equipment. The higher the capital coefficient, the larger would be the increase in investment as a result of a given increase in consumption and conversely. Similarly, the greater the durability of the capital equipment, the larger would be the degree of magnification of the derived demand; when there are no durable means of production, there is no magnification at all.

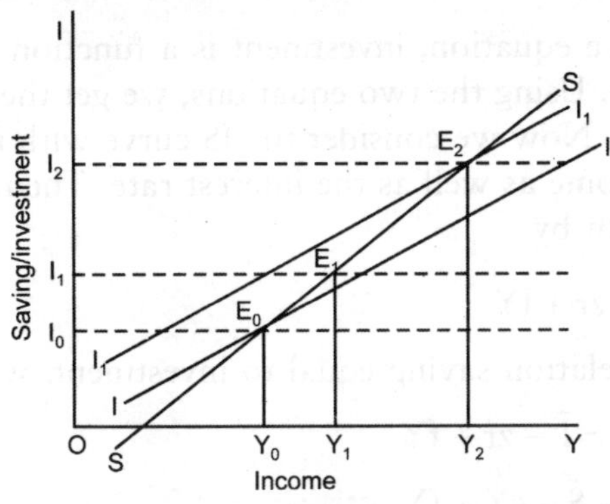

Fig. 13.4

The figure given above illustrates the principle of acceleration. Since investment depends upon the level of national income, investment would be high when national income is high and investment would be low when national income is low. The investment schedule (I I), therefore, is drawn in such a way that it is higher at a higher level of income. The investment may be negative at a very low level of income. If the investment schedule shifts upward from I I to I_1I_1 because of an exogenous increase in investment, the multiplier effect would be greater than it would be if the investment were purely exogenous. If there were only exogenous investment (i.e. increase in income does not induce any investment) as shown by the dotted I I which is parallel to the horizontal axis, the multiplier effect would have been only Y_0Y_1. But when there is induced investment as shown by rising I I, super-multiplier effect or total multiplier-acceleration effect would be Y_1Y_2 which consists of Y_0Y_1 (multiplier effect) and Y_1Y_2 (acceleration effect). If there were no acceleration effect, Y_0Y_2 increase in income would have been obtained by I_1I_2 exogenous investment.

INCOME AS A DETERMINANT OF INVESTMENT

The absolute slope of the IS curve is reduced when we include income as a determinant of investment and this also increases the impact of monetary policy.

The saving and investment functions are given by

$$S = \overline{S} + sY$$

$$I = \overline{I} - zr$$

In the above equation, investment is a function of interest rate but not income. Using the two equations, we get the slope of the IS curve as (– s/z). Now we consider the IS curve with investment as a function of income as well as the interest rate. Then the investment function is given by

$$I = \overline{I} - zr + fY$$

From the relation saving equal to investment, we have

$$\overline{S} + sY = \overline{I} - zr + fY$$

or, $$zr = \overline{I} - \overline{S} - sY + fY$$

or, $$r = \frac{\overline{I} - \overline{S}}{z} - \frac{(s - f)}{z} Y$$

Thus, the absolute value of the slope of the IS curve is reduced from s/z to (s – f)/z. Since, the accelerator results in a decrease in the slope of IS curve relative to LM curve, an increase in the money supply has a greater effect on aggregate demand, which has been shown in Fig. 13.5.

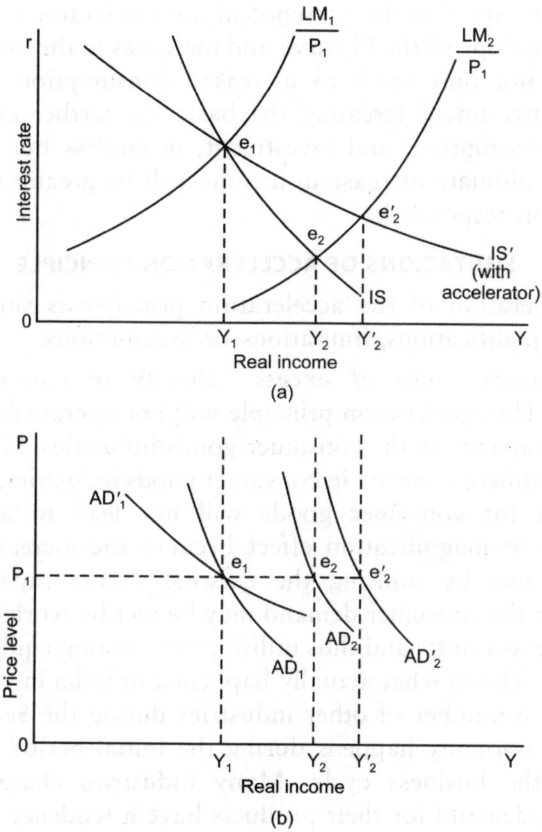

Fig. 13.5

In panel (a) of the Fig. 13.5, we have drawn two IS curves, one with an accelerator and one without it, with a given LM curve at an initial output level of Y_1. An increase in the money supply shifts LM curve rightward. This results in the increase in output. Increase in output is greater $(Y'_2 - Y_1)$ for the case with the accelerator than for the model without the accelerator $(Y_2 - Y_1)$.

In Panel (b) of the Fig. 13.5, the intersection of the IS curves and LM_1 in Panel (a) represents the point e_1 on two aggregate demand curves. AD_1 corresponds to IS, and AD'_1 corresponds to IS′. The increase in the money supply shifts aggregate demand rightward to AD'_2 for the case with the accelerator and to AD_2 without the accelerator. The accelerator increases the rightward shift in aggregate demand from an increase in the money supply.

Thus, we see that the presence of an accelerator effect reduces the absolute slope of the IS curve and increases in the income. A rise in income not only leads to increased consumption but also to increased investment (creating the basis for further expansion of income, consumption, and investment, in endless but diminishing chain), the ultimate increase in income will be greater than if only consumption responded.

LIMITATIONS OF ACCELERATION PRINCIPLE

The operation of the acceleration principle is subject to the following qualifications, limitations or assumptions.

(a) Non-existence of excess capacity in consumer goods industries: The acceleration principle will not operate if there exists unutilised capacity in the consumer goods industries. When there is enough unutilised capacity in consumer goods industries, an increase in demand for consumer goods will not lead to any induced investment or magnification effect because the increased demand would be met by utilising the existing excess capacity. Many increases in the consumer demand may be met by working overtime or adding extra shifts and thus utilising the existing equipment more intensively. This is what actually happened in India in paper, sugar, textile and a number of other industries during the Second World War. This normally happens during the initial period of recovery phase of the business cycle. Many industries characterised by fluctuating demand for their products have a tendency to maintain excess capacity as a normal condition. Thus the working of accelerator assumes that there is no excess capacity and devices like double shift or overtime are not possible.

(b) Excess capacity in investment goods industries: In the capital goods industries, on the other hand, it is assumed that there exists unutilised capacity. If there were no excess capacity in investment goods industries, an increase in the derived demand for equipment would not lead to an increase in the supply of equipment and thus the operation of the accelerator would be impaired. The working of the accelerator, therefore, is conditioned by the tough assumption that there exists excess capacity in the investment goods industry but no excess capacity in the consumer goods industry.

(c) Fluidity: The operation of the accelerator assumes that the industry is in a fluid condition. It presumes that "....finished goods

are turned out as fast as wanted and materials and means of production are instantly supplied as fast as the process of finishing requires them."[2]

(d) Nature of demand: The principle of acceleration will work only if the additional demand for consumer goods is of a lasting nature. If the entrepreneurs feel that the increase in demand is of a purely temporary character, they will not add to their capital equipment for meeting this demand. This also shows that the principle of acceleration is based not only on technological factor but also on profit expectation.

(e) Constant capital-output ratio: The principle assumes that there is a constant ratio between the output of consumer goods and the capital equipment required for their production, or in other words, that there is constant capital-output ratio. In the real world, this ratio is not constant. In addition to inventions and improvements in techniques of production which change the output per unit of capital equipment, the existing capital equipment may be used more or less intensively. Further, changes in the expectations of businessmen in regard to future trends in wages, interest, and demand, may lead to changes in the proportions in which the different factors are combined. The capital-output ratio thus varies in different phases of the business cycle.

(f) Elastic supply of resources: The operation of the principle of acceleration is conditioned by the elastic supply of resources and the ability of the capital-equipment industry to expand its production. The capital-equipment industry would be able to expand its production in response to an increase in demand for its product only if adequate unemployed resources are available to it for employment. But once the full employment level is reached, it would not be possible to expand the production of capital equipment which would put a break to the working of the acceleration principle.

(g) Elastic supply of credit: An elastic supply of money and credit facilitates the smooth working of the acceleration principle. Whenever there is induced investment, money and credit should be forthcoming in adequate quantities for investment in investment goods industries. A shortage of money and credit would raise the rate of interest and thereby the cost of investment financed by

borrowed funds which would in turn inhibit investment. For the free and unhindered operation of accelerator, it is essential that sufficient funds are always available for investment purposes.

(h) Inability of investment demand to fall below the value of depreciation: Though accelerator works in the period of rising demand as well as in that of declining demand, its effect may be limited in the latter period. A decline in the demand for capital equipment (or disinvestment) is necessarily limited to replacement. An entrepreneur cannot reduce his demand for capital equipment below zero. The maximum that he can do in response to a decline in the demand for his product is to curtail replacement of his capital equipment and this cannot go below zero. Suppose the decline in demand for the finished product requires a 25 percent reduction in the capital equipment but replacement demand in any year amounts to only 10 percent of the capital equipment. In this case the accelerator cannot operate with full strength and its operation would be limited to a 10 percent decline in capital equipment. The restraint on the free working of the accelerator in such a situation would be reflected in the generation of excess idle capacity.

(i) Marginal efficiency of investment and the rate of interest: The acceleration principle does not take into account of the role of marginal efficiency of investment and the rate of interest in determining the level of investment.

(j) Expectations: The role of expectations in investment decision is neglected in this theory. But investment is done on the basis of expectation. This vital part is omitted in this theory.

(k) Divisibility of capital: The vital leakage of this theory is that capital is completely divisible. But in reality, capital good is not perfectly divisible and many times it is indivisible.

MULTIPLIER-ACCELERATION INTERACTION

The most famous exposition of the multiplier-accelerator interaction was put forward by Paul Samuelson. He showed that, given a change in autonomous expenditure, income will follow different paths (including regular, damped and explosive) for different combinations of the marginal propensity to consume and the accelerator coefficient. The multiplier-accelerator model has been combined with Hicks's analysis of 'ceilings' and 'floors' to form a central element of the Keynesian approach to business cycles. As such, it can account for both upper and lower turning points in the business cycle.

We use the ceiling and floor version of the accelerator multiplier interactions that were developed in the 1950s as a simple prototype model, which endogenously can generate unsatisfactory states but which can be constrained by interventions to generate satisfactory states. We postulate that institutions and interventions thwart the instability breeding dynamics that are natural to market economies by interrupting the endogenous process and starting the economy again with non-market determined values as initial conditions. It follows that the observed behaviour of the economy is not the result of market mechanisms in isolation but is due to a combination of market behaviour and the ability of institutions, conventions and policy interventions to contain and dominate the endogenous economic reactions that breed instability if left alone.

A Keynesian endogenous explanation of business cycles received a mathematical statement in the formalization of the interaction of the accelerator and multiplier as a second-order linear difference equation. As it could generate only four types of time paths (oscillatory and damped, oscillatory and explosive, non-oscillatory and damped and non-oscillatory and explosive) none of which would do for business cycle analysis, this simple form was unsatisfactory except as an expository device.

Starting with a Samuelson type multiplier-accelerator interaction and assuming that the parameter values lead to explosive (monotonic or cyclical) paths, Hicks added ceiling and floors that had the effect of constraining the economy to acceptable paths. This model was extended by Minsky who motivated the ceilings and floors by referring to the behaviour of monetary and financing relations and interpreted the ceilings and floors as the imposition of new initial conditions. This allowed the endogenous dynamics to be such that unsatisfactory performance would be generated by the unconstrained economy even as the constrained behaviour is acceptable. As policy can be interpreted as the imposition of new initial conditions in Minsky's formulation policy can play a positive role.

In particular, the multiplier does not pretend to give the relation between total national income induced by governmental spending and the original amount of money spent. This is clearly seen by a simple example. In an economy where any rupee of governmental deficit spending would result in a hundred rupee less of private investment than would otherwise have been undertaken, the ratio of total induced national income to the initial expenditure is overwhelmingly negative, yet the multiplier in the strict sense must be positive. The answer to the puzzle is simple. What the multiplier does give, is the ratio of the total amount of investment, governmental and private. In other words, it does not tell us how much is to be multiplied. The effects upon private investment are often regarded as tertiary influences and receive little systematic attention.

In order to remedy the situation in some measure, Professor Hansen has developed a new model sequence which ingeniously combines the multiplier analysis with that of the acceleration principle. This is done by making additions to the national income consist of three components—(a) government deficit spending, (b) private consumption expenditure induced by previous public expenditure, and (c) induced private investment, assumed according to the familiar acceleration principle to be proportional to the time increase of consumption. The introduction of the last component accounts for the novelty of conclusions reached and also the increased complexity of the analysis. A numerical example may be cited to illuminate the assumption made.

In Table 13.2, it is assumed that in each income period, there is an autonomous investment of Rs. 100, that the marginal propensity to consume is ½, and that the accelerator is 2.

Table 13.2

(Figure in Rupees)

Period	*Autonomous Investment*	*Increase in Consumption*	*Induced Investment*	*Total Increase in Income*
1	100	.00	.00	100.00
2	100	50.00	100.00	250.00
3	100	125.00	150.00	375.00
4	100	187.50	125.00	412.50
5	100	206.25	37.50	343.75
6	100	171.87	–68.76	203.11
7	100	101.55	–140.64	60.91
8	100	30.45	–142.20	–11.75
9	100	54.87	–72.64	21.60
10	100	10.80	33.34	144.14
11	100	72.07	122.46	294.53
12	100	147.26	150.38	397.64

Since there is a lag of one period, the rise in investment by Rs. 100 in the first period increases income in this period only by Rs. 100. In the second period, Rs. 100 income of the first period induces a rise of Rs. 50 in consumption because the marginal propensity to consume is assumed to be ½; this rise of Rs. 50 in consumption induces investment of Rs. 100 as the accelerator is assumed to be 2. Thus in this period the income rises by Rs. 100 + Rs. 50 + Rs. 100 or Rs. 250. In the third period, this income of Rs. 250 induces a rise of Rs. 125 in consumption. Since this Rs. 125 constitutes a rise of Rs. 75 over the previous period, a new investment of Rs. 150 is induced. Thus in this period, the increase in income amounts to Rs. 375. In the same manner the increase in income is calculated for the succeeding periods.

Table 13.2 shows that the investments in income fluctuate widely. The increments in income rise up to the fourth period; thereafter they decline and become even negative in period 8. After the 8th period, they start rising again. Even the rates of changes are different in different periods. This explains the cyclical changes which take place in the economy as a result of the interaction of the multiplier and accelerator. It may be mentioned that different values of the marginal propensity to consume and of the accelerator would give rise to different cycles or patterns of series of increment in income shown in the last column of Table 13.2.

If both the marginal propensity to consume and the accelerator are very high, the process of expansion will go on to higher and higher levels until the ceiling of full employment is reached. At this level, the output will flatten out and induced investment will come to a stop. Besides this case, so long as the MPS is positive, the rise in income will be slowed down progressively as a continuously large part of the increase in income is saved. Ultimately there would occur a decline in induced investment. When this decline in induced investment exceeds the rise in consumption, a decline in income will start. Thus inspite of the acceleration effect, a positive marginal propensity to save will ultimately put a stop to the process of income propagation. Further, a continuous increase in investment tends to lower the MEC until further investment no longer remains profitable.

SAMUELSON MODEL

Prof. Samuelson shows that it is possible to have different types of business cycles or fluctuations from a continued injection of public investment by assuming different values of the marginal propensity to consume (α) and the acceleration coefficient (β).[3] The model sequence of national income for selected values of α and β are shown in Table 13.3.

Table 13.3

(unit: one dollar)

Period	$\alpha = .5$ $\beta = 0$	$\alpha = .5$ $\beta = 2$	$\alpha = .6$ $\beta = 2$	$\alpha = .8$ $\beta = 4$
1	1.00	1.00	1.00	1.00
2	1.50	2.50	2.80	5.00
3	1.75	3.75	4.84	17.80
4	1.875	4.125	6.352	56.20
5	1.9375	3.4375	6.6256	169.84
6	1.9688	2.0313	5.3037	500.52
7	1.9844	0.9141	2.5959	1,459.592
8	1.9922	–0.1172	–0.6918	4,227.704
9	1.9961	0.2148	–3.3603	12,241.1216

1. α = 0.5 and β = 0. This gives us purely multiplier effects with income approaching the peak. Here acceleration coefficient is zero.

2. α = 0.5, β = 1. This gives us damped fluctuations, falling in value as they fluctuate about the multiplier level, gradually subsiding to that level. In this case, a constant continuing level of public expenditure will result in damped oscillatory movements of national income, gradually approaching the asymptote $\frac{1}{1-\alpha}$ times the constant level of public expenditure.

3. α = 0.5, β = 2. This gives regular cycles about the multiplier level more or less unchanged values repeating themselves indefinitely.

4. α = 0, β = 2. This gives us explosive cycles with variations about the multiplier level becoming larger and larger. In this case, a constant level of public expenditure will result in explosive ever-increasing oscillations, i.e., the amplitude increases from cycle to cycle.

5. $\alpha = 0.8$, $\beta = 4$. This gives us an ever-increasing income gradually approaching a compound rate of growth. In this case, a constant level of public expenditure will result in an ever-increasing national income (compound rate of interest growth) without oscillations.

Since even very simple models lead to entirely different results if we change our assumptions in regard to the coefficient of acclerator and the marginal propensity to consume, it is quite obvious that predictions as to the combined leverage effect of multiplier and acceleration principle in concrete circumstances is more or less impossible.

HICKSIAN MODEL

John Hicks is credited for trying to reveal proper macroeconomic cycles in a linear multiplier accelerator model by essentially aiming for unstable oscillation and adding floors and ceilings to constrain them. However, Hicks proposed a slightly different model. Instead of having the accelerator related to past consumption changes, he had it related to past output changes. The Hicksian 'floor' is related through a depreciation factor to the actual capital stock that results from the successive investments generated by the model. This seems to be a most reasonable assumption, as the 'floor' is defined to be maximum disinvestment when there is no reinvestment at all. Unlike the traditionally assumed fixed, 'floor' can result in unbounded deviation of all variables, a new method of relative dynamics is suggested. The strategy is based on relative growth rates instead of the variables themselves. Using this we find that the model proposed can produce growth rate cycles of any periodicity. These growth rate cycles are always bounded (even without any 'ceiling'), whereas the income variable itself shows exponential growth (with cyclic deviations). The method therefore also provides a synthesis between growth theory and business cycle theory. With a view to simplify the argument, we also assume:

(a) that disinvestment induced by a fall in output has the same time-shape as the investment induced by an equal rise in output;

(b) that the 'tail' of the stream of induced investment is of negligible importance so that only the initial hump or through needs to be taken into account;

(c) that the initial hump or trough covers one period, namely that immediately following the one in which the rise in output occurs; and

(d) that consumption is lagged one period behind income.

This model is based on two interacting principles—consumers spending a fraction of c of past income, $C_n = cY_{n-1}$, and investors aiming at maintaining a stock of capital K_n in given proportion v to the income Y_n to be produced. With an additional time lag for the construction period for capital equipment, net investments, by definition the change in capital stock, $I_n = K_n - K_{n-1}$, become $I_n = v(Y_{n-1} - Y_{n-2})$. As income is generated by consumption and investments, we have

$$\begin{aligned} Y_n &= C_n + I_n \\ &= cY_{n-1} + v(Y_{n-1} - Y_{n-2}) \\ &= (1 - s)\, Y_{n-1} + v(Y_{n-1} - Y_{n-2}) \\ &= (1 - s + v)\, Y_{n-1} - vY_{n-2} \end{aligned}$$

It could generate growth or oscillations in income. The consumption component is referred to in terms of the 'multiplier' and the investment component in terms of the "principle of acceleration". Two points should be noted, first, Samuelson applied the accelerator to consumption expenditures only; the above described application to all expenditures is due to Hicks (1950), discussed in more detail below. The difference in terms of substance is marginal. Second, all these models contain an additional term called "autonomous expenditures" (i.e., government expenditures, any consumption independent of income, and investments not dependent on the business cycles generated by the model). The multiplier, $1/(1 - c)$, (i.e., the multiplicative factor applied to such autonomous expenditures), resulted in an equilibrium income, or a particular solution to the difference equation. Income could then be redefined as a deviation from this equilibrium income, and the original equation regained, though now in income deviations from the equilibrium. This makes sense of negative values of income that inevitably result from the above difference equation.

Hicks realised that there must be limits to the accelerator-based investment function. In a depression phase, $I_n = v(V_{n-1} - Y_{n-2}) < 0$, and it can even happen that income (= production) decreases at a pace so fast that more capital can be dispensed with than disappears through natural wear. As nobody actively destroys capital to such an end, there is a lower limit to disinvestment, the so-called 'floor', fixed at the (negative) net investment that occurs when no worn out capital is replaced at all.

At the same time, Hicks suggested that there be a 'ceiling' at full employment, when income could not be expanded any more. Hicks never assembled the pieces to a complete formal model. It is clear that the floor constraint is applied to the investment function, so it becomes something like $I_n = \max\{v(Y_{n-1} - Y_{n-2}), I_f\}$, where I_f is the absolute value of the floor disinvestment. On the other hand, it is not quite clear what the ceiling is applied to. Most likely Hicks thinks of it as applied to income, so that the income formation equation is changed to $Y_n = \min\{(cY_{n-1} + I_n), Y_c\}$, where Y_c is the full employment capacity income.

Here, the question arises, which agents cut their expenditures when the ceiling is reached. As an alternative one might incorporate it in the investment function, along with the floor, thereby implying that it is the investors who abstain from further investment when they realise that full employment is reached.

The autonomous expenditure, in this model, can be constant, or growing. Hicks was in favour of exponentially growing autonomous expenditures, as he wanted to model both growth and cycles around a growing trend. Growth, however, was not created endogenously by the model, as the cycles were, but introduced ad hoc. To make this type of model suitable for analysis, the floor and ceiling must be assumed to be growing too, at the same rate as the autonomous expenditures, and this seems to have been Hicks's own tacit assumption. The assumption of equal growth rates is arbitrary.

Hicks identifies the following alternative ways, depending upon the values of v, in which output would react to the disturbance.

(a) If the value of v is less than what Hicks calls floor, output may continue to increase for a few periods and then converge to the equilibrium level and stay there. The sequence is thus similar to the Kahn process (which, in fact, is the case where v = 0) except that there is the possibility of the initial rise.

(b) If v is above the floor but below the middle point, there is a large initial rise than in the first case and damped oscillations (with decreasing amplitude) thereafter, so that equilibrium is reached at the end.

(c) If v is above the middle point but below the ceiling, the initial rise is not only larger than in the previous case but is also followed by fluctuations with increasing amplitude. Thus, there will be an oscillation about the equilibrium position and no tendency to settle at it. All the while, as v increases, the initial swing is getting larger and larger.

(d) If v is above the ceiling, the initial upward movement becomes so large that it fail to turn round at all and the system moves relentlessly away from equilibrium.

The assumed growth of the floor along with the autonomous expenditures is particularly problematic. A growing capital stock, as a result of growing autonomous expenditures, should increase the absolute value of maximum disinvestment, so it is not only arbitrary to assume the floor to grow at the same rate as the autonomous expenditures, but the change even goes in the wrong direction. The floor would rather be decreasing with capital accumulation. For this reason it seems to be important to make capital an explicit variable in the model, and to relate the floor directly to capital stock; put $I_{fn} = rK_n$, where K_n is capital stock and r is the rate of depreciation. Just to avoid misunderstanding, it should be understood that, although the income variable, as we have seen, can be negative in the sense of a negative deviation from equilibrium, capital by necessity always is nonnegative. The points, which distinguish the four alternatives mentioned above, can be easily defined in terms of the value of s (the marginal propensity to save). Under the assumptions we have made, the middle point is to be always found where v = 1. The floor is where $v = \left(1 - \sqrt{s}\right)^2$ and ceiling, where $v = \left(1 + \sqrt{s}\right)^2$. Thus, making changes to the model, we get the extra benefit that the growing trend need not be introduced exogenously. It would result within the model through capital accumulation. The model hence explains both the growth trend and the business cycles that take place around it.

With accumulating capital, the floor is no longer fixed, and the growth of capital stock allows increasing amplitude swings around the growth trend for which it is also responsible. Growth is something that economists regard as a good feature for a model, but it is no good for the use of mathematical methods, which favour the study of fixed points and their destabilization, stationary cycles, quasi-periodicity, and chaos. To make the model suitable for standard analysis, we focus on relative dynamics, the rate of growth of income, and of the actual capital/output ratio.

The above conclusions remain essentially valid under assumptions, which are less rigorous than those made in the simplified case. This is so, for instance, when it is assumed that the initial hump of induced investment is spread out over a number of periods or is postponed to a period later than the one immediately following that which experiences the increase in output, or that consumption lags longer than one period, or that allowance is made for the 'tail'.[4] The intersection of multiplier and accelerator obviously holds the possibility of cyclical fluctuations. This possibility remains even under less rigorous assumptions though in this case the cycle would be less regular. Fig. 13.6 summarizes the Hicks parameter regimes for trade cycle.

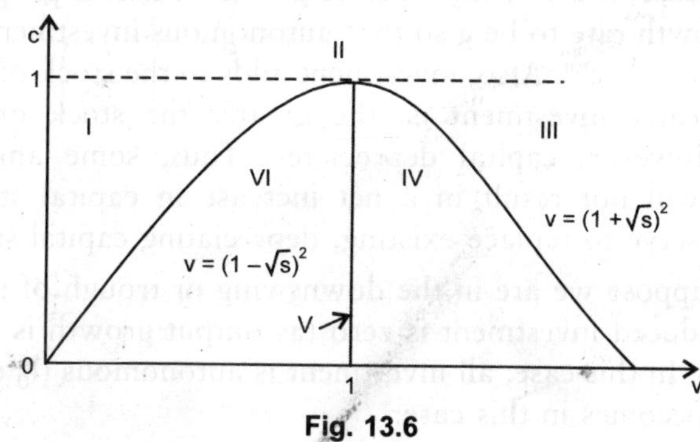

Fig. 13.6

We have six areas of parameter constellations for different dynamics.

I – damped monotonic
II – constant monotonic
III – explosive monotonic
IV – explosive oscillations
V – constant oscillations
VI – damped oscillations

Again like Samuelson case, it is only when parameter values (v, c) fall in region V that we obtain regular cycles. Note, however, that to obtain V, all we have to do is obtain the value v = 1 for any c will be compatible with that. In Samuelson's multiplier-accelerator model, we were forced to obtain precise values of both c and v to get case V of constant oscillations.

Hicks' multiplier-accelerator model remains equally insufficient as a theory of the cycle. Constant cycles can be obtained, but they will not be structurally stable (as any slight movement of v above or below 1 will lead to explosion or stability). However, Hicks (1950) proposed that we add several things to our basic multiplier-accelerator model—namely, ceilings, floors and a exogenous constant growth rate of autonomous investment. This enables us to obtain growth with cycles.

The logic is simple. Investment, as we know, is composed of two parts—autonomous investment, I_0, and induced investment (induced by the accelerator, $v(Y_{n-1} - Y_{n-2})$. Now, Hicks proposed that for a growing economy, "autonomous investment itself will have to increase at a constant rate of growth". Let us propose this constant growth rate to be g so that autonomous investment at any time period n is $I_0\ e^{gn}$. Also, investment adds to the stock of capital, thus the greater investment is, the greater the stock of capital becomes. However, capital depreciates. Thus, some amount of investment will not result in a net increase in capital stock but rather only serve to replace existing, depreciating capital stock.

Now, suppose we are in the downswing or trough of the cycle such that induced investment is zero (as output growth is negative or constant). In this case, all investment is autonomous ($I_0\ e^{gn}$). Net investment becomes in this case:

$$I_n = I_0\ e^{gn} - \delta$$

where, δ is depreciation (level, not rate, and assumed constant).

Now, for the capital stock not to start decreasing (and thus the multiplier not to amplify negative effects), then $I_n > 0$. Thus, we can assume that this places a "floor" on the system. Actual investment cannot fall below δ . But, as there is an exogenous rate of growth of autonomous investment, then that floor is not constant. Simply, as $I_0\ e^{gn}$ is growing over time (and δ is not), then I_n at its minimum must also be growing at rate g.

Hicks then also proposes a ceiling. Output cannot grow indefinitely due to restrictions in factor supplies. Greater output may be demanded, but if one is at full employment, the only possible result is that the prices of these factors will rise—more supply will not be forthcoming. Assuming factor supplies also grow at the exogenous rate g, then the maximum output level also grows at rate g. What Hicks proposes is then quite simple to explain. Namely, suppose v and c assume values such that we obtain explosive oscillations (case VI). With floor and ceiling imposed, both growing at rate g, then oscillations in output are confined within ranges of values between max Y and min Y— both of which are growing at the exogenous rate of g. Similarly, the equilibrium level of output is also growing at rate g.

Interaction in a Dynamic Economy

Let us now turn to the interaction of the multiplier and the accelerator in a dynamic economy. With a view to simplify the argument we consider the simplest form of such an economy, namely, what Hicks calls the regularly progressive economy in which output increases at a constant geometrical rate so that in the nth period it is (1 + g) of that in the (n + 1)th period where g is a positive constant. Assuming a constant v and s, an essential condition of such an economy is that the rate of growth of autonomous investment must be the same as that of output so that the latter always bears a constant ratio to the former.[5] Hicks calls this ratio the super-multiplier.[6] Obviously in such an economy, given the level of autonomous investment at a given time and the constant rate of growth of such investment, the level of autonomous investment can be determined at different times. By applying the super-multiplier to the latter, the level of equilibrium output at different times can be obtained. In this way, we can determine the moving equilibrium path adjusted to the growth of autonomous investment along which output increases at a constant rate. The system can move along it if it is not disturbed. But if it is disturbed the results will be similar to those in the stationary case analysed above. This may be illustrated with reference to the elementary case mentioned above.

We have

Actual current output = current autonomous investment + current induced investment + current consumption.

or, $$Y_n = A_n + v(Y_{n-1} - Y_{n-2}) + (1 - s)\, Y_{n-1}$$

If equilibrium output of the current period is E_n, we have

$$E_n = A_n + v(E_{n-1} - E_{n-2}) + (1 - s)\, E_{n-1}$$

$$Y_n - E_n = v(Y_{n-1} - E_{n-1}) - v(Y_{n-2} - E_{n-2}) + (1 - s)\,(Y_{n-1} - E_{n-1}).$$

Since, $Y_n - E_n$ is the deviation from the equilibrium output in the period n, we may write it as in the stationary case as y_n. We then have

$$y_n = v(y_{n-1} - y_{n-2}) + (1 - s)\, y_{n-1}$$

$$= (1 - s + v)\, y_{n-1} - vy_{n-2}$$

This is the same relation as was obtained in case of a stationary economy. In other words, the deviation of the actual output from equilibrium output has precisely the same properties whether we have a stationary equilibrium or a regularly progressive economy. The results are, therefore, the same if the latter is disturbed, namely, convergence to the equilibrium path if v is below the Lower Point, damped oscillations about the equilibrium path if v is between the Lower and the Middle Point, a regular cycle if v is at the Middle Point, explosive oscillations if v is between the Middle and the Higher Points, and relentless upwards divergence from equilibrium if v is higher than the Higher Point.

HICKS' REAL THEORY OF TRADE CYCLE

We have seen above that if the investment coefficient (v) is at the Middle Point, any initial disturbance will generate regular fluctuations about the equilibrium path. But it would not be realistic to assume that v would always be at this point. Any realistic theory of trade cycle must show how cyclical fluctuations could arise and continue even when v had some other value.

Hicks believes that the cycle can be realistically explained only on the hypothesis of v being, as a rule, above its Middle Point.[7] This hypothesis does not appear to be inconsistent with the available statistical evidence.[8] There is, however, the consideration that on this hypothesis, a single disturbance should produce an explosive cycle. But, throughout the 19th century, the trade cycle was not of this nature. The logical results of the hypothesis may, however, be made consistent with observed reality if there could be discovered some check which prevents the fluctuations from crossing certain limits. "The system", remarks Hicks, "might then continue periodically breaking its head against these limits without running away altogether." Hicks believes that this hypothesis to a large extent corresponds to reality and, on its basis, proceeds to explain the cycle in outline.

Hicks' theory of trade cycle is based on the following assumptions:

(a) that v (the ratio of induced investment to changes in output which called it forth) lies above its middle point so that an upward displacement from the equilibrium path results either in explosive fluctuations about it or in relentless divergence from it;

(b) that the value of the multiplier (determined by the marginal propensity to consume) and the accelerator (which in Hicks' model is the ratio of induced investment to the increase in output or income) are constant and are such as to give a strong tendency to instability as a reaction to any disturbance so that any upward displacement from equilibrium will not be self-contracting (i.e. the equilibrium is not stable) but will cause continuing movement of the explosive variety away from equilibrium;

(c) that there is a ceiling to the expansion of output in response to increase in effective demand on account of employable resources;

(d) that the accelerator operates differently in response to decline in output because of the existence of a ceiling to the rate of disinvestment; and

(e) that (i) autonomous investment is increasing at a constant (geometrical) rate so that the system, if not disturbed from its equilibrium path, could remain in progressive equilibrium (with output increasing at the same constant percentage rate at which autonomous investment increases), and (ii) that the rise in equilibrium output and in the output ceiling consequent on the steady increase in the rate of investment proceeds at the same rate as the latter.

The above assumptions are incorporated in Figure 13.7.

Upswing and boom: Suppose that an economy while proceeding along its equilibrium path experiences an upward displacement at P_0, say, owing to an abnormal burst of autonomous investment generated by an exceptional flow of new inventions. After the burst, autonomous investment returns to its old path. But on our 'explosive' assumption of v being above its Middle Point, output will experience, perhaps after a lag, either explosive oscillations about, or relentless divergence from, the equilibrium path. It must, therefore, in due course touch the ceiling. The path P_0P_1 represents the particular upward movement which thus touches the ceiling. After output touches the ceiling at P_1, it can at best only creep along the ceiling. The phase in which output moves from the equilibrium path upward towards the ceiling may be termed the upswing, and that during which it creeps along the ceiling as the boom.

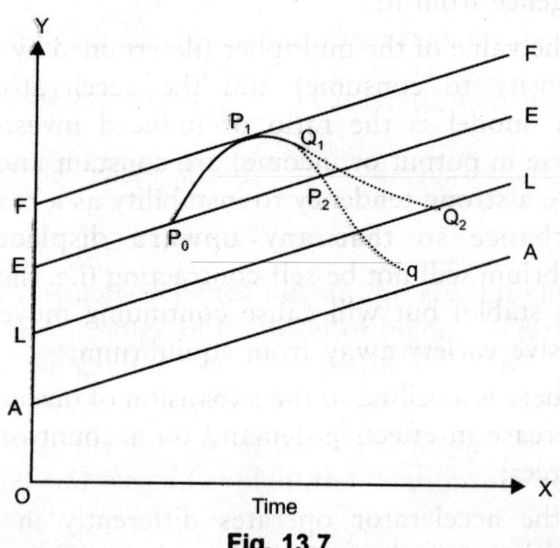

Fig. 13.7

Downturn: The output can creep along the ceiling only for a limited period, ultimately it must start converging towards the equilibrium path. With the end of the assumed shortlived burst of autonomous investment, such investment would return to the normal level. This may be taken to happen at some point on the upper part of the path P_0P_1. After that the continued upward divergence of output from its equilibrium path would be entirely owing to investment induced by the previous rises in output above its equilibrium level. But once the path hits the ceiling and starts creeping along it, there is no further increase in the relative deviation from the equilibrium path. Now the induced investment which this rate of increase in output can induce can support a growth of output not along FF but EE. Output will, therefore, converge to EE. This conclusion remains valid even if induced investment is lagged, contrary to the assumption made above for more than one period. The effect of a longer lag is simply that induced investment remains larger than would support a growth of output no higher than along EE longer than previously so that the path may creep along the ceiling for a longer distance. Eventually, however, the time must come when even the longest lagged induced investment effect of rises in output during the P_0P_1 part of the path is over so that the current induced investment is entirely the result of changes in output represented by that part of the path where it creeps along the ceiling. When this happens, as pointed out above, induced investment will be no more than can support an increase in output along EE. The path, therefore, must start converging towards EE. In practice the path will most certainly start downwards before all the lagged investment effects of rises in output along the P_0P_1 part of the path are over.[9] Hicks thus attributes the downturn to the collapse of the accelerator.

Slump and depression: The decline in output relatively to the equilibrium level as a result of the collapse of the accelerator will not stop on touching this level but, for the following reason, will go further. At P_2, when output declines to the equilibrium level, current induced investment possibly will be the result of changes in output over three distinct parts of the path: (a) the stretch when output was falling relatively to its equilibrium rate of growth, (b) the stretch where the path crept along the ceiling indicating a rate of growth of output equal to equilibrium rate of growth, and (c) the stretch when output was rising relatively to its equilibrium rate of growth. The induced investment generated by (b) might be sufficient to play its part in maintaining output at the equilibrium path, but that resulting from (a) would fall short of this requirement. This deficiency is not likely to be covered by investment in excess of this requirement coming from (a) because the stretch (a) being the farthest away from P_2, the relevant induced investment effect of rises in output during the period would be very much milder. The total current induced investment would, therefore, be insufficient to maintain output, when it reaches P_2, at the equilibrium path. There must be decline in output relatively to the equilibrium rate of growth.

In case the rate of growth is so large that output continues to increase in absolute terms even inspite of the above relative decline, the slump experienced by the system would be no more than slackening of the rate of progress. The system would then experience only mild 'cycles'. But such a high rate of growth is not realistic. The relative decline is thus most likely to involve absolute decline in output. Once that happens, on the 'explosive' assumption made above, if the accelerator operated during the downswing in the same manner as during the upswing, the contraction could not end (if at all) until output had fallen to a very low level. But the accelerator does not work in this manner. As stated earlier, there is a ceiling to the rate of disinvestment in fixed capital. Once the ceiling is reached, the rate of disinvestment becomes inelastic to further declines in output, i.e., it becomes a constant. Total investment now being equal to autonomous investment minus a constant, disinvestment may properly be treated as but a downward adjustment in autonomous investment and represented by a downward shift of the AA line. We then have a situation in which AA line is somewhat depressed below its normal position while induced investment is zero. This gives a situation where the ordinary multiplier works free from the simultaneous operation of the accelerator. As such there will exist a moving equilibrium path corresponding to the adjusted AA line. In the above figure, this is shown by LL which may be called the slump equilibrium line. Since the adjusted AA line lies below the original AA line, LL will lie below EE. The existence of the slump equilibrium line sets a floor to the slump.

From the point the negative rate of investment reaches the ceiling shown by Q_1, in Figure 13.7, there must be a steady decline in output till it reaches the slump equilibrium line at P_2. The path Q_1Q_2 must lie above Q_1q (the path which would have been followed if the ceiling to the rate of disinvestment had not transformed the accelerator).

The above result would have to be slightly modified when we take into consideration also the induced disinvestment in working capital and stocks resulting from the fall in output. For the rate of such disinvestment has no technical ceiling. The accelerator continues working during the downswing to the extent of this part of capital stock. But when disinvestment in fixed capital has reached its ceiling, the investment coefficient relevant to further declines in output, being based only on additional disinvestment in working capital and stocks induced by such declines, will be rather small. And, as seen earlier, a small coefficient rules out the "explosive" possibility. Thus even when allowance is made for disinvestment in working capital and stocks, the path is likely to converge to the Slump Equilibrium.

After touching the Slump Equilibrium path, output starts creeping along it. Hicks calls this phase as 'Depression'. This phase is brought to a close by what Hicks calls 'Recovery' which marks the movement of output upwards from LL to EE.

Upturn or recovery: Recovery is inevitable provided autonomous investment maintains its upward trend (i.e. has the time-shape given by an upswing AA curve as in figure 13.7). For, given such a trend of autonomous investment, the LL line deduced from it would be up-sloping. As such when after reaching the LL line, output path starts creeping along this line the system experiences an absolute increase in output which must, after sometime, bring the old accelerator once again into operation. Once this happens, the equilibrium line is not LL but EE. The output must, therefore, after sometime, start rising to EE. This development marks the beginning of Recovery.

The exact point at which recovery begins is influenced by the speed of the slump and the slope of the Slump Equilibrium line. The speed of the slump is to a great extent influenced by consumption lags: the larger and longer the consumption lags, the slower will be the speed of the slump. The greater the speed of the slump, the larger will be the surplus capital stock (including both fixed capital and stocks) and Q_2 and, the longer will the system creep along the LL line before lack of replacement helps to work off the 'surplus' capital stock. The slope of the LL line depends upon the slope of the *AA* line as the former line is deduced from the latter. The larger the slope of LL, the speedier will be the absolute increase in output as the system creeps along this line, and hence less will be the time required to absorb the 'surplus' capital stock. Slower speed of the slump and larger slope of the LL line thus cut down the time required to work off and absolve the 'surplus' capital stock adequately to make the accelerator strong enough to make the system start rising from LL to EE. In contrast, the higher the speed of the slump and smaller the slope of the LL line, the slower would be the adjustment and hence the longer the duration of the depression.

Thus, Hicks attributes Recovery to the revival of the accelerator just as he attributed the downturn to the latter's collapse.

The upswing again: When the new upswing reaches the upper equilibrium EE, it cannot possibly stop there because output is necessarily expanding more rapidly than it would do along EE. The boom will therefore continue, apparently until it reaches the ceiling. Thereafter, the whole cycle goes on being repeated.

In case of actual cycle, the downturn often occurs before the system touches the Full Employment ceiling. The downturn may thus be experienced again and again without the ceiling ever becoming operative. Hicks feels that it is possible to reconcile this observation with the 'explosive' assumption that v is above its Middle Point. His reasoning is like this. If the investment coefficient were only slightly above its Middle Point, and if the initial displacement were small, there would be, to begin with, a series of small 'free' cycles of increasing amplitude. The ceiling will be touched only when the amplitude has grown long enough. The above discussion of the course of the cycle started precisely at this point. Suppose on one of the earlier swings that are reversed before they touch the ceiling, the absolute decline in output during the downswing is large enough to transform the accelerator in the manner given above. The output would then fall to its slump equilibrium level and start creeping up along it. Recovery that begins, in due course, grows into boom, i.e., the rise in output beginning as an upward movement from the slump equilibrium level (LL) will overshoot the equilibrium path (EE). The fact that the 'free' cycle is explosive means that the divergence above EE would be longer than the distance between EE and the LL line. It may, however, be reversed before touching the ceiling if the latter is high enough. The transformation of the accelerator during the downswing once again brings the latter to an end when the slump equilibrium level is reached. Recovery once again starts at a point where the relative divergence from EE is the same as in the previous upswing; the relative divergence at the corresponding peak will, therefore, be exactly the same and so on. The cycle is thus kept going indefinitely even while v is above its Middle Point without ever touching the Full Employment ceiling.

A snag in Hicks' model: In actual practice, while recovery starts in a slow and imperceptible manner, the downturn involves a rapid decline in output. But Hicks' model suggests quite the reverse. If the accelerator operated identically during the upswing and the downswing, the process must take almost the same number of periods to drop from ceiling on to EE that it would take to rise from LL to EE. But, as discussed above, during the downswing, there is transformation of the accelerator in a way that the decline in output proceeds at a rate slower than it would be if the accelerator were free from constraint as in the upswing. Actual experience thus is contrary to the conclusions that logically follow from Hicks' analysis. To resolve the conflict between the two, Hicks puts forward the view that though the downswing takes a larger number of periods yet the calendar time taken is shorter because of the shortening of the 'period' during this phase of cycle. Financial difficulties and the fear of heavy-losses compel businessmen to try to avoid surplus stocks. This necessitates reduction in output much below the level that would correspond to reduced demand. To affect this much decline in output in the near future requires a rapid decline in inputs. Thus there is rapid decline in the goods-in-process, which means a high rate of disinvestment in working capital. Since the 'period' measures the span of calendar time by the end of which, in case of increase in the demand for output, investment in working capital becomes large enough to offset the accumulation of stocks, or in case of decline in the demand for output, disinvestment in working capital becomes large enough to offset the accumulation of stocks, a higher rate of disinvestment in working capital during the recovery means that in the first case the length of the period in calendar time is shorter. Thus the downswing, even while taking a larger number of periods, takes less calendar time.

Thus, Hicks provides a fairly satisfactory explanation of turning points as well as the periodicity of the cycle. As the system has a ceiling and a floor, changes in income and output oscillate between these two limits like the pendulum of the clock which moves between the two limits. At the lower turning point Hicks makes a significant contribution to the theory of trade cycle by showing how the existence of excess capacity in capital equipment tends to delay the upswing.

Hicks' theory also pinpoints the fact that in the absence of technological development and other powerful growth factors the economy will tend to languish in depression for long periods of time. There are two reasons for this. In the first place, without technological change, autonomous investment may not rise over time, and thus a positive change in output, required to set the accelerator in motion will not take place until equipment has worn out to the point where some replacement investment is necessary. Secondly, if there is no technological change, the time at which this replacement is necessary will be deferred because no help is obtained from the obsolescence of existing equipment. The entire burden of setting the accelerator going is thus placed on the wearing out (or depreciation) of equipment. It is not surprising, therefore, that depressions are more severe and long-lasting during periods when long-run growth factors appear to be in abeyance.

CRITICISM OF HICKS' THEORY

The major weakness of Hicks' theory lies in treating the multiplier and accelerator as having fixed values (i.e. constant coefficients) during the different phases of the cycle. The constant multiplier is derived from the constant propensity to consume out of income. Recent studies, however, show that the marginal propensity to consume does not remain constant over different phases of the trade cycle, although permanent consumption is a stable function of permanent income. As Friedman has shown, there is no certain and predictable relation between the transitory income and consumption elements.

Similarly, the fixed value attached to the accelerator, a powerful tool in Hicks' apparatus, is not very appropriate. The relation between capital and output need not necessarily remain constant over time. There are large variations in this relation as between various sectors of the economy and these various sectors do not expand at a uniform rate. Further, the gestation periods for different types of capital goods differ. For example, while a plan to expand inventories might be completed soon, the construction of a steel plant takes a long time before it starts yielding production. While some upturns may be dominated by an initial expansion of durable goods industries, the dominant place might be occupied by agriculture or consumer goods industries in others. The expansion in output will invoke different investment responses and the assumed constant relation as employed by Hicks is subject to criticism.

Prof. Hutt remarks:

> I maintain that we cannot find in the relation between demand for goods of a lower order [consumption goods] and the demand for goods of a higher order [Investment goods] [and the supposed derivation of the latter from the former], an explanation of cyclical variation in the demand for growth. Nor can we find in those factors the source of great cyclical changes in entrepreneurial optimism affecting prospective yields, the rate of interest offered and the flow of savings. We can not even observe those factors to be influences which induce the cyclical withholding and release of capacity. In the study of all these issues, the relationship which the acceleration principle tries to express is wholly irrelevant.[10]

Another weakness of Hicks' theory is that the full employment ceiling as defined by him is independent of the path of output.[11] It depends rather on the population growth, technological progress etc., and is thus assumed to grow at the same rate as autonomous investment. But the full-employment level of output depends on the magnitude of the resources which are available to the economy. The capital stock is one such resource. This means that the ceiling is raised in any period during which the capital stock is increasing. Since the rate at which output increases determines the rate at which the capital stock changes, the ceiling level of output will vary depending upon the time path of output. It is not, therefore, possible to separate the long-run full-employment trend from what happens during a cycle.

A third important drawback of Hicks' theory is that in it autonomous investment plays a passive role. To cite Dernberg and McDougall[12]:

> It can, however, be argued that in a highly progressive capitalist economy the driving force may be the periodic disruptions introduced by technical progress. Indeed, there is reason to believe that the placing of primary emphasis on

induced investment, while ignoring fluctuations in autonomous investment can be compared to the tail that wags the dog.

NOTES

1. P.A. Samuelson, *Economics*, p. 191.
2. J.M. Clark, "Business Acceleration and the Law of Demand: A Technical Factor in Economic Cycles" in The American Economic Association, *Readings in Business Cycle Theory* (London, 1950), p. 239.
3. Paul A. Samuelson, "Interaction Between the Multiplier Analysis and Principle of Acceleration", *Review of Economic Statistics,* 1939, pp. 75-78.
4. J.R. Hicks, *A Contribution to the Theory of the Trade Cycle,* (London 1951), pp. 74-82.
5. *Ibid.*, p. 59.
6. *Ibid.*, p. 62.
7. *Ibid.*, p. 92.
8. *Ibid.*, pp. 92-94.
9. *Ibid.*, p. 100.
10. Hutt, *Keynesianism: Retrospect and Prospect,* p. 338.
11. Thomas F. Dernberg and Duncan M. McDougall, *Macro-Economics* (New York, 1960), p. 218.
12. *Ibid.*, p. 219.